IT DID HAPPEN HERE

Studies in Critical Social Sciences Book Series

Haymarket Books is proud to be working with Brill Academic Publishers (www.brill.nl) to republish the *Studies in Critical Social Sciences* book series in paperback editions. This peer-reviewed book series offers insights into our current reality by exploring the content and consequences of power relationships under capitalism, and by considering the spaces of opposition and resistance to these changes that have been defining our new age. Our full catalog of *SCSS* volumes can be viewed at https://www.haymarketbooks .org/series_collections/4-studies-in-critical-social-sciences.

IT DID HAPPEN HERE

The Rise of Fascism in Contemporary Society

MILAN ZAFIROVSKI

Haymarket Books
Chicago, IL

First published in 2023 by Brill Academic Publishers, The Netherlands
© 2023 Koninklijke Brill NV, Leiden, The Netherlands

Published in paperback in 2024 by
Haymarket Books
P.O. Box 180165
Chicago, IL 60618
773-583-7884
www.haymarketbooks.org

ISBN: 979-8-88890-231-8

Distributed to the trade in the US through Consortium Book Sales and
Distribution (www.cbsd.com) and internationally through Ingram Publisher
Services International (www.ingramcontent.com).

This book was published with the generous support of Lannan Foundation,
Wallace Action Fund, and the Marguerite Casey Foundation.

Special discounts are available for bulk purchases by organizations and
institutions. Please call 773-583-7884 or email info@haymarketbooks.org for more
information.

Cover design by Jamie Kerry and Ragina Johnson.

Printed in the United States.

Library of Congress Cataloging-in-Publication data is available.

Contents

Tables and Figures

Tables

Figures

Introduction

> This is a Reichstag moment. The gospel of the Führer.
> MARK MILLEY, Chairman of the US Joint Chiefs of Staff

∴

Fascism evidently happens while writing these lines in America contrary to some earlier observations and optimistic expectations that it did not and 'can't happen here'[1] ever in the 'land of freedom' in contrast to the despised authoritarian, fascist 'old world' of Europe and other societies. Specifically, while germinating and originating during the 1980s and 1930–50s—and perhaps earlier such as the 1890s—fascism overtly rises and advances in post-2016 America following the 2016 elections and the resulting autocratic and extreme-right regime, as well as in other countries, such as Brexit Great Britain and others,[2] via a global contagion from or convergence with the American source and center.[3] The aftermath of the 2020 elections involving unprecedented autocratic and conservative attempts (including the January 2021 insurrection and destruction of the Capitol)[4] to overturn the electoral results and subvert democratic institutions dispels any doubts in this respect, just as

---

1 This refers to Sinclair Lewis's 1935 novel *It Can't Happen Here*.
2 Gethin, Martínez-Toledano, and Piketty (2022, p. 2) observe that 'Western democracies have undergone major transformations in recent years [including] the growing success of antiestablishment authoritarian movements (Trump, Brexit, Le Pen, etc.).'
3 Berezin (2019, p. 346) notes that in the 1920s, the 'historian Benedetto Croce famously described Italian fascism as a parenthesis in his nation's history. The election of Donald Trump in the United States and the electoral success of right-wing parties in Europe suggest an inflection point that bears a family resemblance to Croce's parenthesis.' Berezin (2019, p. 346) adds that 'current events in the United States and abroad signal the erosion of democratic institutions and the attenuation of democratic practices pointing toward a new age of illiberalism and authoritarianism. Interest in fascism and populism spiked around 2016, corresponding to the US presidential election.' More broadly, Gethin et al. (2022, p. 2) point to the 'rise of 'populism' in Western democracies.'
4 Brandmayr (2021, p. 112) refers to the '2021 storming of the US Capitol' by the conservative right. Bonikowski, Feinstein, and Bock (2021, p. 533) register the Republican Party's 'widespread support of the Capitol insurrection [and] the party elites' continued fealty to Donald Trump.'

does the radical-right's insurgency at the state level by the suppression of polit-ical, civil, and individual rights.

Future US scholars may well trace the rise and advance of fascism as a dom-inant ideology, political system, cultural climate, and socio-psychological dis-position in America, primarily its anti-liberal conservative and religious pole implying the existence of 'two Americas', to the 2016 elections and post-2016 autocratic regime and its attempts to overturn the results of the 2020 elec-tions, just as their postwar German counterparts traced that of Nazism to the 1933 elections and post-1933 autocracy. Therefore, they may probably associ-ate the disappearance of celebrated 'American exceptionalism' in the sense of America's presumed exceptional immunity from and resilience to fascism as a 'foreign', European affliction and thus the failure of the 'American experiment' in democracy and free society to this period and its social structures, processes, events, and personalities. Conversely, they may trace the beginning of the end or grave protracted crisis of American democracy and of the 'American exper-iment' to this time, including the autocratic and conservative subversion of democratic processes after the 2020 elections, from the January 2021 insurrec-tion to the radical-right's state suppression of political, civil, and individual rights, just as their postwar German colleagues traced the equivalent outcome in Germany to the events of 1933 and its aftermath.

Future US analysts hence may describe post-2016 years[5] as the times of a slow but steady and sustained process of dying or crisis-ridden democracy in America and the 'American experiment' due to the resurgence, expansion, and dominance of fascism even if it assumes an all-American nativist and faith-based form and if fascist history does not repeat itself in all societies since the 1920–30s through the 2010–20s. Even if they optimistically envision the democratic happy end, in their accounts post-2016 years are likely to figure

---

5 Levitsky and Ziblatt (2018) alert that post-2016 may initiate the dying of American democ-racy. Romero (2020, p. 1) states that post-2016 is 'a time when authoritarian heads of states have been elected around the world; empires are arising, borders are hardening; people are torn from their homes to become stateless refugees; and racism and xenophobia are all over social media. We have [such] a US president.' Caren, Andrews, and Lu (2020, p. 451) recount that the US fascist or far right launched 'a new wave of electoral and movement activism, spurred by the reaction to the presidency of Barack Obama and the 2016 election of Donald Trump.' Acemoglu et al. (2022, p. 1234) remark that 'there is renewed interest in fascism, partly as a result of the rise of right-wing populist movements around the world [including] the United States under Donald Trump.' Acemoglu et al. (2022, p. 1234) add that such neo-fascist movements are 'threatening democratic institutions, media freedom, and some key aspects of state capacity' and suggest that 'understanding the factors that fueled the rise of fascism during the interwar years can shed light on the dangers ahead and the implications of these movements for economic policy and political dynamics.'

as the times of the most lethal threat through resurgent fascism and more broadly inherently authoritarian conservatism or the radical right to democracy, human freedom, and life in America since the Revolution or the Civil War.

Fascism ascends and expands in post-2016 America, more precisely its conservative-religious pole such as the former Southern Confederacy and similar spaces, in multiple, intertwined, and consistent syndromes, means, and ways.[6] These syndromes express virtually all the essential elements and properties of fascism that are therefore in abundant evidence and full display in post-2016 America, such as its conservative-religious pole. While fascist history does not repeat itself exactly, almost no essential and even peripheral, grave and grotesque, ingredient of fascism and trait of its autocratic leaders from Mussolini to Hitler is missing in post-2016 conservative-religious America and its own would-be autocrats, with certain adaptations to and variations in the American context. In this regard, the resurgence and prevalence of fascism in post-2016 America, at least its conservative-religious pole, leaves the taste of déjà vu compared with prior fascist episodes, looking as if the 'new nation', at least its section dominated by conservatism, coercive capitalism, religion, and theocracy, learned nothing from the fascist experience in the 'old world' during the 1920–30s.

In essence, post-2016 years in America, namely its conservative-religious pole, have a similar ambiance, feeling, or zeitgeist as the 1930s in Germany, Italy, and Europe—that of fascism and generally anti-democratic rightism, including rightist autocracy, or conservative authoritarianism. In this sense, fascist history virtually, even if not exactly, replicates itself in a new American form, manner, and context and with a time lag of about a century (that the

---

6 In retrospect, the title *It Can't Happen Here* was seemingly premature and overly optimistic but can also appear as sarcastic and predictive of the opposite, namely that fascism actually can and indeed will eventually happen in America, as also other earlier analysts warn and envision. Gross (1980, p. 3) remarks that 'in 1935 Sinclair Lewis wrote a popular novel in which a racist, anti-Semitic, flag-waving, army-backed demagogue wins the 1936 presidential election and proceeds to establish an Americanized version of Nazi Germany. The title, *It Can't Happen Here*, was a tongue-in-cheek warning that it might.' Alpers (2003, p. 254) comments that 'Sinclair Lewis's *It Can't Happen Here* sees little prospect for political change once America has fallen victim to dictatorship.' Alpers (2003, p. 273) notes that 'blaming Nazism on German-ness usually entailed denying that it could happen in America', while citing 'Hayek's overdetermined and self-contradictory analysis [that] simultaneously saw totalitarianism as transnational and as essentially foreign'. Alpers (2003, p. 273) adds that Hayek's *The Road to Serfdom* 'would become enormously important for the libertarian strain of postwar American conservatism, which saw a slippery slope leading from any state intervention in the economy straight to totalitarianism.' Paxton (1998, pp. 3, 23; also, 2004) about two decades ago envisioned the rise of 'an authentic fascism in the United States.'

alternative meaning of *It Can't Happen Here* predicts). This reverses the (Churchill) description of Americans to the effect that they will do eventually the extremely 'wrong' thing after trying all 'good' or typical things within Western modernity—embracing fascism and more broadly authoritarian conservatism, theocratic religion, and conservatives as intrinsic authoritarians after trying liberalism, liberal democracy, secularism, rationalism, progressivism, egalitarianism, universalism, cosmopolitanism, pacifism, and liberals as liberty-defined personalities. This seems a gloomy but mostly correct inference especially for Americans in the conservative-religious pole of America, such as the South and similar regions.

The preceding yields the diagnosis of the rise, escalation, and metastasis of fascism in its multiple facets in post-2016 America, at the minimum its conservative and religious or theocratic pole comprising approximately half of it. As it stands, this seems an accurate detection of a social pathology that is an ultimate and lethal antagonist and destroyer of American democracy, liberty, and society, thus leading to the ultimate failure and effective end of the 'American experiment' in these terms, and eventually a primary barbarian threat, reinventing or reminiscent of Nazism, to civilization and life.[7]

Fascism rises in post-2016 America, such as its conservative-religious half, because of the existence, operation, and influence of certain social factors causing it to surge and expand direct or indirectly, overtly or covertly, manifestly or latently. This opens the question of the causation of fascism in this specific social setting and historical time following that of its diagnosis and consisting of its underlying causes. Etiology and hence explanation of fascism as a social pathological condition appears more complex and difficult than its diagnosis and description as a probably simpler task. Fascism's underlying causes are less probable to be manifest and evident, thus being more likely to be denied or disputed, than its apparent symptoms such as autocratic tendencies and the subversion of democratic processes visible in post-2016 America.

Generally, fascism's rise and advance in post-2016 America, namely in one of the 'two Americas', is the outcome of intricate and encompassing social causation or structuration involving multiple and intertwined factors or structures in society. They involve economic, political, cultural, and related social

---

7 If, as Habermas (2001, p. 45) remarks, the 'force of barbarism' defining Nazism 'had broken through the very foundations of civilization in Germany', the barbarian forces of American fascism threaten to do and to a larger extent has already done this in post-2016 America. Thus, the news media reported that 'before the Jan. 6 [2021] riot at the Capitol, the chairman of the Joint Chiefs of Staff Milley saw ominous parallels between the political turmoil in the United States and the rise of the Nazi party in Germany.'

causes of the emergence, growth, and dominance of fascism in post-2016 America, such as its predominant conservative and religious or theocratic pole versus its weaker liberal-secular opposite. Especially, fascism resurging and expanding in post-2016 America results from the ascendance and predominance of conservatism due to its intrinsic authoritarianism rooted in medieval despotism, in typical association, eventually fusion, and mutual reinforcement with unrestrained coercive capitalism, ubiquitous religion, and theocracy, as it did in Europe, including Italy and Germany, during the 1920–30s. Fascism happens in the 'land of freedom' primarily because of the presence and prevalence of inherently authoritarian conservatism associated, fused, and mutually reinforced with coercive capitalism, pervasive religion, and theocracy (as *It Can't Happen Here* already implies).

Diagnosis and causation of the social pathology of fascism in post-2016 America leads to the question of its remedy or prevention through its antidotes or opposites such as countervailing social structures and processes. Fascism rises and prevails in post-2016 America that is ruled by authoritarian conservatism in conjunction with coercive capitalism, pervasive religion, and theocracy, because it attacks, defames, defeats, and reverses anti- and non-fascist social forces, as it did in Germany and Europe during the 1920–30s. Such counteracting forces to fascism consist of liberalism, liberal democracy, secularism, rationalism, progressivism, egalitarianism, universalism, cosmopolitanism, pacifism, and liberals as liberty-induced persons and groups in American society, more precisely liberal America. Conversely, these countervailing social forces if they reassert themselves can counter, remedy, and reverse fascism and prevent its future recurrence, expansion, and dominance in post-2016 America. This is an empirical problem and statement of fact rather than a normative prescription or value judgment—which social conditions and processes factually operate or can potentially function as countervailing societal powers against fascism. Just as fascism surges and advances in post-2016 conservative-religious America as the nemesis of liberal-democratic, secular, rationalist, progressive, egalitarian, universalist, cosmopolitan, and pacifist social forces, these, if reassert themselves, can act as the remedy to the fascist degeneration of American democracy, liberty, society, and life. Hence, this is the problem of identification and consideration of those social forces and structures that fascism discredits, perverts, and weakens in post-2016 America, but which, if they revitalize themselves, can become countervailing powers to fascist resurgence and dominance in the foreseeable future. It is a matter of plausible prediction or reasonable expectation of the course of fascism in post-2016 America in relation to certain counteracting forces in society.

Overall, the adverse inference for liberal democracy, liberty, equality, human reason and rationality, social progress, wellbeing, and life is that fascism rises and advances in America post-2016 while writing these lines. By contrast, the positive expectation is that countervailing social forces, if reasserting themselves, can overcome fascism and prevent its future recurrence and prevalence, acting as the antidote to fascist lethal pathology. Fascism's rise and expansion in post-2016 America's ultra-conservative and religious-theocratic pole such as the South and similar regions looks like an established reality or a likely probability for many observers.[8] Counteracting and overcoming fascism is also a realistic empirical possibility so long as its principal countervailing social forces, above all, liberalism and liberal democracy, persist and reaffirm themselves. In short, fascism as extreme anti-liberalism and anti-democracy comes to America post-2016, but liberal-democratic social forces may counter and ultimately overcome it, as they did in Europe after WW II.

In summary, this introduction diagnoses the resurgence and expansion of fascism in contemporary American and Western society. It specifically argues that fascism happened in America during post-2016 times contrary to some earlier observations and optimistic predictions that it did not and 'can't happen here'. Notably, it suggests that fascism arose as a dominant or salient ideology, political system and cultural climate in America's anti-liberal conservative and religious pole as opposed to its liberal and secular opposite. The introduction also draws parallels between these tendencies and the rise of fascism in interwar Europe, including Germany. It proposes that fascism happens in post-2016 America in many and various syndromes and means that replicate common fascist elements and properties since interwar Europe. It holds that fascism happens in post-2016 America as the aggregate effect of the existence and influence of certain social factors causing it to rise, expand, and dominate

---

8   For example, former US labor secretary Robert Reich warns in 2021 that the 'greatest danger we face today is not coming from China. It is our drift toward proto-fascism' in the form of 'Trumpism' within the Republican party and generally authoritarian conservatism. Similarly, according to the news media, a former Trump administration official stated in 2021 that the 'Republican party is the top national security threat to the US, as the party's rank-and-file lawmakers continue to support former President Donald Trump's baseless claims of election fraud that incited the Jan. 6 insurrection and use it as a rationale to impose voting restrictions.' Moreover, according to the reporting by the news media in 2021, the chairman of the Joint Chiefs of Staff Mark Milley 'had earlier described to aides that he kept having a stomach-churning feeling that some of the worrisome early stages of 20th-century fascism in Germany were replaying in 21st-century America. He saw parallels between Trump's rhetoric about election fraud and Adolf Hitler's insistence to his followers at the Nuremberg rallies that he was both a victim and their savior. "This is a Reichstag moment," Milley told aides. "The gospel of the Führer"'.

in the conservative-religious pole. It posits that these social causes of fascism in post-2016 America exist and operate in association and mutual reinforcement. In addition, the introduction points to the presence of certain countervailing social forces to fascism in post-2016 America. It suggests that fascism rises in post-2016 America because it attacks, discredits, and defeats these anti- and non-fascist social forces.

Consistent with these preliminary observations, the structure of this book is as follows. Following this introduction, Chapter 1 classifies and considers the essential elements and features of fascism. These elements are probably well-known, but their summary is useful because it relates to the diagnosis of fascism in post-2016 America and other contemporary societies. This diagnosis will examine whether and which of these elements of fascism reappear as resurgent fascist syndromes in post-2016 America and other societies. More specifically, Chapter 1 examines the following general fascist elements and features. They are, first, extreme conservatism or the radical right, second, extreme anti-liberalism, third and as a corollary, extreme anti-democracy, fourth, extreme anti-secularism, fifth, extreme irrationalism and anti-rationalism, sixth, extreme anti-egalitarianism, anti-universalism and anti-cosmopolitanism, including anti-globalism, seventh, a system of absolute rule, unconstrained power and domination, eighth, a system of encompassing and severe coercion, repression, violence and terror of society, ninth, extreme anti-pacifism, militarism, war and conquest in relation to other societies, and tenth, an aggregate of extreme conservative or radical-right authoritarian agents. The chapter suggests that these dimensions of fascism typically emerge, exist and operate in conjunction and mutual dependence and reinforcement. The purpose of the above classification and consideration is to see and assess whether and to what extent these elements and features of fascism reveal and replicate themselves in America and other contemporary societies during post-2016 and to some degree earlier times. The chapter then examines in more detail each one of the ten essential elements of fascism, starting with extreme conservatism or the radical right as an ideology and politics and ending with conservative or radical-right authoritarians as personalities.

Chapter 2 identifies fascism's syndromes and tendencies especially in post-2016 America. This identification connects and compares these indications of fascism in such a specific social space and time with its general elements considered previously. Thus, it helps ascertain whether and to what extent certain apparently fascist and generally authoritarian trends, events, and actors in post-2016 America reveal and replicate the essential components, properties, and figures of fascism. In other words, it explores if and how fascism rises and advances in America during post-2016 times by identifying and examining prevalent fascist syndromes in this setting and period. Specifically, Chapter 2 investigates the following syndromes of fascism in America post-2016. They are syndrome 1: fascism as extreme conservatism, syndrome 2: fascism as extreme anti-liberalism, syndrome 3: fascism as extreme anti-democracy, syndrome 4: fascism as extreme anti-secularism, syndrome 5: fascism as extreme irrationalism, anti-rationalism, and anti-progressivism, syndrome 6: fascism as extreme anti-egalitarianism, anti-universalism, and anti-cosmopolitanism, syndrome 7: fascism as absolute rule, power, and domination, syndrome 8: fascism as extreme coercion, repression, violence, and terror, syndrome 9: fascism as extreme anti-pacifism, militarism, offensive war, and conquest, syndrome 10: fascism as an aggregate of extreme authoritarian agents. The chapter infers that all these syndromes reveal and replicate the essentials of fascism in general considered in the previous chapter. They therefore prove that fascism indeed surges and expands in America post-2016, including after 2020, and to some degree earlier periods, such as the 1950s with McCarthyism, the 1980s with Reaganism, and the early 2010s with the Tea Party. In turn, these specific syndromes of fascism in America post-2016 usually exist and function in interconnection and reciprocal intensification, with some minor variations, just as do universal fascist elements and properties.

Chapter 3 identifies and examines the probable causes of the rise and advance of fascism in post-2016 America. It especially detects and focuses on authoritarian conservatism, coercive capitalism, extremist religion, and effective theocracy as the intertwined primary causes of fascism's resurgence in post-2016 America. Generally, this chapter examines why fascism rises in America post-2016 and earlier by exploring its social causes. It suggests that what caused fascism to rise in America post-2016 and before is a set of multiple societal, including ideological-political, economic, and cultural, factors. More specifically, Chapter 3 identifies the crucial social causes of fascism in, first and foremost, conservatism or the right, second, unfettered, coercive, and inegalitarian capitalism, third, ubiquitous repressive religion or religious extremism, and fourth, theocracy. It proposes that these crucial societal causes of fascism are typically interrelated and mutually reinforcing. The chapter infers that they form an integral chain of causation of fascism in post-2016 America and to some degree earlier times, as during the 1950s, the 1980s and the early 2010s. First, it identifies conservatism as the primary and perpetual ideological-political cause and hence predictor of fascism in post-2016 America, as is in other social settings and historical periods. Second, it finds that unrestrained, coercive and inegalitarian capitalism is the prime economic factor and driver of fascism in America post-2016 and to some degree earlier. Third, it uncovers ubiquitous repressive religion, especially religious extremism, as the cardinal cultural, spiritual cause or sanctification of fascism in America post-2016 and to some degree before. Fourth, it detects evangelical and other theocracy as a related cause or covariate, indeed religious equivalent, of fascism in America post-2016 and earlier times, as in other social settings and periods.

Chapter 4 explores, identifies, and examines countervailing social forces to fascism in post-2016 America and other contemporary societies. It classifies primary countervailing, anti-fascist social forces into liberalism, liberal democracy, secularism, rationalism, progressivism, egalitarianism, universalism, cosmopolitanism or globalism, pacifism or non-militarism, and liberal persons and groups in socio-psychological terms in American society and other societies. It considers whether and how these social forces can effectively counter and ultimately prevail over fascism in post-2016 America. The chapter proposes that such anti-fascist social forces typically emerge, exist, and operate in interaction and reciprocal reinforcement. Specifically, it suggests that especially liberalism interconnects with and mutually reinforces democracy, secularism, rationalism progressivism, egalitarianism, universalism, cosmopolitanism, pacifism, and liberal personalities. The chapter infers therefore that liberalism manifests the functioning of all other anti-fascist social forces and functions as the principal countervailing social power to fascism, as well as authoritarian conservatism and theocracy, in America post-2016 and earlier, as in other social contexts and historical periods since fascist Italy and Nazi Germany. Relatedly, it suggests that these countervailing anti-fascist forces are essentially non-conservative social processes and structures considering that fascism in America and everywhere else arises above all as the product or ally of conservatism, in conjunction and mutual reinforcement with unrestrained coercive capitalism, repressive religion and theocracy. The chapter thereby infers that anti-fascist social powers are essentially those societal processes, changes and institutions that overcome and supplant conservatism.

Chapter 5 constructs and elaborates a substantive composite index or approximation of fascism and generally conservative or right-wing authoritarianism whose components are fascist indicators and proxies. In addition, it calculates quantitative aggregate indexes or approximations of fascism and generally right-wing authoritarianism for Western and comparable societies such as OECD countries. This is an exercise in the operationalization and quantification of fascism or right-wing authoritarianism that is essentially a qualitative phenomenon, and hence a tentative estimation and proximate measurement rather than an exact calculation in this respect. The substantive composite index's components include specific indicators and proxies of fascism and broader right-wing authoritarianism that are obtained from or implicit in its main elements and features from the main body of the book.

For this purpose, these index components are classified into political, cultural, civil-society and economic indicators and proxies of fascism and more broadly right-wing authoritarianism. The results show Western and similar societies with the highest, lowest, and intermediate aggregate indexes of fascism or right-wing authoritarianism. The results provide suggestive evidence that fascism or right-wing authoritarianism indeed rises and advances in America post-2016 through a fascist-style radical-right autocracy and to some extent earlier, but not in most other Western societies, especially Western Europe and within it most notably Scandinavia. The chapter also incorporates an Appendix on the US's military expenditure and its societal consequences.

The final part of the book constitutes a conclusion. It offers tentative predictions[9] about the future of America in terms of democracy and free society considering the rise, advance, and potential perpetuation of fascism that conservatism generates and sustains in conjunction with coercive capitalism, religion, and theocracy in this and other contemporary Western and comparable societies. On one hand, it predicts that the future of America in respect of democracy and free society looks bleak and hopeless post-2016 and even post-2020 because of the explosion, contagion, dominance, and obstinacy of fascism. Furthermore, it posits that the future of democratic America appears bleak overall because fascism not only did happen post-2016 but it threatens to continue happening in America by recurring, persisting, solidifying, and expanding in the foreseeable future or in short to medium terms, as through the 2030s. More broadly, the chapter proposes that the prospect of democratic America currently looks dark and dim so long as the crucial causes and predictors of fascism persist, dominate, and operate, thus causing fascist reproduction in at least one of the two overarching poles of modern American society. Therefore, it infers that the future of America in democratic, freedom terms looks at this point bleak and irremediable so long as the compound of conservatism, unfettered capitalism, religion, and theocracy persists, prevails, and functions and hence reproduces fascism in at least one pole of current American society, namely 'conservative-religious America.' On the other hand, the chapter predicts that democratic and free America's future appears less dark and gloomy and instead brighter and more joyous so long as fascism does

---

9   This is a book of an observer and outsider rather than a participant and insider, without any ideological, political, and party affiliation, association, interest, and investment. This ensures a necessary degree of impartiality and neutrality according to the Weberian ideal of value-free scientific analysis, although it may be difficult and even impossible to remain totally neutral when considering a phenomenon that is an ultimate, lethal danger to human liberty, dignity, wellbeing, and life.

not happen again or recur continuously in the foreseeable future because of its countervailing social powers surviving and reasserting themselves over their fascist and broader conservative opposites. Consequently, it infers that the future of democratic and free America looks less bleak and relatively bright so long as the complex of liberalism, liberal democracy, secularism, rationalism and progressivism, egalitarianism, universalism and cosmopolitanism or globalism, pacifism or non-militarism, and liberal persons and groups survives, functions, and prevails over fascism and broader conservatism and other fascist causes.

What Happened? Essential Elements of Fascism

This chapter classifies fascism's essential elements into ten for convenience. They include, first, extreme conservatism or the radical right, second, extreme anti-liberalism, third and as a corollary, extreme anti-democracy, fourth, extreme anti-secularism, fifth, extreme irrationalism and anti-rationalism, sixth, extreme anti-egalitarianism, anti-universalism, and anti-cosmopolitanism, including anti-globalism, seventh, a system of absolute rule, unconstrained power, and encompassing domination, eighth, a system of severe coercion, repression, violence, and terror of society, ninth, extreme anti-pacifism, militarism, war, and conquest in relation to other societies, and tenth, an aggregate of extreme conservative or radical-right authoritarian agents (see Table 1.1).

These dimensions of fascism typically emerge, exist, and operate in conjunction and mutual dependence and reinforcement, with some variations. The purpose of this classification and consideration is to assess whether and what extent these elements and features of fascism reveal and replicate themselves in America during post-2016 and to some degree earlier times. The following examines in more detail fascism's ten essential elements.

1   Extreme Conservatism

Fascism is invariably a species of extreme, radical conservatism. In other words, fascism is an invariant form of the extreme, radical right. Hence, fascism is universally an extreme conservative, radical-right ideology, social movement, political regime, and cultural ambiance.[1] Fascists are thus everywhere and

---

1   Witnessing the rise of interwar German and other fascism, Mannheim suggests that the latter is basically a species of conservatism in several respects—irrationalism, Machiavellianism, anti-liberalism, and so anti-democracy. Mannheim (1936, pp. 134–5) observes that fascism inherits 'complete irrationalism', even if making it of a somewhat different 'kind', from conservatism. In addition, Mannheim (1936, pp. 140, 230) notes that the fascist theory of politics 'has its roots in Machiavelli, who already laid down its fundamental tenets', and that conservatism is the 'ideology of absolutism' that applies the 'technique of domination' in the style of 'Machiavellianism'. Further, Mannheim (1986, p. 91) states that conservatism attacks the liberal 'principle of liberty upon which [freedom] rests', as it does democracy, and suggests that fascism follows such a conservative-style attack. As a personal note, Mannheim implies a continuity and near-equivalence between the Bavaria pre-Nazi conservative ministry and

TABLE 1.1   Essential elements and features of fascism

---

1   Extreme conservatism, the radical right
     extreme conservative, radical right ideology, movement, regime and
     zeitgeist
     extreme conservative authoritarianism, totalitarianism of conservatism
     radical-right dictatorship, including autocracy, within the broader family
     of authoritarian rightism destination of conservatism
2   Extreme anti-liberalism
     extreme anti-liberal ideology, movement, regime and zeitgeist in an
     extremely conservative, radical-right variant ultimate antithesis and
     lethal poison of liberal modernity, most extreme form of anti-liberalism
     genocide and social hatred versus liberals anti-liberal nihilism and
     societal self-destruction—extreme form of antagonism to and
     destruction of universal liberty, equality, justice and inclusion
3   Extreme anti-democracy
     extreme anti-democratic ideology, movement, regime and zeitgeist in a
     conservative, radical-right version
     most extreme variation of anti-democracy—extremely intense and
     implacable antagonism and nihilism toward liberal democracy
     negation and suppression of political freedoms and rights—voting
     rights, electoral freedom, right to seek and hold power, pluralism, voice,
     open government, etc.
     subversive, putschist anti-democratic ideology and movement, extreme
     Machiavellianism in the function of seizing power
     history as the circulation of elites and elite dictatorship—state of
     nature/anarchy for fascists and conservatives, Leviathan for liberal-
     democrats and non-fascists
4   Extreme anti-secularism
     extreme anti-secular ideology, movement, regime and zeitgeist
     elimination or perversion of secular democracy, for example, the
     differentiation between religion and politics or the separation of church
     and state religious extremism extreme and coercive or socially controlled
     religiosity, merger or linkage with theocracy, theocracy as prototypical
     fascism

---

government 'opposing the grant of citizenship' to such 'foreign bodies', 'alien in culture' as
Karl Mannheim himself (born in Hungary) and Nazism, including 'Hitler's designation as
[German] Chancellor', as Kettler and Meja (1984, pp. 76, 82) suggest.

TABLE 1.1   Essential elements and features of fascism (*cont.*)

5   Extreme irrationalism, anti-rationalism and anti-progressivism
    extreme irrational, anti-rational and anti-progressive ideology,
    movement, regime and zeitgeist
      most complete irrationalism, anti-rationalism and anti-progressivism
      religious and other superstitions, fanaticism and fantasies
      extreme anti-science, anti-art, anti-theory antagonism and
      anti-intellectualism
6   Extreme economic and social anti-egalitarianism, anti-universalism, and
    anti-cosmopolitanism
      extreme economic and social anti-egalitarian, anti-universalist, and anti-
      cosmopolitan, including anti-globalist, ideology, movement, regime and
      zeitgeist
      extreme economic and social inequality, rigid hierarchy, particularism,
      elitism, monopolistic closure, and exclusion within society and in
      relation to other societies
      economic inequalities, closure, deprivation and exclusion—extreme
      wealth concentration, income inequality, material degradation, poverty,
      work hardship, lack of economic-social protection
      extreme conservative aggressive nationalism, nativism, social hatred,
      xenophobia
      economic nationalism, protectionism and irrationalism.
      conservative master-race and master-caste racism
7   Absolutism through absolute rule, power and domination
      ideology and regime of absolute rule and control, total, unconstrained
      and arbitrary maximum power and all-embracing control and
      domination through autocracy, dynasty, oligarchy and other dictatorship
      conjunction of absolutism with Machiavellianism—absolute autocratic
      or oligarchic and plutocratic rule of Machiavellian fascist leaders
      legal arbitrariness, insecurity, and lawlessness, uncontrolled corruption
      and other criminality
      institutional nihilism or radicalism, counterrevolution, conservative anti-
      institutionalist, anti-system populism
8   Extreme coercion, repression, violence and terror
      ideology, movement and regime of total and severe state coercion and
      repression of society, combined with populist deception, misinformation
      and manipulation
      systematic, all-embracing and intense violence and terror—non-
      peaceful conflict resolution in society

TABLE 1.1   Essential elements and features of fascism (*cont.*)

---

   pro-capital and anti-labor coercion, repression, violence and terror,
   including mass murder
   mass imprisonment, indefinite detention, torture, and widespread death
   sentences and executions of lower classes
9 Extreme anti-pacifism, militarism, offensive war and conquest.
   extreme ideology and system of anti-pacifism and militarism—
   continuation and intensification to conservatism's anti-pacifism and
   militarism
   extreme rearmament, arms races and preparation for offensive war
   through exorbitant military expenditure, militarist mobilization and a
   large standing army
   aggressive wars against and imperial conquest and subjugation of other
   societies
   mass death, destruction and self-destruction
10 Aggregate of extreme authoritarian personalities
   collection of extreme authoritarian leaders and the rank-and-file (base)
   extreme sadism and masochism, sadistic-masochistic character
   structures
   mix of grave seriousness and utter grotesqueness
   cult of autocratic leaders by the fascist rank-and-file in combination with
   illusions, delusions, fantasies and fictions and collective suicide

---

always extremist conservatives or allying and blending with them within a broader family of conservatism, simply radical rightists.

Fascism is essentially conservatism, the right at its most intense level or its ultimate point and destination, so fascists are conservatives or rightists turned into extremists or radicals. This makes non-conservative, non-right fascism and non-rightist fascists a non-sequitur and empirical fiction that conservatism creates and sustains to obscure its reproduction of and affinity,[2]

---

2 Parsons (1949, p. 268) states that Nazism was a radical version of 'Prussian conservatism' as a proxy 'official ideology' in old Germany and thus the 'institutionalization of the conservative patterns' in the latter. Lipset (1955, p. 204) characterizes Fascism as an 'extreme version of conservatism', registers that fascism and right authoritarianism 'have received their backing' from conservatives, and predicts that 'under certain conditions part of the conservative group will become Fascists.' Dahrendorf (1979, p. 96) notes that 'there is an extreme version' of conservatism in the form of fascism. Bourdieu (1998, p. 35) characterizes fascist revolutions as 'conservative revolutions, [including] that in Germany in the 1930s', and fascists as

alliance,[3] and eventual merger with fascism. Fascism is what it is precisely because it invariantly constitutes consummate conservatism or the consummation of the right. Fascists are what they are because they are always conservative extremists or rightist radicals, and conversely, extreme conservatives or radical rightists intrinsically are or eventually become fascists.

Therefore, identifying and observing extreme conservatism or the radical right predicts the identification of fascism—whenever and wherever the first exists and prevails, so will eventually the second as a rule, with minor exceptions or secondary variations. This characterization therefore does complete conceptual justice to fascism whose core is universally conservatism or the right, while any attempts to characterize it in non-conservative, non-rightist terms misconstrue it and define a different, non-fascist phenomenon. In this sense, the conceptualization and definition of fascism stands or falls with conceptualizing and defining it in terms of conservatism/the right or otherwise.

The preceding need be reiterated and emphasized because especially postwar American conservatism or the right by deception or delusion denies and hides the generalized fact that fascism, including, Nazism, is invariably extreme

---

the 'conservative revolutionaries of the 1930s'. Paxton (1998, p. 7) recounts that 'early fascist ideas helped amplify the disrepute of the liberal values to which the broad middle classes had largely adhered before World War I. But it is only by distancing themselves from those elements of the early radical programs that were threatening to conservatives that certain fascist movements have been able to gain and exercise power.' Ferguson and Voth (2008, p. 15) observe that 'promising a broad coalition of the right, Hitler was appointed as head of government by the President on January 30, 1933.'

3   Paxton (1998, p. 16) finds that the 'success of fascist movements in assembling new, broad catch-all parties that attract a mass following across classes and hence seem attractive allies to conservatives looking for ways to perpetuate their shaken rule. At later stages, successful fascist parties prove adept at the formation, maintenance, and domination of political coalitions with conservatives. The only route to power available to fascists passes through cooperation with conservative elites. The most important variables, therefore, are the conservative elites' willingness to work with the fascists (along with a reciprocal flexibility on the part of the fascist leaders) and the depth of the crisis that induces them to cooperate.' Paxton (1998, pp. 16–17) illustrates that Hitler and Mussolini 'each was invited to take office as head of government by a head of state in the legitimate exercise of his official functions, on the advice of his conservative counselors, under quite precise circumstances: a deadlock of constitutional government (produced in part by the polarization that the fascists abetted); conservative leaders who felt threatened by the loss of their capacity to keep the population under control at a moment of massive popular mobilization [and who felt] unable to continue to rule without further reinforcement [by fascists]' (see also Paxton 2004). Acemoglu et al. (2022, p. 1245) recount that 'in late October 1922, Mussolini organized a march on Rome, which gathered about 25,000 black shirts. Prime Minister Luigi Facta wanted to send the troops to stop them, but King Victor Emmanuel III did not agree, and Facta resigned. On October 29, 1922, the king asked Mussolini to form a new government and assemble a right-wing coalition'.

conservatism or the radical right, and thus purifies it from any conservative-rightist features. As a result of conservative deceptions, most Americans do not seem aware that fascism, including Nazism, is fundamentally a conservative, rightist phenomenon and do not suspect that conservatism, a dominant American ideology since the 1980s, is the universal fascist core, in contrast to Europeans who know well this notorious fact since the 1920–30s.

1.1   *Fascism as Conservative Totalitarianism*

As a corollary, fascism is invariantly extreme conservative authoritarianism,[4] more accurately, conservatism's totalitarianism. In other words, it is radical-right dictatorship, including autocracy, dynasty, and oligarchy. Fascists are everywhere and always extreme conservative authoritarians, more precisely, totalitarians within the broader framework of conservatism, or radical-rightist dictators and rank-and-file members, including autocratic leaders and followers, arising, persisting, and perishing in the extended family of authoritarian rightism.[5] Fascism embraces and takes the inherent or latent medieval-rooted authoritarianism of conservatism[6] to the extreme to make it explicit

---

4   Dewey (1940) notes that fascism and generally authoritarianism connoted a 'dictatorial system of the type of the German or Italian one', adding that the 'German system in particular [is] Nazism.'

5   Lipset (1955, p. 184) observes that 'Fascism was a rightist movement [reflecting] conservative forces.' Giddens (1979, p. 144) suggests that fascism is 'right totalitarianism' and a 'type of system degeneration' in modern capitalism. Mann (2004, p. 237) finds that interwar 'fascism diffused widely–not only as a distinct movement, but also as a corrosive radical force within more conservative authoritarian regimes. For authoritarians here remained through the interwar period as a fractious family whose reactionary [conservative], corporatist [capitalist], and fascist members struggled noisily for overall dominance.' Mann (2004, p. 353) infers that fascism was part of the 'forward surge of a broader family of authoritarian rightists who swept into power across one-half of interwar Europe, plus a few swaths in the rest of the world. In Europe the surge carried regimes further across the spectrum, from semi-authoritarianism to semi-reactionary and thence to corporatist. A few then went further, to fascism.' Brouwer (1998) alerts to the 'similarities' between the New Right in America and the European 'Conservative Revolutionaries' of the early 1900s who were instrumental in the rise of fascism, by being, first, extreme nationalistic, patriotic, and authoritarian, second, anti-secular and anti-humanist inspired by revived traditional religion, and third anti-liberal and attempting to restore ancient morality.

6   Michels (1968, p. 11) suggests that conservatism is inherently authoritarianism in that he identifies the 'conservative spirit of the old master-caste', adding that 'however deeply rooted it may be, is forced to assume, at least during times of election, a specious democratic mask.' Miliband (1969, pp. 265–72) observes that 'capitalist societies are subject to strains and their inability to resolve these strains makes their evolution towards conservative authoritarianism more rather than less likely [i.e.] the transition from 'bourgeois democracy' to conservative authoritarianism.' Dahrendorf (1979, p. 98) identifies the inherently

conservative totalitarianism[7] as its maximal intensification. In brief, fascism brings radical-right intrinsic authoritarianism to the conclusion in the form of dictatorship, including autocracy. Fascists always and everywhere adopt and carry conservatives' inner authoritarianism to the ultimate point of totalitarianism or adopt and take radical rightists' innate authoritarian tendencies to the final stage of dictatorship.

Fascism and conservatism therefore differ in different quantities or statistical-like degrees of unfreedom rather than in substance, namely freedom versus unfreedom. Specifically, this is the quantitative difference between higher and lower degrees of unfreedom in totalitarianism and authoritarianism.[8] It is not a qualitative difference between different qualities, such as unfreedom in fascism and the opposite in American conservatism that de facto eliminates freedom and liberal democracy in the name of 'freedom' and 'democracy' via 'holy' war against 'un-American' liberalism and thus admits

---

'conservative-authoritarian movement by way of law-and-order slogans' as among 'collectivist threats' to developed democratic societies. Dahrendorf (1979, p. 103) elaborates that 'right conservatism has elements of social and political control which do not even stop short of freedom of the press, and general praise for the good old values of authority, discipline, order, punishment [and so] finds itself in a position of confrontation with prevailing conditions.' Kinloch (1981, pp. 20–2) detects conservatism's inherent authoritarianism observing that it 'reacts to societal confusion by attempting to maintain or restore the old order by imposing social conformity, resulting in authoritarian political arrangements.' Bourdieu (1984, p. 366) remarks that 'old-style conservatism [is] based on an overtly authoritarian image of the hierarchical relations between the classes, generations or sexes.'

7   Horkheimer and Adorno (1993, p. 152) remark that fascism is 'also totalitarian in seeking to place oppressed nature's rebellion against domination directly in the service of domination.'

8   Habermas (1975, p. 12) distinguishes a 'conservative-authoritarian welfare state that reduces political participation of citizens to a harmless level' and 'a fascist-authoritarian state that holds the population by the bit at a relatively high level of permanent mobilization without having to overdraw its account through welfare-state measures.' This distinction is essentially identical to that between conservative authoritarianism and fascist totalitarianism or hyper-authoritarianism. Giddens (1981, p. 5) proposes that the 'concentration of surveillance activities of the state in modern times is the chief basis of the looming threat of totalitarianism [as] distinguished from the 'despotism' of non-capitalist states.' Giddens (1991, p. 8) elaborates that fascist and any 'totalitarianism is distinct from traditional despotism, but is all the more frightening as a result. Totalitarian rule connects political, military, and ideological power in more concentrated form than was ever possible before the emergence of modern nation-states.' Riley and Fernández (2014, p. 433) state that dictatorships are 'all nonliberal democratic regimes' and that types of dictatorship include 'totalitarian or authoritarian', invoking Italy (1922–43) as a 'key empirical example of totalitarianism, and Spain (1939–75) [for] authoritarianism.'

that the latter is the ideal of universal liberty.[9] In short, the difference between fascism and conservatism is equivalent to that between rightist totalitarianism and right authoritarianism, which is what fascism and conservatism intrinsically are, respectively.

In this context, it is more accurate or precise to designate and consider fascism as rightist, conservative totalitarianism rather than just right authoritarianism because the latter is what conservatism intrinsically and persistently is since its emergence in France/Europe in vehement revolt against the Enlightenment and French Revolution through the 2020s and likely will remain, especially in the anti-liberal pole of America. Conversely, designating and considering fascism as right authoritarianism lacks accuracy, precision, or specificity so long as this conflates it with inherently authoritarian conservatism instead of treating it as the extreme variation of the latter through conservative, rightist totalitarianism. (If the book occasionally describes fascism as or links it with 'right authoritarianism', this is for conventional purposes or convenience.) Such a designation does not do full conceptual justice to the right-totalitarian nature and closure of fascism insofar as authoritarianism features lower quantitative degrees of unfreedom or less severe control, coercion, and oppression than totalitarianism. Since conservative and any totalitarianism is the extreme variant of authoritarianism, this characterization of fascism is consistent with characterizing it as extreme conservatism. While being extreme conservatism, fascism is conservative totalitarianism, and not just authoritarianism which conservatism originally is and continuously remains in Europe, America, and beyond from the late 18th to the early 21st century.

1.2   *Fascism as the Destination of Conservatism*
Therefore, fascism is ultimately the destination, last phase, culmination, and in that sense vanishing act of conservatism that allies, associates,[10] and eventually merges with, and in that sense vanishes in fascism which occasionally

---

9   Mannheim (1986, p. 91) considers liberalism the 'principle of liberty upon which [freedom] rests', observing that conservatism assaults this principle and thus arises as and constitutes vehement anti-liberalism.

10   Paxton (1998, p. 18; also 2004) infers that the 'fascist leaders who have reached power, historically, have been condemned to govern in association with the conservative elites who had opened the gates to them'—and often literally, as German conservatives did to the Nazis and their US counterparts to neo-Nazis post-2016, including opening the gates of Congress in one way or another to the January 6, 2021 fascist insurrection. Further, Paxton (2004, p. 68) suggest that the '[Nazi] movement might have ended as a footnote to history had it not been saved in the opening days of 1933 by conservative politicians who wanted to pilfer its following and use its political muscle for their own purposes.'

subdues[11] or assimilates it by rendering it from intrinsically authoritarian into overtly totalitarian—simply, fascist. In turn, the origin of conservatism is medievalism, namely the medieval compound of feudal bondage,[12] monarchy, aristocracy, and theocracy, and in that sense the Dark Middle Ages that it seeks to retrieve from the 'dead past'[13] and perpetuate in revolt against liberal modernity, such as the rationalistic Enlightenment and the democratic French Revolution,[14] just as the conservative offspring fascism, notably Nazism, does. To that extent, conservatism originates in medievalism and feudalism and ends in fascism, including Nazism, linking the old and new dark ages.

---

11   Brown (1987) reports that in Germany's 'realigning' election of July 1932, electoral support for non-Catholic 'moderate' parties moved to the extreme rightist parties such as the Nazis, which implicitly defines Nazism and thus fascism generally as extremist rightism/conservatism. Blinkhorn (2003, p. 13) notes that in Nazi Germany the 'conservative right [came] close to being devoured by the [fascist] tiger it had chosen to ride.' Barnett and Woywode (2004, pp. 1490–91) imply this for Austria reporting that in Vienna during 1918–38, the 'environment of political opportunity shifted in such a way as to give apparent support for the claims of the extreme right [and] the Austrian right wing remained extreme and unaccommodating throughout the period. As political, social, and economic developments worked to give credibility to the claims of the right, however, the right-wing's approach came into favor. Under these circumstances, victories by the right came at the expense of their [conservative] ideological neighbor.' Hitchens (2009, p. 81) recounts that the 'extreme right-wing military coup in Hungary, led by Admiral Horthy, was warmly endorsed by the church, as were similar fascistic movements in Slovakia and Austria.' Acemoglu et al. (2022, p. 1234) suggest that in Italy the 'support of the traditional right' formed the 'basis of fascist success after 1920', together with the 'military organization of a political party [as] the novelty of Fascism.' Acemoglu et al. (2022, pp. 1235–36) find that in Italy by 1924, 'a significant fraction of the right-wing and center-right vote shifted to the Fascist Party [and so] the consolidation of right-wing and center-right votes under the auspices of the Fascist Party.' Acemoglu et al. (2022, pp. 1245–46) add that once in power Mussolini incorporated 'fascist paramilitary organizations into the state apparatus [while] dissolving all remaining socialist local councils, [securing] most right-wing support in fascist hands, [and co-opting] the center-right.'

12   Noakes (2003, p. 81) points to the 'neo-feudalism of the Young Conservatives' as a branch of the 'revolutionary conservative' movement in interwar Germany, which generally holds true for most conservatives in this and other European countries, as well as the US, especially the South.

13   Mannheim (1936, p. 108) uses the phrase 'a flight into the security of a dead past' primarily with reference to conservatism, including fascism. Also, Keynesian economist Harrod (1956) adopts the expression the 'dead hand of the past' by implicit reference to conservatism or orthodox economics.

14   Mannheim (1986, p. 83) states that modern conservatism differs from traditionalism in general in that the first 'is a function of one particular historical and sociological situation [i.e., negative] reaction to the Enlightenment and the French Revolution.'

Accordingly, fascism, including Nazism, constitutes the 'new', reinvented, and definitive conservatism, thus the ultimate form of conservative counter-revolution against liberal-democratic revolutions and institutions.[15] In other words, fascism is the complete implementation and absolute rule of the radical right. Fascists are everywhere the last remaining, 'new', 'only true' conservatives or radical rightists who submerge others, especially moderates who are otherwise a rare species within conservatism as inherent authoritarianism or in the authoritarian right. It follows that fascism is conservative, rightist totalitarianism because of being extreme conservatism or the radical right. Fascism adopts and brings conservatism's intrinsic authoritarianism inherited from medievalism to the extreme and closure of totalitarianism, which affirms that the difference between fascist and conservative regimes is in degrees of unfreedom rather than in substance.

The above ought to be reiterated and emphasized because American conservatism or the right distorts and disguises through its typical deceptions and delusions the core and reality of fascism, including, Nazism, as invariantly conservative, rightist totalitarianism. Subjected to such distortions and deceptions by conservatism, most Americans do not seem cognizant or appreciative of the fact that fascism, including Nazism, is universally conservative, rightist totalitarianism unlike Europeans who know or appreciate this moment well. Relatedly, by its 'freedom' deceptions and delusions conservatism denies and hides—inflicting most Americans with ignorance rationalized as the 'all-American' resistance to 'un-American' liberalism according to McCarthyism and Reaganism—that fascism inherits and intensifies conservatism's intrinsic medieval-rooted authoritarianism[16] in the form of conservative totalitarianism

---

15   Bourdieu (1998, p. 35) observes that 'it is characteristic of conservative revolutions, [including] that in Germany in the 1930s [etc.], that they present restorations as revolutions.' Manent (1998, p. 218) points to the conservative 'partisans of an antidemocratic regime, whose enmity climaxed in the Nazi challenge that was decisively disposed of in Dresden's and Berlin's fire and rubble.' Hodgson (2002, pp. xiii) refers to the 'rubble of fascism and war.' Noakes (2003, p. 81) suggests that the 'revolutionary conservative' movement [including the 'Young Conservatives'] in Germany advocating 'a conservative revolution on such a scale as the history of Europe has never known' regarded Nazism as such a revolution and so a 'new Conservatism.' Noakes (2003, p. 81) cites a German conservative's statement that the 'mass rule' of liberal democracy must be 'overcome by a new Conservatism, freedom by integration, leadership and subordination, with rights according to achievement, the inequality of men, hierarchy and order', notably that the Nazis had the 'historic honour of having liquidated the [Weimar democratic Republic], such a tremendous feat that the gratitude of the Conservatives is assured'.

16   Berlin (1990a, p. 5) proposes that early conservative philosopher Maistre's 'famous, terrible vision of life [i.e.] violent preoccupation with blood and death [has] an affinity with the paranoiac world of modern fascism, which it is startling to find so early in the nineteenth

or right dictatorship, including autocracy and oligarchy. (In turn, fascism in Europe and America coopts conservatism's 'freedom' and 'liberty' deceptions and delusions by forming 'Freedom' Parties, 'Freedom' Caucuses, 'Liberty' Universities, etc.) And this process is what Americans are precisely witnessing and those in the conservative-religious pole of America joining and rejoicing post-2016 and Europeans, including Germans, witnessed in respect of their conservatism and fascism during the 1920–30s.

2   Extreme Anti-liberalism

Second and as a corollary of being extremist conservatism and conservative, rightist totalitarianism or dictatorship, fascism is invariably a species of extreme anti-liberalism. Alternatively, fascism is extreme anti-liberalism in the special form of extremist conservatism as a vehemently anti-liberal[17] entity and of conservative totalitarianism as the destructive antithesis of liberalism[18]

---

century.' Berlin elaborates that Maistre's is 'not authoritarianism [but] approaching the worlds of the German ultra-nationalists, of the enemies of the Enlightenment, of Nietzsche, Sorel and Pareto, [etc.] *Blut und Boden*, far beyond traditional authoritarianism.' Generally, Berlin observes that conservatism's 'great counterrevolutionary movement' against the Enlightenment and the French Revolution 'culminated in fascism'. Hence, by identifying the distant origins of fascism in Maistre Berlin implicitly uncovers its origin in early conservatism. Berlin (1990b, p. 1) elaborates that Maistre's political theory is a 'dominant influence on reactionary, obscurantist, and, in the end, fascist ideas in the years that followed [his] violent hatred of free traffic in ideas, and his contempt for all intellectuals' both 'echoes the fanatical voices of the Inquisition and sounds what is perhaps the earliest note of the militant antirational fascism of modern times.'

17   Mannheim (1936, p. 234) observes that conservatism defines liberalism 'translated into rationalistic terms' as its 'immediate antagonist'. He elaborates that at the outset conservatism is 'nothing more than traditionalism become self-reflective' in vehement opposition to emergent liberalism (Mannheim 1986, p. 88). Kettler and Meja (1984, pp. 76–78) comment that Mannheim shows 'intellectual and social affinities' between '[German] conservatism and the anti-liberal aristocracy' and that conservatism is originally rooted 'in strata hostile to capitalist and liberal rationalism'. Esping-Andersen (1990, p. 40) finds that in Germany under Bismarck and Austria—two future Nazi-ruled societies—conservatism's 'ulterior motives [in granting social welfare rights] were social integration, the preservation of authority, and the battle against socialism [while] also motivated by an equally strong opposition to individualism and liberalism.'

18   Dahrendorf (1979, p. 96) states that as an 'extreme version' of conservatism, fascism, 'is at the opposite end of the scale of political attitudes from liberalism.' Brouwer (1998) remarks that the New Right in America and the European 'Conservative Revolutionaries' of the early 1900s leading to fascism both were 'anti-liberal.' Paxton (1998, p. 9) describes fascist regimes as 'hard, violent, antiliberal and antisocialist nationalist dictatorships.' Paxton (1998, p. 16–17) notes that while neither took power by force, both Mussolini and

and more broadly modernism. In short, fascism is the ultimate enemy and lethal poison of liberal modernity and its ideal of liberty and democracy of which conservatism is the original and perpetual antagonist.

Hence, fascism is universally and unconditionally an extreme anti-liberal ideology, social movement, political regime, and cultural zeitgeist specifically in an extremely conservative, radical-right variant.[19] Fascists are everywhere and always extremist anti-liberals concretely in the conservative, radical-right face. Moreover, fascism is the most extreme form of anti-liberalism among all forms of the latter, and fascists are the most radical group of anti-liberals of all anti-liberal groups. In other words, fascism is the most intense anti-liberal extremism and fascists foremost anti-liberal extremists. Not every anti-liberalism is fascist and more broadly conservative, but all fascism is extreme anti-liberalism, as is generally conservatism with secondary variations and minor exceptions like 'moderate' conservatives becoming an extinct or rare species especially in America since 2016 and before.

Conversely, the label 'liberal' fascism and fascists is a logical non sequitur and empirical fiction that especially American conservatism, ever-eager to disguise the conservative-fascist attraction, link, and eventual osmosis, creates in that it attributes 'fascism' to 'un-American' liberalism. American conservatism condemns liberalism as supposedly harboring 'fascist' intentions and tendencies through liberal democracy—as if, in conservative minds, fascism and the latter were the same—secularism, rationalism, progressivism, egalitarianism,

---

Hitler 'used force earlier to destablize the liberal regime and later to transform their governments into dictatorships' (see also Paxton 2004). Boltanski and Chiapello (2005, p. XL) propose that some social groups in Europe (small employers, self-employed people occupants of intermediate posts in firms) 'regarded fascism as the sole bastion against the excesses of liberalism in the second half of the 1930s.' Habermas (2001, pp. 44) distinguishes conservative-fascist and other 'forces of totalitarianism and their liberal enemies.' Berezin (2019, p. 348) suggests that 'fascism, in contrast to liberalism, which draws a sharp boundary between public and private spheres, demands a fusion of the two spheres in the fascist or corporate state.'

19 Noakes (2003, p. 81) notes that in Germany the 'revolutionary conservative' movement's members 'shared two broad convictions: hostility to the Weimar Republic and what they saw as the hegemony of liberalism, by which they meant the secular, rational, moral tradition of the West; and a vision of national redemption through a new 'Third' Reich containing a new post-bourgeois order.' Noakes (2003, p. 81) adds that 'whilst also differing in the extent of their sympathy for Nazism, all [conservatives] welcomed the political energies which it had unleashed against the Republic.' Acemoglu et al. (2022, p. 1243) confirm that in Italy fascist violent 'antisocialist actions gained the approval and support of many conservatives.' Overall, Acemoglu et al. (2022, p. 1245) recount that Italian conservatives during the early 1920s sought to form 'a unified conservative and nationalist coalition, including the fascists.'

universalism, cosmopolitanism, pacifism, and liberals as personalities. As they stand, all these supposed 'fascist' properties are polar opposites to fascism that invariably condemns and eliminates them, including liberal democracy, as the typical features of liberalism, just as does conservatism originally. Universally, when fascism appears and prevails, it immediately attacks and eradicates liberalism,[20] while arising as the 'new', 'true' conservatism or allying and merging with, by subduing or assimilating, preexisting conservatism. Fascists always and everywhere know what their principal antidote and adversary, and conversely their main source and support are—liberalism and conservatism, respectively—and act accordingly and consistently.

As a result, while its positive connotation being extreme conservatism or the radical right, the negative sociological designation of fascism is ultimate anti-liberalism or anti-liberal extremism. While fascists' positive identification is extremist conservatives or radical rightists, their negative designation is extreme anti-liberals or anti-liberal extremists, thus never being non-conservatives or non-rightists and liberals, contrary to American conservatism's deceptive or delusionary assertions. While not all anti-liberals are fascists and generally conservatives, fascists are always anti-liberals, as are most conservatives, aside from rare or rarifying exceptions such as conservative 'moderates' especially in America since 2016.

2.1   *Fascism, Conservatism, and Liberalism*

Fascism inherits and carries the original vehement anti-liberalism of conservatism[21] or the right to the limit to make it the most extreme and utterly implacable. Fascists emulate and intensify conservatives' or rightists' inner, strong, and persistent anti-liberal propensities to become the most extremist anti-liberals

---

20   Paxton (1998, p. 6; also, 2004, p. 41) includes in the 'mobilizing passions' of fascism 'dread of the group's decadence under the corrosive effect of individualistic and cosmopolitan liberalism.' He elaborates that early fascism 'helped amplify the disrepute of the liberal values' that prevailed before World War I, though it succeeded to take and exert power only by rejecting those liberal (or radical) program elements that were 'threatening to conservatives' (Paxton 1998, p. 7). Overall, Paxton (2004, pp. 39–42) notes 'fascism's rivals, the previously ascendant bourgeois liberalism and the powerful reformist socialism of pre-1914 Europe,' with fascism standing 'against liberal individualism and constitutionalism and against Leftist class struggle [as] a mass movement directed against the Left.'

21   Paxton (2004, p. 32) observes that 'deeper preconditions of fascism lay in the late-nineteenth century [conservative] revolt against the dominant liberal faith in individual liberty, reason, natural human harmony, and progress. Well before 1914 newly stylish anti-liberal values, more aggressive nationalism and racism, and a new aesthetic of instinct and violence began to furnish an intellectual-cultural humus in which fascism could germinate.'

within the extended family of conservatism or the right and beyond. Fascism follows, perpetuates, and escalates conservatism that develops, functions, and remains as fervent and uncompromising anti-liberalism by arising in vehement and violent revolt against emergent liberalism and modernism beginning with the Enlightenment and its product the French Revolution. As in most respects, with respect to anti-liberalism, fascism imitates and exceeds, emulates and escalates conservatism in that it does the same but doing so to the extreme point of no return, by intensifying conservative intrinsic authoritarianism into right totalitarianism[22] as the ultimate, most effective means of eradicating liberalism and so the ideal of liberty. Fascists behave as and surpass conservatives or rightists in relation to liberals in that they act to the latter in the same manner but extremely so without bounds by moving from the conservative authoritarian repression to the right totalitarian persecution and destruction of liberal forces and institutions as 'anti-German', 'un-American', and so on.

Fascism is extreme anti-liberalism in that it, following and escalating anti-liberal conservatism, defines, attacks, and seeks to destroy liberalism that it identifies as its perceived antidote and main adversary within Western society. Fascists are the most radical anti-liberals by, while emulating and intensifying conservatives' anti-liberal proclivities, targeting and persecuting liberals whom they identity as their chief opponents among Western societies. Moreover, following conservatism, fascism negates the legitimacy and right of coexistence, let alone ideological, political, and cultural competition, of liberalism by denouncing and attacking it as the 'enemy' of the people,

---

22   Paxton (2004, p. 11) states that 'one cannot consider fascism simply a more muscular form of conservatism, even if it maintained the existing regime of property and social hierarchy.' However, as the later part of the statement implies, Paxton (2004, p. 22) suggests that fascism essentially embraced and maintained all that conservatism cherished, defended, and perpetuated, including the 'inherited hierarchies of wealth and birth', 'obedience and deference', and traditional elite rule 'through property, churches, armies, and inherited social influence'. Conversely, fascists attacked and destroyed precisely what, as Paxton (2004, p. 22) observes, 'conservatives in Europe still rejected in 1930 [namely] the main tenets of the French Revolution, preferring authority to liberty, hierarchy to equality, and deference to fraternity'. To that extent, fascism emerged as 'simply a more muscular form of conservatism.' Further, Paxton (2004, p. 22) notes that 'where simple authoritarianism sufficed, conservatives much preferred that' to fascism and 'would work with fascists if the Left looked otherwise likely to win [and] made common cause with the fascists' for that purpose. This reaffirms that conservatism is intrinsic authoritarianism, while fascism being totalitarianism. Yet, the difference between authoritarianism and totalitarianism, so between conservatism and fascism, is one of different degrees of unfreedom and oppression rather than of substance, with the second system just being more oppressive and so 'muscular' than the first. This demonstrates again that fascism is indeed 'simply a more muscular form of conservatism.'

nation, or state: 'anti-German' for Nazism and 'un-American' for its American equivalent. In the initial manner of conservatives revolting against liberalism, fascists deny that liberals are legitimate members of society by condemning and assaulting them as the 'enemies' of the people, nation, and state ('anti-German', 'un-American').

In this respect, embracing and intensifying religious conservatism's genocidal and hateful tendencies to subordinate groups in society—for example, Puritanism's religiously driven proxy genocide of 'pagan' Native Americans— fascism is the system and fascist are agents of genocide in intra-societal terms and of social hatred (Simmel's term[23]) versus liberalism and liberals and other non-conservative forces. This demonstrates the extent to which fascism poses the grave danger, indeed the mortal threat to the fabric, functioning, and existence of the society in which it arises and prevails in the past or present, including Germany, Italy, and the US, just as to other societies that it invades and subjugates as 'enemies.' While liberalism, liberals, and other non-conservative actors are the initial victims, the ultimate victim of fascism and broader anti-liberal conservatism is society,[24] including the fascist and conservative rank-and-file paying the final price for false fascist-conservative populism, as well as other societies attacked by its offensive wars (in Spencer's words). Escalating conservatism's original tendencies to collective suicide rooted in apocalyptic medievalism and religion, fascism is ultimately a suicidal

---

23   Simmel (1955, p. 48) identifies the 'peculiar phenomenon of social hatred', though in the sense of in-group hatred directed to some members perceived as within-group enemies rather than out-group hatred displayed for other social groups and whole societies, as presently understood. Relatedly, Arendt (1951, p. 345) observes that 'more specific in totalitarian propaganda, however, than direct threats and crimes against individuals is the use of indirect, veiled, and menacing hints against all who will not heed its teachings and, later, mass murder perpetrated on 'guilty' and 'innocent' alike. To this rationally conducted torture another, irrational, sadistic type was added in the first Nazi concentration camps and in the cellars of the Gestapo [and] behind the blind bestiality of the [Nazi] SA, there often lay a deep hatred and resentment against all those who were socially, intellectually, or physically better off than themselves, and who now, as if in fulfillment of their wildest dreams, were in their power.'

24   Collins (2012, p. 7) cites a well-known 1930s poem from Germany under Nazism: 'They came first for the Communists, and I didn't speak up because I wasn't a Communist. Then they came for the trade unionists, and I didn't speak up because I wasn't a trade unionist. Then they came for the Jews, and I didn't speak up because I wasn't a Jew. Then they came for me and by that time no one was left to speak up' and comments that the 'poem implies that if we do not take action, we will end up in a Nazi concentration camp.' More broadly, the poem implies that 'true' Germans (the 'master race' of 'Aryans') and in extension 'real' Americans ('patriots'), simply the people, are the ultimate victims of fascism in Germany and America after its purging of 'non-German' and 'un-American' populations.

social system beginning as anti-liberal nihilism and ending as societal self-destruction that follows or evokes the pattern of mass suicides of Christian and other religious cults and sects. Carrying the conservative suicidal tendency to its conclusion, most fascist leaders and masses tend to kill themselves Hitler-Goebbels' style when facing defeat by liberalism and generally anti-fascism or in the religious-style quest for salvation via annihilation after eliminating liberals and destroying society.

2.2 Fascism versus Liberalism

Fascism is, together with its root and ally conservatism, definitive anti-liberalism and defines liberalism[25] as its main adversary because it is well-aware and resentful of the social fact and knowledge that the latter is the ideal and system of universal liberty in society, combined with equality, justice, and inclusion, which fascism fanatically and systematically destroys. Fascism inherits and carries conservatism's original obsessive fear[26] of and intense anger and hostility toward liberalism as such an ideal and complex of liberty, thus liberalization and modernization, to the extreme of anti-liberal social hatred, madness, and paranoia. Fascists are extreme anti-liberals and define

---

25   Mannheim (1986, p. 91), defining liberalism as the 'principle of liberty' that conservatism attacks and on which freedom rests, adds that the liberal 'concept of freedom can only be understood in conjunction with its complement, the idea of [political] equality.' Knight (1967, p. 789) observes that the 'Liberal Revolution, establish[ed] free society, that is, democracy in the broad meaning, especially a political order minimizing compulsory law as well as exercise of arbitrary power, and restricting the latter to acts by lawful agents of the society, approved or accepted by public opinion.' Dahrendorf (1979, pp. x, 95) notes that the idea of liberty relates with the 'political force of liberalism' and in that sense is a 'partisan programme even in a free society.' Dahrendorf (1979, p. 100) suggests, however, that the 'marriage of liberalism and capitalism has to be dissolved' by decoupling the first from the second. He notes that liberalization through the 'liberation of a new potential by modernization, symbolized by the French Revolution, meant unheard-of progress of life chances for many people. This was a dynamic process which began with the rule of law [i.e.] the protected formal status of the citizen, and ended with the welfare state [via] comprehensive and substantive citizenship rights' (Dahrendorf 1979, p. 100). Nisbet (1966, p. 9) admits that the 'hallmark of liberalism is devotion to the individual; especially to his political, civil, and social rights. What tradition is to the conservative and the use of power is to the radical, individual autonomy is to the liberal. The touchstone was individual freedom, not social authority.' Kinloch (1981, p. 20) proposes that liberalism 'is aimed at maximizing individual autonomy, knowledge and intelligence through rational constitutional safeguards in a democracy.' Following J. S. Mill, Mueller (2009, p.17) defines liberalism as the 'liberty to do, think and say what one wants so long as the exercise of such liberty does not do undue harm to others.'

26   Calder (2020, p. 336) refers to religious conservatism's 'angry, fearful response' to liberalization and modernization, along with economic rationalization.

liberals as their principal adversaries (along with socialists) because they know that these protect universal social liberty, equality, justice, and inclusion, which they assault and eliminate.

In consequence, fascism is the extreme mode of fanatical antagonism to and of effective destruction of universal liberty, equality, justice, and inclusion in society, expressing its anti-liberal and to that extent societal nihilism versus liberal modernity. Fascists are extreme antagonists to and destroyers of these and related liberal values and institutions, simply anti-liberal and anti-modernist societal nihilists. By attacking and destroying liberalism and liberals, fascism and fascists attack and destroy universal liberty, equality, justice, and inclusion in society. Conversely, following the Machiavellian tactics of anti-liberal conservatism and conservatives, fascism and fascists couch their attack on and destruction of social liberty, equality, justice, and inclusion as the patriotic, 'holy' war on and the elimination of liberalism and liberals whom they denounce as illegitimate, the 'enemy' of the people, or 'foreign' ('non-German',[27] 'un-American').

3   Extreme Anti-democracy

Third and as a dual corollary of being extremist conservatism and anti-liberalism, fascism is invariably a species of extreme anti- and non-democracy. Hence, fascism is universally an extreme anti-democratic ideology, social movement, political regime, and cultural zeitgeist in a specific conservative, right version. Fascists are everywhere and always extremist anti-democrats or anti-democratic extremists in concrete conservative, right faces. Moreover, fascism is the most extreme variation of anti-democracy among all variations of the latter, and fascists are the most radical anti-democrats of all anti-democratic groups, within the broader family of conservatism or the right and

---

27   Parsons (1951, p. 352) notes that 'for a variety of reasons 'liberalism' had been considerably weaker in Germany than in the rest of the Western world, and this, plus the existence of a strong Communist movement as a foil, created a highly favorable situation from the propaganda point of view' for the Nazi movement. Also, recall Noakes' (2003, p. 81) observation that German revolutionary conservatives were hostile to 'what they saw as the hegemony of liberalism, by which they meant the secular, rational, moral tradition of the West', thus implicitly anti- or non-German so long as they did not see Germany as part of the latter but as a unique country. In a similar vein, American extremist, revolutionary conservatives from Reagan, Goldwater and McCarthy through the proto-fascist Tea Party and the post-2016 autocracy denounce liberalism as 'foreign', Western European attaching to it a pejorative meaning (the 'L-word') and US liberals as 'un-American'.

beyond. While not every anti- or non-democracy being fascist and conservative generally, all fascism is an extreme form of anti-democracy, just as most conservatism is anti- or non-democratic with minor variations or 'democratic' and 'libertarian' deceptions, masks, and pretensions.[28] In terms of modern democracy, this is the true sociological designation and name of fascism and fascists—anti-democracy and anti-democrats—as is of most conservatism and conservatives, aside from secondary variations and rare exceptions.

As a consequence of its extreme anti-liberalism, fascism is the most radical form of anti-democracy in the sense of extremely intense and implacable antagonism and nihilism toward liberal and thus genuine modern democracy and its ideal and system of universal liberty.[29] Fascists are the most extreme, destructive opponents of liberal-democratic ideas, processes, and institutions. For fascism and fascists, liberal democracy, notably the 'liberal' component, is the 'enemy' of or an alien element in society and liberal-democratic actors are 'enemies' of the people, nation, and state. Consequently, fascism attacks and dissolves the integration of liberalism and democracy in society as an 'evil', illegitimate, and 'foreign' conspiracy ('non-German', 'un-American'). Especially, fascists assault and eliminate democracy and thus universal political, civil, and individual liberties under the pretext of countering and eliminating liberalism as a supreme national 'enemy' and 'foreign' threat. Emulating conservatives as their role models and allies, however, even modern fascists sometimes do not dare openly declare their attacking and destroying democracy. Like conservatives, they resort to 'democracy', 'people', 'freedom', 'liberty' populist and libertarian deceptions and couch their anti-democratic activities as the patriotic 'defense' and 'sacred' warfare on 'unpatriotic' and 'godless' ('non-German', 'un-American', 'anti-Christian') liberalism.

Specifically, when in opposition to liberal-democratic institutions and thus not yet seizing and exerting total state power, fascism is essentially a subversive, putschist anti-democratic political ideology and social movement, hence

---

28   Michels (1968, p. 8) remarks that 'even conservatism assumes at times a democratic form. Before the assaults of the democratic masses, it has long since abandoned its primitive aspect, and loves to change its disguise.' He elaborates that the 'conservative spirit of the old master-caste, however deeply rooted it may be, is forced to assume, at least during times of election, a specious democratic mask [and] the conservative currents flow over the plain of democracy, occasioning there disastrous floods and rendering the plain unrecognizable' (Michels 1968, pp. 11, 20).

29   Colantone and Stanig (2019, p. 148) characterize neo-fascism or the new extreme right by 'radicalism, meant as a criticism of the established order, in particular of liberal democracy and its system of institutional checks on the will of the majority', along with other characteristics like 'exclusionary nationalism and nativism' and 'populism.'

fascists are putschists.[30] Fascism is the movement and fascists are agents of putsches or state coups as the forcible mechanism of seizing power, when failing to prevail in democratic procedures like elections which it uses, when fascist pretenders are victorious, effectively against and indeed to end democracy. Simply, fascists capture power ultimately by the force of the 'bullet' after they attempt and often fail to do so by the liberal-democratic ballot which they terminate if victorious, aside from notable exceptions like Italian fascism's 1924 sham election triumph[31] and Nazism's 1933 partial electoral victory, both victories ending democracy in Italy and Germany. Alternatively, they may seize power through democratic elections—which they immediately terminate after their victory—following their partly successful state coups, for example, Mussolini's Italian fascists' march on Rome,[32] or unsuccessful putsches, such as the Nazi Hitler putsch, as during the 1920s.

---

30   Mannheim (1936, p. 141) observes and indeed personally witnesses during the 1920–30s that from a sociological viewpoint, fascism is the 'ideology of 'putschist' groups [trying] to seize power by exploiting the crises [of] modern society', including economic and political crises. Mueller (1996, pp. 263–4) reaffirm Mannheim's observation in that he suggests that fascist dictatorships 'occur most frequently in 'crisis' situations, which the democratic government seems incapable of resolving. Adolf Hitler's rise to power in Depression-plagued Germany is an obvious example.' Mueller (1996, p. 272) adds that the 'inability of Germany's multiparty government to deal with the severe economic crisis of the early 1930s, with Communists pulling one way and the Nazis the other, is just the kind of paralysis that many fear of multiparty parliamentary democracy. Germany's president, Hindenburg, responding to pressure to resolve the crisis, named Adolf Hitler chancellor. Hitler did act decisively to the ultimate destruction of both himself and his country.' Beck (2000, p. 111) observes that in 'Germany, where [the Great Depression and] the resulting mass unemployment was blamed on a 'systematic breakdown' of democracy, [Nazism] became a mass movement virtually overnight, eventually enabling Hitler to capture power.' Confirming Mannheim, Colantone and Stanig (2019, p. 143) register the 'rise of radical-right parties in Europe in the 1920s and 1930s, as linked to the Great Depression [and from 1870 to 2014], a positive and distinctive effect of financial crises on extreme-right support.' Autor et al. (2020, pp. 3143–4) also confirm Mannheim by noting that US 'populist movements tend to arise during times of economic hardship', as well as that during the Great Depression, 'far-right movements had greater success in European countries that had more prolonged downturns.'

31   Acemoglu et al. (2022, pp. 1246–7) relate that 'Mussolini exclaimed on the eve of the [1924] elections, "This is the last time that we run the elections in this way. Next time I'll vote for everyone." Mussolini soon banned local council elections and set up a single-party system, outlawing all other political movements. From 1938 onward, elections were entirely abolished.'

32   Gross (1980, p. 12) reports that on 'October 26, 1922, as his Fascist columns started their March on Rome, Mussolini met with a group of industrial leaders to assure them that the aim of the impending Fascist movement was to reestablish discipline within the factories and that no outlandish experiments would be carried out.' Gross (1980, p. 12) adds that

While not every subversive anti-democratic ideology and movement is fascist and not all putschist groups are fascists, fascism is invariably a force of
subversion of democracy, and fascists are everywhere putschists in the sense
of agents of state coups when failing to seize or retain power through democratic methods. While using these methods, fascists typically do not accept
and honor democratic outcomes like electoral results if they are the losing side
and attempt to overturn them by state coups and related forcible actions, thus
intensifying conservatives' hostility toward liberal democracy's rules and procedures. Conversely, fascists only accept electoral and similar results if they
are victorious in elections and other political contests, carrying to the extreme
the tendency of conservatives from aristocrats to later ruling classes to adopt
democracy only if it secures their dominance.[33]

Once subverting liberal-democratic institutions and seizing total power, fascism operates as an extreme anti-democratic regime, and fascists act as extremist anti-democrats, eliminating democracy, so political, civil, and individual
liberties and rights. Taken together, when in opposition, fascism demands
political liberties and rights for its adherents and uses liberal-democratic institutions and processes like a free polity and elections to capture the state, or, if
failing to do so, it undertakes coups. Once in power fascism eliminates what it
vehemently demanded and used, namely freedom and democracy, thus effectively using the latter against themselves by terminating them. This demonstrates that fascism poses an extreme gravity of danger and destruction for
liberal democracy and fascists are deadly poisons to it by playing the democratic
game to seize and exert power and ending the process permanently by the ballot
of elections or the bullet of putsches. Even when playing the democratic game
to seize and solidify total power fascists never abide by the rules of this and all
peaceful social games but blatantly and systematically violate them through a

---

just 'a few days after the march on Rome, a close associate of Hitler, Herman Esser, proclaimed in Munich among tumultuous applause: 'What has been done in Italy by a hand-
ful of courageous men is not impossible here. In Bavaria too we have Italy's Mussolini. His
name is Adolf Hitler.' Adolf Hitler became [the] most powerful orator against Slavs, Jews,
Marxism, liberalism, and the Versailles treaty.' Berezin (2019, p. 348) notes that fascism 'as
a historical and political entity began in 1922 with Benito Mussolini's coming to power in
Italy.' Berezin (2019, p. 349) elaborates that 'Benito Mussolini, who ruled Italy from 1922 to
1943, coined the term to describe both the ideological underpinnings and the form of government that he was installing in interwar Italy. Fascism began to assert itself as ideology
and political practice in the 1920s. Nazism quickly overtook fascism as an area of interest
when Hitler came to power in Germany in 1933.'

33   Dahrendorf (1979, p. 108) observes that in capitalism the 'ruling classes and parties welcomed democracy only so long as it guaranteed their predominance.'

myriad of Machiavellian practices of deception, disinformation, and manipulation, compounded with intimidation and force.

Hence, fascists' Machiavellian play of the ballot of democratic procedure, if it fails to attain their objective, prefigures their use of the bullet of force to seize power through putsches and similar forcible counter-state actions. In this regard, fascism is extreme Machiavellianism in the function of capturing the state and fascists are consummate Machiavellians using any effective means to attain their end of absolute power. Fascism inherits and intensifies the Machiavellianism of conservatism[34] that, while being the ideology of anti-democratic, anti-liberal absolutism, assumes under certain conditions such as elections a mask and posture of 'democracy' and 'freedom' to seize power but actually eliminates democracy and liberty in the name of fighting liberalism and of 'God'.

Fascism is an extreme mode of escalation and intensification of conservatism's original opposition and persistently attempted elimination of liberal democracy,[35] by inheriting and carrying this old conservative anti-democratic trait to the extreme of destruction through the anti-democratic counterrevolution of nihilism.[36] Fascists are extremely anti-democratic nihilistic conservatives who overtly declare and vehemently attack democratic forces, processes,

---

34   Mannheim (1936, pp. 140, 230) stating that the fascist theory of politics 'has its roots in Machiavelli, who already laid down its fundamental tenets', suggests that conservatism is the 'ideology of absolutism [which] shows an outlook originally oriented towards the mastery of a life-situation, acquiring the tendency to reflect in a rather cold-blooded way on the technique of domination—in the manner of [classical] Machiavellianism.'

35   Michels (1968, p. 9) observes that conservatism as an aristocratic ideology seeks that 'democracy must be eliminated by the democratic way of the popular will. The democratic method is the sole one practicable by which an old aristocracy can attain to a renewed dominion. Moreover, the conservatives do not usually wait until they have been actually driven from power before appealing to the masses.' Michels (1968, p. 9) adds that during 'periods and among nations where the old conservative elements have been expelled from direct participation in power, and have been replaced by innovators fighting under the banner of democracy, the conservative party assumes an aspect hostile to the existing order of the state, and sometimes even a revolutionary character. Thus, however, is effected a metamorphosis of the conservative party, which, from a clique cherishing an aristocratic exclusivism at once by instinct and by conviction, now becomes a popular party.'

36   Slater and Smith (2016, p. 1473) identify the 'most decidedly counterrevolutionary case: fascist Germany'. They elaborate that in 'Europe, counterrevolution has left faint institutional traces because it was ultimately defeated, destroyed, and discredited [including] 20th-century cases like Hitler and Mussolini' and conclude that 'European counterrevolution found its ultimate expression in fascist parties' (Slater and Smith 2016, pp. 1474).

and institutions as liberal 'evils', 'enemies', and 'conspiracies', couching their anti-democracy actions as a patriotic defense and holy warfare against 'alien' and 'godless' liberalism. As typical, fascism therefore completes what conservatism initiates and fascists finalize what conservatives start. This is the elimination of liberal democracy and thus political, civil, and individual liberties under the cover of national 'defense' from and 'holy' war on 'foreign' and 'ungodly' liberalism.

Fascism thus shares with conservatism the common enemy—liberal democracy—and acts accordingly as the continuation and culmination of conservative anti-democratic politics by analogy to the (Clausewitz) concept of war and policy. Fascism and conservatism still assault more overtly 'liberal' than 'democracy' in a Machiavellian calculation that assaulting liberalism, as a 'patriotic' ('German', 'all-American') duty, is more acceptable to the fascist and conservative rank-and-file than attacking democracy that exists and thrives in the imagination of the base, expressing deceptive populism. Following conservatism, fascism manipulates deceptive populism to rationalize its destruction of 'liberal' in liberal democracy and thus its anti-liberalism as 'democratic' and 'anti-elitist' in the sense of illiberal populist 'democracy' and spurious 'anti-elitism.'

Following conservatism's ideal of aristocratic rule, fascism construes society and its history as the 'circulation of elites'[37] (a la Pareto) and, like their conservative allies, fascist leaders are actual elites. Just as conservatism arising as the defense of feudal aristocracy, fascism is essentially elitism and thus contradicts and eventually disposes of rank-and-file populism consistent with the fact that the ultimate victims of fascist leaders are the fascist-conservative masses as eventual sacrificial materials after eliminating liberal-democrats and other anti-fascists and non-conservatives. Fascist leaders use their rank-and-file populism

---

37   Mannheim (1936, p. 143) points out that fascism 'regards history as a circulation of elites' and thus implies that fascists seek and claim to be the new permanent elite, exposing fascist populism or anti-elitism as a deception and manipulation of the masses. Piketty (2014, p. 260) remarks that 'in the interwar years, the Italian Fascists adopted Pareto as one of their own and promoted his theory of elites. Although they were no doubt seeking to capitalize on his prestige, it is nevertheless true that Pareto, shortly before his death in 1923, hailed Mussolini's accession to power.' Relatedly, Parsons (1949, p. 268) identifies the 'tendency for elite elements whose main patterns go far back into the older traditional society to become susceptible to the fascist type of appeal—such as the landed nobility and higher clergy in Spain, or the Junker class in Germany. Fascism [stood], in the logic of the sentiments, for 'sound' traditional values and constitute[d] a bulwark against subversive radicalism.' Mann (2004, p. 177) observes that, 'like the Italian fascists, the Nazis actually seized power with help from the country's elites.'

to depose the old elite as a manifestation of anti-elitism and become, in alliance and merger with conservatives, the new permanent elite, manifesting their elitist propensity. This holds true, even though the fascist rank-and-file, for example, the Nazi 'blind herd', seems unable or unwilling in its total submission to and cult of the 'natural' leader[38] to experience this replacement as another form of elitism in fascism but regards it as anti-elitist and populist. In this respect, fascism is an ultimate form of conservative, right 'elite dictatorship'[39] as the extreme anti-democratic and illiberal rule of elites, revealing its elitism and false populism. And while not all anti-democrats versus liberal democracy are fascists and conservatives, fascists are always ultimate anti-democrats, as are most conservatives, aside from few 'moderate' exceptions or 'democratic' disguises and pretensions.

Fascism constitutes an extreme variant of anti-democracy and eliminates liberal democracy because it is well-aware of that the latter is the principle and system of universal political, civil, and individual liberties and rights[40]

---

38   Paxton (1998, p. 6) invokes as one of the 'mobilizing passions' of fascism 'authority of natural leaders' of society, 'culminating in a national chieftain who alone is capable of incarnating the group's destiny.'

39   Acemoglu, Egorov, and Sonin (2018, p. 1043) define fascist or radical-right and other 'elite dictatorship' by a regime in which 'all political decisions are made by the rich.' In this sense, this dictatorship is equivalent to what Olson (2000) calls 'capitalist dictatorships' and Frank (2007) names plutonomies in the sense of plutocracies.

40   Bruce (2002) observes that the 'context of liberal democracy' encompasses individualism, diversity, and egalitarianism. Bruce (2004, p. 18) also states that the 'core principle of liberal democracy is that each citizen's vote counts the same; for that to be the case rights must be distributed irrespective of religion.' Einolf (2007, p. 104) observes that, alongside free elections, 'minority rights, the rule of law, and an independent judiciary' are additional 'features of liberal democracy.' Mueller (2009, p. 1) remarks that the 'rich countries today, with very few exceptions, are liberal democracies. They are liberal in the sense that their citizens have freedoms to go and to do as they wish. They are democracies in that their citizens exercise a significant control over the state.' He elaborates that 'in a liberal democracy citizens not only participate in a democratic process but also get great freedoms to think and do as they please. Thus, liberal democracy requires two sets of institutions, voting rules and electoral laws that enable the state to provide goods and services that benefit the citizen, and constitutional rights and a judiciary that protects certain individual freedoms from the state' (Mueller 2009, p 13). Marks, Mbaye, and Kim (2009, p. 632) note that 'today, civil rights and universal suffrage are considered components of a single phenomenon, liberal democracy.' They add that 'most contemporary authoritarian regimes with revolutionary oppositions are politically inclusive but not liberal—they allow citizens to vote but deny them liberty. [So] basic liberties—the right to organize and freely communicate political opposition—are decisive because they establish the conditions under which political citizenship is meaningful' (Marks et al. 2009, p. 632). Bergemann (2017, p. 402) contrasts a fascist and generally 'totalitarian state' with a 'liberal democracy.'

that it negates and destroys. Fascism adopts and takes conservatism's fear of and hostility to liberal democracy as the ideal of liberty to the extreme of anti-democratic hatred, madness, and hysteria. Fascists are extremely hateful and hysterical conservative, illiberal anti-democrats—'madmen'[41] in both implacable opposition to liberal democracy and total state power. They attack liberal-democratic actors because they know that the latter establish and sustain universal political, civil, and individual liberties and rights, which they instead deny to and suppress for others and monopolize for themselves to the point of license, while engaging in severe repression and elimination of liberals and other anti-fascists.

In Hobbesian terms, emulating and intensifying conservatism to the extreme, fascism is the regime of the state of nature and anarchy for fascists and conservatives, notably their leaders and to some degree the rank-and-file, and Leviathan against and thus coercion of liberal-democrats and all anti-fascists and non-conservatives. It hence combines the absolute freedom or license of fascist-conservative rulers and followers, including that to kill—as through their mass possession of and murders by firearms—with the utmost oppression and persecution of liberals, democrats, and other non-fascists.

4 Extreme Anti-secularism

Fourth, as another double corollary or corelate of being extremist conservatism and anti-liberalism, fascism is typically a species of extreme anti-secularism. It follows that fascism is typically an extreme conservative, radical right anti-secular ideology, social movement, political regime, and cultural zeitgeist, with secondary transient variations. Fascists are usually extremist conservative, radical-right anti-secularists, aside from few and temporary 'secular' exceptions or superficial appearances. Not every anti-secularism is fascism and not all anti-secularists are fascists, yet fascism is extreme anti-secularism, in conjunction and mutual reinforcement with anti-liberalism, and fascists are extremist anti-secularists, just as anti-liberals, with minor variations.

---

41 Keynes (1960, p. 383) alerts to 'Madmen in authority, who hear voices in the air, are distilling their frenzy from some academic scribbler of a few years back'. This especially holds true for fascists who, as Mannheim (1936, pp. 143, 134) suggests, distil their madness from Pareto's and other 'irrationalist philosophies and political theories', notably the theory of society's history as 'a circulation of elites' whom they consider themselves or seek to become through putsches and violence overall.

Extreme anti-liberalism renders, ceteris paribus, fascism and fascists extremist anti-secularism and anti-secularists so long as liberalism typically interconnects with secularism and liberals are mostly secularists[42] within Western society, aside from certain variations and exceptions. Conversely, extreme antisecularism sustains and reinforces, all else being equal, fascism and fascists as extreme anti-liberalism and anti-liberals insofar as secularism[43] usually interacts with liberalism and most secularists are liberals within Western society, with some variations and exceptions. Consequently, due to being extreme conservatism and anti-liberalism, secular fascism is a non-entity or extreme rarity, and secularist fascists are a non-existent or rare species, despite some 'secular' fascist, including Nazi, disguises, pretensions, or imputations by conservatives

---

42   Rawls (2010, p. 265) proposes that liberal, constitutional democracy is a secular system by being 'realized in institutions by the separation of church and state.' Habermas (2001, p. 127) also suggests that democracy or autonomy 'implies a secularized political authority uncoupled from religious or cosmological worldviews. In the view of Islamic, Christian or Jewish fundamentalists, their own truth claim is absolute in the sense that it deserves to be enforced even by means of political power, if necessary. [Fundamentalist] outlook has consequences for the exclusive character of the polity; legitimations based on religions or worldviews of this sort are incompatible with the inclusion of equally entitled nonbelievers or persons of other persuasions.' Bruce (2004, p. 18) proposes that 'religion taken seriously is incompatible with democracy. Either the will of God or the will of the people is sovereign. Essential to the liberal democratic character of western European polities is the fact that they are secular. Either few people are seriously religious or the seriously religious (and their churches, sects and denominations) accept that religious imperatives be confined to the home, the family and the voluntary sector. Religion is confined to the realm of personal preference.'

43   Parsons (1949, p. 119) comments that for Nazism 'anti-religious secularism' belongs to the 'class of things to be energetically combatted.' Helm (2008, p. 11) notes the 'rise of the Nazi Party in Germany and its creation of 'German Christianity', a sort of religion of the German nation.' Bendix (1984, pp. 44–5) states that 'fascism and communism are two versions of the utopian mentality. In both cases the consequences of utopia have been so abhorrent as to inspire a fundamental distrust of utopianism.' As it stands, this statement seems to make too facile an equivalence, or fails to make a precise differentiation, between fascism and communism (for such a distinction see Mannheim 1936). Brubaker (2015, p. 6) claims that the 'exhaustion of communism and fascism has reduced the salience of conflict driven by comprehensive secular ideological commitments, but moral crusades, social movements, and other forms of political contestation continue to be driven by secular as well as religiously informed moral commitments and understandings of right order.' This claim overlooks that, unlike communism, fascism essentially represented comprehensive anti-secular rather than secular ideological commitments, including the findings of the role of religious and related 'grassroots associations in the rise of the Nazi party in Germany' (Portes and Vickstrom 2011, p. 473) and that indeed 'Nazi Party success correlated with religion' (Satyanath et al. 2017, p. 479).

attempting to obscure the conservative-fascist mutual attraction, linkage, and osmosis.

Following conservatism's original and persisting anti-secularism descending from pre-secular medievalism and its theocracy, fascism typically assaults and destroys secular social institutions and fascists attack and persecute their representatives. Fascism eliminates secular democracy by eliminating the differentiation between religion and politics, such as the separation of church and state, and fascists and other conservatives like theocrats attack and persecute secularists as 'godless' and 'infidels' ('anti-Christian', 'anti-Islamic'). In consequence, once seizing and exerting total state power, fascism develops and functions as an extremely anti-secular political and social system eventuating in theocracy, aside from minor and transient variations, and fascists rise and act as anti-secularist extremists qua 'holy' warriors, with rare exceptions.

In this regard, fascism operates in the same manner inherently authoritarian conservatism has operated since the 18th century—and through traditionalism such as medievalism from the Dark Middle Ages—and fascists behave as most conservatives have behaved for centuries. The only difference is in degrees of anti-secular repression and persecution and of suppression of freedom by fascism and conservatism. Fascism operates as a totalitarian form of, and fascists act as totalitarians in, this process, while conservatism operating as authoritarianism and conservatives acting as authoritarians, consistent with that totalitarianism is the ultimate intensification of authoritarianism. Both fascism and conservatism dissolve the differentiation between religion and politics, notably the separation of church and state, as a necessary condition and essential element of liberal-secular democracy, a fact that they seem to know well by attacking the former and thus assaulting the latter as their targeted 'evil' and common 'enemy'. The difference in degree is that fascism engages in the totalitarian destruction of this condition of liberal-secular democracy and the murderous elimination of its defenders while conservatism engaging in the authoritarian subversion of it and repression or exclusion of its advocates from political power and process. Fascism continues, intensifies, and finalizes what conservatism initiates and perpetrates, and fascists complete what conservatives start—the revolt against and elimination of secular democracy and other social institutions and rules. In terms of anti-secularism, fascism displays conservative 'iron consistency',[44] manifesting itself as consistent conservatism

---

44 Weber (1976, p. 137) uses the expression 'iron consistency' with reference to repressive Calvinism, including Puritanism, but it evidently applies to fascism, also because the latter, particularly its German version Nazism, has religious origins or precedents in the

even if carried to the extreme but logical conclusion from the authoritarian repression to the totalitarian persecution of secular social forces.

Conversely, connecting to its extreme anti-liberalism and anti-secularism, fascism typically is an extremely religious ideology, movement, regime, and zeitgeist, with minor and transient variations, and fascists are usually extremist religionists, aside from few exceptions. Fascism allies and ultimately merges with coercive, exclusionary religion, fascists allying and merging with religious figures, in a joint 'holy' warfare against democratic secular and liberal social institutions and actors.[45] Specifically, fascism embraces and uses coercive and exclusionary religion to capture, exert, and perpetuate total state power through religious support and sanctification of its totalitarian rule and oppression. Fascism adopts and nurtures religion as the most secure, enduring, indeed eternal 'divine' and so 'sacred' instrument of its totalitarian conquest and domination of society and its perpetuation into infinity or millennial time, for example, the Nazi one-thousand year Third Reich expressing Christian millennialism.

Conversely, religion supports[46] and consecrates fascism as an effective mechanism of or ally in religious compulsion, exclusion, and dominance in

---

former and Lutheranism, as sociologists and other scholars show (e.g., Adorno 2001; Fromm 1941; Harrold 1936; McLaughlin 1996; Merton 1939).

45   Paxton (1998, p. 5) while suggesting that the first European fascism was 'pagan for contingent historical reasons' recognizes that 'in practice, however, fascisms can be close to churches identified with the national cause, as in Croatia'. Further, Bruce (2004, p. 5) observes that of interwar Europe's 'fascist regimes, almost all were Catholic: Italy, Spain, Portugal, Slovakia, Croatia, Austria and Lithuania. Germany was two-thirds Catholic. And there were three Lutheran examples: the Quisling regime in Norway and the rather moderately right-wing dictatorships in Estonia and Latvia.' He adds that 'additional examples could be drawn from a very different setting: Latin America. In the twentieth century oppressive regimes of the right were Catholic. [But] even in the twentieth century, militant Protestantism has produced its own authoritarian movements. In 1930s Scotland, the Scottish Protestant League in Glasgow and Protestant Action in Edinburgh won local council seats on an anti-Irish and anti-Catholic platform. In the USA, the Ku Klux Klan and various other nativist movements presented a similarly curtailed notion of freedoms and rights: democracy was to be restricted to white Anglo-Saxon Protestant males. And the two contemporary examples of Protestants in power—Northern Ireland from 1921 to 1972 and apartheid South Africa—hardly offer models of liberal democracy' (Bruce 2004, p. 6). Dawkins (2006, p. 237) recalls that 'Nazi belt buckles were inscribed with *Gott mit uns* (God with us)'. He adds that 'Hitler didn't carry out his atrocities single-handed. The terrible deeds themselves were carried out by soldiers and their officers, most of whom were surely Christian [extolling] the Christianity of the German people' (Dawkins 2006, p. 276).

46   Dawkins (2006, p. 277) suggests that 'Hitler felt that he had to display some token sympathy for Christianity, otherwise his regime would not have received the support it did from the Church. This support showed itself in various ways, including Pope Pius XII's

society. Moreover, religion endorses and sanctifies fascism as the best instrument for imposing and maintaining religious totalitarianism or encompassing dictatorship via theocracy. Theocratic religionists from interwar dogmatic Catholics and Protestants in Europe, including Italy and Germany, to today's US evangelicals and other fundamentalists seem to realize that they can institute and sustain their total religious rule via theocracy by reversing liberal-secular democracy most effectively by the agency and assistance of fascism and its totalitarian destruction of the latter.

Taken together, fascism and coercive-exclusionary religion exhibit their deep and strong mutual attraction or elective affinity that is crucial to ensure their domination and perpetuation but fatal to secular democracy and lethal to society. This linkage and ultimately merger between fascism and religion virtually replicates or resembles the 'holy' alliance and blend between the medieval nobility (including monarchy) and the clergy as the first and second estate, respectively, in feudalism. Just as the medieval clergy consecrated and perpetuated aristocratic rule as 'divinely ordained' and endowed kings with 'divine rights', later religion typically sanctifies and perpetuates fascism as a 'Divine plan' and fascist leaders as 'chosen by God'. Conversely, just as aristocracy and kings allowed the medieval clergy to exert religious compulsion and repression over 'infidels', fascism allows and through state control and oppression enables religion to repress, exclude, and discriminate against non-believers, secularists, and liberals and impose 'faith' and 'godliness' on society. (An example is the mandated 'recognition of Divinity' and similar 'faith-based' stipulations as the precondition and qualification for seeking and holding political power or public office at federal and state levels in the US.)

In other words, fascism typically epitomizes or approximates religious extremism, with certain variations, thus fascists exemplifying or approaching

---

persistent refusal to take a stand against the Nazis—a subject of considerable embarrassment to the modern Church. Either Hitler's professions of Christianity were sincere, or he faked his Christianity in order to win- successfully—co-operation from German Christians and the Catholic Church.' Hitchens (2009, p. 81) observes that the 'Catholic Church was generally sympathetic to fascism as an idea. Benito Mussolini had barely seized power in Italy before the Vatican made an official treaty with him, known as the Lateran Pact of 1929. Under the terms of this deal, Catholicism became the only recognized religion in Italy, with monopoly powers over matters such as birth, marriage, death, and education, and in return urged its followers to vote for Mussolini's party. Pope Pius xi described ii Duce ('the leader') as "a man sent by providence."' He adds that 'across southern Europe, the church was a reliable ally in the installment of fascist regimes in Spain, Portugal, and Croatia. The very first diplomatic accord undertaken by Hitler's government was consummated on July 8, 1933, a few months after the seizure of power, and took the form of a treaty with the Vatican' (Hitchens 2009, p. 82).

religious extremists, apart from rare exceptions. Therefore, fascism presents itself as the grave threat to liberal democracy also due to its religious extremism as profoundly and vehemently illiberal and anti-democratic,[47] along with its extreme anti-liberalism as the correlate. Fascists are ultimate illiberal and anti-democratic forces because of being religious extremists as well, just as extreme anti-liberals. This suggests that the compound of religious extremism with anti-liberalism renders fascism into the lethal dual threat to liberal democracy and liberty and makes fascists a double agent provocateur via anti-democracy, anti-democratic chaos and madness, and illiberty. Fascism is what it is—a conservative totalitarian antithesis of liberal democracy—and fascists act as they do, rightist anti-democratic totalitarians, because also of religious extremism compounded with anti-liberalism. And these properties form fascism's inheritance from conservatism or the old right as religiously extremist and vehemently anti-liberal.

While not every religious extremism is fascism, the second is typically an instance of the first, and even if not all religious extremists are fascists, these usually exemplify them. Virtually every religious extremism is conservatism and almost all religious extremists are conservatives or rightists considering the historical and continuing symbiosis of conservative ideology and coercive religion since arch-conservative Edmund Burke[48] and his vehement attack on the secular and liberal-democratic French Revolution, putting aside minor variations and few exceptions.

In particular, fascism typically associate and ultimately blends with theocracy, thus fascists associating and blending with anti-democratic theocrats. Consistent with conservatism's 'divine' design and system of theocracy, fascism eventuates in or approaches a theocratic regime and fascists, especially their leaders, act like or resemble theocrats. Fascism usually enables establishment of a state religion or official church, enforces, and spreads religious belief, and suppresses and sanctions non-belief and other secular ideas, and represses

---

47   Mueller (2009, p. ix) alerts that there is the 'incompatibility of strong religious views and liberal democracy. Wherever extremist religious beliefs exist, liberalism is at peril'. He identifies the 'growing importance of religious extremism in the United States' and Islamic countries and suggests that 'liberalism and democracy are [vulnerable] to attack from religious extremists' (Mueller 2009, p. ix.). Glaeser, Ponzetto, and Shapiro (2005, p. 1283) find 'a nonmonotonic relationship between religious [and political] extremism and religious attendance.'

48   Acemoglu and Robinson (2013, p. 359) recognize that Hayek et al.'s conservative hero 'Burke was wrong on the big picture. The French Revolution had replaced a rotten edifice and opened the way for inclusive institutions not only in France, but throughout much of Western Europe.'

and persecutes non-believers and secularists. Fascism typically requires religious qualifications, such as 'faith' and recognition of 'Divinity', for seeking and holding political power or public office as a defining trait and diagnostic criterion of theocracy, thus excluding and oppressing secular actors, and fascist leaders act as driven by and saturated with 'faith' and 'godliness.'

Fascism eventuates in or merges with theocracy because it claims to be—and compulsory religion consecrates it as—'divinely ordained', with its leaders claiming and the fascist rank-and-file believing them to be 'chosen by God.'[49] Furthermore, fascism seeks to become or establish a new compulsory religion,[50] just as becoming the 'new conservatism', thus theocracy in its own right, and its leaders act as if they were equivalents of gods, so as effective theocrats qua 'agents of God'. Religious extremism in fascism and more broadly conservatism, such as dogmatic Catholicism, evangelical Protestantism, their alliance in the Christian Right, and fundamentalist Islam,[51] therefore generates fascist-conservative theocracy and theocrats. Due to its religious extremism, fascism and generally conservatism operates as the highly effective and

---

49   Dawkins (2006, p. 277) recounts that 'Hitler never ceased using the language of Providence: a mysterious agency which, he believed, had singled him out for a divine mission to lead Germany. He sometimes called it Providence, at other times God. After the Anschluss, when Hitler returned in triumph to Vienna in 1938, his exultant speech mentioned God in this providential guise: "I believe it was God's will to send a boy from here into the Reich, to let him grow up and to raise him to be the leader of the nation so that he could lead back his homeland into the Reich"'. He adds that after a 'failed assassination the Archbishop of Munich, Cardinal Michael Faulhaber, ordered that a *Te Deum* should be said in his cathedral, "To thank Divine Providence in the name of the archdiocese for the Fuhrer's fortunate escape"' (Dawkins 2006, p. 277).

50   Dawkins (2006, p. 277) notes that 'some of Hitler's followers, with the support of Goebbels, made no bones about building Nazism into a religion in its own right. The following, by the chief of the united trade unions, has the feel of a prayer, and even has the cadences of the Christian Lord's Prayer ('Our Father') or the Creed: Adolf Hitler! We are united with you alone! We want to renew our vow in this hour: On this earth we believe only in Adolf Hitler. We believe that National Socialism is the sole saving faith for our people. We believe that there is a Lord God in heaven, who created us, who leads us, who directs us and who blesses us visibly. And we believe that this Lord God sent Adolf Hitler to us, so that Germany might become a foundation for all eternity.' Hitchens (2009, p. 81) recalls that 'Pope Pius XI described Il Duce ('the leader') (Mussolini) as "a man sent by providence."' Mueller (2013, p. 4) includes fascism among "political religions".

51   Bazzi, Koehler-Derrick, and Marx (2020, p. 846) observe that 'legal institutions that provide permanent and inalienable protection to religious schools and houses of worship can empower religious actors and transform these organizations into effective venues for political activism', citing the use of 'Islamic charitable trusts' in the Muslim world—and by implication their Christian counterparts in the US—'to mobilize political support and wage ideological warfare against secular forces.'

extremely coercive mechanism of establishing and imposing theocracy as religious dictatorship complementing fascist political totalitarianism, and fascists and other conservatives ally with and indeed often act like theocrats.

Accordingly, fascism and conservatism as a whole ultimately become or move toward theocracy, with fascist leaders and conservative rulers becoming or resembling theocrats, save in name and dress. Consequently, theocracy and theocrats, theocratic religion and religionists appreciate and embrace totalitarian fascism, along with authoritarian conservatism, as the strongest 'defense', ultimate weapon, and most loyal ally in the 'divine' warfare against 'ungodly' liberal-secular democracy. Ultimately, they form and nurture a 'holy' religious-fascist-conservative alliance, as in the case of the Vatican's pacts with Mussolini and Hitler and the US Christian Right.

Conversely, theocracy is a prototypical or proximate fascism and generally proto-totalitarianism— 'religious slavery' in Jefferson's description—owing to its totalistic compulsion, control, and repression of society, thus making theocrats arch-fascists. Owing to these features, theocracy leads to and enables fascism and theocrats prefigure and inspire fascists, as the historical link and affinity of theocratic Catholicism and Calvinism,[52] including Puritanism, with fascism, in particular Nazism, shows, as does the attraction and interconnection between evangelicalism and neo-fascism.[53] Catholic, Calvinist-Puritan, and other Christian theocracy looks as primordial or proto-fascism, generally totalitarianism, in substance and outcome, if not in form and name (the 'Biblical commonwealth', 'Christian polity', 'Christian republic', 'Holy commonwealth').

---

52   McLaughlin (1996, p. 248) comments that 'Fromm argues that the Weberian theoretical tradition ignores Luther's and Calvin's "emphasis on the fundamental evilness and powerlessness of men"'. McLaughlin (1996, p. 249) ads that 'Calvinism served the same [anti-life] sociological function for Anglo-Saxon countries [as fascism]. Protestantism was [not only] linked with political freedoms and economic progress [but also] to Nazism.' Hitchens (2009, p. 80) reminds that 'Calvin's Geneva was a prototypical totalitarian state, and Calvin himself a sadist and torturer and killer, who burned Servetus (one of the great thinkers and questioners of the day) while the man was still alive.'

53   Stivers (1994, p. 23) remarks that Puritanism in early America 'was the most totalitarian form of Calvinism [which] not satisfied with a minimalistic morality, searched for a rigorous moral discipline.' Bauman (1997, p. 184) suggests that the 'Islamic integrisme of ayatollahs [and] evangelist churches of the Bible Belt belong to a wider family of [proto] totalitarian solutions offered to all those who find the burden of individual freedom excessive and unbearable.' Dawkins (2006, pp. 292–3) holds that the US evangelical 'ambition to achieve what can only be called a Christian fascist state is entirely typical of the American Taliban. It is an almost exact mirror image of the Islamic fascist state so ardently sought by many people in other parts of the world.'

Taken together, theocracy predetermines, prefigures, and predicts fascism, and the latter perpetuates, restores, and enforces the former, with certain adaptations and modifications. This makes theocracy and fascism the most totalitarian, severe, persistent, or obstinate political regimes and social systems overall. Theocracy is such a system since it is proto-fascism too, while fascism being this because it becomes eventually a theocratic regime as well, thus being dual and indeed total dictatorships. This helps explain the totality, severity, persistence, or obstinacy of theocracy and fascism, theocrats and fascists, as 'Divine' and so eternal and immutable systems and rulers, versus secular-liberal democracy, contrasting with the more transient and less persistent or obstinate character of non-religious and non-fascist dictatorships.[54]

5   Extreme Irrationalism, Anti-rationalism, and Anti-progressivism

Fifth and related to its extreme conservatism, anti-liberalism, and anti-secularism, fascism is invariably a compound of extreme irrationalism, anti-rationalism, and anti-progressivism. In consequence, fascism is unconditionally an extreme conservative, radical-right irrational, anti-rational, and anti-progressive ideology, social movement, political regime, and cultural zeitgeist. In other words, it represents conservative, right irrationalist, anti-rationalist, and anti-progressive radicalism,[55] notably a nihilistic counterrevolution of extreme irrationalism, anti-rationalism, and anti-progressivism. Fascists are everywhere extremist conservative, rightist irrationalists, anti-rationalists, and anti-progressives, including nihilistic counterrevolutionaries espousing extreme irrationalism, anti-rationalism, and anti-progressivism. While not every irrationalism, anti-rationalism, and anti-progressivism is

---

54 Hume (1983) classically detects the 'unreasonable obstinacy' of Puritanism in respect of its imposition of proto-totalitarian theocracy by obstinately establishing itself as the 'only true' religion by law. Juergensmeyer (2003, p. 217) relatedly remarks that the 'absolutism of religion has been revealed especially in the notion of cosmic war. Although left-wing movements subscribe to what may seem a similar idea—the concept of class conflict—ordinarily this contest is thought to take place only on a social plane and within the temporal limitations of history. Religious concepts of cosmic war, however, are ultimately beyond historical control, even though they are identified with this-worldly struggles. A satanic enemy cannot be transformed; it can only be destroyed. The vast time lines of religious struggles also set them apart from secular conflicts. Most social and political struggles have sought conclusion within the lifetimes of their participants. But religious struggles have taken generations to succeed.'

55 Parsons (1949, p. 117) identifies the 'revolutionary radicalism in the Nazi movement.'

fascism, the latter is an invariant epitome of the former, and even if not all irra-tionalists, anti-rationalists, and anti-progressives are fascists, the second are always examples of them.

Furthermore, fascism is the most total and intense compound of irratio-nalism, anti-rationalism, and anti-progressivism, and fascists the most ata-vistic non- and anti-rationalists and anti-progressives, along and in alliance with religious extremists like Catholic dogmatics, Protestant evangelicals, and Islamic fundamentalists, usually blending with each other in irrational-ist, anti-rationalist, and anti-progressive blindness, exaltation, and apocalyptic myths.[56] Fascism perpetuates and intensifies the inherently 'complete' irratio-nalism,[57] anti-rationalism, and by implication anti-progressivism of conserva-tism, reaching the point of societal madness and chaos, combined with cynical manipulation and deceitful propaganda by and imitation of its leaders.[58]

---

56   Mannheim (1936, p. 145) notices that fascism is 'living in the blind glare of the irrational' linked or similar to the 'religious exaltation of [Anglo-American] sectarians' that is 'sus-tained by apocalyptic myths'. He adds that fascism, including Nazism, and more broadly conservatism treats the fascist and conservative rank-and-file and people overall as the 'blind herd' in contrast to the 'élan of great leaders and elites' (Mannheim 1936, pp. 42–3). This exposes fascist-conservative populism as a deceit and trickery to attract the masses which ultimately pay the price by their own destruction and death.

57   Mannheim (1936, pp. 134–5) suggests that fascism links itself with the 'irrationalist philos-ophies and political theories', such as those of Bergson, Sorel and Pareto, and 'is a com-plete irrationalism but not the [conservative] kind [viz.] not the folk spirit, not silently working forces, not the mystical belief in the creativeness of long stretches of time, but the irrationalism of the deed which negates even interpretation of history'. Becker (1945, p. 80) suggests that the 'black-shirted adherents of the Fascist faith' embrace and perpet-uate 'traditional irrationality [which] then, is not a matter of the remote, the faraway, the medieval, or the so-called primitive; the modern world affords many instances.'

58   Horkheimer and Adorno (1993, p. 152) observe that the 'purpose of the fascist cult of formulae, the ritualized discipline, the uniforms, and the whole allegedly irrational appa-ratus, is to make possible mimetic behavior. The elaborate symbols proper to every coun-terrevolutionary movement, the death's heads and masquerades, the barbaric drumming, the monotonous repetition of words and gestures, are so many organized imitations of magical practices, the mimesis of mimesis. The Fuhrer, with his ham-actor's facial expres-sions and the hysterical charisma turned on with a switch, leads the dance. In his perfor-mance he acts out by proxy and in effigy what is denied to everyone else in reality.' Adorno (2001, p. 222) suggests 'cynical soberness is probably more characteristic of the fascist mentality than psychological intoxication. [So] even those stages of collective enthusi-asm to which the term 'mass hypnosis' refers have an element of conscious manipulation, by the leader and even by the individual subject himself, which can hardly be regarded as a result of mere passive contagion [i.e.] the ego plays much too large a role in fascist irra-tionality to admit of an interpretation of the supposed ecstasy as a mere manifestation of the unconscious. There is always something self-styled, self-ordained, spurious about fascist hysteria [and] the irrational slogans which Fascism itself promotes.'

Fascists inherit and carry conservatives' intrinsic irrationality, anti-rationality, and anti-progressivity to the outer limit to become and act as irrational yet manipulative 'madmen' in total power—a mixture of passions and cynicism, madness, and manipulation.[59]

Fascism is a species of extreme irrationalism especially in that it forms a compound of religious and other superstitions, fanaticism, and fantasies, and fascists tend to hold and propagate these superstitious and fantastic beliefs. Fascism typically holds the mass belief in the existence of 'Satan' and by association 'witches' and engages in corresponding practices of 'exorcism' and witch-trials, thus fascists enforce and spread such beliefs and fervently participate in these rituals, just as religious conservatism does and fundamentalists like evangelicals and Islamists do. Fascism inherits and continues the superstitions, fanaticism, and fantasies of religious conservatism, for example, dogmatic Catholicism,[60] theocratic Calvinism/Puritanism, and Islam, including the mass belief in 'Satan' and 'witches', 'exorcism', and witch-trials. Fascists are as religiously superstitious, fanatical, and fantasy-believing as religious conservatives who inherit and perpetuate these properties from irrational medieval traditionalists like Christian (Catholic, Protestant, Orthodox) and Islamic irrationalists. In this sense, fascists create the New Dark Ages of superstitions, fanaticisms, and fantasies, just as religious conservatives recreate the superstitious, fanatical, fantasy-saturated Dark Middle Ages.

Relatedly, fascism represents a species of extreme anti-rationalism and anti-progressivism by being an ultimate expression of anti-science and of

---

59   Recall Keynes (1960, p. 383) uses the term 'Madmen in authority' and characterizes them as those 'who hear voices in the air', which seemingly applies to fascists and, as Mueller (2009) suggests, religious extremists, like US Southern and other evangelicals, along with Islamic fundamentalists. Paxton (1998, pp. 6–7) identifies the following 'mobilizing passions' of fascism: '1. The primacy of the group, toward which one has duties superior to every right, whether universal or individual. 2. The belief that one's group is a victim, a sentiment which justifies any action against the group's enemies, internal as well as external. 3. Dread of the group's decadence under the corrosive effect of individualistic and cosmopolitan liberalism. 4. Closer integration of the community within a brotherhood (fascio) whose unity and purity are forged by common conviction, if possible, or by exclusionary violence if necessary. 5. An enhanced sense of identity and belonging, in which the grandeur of the group reinforces individual self-esteem. 6. Authority of natural leaders (always male) throughout society, culminating in a national chieftain who alone is capable of incarnating the group's destiny. 7. The beauty of violence and of will, when they are devoted to the group's success in a Darwinian struggle.'

60   Squicciarini (2020, p. 3461) notes that the 'French Revolution (1789) marked a turning point in the relationship between Catholicism and science' in which the first became growingly hostile to the second.

antagonism to scientific progress, as well as anti-art, anti-theory, and more broadly anti-intellectualism. Fascists are everywhere and always anti-scientific, anti-artistic, anti-theoretical, and generally anti-intellectual, aside from few exceptions. Fascism is the ultimate antithesis and lethal poison of science and scientific knowledge and education, as well as artistic creativity and freedom, social theory, and other autonomous intellectual activities. Fascists are implacable enemies of scientists and scientific educators, creative and free artists, social theorists, and other intellectuals as drivers of cultural and social progress.

While not every anti-science and antagonism to scientific progress and generally anti-progressivism and anti-intellectualism is fascism, the second forms invariantly a paradigmatic instance of the first.[61] Not all anti-scientific and generally anti-progressive and anti-intellectual forces are fascists, but the latter are everywhere examples of the former. Whenever and wherever fascism rises and prevails and fascists rule, science and scientific knowledge, progress, and education decline and ultimately disappear, just as artistic creativity and freedom, social theory, and all free intellectual activities do. Fascism adopts and takes to the nihilistic extreme the original and intrinsic anti-science, anti-art, anti-theory, anti-progressivism, and anti-intellectualism of conservatism which inherits these features from medievalism's overarching darkness, with secondary variations, as its irrational origin and ideal.[62] Fascists continue, intensify, and complete conservatives' initial anti-scientific, anti-artistic, anti-progressive, and anti-intellectual revolt and 'crusade' that they embrace from medieval traditionalists and resume.

---

61   Mannheim (1936, pp. 138, 145) remarks that fascism has the 'profound skepticism toward science and especially the cultural sciences [and] designates all scientific social-political thought as illusion.' Bourdieu and Haacke (1995, p. 10) remind that the Nazis 'purged German museums of 'degenerate art''. Dahrendorf (1979, p. 158) singles out the 'anti-philosophy of fascism' as a symptom of its anti-intellectualism. Paxton (1998, p. 4) notes that 'fascism does not base its claims to validity on their truth. Fascists despise thought and reason, abandon intellectual positions casually, and cast aside many intellectual fellow-travelers.' Paxton (1998, pp. 4–5) elaborates that fascists 'subordinate thought and reason not to faith, as did the traditional Right, but to promptings of the blood and the historic destiny of the group.' Paxton (1998, p. 6) adds that 'feelings propel fascism more than thought does', which operate as 'mobilizing passions' both fascist movements for follower recruitment and in fascist regimes for welding the fascist "tribe" to its leader.'

62   Kettler and Meja (1984, pp. 73–4) comment that in Mannheim's seminal account, conservatism 'stands against all constructions of human relations [seen] as governed by rationalistic universal norms [and rights]', and especially that it 'enter[s] into the contemporaneous oppositions to the predominance of natural science models in intellectual life and liberal-capitalist rationalizations in social knowledge.'

Irrationalism, anti-rationalism, and anti-progressivism of fascism are so extreme, intense, and pure that the latter produces the New Dark Ages[63] of superstition, fanaticism, madness, anti-science, and anti-knowledge. In so doing, fascism effectively restores the Dark Middle and indeed primeval Ages[64] that conservatism arising from the darkness of medievalism attempts to per-petuate in vehement revolt against rationalism, progressivism, liberalism, and secularism which the Enlightenment epitomizes. Fascism therefore finalizes what medieval-rooted conservatism initiates—reassertion of extreme irra-tionalism, anti-rationalism, and anti-progressivism through the restoration of the Dark Middle Ages. Fascists are everywhere so intensely irrationalist, anti-rationalist, and anti-progressive forces that they act as the main agents and faces of the New Dark Ages. They hence cause society to descend to the Dark Middle Ages, completing irrationalist, regressive, and illiberal conservatives' attempts a la Burke and Maistre[65] to perpetuate and sanctify these times of darkness in revolt against Enlightenment rationalism, knowledge, science, and progress, as well as the liberal-democratic French Revolution.

6   Extreme Anti-egalitarianism, Anti-universalism, and
       Anti-cosmopolitanism

Sixth and related especially to its extreme conservatism and anti-liberalism, fas-cism is invariably a species of extreme anti-egalitarianism, anti-universalism,

---

63   Bauman (2001, p. 84) refers to the 'coming of the New Dark Ages' and implicitly connects
      them with the rise of neo-fascism and generally religious-political conservatism, such as
      American evangelicalism and Islamic fundamentalism.
64   Horkheimer and Adorno (1993, p. 9) imply that fascism leads to the New Dark Ages such
      that the 'fake myth of fascism reveals itself as the genuine myth of prehistory, in that
      the genuine myth beheld retribution while the false one wreaks it blindly on its victims.'
      Relatedly, they add that 'so blind is the murderous fascist colossus in face of nature that
      he conceives of animals only as means of humiliating humans [and] that they knew how
      to disguise [their] hatred of certain men and things as pity toward animals, applies truly
      to the fascist butcher. The precondition of the fascists' pious love of animals, nature, and
      children is the lust of the hunter. The idle stroking of children's hair and animal pelts
      signifies: this hand can destroy' (Horkheimer and Adorno 1993, p. 210).
65   Berlin (1990a, p. 1) remarks that conservative Maistre's works are regarded as the 'last
      despairing effort of feudalism and the Dark Ages to resist the march of progress.' Mueller
      (2007, p. 26) describes Edmund Burke as 'awkwardly born into the Enlightenment' but
      opposed to it due to being the 'perfect embodiment of a traditionalist', more precisely
      arch-conservative, specifically medievalist obstinately devoted to the pre-Enlightenment
      of the Dark Middle Ages.

and anti-cosmopolitanism, including anti-globalism, except in the perverted, aggressive form of globalism as fascist conquest and imperialism. It follows that fascism is invariantly an extreme anti-egalitarian, anti-universalist, and anti-cosmopolitan, including anti-globalist, ideology, social movement, political regime, and cultural ambiance. Fascists are always and everywhere anti-egalitarians, anti-universalists, and anti-cosmopolitans, including anti-globalists. More precisely, fascism represents the extreme form of conservative anti-egalitarianism or inequality and anti-universalism[66] or non-inclusion within society and of anti-cosmopolitanism or anti-globalism in relation to other societies.

Accordingly, fascism is an extreme conservative, radical-right anti-egalitarian, anti-universalist or non-inclusive ideology, movement, system, and climate in the society that it rules and an anti-cosmopolitan and anti-globalist entity versus other societies. Fascists are radical-rightist anti-egalitarian, anti-universalist, and exclusionary groups within society and anti-cosmopolitans and anti-globalists in relation to other societies. In other words, fascism is universally conservative anti-egalitarian, anti-universalist, and anti-cosmopolitan extremism, fascists everywhere being right extremists in these terms. Altogether, owing to its intra-societal anti-egalitarianism and anti-universalism and its trans-societal anti-cosmopolitanism and anti-globalism, fascism amounts to an extreme conservative variant of the new tribalism[67] and in that sense reinvented savagery or barbarism[68] and

---

66   Horkheimer and Adorno (1993, p. 181) observe that 'bourgeois reason is not only particularistic but also, indeed, universal, and in denying its universality fascism defeats itself.' Habermas (1975, p. 84) remarks that 'universalistic morality and other cultural barriers have arisen that could only be broken at a psychological cost of regressions', which German fascism exemplifies. Rydgren (2007a, p. 243) notes that neo-fascism or 'political monism of the extreme right is expressed in two ways: as a rejection of the democratic political system and/or a rejection of universalistic and egalitarian, sometimes called democratic, values.'

67   Paxton (1998, p. 6) proposes that the 'mobilizing passions' of fascism 'function in fascist movements to recruit followers and in fascist regimes to "weld" the fascist "tribe" to its leader.'

68   Horkheimer and Adorno (1993, p. 9) suggest that Hitlerism like the Hitler Youth organization is not just 'a relapse into the old barbarism' but a reinvention of its new forms. Horkheimer and Adorno (1993, pp. 173, 180) simply describe Hitler et al. as 'barbarians' and identify the 'worship of fascist barbarism'. Habermas (2001, p. 45) reminds that the 'force of barbarism [by Nazism] had broken through the very foundations of civilization in Germany.'

primordialism, including social Darwinism,[69] and fascists reappear as radical-right tribalists and savages or barbarians.

Furthermore, fascism is the most extreme form of anti-egalitarianism and anti-universalism in society and of anti-cosmopolitanism and anti-globalism versus other societies, and fascists are foremost anti-egalitarians and anti-universalists in relation to other social groups and anti-cosmopolitans and anti-globalists against diverse nations. In this regard, fascism appears as the most extreme case of the new tribalism and to that extent of savagery or barbarism and primordialism, including social Darwinism, and fascists ultimate tribalists and savages or barbarians. Not every anti-egalitarianism, anti-universalism, and anti-cosmopolitanism or anti-globalism is fascism, but the latter is unconditionally extremely anti-egalitarian, anti-universalist and anti-cosmopolitan or anti-globalist (or globalist in the perverted form of conquest and imperialism). Fascism adopts and carries to the extreme conservatism's inherent and persistent anti-egalitarianism or inequality and anti-universalism or non-inclusion within society and anti-cosmopolitanism and anti-globalism or perverse globalism as conquest and imperialism versus other societies.[70] Fascists inherit and intensify conservatives' intrinsic anti-egalitarian, anti-universalist, and anti-cosmopolitan, including anti-globalist, propensities and actions by becoming and acting as extremely hierarchical ('superior'), closed, exclusionary, hateful, and isolated cliques. Fascism continues and completes to the maximum what conservatism, especially its religious form,[71] begins, thus fascists finalizing what conservatives start. This is the compound of anti-egalitarianism and anti-universalism in society and anti-cosmopolitanism versus other societies—in revolt against and reversal of liberalism, egalitarianism,

---

69   Fromm (1941, p. 192) remarks that 'in connection with this crude Darwinism the 'socialist' (actually capitalist) Hitler champions the liberal principles of unrestricted competition.' Paxton (1998, p. 5) emphasizes that fascists' 'only moral yardstick is the prowess of the race, of the nation, of the community. They claim legitimacy by no universal standard except a Darwinian triumph of the strongest community.' He adds that fascists' 'mobilizing passions' include the 'beauty of violence and of will, when they are devoted to the group's success in a Darwinian struggle' (Paxton 1998, p. 7).

70   Kettler and Meja (1984, pp. 73–4) comment that in Mannheim's account, conservatism attacks 'all constructions of human relations' regarded as regulated by universal rationalistic norms and rights.

71   Friedland (2002, p. 419) implies fascism's and religious nationalism's anti-globalism stating that 'Nazism, whose semiotic print matches that of the [US] religious nationalists, also eroticized the political economy as a project of body-making and pointed to the feminizing powers of global money.'

universalism, and cosmopolitanism, especially its genuine liberal form.[72] In this sense, fascism intensifies and consummates religious conservatism's original medieval-rooted tribalism, savagery, barbarism, or primordialism[73] and fascists emulate and reinforce conservative or traditional tribalists, savages, barbarians, or primitives from the Dark Middle and primeval Ages.

Conversely, fascism is invariably a species of extreme inequality, rigid hierarchy, particularism, specifically elitism, monopolistic closure, and exclusion within society and in relation to other societies. It manifests and implements its anti-egalitarianism and anti-universalism into intra-societal inequality, elite rule, hierarchy, closure, and exclusion, and realizes and translates its anti-cosmopolitanism into inter-societal hostility and isolation. It thereby creates and perpetuates internally an extremely unequal, hierarchical, closed, and exclusionary and externally an intensely hostile and isolated society. Fascism is hence universally an extreme conservative hierarchical, elitist, particularistic, closed, and exclusionary ideology, movement, regime, and zeitgeist in both intra- and trans-societal terms. It is the extreme conservative vision and realization of a severely unequal, hierarchical, closed, exclusionary, and oppressive society and fascists are radical-rightist agents of severe societal inequality, elite rule, hierarchy, closure, exclusion, and oppression. Consequently, fascism is the extreme conservative antithesis and destruction of an egalitarian, open, inclusive, and free society, and fascists are ultimate rightist enemies and destroyers of societal, including economic and political, equality, openness, universal inclusion, and freedom.

---

72   Recall that Paxton (1998, p. 6) includes 'dread of the group's decadence under the corrosive effect' of cosmopolitan liberalism in fascism's 'mobilizing passions'.

73   Hitchens (2009, p. 80) describes Christian Augustine-Calvin's predestination [election] doctrine as a 'primordial sentence'. He elaborates that 'it is not possible, in the religious totalitarian vision, to escape this world of original sin and guilt and pain. An infinity of punishment awaits you even after you die. According to the really extreme religious totalitarians, such as John Calvin, who borrowed his awful doctrine from Augustine, an infinity of punishment can be awaiting you even before you are born. Long ago it was written which souls would be chosen or 'elected' when the time came to divide the sheep from the goats. No appeal against this primordial sentence is possible, and no good works or professions of faith can save one who has not been fortunate enough to be picked' (Hitchens 2009, p. 80). Rawls (2010, pp. 265) warns that 'Christianity [if] taken seriously could have deleterious effects on one's character. Christianity is a solitary religion: each is saved or damned individually, and we naturally focus on our own salvation to the point where nothing else might seem to matter, whereas actually our own individual soul and its salvation are hardly important for the larger picture of civilized life [e.g.] how important is it that I be saved compared to risking my life to assassinate Hitler, had I the chance? It's not important at all.'

In this respect, fascism is a restored caste society and fascists become the new conservative 'master caste' and thus a ruling elite, consistent with proclaiming to being the 'new' conservatives, such as the Nazis in interwar Germany. Fascism inherits, revives, and perpetuates the 'conservative spirit of the old master caste' and so elite rule, by making fascist leaders masters and elites of society and others, including eventually their rank-and-file, subjugated and indeed sacrificed, slave-like castes. In this sense, fascism realizes conservatism's design of restoring caste society, notably the dream of reinstituting the conservative 'master caste', in revolt against and reversal of liberalism and democracy, though the new fascist masters tend to eventually subdue or assimilate their conservative allies within the extended family of rightist authoritarianism. While not every extreme societal inequality, hierarchy, particularism, including elitism, monopolistic closure, and exclusion are fascist, fascism universally is extremely unequal, hierarchical, particularistic, notably elitist, closed, and exclusionary both within society and versus other societies, just as is conservatism.

In particular, fascism is extreme conservative economic anti-egalitarianism and anti-universalism, in addition to and conjunction with their non-economic, including political and cultural, forms, while extolling the 'survival of the fittest'[74] within capitalism. Fascism is typically an ideology and system of extreme economic inequality, exclusion, hierarchy, and subordination, just as of social non-economic, including political and cultural, inequalities, exclusions, hierarchies, and subjugations.[75] Fascism usually is an economic structure of extremely unequal distribution, concentration, and ultimately monopolization of wealth by the ruling fascist-conservative elite, such as the extremely high wealth share of the top one percent of society. Relatedly, fascism is an economy of extreme income inequality favoring fascist-conservative rulers, for example, high Gini coefficients of income distribution. Because of its extreme wealth/income concentration and in economic terms, fascism is essentially oligarchic plutocracy, including extremely rich autocracy and dynasty, or plutocratic oligarchy.[76]

---

74   Mannheim (1936, p. 146) quotes Mussolini's anti-egalitarian, anti-universalist social-Darwinist statement that 'capitalism is not just a system of oppression—on the contrary [is] the choice of the fittest, equal opportunities for the most gifted, a more developed sense of individual responsibility.'

75   Noakes (2003, p. 81) cites a German conservative with strong Nazi credentials or sympathies who states the 'mass rule' of liberal democracy must be 'overcome by a new Conservatism, freedom by integration, leadership and subordination, with rights according to achievement, the inequality of men, hierarchy and order.'

76   Besley and Kudamatsu (2006, p. 313) characterize fascist and other autocracy as a 'dictatorship of the rich', which is thus equivalent to plutocracy.

As a corollary of extreme wealth/income concentration, fascism is typically an ideology and system of material deprivation, degradation, hardship, and economic non-protection and insecurity, with some minor 'welfare' variations or deceptive simulations. Putting aside rare and transient exceptions, fascism usually exhibits chronic and widespread poverty, material deprivation, and degradation of vast segments of the population, especially labor and lower classes. In addition, fascism is an economic system of directly or indirectly compulsory hard or long work and conversely non-existent or short paid vacations and paternity leave, with minor 'welfare' variations. Related to the previous, fascism is a system of absent or weak employment protection, non-existent or low unemployment benefits and the absence or weakness of social protection and economic security, aside from secondary 'welfare' exceptions.

In addition, fascism is invariantly a species of extreme conservative nationalism, nativism, and xenophobia or anti-immigration sentiment[77] as an aggressive and ultimate form of anti-universalism, specifically anti-cosmopolitanism, and monopolistic closure, and fascists are radical-right nationalists, nativists and xenophobes. In short, it is conservative nationalist, nativist, and xenophobic extremism, and they are rightist radicals. Fascism's extreme nationalism, nativism, and xenophobia are extended forms of its tribalism, savagery or barbarism,[78] and primordialism, and fascists' nationalist, nativist and xenophobic tendencies reveal their tribalist, savage, or barbarian attributes. Conversely, fascism's tribalism, savagery or barbarism and primordialism express and release themselves in extreme nationalism, nativism and xenophobia, and fascists' tribalist and savage or barbarian attributes translate into nationalist, nativist, and xenophobic attitudes and acts. Fascism perverts the nation-state and patriotism into unreasonable chauvinism and maximalist nationalism, nativism, and xenophobia, ultimately into nationalist madness seeking its release in war, destruction, and self-destruction, expressing its irrationalism that it inherits and intensifies from conservatism.

At this point, fascism reappears as extremely nationalist, nativist, and xenophobic conservatism, and conversely, the second typically amounts to the first. Even if not every extreme nationalism, nativism, and xenophobia are fascist, fascism is universally extremely nationalist, nativist, and xenophobic and fascists are radical nationalists, nativists, and xenophobes. In its evolution, fascism's nationalism, nativism, and xenophobia initially supply the alchemy or

---

77   Dorn and Zweimüller (2021, p. 50) observe that hostility or skepticism toward immigration is a 'signature issue of right-wing' European and other fascist populism.

78   Habermas (1975, p. 84) holds that German fascism involves 'extraordinary motivational burdens', such as 'a psychological cost of regressions' into barbarism.

most efficient formula of its rise, advance, and domination. Yet, they ultimately prove to be fascism's undoing and self-destructive weapon through defeats in aggressive wars and self-destruction, as during ww II which ww I prefigures in that German conservatism (Bismarck) by the nationalist recipe precedes and inspires Nazism (Hitler)[79], suffering the same fate.

Relatedly, fascism is invariably a mode of master-race and similar racism as another aggressive and ultimate form of anti-universalism or anti-cosmopolitanism, particularism, and monopolistic closure that are intertwined with extreme nationalism and nativism. Fascism's master-race racism is typically a variation of white supremacy in the reduced form of 'Aryan'[80] or 'Nordic' superiority over and mastery of other races and ethnicities as 'inferior', including most of the white population as the ultimate victim, for example, what Weber' observes as the 'poor white trash' in the US South, along with non-white populations as initial victims. Simply, fascists, notably their leaders, claim to be the 'master race' and reduce all other races, including most of the white race, to their effective slaves or subordinates, thus acting as white supremacists in this narrow sense. As a result, fascism is a system of institutional racism and fascists are extreme racists in relation to both non-white races and the non-Arian or non-Nordic majority of the white race as fascists define it. This especially holds true for such variants of fascism as Nazism and neo-Nazism whose leaders and rank-and-file consider themselves the 'Arian' master-race seeking and exerting mastery over the rest of the white population and non-white populations. Consequently, the victims of the racial purification of fascism such as Nazism are initially non-white populations and ultimately, after these being purged, the non-Arian or non-Nordic majority of the white race in fascist-ruled societies (e.g., most Germans and Americans in Nazi Germany and conservative America).

---

79   Horkheimer and Adorno (1993, p. 197) propose that there is a short 'distance between the individuality of Bismarck and of Hitler'. Esping-Andersen (1990, p. 40) observes that during the 1930s, the Nazis 'actually began implementing Bismarck's old notion of militarized labor, through work conscription, a policy against women's employment, and compulsory membership in Robert Ley's hyper-corporativist Labor.' Hedges (2004) notes that 'Bismarck used "values" to energize his base at the end of the 19th century and launched *Kulturkampt*, the word from which we get "culture wars". Bismarck 's attacks split the country, made the discrediting of whole segments of the society an acceptable part of the civil discourse and paved the way for the more virulent racism of the Nazis.'

80   Habermas, Cronin and De Greiff (1998, p. 116) alert to the 'racist policies of the Nazis.' Brubaker (2009, p. 32) registers that the 'most notorious cases [of racism] are the official schemes of racial classification and identification employed by Nazi Germany.' Tetlock, Mellers, and Scoblic (2017, p. 98) refer to the link between 'Nazism and Aryan supremacy.'

Fascism, in particular Nazism, inherits and reinvents the 'conservative spirit of the old master-caste' as master-race racism and total mastery over 'inferior' groups. Fascism, particularly Nazism, perpetuates the conservative ghost of the 'master-caste' in a blatantly and officially racist form through narrow white supremacy, and fascists, notably their leaders, claim to be masters of others by acting as racial supremacists. The spirit of conservatism and the propensity of conservatives are the root and core of the nature of fascism and the proclivity of fascists, including Nazism and Nazis. Specifically, fascism, including Nazism, through master-race racism and mastery over 'inferior' racial groups reproduces the conservative 'old master-caste' consisting of slave masters, feudal aristocrats, and ruling castes. As a result, fascism, especially Nazism, amounts to or approaches a new system of racial slavery in the form of a reduced-form white supremacy, and fascist leaders seek to become modern-day slave masters acting as racist supremacists. It follows that the conservative 'old master-caste' determines and predicts the fascist essence of master-race racism, which reaffirms that fascism makes explicit and extreme what is implicit and standard in conservatism, finishing what the latter initiates.

7   Absolute Rule, Unconstrained Power, and All-Encompassing Domination

Seventh and as a corollary of being conservative totalitarianism and extreme anti-liberalism and anti-democracy, fascism is invariably a social system of absolute rule, unconstrained power, and all-encompassing domination. Accordingly, fascism is universally an extreme conservative, radical-right ideology, regime, and climate of absolute rule and control, total unrestrained and arbitrary power, and all-embracing and severe domination of society in the form of autocracy, dynasty, oligarchy, and other forms of dictatorship, including fascist police states and military dictatorships. It is the absolute rule of a single conservative, radical-right person and family, thus autocracy[81] and dynasty, or of a closed narrow clique within the broader filiation of authoritarian conservatism or rightist authoritarianism and so oligarchy, including

---

81   Acemoglu, Egorov, and Sonin (2018, p. 1043) refer to right or 'elite dictatorship, where all political decisions are made by the rich', thus essentially plutocracy or wealthy oligarchy.

military juntas, and in the setting of capitalism,[82] thus plutocracy or capitalist aristocracy and dictatorship.[83]

Fascist leaders are everywhere rightist absolute rulers, total unconstrained and arbitrary power-holders and all-embracing dominators as autocrats, oligarchs, and in part plutocrats, and the fascist rank-and-file their loyal, indeed blind followers totally submissive, subordinate, and willing and ready to sacrifice their property, life, and family to the cult and worship of the leader. This absolutism of societal rule and totality of power and domination defines fascism as conservative totalitarianism and extreme anti-liberalism and fascists as radical-right totalitarians and anti-liberal extremists.

As a typical patten, fascism inherits and takes conservatism's intrinsic authoritarianism through absolute rule, control, and power to the extreme level of absoluteness, totality, lack of constraints and limits, and arbitrariness.[84] Fascism embraces, continues, and reinforces the illiberal and anti-democratic ideology of absolutism which typifies conservatism,[85] together with the latter's

---

82   Habermas (1989, p. 54) registers 'authoritarian corporatism', essentially still capitalism, in fascism, including 'in Fascist Italy, in Nazi Germany, and in Falangist Spain,' as corporate-capitalist economies. Hirschman (1994) contrasts 'Socialism-Communism' to 'Corporatism-Fascism'. Brustein (1991, p. 652) finds that in the critical 1921 Italian national legislative election the 'growth of the Fascists came at the expense of the Socialists [i.e.] was the result of voters switching from the Socialists to the Fascists' and generally private property rights are 'major determinants of fascism's popular support', which suggests that fascism opposed socialism and embraced capitalism. For example, Acemoglu et al. (2022, p. 1234) confirm that the '(perceived) threat of socialism was critical to the rise of fascism in Italy.' Specifically, they estimate that the 'bulk of fascist violence in the early 1920s and about a quarter of the increase in the vote share of the fascist lists from 1919 to 1924 [are] related to this "red scare" mechanism' (Acemoglu et al. 2022, p. 1235).

83   Riley (2005, p. 288) describes fascist Italy and Spain as 'economic-corporate' and in that sense capitalist dictatorships since capitalism was the dominant type of economy in these countries.

84   Adorno (2001, p. 222) recounts that fascist 'totalitarianism means knowing no limits, not allowing for any breathing spell, conquest with absolute domination, complete extermination of the chosen foe. With regard to this meaning of fascist 'dynamism,' any clearcut program would function as a limitation, a kind of guarantee even to the adversary. It is essential to totalitarian rule that nothing shall be guaranteed, no limit is set to ruthless arbitrariness.' Berezin (2019, p. 349) notes that 'today, fascism [is] a bridging metaphor [i.e.] a term used independently of historical or definitional context to describe arbitrary violence or authoritarianism in political and, in some instances, social life.'

85   Mannheim (1936, pp. 140, 230) observes that conservatism is the 'ideology of absolutism [in that it] shows an outlook originally oriented towards the mastery of a life-situation' through absolute rule of society and power and domination over its opponent, liberalism. Esping-Andersen (1990, p. 41) implies that feudal-rooted conservatism comprises 'absolutist systems of labor control.' Bourdieu (2000, p. 228) states that 'absolute power is the power to make the world arbitrary, mad' and invokes Nazism as the exemplar. Cooney and Burt (2008, p. 492) adopt the [Durkheim] proposition that the 'severity of punishment increases with political absolutism.'

also characteristic Machiavellianism. Fascists are everywhere extreme conservative Machiavellian absolutists, total unconstrained, and arbitrary radical-rightist power-seekers and rulers.

With respect to absolute rule, total unconstrained and arbitrary power, and all-encompassing domination, fascism intensifies and completes what conservatism initiates and performs, thus fascists escalating and finalizing what conservatives start. Fascism operates as the agent or continuator of conservatism as the principal or initiator of absolute rule, control, and power, since the first invariably develops within the broader setting of the second, namely conservative authoritarianism or authoritarian rightism, thus objectively operating on its behalf. The above holds true up to the stage of the process at which the monster of fascism submerges or assimilates its creator conservatism, or the latter blends with or disappears in the former. This outcome occurs in an endogenous evolution of rightism from authoritarianism to totalitarianism, or through intra-group contestation as a family contest in which the 'new conservatism' such as totalitarian Nazism prevails over or assimilates the old, for example, German Bismarck-style traditional authoritarian conservatism. Fascists universally act as agents or reinforcers of conservatives as absolutist principals or initiators given that the former always rise and grow within the extended family of conservative, rightist authoritarians, thus directly or indirectly acting on the behalf of the latter. This applies up to the point at which fascist monsters subdue their creators, conservatives—or the second coalesce in the first—in an internal mutation of rightists from authoritarians to totalitarians, or via all-in-the-family feuds in which the 'new' conservatives like Nazis replace the old.

Continuing and intensifying conservative absolutism, fascism is a social system of absolute rule, total unconstrained and arbitrary power, and encompassing domination in that it seeks by subversion or abuse of democracy to capture, control absolutely, and dominate totally all social domains and structures, including society's polity, economy, civil society, and culture. Within the polity, it attempts to seize and control legislative, executive, and judicial branches of the state in order to attain and exert absolute rule, total power, and encompassing domination in society, while abolishing any separation of powers and independence of the legislature and judiciary from the executive branch. As a result, fascism is a regime of abolished, non-existent power constraints and limits, essentially the boundless autocratic, dynastic or oligarchic, and plutocratic rule of fascist leaders relying on and blindly followed by the submissive rank-and-file of fascists and most other conservatives. Furthermore, fascism does not confine itself to seizing and controlling polity in its various branches but also seeks to capture and control economy, civil society, culture, and all other social systems, thus displaying and intensifying conservative-style absolutism and implementing its totalitarianism.

As a consequence of total unconstrained and arbitrary power by its leaders, fascism is the regime of legal arbitrariness and insecurity to the point of chaos and lawlessness. It is essentially an arbitrary, indeed lawless system, even while extoling the 'rule of law' and resorting to 'law and order' threats.[86] Fascists respect no laws, especially fascist leaders are above any law, while deceptively proclaiming the 'rule of law' and enforcing 'law and order' on non-fascists and other non-conservatives only, by inflicting them with arbitrary severe punishment, including mass imprisonment, death, torture, and other state terror. Fascism adopts conservatism's 'law and order' that is enforced only on non-conservatives and so bordering on lawlessness,[87] and makes it an instrument of the absolute rule and total power of fascist leaders and the manipulation and blind obedience and following of their rank-and-file. Fascism is hence the system of legal arbitrariness, lawlessness, and lenience for fascists and conservatives overall, especially fascist leaders and their conservative allies—until the first eventually subdue the second within the broader family of authoritarian rightists—and of 'law and order' and Draconian punishment for non-fascists and other non-conservatives.

As another consequence of total unconstrained and arbitrary power by its leaders, fascism is the regime of extreme and uncontrolled corruption in the

---

86   Hayek (1960, p. 350) states that 'in Hitler Germany and in Fascist Italy, as well as in Russia, it came to be believed that under the rule of law the state was 'unfree,' a 'prisoner of the law,' and that, in order to act 'justly,' it must be released from the fetters of abstract rules'. Yet, he grossly overlooks that Nazism and fascism following their creator and source conservatism claimed to establish the 'rule of law' or 'law and order' while actually all three functioned as lawless regimes. Contradicting Hayek, Mueller (1996, p. 43) notes that even fascist and other dictatorships 'have a constitution.' Also, Rydgren (2007a, pp. 242–3) suggests that neo-fascist or the 'new radical rightwing parties share a core of ethno-nationalist xenophobia and antiestablishment populism [that] is embedded in a general sociocultural authoritarianism that stresses themes such as law and order and family values.'

87   Simpson (1934, p. 157) observes that in the US the conservative 'whole decade from 1920 to 1930 was a period of conspicuous governmental incompetence, with a consequent increase in lawlessness and crime, the development of vicious types of business organization and crime, the development of vicious types of business organization and methods, and the growth of a deep penumbra of racketeering practices around the ragged fringe of corrupt and incompetent government [as before].' Dahrendorf (1979, p. 98) alerts to the 'conservative-authoritarian movement by way of law-and-order slogans' as one of the 'collectivist threats' to advanced societies. Perelman (2000, p. 20) finds that within a conservative and early capitalist 'contrived law and order, workers found their rights to organize unions and even to act politically severely restricted.'

broadest sense to encompass both its economic and non-economic forms, such as systematic abuses of power with impunity. It is a profoundly corrupt regime broadly understood to include both economic corruption and power abuses, specifically autocracy and dynasty, as well as conservative oligarchy and capitalist plutocracy.[88] In fascism, absolute rule/power really corrupts and degenerates absolutely its fascist holders—and conversely, the latter corrupting and degenerating the state and society—and even their rank-and-file vicariously experiencing or rejoicing over their leaders' extreme corruption, arbitrariness, and lawlessness in attacking ('owning') anti-fascists like liberals.

Relatedly, fascism constitutes institutional nihilism in the sense of antagonism to and destruction of existing liberal-democratic, secular, rationalist, egalitarian, and universalistic social institutions and rules, simply anti-institutionalism[89] or anti-system. In this sense, fascism arises and advances as the counterrevolution of institutional and overarching societal nihilism and hence destruction of society. Fascist institutional nihilism typically assumes the form of spurious, deceptive conservative, radical-right populism[90] expressing bogus and perverting genuine popular sovereignty in the sense of people's choice, voice, and power. Such nihilism manifests itself through anti-institutionalist or anti-system populism as the revolt and attack against

---

88   Michels (1968, p. 188) remarks that the 'unrestricted power of capital [in the US] necessarily involves corruption.'

89   Parsons (1949, p. 123) proposes that Nazism 'constitutes a mobilization of the extremely deep-seated romantic tendencies of German society in the service of a violently aggressive political movement, incorporating a 'fundamentalist' revolt against the whole tendency of rationalization in the Western world, and at the same time against its deepest institutionalized foundations.' Bahr (2002, p. 820) notes that Nazism was 'adept in mobilizing 'fundamentalist' feelings' like 'cherished sentiments and commitments.'

90   Habermas (2001, pp. 50–1) points to the 'sentiments of right-wing populism' as forces 'eroding the legitimacy of democratic procedures and institutions themselves.' Alpers (2003, p. 7) registers 'a variety of individuals and groups often accused (fairly or unfairly) of representing the beginnings of American fascism, including various proponents of reactionary populism, most famously Huey Long and Father Coughlin; fundamentalist leaders of the old Christian right like Reverend Gerald Winrod; and even a small number of self-identified fascists, such as Lawrence Dennis.' Rodrik (2018, p. 198) refers to the 'fascistic Father Charles Coughlin, with tens of millions of followers on the radio,' as an early face of Christian fascism in America during the 1930s. Rydgren (2007a, pp. 242) observes that neo-fascism and generally the new radical right-wing 'promote xenophobia (and sometimes racism), ethno-nationalism, sociocultural authoritarianism, and antisystem populism. They generally view individual rights as secondary to the goals of the nation.' Berezin (2019, pp. 351, 356), however, suggests that 'in contrast to fascism, populism is less connected to national histories [and] typically represents a shifting aggregate of popular preferences without a clear ideology that unites them.'

established and legitimated social institutions, norms, and actors condemned and eliminated as the 'establishment', 'elitism', or 'elites' in opposition to the purity and 'spirit of the people'[91] (*Volksgeist* originally in German conservatism and latter in Nazism). Fascist institutional nihilism attacks and displaces existing social structures and powers, including those of liberal democracy, as 'elitism' while fascists becoming the new elites consistent with fascism's construing the history of society as the 'circulation of elites' (a la Pareto). Fascism thereby renders deceptive, specious populism into a mass weapon of fascist absolute rule and control, and perverts classical popular sovereignty eventually into its own negation and destruction, as the 'people' is the ultimate victim of fascist leaders who invariably despise and subjugate the masses as their blindly submissive rank-and-file (the 'blind herd' in Mannheim's firsthand observation). While not every populism is fascist, fascism is universally populist by deceptively espousing ersatz and eliminating true popular sovereignty and oppressing, persecuting, and subjugating the people, with minor variations. Not all populists are fascists, but fascists are everywhere deceitful, false populist actors destroying genuine popular sovereignty and sacrificing the people, including the fascist rank-and-file, to the cult of leaders, aside from rare exceptions.

8   Extreme Repression, Violence, and Terror

Eighth and as another corollary of representing conservative totalitarianism and extreme anti-liberalism, fascism is invariably a system of all-embracing and severe coercion, repression, violence, and terror inflicted on society. It is hence universally an extreme conservative, radical-right ideology, social movement, political regime, and cultural ambiance of total and intense state compulsion and oppression of society, while combined and reinforced with the populist, anti-elitist deception, disinformation, and manipulation qua the 'spirit of the people'. Fascism inherits and takes conservatism's inherent, medievalrooted coercion and repression of society to the all-embracing and maximally intense level. Fascism is the totality and maximum of conservatism's or the radical right's intrinsic coercion and repression of society consistent with the pattern that fascist totalitarianism continues and intensifies inner conservative authoritarianism. Conversely, conservatism's permanent coercion and

---

91   Habermas (2001, p. 4) warns that a conservative/fascist 'spirit of the people', 'a *Volksgeist* always directed toward a real or imagined past poses insurmountable difficulties for the future-oriented republicanism.'

repression of society reaches its totality and maximum in fascism compatible with the tendency for inner conservative authoritarianism or authoritarian rightism to culminate in fascist totalitarianism. Fascists, notably their leaders, are everywhere and always extremely coercive and repressive conservative/ rightist agents seeking to, as soon as they capture total state power, completely subjugate and essentially enslave and eliminate non-fascists and more broadly non-conservatives from polity and society as a whole. Fascism invariantly establishes and perpetuates itself, notably its leaders exert absolute rule and maintain total power and encompassing domination, through severe coercion and repression once capturing the state by force or abuses of democratic processes like elections.

In this sense, fascism is substantively the equivalent of slavery or bondage, and its leaders act as equivalents of slave or caste masters. Leaders in fascism attempt to reduce all others, including the 'people' (the *folk*) and the blindly submissive fascist and conservative rank-and-file and exposing their populist slogans as deceits, to slaves or inferiors subjected to slave-like labor, including compulsory long work, and treatment.[92] Given its core of extreme conservatism, fascism amounts to the new conservative slavery or bondage and fascist leaders are or pretend to be novel radical-rightist slave or caste masters. Fascism continues, escalates, and intensifies conservative slavery[93] or bondage, because conservatism arises and operates as the medieval-rooted aristocratic ideology, movement, and regime of enslavement in the broadest sense or of serfdom through the master-servant system[94] that medieval common law

---

92   Ironically, Pareto (2000, p. 55) while inspiring and endorsing the rise of fascism predicts that the latter like Nazism will result in slavery, stating that German religious conservatism 'preaches militarism, war and extermination against the enemies of Germany and also against those who, though not her enemies, refuse to be her slaves.'

93   Michels (1968, p. 147) refers to the conservative and religious or religion-using 'slave owners of the southern states' in America. Savelsberg and King (2005, p. 581) remark that conservative 'American law [does] not place special emphasis on the protection of victims of national inhumanity such as the near extinction of the Native American population, the slave trade, and the slavery system, despite regular references to foreign atrocities.' Hitchens (2009, p. 81) observes that, as in colonial America's Puritan theocracy (as narrated in the novel *the Scarlet Letter*), the Christian 'state religion supplied a complete and 'total' answer to all questions, from one's position in the social hierarchy to the rules governing diet and sex. Slave or not, the human was property, and the clergy was the reinforcement of absolutism [by] Christian sadists.'

94   Naidu and Yuchtman (2013, p. 107) report that 'Master and Servant law gave employers the ability to criminally (as opposed to civilly) prosecute and severely punish a majority of employees across industries for breach of contract in Great Britain.' They add that 'criminal prosecution of workers, rather than being a vestige of medieval common law, was actively used in the leading industrial sectors of nineteenth century Britain [and so]

legitimized in Anglo-Saxon societies like England and the US and which conservatism, including false 'libertarianism', adopts from feudalism and perpetuates as 'free enterprise'. Fascists therefore merely inherit, continue, and carry to the extreme conservatives' practice and spirit of the 'old master caste' of slave or servant masters.

Relatedly, given its extreme anti-secularism and merger with theocratic religion, fascism represents or resembles a new variant of what Jefferson denotes 'religious slavery' as the essence of theocracy through the enslavement of non-fascists and other non-conservatives as mostly non-believers or moderate believers. As extreme anti-secularists allied and blended with theocrats, fascists are or act as the new religious slave masters[95] seeking to enslave non-believers comprising largely non-fascists and other non-conservatives, such as liberals and scientific rationalists. In essence, fascism is the most extreme contemporary exemplification or approximation of slavery and fascists are the closest recent examples or proxies of and pretenders to slave masters. To that extent, fascism exemplifies or approximates conservative-religious slavery in the sense of Jefferson and fascists are examples of or pretenders to conservatives-slave masters in the meaning of conservatism's 'old master caste'. Overall, while not every ideology, regime, and agent of total and intense state coercion and repression, including enslavement or subjugation, is fascism, the second is universally the first, and fascists are everywhere extremely coercive, repressive, enslaving, or subjugating, agents.

Consequently, fascism is invariably an extreme conservative, radical right ideology, movement, system, and atmosphere of systematic, all-embracing, and intense violence and terror.[96] Following and intensifying to the extreme

---

labor market coercion—the criminal prosecution of workers for breach of contract, with punishments including imprisonment, forced labor, whipping, and orders of specific performance—was commonplace in Victorian British industry [as] criminal prosecutions were widely applied across nineteenth century Britain' (Naidu and Yuchtman 2013, pp. 108–9).

95   Horkheimer and Adorno (1993, p. 79) state that by 'elevating the cult of strength to a world-historical doctrine, German fascism took it to its absurd conclusion. As a protest against civilization the master morality perversely upheld the oppressed: hatred of stunted instincts objectively exposes the true nature of the slave masters, which reveals itself only in their victims. But, in the guise of a great power and a state religion, the master morality places itself entirely in the service of the civilizing powers that be, of the solid majority, of resentment and everything it once opposed.'

96   Dunn and Woodard (1996, p. 77) remark that the 'practice of terror, propaganda and rulership by a single political party has characterized dictatorships in the twentieth century of both the Right and Left, by the fascists, Nazis, and communists', which admits that fascism/Nazism is conservative, rightist authoritarianism vs. communism as the leftist.

conservatism's old and continuing forcible, violent, and terrorist tendency, fascism glorifies and always resorts to force, violence, and terror as the first resort and instrument of capturing, exerting, and retaining state power. Like conservatism and its root medievalism, fascism is impossible to rise, advance, and persist in long terms without the use of force, violence, and terror, compounded with and disguised by manipulation and propaganda. Fascists, including leaders and the rank-and-file, are everywhere and always extremely forcible, violent, and terrorist, living and acting, like their theocratic allies for the 'glory of God', by the force of the 'sword'. Yet, fascists deny or overlook, along with 'holy' religious warriors, that this is a double-edged lethal weapon that can cause their own destruction too, and not only of liberal, secular, and rationalist dissenters as enemies or 'heretics', and so they 'live and die by the sword', as their military defeat in ww II shows. Like Christian[97] (and Islamic) theocracy of which it is a substantive equivalent or historical descendant, fascism is the system of constant use of the deadly 'sword' against countervailing non-fascist and non-conservative, notably liberal, secular, and rationalist social forces, and ultimately the fascist base and 'people', revealing its bogus populism, along with the collective suicide of its leaders Hitler/Goebbels-style.

Specifically, fascism whenever in opposition to and outside of state power resorts to the 'sword' of counter-state force, violence, and terror, thus fascists when opposing established institutions and actors act as anti-state violent agents and terrorists.[98] Conversely, fascism whenever capturing and exerting

---

97   Rawls (2010, p. 264) observes that the 'great curse of Christianity was to persecute dissenters as heretics.' He elaborates that the 'history of the [Christian] Church includes a story of its long historical ties to the state and its use of political power to establish its hegemony and to oppress other religions. [The] Church saw itself as having justification for its repression of heresy [but] the denial of religious freedom and liberty of conscience is a very great evil' (Rawls 2010, pp. 264–5).

98   Gross (1980, p. 11) recounts that after the 1922 electoral defeat of the Fascists Mussolini 'countered with a nationwide wave of terror that went far beyond ordinary strikebreaking. Mussolini directed his forces at destroying all sources of proletarian or peasant leadership. They enjoyed the passive acquiescence-and at times the direct support-of the police, the army, and the church. Above all, business groups supplied Mussolini with an increasing amount of funds. In turn, Mussolini responded by toning down the syndicalism and radical rhetoric of his followers, and, while still promising to 'do something for the workers,' began to extol the merits of private enterprise.' Acemoglu et al. (2022, pp. 1242–4) recount that in Italy 'fascist violence against leftists that came to define the early 1920s [and] fascist organizations were extremely violent, and used "punitive expeditions" against worker associations and socialists to restore the control of landowners in the countryside [as] the fascist black shirts attacked, intimidated, and killed workers, laborers, and socialists.' They add that 'episodes of intimidation, violence, and vote rigging were denounced at the opening of the new parliament [in 1924] by Giacomo Matteotti, the leader of the Unitary

total power relies on the 'sword' of state force, violence, and terror and thus ruling fascists act as official forcible, violent, and terrorist agents.[99] While not every ideology, movement, system, and climate of the pervasive and systematic use of force, violence, and terror being fascism, the latter is universally an epitome of the former, thus not all extremely forcible, violent, and terrorist forces are fascists, but the second are always exemplars of the first. In short, fascism is terrorism and fascists are terrorists both in the form of state and counter-state terror depending on being in or out of political power.

Due to its maximal utilization of force, violence, and terror, fascism inherently constitutes or eventually becomes a regime of mass murder and destruction of human life and society. Its victims are initially anti-fascist and non-conservative social groups and ultimately the fascist rank-and-file, simply the 'people' (*folk* in Nazism, its 'people' in its American proxy) that pays the final price for its blind obedience to and following of fascist leaders, manifesting the perversity of fascism's populism. When in violent opposition and outside of state power, fascism operates as an ideology and movement of counter-state mass murder of state representatives and indiscriminate destruction of existing institutions, and fascists act as murderers[100] of anti-fascist and non-conservative officials and related actors. Once seizing and exerting total power, fascism functions as an ideology and system of state mass murder of its opponents and even neutrals, and fascists become murderers of anti-fascists and non-conservatives, such as liberals, secularists, and rationalists whose murder

---

Socialist Party. Ten days later, Matteotti was kidnapped and killed. The murder provoked a constitutional crisis, resulting eventually in the establishment of the fascist dictatorship' (Acemoglu et al. 2022, p. 1246).

99   Horkheimer and Adorno (1993, p. 68) state that 'after the brief interlude of liberalism in which the bourgeois kept one another in check, power is revealing itself as archaic terror in a fascistically rationalized form.' Adorno (2001, p. 221) alerts that 'with regard to terror and repressive measures, Fascism habitually goes *beyond* what it has announced.' Arendt (1951, p. 30) states that the nature of fascist totalitarianism is the 'combination of its essence of terror and its principle of logicality', invoking Nazi Germany's legal system as a 'terroristic police force'. Lemert (1991) registers the 'eve of the Nazi terror', the time when Mannheim published *Ideology and Utopia*. Burawoy (2005, p. 5) reminds of the 'terrorist storm' of fascism. Savelsberg and King (2005, p. 596) point to the 'terror of Nazism'. Rydgren (2007b, pp. 234–6) gives the example of the 'Ustasa terror' in Croatia when ruled by the 'proto-Fascist Ustasa.' Blee and Creasap (2010, p. 210) note that some contemporary 'right-wing' groups, including the US Christian Right and Haider's Freedom Party in Austria, show the 'growing tendency' to embrace the 'organization, goals, and strategies that are commonly associated with terrorism.'

100   Arendt (1951, p. 345) alerts to 'mass murder perpetrated on 'guilty' and 'innocent' alike' in German fascism. Horkheimer and Adorno (1993, p. 181) admonish that 'when fascist murderers are waiting, one should not incite the people against the weak government.'

or persecution equals or resembles that in theocracy and religious conservatism.[101] In this regard, fascism both outside of and in state power is a murderous extreme conservative, radical-right ideology and relatedly, a mostly
religious or theocratic movement and regime.

Especially, fascism is an ideology and system of pro-capital and anti-labor
coercion, repression, violence, and terror, including mass murder, with minor
variations. In essence, it is the combined capitalist-conservative movement and
regime of total and intense coercion, repression, violence, and terror directed
against labor and its collective organization and action and of mass murder or persecution of its members like union leaders. Fascism is vehemently
and violently anti-union in that it attacks and abolishes labor movement,[102]
such as independent, as opposed to pro-fascist, trade unions, and murders
and persecutes their figures as enemies and threats to fascist rule,[103] aside
from rare exceptions. On this account, it finishes what coercive capitalism

---

101   Hedges (2004) notes that the 'Christian Right finds its ideological justification in a narrow
      segment of the Gospel, in particular the letters of the Apostle Paul, especially the story of
      Paul's conversion on the road to Damascus in the Book of Acts. It draws heavily from the
      book of Revelations and the Gospel of John. These books share an apocalyptic theology.
      The Book of Revelations is the only time in the Gospels where Jesus sanctions violence,
      offering up a vision of Christ as the head of a great and murderous army of heavenly
      avengers.' Savelsberg (2006, pp. 391–3) reminds of the 'murderous abuse of government
      power during the Nazi regime' as well as that 'major sections of the Protestant Church had
      been incorporated into the Nazi state', aside from 'an important opposition movement'.
      Hitchens (2009, p. 82) recounts that Nazi 'fugitive torturers and murderers like Klaus
      Barbie often found themselves second careers as servants of (extreme-right dictatorships
      in the Southern Hemisphere), which until they began to collapse in the last decades of
      the twentieth century had also enjoyed a steady relationship of support from the local
      Catholic clergy. The connection of the church to fascism and Nazism actually outlasted
      the Third Reich itself.' Satyanath, Voigtländer, and Voth (2017, 479) report that 'Nazi Party
      success correlated with religion'.
102   Paxton (1998, p. 6) observes that the 'most important common interest [between German
      capitalists and the Nazi regime], of course, was the emasculation of the labor movement'.
103   Ferguson and Voth (2008, pp. 105–6) recall that 'promising a broad coalition of the right,
      Hitler was appointed as head of government by the President on January 30, 1933. Using
      the pretext of the Reichstag fire, the new government cracked down on the Communist
      party and suspended civil liberties. The enabling law, passed with the votes of all parties
      except the Social Democrats, changed the constitution and allowed laws to be passed
      without parliamentary approval. The unions were dissolved in early May, and numerous
      members jailed. By the summer of 1933, all parties except the [Nazi party] had been dis-
      solved.' Spenkuch and Tillmann (2017, p. 14) recount that, except for the Nazi party, all
      political parties in Germany were banned by the Nazi government in 1933 following the
      Enabling Act by which conservative/rightist parties enabled Hitler's rule as expressing the
      dominance of authoritarian rightism.

and authoritarian conservatism start and attempt in unison—prevention or destruction of worker organizations and actions—and represents a 'final solution' to the supposed labor or union anti-capital and anti-conservative 'problem'.

Conversely, fascism is typically pro-capitalist by being the 'exponent of bourgeois groups'[104] against working classes and labor movement, although it initially while in opposition strategically deploys some anti-capitalist 'national socialist' appeals and slogans to attract, recruit, or deceive workers and other lower or middle strata who ultimately become its main victims, and to neutralize their associated political parties. Once seizing and exerting total political power, fascism, including Nazism, becomes and functions as pro-capitalist, 'antisocialist' dictatorship.[105]

Furthermore, fascism arises, acts as, and promises to be the last and strongest defense of capitalism against the threat of socialism and other forms of anti-capitalism. Crucially, when capturing and exercising total state power,

---

104   Mannheim (1936, p. 146) observes that 'fascism is the exponent of bourgeois groups [so it seeks] only of substituting one ruling group for another within the existing class arrangements.' Paxton (1998, p. 7) notes that 'fascist militants proclaim themselves antibourgeois; what they hate in the bourgeoisie, however, is not exploitation but softness'—and in that sense they look like would-be violent bourgeois.

105   Parsons (1951, p. 352) remarks that the 'inclusion of socialism in the ideological formula [of Nazism] served to neutralize the left and to mobilize the immense reservoir of anti-capitalistic sentiment from the right and large parts of the left behind the single movement.' Gastil (1989, p. 4) notes that 'it is surprising how many well-informed persons believe that since the 'German Democratic Republic' also uses the term democracy in its label, we must include regimes of this type within our definition. It would be like saying that since the German fascists called their party 'National Socialist,' discussions of socialism must use definitions that would include the Nazis', which implies that Nazi 'socialism' was bogus or deception deceiving some economists about the 'alliance of Nationalism and Socialism' (Clark 1957). Paxton (1998, p. 5) cautions that early fascist social-economic programs are 'poor guides to later fascist policy', including the economic-social changes 'proposed by Mussolini's first Fascist program of April 1919' contradicted by his 'deals with conservatives'. Also, Paxton (1998, p. 5) remarks that the 'hostility' of early Nazism (e.g., the Nazi Twenty-Five Points of 1920) toward capitalism (minus that of artisan producers) 'bears little relation to the sometimes strained though powerfully effective collaboration for rearmament between German business and the Nazi regime.' He elaborates that 'in fact, most business leaders, whose negative memories of Weimar and the Depression were still fresh, swallowed their reluctance about Nazi autarky and thrived handsomely on rearmament. Daimler-Benz enjoyed particular favor with the regime' (Paxton 1998, pp. 5–6). Overall, Paxton (1998, p. 9) characterizes fascist regimes as 'antisocialist nationalist dictatorships.' Acemoglu et al. (2022, pp. 1243–4) reaffirm that 'Mussolini soon managed to refashion the [fascist] party as a robust antisocialist force, attracting new members more committed to violent, antisocialist action.'

fascism invariably allies and merges with coercive capitalism[106] by defending capitalist interests and oppressing and eliminating organized labor, such as unions and their leaders and members.

In economic respect, hence fascism is a totalitarian rendition and degeneration but not opposition to and supersession of capitalism[107] and an extreme

---

106   Friedman (1982, p. 9) admits that 'Fascist Italy and Fascist Spain, Germany at various times in the last seventy years, Japan before World Wars I and II, tzarist Russia in the decades before World War I—are all societies that cannot conceivably be described as politically free. Yet, in each, private enterprise was the dominant form of economic organization. It is therefore clearly possible to have economic arrangements that are fundamentally capitalist and political arrangements that are not free. Burawoy (2005, p. 4) diagnoses 'capitalism-become-fascism' during the 1930s. Ferguson and Voth (2008, p. 101) find that 'many more large firms had ties with the National Socialist German Workers' Party (NSDAP) to the extent that weighted by capitalization in 1932, more than half of listed firms on the Berlin stock exchange enjoyed close links with the Nazi movement. Affiliated firms outperformed the stock market by 5% to 8% and account for a large part of the market's rise. Investors recognized value where they saw it and rewarded firms with preestablished ties handsomely.' Notably, they point to the 'conviction of influential industrialists such as Friedrich Karl Flick, Alfried Krupp, and I. G. Farben executives in the Nuremberg trials, [as] major German firms had financed the Nazi party's rapid rise after 1930', citing Fritz Thyssen's statement 'I Paid Hitler' (Ferguson and Voth 2008, p. 102). Huber, Lindenthal, and Waldinger (2021, p, 2457) refer to '655 German firms listed on the Berlin Stock Exchange' under Nazism. They also note most German capitalist firms' 'connections to the Nazi Party' (Huber et al. 2021, p, 2458).

107   As typical of Austrian economics, including his colleague Hayek, Mises (1951, p. 578) misconstrues fascism in that he equates it with socialism, stating that the two 'are in concert: they reprobate private property and aspire to create a social system based on collective economy'. This overlooks that Nazism, along with Italian fascism, approved of private property and maintained capitalism, including large-scale private capitalist enterprises a la Krupp et al. that in fact financed Hitler's rise and rule, as well as the private stock market, as Ferguson and Voth (2008) show. Also, contradicting Mises, Steinmetz and Wright (1989, p. 973) note that, along with Wilhelm II in Imperial Germany, the Italian and German fascists 'have promulgated laws to prop up small businesses [so private property] in order to consolidate political support.' In a way, most Austrian economists, at least Hayek and Mises, along with Schumpeter, hide or obscure their Nazi or pan-German sympathies, as well as aristocratic conservative backgrounds, biases, and prejudices, with dogmatic and vehement anti-socialism, compromised laissez-faire capitalism, and bogus 'libertarianism'. Herman (1945, pp. 15–16) describes Hayek's The Road to Serfdom as the 'road to reaction' against democracy and the 'reactionary manifesto' linked with fascism, observing that that 'here is a joy for all conservatives. In spite of the world's desperate travail to overthrow Hitler and Mussolini and what they stood for, many conservatives need the new joy because secretly they have just lost the old [fascist] one. We now live in a world without Hitler. His removal has swept away the inhibition against open avowal of his doctrines of contempt for the majority and equality and popular sovereignty.' Herman (1945, pp. 15–16) predicts that 'there will be a babel of antidemocratic statements within a few months; murmurings can already be heard [such as Hayek]. For a time the bitterness

system of labor coercion, repression, violence, and terror, including mass murder and persecution of workers or union leaders and members.

Fascism engages in labor repression through the prohibition or suppression of trade unions, as Nazism demonstrates by its dissolution of unions and persecution of their leaders and members. Relatedly, fascism or authoritarian conservatism exerts such repression by the prohibition or suppression of collective bargaining between employers and workers and labor participation in management and other forms of economic democracy.[108]

More broadly, fascism is invariably an extreme conservative or radical right ideology and system of mass imprisonment, indefinite detention, torture, police brutality, violence, and other abuses and violations of elementary human rights as elements of state repression and terror. Relatedly, it is an extreme conservative regime of mass or widespread death sentences and executions, pervasive and chronic murders by the police, and other acts of murderous state and state-sponsored 'political terror'.[109] Furthermore, following and escalating conservatism's old repressive pattern to the extreme, fascism perverts civil society into an open prison or overarching monastery through total surveillance, vigilantism, denunciation,[110] and reporting of people's

---

of the reactionaries has been merely bridled, out of expediency, while the power and repute of the majority have been magnified, because it is the majority that fights world wars.' Also, Piketty (2020, p. 14) describes some of Hayek's work as 'semi-dictatorial' and thus by implication semi-fascist or radical right due to being ultra-conservative.

108   Rogers and Streeck (1995, p. 15) point to Germany's economic democracy 'aborted by the Nazis'.

109   Besley and Persson (2009, p. 292) characterize 'a political terror scale' by that 'civil and political rights violations such as execution, imprisonment and political murders/ brutality are widespread. In the worst cases, leaders of society place no limit on the means or thoroughness with which they pursue personal or ideological goals [e.g.] purges: systematic murders and eliminations of political opponents within regimes.'

110   Hitchens (2009, 80) asks 'what is a totalitarian system if not one where the abject glorification of the perfect leader is matched by the surrender of all privacy and individuality, especially in matters sexual, and in denunciation and punishment—"for their own good"—of those who transgress? The sexual element is probably decisive, [which] Nathaniel Hawthorne captured in The Scarlet Letter: the deep connection between repression and perversion' in theocratic Puritan society. Bergemann (2017, p. 384) finds that in 'Nazi Germany, for example, the Gestapo gathered most of their intelligence through the widespread participation of Germans willing to report deviance within their local communities. This is what led the Gestapo to be perceived as 'omniscient, omnipotent, and omnipresent', despite there being only one officer for every 10,000 residents. [For example] there were more than 17,000 denunciations in 1937 alone for violations against one of the many laws that a person could be denounced for violating.' Also, a law in the Bible-Belt, ultra-conservative state of Texas resulting from a tacit coalition between religious conservatives and radical feminists mandates its residents under the threat of

private activities, notably sexual behaviors and even intentions, to fascist and theocratic authorities who punish them with standard Draconian cruelty and severity.

In short, completing conservatism, fascism amounts to an Orwellian dystopian world of non-existent or less actual crime and more cruel and severe punishment,[111] including mass imprisonment, pervasive death sentences, and widespread police brutality, violence, and murders. Furthermore, taking to the extreme conservatism's and theocratic religion's death penalty application or defense, fascism becomes the system of mass death and extermination of its anti-fascist and non-conservative opponents, such as liberals, democrats, secularists, rationalists, including scientists and educators, progressives, egalitarians, cosmopolitans, socialists, communists, labor leaders and union members, as well as ethnic-racial minorities. Yet, ultimately, fascism leads to the mass death and destruction of its own blindly following rank-and-file and thus the majority and the 'people' as the ultimate and largest victim of fascism's deceptive populism as the negation or perversion of classical popular sovereignty and hence democracy, together with the collective suicide of its leaders a la Hitler et al.

9   Extreme Militarism, Offensive War, and Conquest

Ninth and yet another corollary of being conservative totalitarianism and anti-liberalism, fascism is invariably a complex of extreme anti-pacifism, militarism, aggressive war, and imperial forcible conquest, with secondary variations. Fascism is therefore universally an extreme conservative, right ideology, social movement, political regime, and cultural zeitgeist of the most intense

---

severe punishment to monitor, denounce, and report to the police the sexual activities, intentions, or transgressions (couched as 'sexual assaults') of neighbors, acquaintances, friends, spouses, and everyone else in the best Puritanical proto-fascist tradition (on elements of fascism in Puritanism see Adorno 2001; Fromm 1941; Harrold 1936; Merton 1939). Such Bible-Belt laws thus combine the Puritan-style witch-hunts of sinners—most acts denounced as crimes-sins are as much 'sexual assaults' as the victims of Puritan terror were 'witches'—with Nazi vigilantism for deviance, along with radical feminism's gendered 'social hatred' that highlights its ironic 'femi-Nazi' label by US conservatives as intrinsic or 'closet' proto-fascists. They just continue the shared Puritan-Nazi morbid obsession with sin like sex and reproduce a Bible-Belt religious-vice police state of mass imprisonment and other punishment of sinners in Texas and the South overall even five centuries since the arrival of Puritanism and one century after the rise of Nazism.

111   Cooney and Burt (2008) report 'less crime, more punishment' in the US during the conservative 'war on crime', especially the Reagan-style Puritanical 'war on drugs.'

anti-pacifism and militarism, with minor and temporary variations. Aside from rare exceptions, fascists, including leaders and rank-and-file members, are everywhere and always extreme rightist anti-pacifists and militarists who attack and subjugate other peoples and societies that they, as the self-deluded and self-declared superior 'master' nation, regard and mistreat as 'inferior'.

Fascism exalts and pursues extreme militarism as the proof of strength, superiority, and mastery over 'inferior' peoples, races, and societies that supposedly cannot exist and function without being ruled by fascist 'masters' and 'superiors'. Conversely, fascists denounce and despise pacifism[112] as the trait of 'inferior', weak peoples and societies and thus associate it with national and racial 'inferiority' and weakness, the abject lack of strength of nations and races.

Hence, master-race nationalism and racism operate as the driving force and rationale of fascism's composite of anti-pacifism and militarism, and consequently conquest and offensive war expressing imperialism. The latter especially holds true for the Western colonial and imperial 'great powers' (allied in NATO as an expansionary military alliance in the function of American imperialism and Western neocolonialism), as distinct from weaker fascist states that are their allies via various warlike alliances (from the Axis during WW II to NATO in postwar times). What drives and, in their own minds, rationalizes fascists, notably their leaders, in acting extremely anti-pacifist and militarist is the 'fantastic notion'[113] that they are the master, superior race or nation and all others their slaves or inferiors. Fascism thereby provides the foremost proof that aggressive nationalism eventually generates and predicts anti-pacifism

---

112   Mannheim (1936, p. 136) cites Mussolini stating that 'I have no great confidence in these ideals' of pacifism.

113   US President Franklin T. Roosevelt described as the 'fantastic notion' Nazism's claim to the German 'superior race'. Critics may object that even the most consequential, benevolent, and respected 20th century President overlooked that American conservatives had held precisely such a notion or its variations for long since the Divine 'manifest destiny' sanctification of the genocide or persecution of Native Americans by Puritanism and its ramifications to neo-fascist white supremacists, including US Presidents from Andrew Jackson's violent nationalism to the post-2016 autocracy emulating it. Tocqueville (1945, p. 624) classically remarks that 'it has been imagined that General Jackson is bent on establishing a dictatorship in America, introducing a military spirit, and giving a degree of influence to the central authority that cannot but be dangerous to provincial liberties' and comments that 'in America the time for similar undertakings, and the age for men of this kind, has not yet come'. Today's observers may add that the time for a Jacksonian nationalist and militarist 'dictatorship in America' eventually came in post-2016 and even the 1980s. Bonikowski and DiMaggio (2016, p. 953) identify in the US 'a xenophobic counter-narrative, often associated with conservative Protestantism and the tradition of Jacksonian nationalism.'

and militarism, as well as imperialism via conquest and offensive war especially among the Western colonial and imperial 'great powers' (e.g., the
US/NATO's wars after WW II or the Cold War qualify as offensive, from South
America through Vietnam to Yugoslavia and Iraq). Fascists are the ultimate
examples of intense nationalists being typically extreme anti-pacifists and
militarists, as well as imperialists and bellicose forces when arising and acting
within these 'great powers.' It follows that the compound of master-race racism
and nationalism drives both fascism's anti-pacifism and militarism and eventually its aggressive wars and conquest and thus imperialism especially among
the colonial and imperial Western 'great powers'. Specifically, white supremacy
is the prime mover of fascist anti-pacifism and militarism, particularly aggressive war and conquest, and so imperialism among the Western 'great powers',
which particularly holds for Nazism.[114]

Conversely, fascism as pacifism and non-militarism, just as a liberal-
democratic system, is a logical non sequitur and empirical fiction or rarity,
with minor and transient variations, especially during its early stages of capture and consolidation of absolute power within society and brief isolationism
from other societies, for example, Italian fascism in the 1920s, Nazism before
1936, the US post-2016 regime in its first years. Pacifist and non-militarist, just
as liberal-democratic, fascists are self-contradictions and non-entities, or
impossible and do not exist in reality for long, aside from rare transient exceptions during their rise and seize of power in society and taking an isolationist
posture temporarily and tactically in the aim of consolidation of their absolute rule.

The above indicates that fascism poses a dual lethal threat to liberal-
democratic modernity, initially to the society in which it rises, captures power,
and dominates and ultimately to all other societies through its intense anti-
pacifism and militarism. To that extent, the rise and dominance of fascism in a
certain, especially major, society is a warning signal, panic alarm for all liberal-
democratic societies. Fascism not only destroys liberal democracy and liberty
in a society, indeed the societal fabric, in which it rises and prevails but also
ultimately threatens to destroy those in other societies and even these as such
due to its extreme anti-pacifism and militarism. The power capture and rule
of fascism is not just an internal, intra-societal phenomenon affecting a single

---

114   Fischer (2003, p. 27) alludes to fascism, especially Nazism, by referring to the 'projects and
        politics of militarism and imperialism' in interwar Europe. Satyanath et al. (2017, p. 480)
        single out the 'Nazis' racist, militaristic, expansionist ideology.' More broadly, Acemoglu
        et al. (2022, p. 1234) concur with the view that in Italy 'the novelty of Fascism lay in the
        military organization of a political party'.

society but also, after its initial adaptation and transient tactical isolationism, an inter-societal threat to other liberal-democratic societies because of intense fascist anti-pacifism and militarism. Fascists are lethally dangerous agents not only to their own pre-fascist society but also eventually, after being temporarily and tactically isolationist, to other liberal-democratic societies because of being extremely anti-pacifist and militarist. In short, fascism initially ends liberal democracy in a society in which it seizes power and eventually by its anti-pacifism and militarism disturbs peace among other societies. Generally, while not every anti-pacifism and militarism is fascist, fascism is universally extremely anti-pacifist and militarist, thus not all anti-pacifists and militarists being fascists, but the latter are always extreme instances of the former.

Fascism inherits, continues, and takes conservatism's characteristic anti-pacifism and militarism[115] to the extreme of anti-pacifist and militarist frenzy and madness, culminating in aggressive wars, mass death, destruction and finally self-destruction in the form or image of MAD, mutually assured destruction. Counterfactually but perhaps realistically, Nazism would have probably caused MAD during WW II if it succeeded to invent and produce a nuclear bomb and did not expel those who, along with others, invented it for the US, as scientists-immigrants whom American conservatism and fascism depreciate and demonize as both scientists and immigrants. Like Clausewitz's war, fascism is the continuation and maximum intensification of conservatism's original and persistent anti-pacifism and militarism by other or identical means.

Alternatively, conservatism's intrinsic anti-pacifism and militarism persist and culminate in fascism's anti-pacifist and militarist hysteria and madness. In longer historical terms, conservative anti-pacifism and militarism originate in and perpetuate militarist feudalism and primitive, medievalist warlike religion, for example, crusading Christianity, especially bellicose Calvinism/Puritanism as the 'Church Militant' (Weber's words), and jihadist Islam, and continue through and evolve in those of fascism as their culmination. At this point, fascism links with medievalism through medieval-rooted conservatism that connects Nazism with medievalist German romanticism and the First Reich or the Germanic empire.

Accordingly, fascists, including fascist leaders and followers, are everywhere and always extreme conservative, radical-rightist anti-pacifists and militarists.

---

115   Paxton (2004, p. 31) reports that after WW I 'conservatives said little in 1918, but tried quietly to restore a world in which armed force settled relations among states,' thus displaying strong militarism and warlike propensities. He adds that the 'fascists' new formula promised, like that of the conservatives, to settle territorial conflicts by allowing the strong to triumph' (Paxton 2004, p. 32).

Conversely, most conservative anti-pacifists and militarists eventually become fascists who possess such traits, with the result that the two groups are substantively almost indistinguishable in respect of anti-pacifism and militarism. The difference between them is formal or quantitative, as in relative degrees of anti-pacifism and militarism, and not in substance or kind, as in the presence or absence of these elements, with fascists displaying just a higher anti-pacifist and militarist intensity compared to other conservatives or rightists.

Specifically, fascism is the system of extreme rearmament,[116] arms races, preparation for offensive war through exorbitant expenditure of societal resources on wars, militarist, political and economic mobilization, and a large standing army. In this sense, fascism amounts to a Leviathan-like[117] ever-growing and aggressive military-industrial complex[118] as the instrument of extreme fascist and generally conservative anti-pacifism, militarism, and ultimately offensive war, conquest, and imperialism. Just as being a constant conservative counterrevolution of anti-liberal nihilism in society, fascism is a compound of perpetual frantic rearmament, arms races, and militarist political-economic mobilization and preparation for wars of aggression[119]

---

116   Galbraith and Parker (2017, p. 243) state that 'civil works expenditure was followed only later by that for arms' in Nazism but this seems to overlook that mass and threatening rearmament was the initial element of the Nazi program, notably its opposition to the Versailles treaty ending WW I by unjustly, in Hitler's view, harming, Germany. Galbraith and Parker (2017, p. 242) placing Adolf Hitler among 'Keynesians well before Keynes' seems exaggerated, because the latter dismissed Nazism and its militarism (Fischer 2003). Cohen (2003, p. 51) notes Nazism's 're-armament program of 1936'.

117   Steinmetz (2005, p. 358) describes the 'global American military machine' as 'martial Leviathan.'

118   Lloyd (2012, p. 487) registers the 'location of the postwar military industrial complex in the Southeast (and far West)' US and the 'postwar relocation of German scientists, including decorated Nazi war hero turned NASA pioneer Wernher von Braun, to Huntsville (Alabama), where rockets were developed in service of both American airborne military capacity and the US space program.' It seems as if the US postwar conservative government could not develop this program without the help of such decorated Nazi war heroes, displaying and indeed reaffirming the covert or latent 'fatal attraction' and 'affair' between 'all-American' conservatism and foreign Nazism.

119   Parsons (1949, p. 140) points to the 'fascist tendency immediately to mobilize the economy in preparation for war' in Germany. Habermas (1975, p. 12) refers to a 'fascist-authoritarian state that holds the population by the bit at a relatively high level of permanent mobilization.' Braverman (1998, p. 198), suggests that, along with 'other aspects of monopoly capitalism', a 'permanent war mobilization' was 'pioneered by Germany (during the Nazi era in the 1930s) and has been practiced on a grand scale by the United States since World War II.' Agamben (1998, p. 88) registers the 'incessant political mobilization' of Nazism.

against other societies that it defines, attacks, and subjugates as 'enemies' and 'inferior' nations. Fascists everywhere are heavily armed groups, including counter-state and state militias when outside of and in political power, wielding the most lethal weapons through unrestricted gun ownership and assaulting liberals and other anti-fascists, plus ethnic-racial minorities, within society and 'inferior' peoples and races in other societies.

Ultimately, fascism is a system of aggressive wars against and conquest and subjugation of other societies that it condemns and attacks as 'inferior' to be ruled by the fascist 'master race', which especially applies to Nazism. Exactly like in Clausewitz's setting, fascism's aggressive war is really the continuation and escalation of its politics of extreme anti-pacifism and militarism by other or identical means consisting of brute military force acquired through frenzied rearmament, exorbitant military expenditure, and permanent militarist mobilization. Hence, fascism, notably Nazism, constitutes the aggressive warfare state[120] in relation to other societies, that is conjoined and mutually reinforced with the police state within society.

Consequently, fascism turns out to be a complex of mass death, destruction, and ultimately self-destruction, literally MAD, through mutually assured destruction in the scenario of nuclear war that fascism, along with apocalyptic

---

Bahr (2002, p. 811) notes that Nazi totalitarianism 'describes a type of regime that, no longer satisfied with the limited aims of classical despotisms and dictatorships, demands continual mobilization of its subjects and never allows the society to settle down into a durable hierarchical order.' Barnett and Woywode (2004, p. 1455) remark that 'by the early 1930s the forces of right and left in Vienna were mobilized, and, until the *Anschluss*—the annexation of Austria by Hitler's Germany on March 13, 1938—fervent ideological competition continued throughout Austria.' Rydgren (2007a, pp. 253) notes the 'new radical right-wing parties' voter mobilization.' Blee and Creasap (2010, p. 276) characterize the rise of German Nazism as 'a prototype of right-wing mobilization.'

120   Esping-Andersen (2003, p. 8) registers that in its 'English usage, the welfare state was coined by the Archbishop of York during World War Two as a programmatic antidote to the Nazi warfare state.' He adds that many 'would date the arrival of welfare states to the moment when a basic repertoire of social policies was in place. In this case, Britain was a welfare state in 1920, as was Nazi Germany, and Franco's Spain in the 1960s. But if it is to have any meaning at all, the welfare state is more than social policy; it is a unique historical construction, an explicit redefinition of what the state is all about' (Esping-Andersen 2003, p. 34). Esping-Andersen (2003, p. 81) observes that the 'passage from origins to postwar welfare capitalism has, in (Catholic dominated) countries, been guided primarily by Christian democratic or conservative coalitions (in some cases with a Fascist interregnum)', with the last part intimating a connection of Catholicism and conservatism with fascism. Esping-Andersen (2003, pp. 81–2) adds that 'most Continental European countries emulated Imperial Germany's social insurance reforms and, like Bismarck, their original aims were far removed from any egalitarianism. The early social reformers were typically authoritarian', which implies intrinsic or typical conservative authoritarianism.

Christian evangelicalism,[121] would likely start—and would have probably launched if Nazism had nuclear weapons during ww ii—and thus self-destructive societal madness. The latter is the outcome of fascist 'madmen' seizing and exercising absolute state power and total control and domination of society. The last stand of fascism is the destruction of other societies and peoples, together with anti- and non-fascist social forces, and the self-destruction of its own society and its 'people' as a perverse ultimate result of fascist bogus populism that effectively eliminates popular sovereignty by eliminating liberal democracy. The final act of fascists is destroying or harming other nations, along with anti-fascists within society, and self-destroying their nation and eventually themselves Hitler-Goebbels' style.

On this account, fascism is an equivalent of murderous and suicidal religious sects and cults,[122] and fascist leaders and followers are counterparts of those of the latter. Ultimately, fascism is bent on and ends in mass suicide through self-destruction of society in the manner of suicidal Christian fundamentalist and other religious sects and cults destroying others and themselves. Fascist leaders sacrifice the lives of their rank-and-file to their absolute power, just as those of suicidal religious sects and cults sacrificing their followers to their personal 'salvation'[123] ('heaven', 'rapture', the 'second coming'). In the end, fascist leaders destroy themselves as the final act, just as do those of suicidal religious sects and cults, both probably seeking to attain some variant of salvation via total annihilation of society.[124] This illustrates the immense gravity that

---

121   Dawkins (2006, p. 132) observes that 'some rapture [US] Christians go further [than to wait] and actually yearn for nuclear war because they interpret it as the "Armageddon."'

122   Recall that Dawkins (2006, p. 277) notes that 'some of Hitler's followers, with the support of Goebbels, made no bones about building Nazism into a religion in its own right', thus a religious sect or cult.

123   Referring to today's Calvinists going by the 'softer names of Presbyterians and Baptists', Hitchens (2009, p. 80) suggests that the 'urge to ban and censor books, silence dissenters, condemn outsiders, invade the private sphere, and invoke an exclusive salvation is the very essence of the totalitarian.'

124   Adorno (2001, p. 230) observes that destructiveness is the 'psychological basis of the fascist spirit. The programs are abstract and vague, the fulfillments are spurious and illusory because the promise expressed by fascist oratory is nothing but destruction.' He elaborates that hence 'all fascist agitators dwell upon the imminence of catastrophes of some kind. Whereas they warn of impending danger, they and their listeners get a thrill out of the idea of inevitable doom, without even making a clear-cut distinction between the destruction of their foes and of themselves. This mental behavior [was] clearly observed during the first years of Hitlerism in Germany, and has a deep archaic basis. One of the [US] West Coast demagogues once said: 'I want to say that you men and women, you and I are living in the most fearful time of the history of the world. We are living also

fascism represents for society and human life because of its anti-pacifism, militarism, consequently aggressive wars, and conquest—a grave, indeed lethal danger both to the 'superior' nation in which it rises and dominates and to other 'inferior' nations that it attacks and subjugates, ultimately all societies.

10   Aggregate of Extreme Authoritarians Agents

Tenth and as a corollary of all the preceding elements, fascism represents invariably an aggregate of extreme authoritarian agents in socio-psychological terms. It follows that fascism is universally an extreme conservative, radical-right collection of authoritarian personalities.[125] Fascists, including both fascist leaders and their blindly submissive rank-and-file, are everywhere and always extremely illiberal, anti-democratic subjects typifying an authoritarian personality, simply extreme authoritarians.[126]

Specifically, fascist leaders are extreme authoritarian rulers by pursuing and holding absolute power and seeking and exercising total control and domination of society. This tendency ultimately reaches the point of fascist leaders having the 'license to kill' literally or figuratively, which makes fascism descend into Hobbesian anarchy and the state of nature governed by the law of the strongest or the jungle, thus the extreme of lawlessness. The law of the strongest in the primeval state of nature is the only law that fascist leaders recognize and observe, thus making and perpetuating fascism as a lawless social system. The fascist rank-and-file form extreme authoritarian followers by following and submitting to, indeed demanding, their leaders' absolute power and total control and domination of society, including themselves. Such a tendency eventually reaches the stage of the fascist rank-and-file exhibiting blind obedience,

---

in the most gracious and most wonderful time.' This is the agitator's dream, a union of the horrible and the wonderful, a delirium of annihilation masked as salvation [i.e.] its self-destructive implications. The unconscious psychological desire for self-annihilation faithfully reproduces the structure of a political movement which ultimately transforms its followers into victims.'

125   Miller, Slomczynski, and Kohn (1987) propose the 'concept authoritarian conservatism' defined in terms of an 'unreflexive, rigid thought process' but as distinct from 'Adorno et al.'s psychoanalytic interpretation of an authoritarian personality'.

126   Mann (2004, p. 237) observes that 'authoritarians here remained through the interwar period as a fractious family whose reactionary [conservative], corporatist [capitalist], and fascist members struggled noisily for overall dominance.' Altemeyer (2007, p. 257) creates the 'unidirectionally-worded measure of authoritarianism called the Fascism Scale'. Altemeyer (2007, pp. 246–7) observes that no 'fascist dictatorship lies just over our horizon [yet] we are [not] well protected against one. [Indeed] the threat is growing.'

submission, and sacrifice (the Nazi 'blind herd') of their property, family, and life to the cult of their leaders and their absolute power. By so doing, fascist followers also only respect the law of the strongest in the state of nature.

Taken together, the above creates a circle of authoritarian rule and follow-ing, control and obedience, domination and subjection, a conglomerate of authoritarians in total power and blind submission alike. In short, fascism is a socio-psychological aggregate of extreme authoritarians-leaders and authoritarians-followers in interplay and mutual reinforcement. Fascist lead-ers need and create, although profoundly despise and systematically degrade, their authoritarian followers, and conversely, the second want and sustain the first so long as these prove themselves according to the law of the strongest, with some variations. However, compatible with fascism's elitist interpretation of social history as a 'circulation of elites', fascist authoritarian leaders ulti-mately discard and make their mass and blindly loyal followers into despised and helpless victims, who hence want or need more for their expression and preservation their absolute rulers than conversely.

Fascism as a social system both reproduces and attracts authoritarian actors and forces in society. On one hand, it generates and sustains authoritarian personalities in society by perverting normal human actors into pathological characters such as extreme authoritarians as fascist leaders and followers. On the other hand, it attracts, preselects, and incorporates for its totalitarian goals preexisting authoritarian and related forces, such as 'explosive irrational ele-ments',[127] from society. Taken together, fascism is both the cause and effect of authoritarian forces, with authoritarians being its products and prerequisites. While not all authoritarian actors are fascist, fascists are universally extreme authoritarians as leaders and followers in socio-psychological terms.

Specifically, fascism is universally a compound of extreme sadism and masochism in the face of sadistic-masochistic actors and traits.[128] Fascists everywhere and always manifest compounded extreme sadistic-masochistic characters, acting sadistically toward some groups and masochistically when

---

127   Mannheim (1936, p. 141) witnesses that fascism 'attracts the explosive irrational elements in the modern mind.'

128   Fromm (1941, p. 255) proposes that 'with regard to Fascism the same principle of explana-tion [applies as to Calvinism]: the lower middle class reacted to certain economic changes, such as the growing power of monopolies and postwar inflation, with an intensification of certain character traits, namely sadistic and masochistic strivings; the Nazi ideology appealed to and intensified these traits; and the new character traits then became effec-tive forces in supporting the expansion of German imperialism.' Arendt (1951, p. 30) finds that the 'irrational, sadistic type [of torture] was added in the first Nazi concentration camps and in the cellars of the Gestapo.'

facing others. Fascist leaders everywhere display extreme sadism in relation to their subordinates, rank-and-file, and the masses overall. Notably, the supreme fascist leader acts in an extremely sadistic manner toward all other persons— perhaps minus close family members—acting as the foremost sadist in fascism. Furthermore, the fascist rank-and-file also manifest extreme sadism in relation to other persons than their leaders, acting sadistically toward anti-fascists and non-conservatives like liberals, as well as lower social strata, including working classes, and ethnic minorities. On this account, all fascists from the single supreme fascist leader through subordinate intermediate leaders and the rank-and-file are essentially sadists, even if in different degrees and ways.

In turn, fascist rank-and-file members exhibit extreme masochism in relation to their leaders by willingly and joyfully subjecting themselves to their sadistic treatment. Moreover, all fascists display such masochism in relation to the supreme fascist leader by submitting with masochistic pleasure and nationalist pride to the latter's sadistic treatment of them. All fascists, including the fascist rank-and-file and subordinate intermediate leaders, appear as masochists, although in varying degrees and ways, with even the supreme fascist leader showing masochistic or self-destructive traits in certain situations like Hitler's suicide when Nazism was defeated.

Owing to its compound of sadism and masochism, its aggregate of sadists and masochists, fascism is what its precursor and inspiration Pareto denotes referring to religion, such as Christian theological disputes,[129] the 'cage for the insane' so long as sadistic-masochistic tendencies typify the latter. The 'cage for the insane' with such a referent seems—contrary to Pareto's expectations— a proper metaphor for fascism given its extreme anti-secularism, religious extremism, and merger with theocracy. Fascism produces and perpetuates sadism and masochism in society in that it perverts human personalities, including those perfectly normal, into sadistic-masochistic characters. In this

---

129 Glaeser (2004, p. 409) remarks that 'in the wake of World War II, a series of psychological experiments showed that normal Americans could be induced to act barbarically [i.e.] are willing to follow orders from an authority figure to cause pain to an innocent bystander [and] adopt the identity of sadistic guards. These experiments refute the view that Nazi-like behavior could not happen here, but they do not explain why Nazism occurred in Germany but not in the US.' Dawkins (2006, p. 252) identifies the 'sado-masochism of the Christian religion in that God incarnated himself as a man, Jesus, in order that he should be tortured and executed in atonement for the hereditary sin of Adam. Ever since Paul expounded this repellent doctrine, Jesus has been worshipped as the redeemer of all our sins. Not just the past sin of Adam: future sins as well, whether future people decided to commit them or not!' Hitchens (2009, p. 80) alerts to 'Christian sadists' especially in the US.

sense, fascism creates, multiplies, and sustains the 'insane' to inhabit the 'cage'. On the other hand, fascism attracts preexisting sadism and masochism from society in that it preselects and embraces for its purposes sadistic-masochistic personalities who join and find their natural environment in the fascist system. In this regard, fascism builds, expands, and maintains the 'cage' for containing the 'insane'. Taken together, this process forms a perpetual cycle of compounded sadism-masochism, mixed sadists-masochists in fascism. In sociopsychological terms, the compound of sadism and masochism, thus personal destruction and self-destruction, demonstrates the insanity of fascism, and the mix of sadists and masochists exemplifies fascist 'madmen' in power.

In addition, fascism's authoritarian leaders display both grave seriousness and extra-ordinary actions and grotesqueness and ordinary presence, as their followers do. On one hand, fascist leaders act as deadly serious, decisive, cruel, including sadist-masochistic, pompous, charismatic, and seemingly 'highly efficacious expressive',[130] with their authoritarian followers blindly adopting or imitating these traits and behaviors. Furthermore, fascist leaders pretend to be superhuman, Divine-like creatures or chosen by God, deluding themselves and others, pretending to have 'divine' origins or rights, with their authoritarian followers blindly subscribing to these delusions and pretensions.

On the other hand, fascist leaders appear and behave as grotesque, cowardly, ridiculous, laughable, and ordinary as if playing in a mix of tragedy and comedy,[131] for example, Mussolini's buffoonery, Hitler's clown-style gestures, Chaplin's *the Great Dictator*, etc., and in that sense as tragic-comic actors. Relatedly, they look like all other humans rather than as superhuman, Divine-like creatures, which their followers, due to their blind adulation and

---

130   Parsons (1951, p. 352) suggests that 'resting partly on German military and authoritarian [conservative] traditions, the [Nazi] movement developed a very tight internal organization and soon there emerged a highly efficacious expressive leader in the person of Hitler [etc.].' Aron (1998, p. 302) comments that Weber's 'philosophy of commitment, does not necessarily offer a better protection against barbarians. The charismatic leader was to provide a refuge against the anonymous domination of the bureaucracy, but we have learned to fear the promises of demagogues more than the banality of rational organization' with apparent reference to Hitler and other fascist leaders.

131   Panunzio (1945, p. 642) describes Mussolini as the 'Buffoon of Palazzo Venezia' and points to his 'demagogy.' Horkheimer and Adorno (1993, p. 152) note that 'Hitler can gesticulate like a clown, Mussolini risk false notes like a provincial tenor [and] Coughlin preach love like the Savior himself, whose crucifixion he impersonates for the sake of yet more bloodshed.' Wang (2021, pp. 3065–66) finds that US Catholic priest Father Coughlin while accusing Franklin D. Roosevelt of being 'anti-God' displayed 'fascist sympathies' and that cities with 'higher exposure to Father Coughlin's radio program' during the late 1930s' were more likely to have a 'local branch of the pro-Nazi German-American Bund.'

obedience, are incapable of realizing. Upon the demise and final act of fascism, fascist leaders losing their sinister charisma and defeated in wars reveal themselves as pedestrian as their authoritarian followers, for example, like talkative street barbers[132] and peddlers, used car dealers, or house and estate sellers.

Relatedly, fascism creates, propagates, and cultivates the cult and worship of autocratic leaders by the fascist rank-and-file. In this respect, fascism is equivalent or comparable to religious cults and worships to the point of fascist and conservative followers sacrificing their property, family, and even life to the cult, glory, honor, and worship of their leader. Like all religious-type cults,[133] the cult and worship of fascist leaders rest on a variety of illusions, delusions, fantasies, fictions, or hallucinations that they and their followers hold and thus create and live in an alternative universe versus the real world. Both fascist leaders and followers tend to be extremely delusionary about themselves, society, and life. Fascist leaders are delusionary about their supposed greatness, ability, and power, the adulation and devotion[134] of their followers, and society and life. Similarly, the fascist rank-and-file are delusionary about their leaders' greatness, ability, power, and love for authoritarian followers, just as themselves and their importance in fascism, society, and life, producing or being extremely susceptible to delusions and fantasies, as well as disinformation and misinformation.

In this respect, both fascist leaders and followers create and live in a parallel universe or alternative reality perpetuating itself during the rule of fascism, which the end of the cult through military and other defeat exposes as a fantasy and delusion. Finally, like all religious-like cults, the cult and worship[135] of fascist autocratic leaders is suicidal and ends through collective suicide, including that of the supreme leader, and mass self-destruction of authoritarian 'people'

---

132 Horkheimer and Adorno (1993, p. 197) advise that 'in the struggle against fascism, not the least concern is to reduce the bloated leader images to the true scale of their insignificance. At least in the similarity between the ghetto barber and the dictator, Chaplin's film [*The Great Dictator*] hit on something essential.' Adorno (1991, p. 172) also remarks that the fascist dictator is 'a bad, pompous and cowardly man [acting] with extreme stupidity', although there is the 'objective dynamics of dictatorship' in fascism.

133 Phillips (2006, pp. 5–6) points to the 'apocalyptic mindset of many in the Christian Right.'

134 Olick (1999, p. 344) comments that 'Adorno worried about the persistence, for instance, not of fascist tendencies against democracy but within democracy, which he believed resulted from a failure of Germans to 'work through' their past [viz.] a collective (or collected) neurosis deriving from German people's 'inability to mourn' the loss of their all-powerful leader. That inability to mourn prevented an honest and therapeutic confrontation with the legacies of their devotion.'

135 Steinmetz (2005, p. 342) registers 'a kind of emperor worship' in Nazi Germany, following the 'Germany of Kaiser Wilhelm.'

followers who become ultimate victims of fascism and its bogus populism. They all drink and end by 'Kool-Aid', or 'live and die by the sword', in the manner reminiscent of US Christian fundamentalist cults and sects.

CHAPTER 2

How Did It Happen? Syndromes of Fascism

1 It Happens Here and Now: Fascism's Return

What happens in America post-2016,[1] including after 2020, and by a global contagion or convergence other countries from Brexit Great Britain through Hungary and Poland to Brazil essentially reveals and replicates in certain degrees and ways all the essential elements of fascism identified and considered previously. In this respect, fascism rises in substance, save in name, and then advances and prevails in America post-2016, while having its origins in the 1920–50s with the Ku Klux Klan, the anti-New Deal conservative reaction, McCarthyism, in the 1980s with Reaganism as their sequel through the early 2010s with the proto-fascist Tea Party.

Accordingly, what is occurring post-2016, including after 2020, literally now, epitomizes and reveals the essential ten properties, hence the core of fascism. Fascism in post-2016 America shows virtually no reverse 'American exceptionalism' in these terms and completely conforms to the rule, namely the pattern of original fascism in Europe, including Nazism in Germany. Contrary to 'American exceptionalism' claims, fascism in America appears as hardly different from its European, including German variant, in substantive sociological terms, aside from secondary geographic 'new nation' and 'old world' differences that globalization—which US fascists and conservatives seek to reverse into total nativism or tribalism[2]—practically erases or makes irrelevant.

---

1 Berezin (2019, pp. 356) observes that the 'resurgence of interest [in fascism] is arguably a response to a nondemocratic or illiberal turn in the United States and Europe—although the reach of illiberal politics is global. The October 2018 presidential election in Brazil and the right-wing government in India are two non-Eurocentric examples of global reach.' Berezin (2019, pp. 356) also points to 'fascistic practices and processes today—Hungary, Poland, and Turkey.' Bonikowski, Feinstein, and Bock (2021, p. 493) alert to the rise and even mainstream infiltration of fascism via 'radical-right politics—a category that subsumes most European far-right parties but also Donald Trump's presidency and the Brexit referendum.' Recall that Paxton (1998, p. 3) envisaged several decades earlier 'an authentic fascism in the United States'.

2 This is consistent with that, as Paxton (1998, p. 6) observes, the 'mobilizing passions' of fascism function in fascist states to "weld' the fascist 'tribe' to its leader', manifesting fascist tribalism.

Moreover, while initially derivative and imitating, American fascism revital-
izes, inspires, and allies with its European original or its facet of conservative,
radical-right populism through an inter-continental contagion, convergence,
and formal or informal alliance[3] temporarily or persistently, as with Brexit
Great Britain, Hungary, Poland, Brazil, and other countries ruled by neo-fascist
or right-wing, conservative elites.[4] Instead of European fascism 'coming to
America',[5] as in most earlier predictions, American fascism post-2016 to a certain degree moves to and penetrates Europe through such processes, including
its regions long considered immune to fascist tendencies given their history of
nominal anti-fascism but of religious extremism and repression through theocracy or its equivalent, for example, Great Britain and Poland.

Notably, the proxy fascist autocracy in post-2016 America shapes and
inspires those or their extreme-right proxies in Eastern, Western Europe,
and beyond, especially Hungary, Poland, Brexit Great Britain, and Brazil. For
example, such an autocratic regime essentially replicates itself in Brexit[6] Great

---

3   Blee and Creasap (2010, p. 280) point to 'new efforts by the US Christian Right to develop
    transnational religious alliances', such as with Haider's Fascist 'Freedom Party' in Austria.
    Apparently, the ultimate enemy and destroyer of freedom to deceive the electorate and pop-
    ulation while deluding its adherents now rebrands itself as the 'Freedom Party' in Europe and
    the US, the 'Liberty' states in the 'Bible Belt', and the like. Yet, the only 'freedom' in fascism
    is the 'license to kill', mistreat, and oppress non-fascists and non-conservatives by fascist-
    conservative leaders and their rank-and-file since Hitler and Mussolini and their followers to
    their US equivalents and their own base enabled by their almost exclusive mass possession
    and use of guns, including military-style firearms, to commit and perpetuate mass murders
    and terror for long.
4   Gethin et al. (2022, p. 3) include 'Christian democratic and anti-immigration parties' into
    'right-wing' or 'conservative and affiliated' parties.
5   For example, Sinclair Lewis's novel *It Can't Happen* seemed more about European fascism
    possibly coming to America than vice versa.
6   Lamont (2018, p. 423) notes 'Trump's election', in connection to 'Brexit and to [conservative]
    populism more generally'. Lamont (2018, p. 434) also alerts to the 'ideological 'silos' (or 'bub-
    bles') that have come to define the US public sphere, particularly since the Trump election.'
    Edwards (2019, pp. 95–6) remarks that 'Donald Trump's rallies [included] the fierce attacks
    and mocking of political rivals, the antiglobalization rhetoric, and the criticism of the elites
    and the establishment [along with] severe denunciations of traditional institutions. Before
    the 2016 election, Trump hinted that he might not feel bound to acknowledge the results
    if they went against him.' Margalit (2019, p. 152) observes that the 'rise of populist forces in
    many established democracies is undoubtedly one of the most notable political develop-
    ments in recent years', invoking 'Donald Trump's victory in the US presidential election of
    November 2016 and the Brexit vote in June 2016.' Great Britain's Brexit Prime Minister was
    forced to resign in the summer of 2022 because of moral sins (alcohol drinking and party-
    ing, etc.) rather than neo-fascist autocratic and other undemocratic tendencies, as well as
    disastrous policies and failing politics. This confirms that the ghost of Puritanism is still alive

Britain's would-be conservative, populist autocracy—or conversely, the second emulates the first—in most respects, including the mix of illiberal gravity and grotesque buffoonery, as in Australia under radical-right rule via an Anglo-Saxon contagion or convergence.

To that extent, the rise and growing power of fascism in post-2016 America, at the minimum its conservative and religious pole, and its contagion into or confluence with Brexit Great Britain and Australia marks a partial Anglo-Saxon sociological tragedy, while only Canada and New Zealand seem resistant to this autocratic and authoritarian tendency. This holds true given that these societies always proclaim to be the most genuine democracies and free societies and their leaders lecture other countries on and preach to the world the superior virtues of 'democracy' and 'freedom' (and 'anti-fascism') in their countries. During post-2016, these two putatively most, even sole 'democratic' and 'free' countries are closer to becoming fascist social systems than any other major Western societies, thus excluding Brazil, Hungary, Poland, Turkey, Russia, China, and others. The undisputed leaders of 'democracy' and 'freedom' (the 'free world') turn out to be the genuine vanguards of fascism via radical-right autocracy and broader authoritarian conservatism and thus dictatorship among Western societies, albeit this does not deter American, British, and other Anglo-Saxon conservatives to continue to lecture other countries on and preach democracy and freedom to the world. Their two would-be autocrats and saviors more than do any other presidents or prime ministers among Western societies consciously or subconsciously emulate or resemble the fascist leaders of the 1920–30s, including Mussolini's buffoonery[7] and Hitler's clown-style gesturing. This indicates the mutation of intrinsically authoritarian Anglo-Saxon conservatism since Reaganism and Thatcherism into fascism and exposes America's and Great Britain's shared legacy of (in Weber's words) the 'pure hypocrisy' of Puritanism, as perhaps its only 'purity', by performing the

---

in Great Britain, just as even more in conservative America, and treats moral sins as graver transgressions than fascist and other anti-democratic acts.

7 Jouet (2017, pp. 28–9) notes that 'Trump tweeted a quote from Benito Mussolini—whose Fascist regime fought against America in World War II—insisting that it was "a very good quote" and "I know who said it" [and] alleged that it would be "rigged" and suggested that he might not accept the democratic process: "I will totally accept the results—if I win."' Jouet (2017, p. 29) concurs that 'even though Trump is not a traditional fascist in Mussolini's mold, his campaign had neofascist dimensions [and] shows a rather alarming willingness to use fascist themes and fascist styles.' At the minimum, even if these post-2016 leaders are not overt, pure fascists by their demeanor and ideas alike they consciously or not resemble Mussolini and Hitler and thus embody and transmit many features of classic European fascism to American and Brexit-British contexts during the 2010–20s.

simulation, cheap talk, or placebo of 'democracy' and 'liberty' Puritan-style while effectively eliminating or perverting them.

Above all, what is happening in post-2016 America looks like a sociological version of Dreiser's literary individual *American Tragedy*. This holds true because fascism save in name yet in essence seems more pervasive, intense, and powerful in post-2016 America, notably dominating its conservative and religious pole, than in other Anglo-Saxon and Western and comparable societies, excluding probably Hungary and Poland. This looks like a sociological tragedy in Tocqueville's historical and comparative framework of 'democracy in America' and Jefferson's liberal Enlightenment principle of universal 'liberty and justice', since both would categorically rule out a fascist, including autocratic, thus undemocratic and anti-liberal involution of the 'land of freedom'. Moreover, it threatens to become a Western and global sociological—as is partial Anglo-Saxon—anti-liberal and anti-democratic tragedy. This applies so long as post-2016 America growingly mutates from a presumed model of democracy and the 'leader of the free world' to that of fascist and generally radical-right autocracy and broader authoritarian rule for the West and the rest of the world, a trend which the 2020 Presidential elections probably just partly and temporarily interrupted.

The argument and observation at this stage is that fascism rises in substance, even if not in name, in America post-2016 and moreover advances and spreads as if by global metastasis, epidemic, or convergence beyond to certain Western and other societies, especially Anglo-Saxon, Eastern European, and South American countries. The indication that the fascist phenomenon happens in this American setting and time is that post-2016 events and tendencies— of which the 2020 Presidential Elections are perhaps merely a partial and transient interregnum—clearly reveal and completely replicate fascism's essentials. In essence, what is happening in America post-2016, primarily its conservative-religious pole, displays the same syndromes as the essentials and thereby yields the substantive diagnosis of the rise of fascism, except in name. Conversely, by displaying such syndromes, this trend does not exempt itself from or overcome any one of these essentials of fascism and hence fails to show non-fascist democratic 'American exceptionalism'. Instead, what happens now moreover appears as a strong confirmation of the fascist rule and an epitome of fascism, including that in non-American settings. In sum, what occurs in post-2016 America is fascism in substance with its pathology of syndromes, except in name and with minor variations in geographic context and personalities. Consequently, this should be substantively considered and clearly denoted what it essentially is or exponentially approaches—'all-American' fascism[8] as a more accurate concept or precise designation than other more generic and vague ones, 'authoritarianism', 'populism', the 'right wing', the 'far right', etc.

In this sense, fascism in post-2016 America is déjà vu in relation to that in other historical and comparative settings, such as interwar fascist Italy, Nazi Germany, and the rest of Europe under authoritarian rightism, thus showing no substantive novelty or exceptionality, aside from secondary formal, geographic, and individual differences. The history of fascism, including fascist autocracy, dynasty, oligarchy, and plutocracy, seems to substantively, though not exactly and formally, repeat itself both in its grave and grotesque aspects, for example, repression, terror, Mussolini's buffoonery, and Hitler's clown-like gesturing in their US post-2016 and British-Brexit autocratic replications or evocations. This holds good even if it happens in a different, indeed mostly unexpected geographic and social space of the foremost and sole 'land of freedom' and via contagion and metastasis much of the Anglo-Saxon 'free world' preaching 'democracy' and 'liberty' and previously deemed supremely, indeed solely, impervious to fascist and other autocratic and anti-democratic dangers.

Specifically, what happens, spreads, and prevails while writing these lines in post-2016 America, above all, its conservative-religious pole, reveals and replicates the same syndromes as the essentials of fascism, as specified earlier (see Table 2.1).

As the revelation of the first essential of fascism, this post-2016 trend reveals extreme conservatism or the radical right, and conversely, conservatism revealing itself as embellished fascism. It especially replicates extreme conservative authoritarianism or radical-right dictatorship, including autocracy, dynasty, oligarchy, and plutocracy.

In a related revelation of the second essential of fascism, the post-2016 trend reveals extreme anti-liberalism and anti-modernism generally. Specifically, consistent with its conservatism, it replicates an extreme conservative, radical-right form of anti-liberalism and anti-modernism.

A corollary revelation of the third essential of fascism is that the post-2016 trend reveals extreme anti-democracy. Specifically, consistent with its conservatism and anti-liberalism, it replicates an extreme conservative variant of anti-democracy in the form of radical-right antagonism to and destruction of liberal democracy.

8　Johnson (2017) suggests that since 2016 and even to some extent earlier the United States has moved toward 'a new form of fascism.'

TABLE 2.1   Syndromes of fascism in America

---

extreme conservatism, the radical right
extreme anti-liberalism
extreme anti-democracy
extreme anti-secularism
extreme irrationalism and anti-rationalism.
extreme anti-egalitarianism, anti-universalism and anti-cosmopolitanism,
including anti-globalism
absolute rule, total, unconstrained and arbitrary power and all-
encompassing domination
encompassing and severe coercion, repression, violence and terror of
society
extreme anti-pacifism, militarism, war and conquest.
aggregate of extreme conservative or radical-right authoritarian agents

---

A corollary revelation of the fourth essential of fascism consists in that the post-2016 trend reveals extreme anti-secularism. Specifically and consistent with fascism's conservatism and anti-liberalism, it replicates an extreme anti-secular ideology, movement, regime, and ambient eliminating secular democracy, involving religious extremism, and leading to or merging with theocracy.

Indicating the revelation of the fifth essential of fascism, the post-2016 trend reveals extreme irrationalism, anti-rationalism, and anti-progressivism. Particularly, it replicates religious and other superstitions, fanaticism, fantasies, and extreme anti-science and anti-intellectualism.

As the revelation of the sixth essential of fascism, the post-2016 trend reveals extreme anti-egalitarianism, anti-universalism, and anti-cosmopolitanism, including anti-globalism, and alternatively severe inequality, rigid hierarchy, particularism, elitism, monopolistic closure, and exclusion within society and in relation to other societies. In particular, it replicates extreme conservative, rightist political, cultural, and economic nationalism and irrationalism, nativism, xenophobia, and master-race racism.

In the revelation of the seventh essential of fascism, the post-2016 trend reveals a system of absolute rule, total, unconstrained and arbitrary power and encompassing domination through autocracy, oligarchy, and other dictatorship. Particularly, it replicates absolutism, Machiavellianism, legal arbitrariness, lawlessness, uncontrolled corruption, and counterrevolutionary institutional nihilism to liberal-democratic and related social institutions, including anti-institutionalist spurious rightist populism.[9]

The revelation of the eighth essential of fascism is that the post-2016 trend reveals a system of encompassing and severe coercion, repression, violence, and terror of society, combined with populist deception, misinformation, and manipulation. In particular, it replicates pro-capital and anti-labor coercion and repression, including mass imprisonment and widespread executions of lower classes.

The revelation of the ninth essential of fascism consists in that the post-2016 trend reveals extreme anti-pacifism, militarism, wars of aggression, and conquest. Particularly, it replicates extreme rearmament and preparation for offensive war, imperial conquest, and subjugation of other societies through exorbitant military expenditure, militarist mobilization, and a large standing army, leading to mass death, destruction, and ultimately self-destruction.

Showing the revelation of the tenth essential of fascism the post-2016 trend reveals an aggregate of extreme conservative or radical-right authoritarian agents in socio-psychological terms. In particular, it replicates a collection of sadistic-masochistic actors, a mix of grave morbid seriousness and utter grotesqueness, and the cult of autocratic leaders by the rank-and-file that are characteristic of fascism.

These specific syndromes of fascism in America post-2016 usually exist and function in interconnection and reciprocal intensification, with some minor variations, as do general fascist properties. Taken together, such concrete syndromes reveal and replicate all the universal essentials of fascism.[10] To that

---

9   Kaltwasser (2018, p. 206) observes that rightist or exclusionary expressions of populism 'are predominant in various places of the world today.' He adds that 'exclusionary populism advances a radical right agenda due to its reliance on nativism, i.e., the idea that states should be inhabited exclusively by members of the native group ('the nation'), and that non-native ('alien') are threatening to the alleged homogeneity of the nation-state. Because of their nativism, populist radical right forces are at odds with economic immigration and defend welfare chauvinism. Paradigmatic examples of this type of populism can be found in the United States (Trump) and France (Marine Le Pen)' (Kaltwasser 2018, p. 206). Also, Levy, Razin, and Young (2022, p. 928) remark that the 'more recent incidences of populism in the western world seem to be centered on a simple ethos of "the people" versus the "elite." They elaborate that the defining features of recent populism movements [are] anti-expert, anti-science, and against the rule of law, all complex features of liberal well-functioning democracies. Anti-pluralism, anti-immigration and nationalist views espoused by populists also necessitate a simple definition of group identities' (Levy et al. 2022, p. 929).

10   The above syndromes reveal and replicate in varying degrees and ways what Paxton (1998, p. 5) calls, the 'mobilizing passions' of fascism. Recall these passions of fascism are '1. The primacy of the group, toward which one has duties superior to every right, whether universal or individual. 2. The belief that one's group is a victim, a sentiment which justifies

extent, they prove that fascism definitely happens and spreads in America post-2016, while probably originated and germinated during earlier times, such as the 1920–1950s, 1980s, and early 2010s.

2   Syndrome 1: Fascism as Extreme Conservatism and Conservatism as Latent Fascism

First and foremost, fascism in America post-2016 reveals and thus replicates extreme conservatism or the radical right as a universal fascist essential in all societal spaces and times, while conversely conservatism exposing itself as disguised, hidden, or latent fascism or its equivalent. Accordingly, American fascism manifests itself as an extreme conservative, radical right[11] ideology, social movement, political regime, and cultural zeitgeist. In this sense, fascism in post-2016 America happens and spreads as extreme conservatism or the radical right, as it did in interwar Europe, including Italy, Germany[12] and Spain in the 1920–30s,[13] postwar South America, post-socialist Hungary, Poland, and other parts of Eastern Europe during the 2010s, Brexit Great Britain, Brazil, and Italy[14] after 2018, and all other settings and times.

---

any action against the group's enemies, internal as well as external. 3. Dread of the group's decadence under the corrosive effect of individualistic and cosmopolitan liberalism. 4. Closer integration of the community within a brotherhood (fascio) whose unity and purity are forged by common conviction, if possible, or by exclusionary violence if necessary. 5. An enhanced sense of identity and belonging, in which the grandeur of the group reinforces individual self-esteem. 6. Authority of natural leaders (always male) throughout society, culminating in a national chieftain who alone is capable of incarnating the group's destiny. 7. The beauty of violence and of will, when they are devoted to the group's success in a Darwinian struggle' (Paxton 1998, pp. 5–7).

11   Lipset (1955, p. 185) divides American conservatism 'into moderate conservatives and the radical right [as extreme conservatism]. The radical right wants to turn the clock back all the way [by opposing] (1) the labor movement, preferring to see unions eliminated, (2) the income tax, (3) the welfare state'. Rydgren (2007a, p. 246) observes that the fascist myth of moral and cultural 'decadence has been a recurrent ideological and rhetorical theme of some of the new radical right-wing parties', including those in the US.

12   Brown (1987) exemplifies the 'extreme rightest parties' in Germany by the Nazis.

13   Bourdieu (1998, p. 35) treats interwar fascist revolutions as 'conservative revolutions, [including] that in Germany in the 1930s', along with 'those of Thatcher, Reagan', and fascists as the 'conservative revolutionaries of the 1930s'. Bourdieu (1998, p. 35) elaborates that a characteristic of 'conservative revolutions' from the Nazi Revolution in Germany in the 1930s to those of Thatcherism and Reaganism is that 'they present restorations as revolutions.'

14   Colantone and Stanig (2019, p. 147) report that the 'populist government of Italy, formed in 2018 and led de facto by the radical right, collapsed after slightly more than one year.'

In consequence, fascism in post-2016 America completely conforms to the general rule, namely the universal pattern of fascism, rather than being a special and sole exception in the form of supposed conservative 'American exceptionalism' in superior and sole 'democracy' and 'freedom'. Indeed, it is a consummate example of extreme conservatism, an epitome of the radical right, rather than something new and different, such as 'non-conservative', 'non-rightist'. Fascism in post-2016 America is as American-conservative or the radical right as the 'apple pie.' Fascism does not come to America from some foreign lands such as the old fascist Europe via a visible invasion, immigration, or contagion but coming from 'all-American' conservatism or the right through an almost invisible process—it is completely and proudly 'made in the USA'.

Fascists surge in post-2016 America as extreme conservatives or radical rightists, as they did everywhere else, including interwar Europe, postwar South America, post-socialist Eastern Europe, and Brexit Great Britain. They hence confirm the universal tendency that genuine fascists are always extreme conservatives or radical rightists, with virtually no exceptions. Fascists in post-2016 America are 'all-American' extreme, 'true' conservatives or radical rightists, including most religious fundamentalists like evangelicals or the majority of the Christian Protestant-Catholic Right, as were those in Europe, including Nazis as the 'new' German conservatives and Christians, and elsewhere and later. They hence do not come to America from the old fascist Europe by invading or immigrating to the 'new nation' from distant foreign lands, instead coming from the extended, even if occasionally feuding, family of 'all-American' conservatives or radical rightists, including religious fundamentalists or the Christian Right—they are all with maximally intense joy and immense pride 'born in the USA'.

In other words, fascism rises and advances in post-2016 America through American extreme conservatism or the radical right evolving or coalescing into fascism as its culmination and final point. Since the 1920–50s with the Ku Klux Klan, the anti-New Deal conservative opposition and McCarthyism[15] through Goldwater and Reaganism to the Tea Party, American extreme conservatism or the radical right[16] moves inexorably in the direction of fascism

---

15   Lipset (1955, p. 200) exemplifies the postwar US 'radical right' by McCarthyism. Lipset (1996, p. 176) also includes McCarthyism into 'waves of xenophobia and of heightened nationalism.' Rydgren (2007a, pp. 242) refers to 'interwar fascism in Europe and early postwar right-wing radicalism in the US.'

16   Bell (2002, pp. 462, 466) remarks that for American conservatism the 'crux of the problem is the nature of individualism' and what united conservatives 'was the emphasis on the theme of moral decay and the role of liberalism in [it].' Consequently, Bell (2002, p. 485) envisions the 'prospect of the continuing involvement of the radical right in politics.'

and finally metastasized into it post-2016. This confirms the tendency that the destination or ultimate outcome of conservatism or the radical right almost inevitably is fascism, with minor variations which temporarily postpone such a development, as Brexit Great Britain also shows by the eventual conservative-to-fascist metastasis from Thatcherism to rightist populism. Extreme conservatism or the radical right makes fascism happen in America, just as making it occur in other social spaces and times from interwar Italy and Germany through postwar South America to post-socialist Eastern Europe, confirming the generalized pattern.

Fascists emerge and multiply in post-2016 America as extreme conservatives or radical rightists who blend with them as their products or members of the same family of conservative authoritarianism or authoritarian rightism. Since the 1920–50s with the Ku Klux Klan, anti-New Deal conservatives,[17] and McCarthy through the 1960–80s with Goldwater and Reagan[18] to the 2010s with Tea Partiers, US extreme conservatives or radical rightists display or harbor fascist propensities and mutate in fascists post-2016. They reaffirm the tendency

---

Plotke (2002, pp. xxxi, xxxii) notes that the overall US 'political spectrum has shifted notably to the right. [So] a range of radical right ideas (opposition to virtually all government regulation, rejection of the entire welfare state) has grown in significance and now appears across a large part of the political spectrum. Many of the substantive positions of the postwar radical right now extend much further toward the political center than (before 1964 and Goldwater).' Autor et al. (2020, p. 3140) register a 'sizable rightward shift among the GOP [vs] a modest leftward shift among Democrats [as] Tea Party and like-minded conservatives have risen to prominence in the GOP.' Caren, Andrews, and Lu (2020, p. 451) observe that even though the US 'far right has a long history in the margins of online and offline spaces, the late 2010s saw a new wave of electoral and movement activism, spurred by the reaction to the presidency of Barack Obama and the 2016 election of Donald Trump.'

17   Parsons (1949, p. 117) distinguishes Nazi Germany's 'conservative leanings' from the 'leftward leanings' of the American New Deal and British Labor. Rodrik (2014, p. 2014) observes that the 'Great Depression spawned the New Deal in the United States, fascism in some parts of Europe, and socialism in some other parts of Europe.' Bernstein (2014, p. 115) recounts that 'Republicans viewed with satisfaction the imminent opportunity to dismantle the most objectionable manifestations of the New Deal and the Fair Deal. The blurring of party differences wrought by the beginnings of the cold war, the marginalization of the Right by the victory of the Grand Alliance over fascism, the suppression of the Left by the gathering momentum of McCarthyism—all this emboldened the enemies of federalism, primarily but not solely Republicans, to settle accounts.'

18   Gross (1980, p. xiii) states that 'Ronald Reagan must be the nicest president who ever destroyed a union, tried to cut school lunch milk rations from six to four ounces, and compelled families in need of public help to first dispose of household goods in excess of $1,000. If there is an authoritarian regime in the American future, Ronald Reagan is tailored to the image of a friendly fascist.'

for most extreme conservatives or radical rightists ultimately to become or ally with fascists, aside from rare and transient exceptions that delay or disguise the conservative-to-fascist transformation, as the UK Conservative Party from Thatcherism to Brexit Great Britain also shows. US extreme conservatives or radical rightists, including most religious fundamentalists or the majority of the Christian Right, reappear as fascists in post-2016 America, as their counterparts do everywhere else from fascist Italy and Nazi Germany through neo-fascist South America (Chile) to partly fascist Eastern Europe (Hungary, Poland) and Brexit Great Britain and beyond. Simply, 'all-American' true conservatives, including most evangelicals or the Christian Right, make fascism happen in post-2016 America, with their equivalents in other societies making it occur in various social settings.

Especially, fascism in post-2016 America reveals and replicates extreme conservative authoritarianism and ultimately conservatism's totalitarianism or radical-right dictatorship, particularly rightist autocracy, as a universal feature of fascism in all societal spaces and times. In this sense, fascism in post-2016 America reemerges as extreme conservative authoritarianism or radical-right dictatorship, specifically rightist autocracy, as it does in all other social contexts and periods from interwar Italy and Germany through postwar South America to post-socialist Eastern Europe and Brexit Great Britain. Consequently, what is happening in post-2016 America completely accords with the general rule of fascism rather than being an exception in the sense of conservative 'American exceptionalism' by the best and only 'democracy', 'freedom'. Moreover, American fascism is an exemplar of extreme conservative authoritarianism, radical-right dictatorship, such as ultra-conservative, rightist autocracy, rather than novel and distinct, namely supposedly 'non-authoritarian', 'dictatorial', and 'non autocratic'. At this juncture, fascism in post-2016 America appears again as American conservative-authoritarian as the 'apple pie.' Fascism does not come to America from the old world via European conservative authoritarianism or radical-right dictatorship, including rightist autocracy, instead coming through its native 'all-American' equivalent, so from home (especially the 'sweet home' of Alabama and the South or 'Bible Belt' overall).

Fascists erupt and proliferate in post-2016 America as extreme conservative authoritarians, radical-right dictatorial leaders and followers, specifically rightist autocrats and their rank-and-file, as they do in all other social settings and periods. They illustrate the pattern of fascists being universally extreme conservative authoritarians, radical-right dictatorial leaders, including rightist autocrats, and followers, with almost no exceptions. Fascists in post-2016 America look as 'all-American' extreme conservative authoritarians or radical-right dictatorial leaders, such as rightist autocrats, and followers, including most religious fundamentalists or the Christian Right, as do those in interwar Europe, including Nazis. They hence do not come to America from distant foreign lands like the old fascist Europe by invasion or immigration, instead coming from the broader, even if internally contending, family of 'all-American' conservative authoritarians or authoritarian rightists, including religious fundamentalists or the Christian Right—simply, 'born in the USA'.

Conversely, fascism rises and spreads in post-2016 America through American extreme conservative or radical-right authoritarianism, especially rightist autocracy. Since at least the Ku Klux Klan and McCarthyism[19] through Reaganism[20] and the Tea Party, American extreme conservative, radical-right authoritarianism steadily moves toward or converges with, and ultimately culminates in fascism post-2016. This long, steady movement reaffirms the tendency for the mutation of extreme conservative authoritarianism or radical-right dictatorship, including rightist autocracy, into fascism. In short, extreme conservative, radical-right authoritarianism, especially rightist autocracy, makes fascism happen in America, just as making it occur in other spaces and times.

Fascists hence explode and multiply in post-2016 America through the agency of extreme conservative authoritarians or radical-right leaders, including rightist autocrats, and followers, becoming or merging with the former as their ultimate variants or allies. US conservative authoritarians or radical-right leaders, including rightist autocrats, and followers, from the Ku Klux Klan[21] through McCarthy, Goldwater and Reagan, to Tea Partiers,[22] always verge on

---

19   Hechter (2004, p. 401) remarks that 'McCarthyism cast a pall on political dissent in all walks of life in the United States for decades.'

20   Bourdieu (1998, p. 35) observes 'if this conservative [Thatcher and Reagan] revolution can deceive people, this is because it seems to retain nothing of the old Black Forest pastoral of the conservative revolutionaries of the 1930s [fascists]; it is dressed up in all the signs of modernity.' Cohen (2003, pp. 50, 113) suggests that fascism's 'totalitarian temptation seemed irresistible, at the time playing the role held today' by neo-conservatism ('neoliberalism'), specifically the 'ideology of Margaret Thatcher and Ronald Reagan', thus almost equating Nazism with Thatcherism and Reaganism.

21   Bruce (2004, p. 6) notes that 'in the USA, the Ku Klux Klan and various other nativist movements presented a similarly curtailed notion of freedoms and rights: democracy was to be restricted to white Anglo-Saxon Protestant males.'

22   Altemeyer (2010, p. 4) remarks that 'while Tea Partiers overwhelmingly take conservative economic stands, which bind them together most, many seem to be strong 'social conservatives' as well. Local groups often speak of wanting only 'pure conservatives' or '100 percent' conservatives as candidates. as a group, social conservatives share the psychological trait of being authoritarian followers. And you can hardly miss the authoritarian follower tendencies in the behavior of the Tea Partiers.' Hahl et al. (2018, p. 8) observe that the Ku Klux Klan in the 1920s and the Tea Party after 2008 are conservative movements that are 'driven by a mix of status, economic, and political changes that sow fear of

being or acting as and eventually become fascists post-2016. They confirm the pattern that extreme conservative authoritarians or radical-right autocrats and followers ultimately become or ally and merge with fascists. 'All-American' extreme conservative authoritarians or radical-right autocrats and followers, including religious fundamentalists or the Christian Right, thus reappear as fascists in post-2016 America, as do their equivalents beyond since fascist Italy and Nazi Germany. In sum, 'all-American' conservative authoritarians, including most evangelicals or the Christian Right, make fascism happen in post-2016 America, just as their equivalents elsewhere making it occur in all other social contexts and periods.

3   Syndrome 2: Fascism as Extreme Anti-liberalism

Second and as a corollary of the previous, fascism in America post-2016 reveals and replicates extreme anti-liberalism as another universal fascist element in social space and time. Consequently, American fascism represents an extreme anti-liberal ideology, social movement, political regime, and cultural zeitgeist in a conservative, radical-right[23] version as the primary form, as distinct from other, secondary forms, of anti-liberalism.

Fascism in post-2016 America emerges and advances as extreme anti-liberalism or illiberalism in a conservative, radical-right form, as it does in

---

power-devaluation among those who previously felt they were part of the establishment'. Caren et al. (2020, p. 451) note that a 'precursor of the far-right movement is the eruption of the 2010 Tea Party protests in the United States, which saw immense electoral mobilization from middle-class conservatives against the Obama presidency.'

23   Bourdieu and Haacke (1995, p. 44) remark that the US 'old Right [is] anti-intellectual, xenophobic, and isolationist [i.e.] conservative Middle America, the natural constituency of Republicans. Aside from this stripe of traditional conservatives (the paleo-conservatives), most of whom are anti-Semitic, racist, and authoritarian, there is another camp: the neo-conservatives who are at least as influential. However, despite their internal conflicts, they have succeeded, since Reagan's arrival in the White House, in framing the political debate of the nation. Liberal (in the American sense) ideas are being called into question not only by the Government but also in the media. [American neo-conservatism] is financed by right-wing foundations. It is this network of the neo-conservative movement that produces and supplies political ideas and strategies for Republican Presidents.' In short, they diagnose 'a political climate where the word *liberal* (in the American sense) already poses a problem [and] the neo-conservatives are well aware of this—and make use of it' (Bourdieu and Haacke 1995, p. 50).

all other social spaces and times from Europe[24] during 1920–30s, including Italy and Germany, South America (Chile, etc.) in the 1970s, post-socialist Eastern Europe (Hungary, Poland, Croatia, the Baltics) after the 1990s, Brexit Great Britain, Brazil, etc. Fascism in post-2016 America entirely accords with fascism's antiliberal or illiberal essence rather than being a unique exception to the fascist universal pattern of anti-liberalism through alleged 'American exceptionalism' in superior 'democracy' and 'freedom'.

Moreover, American fascism is a foremost exemplar of extreme anti-liberalism or illiberalism in the primary conservative, rightist shape rather than being an exceptional and opposite phenomenon, contrary to conservatives' denial to obscure the linkage and ultimate osmosis of anti-liberalism in the form of conservatism with fascism. Fascism in post-2016 America is as American-antiliberal—if liberalism is 'un-American' according to conservatism since McCarthyism through Reaganism and its derivations—as the 'apple pie.' Fascism does not come to America from the old fascist Europe via external routes, instead coming from 'all-American' extreme anti-liberalism[25] in the primary conservative, radical-right form through an internal route and in that sense from conservative illiberal America,[26] so with enormous national pride and joy is totally 'made in the USA'.

As a result, fascism in post-2016 America couches and embellishes itself as home-grown anti-liberalism or illiberalism in the conservatism or radical-right form through a religious-style crusade against 'foreign' European,

---

24   Horkheimer and Adorno (1993, p. 68) state that 'after the brief interlude of liberalism in which the bourgeois kept one another in check, power is revealing itself as archaic terror in a fascistically rationalized form.'

25   Lipset (1955, pp. 190–1) reports that in 'distinguishing between greater or less liberalism in civil liberties among the lower classes, the principal differentiating factor [is] party allegiance. In the US and [UK] the conservative workers, those who back the Tory or Republican parties, tend to have the most intolerant attitudes.' Brouwer (1998) registers the 'similarities' between the New Right in America and the European 'Conservative Revolutionaries' of the early 1900s who were instrumental in the 'rise of fascism', such as both being vehemently and violently anti-liberal. Bell (2002, p. 466) observes that what united American conservatism since the 1960s 'was the emphasis on the theme of moral decay and the role of liberalism in [it]', simply anti-liberalism.

26   Jouet (2017, p. 28) observes that the 'gulf between conservative and liberal America worsened in the 2016 campaign'. Jouet (2017, p. 29) adds that the 'intensity of America's regional divide is exceptional. There are obviously rather liberal and conservative regions in other Western nations, but their citizens are not sharply divided over such basic issues as whether people should have a right to medical treatment. Besides, the extraordinary polarization of American society is not merely between blue and red states, as a major partisan rift has occurred nationwide. Republican leaders in blue states typically join their counterparts in red states in defending hardline positions on essentially all issues.'

'un-American' liberalism. Post-2016 American fascism strategically calculates that presenting itself as native 'all-American' anti-liberalism or 'true' conservatism is the winning formula of its mainstream legitimacy, penetration, and dominance in America, especially its conservative-religious pole, thus a social alchemy of converting its authoritarianism and dictatorship such as autocracy into illiberal 'democracy' and 'freedom'. This replicates fascism's tendency to present itself, expand, and dominate as extreme anti-liberalism, indeed the national 'savior' from 'foreign' and 'dangerous' liberalism, which implacably anti-liberal Nazism particularly demonstrates by its destruction of liberal institutions and values, as does neo-fascism in South America, post-socialist Eastern Europe, and elsewhere.

In this sense, fascism post-2016 hardly invents anything substantively new. Instead, it adopts an old, notably Nazi Machiavellian, strategy and tactic of societal presentation, legitimation, expansion, and domination as widely acceptable, innocuous, and hyper-patriotic anti-liberalism or illiberalism,[27] which, in its calculations, most of American society does not suspect ultimately produces fascist and thus totalitarian outcomes, just as most of Germany did not during the 1930s. By covering itself as anti-liberalism or illiberalism, American fascism looks as old and clever in the Machiavellian sense as Nazism and other fascism in interwar Europe and beyond, including postwar South America, post-socialist Eastern Europe, Brexit Great Britain, and elsewhere. Conversely, aside from rare admissions, this fascism, especially the post-2016 autocracy, refrains from overtly and publicly stating what truly it is—the latest 'all-American' variation of the old European fascism such as fascist autocracy—because it calculates that most of American society would find such a description unacceptable due to its adverse reputation or initially foreign origin.

It follows that fascists erupt and proliferate in post-2016 America as extreme, implacable antiliberals in the specifically conservative or radical-right face, just as they do in all other societies and times. They conform to the generalized rule that fascists are universally extreme antiliberals precisely in the conservative, radical-right shape, rather than being 'all-American' superior exceptions in 'freedom'. Fascists post-2016 are 'all-American' extreme, implacable, 'true' antiliberals of the conservative, radical-right lineage, which includes most evangelicals and other religious fundamentalists or the majority of the Christian Right, as were those in interwar Germany and Europe, with Nazis being ultimate antiliberal forces as the 'new' conservatives, and beyond. As before, fascists do not

---

27   Berezin (2019, p. 346) suggests that 'current events in the United States and abroad signal the erosion of democratic institutions and the attenuation of democratic practices pointing toward a new age of illiberalism and authoritarianism.'

come to America from the old fascist Europe and other distant foreign lands through outside channels, instead coming from the extended, if partly contending and dysfunctional, family of 'all-American' antiliberals in the conservative, radical-right face, including religious fundamentalists or the Christian Right, by an internal home-made channel—all 'born in the USA'.

Consequently, these fascists disguise and present themselves as proud home-born conservative antiliberals waging a patriotic and 'holy' warfare against liberals as 'un-American' since McCarthy and Reagan et al. through the Tea Party and the post-2016 autocracy. Apparently, they see and use the presentation of themselves as 'holy' warriors against liberals as the winning formula in their quest for gaining acceptance and mainstream legitimacy among Americans and seizing, retaining, and exerting absolute power in America. Therefore, they behave and appear in the way fascists of all social spaces and times do, notably Nazis behaving and appearing as the ultimate 'new' conservative antiliberals and national 'saviors' from 'anti-German' liberals and liberal democracy as their conservative allies praised them. Conversely, aside from few admissions, these new fascists, especially fascist leaders such as post-2016 US and Brexit Great Britain would-be-autocrats, do not have dare to publicly admit what they really are or plan to become, because they calculate that most of Americans and Britons would not accept 'fascists' due to their negative names or originally foreign roots.

In other words, fascism rises and spreads in America through the development and coalescence of American extreme anti-liberalism or illiberalism of a conservative, radical-right lineage into fascism as its inexorable ultimate outcome. Since the Ku Klux Klan and the anti-New Deal conservative opposition[28] during the 1920–30s and McCarthyism in the 1950s through Reaganism to the Tea Party, American extreme conservative, rightist anti-liberalism long and steadily moves to and eventually develops and coalesces into fascism during post-2016. This development in post-2016 America reaffirms extreme conservative anti-liberalism's universal rule of ultimately developing and coalescing into fascism in all social spaces and times from interwar Italy, Germany, and Europe to postwar South America, much of post-socialist Eastern Europe, Brexit Great Britain,[29] Brazil, and beyond. Reaffirming the rule, extreme anti-liberalism

---

28   Commons (1931) implies that since the 1920–30s American conservatism/fascism opposes the 'philosophy of liberalism and regulated capitalism' in favor of pre-liberalism, essentially medievalism, and primitive laissez-faire, unfettered capitalism.

29   Colantone and Stanig (2019, p. 148) suggest that the rise of fascism or the radical right in Western Europe, including especially the British Brexit referendum of 2016, is a reversal of 'embedded liberalism' in economic and political terms.

or anti-liberal extremism[30] of a conservative, rightist lineage makes fascism rise in America, just as making it occur in all other social settings and periods noted above. Extreme conservative anti-liberalism through its warfare against liberalism in America after a long and steady movement in the fascist direction finally erupts and overly expresses itself in the form of fascism post-2016, as it did in Germany during the 1930s and beyond.

Accordingly, fascists resurge and multiply in post-2016 America as extreme, implacable antiliberals in the conservative or radical-right face by becoming or mixing with the first, as they do in all other social spaces and times. Since the Ku Klux Klan, anti-New Deal opponents, McCarthy, and Goldwater to Reagan et al. and Tea Partiers, US extreme conservative antiliberals display or harbor fascist tendencies and eventually become or merge with fascists post-2016. Far from being the faces of 'American exceptionalism', they only accord with and exemplify conservative antiliberals' tendency to ultimately become or join fascists, from interwar Europe through postwar South America to post-socialist Eastern Europe, Brexit Great Britain, Brazil, and elsewhere. 'All-American' extreme, implacable, and proud antiliberals of the conservative lineage, including most evangelicals and other religious fundamentalists[31] or the majority of the Christian Right, hence look as fascists in post-2016 America, as do their equivalents in other social settings and times. In sum, American antiliberal political and religious extremists make fascism happen in post-2016 America, while their 'brothers in arms' elsewhere making it occur in other settings.

4   Syndrome 3: Fascism as Extreme Anti-democracy

Third and as a corollary of its anti-liberalism, fascism in post-2016 America reveals and replicates extreme anti-democracy in the sense of antagonism to and elimination of liberal democracy, as another universal fascist essential in all social spaces and times.[32] American fascism reappears as an extreme

---

30   Berezin (2019, p. 348) notes that the 'extremism and violence [are] constitutive of fascist and populist politics' in both Europe and the US.

31   Munch (2001, p. 270) points to US 'internal fundamentalist Protestant movements against the reality of a liberal and pluralist society.'

32   Parsons (1949, p. 108) suggests that 'a divergence of political orientation so fundamental as that at present developing between the fascist and the liberal-democratic societies must go back to deeper structural sources.' He adds that the 'main line of the evolution of Western society [is] the progressive approach to the realization of 'liberal-democratic' patterns and values' (Parsons 1949, p. 116). Parsons (1949, p. 117) proposes that German fascism 'arose in a situation [producing] a strong nationalistic and conservative reaction [in]

anti-democratic ideology, social movement, political regime, and cultural zeit-geist in a conservative, radical-right variant as the predominant and resurging form of anti-democracy by vehement opposition to and violent destruction of liberal democracy in modern society during the early 21st century. Furthermore, it arises as the most extreme variation of anti-democracy within modern Western society through its extremely intense and implacable antagonism and nihilism to liberal democracy as the ideal and social system of universal liberty, complemented with equality, justice, and inclusion. Especially, fascism erupts as subversive, putschist anti-democratic ideology and movement and adopts extreme Machiavellianism in the function of destroying liberal democracy and its complex of liberty and of seizing and retaining absolute power. Relatedly, it embraces the fascist elitist interpretation of societal history as the circulation of elites and operates as elite dictatorship through autocracy, dynasty or oligar-chy, plutocracy, and other opposites of liberal democracy.

In this regard, fascism in post-2016 America rises as extreme anti-democracy in a conservative, radical-right form through vehement and violent revolt against liberal democracy, just as does in all other social settings and periods from interwar Italy, Germany, Spain, and the rest of Europe, postwar South America, post-socialist Hungary, Poland and other parts of Eastern Europe, Brexit Great Britain (with minor qualifications), Brazil after 2018, and beyond. This 'all-American' entity is therefore entirely consistent with fascism's anti-democracy universalized pattern of antagonism and nihilism toward liberal democracy rather than being an exception through supposed conservative 'American exceptionalism' in superior 'democracy' and 'freedom'. Indeed, fascism in post-2016 America is an epitome of anti-democracy in the con-servative, radical-right rendition by opposition to and subversion of liberal democracy rather than a unique 'all-American' exception to the fascist anti-democratic rule. Consequently, American fascism renders the conservative-religious, as distinct from liberal-secular, pole of America into the model of anti-democracy, as of anti-liberalism as the primary cause, in the form of an antithesis and reversal of liberal democracy within modern Western society rather than, as its leaders and devotees allege, an exceptional and sole space of 'democracy' and 'freedom.' Fascism hence does not come to America from the old fascist Europe via exogenous processes but rather comes from an 'all-American' extreme anti-democracy ideology, movement, regime, and climate

---

conflict with the leftward elements of the 'liberal-democratic' tradition of the Western world'. Schumpeter (1950, p. 352) laments that 'we have traveled [far] from the old moor-ings of liberal democracy [and] to exalt national unity into a moral precept spells accep-tance of one of the most important principles of fascism.'

in the resurgent conservative,[33] radical-right form through an endogenous process of opposition to and perversion of liberal democracy—proudly and joyfully 'made in the USA'.

It follows that fascists erupt and proliferate in post-2016 America as extreme antidemocrats specifically in conservative, rightist faces opposing and subverting liberal democracy, as they do in all other social spaces and times. In so doing, rather than being 'all-American' exceptions, they exemplify the universal pattern that fascists are always extreme antidemocrats in conservative, radical-right faces as the implacable and perpetual enemies of liberal democracy. Simply, post-2016 (and earlier) American fascists are vehement, though often disguised, antidemocrats of the conservative, rightist lineage, just as were those in interwar Europe and other societal settings and historical periods since fascist Italy and Nazi Germany. This lineage thus includes extreme political conservatives or radical-rightists and religious fundamentalists like theocratic evangelicals or the main segment of the Protestant-Catholic Christian Right. Fascists thus do not come to America from the old fascist Europe via intercontinental journeys but hail from the broader unified, even if occasionally contentious and dysfunctional, family of American antidemocrats in conservative, radical-right faces, including political conservatives and theocratic fundamentalists within the Christian Right, through an internal journey—with immense joy and pride 'born in the USA'.

In other words, fascism rises and spreads in America via the escalation and intensification of an American variation of antidemocracy by opposition to and subversion of liberal democracy[34] through a conservative, radical-right reaction into a fascist regime as its final stage. Since the 1920–50s and through the Ku Klux Klan, the anti-New Deal opposition, McCarthyism, Reaganism, and the Tea Party,[35] various American anti-democracy ideas and forces of a conservative, radical-right lineage against liberal democracy consistently move toward and finally ensue in or blend with fascism post-2016. Such an outcome confirms the tendency that the extreme anti- democracy ideology, movement, or regime of a conservative, radical-right type by opposing and eliminating

---

33 Mueller (2009, p. x) alerts to the 'dangers' that conservatism ('traditionalism'), along with religion, poses for 'liberal democracy' in America and beyond that conservatism and dictatorship, thus by implication fascism, 'go hand in hand'.

34 Berezin (2019, p. 346) observes that post-2016 'events in the United States and abroad signal the erosion of democratic institutions and the attenuation of democratic practices pointing toward a new age of illiberalism and authoritarianism.'

35 Caren et al. (2020, p. 451) note that a 'precursor of the far-right movement is the eruption of the 2010 Tea Party protests in the United States, which saw immense electoral mobilization from middle-class conservatives against the Obama presidency.'

liberal democracy ultimately ensues in or blends with fascism in diverse societies and times from Italy and Germany during the 1920–30s through South America in the 1970s and post-socialist Eastern Europe to Brexit Great Britain, and post-2016 America. By confirming rather than being an American exception to the rule, anti-democracy extremism of a conservative, radical-right lineage antithetical to liberal democracy makes fascism happen in America, just as making it occur in all other social spaces and times above.

Fascists hence explode and march in post-2016 America as extreme, vehement antidemocrats in conservative or radical-right faces escalating and intensifying their attacks on and elimination of liberal democracy as to become or act as fascist agents. Since the Ku Klux Klan, New-Deal opponents, McCarthy, Goldwater, and Reagan through Tea Partiers, various American conservative or rightist antidemocrats opposing liberal democracy exhibit fascist propensities, symptoms, and sympathies, and finally act on them by becoming or acting as fascists post-2016, as do their functional equivalents[36] everywhere else since interwar Italy and Germany. Multiple American conservative, radical-right antidemocrats, including political and religious conservatives, by attacking and subverting liberal democracy thus make fascism rise in post-2016 America, with their equivalents making it occur in all other social settings and periods.

Furthermore, precisely because of being an anti-democratic ideology, movement, regime, and zeitgeist of a conservative, radical-right form, fascism in post-2016 America reemerges as the most extreme variation of anti-democracy within Western society. Due to this property, American fascism rises and advances as the most intense and implacable mode of antagonism to and destruction of specifically liberal and thus genuine democracy—as distinct from illiberal bogus 'democracy'—by seeking to destroy it as the principle and system of universal political and civil liberties and rights, just as this happens in other social settings and periods since fascist Italy and Nazi Germany. Therefore, this post-2016 constellation epitomizes fascism's essence as the ultimate variant of anti-democracy and the maximal antagonism and destructiveness toward liberal democracy rather than being an exceptional situation

---

36   Paxton (1998, p. 22) remarks that the 'most interesting cases today, however, are not those that imitate the exotic colored-shirt movements of an earlier generation. New functional equivalents of fascism would probably work best (as Orwell envisioned) clad in the mainstream patriotic dress of their own place and time. An authentically popular fascism in the United States would be pious and anti-Black; in Western Europe, secular and antisemitic, or more probably, these days, anti-Islamic', with for example, the skinheads being 'functional equivalents of Hitler's SA and Mussolini's squadristi'.

expressing presumed conservative democratic and libertarian 'American exceptionalism' in relation to the 'old' Europe. Such antagonism toward genuine, liberal, as distinct from ersatz, illiberal, democracy illustrates the fact that fascism in post-2016 America rises and expands as a double entwined compound of 'all-American' anti-liberalism and anti-democracy of a conservative or radical-right variant. It also reaffirms the fact that fascism universally is a compound of extreme conservative anti-liberalism and radical-right anti-democracy spanning from interwar Italy and Germany to postwar and present times and settings. Post-2016 US fascism's inner core as extreme 'all-American' conservatism determines and predicts its implacable hostility and total destructiveness to liberal democracy given that conservatism emerging out of medievalism arises in vehemently hostile reaction to liberalism and its project of democracy according to its ideals of universal liberty.[37]

Fascists hence surge and march in post-2016 America as the most extreme anti-democrats in conservative, rightist faces assaulting and reversing liberal democracy. Since the Ku Klux Klan, New-Deal opponents, McCarthy, Goldwater, and Reagan through Tea Partiers, these conservative agents are not just nondemocratic but the most extreme anti-democrats in America by opposing and subverting liberal democracy and attacking and repressing its representatives as 'un-American' in McCarthyism-Reaganism's definition. Rather than being 'all-American' exceptions, they conform to all fascists' nature and designation as the most extreme anti-democrats and anti-liberals, ultimate antagonists to and destroyers of liberal democracy and enemies of liberals-democrats. Post-2016 US fascists' character as extreme 'all-American' conservatives determines and predicts their implacable hostility to and systematic subversion of liberal democracy, since conservatives generally (a la Burke[38] et al.) originating in medievalists erupt in rebellion against emergent liberal-democratic ideals and values.

Particularly, fascism in post-2016 America rises and spreads as a subversive anti-democratic ideology and movement adopting extreme Machiavellian means and tactics for attaining the end of total power seizure and elimination of liberal democracy, as it does in other social settings and times since fascist

---

37   Bruce (2004, p. 18) states that the 'core principle of liberal democracy is that each citizen's vote counts the same; for that to be the case rights must be distributed irrespective of religion.' He adds that what is 'essential to the liberal democratic character of western European polities is the fact that they are secular' (Bruce 2004, p. 18).

38   According to Gross, Medvetz, and Russell (2011, p. 327), the 'long history of American conservatism [has] its ideological roots in the writings of thinkers such as Edmund Burke or Alexis de Tocqueville.'

Italy and Nazi Germany. Consequently, this confirms that fascism, including Nazism, typically is a putschist movement and an extreme rendition of Machiavellianism in function of capturing and maintaining total state power and eliminating liberal democracy rather than being a unique exception to this rule in the manner of conservative democratic 'American exceptionalism'. More precisely, fascism in post-2016 America emerges as an anti-democratic ideology and movement using democratic procedures like elections as the Machiavellian means to seize absolute power and against liberal democracy by subverting it through encompassing domination and severe repression, as it happened prior to the 2020 elections that probably just partially or temporarily mitigate this trend.

The above is fully consistent with fascism-conservatism's penchant to wear a 'specious democratic mask' during elections to seize power and to effectively eliminate liberal democracy by the 'popular will' and in that sense populism,[39] thus replicating Italian fascists' and German Nazis' electoral victories. Specifically, the electoral result of the 2016 Presidential elections by its anti-democratic effects replicates or resembles that of the 1933 elections in Germany, with both leading to the perversion of liberal democracy through extreme-right autocracy, aside from some secondary geographic, historical and personality differences. Furthermore, fascism in post-2016 America rises and expands ultimately as a subversive anti-democratic attempt and movement to recapture absolute power by violently overturning the democratic process such as electoral results, as after the 2020 elections and by the unprecedented attack on US Congress in 2021. This is entirely compatible with fascism as a putschist anti-democratic movement attempting to capture power through putsches or state coups when failing to do so via democratic processes.[40] For example, the 2021 radical-right insurrection and siege of US Congress accords with and almost replicates Mussolini's forces' march on Rome and that of Hitler[41] and his followers on Munich in the 1920s. Altogether, in post-2016 America fascism emerges at first via ballot that it abuses in a Machiavellian manner against

---

39   Rodrik (2018, p. 199) warns that American and other post-2016 'populism that undercuts liberal, pluralist, democratic norms [i.e., the political variant of populism] is almost always dangerous.'

40   Jouet (2017, p. 29) recounts that 'Trump alleged that it [the election] would be 'rigged' and suggested that he might not accept the democratic process: 'I will totally accept the results—if I win,' which epitomizes fascists' tendency not to accept and instead to overturn electoral results if they lose elections.

41   Acemoglu et al. (2018, p. 1043) state that the 'rise of Hitler [is] perhaps the most spectacular collapse of a modern democratic system in history.'

democracy and eventually through bullet by attempting to destroy democratic processes, which completely accords with fascism in general since Italian fascists and German Nazis using both means to seize absolute power.

Relatedly, fascism in post-2016 America develops and metastasizes as elite dictatorship in the form of autocracy, family dynasty, oligarchy, and plutocracy, while its autocratic rulers using rhetoric of bogus populism as a Machiavellian deception and delusion to attract and deceive the radical-right rank-and-file and other 'people', just as it does in all other social spaces and times since Italy and Germany in the 1920–30s. This conforms with fascism in general interpreting societal history as the circulation of elites and operating as elite dictatorship through autocracy, dynasty, oligarchy, and plutocracy, while its leaders resorting to deceptive or delusionary populism for their followers. Fascists explode and march in post-2016 America as elite would-be dictators or rulers such as autocrats, oligarchs, and to some extent plutocrats, while recruiting and deceiving their followers and other 'people' by bogus anti-elitist, anti-system, or anti-establishment populism. In the process, fascists leaders become the elite, system, or establishment itself in post-2016 America, which their base approves or is unable and unwilling to realize because of its blind submission (evoking the Nazi 'blind herd') and authoritarian sadistic-masochistic personalities. These all-American new elites emulate fascist leaders as elite rulers and their deceptive anti-institutional populism in the manner of Mussolini and Hitler until capturing and wielding total institutional power.

5   Syndrome 4: Fascism as Extreme Anti-secularism

Fourth and resulting from conservatism and linking with anti-liberalism, fascism in America post-2016 reveals and replicates extreme anti-secularism as an additional universal fascist element in various social settings and periods. American fascism thus develops and metastasizes as an extreme anti-secular ideology, social movement, political regime, and cultural zeitgeist. Consequently, it attempts to eliminate or pervert secular social institutions, most notably liberal-secular democracy and its defining element, the structural differentiation between religion and politics, particularly the separation of church and state, or 'sacred' and secular powers. In short, American fascism surges and operates as, or allies and merges with, religious extremism. Further, it allies and merges with theocracy or its religious equivalent and precedent.

On this account, fascism in post-2016 America—and to some degree earlier, as during the 1980s with Reaganism as evangelicalism[42]—rises as extreme, vehement anti-secularism, as it does in all other social spaces and times starting with fascist Italy and Spain and Nazi Germany through proto-fascist South America in the 1970–80s to neo-fascist or populist Hungary and Poland since the 2000s, Brazil after 2018 and beyond, with minor variations. Specifically, American fascism occurs as an extremely and vehemently anti-secular conservative ideology, movement, regime, and climate in the 'land of freedom' during this period, as in all other lands and periods mentioned above. Therefore, this 'all-American' creation completely accords with and exemplifies the generalized fact that fascism universally is extreme conservative anti-secularism by always arising and functioning as an extremely anti-secular phenomenon, with secondary variations and few transient exceptions. Moreover, post-2016 American fascism is the probably most extreme type of anti-secularism of all fascist varieties or proxies in Western societies while equivalent to such cases in non-Western countries like post-socialist Hungary and Poland, post-2018 Brazil, and Islamic-ruled Turkey. In other words, fascist and broader conservative extreme anti-secularism culminates in post-2016 American fascism within the West and beyond, along with anti-secular Catholic-dominated Poland and Islamic-ruled Turkey. Considering this development, conservative extreme, vehement anti-secularism makes fascism happen in post-2016 America, just as it does in all other societies and times noted earlier. Even if not all American conservative anti-secularism is fascist, fascism in post-2016 America is an extreme and implacable anti-secularist ideology, movement, regime, and ambiance.

---

42   DiPrete et al. (2011, p. 1236) find that 'political conflict between proponents of secular and religiously orthodox values has been especially prominent since the Reagan presidency'. They conclude that especially since and due to Reaganism, religion 'in particular has emerged as a fundamental cleavage in American society at the level of day-to-day interaction. From the perspective of the culture wars that we have seen play out in the American political sphere and the past decade or so, this may not be surprising' (DiPrete et al. 2011, p. 1272). Krasa and Polborn (2014, p. 308) observe that 'Reagan's conservative revolution has created a cultural wedge between the parties that only widened in the 1990s and 2000s.' They add that 'Ronald Reagan's election and the [resulting] contemporaneous integration of evangelicals into the main stream of the Republican party [is] the starting point of a clearer ideological differentiation between parties [and so] a cultural radicalization of the Republican party under Reagan, and similarly later under George W. Bush' (Krasa and Polborn 2014, p. 321).

Fascists hence resurge and march in post-2016 America as extreme and implacable conservative anti-secularists,[43] as they do in all other social spaces and times since fascist Italy by Mussolini's pact with the Vatican and Spain by Franco's alliance with the Catholic church, and Nazi Germany by Hitler's treaty with the Pope and incorporation of most Lutheranism, aside from rare or transient exceptions. These 'all-American' examples therefore fully conform to the extremely anti-secular character and activity of fascists and other conservatives. Indeed, American-born fascists are likely the most extreme and implacable anti-secularists of all fascist actors in Western societies and beyond, together with their counterparts in Catholic-dominated Poland and their proxies in Islamic-ruled Turkey. In other words, US extreme, implacable conservative anti-secularists erupt and become American-born fascists, just as do their equivalents elsewhere in Western and especially non-Western societies, such as Poland, Hungary, and Turkey since the 2000s. In this sense, conservative extreme, implacable anti-secularists make fascism happen in post-2016 America, as they do in all other social settings and periods mentioned previously. While not all American conservative extreme, implacable anti-secularists are fascist, fascists in post-2016 America are extremely and implacably anti-secularist and religiously extremist forces.

Consequently, fascism in post-2016 America and to some extent during the 1980s with Reaganism rises and advances as an ideological design and practical attempt to eliminate or pervert secular social institutions and rules, as it does in all other social settings since fascist Italy and Spain and Nazi Germany through neo-fascist South America to theocratic Poland and Turkey, and neo-fascist Hungary. Especially, American fascism emerges as a vision and endeavor of elimination of liberal-secular democracy and its underlying institutions and rules as the common antidote to fascism and as extreme anti-secularism which it inherits and continues from medieval-rooted conservatism that perpetuates pre-secular medievalism as the Dark Middle Ages of religious superstition, fanaticism, and irrationalism. Specifically, since this involves the dissolution of the differentiation between religion and politics, fascism occurs as the abolition or subversion of the separation of church and state, as it does everywhere else from fascist Italy/Spain and Nazi Germany to Catholic-dominated Poland and Islamic-ruled Turkey. The 'all-American' example hence entirely accords with and epitomizes fascism's and generally religious conservatism's perennial aim and constant action to eliminate or pervert secular social institutions and

---

43 Gorski and Altınordu (2008, pp. 75–6) point to US anti-secular 'culture warriors of the right, who define secularism in such a way as to include everybody except themselves and their closest allies.'

rules, notably liberal-secular democracy and its differentiation between religion and politics, including the separation of church and state. Furthermore, post-2016 American fascism is the probably most extreme instance of the dissolution of the differentiation between religion and politics through the demolition of the separation of church and state in Western and comparable society, along with Catholic-dominated Poland and Islamic-ruled Turkey. In other words, the perennial conservative design and attempt of dissolving the differentiation between religion and politics by demolishing the separation of church and state materializes and culminates in post-2016 American fascism within the mostly secular Western setting.

While conforming with all European, fascisms, American fascism flagrantly and constantly negates and violates the opposite American Jeffersonian principle of the separation of church and state and thus the differentiation between religion and politics as the necessary condition and defining element of liberal, genuine democracy.[44] Post-2016 American fascism looks more 'foreign', European than 'native', American in the sense of Jefferson's liberal-democratic ideal and the US Constitution but remains profoundly 'home-born' rather than coming to America from the old fascist Europe. The designed and attempted elimination of liberal-secular democracy and related social institutions and rules through the demolition of the separation of church and state makes fascism happen in post-2016 America, as it does in other social settings.

Fascists thus explode and march in post-2016 America as extreme conservative forces attempting to eliminate secular social institutions and rules, as they do elsewhere from Mussolini, Franco, and Hitler through their postwar and contemporary descendants in South America, parts of Western and Eastern Europe, and beyond. Especially, US fascists resurge as rightist anti-secular and anti-democratic forces seeking to destroy liberal-secular democracy by dissolving its differentiation between religion and politics through dismantling the separation of church and state, just as they do in all these other instances. They hence entirely follow and implement fascists' and other conservatives' antagonism toward liberal-secular democracy and demolition of the separation of church and state. Moreover, American-born fascists are probably the most extreme, implacable destructive forces against liberal-secular democracy and its separation of church and state among all fascist groups in contemporary Western societies and beyond, along with their equivalents in Catholic-dominated Poland and their proxies in Islamic-ruled Turkey. In this regard, the

---

44   Phillips (2006, p. 5) specifically warns that the US Religious Right is 'actively seeking to dismantle the separation of church and state.'

conservative extreme, implacable enemies of liberal-secular democracy and its separation of church and state makes fascism happen in post-2016 America, as they do in all other spaces and times listed above.

In other words, fascism in post-2016 America, and to some degree during the 1980s with evangelical Reaganism, rises as religious extremism,[45] or allies and eventually merges with the latter, as it does in all other social settings and periods since fascist Italy and Spain and Nazi Germany through neo-fascist South America and Hungary and theocratic Poland. Fascists surge in post-2016 America as religious extremists, or allying and blending with them, as they do everywhere from Mussolini, Franco, and Hitler through their later heirs in South America (Chile's Pinochet) to parts of Europe (Hungary's and Poland's extreme conservative rulers), and beyond.

The 'all-American' fascist form reaffirms the general rule that fascism universally is, or allies and blends with, religious extremism rather than being a unique exception following conservative 'American exceptionalism' in compulsory or fervent 'faith' as 'democracy and freedom'. 'All-American' faces of fascism thus conform to fascists' pattern of being, or allying and blending with, religious extremists. Specifically, post-2016 American fascism's religious extremism primarily assumes the form of or allies and blends with Protestant evangelicalism and related fundamentalism[46] and to some degree dogmatic

---

45 Mueller (2009, p. ix) alerts to the 'incompatibility of strong religious views and liberal democracy' suggesting that wherever 'extremist religious beliefs exist, liberalism is at peril' and invoking the 'growing importance of religious extremism in the United States [where] liberalism and democracy are [vulnerable] to attack from religious extremists.' Mueller (2009, p. 415) elaborates that the 'intensity to which religious beliefs are incompatible with liberal democracy and more generally with rational thought depends on both the nature of these beliefs and the intensity to with which they are held.' Mueller (2009, p. 417) infers that 'it is religious extremists therefore that deserve the closest attention today from those who defend liberal democracy.' Especially, Mueller (2009, p. 392) deplores that evangelical Americans' 'Puritanical beliefs cause hardship, suffering, and often death by denying others the possibility of having safe and cheap abortions [plus] means of birth control.'

46 Mueller (2013, p. 7) observes that 'religious fundamentalists were behind the Prohibition movement in the United States at the start of the twentieth century. Not only did Prohibition infringe on the rights of those with less strong religious convictions, it resulted in a great increase in crime in the United States. More recently, the religious fundamentalists in the United States have turned their attention to preventing abortions. Extremists in this movement have broken US laws by blocking access to public buildings, damaging property, harassing young pregnant women, and workers in abortion clinics and, on occasion, murdering doctors who perform abortions.' Mueller (2013, p. 10) especially laments that 'evangelical Americans, a significant fraction of the population, see the world in terms of good and evil. Evil must be punished. Drugs are evil. Send the users and sellers to jail.' He concludes that there are 'no social benefits that America reaps from

Catholicism, with both coalescing, setting aside their historical enmity and conflict, into the Christian Right that espouses political extremism[47] versus liberal-secular democracy. American-born post-2016 fascists are, or ally and blend with, most evangelicals[48] and other fundamentalists and many orthodox Catholics, while both uniting, apparently setting aside their long-standing hostilities and wars, into the Christian Right as a set of (also) political extremists attacking seculars and liberals.

Moreover, post-2016 American fascism is the probably most extreme instance of religious extremism, or of an alliance and merger with the latter, among all fascist varieties or proxies in Western and comparable societies, together with those in Catholic-dominated Poland and Islamic-ruled Turkey. American-born post-2016 fascists are probably the most implacable cases of religious extremists, or allying and blending with them, within these settings, together with their equivalents or proxies in Poland and Turkey. On this account, religious extremism in the primary form of, or alliance and merger with, evangelicalism and broader fundamentalism and dogmatic Catholicism, briefly the Christian Right,[49] makes fascism happen in post-2016 America, just as it does in all other

---

its greater religiosity compared with Europe. Those with strong religious beliefs are often able to pass laws, which limit the freedoms of individuals in the community thereby harming those who would undertake the forbidden actions' (Mueller 2013, p. 10).

47   Lipset (1955, p. 200) suggests that extreme conservatism 'unites bigots of various stripes. In the South [and elsewhere], fundamentalist Protestant groups back the radical right [such as McCarthyism].' Glaeser, Ponzetto, and Shapiro (2005, p. 1283) report a 'non-monotonic relationship between religious [and political] extremism and religious attendance'. Especially, they find that religious attendance predicts political extremism [Republicanism] in the US and even that the 'estimated [effect] in the US is slightly higher than that for the world as a whole' (Glaeser et al. 2005, p. 1313).

48   Bazzi et al. (2020, p. 845) point to the 'rise of the religious vote in the United States', including the evangelical voting mostly for fascist or radical-right candidates in the 2016 elections resulting in autocracy and generally radical-right rule.

49   Hedges (2004) recounts that 'Dr. James Luther Adams, professor at Harvard Divinity School, [said] we would all be fighting the 'Christian fascists' [as US] radio and televangelists began speaking about a new political religion that would direct its efforts at taking control of all institutions, including mainstream denominations and the government. Its stated goal was to use the United States to create a global, Christian empire.' Hedges (2004) adds that 'it was hard, at the time, to take such fantastic rhetoric seriously, especially given the buffoonish quality of those who expounded it. The Nazis, he said, were not going to return with swastikas and brown shirts. Their ideological inheritors had found a mask for fascism in the pages of the Bible. He was in Germany in 1935 and 1936. He saw in the Christian Right, long before we did, disturbing similarities with the German Christian Church and the Nazi Party, similarities that he said would, in the event of prolonged social instability or a national crisis, see American fascists, under the guise of religion, rise to dismantle the open society.' Hedges (2004) elaborates that 'he despaired of liberals, who

social spaces and times noted above. Religious extremists in the face of most evangelicals, other fundamentalists, and many orthodox Catholics, simply Christian Rightists, make fascism happen in post-2016 America, just as making it occur everywhere else since Mussolini, Franco, and Hitler.

Furthermore, fascism in post-2016 America and to some degree during the 1980s with theocratic Reaganism rises as, or links and ultimately merges with, theocracy,[50] as it does in most other social spaces and times since fascist Italy and Spain and Nazi Germany through parts of neo-fascist South America to Catholic-dominated Poland and elsewhere like Islamic-ruled Turkey among Muslim countries. Fascists erupt and march in post-2016 America as theocrats, or allying and blending with them, as they do in these other settings since Mussolini-Franco-Hitler's pacts with the Vatican and blend with Catholicism and, in Nazi Germany, incorporation of Lutheranism through their heirs in South America, such as Pinochet's mobilization of the Catholic church, parts of Europe like Hungary's and Poland's ultra-conservative rulers' merger with theocratic religion, and beyond.

Far from being a sole exception, the 'all-American' fascist form hence completely confirms fascism's typical character and operation as, or linkage and merger with, theocracy and theocratic religion. It also reaffirms the tendency that theocracy and more broadly theocratic religion due to its inherent proto-totalitarianism is prototypical fascism or its religious equivalent and precedent, just as by being extreme conservatism and anti-liberalism fascism is typically theocratic and religious, with secondary and transient variations. 'All-American' examples of fascism accord with fascists being and acting as or allying and blending with theocrats and theocratic religionists. They also confirm that theocrats and theocratic religionists due to their proto-totalitarian

---

he said, as in Nazi Germany, mouthed silly platitudes about dialogue and inclusiveness that made them ineffectual and impotent. Liberals, he said, did not understand the power and allure of evil nor the cold reality of how the world worked. Two decades later, even in the face of the growing reach of the Christian Right, his prediction seems apocalyptic. And yet the powerbrokers in the Christian Right have moved from the fringes of society to the floor of the House of Representatives and the Senate. Christian fundamentalists now hold a majority of seats in 36 percent of all Republican Party state committees, or 18 of 50 states, along with large minorities in 81 percent of the rest of the states.'

50 Bénabou, Ticchi and Vindigni (2015, p. 347) observe that the 'American regime' allows 'specific exemptions or other policies [e.g., laws regulating behavior] benefiting religious activities and citizens' and 'a rise in income inequality can lead the rich to form a Religious-Right alliance with the religious poor and start blocking belief-eroding discoveries and ideas'. They thus imply that the 'American regime' is essentially, even if not nominally, a 'theocratic regime' that Islamic states formally epitomize in contrast to the 'Secularization or Western-European regime.'

tendencies are prototypical fascists or their religious equivalents and precursors, just as fascists being theocratic or extremely religious.

Specifically, post-2016 American fascism's element of theocracy or theocratic religion assumes primarily the form of or links and merges with its evangelical and other fundamentalist versions and growingly Catholic version, all coalescing in the Christian Right as the 'divine' design, movement, and regime of proto-fascist theocracy cum 'Christian America' eliminating liberal-secular democracy by abolishing the Jeffersonian 'wall of separation of church and state.'[51] American-born post-2016 fascists are, or ally and blend with, most evangelical, other fundamentalist and many orthodox Catholic theocrats, who unite in the Christian Right[52] as a broader, even if often contending, family of theocratic religionists launching a warfare on seculars and liberals.

Moreover, post-2016 American fascism is the probably most extreme instance of theocracy or of a link and merger with it among all fascist varieties or proxies within Western and comparable societies, along with those in Catholic-dominated Poland and Islamic-ruled Turkey. American-born post-2016 fascists are probably the most vehement examples of theocrats, or allying and blending with them, among these societies, together with their counterparts or proxies in Poland and Turkey. On this account, theocracy in its

---

51   Phillips (2006) identifies 'American Theocracy' characterized as the 'Peril and Politics of Radical Religion'. He elaborates by pointing to the Religious Right which is 'actively seeking to dismantle the separation of church and state–indeed, such religious fundamentalists explicitly affirm that the United States is a Christian nation founded on Biblical principles–takes the Bible as the inerrant Word of God' and warning that the 'seriousness and influence of this Religious Right cannot be discounted' (Phillips 2006, p. 5). Dawkins (2006, p. 292–3) remarks the US evangelical 'ambition to achieve what can only be called a Christian fascist state is entirely typical of the American Taliban. It is an almost exact mirror image of the Islamic fascist state so ardently sought by many people in other parts of the world.' Bénabou et al. (2015, p. 347) generally characterize a 'Theocratic regime with knowledge stagnation, extreme religiosity, a Church that makes no effort to adapt since its beliefs are protected by the state, and also high taxes but now used to subsidize the religious sector.' Notably, they suggest that the 'American regime' is a 'Theocratic regime' save in name yet in substance due to its policies and laws 'benefiting religious activities and citizens' and the 'Religious-Right alliance' between the plutocratic rich and the religious poor 'blocking belief-eroding discoveries and ideas' (Bénabou et al. 2015, p. 347).

52   Alpers (2003, p. 7) notes the inclusion of 'fundamentalist leaders of the old Christian right' into the 'beginnings of American fascism'. Hedges (2004) alerts that the 'Christian Right finds its ideological justification [in] a vision of Christ as the head of a great and murderous army of heavenly avengers.' Phillips (2006, p. 5) detects the 'apocalyptic mindset of many in the [US] Christian Right.' Blee and Creasap (2010, p. 280) register 'new efforts by the US Christian Right to develop transnational religious alliances' with fascist parties like Haider's Austria 'Freedom Party'.

evangelical and other fundamentalist versions and growingly its Catholic version, simply the theocratic Christian Right, makes fascism happen in post-2016 America, as it does in other social settings and periods listed earlier. Theocrats in the face of theocratic evangelicals, other fundamentalists, and many orthodox Catholics, simply Christian Rightists, make fascism happen in post-2016 America, while making it occur everywhere else.

American fascism could happen and endure in the sense of its religious perpetuation and consecration only or primarily through theocracy and more broadly theocratic religion coalescing into the Christian Right, thus solely or mainly owing to evangelicals, other fundamentalists, and dogmatic Catholics united as theocrats. Conversely, it is American fascism only or primarily, together with conservatism or the radical right, that can enforce and sustain theocracy and theocratic religion[53] generally in the 'land of freedom', so fascists, along with other conservatives or extreme rightists, solely or mainly being able to impose and maintain theocratic 'Christian America'. This confirms the interdependence, mutual reinforcement, and ultimately osmosis between fascism and theocracy or theocratic religion in all societal settings and times since fascist Italy/Spain and Nazi Germany through current societies and present days.

6   Syndrome 5: Fascism as Extreme Irrationalism, Anti-rationalism, and Anti-progressivism

Fifth and ensuing from conservatism and connecting with anti-liberalism, fascism in America post-2016 reveals and replicates extreme irrationalism, anti-rationalism, and anti-progressivism as a universal fascist element in all social spaces and times. American fascism hence rises and advances as an extreme irrational, anti-rational, and anti-progressive ideology, social movement, political regime, and cultural zeitgeist. Moreover, it develops and metastasizes as the most complete and intense irrationalism, anti-rationalism, and anti-progressivism in Western and comparable societies. In particular, it resurges and spreads as a compound of religious and other superstitions, fanaticisms, fantasies, and ignorance. Relatedly, it emerges and functions as extreme anti-science antagonism and generally anti-intellectualism.

---

53   Mueller (2009, pp. ix–x) observes that conservatism (traditionalism) and theocratic religion 'go hand in hand, as does to a large extent [conservatism] and dictatorship' and infers the 'dangers' that conservatism and religion both 'pose for liberal democracy'.

Fascism in post-2016 America and to some degree before, as during the 1980s with Reaganism emerges as extreme, atavistic irrationalism and vehement anti-rationalism and anti-progressivism, as it does in all other social spaces and times beginning with interwar fascist Italy and Nazi Germany through postwar proto-fascist South America to post-socialist neo-fascist/populist Hungary and Poland, Brexit Great Britain, Brazil after 2018, and other cases. Specifically, American fascism rises as an extremely, atavistically irrational, and anti-rational and anti-progressive conservative—as distinct from other—ideology, movement, regime, and ambiance in America currently, as in all other countries and times. In consequence, this American example entirely confirms and indeed epitomizes rather than exempts—as via alleged 'American exceptionalism'—itself from the rule that fascism everywhere and always emerges and operates as an extremely irrational, anti-rational, and anti-progressive entity and hence is universally a compound of extreme conservative irrationalism, anti-rationalism, and anti-progressivism, with virtually no exceptions. In other words, conservative atavistic irrationalism and implacable anti-rationalism and anti-progressivism make fascism happen in post-2016 America, as they do in all other cases. While not all-American conservative irrationalism, anti-rationalism, and anti-progressivism are fascist, fascism in post-2016 America is an atavistically irrational and implacably anti-rational and anti-progressive movement, ideology, regime, and ambiance, as it is everywhere else.

Fascists hence erupt and march in post-2016 America as extreme, atavistic conservative irrationalists and implacable anti-rationalists and anti-progressivists, as they do in all other social settings and periods since Italy's Mussolini and Germany's Hitler through Hungary and Poland's neo-fascists/populists to those in Brexit Great Britain, Brazil, and elsewhere, with few partial and transient exceptions. In so doing, these 'all-American' examples exemplify rather than being exceptions to fascists' and more broadly conservatives' atavistically irrational and vehemently anti-rationalist and anti-progressive core. To be sure, not all American conservative extreme, atavistic irrationalists and vehement anti-rationalists and anti-progressives are fascist, yet fascists in post-2016 America are always atavistically irrationalist and vehemently anti-rationalist and anti-progressive forces, as they are everywhere else.

Moreover, fascism in post-2016 America rises and expands as the most extreme, atavistic[54] irrationalism and vehement anti-rationalism and

---

54   McMurtry (1999, p. 255) also denotes the 'competitiveness of the beast' as an 'atavistic substratum' of Nazism and other fascism. Relatedly, Bourdieu (1998, p. 50) remarks that US neo-conservatism ('neo-liberalism') rests on an 'atavistic faith in historical inevitability' and thus represents conservative ('neo-liberal') 'fatalism'.

anti-progressivism among all fascist varieties or proxies in contemporary Western societies and non-Western countries, along with post-socialist Poland, Islamic-ruled Turkey, post-2018 Brazil, etc. This means that the fascist and broader conservative compound of anachronistic irrationalism and vehement anti-rationalism and anti-progressivism attains its apex in post-2016 American fascism within the Western world and other settings, together with irrationalist and anti-rationalist Poland, etc. Post-2016 American fascism and more broadly conservatism, as it does in all crises, proves to be the 'leader' of atavistic and nihilistic, including self-destructive, irrationalism, anti-rationalism, and anti-progressivism within the Western world and beyond during the Covid-19 pandemic by denying, virtually alone in this setting, the health crisis and resisting its solutions. No other ideology, movement, and regime in the West and elsewhere shows to be more irrationalist and anti-rationalist in this health crisis than post-2016 American fascism and conservatism. Regarding these crises, post-2016 American fascism/conservatism is virtually the only social force within the Western world and beyond that denies (human causes of) climate change such as global warming[55] and opposes its rational remedies, proving to be the world 'leader' of atavistic irrationalism and nihilistic anti-rationalism and anti-progressivism. Generally, the conservative compound of atavistic irrationalism and vehement anti-rationalism and anti-progressivism precisely makes fascism happen in post-2016 America, as it does in all other cases mentioned previously.

American-born fascists and other conservatives are hence probably the most atavistic irrationalists and destructive anti-rationalists and anti-progressives among all fascist and conservative agents in Western and even other societies, together with their equivalents in Catholic-dominated Poland and their proxies

---

55   Nordhaus (2019, p. 2008) notes that the 'Trump administration announced that the United States will withdraw from the (Paris) agreement' in spite or perhaps—in a conservative tendency to America's and global self-destruction as 'salvation'—because of the 'ominous march of climate change'. Nordhaus (2019, p. 2012) concludes that obstacles to slowing this ominous process are conservative 'ignorance' and the 'distortions of democracy by anti-environmental interests and political contributions' by conservatives, along with 'free-riding among those looking to the interests of their country, and shortsightedness among those who discount the interests of the future.' Further, the post-2016 conservative-dominated, Supreme Court, as the press reports, 'limits federal power to curb carbon emissions' under the Clean Air Act and thus effectively gives US business the license to pollute and exacerbate the grave climate crisis as an existential treat. While America and the planet facing this existential treat, the conservative Supreme Court aligns itself with anti-environmental interests and acts as a major impediment to the rational societal action against the climate crisis, manifesting its lethal irrationalism, ideological fanaticism, and political extremism.

in Islamic-ruled Turkey. Post-2016 American fascists-conservatives prove to be leading atavistic irrationalists and nihilistic, including self-destructive, anti-rationalists and anti-progressives in the Western and entire world during the Covid-19 pandemic by denying it and opposing its rational solutions, such as vaccines, mask wearing, and other measures, more than any others, as they do in all other crises. Regarding these crises, US fascists-conservatives are virtually the only group in Western and other societies denying climate change and its human causes and rational social solutions, proving to be the foremost irrationalists, anti-rationalists, and anti-progressives in the West and beyond. It follows that conservative atavistic and nihilistic irrationalists, anti-rationalists and anti-progressives precisely make fascism happen in post-2016 America, as they do in other cases above.

In particular, fascism in post-2016 America resurges and operates as a compound of religious and other superstitions, fanaticisms, fantasies, and ignorance, as it does in all other social settings and periods commencing with fascist Italy and Spain and Nazi Germany through proto-fascist South America to neo-fascist/populist Hungary, Poland, Brexit Great Britain, Brazil, and others. Specifically, fascism rises in post-2016 America as an extreme conservative compound of religious superstitions and delusions, thus extreme religiosity,[56] as it does in these other cases. These superstitions range from the irrational expectation and precipitation of 'rapture' and the superstitious beliefs in 'creationism' or 'intelligent design' and the existence of 'Satan' to the anti-rationalist opposition to biological evolutionism, vaccinations, stem-cell research, universal health care,[57] and climate science and climate-change causes and remedies.[58] Accordingly, what happens in post-2016 America exemplifies and reaffirms the pattern of fascism as an admixture of religious and other superstitions, fanaticisms, fantasies, and ignorance rather than being an exception

---

56   Bénabou et al. (2015, p. 349) find that religiosity is 'consistently associated with more negative views of scientific progress.' Specifically, they report that 'greater religiosity [is] clearly associated with lower scientific literacy. Across people as well as places, the strength of religious belief is strongly negatively correlated with education (especially for literalist beliefs in miracles, the devil, or the inerrancy of the Bible)' (Bénabou et al. 2015, p. 350). Also, Squicciarini (2020, p. 3454) observes that 'religion can still hamper the diffusion of knowledge and innovation in many regions today.'

57   Saez and Zucman (2020, p. 23) note that all OECD countries 'except the United States have a national program for financing health care'.

58   Nyhan (2020, 220–1) citing the US conservative 'death panel' myth deceptively justifying the opposition to universal health care notices that 'misperceptions threaten to warp mass opinion, undermine democratic debate, and distort public policy on issues ranging from climate change to vaccines,' noting 'highly credible evidence (like the role of humans in climate change)'.

in the sense of supposed conservative 'American exceptionalism' in 'true' faith. In this regard, the conservative compound of religious and other superstitions, fanaticisms, fantasies, and 'blissful' ignorance make fascism happen in post-2016 America, as they do in all other instances mentioned earlier.

Furthermore, fascism in post-2016 America develops and metastasizes as the most expansive, intensive, and persisting admixture of religious and other superstitions, fanaticisms, fantasies, and ignorance among all fascist varieties or proxies in Western and non-Western societies, together with Catholic-dominated Poland, Islamic-ruled Turkey, and post-2018 Brazil. This signifies that the fascist and broader conservative mélange of religious and other superstitions, fanaticisms, fantasies, and ignorance culminates in post-2016 American fascism within Western and other settings, along with growingly superstitious Catholic-dominated Poland, etc. During the Covid-19 pandemic, post-2016 American fascism and broader conservatism proves to be the champion of atavistic and nihilistic, including self-destructive, religious, and other superstitions, fanaticism, fantasies, and ignorance, briefly delusions, within the Western and entire world by alone denying this crisis and opposing its solutions. Conversely, no other ideology, movement, and regime in the West and beyond proves to be more superstitious, fanatical, ignorant, and delusionary in this health crisis than American fascism-conservatism, as it does in all other crises. Concerning the latter, by virtually alone in the Western and global setting denying climate change or its human-social causes[59] and resisting its rational remedies on religious (Biblical) and other superstitious or delusionary grounds, American fascism/conservatism proves to be such a leader in atavistic and nihilistic superstitions and delusions in the West and beyond.

American-born fascists and broader conservatives hence are likely the most religiously and otherwise superstitious, fanatical, ignorant, and delusionary of all fascist and conservative actors in Western and other societies, together with their counterparts in Catholic-dominated Poland and their proxies in Islamic-ruled Turkey. They prove this 'leadership' during the Covid-19 pandemic as they behave as the most superstitious, fanatical, ignorant, and delusionary of all actors in Western and other settings facing this crisis. Furthermore, they prove themselves as the leaders of religious superstitions, fanaticisms, ignorance, and delusions during various other social crises persistently, including climate change by denying it and opposing its rational solutions for religious and other

---

59   Akerlof (2020, p. 414) alerts that 'among the US [conservative] public, there are not only those who view global warming as outright hoax; many more also fail to perceive its urgency. The stories that justify continued inaction, year after year, are as important as the physical reality of global warming itself.'

superstitious or delusionary and nihilistic reasons. In general, American-born fascists and other conservatives display more religious superstitions, fanaticism, ignorance, and delusions, including beliefs in 'miracles', 'rapture', 'creationism', 'intelligent design', 'flat earth', 'Satan', and 'witches', than any other groups in Western and other societies. The belief in the existence of 'Satan' and by association 'witches' is more widespread among US fascists and other conservatives, especially evangelicals, than any other groups in Western and comparable non-Western countries,[60] except only for Islamic-ruled Turkey. This holds true for 'creationism', 'intelligent design', 'rapture',[61] 'flat earth', 'miracles', and related religious and other superstitions, dogmas, and manifestations of ignorance—US fascists-conservatives hold these beliefs and impose them on others more intensely and persistently more than any other groups in Western and comparable settings. This demonstrates fascism-conservatism's unparalleled extent and gravity of extreme and self-destructive irrationalism in post-2016 America.

Relatedly, fascism in post-2016 America and perhaps since the 1980s with Reaganism[62] rises and spreads as extreme anti-science antagonism expressing vehement anti-rationalism, anti-intellectualism, and anti-progressivism regarding scientific progress, as it does in all other social spaces and times since fascist Italy and especially Nazi Germany through neo-fascist/populist Hungary, Poland, Brexit Great Britain, Brazil, and others. Specifically, American fascism emerges as an extremely, conservative, radical-right anti-science, anti-progressive, and anti- or non-intellectual,[63] including anti-art and anti-theory, ideology, movement, regime, and atmosphere in America during this period, as

---

60   Glaeser (2004, p. 408) refers to the finding that '71 percent of Americans believe in the Devil, while only 19 percent of the French and 11 percent of Danes think that there is some sort of Mephistopheles.'

61   Dawkins (2006, p. 132) elaborates that 'some rapture [US] Christians go further [than to wait] and actually yearn for nuclear war because they interpret it as the 'Armageddon' which, according to their bizarre but disturbingly popular interpretation of the book of Revelation, will hasten the Second Coming.'

62   Mooney (2005, p. 5) alters to American conservatism's vehement opposition to the 'dynamism of scientific inquiry—its constant onslaught on old orthodoxies, its rapid generation of new technological possibilities.' Pfeffer, Fomby, and Insolera (2020, p. 86) recount that in 1981, 'President Reagan proposed to cut social science research at NSF by 75%. NSF funding was restored by Congress.'

63   Lipset (1955, p. 196) observes that 'basically the [US] radical right [conservatism] is unintellectual'. Bourdieu and Haacke (1995, p. 44) also note that the US old Right is 'anti-intellectual'. Munch (2001, p. 223) finds that primarily due to Puritan-rooted conservatism and its anti-intellectualism, the US 'lacks the kind of intellectual scene that France enjoys.'

in other social settings and periods mentioned above. Accordingly, American fascism fully confirms and epitomizes fascism's pattern of extreme anti-science antagonism, anti-progressivism, and anti-intellectualism rather than showing supposed conservative 'American exceptionalism' in superior 'science', scientific 'progress', and 'intellectual' activity or capacity. In this respect, conservative anti-science, anti-progressivism, and anti-intellectualism makes fascism happen in post-2016 America, as it does in all other social spaces and times mentioned previously. While not all American conservative anti-science[64] antagonism, anti-progressivism, and anti-intellectualism is fascist, fascism in post-2016 America is an extremely anti-scientific, anti-progressive, and anti-intellectual movement, ideology, regime, and zeitgeist, as is in all other cases noted above.

Fascists hence erupt and march in post-2016 America and act as extreme conservative anti-science antagonists, anti-progressives, and anti- or non-intellectuals,[65] as they do in all other social places and times since Mussolini and Hitler et al. through Hungary's, Poland's, Turkey's, Brexit Great Britain's, Brazil's, and other neo-fascist or populist rulers, with hardly any exceptions. By acting so, these 'all-American' home-grown examples fully exemplify the anti-science, anti-progress, and anti-intellectual essence of fascists and conservatives rather than being exceptions. While not all American conservative anti-science and anti-progress opponents and anti-intellectuals are fascist, fascists post-2016 are universally extreme anti-science antagonists, anti-progressives, and anti-intellectuals, just as are in all other settings and periods.

Moreover, fascism in post-2016 America resurges and expands as the most intense anti-science antagonism, anti-rationalism, irrationalism, anti-progressivism and anti-intellectualism among all fascist varieties or proxies in Western and comparable non-Western societies, along with Catholic-dominated Poland, Islamic-ruled Turkey, and post-2018 Brazil. It follows that

---

64   Gauchat (2012, p. 172) suggests that the religious right and transnational corporations are the 'two key constituencies' of the US anti-science new right and that 'each have vested interests in scientific outcomes. Corporations subject to government regulation often challenge science to undermine federal controls and protect their profit margins. Religious groups clash with science over moral, epistemological, and ontological issues, such as Darwinian evolution, stem cell research, and AIDS research.'

65   Adorno (2001, p. 219) observes that in current [postwar] 'American fascist propaganda' its agitators depict its audience as 'as poor but honest, common-sense but non-intellectual, native Christians. They identify themselves with their listeners and lay particular emphasis upon being simultaneously both modest little men and leaders of great calibre. They often refer to themselves as mere messengers of him who is to come–a trick already familiar in Hitler's speeches.'

the fascist and conservative compound of anti-science antagonism, overarching anti-rationalism, irrationalism, anti-progressivism, and anti-intellectualism culminates in post-2016 American fascism within Western and other settings, together with growingly anti-scientific and anti-rationalist Catholic-dominated Poland and Islamic-ruled Turkey.

Post-2016 American fascism and generally conservatism proves to be the Western and indeed world leader in anti-science antagonism, hence anti-rationalism, irrationalism, anti-progressivism, and anti-intellectualism during the Covid-19 pandemic by denying it and resisting its rational solutions, such as preventive measures, including wearing masks and vaccines.[66] Alternatively, no other ideology, movement, and regime in the West and even beyond demonstrates to be more anti-scientific, anti-rationalist, irrationalist, anti-progressivist, and anti-intellectualist during this crisis than American fascism/conservatism, as the latter does in all other social crises. Among these crises, climate change exposes for long American fascism and conservatism, by denying its occurrence, resisting its societal remedies, and attacking climate science, as the anti-science, anti-rationalism, irrationalism, anti-progressivism, and anti-intellectualism leader second to none in the Western world and beyond, except for Catholic-dominated Poland and Islamic-ruled Turkey. In addition, American fascism-conservatism is the Western leader in opposing and perverting other natural and social sciences ranging from biological evolutionism and scientific medicine, including vaccines, such as the Covid-19 vaccine, and stem-cell research, to social science. This shows American fascism's and broader conservatism's comparatively unrivalled gravity of atavistic and destructive anti-science, anti-rationalism, irrationalism, anti-progressivism, and anti-intellectualism and the grave dangers they pose for science, including the lethal threats to public health and wellbeing, scientific and social progress, and human civilization[67] as by denying climate change and resisting its rational societal solutions.

---

66   Newhouse (2021, p. 102) remarks that the 'COVID-19 pandemic has made prevention highly salient; virtually the entire world has engaged in various forms of preventive behavior, including partial shutdowns of the economy, sheltering in place, wearing face masks, and frequent handwashing', but US conservatives have opposed most of these rational measures and thus behaved extremely irrational.

67   Nordhaus (2019, p. 1992) observes that 'global warming is the most significant of all environmental externalities. It menaces our planet and looms over our future like a Colossus.' American fascism/conservatism dismisses such a menace, as well as its human causes, as a "fake news', 'hoax' or 'liberal conspiracy' and vehemently opposes rational social solutions to this crisis, just as to other social crises, including most recently the Covid-19 pandemic that moreover it denies as being real.

Accordingly, American-born fascists and related conservatives or rightists are leading anti-science antagonists, thus anti-rationalists, irrationalists, anti-progressives, and anti-intellectuals, of all fascist and conservative agents in Western and other societies, along with their analogues in Catholic-dominated Poland and their proxies in Islamic-ruled Turkey. Behaving as the most anti-scientific, anti-rationalistic, irrationalist, anti-progressive, and anti-intellectual forces in Western and comparable societies, they prove to be anti-science, irrationalist leaders during the Covid-19 pandemic by virtually alone denying and resisting remedies to this health crisis, including vaccines and masks, as they do in all other crises. They also prove their anti-science unrivaled atavism for long by emerging and indeed remaining as the major sole opponents of climate science among Western and other societies, denying the process of global warming and its human-social causes and resisting its rational remedies.

Additionally, they are Western and global leading forces in attacking other natural and social science and scientists spanning from biological evolutionism[68] and evolutionary biologists and scientific medicine and physicians, including vaccines and their providers and stem-cell research and researchers, to social scientists. This illustrates the unparalleled comparative destructive threat that American-born fascists and conservatives as implacable anti-science antagonists, anti-rationalists, irrationalists, anti-progressivists, and anti-intellectuals pose to science and scientists, rationalism and rationalists, scientific social progress and progressives, intellectualism and intellectuals, so human wellbeing, health, and civilization, as do their equivalents in other social places and times from Mussolini and Hitler to Hungary's, Poland's, Brexit Great Britain's, Brazil's and other neo-fascist or populist rulers.

7   **Syndrome 6: Fascism as Extreme Anti-egalitarianism, Anti-universalism, and Anti-cosmopolitanism**

Sixth and yet another corollary of its extremist conservatism and connected to its vehement anti-liberalism, fascism in America post-2016 reveals and replicates extreme economic and social anti-egalitarianism, anti-universalism, and anti-cosmopolitanism, including anti-globalism, as a set of additional universal fascist elements in all social settings and historical periods. American fascism

---

68   Gauchat (2012, p. 184) finds that US 'conservatives were far more likely to define science as knowledge that should conform to common sense and religious tradition [and their] unfavorable attitudes are most acute in relation to government funding of science and the use of scientific knowledge to influence social policy.'

thereby develops and functions as an extreme anti-egalitarian, anti-universalist, and anti-cosmopolitan, including anti-globalist, ideology, social movement, political regime, and cultural zeitgeist. Consequently, it resurges as the compound of extreme inequality, including economic inequalities and deprivation, rigid hierarchy, particularism, elitism, monopolistic closure, and exclusion within society and in relation to other societies. In particular, it explodes as extreme conservative nationalism, nativism, social hatred, and xenophobia, including economic nationalism, protectionism, and irrationalism. Relatedly, American fascism erupts as conservative master-race or master-caste and similar racism.

In light of the above, fascism in post-2016 America—and to some degree during the early 2010s with the Tea Party, the 1980s with Reaganism, and the 1950s with McCarthyism—rises and advances as extreme economic and social anti-egalitarianism, anti-universalism, and anti-cosmopolitanism, including anti-globalism, as it does in all other social settings and periods beginning with interwar Italy, Spain, and Germany through postwar South America to current Hungary, Poland, Brazil, Brexit Great Britain, and other countries, with minor variations and few transient exceptions. Specifically, American fascism develops and functions as an extremely conservative anti-egalitarian, anti-universalist, and anti-cosmopolitan, including anti-globalist, social ideology, movement, system, and atmosphere in America during this period, as in all other societies and periods. Consequently, instead of manifesting presumed 'American exceptionalism', this 'all-American' instance fully exemplifies and reaffirms fascism's universal core of extreme conservative economic and social anti-egalitarianism, anti-universalism, and anti-cosmopolitanism, including anti-globalism. To that extent, the compound of conservative inherent, extreme anti-egalitarianism, anti-universalism, and anti-cosmopolitanism, including anti-globalism, makes fascism happen in post-2016 America, as it does in all other historical and present instances. Even if not economic and social anti-egalitarianism, anti-egalitarianism, and anti-cosmopolitanism is fascist, fascism in post-2016 America is an extremely conservative anti-egalitarian, anti-universalist, and anti-cosmopolitan ideology, movement, regime, and ambiance, as is in all other social spaces and times.

Fascists hence surge and act in post-2016 America and to some extent during Reaganism, the Tea Party, and McCarthyism as extreme conservative, rightist economic and social anti-egalitarians, anti-universalists, and anti- or non-cosmopolitans, including anti-globalists, as they do in all other social settings and periods since Mussolini and Hitler et al. through Hungary's, Poland's, Brazil's, Brexit Great Britain's, and other neo-fascist and populist rulers, with hardly any exceptions. Therefore, rather than being exceptional displaying 'American exceptionalism', these 'all-American' examples exhibit fascists' extreme anti-egalitarian, anti-universalist, and anti-cosmopolitan, including anti-globalist, core. In this respect, extreme economic and social anti egalitarians, anti-universalists, and anti-cosmopolitans, including anti-globalists, precisely make fascism happen in post-2016 America, as they do in all other social settings and periods. While not 'all-American' anti-egalitarians, anti-universalists, and anti-cosmopolitans are fascist, fascists in post-2016 America universally are extremely anti-egalitarian, anti-universalist, and anti-cosmopolitan, including anti-globalist, as in other social spaces and times.

Furthermore, post-2016 American fascism and broader conservatism is probably the most extreme subset of economic and social anti-egalitarianism, anti-universalism, anti-cosmopolitanism, and anti-globalism of all fascist and conservative varieties or proxies among Western societies and beyond, along with that in Brexit Great Britain, Hungary, and Poland. Especially, American fascism is ultimate anti-cosmopolitanism and anti-globalism to the point of anti-cosmopolitan and anti-globalist madness, thus surpassing even the old European fascism and conservatism in which these anti-universalism aspects initially originate.[69] Thus, post-2016 'all-American' fascists and broader

---

69   Enke (2020, p. 3682) states that 'Trump's moral language is less universalist (or equiva-
      lently, more communal) than that of any other presidential nominee in recent history'.
      Notably, he finds that 'voting for Trump is always negatively correlated with universalist
      and positively correlated with communal moral values [and] the relationship between
      moral values and voting for Trump is not driven by priming effects from Trump's language
      [but by] moral values from a period when Trump was not even politically active, [which]
      are still strongly related to Trump's vote share.' This implies that anti-universalist and, in
      that sense, proto-fascist moral values were prevalent in conservative America even prior to
      the rise of Trumpism. Relatedly, Bonikowski et al. (2021, pp. 496–502) observe that by 2016
      the 'Republican Party predominantly subscribed to exclusionary, unproud, and chauvin-
      istic conceptions of nationhood [or] ascriptive Americanism. This suggests that demand
      for a candidate like Donald Trump had long been growing among Republican voters [as]
      racist, anti-immigrant, and [related] frames had long been a feature of Republican pol-
      itics and conservative media.' To that extent, this implies that the Republican Party or
      conservatism harbored syndromes of proto-fascism such as 'restrictive or ardent nation-
      alism' long before Trumpism (Bonikowski et al. 2021, p. 530). Bonikowski et al. (2021,
      p. 531) warn that the 'fact that one of the two national parties (the Republican Party)
      has become a party of ethnoracial exclusion, nationalist discontent, and chauvinism is
      unlikely to produce a stable democratic equilibrium, particularly in the context of rapidly
      rising elite polarization, mass negative partisanship, and growing demographic diversity'.
      Slattery and Zidar (2020, p. 90) refer to the 'growing disaffection of noncosmopolitans' in
      America, primarily its conservative part. Edwards (2019, pp. 95–6) remarks that 'Donald
      Trump's rallies [included] the antiglobalization rhetoric', along with the 'fierce attacks
      and mocking of political rivals' and the 'criticism of the elites and the establishment.'

conservatives are likely the most extreme economic and social anti-egalitarians, anti-universalists, anti-cosmopolitans, and anti- globalists among all fascist and conservative agents in Western and comparable societies, together with their equivalents in Brexit Great Britain, Hungary, and Poland. Above all, they are maximalist, implacable anti-cosmopolitans and anti-globalists acting as anti-cosmopolitan and anti-globalist 'madmen' in total power or violent opposition, surpassing the old European fascists and conservatives as original exemplars of these elements of fascism. Western and comparable societies probably contain no more extreme anti-cosmopolitans and anti-globalists than American fascists and broader conservatives or rightists who become leaders in anti-cosmopolitanism and anti-globalism within this setting, along with their counterparts in Brexit Great Britain, Hungary, and Poland.

In consequence, fascism in post-2016 America and to some extent under Reaganism and the Tea Party emerges as the compound of extreme economic and social inequality,[70] rigid hierarchy, particularism, elitism, monopolistic closure, and exclusion within society and in relation to other societies, as it does in all other societies and times since interwar Italy and Germany through postwar South America to present Hungary, Poland, Brazil, Brexit Great Britain, and elsewhere, with secondary variations. In particular, American fascism rises as the complex and rationalization of extreme economic inequalities, closure, exclusion, and deprivation, such as growing wealth concentration[71] and income inequality,[72] pervasive poverty, work hardship, lack of socioeconomic protection, and so on. Specifically, fascism in post-2016 America and

---

70   Solow, Budd, and Weizsacker (1987, p. 182) observe that Reaganism 'cares about the distribution of wealth and its program is and has always been in favour of the redistribution of wealth in favour of the wealthy'—simply, plutocracy. Cohen and Blanchard (1988, p. 196) concur with the view [of Solow] that the 'constituency of the right is wealthy and powerful and does not need the government's protection that the poor and the weak want so much.' Piketty (2014, p. 35) notes that the 'victories of Margaret Thatcher in England in 1979 and Ronald Reagan in the US in 1980 [indicated] the beginning of a conservative revolution.'

71   Piketty (2014, p. 25) envisions that especially [though not solely] in American capitalism, the 'concentration of capital will attain extremely high levels—levels potentially incompatible with the meritocratic values and principles of social justice fundamental to modern democratic societies.' Lamont (2018, p. 421) notices that in the US the 'concentration of wealth is at its highest point since the Great [Depression] of 1929'. Even the US 'Patriotic Millionaires' voice their 'concern about the destabilizing concentration of wealth and power in America.'

72   Piketty, Saez, and Zucman (2018, pp. 604–5) observe that in the US, the 'stagnation of bottom 50% incomes and the upsurge in the top 1% coincided with reduced progressive taxation, widespread deregulation (particularly in the financial sector), weakened unions, and an erosion of the federal minimum wage'.

during Reaganism develops as an extremely conservative inegalitarian, hierarchical, particularistic, elitist, monopolistic, and anti-universalist exclusionary ideology, movement, social system, and cultural ambiance in intra- and inter-societal terms within America post-2016, as in all other societies and times.

Consequently, what emerges in post-2016 America and to some degree during Reaganism and the Tea Party completely accords with fascism's generalized rule of extreme economic and social inequality, rigid hierarchy, particularism, elitism, monopolistic closure, and exclusion within society and in relation to other societies rather than expressing 'American exceptionalism' in these respects. In short, this American example is an epitome of fascism's blueprint and realization of an extremely inegalitarian, hierarchical, closed, exclusionary society instead of being a unique exception to it. On this account, the conservative compound of extreme economic and social inequality, rigid hierarchy, particularism, elitism, monopolistic closure, and exclusion, simply conservatism's 'divine design' of a closed society, makes fascism happen in post-2016 America, as it does in all other social contexts and periods. While not economic and social inequality, hierarchy, particularism, elitism, monopolistic closure, and exclusion in society and versus other societies are fascist, fascism in post-2016 America is an extremely inegalitarian, hierarchical, particularistic, elitist, monopolistic, and exclusionary conservative ideology, movement, social system, and cultural ambiance in intra- and inter-societal terms, as is in other contexts and times.

Fascists hence resurge and march in post-2016 America, in some degree during Reaganism and the Tea Party, as extreme inegalitarian, hierarchical, particularistic, elitist, monopolistic, and exclusionary forces, as they do in all other social places and times since Mussolini and Hitler et al. through Hungary's, Poland's, Brazil's, Brexit Great Britain's, and other neo-fascist and populist leaders, virtually without exceptions. These 'all-American' examples thereby exemplify and reproduce fascists' and conservatives' inegalitarian, hierarchical, particularistic, elitist, monopolistic, and exclusionary core rather than being sole exceptions. In this regard, extreme conservative inegalitarian, hierarchical, particularistic, monopolistic, and exclusionary actors exactly make fascism happen in post-2016 America, as they do in all social spaces and times. Even if not all inegalitarian, hierarchical, particularistic, monopolistic, and exclusionary actors are fascist, fascists in post-2016 America invariably are agents of extreme economic and social inequality, rigid hierarchy, particularism, elitism, monopolistic closure, and exclusion within American society and relative to other societies, as in other exmples

In addition, fascism in post-2016 America and during Reaganism, McCarthyism, and the Tea Party literally explodes and metastasizes through the social body as the compound of extreme economic and social nationalism, nativism, social hatred, and xenophobia, as it does in all other societal spaces and times from interwar Italy and Germany through postwar South America to today's Hungary, Poland, Brexit Great Britain,[73] and other cases, with minor variations. In particular, American fascism erupts and expands as a complex of economic nationalism, protectionism,[74] hatred, and irrationalism through an economy-market closure, self-defeating irrational trade wars harming (by higher prices) American consumers,[75] hateful discrimination and attacks against foreign businesses and immigrants, restriction, and eventually fascist-style termination of legal immigration, and so on.

---

73 Gorman and Seguin (2018, pp. 744) find that 'residents of strong states [such as the US and the UK] emphasize particularistic identities that encourage isolationist and xenophobic tendencies in response to acute threats, this presents an ironic dilemma: the reactions of residents of the same core states that largely constructed and continue to dominate the global order compose the greatest risk to its preservation.' They note, for example, that 'residents of the United Kingdom, one of the world's most powerful countries, recently voted to leave the European Union, while residents of less powerful countries such as Albania, Macedonia, Montenegro, and Serbia remain eager to join' (Gorman and Seguin 2018, pp. 745).

74 Edwards (2019, p. 96) observes that the 'Trump administration implemented protectionist policies [and] Trump disparaged the Federal Reserve—he called its policy "crazy" and "loco" and so on.'

75 Fajgelbaum et al. (2020, p. 5) report 'large consumer losses from the [post-2016] trade war [and] reductions in tradeable real wages [e.g.] an average decline of 1.0%. US import protection was biased toward products made in electorally competitive counties, as measured by their 2016 presidential vote share, suggesting a potential ex ante electoral rationale for the pattern of tariffs increases.' They estimate 'an annual loss for the United States of $51 billion due to higher import prices' Fajgelbaum et al. (2020, p. 52). Flaaen, Hortaçsu, and Tintelnot (2020, p. 2106) find that some trade wars or policy actions 'enacted by the Trump administration [e.g., the tariffs on washing machines] resulted in increased consumer costs of just over US$1.5 billion annually.' More broadly, Amiti, Redding, and Weinstein (2020, p. 541) report that the 'US tariffs continue [since 2018 through 2019] to be almost entirely borne by US firms and consumers.' In passing, the sobering fact that the post-2020 President kept these tariffs in place and thus continued the trade war against China by repeating the nativist insistence on 'buy American' reaffirms that economic nationalism as a facet of nativist Americanism intoxicates in a 'bipartisan' consensus virtually all ideology, politics and presidents in America, as do militarism, war, and imperialism rationalized as 'manifest destiny' via the 'Divine mission' to 'lead' the world and as 'American' interests and values. And a group of 'bipartisan' conservatives and nationalists urged the post-2020 President to keep the tariffs and continue the trade war, thus apparently being so intoxicated by economic nationalism or nativist Americanism, as well as the anti-Chinese hysteria, to abandon any commitment to free trade and so free markets. Regarding the anti-Chinese hysteria, this is one of a long series of conservative-religious hysterias, manias, and witch-hunts since Puritanism through the red scare and McCarthyism to Reaganism's anti-Russian mania and hysterics about Japanese car imports to post-2016 fascist nativism, thus neither the first nor probably the last. This holds since US conservatism and religion seem to need and create objects of

Specifically, fascism resurges and spreads as a conservative extreme economically and socially nationalist, nativist, hateful, and xenophobic ideology, social movement, system, and zeitgeist in America during this period, as in all other social settings and periods. Accordingly, rather than showing 'American exceptionalism', fascism in America demonstrates and indeed epitomizes fascism's and broader conservatism's underlying configuration of extreme economic and social nationalism,[76] nativism, social hatred, and xenophobia.[77] Instead of being exceptional, the American example is a paradigmatic instance of fascism's vision and implementation of an extremely nationalist-nativist, hate-driven, and xenophobic society in economic and social terms. To that extent, the conservative compound of extreme economic-social nationalism, nativism,[78] social hatred, and xenophobia, hence conservatism's 'divine' design of nationalist, nativist, hateful, and xenophobic society, precisely makes fascism happen in post-2016 America, as it does in all other societies and times. Even if not every compound of extreme economic-social nationalism, nativism, social hatred, and xenophobia is fascist, fascism in post-2016 America invariably is an extremely nationalist, nativist, hate-driven or addicted,[79] and xenophobic conservative ideology, movement, regime, and zeitgeist, as in all other societies.

---

such hysterias, manias, and hatred mostly regardless of the real features or actions of the hated countries or groups, simply needing 'someone to hate', as Simmel (1955, p. 31) explains in general stating that hostility is 'among those primary human energies not provoked by the external reality of their object but which create their own objects out of themselves', simply, like love, hatred 'is not a mere reaction evoked by its object but [involves] a need of [hating].'

76   Autor et al. (2020, p. 3141) note that the 'surprise election of Donald J. Trump to the presidency in 2016 has further heightened the partisan divide and injected ethnic nationalism into Republican policy positions.'

77   Piketty (2020, p. 3) warns that 'if we do not radically transform the present economic system to make it less inegalitarian, more equitable, and more sustainable, xenophobic 'populism' could well triumph at the ballot box and initiate changes that will destroy the global, hypercapitalist, digital economy that has dominated the world since 1990.' Especially, Piketty (2020, p. 33) observes the 'rise of xenophobia and identity politics' in Great Britain and the United States and that these 'developments came to a head in 2016, with the British vote to leave the European Union [Brexit] and the election of Donald Trump.'

78   Edwards (2019, p. 96) infers that 'populists in many recent advanced countries are right wing [and] modern populism in the advanced nations—in the United States, the United Kingdom [Brexit], Italy, and Hungary—has been characterized by a high degree of nativism. Immigrants are blamed for crime, unemployment, and the stagnation of wages.'

79   Simi et al. (2017) depict US white supremacists as 'addicted to hate.'

Fascists hence explode and march in post-2016 America as extreme economic-social nationalists, nativists, haters, and xenophobes, as they do in all other social settings and historical periods from Mussolini and Hitler et al. to Hungary's, Poland's, Brazil's, Brexit Great Britain's, and other neo-fascist or populist leaders and followers, with hardly any exceptions. Hence, instead of being putative sole exceptions to the rule, these 'all-American' emanations replicate the extreme nationalist, nativist, hateful, and xenophobic hard core of fascists and other conservatives. On this account, extreme economic-social nationalists, nativists, haters, and xenophobes[80] make fascism happen in post-2016 America, as they do in all other instances. Even if not all economic-social nationalists, nativists, haters, and xenophobes are fascist, fascists in post-2016 America always are extremely nationalist, nativist, hateful, and xenophobic, as in other social settings and periods.

Relatedly, fascism in post-2016 America literally erupts and metastasizes through the social fabric as master-race or master-caste and similar racism, as it does in other social settings and historical periods, especially Nazi Germany, to some degree fascist Italy, neo-fascist or populist Hungary, Brexit Great Britain, and elsewhere, with minor variations and few exceptions. Specifically, American fascism explodes as a distinctly conservative master-race or master-caste and similar racist ideology, movement, regime, and climate in America, as it does in other social spaces, above all Nazi Germany and its puppet, allied fascist-style regimes in Austria and Northern Europe (Denmark, Norway, the Baltics). In this sense, fascism in post-2016 America recurs as neo-Nazism given that master-race/master-caste racism primarily defines Nazism among fascist varieties. As a corollary, what emerges in post-2016 America replicates and sustains the pattern of master-race, master-caste, and related racism in fascism, especially Nazism, and more broadly conservatism, instead of manifesting ostensive 'American exceptionalism'. In brief, the American instance exemplifies Nazism's project and creation of an extremely racist society ruled by a master race/caste rather than an exception to it.

---

80   Piketty (2020, p. 40) observes that the 'white native-born working class succumbed to nativist xenophobia' in especially the United States as well as Great Britain. Bursztyn, Egorov, and Fiorin (2020, p. 3524) find that 'Donald Trump's rise in popularity and eventual victory in the 2016 US Presidential election causally increased individuals' willingness to publicly express anti-immigration [xenophobic] views, as well as the social acceptability of such expression [as] Donald Trump's rise in popularity and eventual victory in the 2016 US Presidential election increased individuals' willingness to engage in public xenophobic behavior.' They find that 'Trump's rise in popularity and eventual electoral victory causally changed social norms regarding the expression of xenophobic views in the United States' (Bursztyn et al. 2020, p. 3527).

Master-race racism in post-2016 and earlier American fascism assumes the form of reduced white (Aryan) biological 'superiority' and societal 'supremacy' over all other races and ethnic groups, including most of the white race/ethnicity that turns out to be the ultimate victim of such a racist ideology and regime, as in Nazism of which most Germans were eventually victims. Post-2016 American fascism appears as the near-exact replica or true descendant of Nazism and its European ramifications in other German and Nordic Nazi puppet and allied states rather than being different and exceptional in alignment with 'American exceptionalism'. Conservative master-race or master-caste and similar racism, conservatism's 'divine' design of racist society[81] therefore makes fascism happen in post-2016 America, as it does in other social settings and periods, most notably Nazi Germany, to some degree fascist Italy and neo-fascist or populist Hungary, Brexit Great Britain, and so on. While not all master-race or master-caste racism is fascist, fascism in post-2016 America and before invariably is an extremely racist ideology, movement, regime, and zeitgeist recreating a society ruled by a narrow master-caste expressing reduced-form white 'superiority' and 'supremacy', as is in other settings since Nazi Germany.

Fascists hence surge and act in post-2016 America and before as extreme master-racists in the sense of claiming to belong to a white master-race or master-caste, as they do in other social places and times since Hitler et al. through Hungary's, Brexit Great Britain's, and other neo-fascist or populist racist masters, aside from rare, partial, and transient exceptions. In this respect, US fascists erupt as neo-Nazis[82] since Nazis are ultimate master-racists and foremost pretenders to the master-caste similar to their archetypes or precursors, Calvinists/Puritans pretending to be of the 'elect'. It follows that such 'all-American' incarnations adopt and reproduce fascists', notably Nazis', and broader conservatives' master-racist core rather than being different. Instead of manifesting 'American exceptionalism', they appear as near-exact replicas

---

81   Savelsberg and King (2005, p. 585) recount that 'longstanding racial hatred gained a new quality and reached new heights during the Reconstruction period. Jim Crow laws, the rise of the Ku Klux Klan, and the history of lynching are well known, as are the antiimmigrant know nothing movement of the late 19th century, anti-Catholicism.' More broadly, Kranton (2016, p. 406) observes that US and other 'politicians and others promote division and hatred as a rational competitive strategy', which primarily applies to fascists or radical-rightists and other conservatives.

82   McDermott and Samson (2005, p. 253) report that contemporary US 'white supremacist formations include the Ku Klux Klan, neo-Nazis (and racist skinheads), and militia movements.' Simi et al. (2017, p. 1168) identify 'four major branches of US white supremacists: Ku Klux Klan, Christian Identity, neo-Nazi, and racist skinheads.'

or true heirs of the Nazis and their European extensions in other German and Nordic Nazi puppet and allied states. To that extent, extreme conservative master-racists and pretenders to the master-caste make fascism happen in post-2016 America, as in other social settings. Even if not all racists and master-caste pretenders are fascist, fascists in post-2016 America are extreme racists in the form of master-race, master-caste, and similar racism as white 'superiority' and 'supremacy', as in these other instances.

8   Syndrome 7: Fascism as Absolute Rule, Unconstrained Power, and All-Encompassing Domination

Seventh and as an aggregate effect of all the preceding, fascism in America post-2016 reveals and replicates absolute rule, total arbitrary unconstrained power, and all-encompassing domination as another set of universal fascist and generally totalitarian or authoritarian elements in all social spaces and times. Therefore, American fascism arises and expands as an extreme conservative ideology, social movement, political regime, and cultural spirit of absolute rule, unconstrained power without institutional constraints, and comprehensive control. Furthermore, American fascism emerges and operates as the combination of absolutism and Machiavellianism through the absolute power/rule of Machiavellian fascist leaders. In addition, American fascism develops and functions as the political regime of legal arbitrariness, insecurity, lawlessness, and uncontrolled corruption. Relatedly, fascism in America literally erupts and metastasizes through the social body as institutional nihilism and rightist counterrevolution, including conservative anti-institutionalist, anti-system false populism.

Taking into consideration the above, fascism in post-2016 America and to some degree during McCarthyism and especially Reaganism[83] and the Tea Party rises and advances as the design and system of absolute rule, power, control, and domination, as it does in all other social spaces and times from fascist Italy/Spain and Nazi Germany to neo-fascist or populist Hungary, Poland,

---

83   Solow et al. (1987, p. 182) witness that Reaganism 'cares' also about the distribution of power and its 'program is and has always been in favour of the redistribution' too of 'power in favour of the powerful'— simply, autocracy and oligarchy. Moreover, Bourdieu (1998, p. 35) observes 'if this conservative [Thatcher and Reagan] revolution can deceive people, this is because it seems to retain nothing of the old Black Forest pastoral of the conservative revolutionaries of the 1930s [fascists]; it is dressed up in all the signs of modernity.'

Brazil, Brexit Great Britain, and other cases, without exceptions. Specifically, American fascism reemerges as an extreme conservative ideology, movement, and regime of absolute rule, maximum arbitrary and unconstrained power lacking relevant institutional and social constraints, and all-embracing control and domination through autocracy, dynasty, oligarchy, plutocracy, and other authoritarian, undemocratic forms in America, as in all other settings. In short, American fascism resurges as extreme conservative authoritarian rule or radical-right dictatorship in post-2016 America, as everywhere else. This shows that this 'all-American' phenomenon is completely consistent with the absolute rule, power, control, and domination universal essence of fascism and conservatism rather than a unique exception expressing 'American exceptionalism' in supreme 'democracy' and 'freedom'.

On this account, the conservative ideology, movement, and regime of absolute rule, unconstrained power, and overarching social control through autocracy, dynasty, oligarchy, plutocracy, and other authoritarianism make fascism happen in post-2016 America, as in all other cases. Any conservative, radical-right ideology, movement, and regime of the absolutism of societal rule, power, and control can only be fascism and related totalitarian systems or dictatorships, such as Puritan-style evangelical and other fundamentalist theocracy a la 'Christian America' as the design of the 'Christian Right'. Conversely, fascism can rise only—just as evangelical theocracy and similar religious dictatorships—through conservative, radical-right absolutism, as it does in post-2016 America and to some degree earlier, such as the 1950s with McCarthyism, the 1980s with its sequel Reaganism, and the early 2010s with the Tea Party.

Fascists hence surge and march in post-2016 America as extreme absolute rulers, unconstrained power-holders, and overarching dominators or dictators,[84] as they do in other social settings and periods from Mussolini, Franco and Hitler to Hungary's, Poland's, Brexit Great Britain's, and other neo-fascist

---

84   Mueller (1996, p. 124) envisions that in the US whereas 'a would-be Hitler could choose to tear up the constitution and introduce a dictatorship in a two-party system, his fellow party members would probably have some advance warnings that this action was about to take place and could, if they so chose, act to prevent it.' He adds that an 'all-powerful president would face no similar checks. The problem more frequently faced in the United States other than that of having candidates like Franklin Roosevelt-whose personality and policies were so popular that he was reelected again and again-is that of having no candidate who seems particularly well qualified and capable' (Mueller 1996, p. 124). He concludes that 'authority to take drastic actions in time of crisis, particularly when the latitude to define a crisis situation is left with the chief executive, opens the door to both the nation-saving actions of a Lincoln and the nation-destroying actions of a Hitler' (Mueller 1996, p. 272). The last statement effectively anticipates the post-2016 would-be autocracy.

or populist leaders, with no exceptions. These 'all-American' emanations thus erupt as absolutists, conforming to the universal character of fascists as 'mad-men' in absolute power, instead of being putative exceptions, who use the mask and pretense of 'democracy', 'freedom' and 'liberty' ('freedom' parties, 'freedom' coalitions, 'liberty' states) to destroy them. To that extent, extreme conservative absolute rulers, power-holders, and dominators exactly make fascism happen in post-2016 America, as they do in all other societies and times. Essentially, any conservative absolutists can only be fascists and related totalitarian agents or dictators like evangelical and other fundamentalists and theocrats, such as absolute rulers of 'Christian America' in the 'Christian Right' design. Conversely, fascists can surge only—along with evangelical theocrats and similar dictators or authoritarians as absolute rulers—through conservative absolutists, as they exactly do in post-2016 America and to some extent during McCarthyism, Reaganism, and the Tea Party.

Furthermore, fascism in post-2016 America rises and spreads as the combination of absolutism with Machiavellianism through the absolute, boundless autocratic or oligarchic and plutocratic rule of Machiavellian fascist leaders in a 'patriotic' and 'holy' alliance with conservative and religious figures, as it does in all other societal settings and historical periods from fascist Italy/Spain and Nazi Germany to neo-fascist and populist Hungary, Poland, Brexit Great Britain and other cases, with no exceptions. Specifically, American fascism develops as an extreme conservative combination of absolutism as an ideology of absolute power and rule and of Machiavellianism as an amoral the end-justifies-the means strategy and technique of encompassing and intense domination in America during this period, as it does in all other examples. In short, fascism emerges as Machiavellian absolutism or absolutist Machiavellianism in post-2016 America, like everywhere else. This suggests that such an 'all American' example epitomizes fascism's and conservatism's blend of anti-democratic absolutism[85] and immoral Machiavellianism and cannot claim 'American exceptionalism'.

To that extent, the conservative combination of power absolutism with Machiavellianism as its effective instrument makes fascism happen in post-2016 America, as in all other examples above. As a corollary, any conservative, radical-right combination of power absolutism with Machiavellianism can only be fascism and similar totalitarian regimes, most notoriously and obstinately evangelical and related theocracy qua 'Christian America'. Conversely,

---

85   Agamben (1998, p. 10) refers to the category opposition 'absolutism/democracy'. Hitchens (2009, p. 81) remarks that under the Christian state religion the 'clergy was the reinforcement of absolutism [by] Christian sadists.'

fascism can occur solely, along with similar dictatorships like evangelical the-ocracy, in post-2016 America by means of the conservative, radical-right mix of power absolutism with Machiavellianism, as it exactly does post-2016 and to a degree during McCarthyism, Reaganism,[86] and the Tea Party

Fascists therefore erupt and march in post-2016 America as conservative absolutists and Machiavellians blended with one another, as they do, without exceptions, in all other examples from Mussolini, Franco, and Hitler as abso-lute Machiavellian rulers to Hungary's, Poland's, Brexit Great Britain's, and other similar neo-fascist or populist leaders. In short, these US cases resurge as Machiavellian absolutists or absolutist Machiavellians, thus conforming to fas-cists' nature as blended absolutists-Machiavellians rather than being unique 'freedom' exceptions. If so, blended conservative absolutists-Machiavellians make fascism happen in post-2016 America, as they do in all other examples. In essence, conservative absolutists-Machiavellians can only be fascists and similar totalitarian or authoritarian agents and dictators, such as evangelical and related theocrats as absolute rulers 'chosen by god', masters of 'Christian America'. Conversely, fascists can only appear, together with similar dicta-tors and totalitarians or authoritarians like evangelical theocrats, in America via blended conservative absolutists-Machiavellians, as they precisely do in post-2016 years and to some degree during McCarthyism, Reaganism, and the Tea Party.

In particular, fascism in post-2016 America, as well as during McCarthyism, Reaganism,[87] and the Tea Party develops and functions as the political sys-tem of extreme legal arbitrariness, insecurity, indeed outright lawlessness, as well as unrestrained corruption and other criminality, as it does in all other social settings from fascist Italy and Nazi Germany to neo-fascist and popu-list Hungary, Poland, Brazil, Brexit Great Britain, and elsewhere, with minor variations and rare exceptions. American fascism specifically emerges as an extreme conservative regime of legal arbitrariness, insecurity, lawlessness and uncontrolled autocratic, dynastic, and oligarchic corruption, and other crimi-nality subverting the rule of law and exposing the fascist 'law and order' slogan as a Machiavellian deceit,[88] as it does in other examples. In short, fascism rises

---

86   Cooney and Burt (2008, p. 492) by implication associate 'political absolutism' with American conservatism and its 'war on crime' and especially drugs [and alcohol] as non-violent moral sins resulting in mass imprisonment of sinners-as-criminals [as prisoners of ethical conscience] since Reagan through later conservatism.

87   Ramirez (2013) identifies American 'lawless' and 'ersatz' capitalism as by implication pri-marily the achievement or legacy of Reaganism.

88   Altemeyer (2010, p. 4) refers to 'law and order' in the proto-fascist or radical-right 'Tea Party movement'.

as an extremely conservative arbitrary, lawless, corrupt, and criminal phenomenon in post-2016 America, as anywhere else. Far from exhibiting 'American
exceptionalism' in the superior 'rule of law' and uncorrupted 'purity' such an
'all American' instance demonstrates the universal core of extreme legal arbitrariness, insecurity, lawlessness, and unrestrained corruption and criminality of fascism and more broadly conservatism, with secondary variations or
Machiavellian deceptions a la 'law and order' as a disguise for lawless severe
oppression and terror. To that degree, the conservative composite of extreme
legal arbitrariness and insecurity, lawlessness, unrestrained corruption, and
criminality exactly makes fascism happen in post-2016 America, as in other
cases. While not all extreme legal arbitrariness, lawlessness, unrestrained corruption, and criminality are fascist, fascism in post-2016 America invariably
is an extremely arbitrary, lawless, corrupt, and criminal regime, as is in other
settings since fascist Italy and Nazi Germany despite 'law and order', 'purity'
slogans.

Hence, fascists explode and act in post-2016 America as extremely arbitrary, lawless, corrupt, and criminal agents, as they do in all other examples
from Mussolini and Hitler as embodiments of legal arbitrariness, lawlessness,
unrestrained corruption and criminality to Hungary's, Poland's, Brexit Great
Britain's, Brazil's, and other neo-fascist or populist leaders, with hardly any
exceptions. These US examples, especially their leaders, surge as lawless rulers, unrestrained corruptors, and unhinged criminals, thus displaying fascists'
lawlessness, corruption, and criminality instead of being exceptional in the
sense of 'American exceptionalism'. To that extent, conservative extremely
arbitrary, lawless, corrupt, and criminal forces make fascism happen in post-
2016 America, as in all other social contexts and times. While not all American
lawless rulers, unrestrained corruptors, and unhinged criminals are fascist,
fascists in post-2016 America always are faces of legal arbitrariness, lawlessness, unrestrained corruption, and criminality, as they are everywhere since
Mussolini and Hitler.

Relatedly, fascism in post-2016 America emerges, expands, and operates as
institutional nihilism and counterrevolution, including populism[89] as anti-
institutionalist, anti-system or 'anti-establishment' revolt against the institutions and system of liberal democracy, as it does in all other instances from

---

89   Lamont (2018, p. 420) notes American 'conservative populism and Donald Trump's elec-
      toral success' driven by it. Berezin (2019, p. 346) observes that 'interest in fascism and
      populism spiked around 2016, corresponding to the US presidential election.' Autor et al.
      (2020, pp. 3143–4) imply that 'conservative' candidates and groups in the US after 2016
      belong to 'right-wing populist' or 'far-right' movements.

fascist Italy and Nazi Germany to neo-fascist and populist Hungary, Poland, Brazil, Brexit Great Britain,[90] and elsewhere, with minor variations and few exceptions. American fascism occurs specifically as extreme conservative institutional nihilism and counterrevolution or insurrection, particularly as rightist anti-institutionalist, or anti-system, specifically anti-liberal and anti-democratic, populism against the institutions of liberal democracy, as it does in all other instances. In short, fascism rises as extreme conservative destructive, counterrevolutionary, and populist anti-institutionalism versus liberal-democratic institutions in post-2016 America, as everywhere else. Such an 'all American' example accords with fascism's and broader conservatism's institutional nihilism or counterrevolution, including anti-institutionalism through anti-liberal and anti-democratic populism against liberal-democratic institutions, instead of displaying 'American exceptionalism' in the pure 'rule of law', 'law and order', 'freedom', 'democracy'.

On this account, conservative institutional nihilism and counterrevolution, including anti-liberal rightist populism, against liberal-democratic institutions, makes fascism happen in post-2016 America, as in other cases from fascist Italy and Nazi Germany to neo-fascist or populist Hungary, Poland, and Brexit Great Britain. Consequently, American conservative institutional nihilism and counterrevolution, in particular rightist anti-liberal populism, revolting against liberal-democratic institutions can only be, ceteris paribus, fascism and related totalitarian regimes, above all evangelical theocracy such as the Southern 'Bible Belt' and 'Christian America'. Conversely, fascism solely can materialize, together with evangelical theocracy and similar dictatorships, in America via conservative institutional nihilism and insurrection, particularly rightist anti-liberal populism, versus liberal-democratic institutions, as it does post-2016 and to some extent during McCarthyism, Reaganism, and the Tea Party.

It follows that fascists erupt and march in post-2016 America as institutional nihilists and counterrevolutionaries or insurrectionists, including anti-institutionalist, 'anti-establishment' populists[91] revolting against

---

90   Edwards (2019, p. 96) registers 'modern populism in the advanced nations [including] the United States the United Kingdom [Brexit], Italy, and Hungary'. Margalit (2019, p. 152) invokes 'Donald Trump's victory in the US presidential election of November 2016 and the Brexit vote in June 2016' to illustrate the 'rise of populist forces in many established democracies.'

91   Edwards (2019, pp. 95–6) notes that 'Donald Trump's rallies [included] the criticism of the elites and the establishment [such as] severe denunciations of traditional institutions. [For example] Trump disparaged the Federal Reserve—he called its policy 'crazy' and 'loco" and so on.

liberal-democratic institutions, as they do in all other examples from Mussolini and Hitler as the ultimate incarnations of nihilism, counterrevolution, and anti-democratic populism to Hungary's, Poland's, Brexit Great Britain's, Brazil's, and additional neo-fascist and populist leaders. These 'all-American' emanations express the nature of fascists as extreme conservative institutional nihilists, counterrevolutionaries, and populists versus liberal-democratic institutions rather than being unique 'freedom' and 'democracy' exceptions. To that extent, conservative institutional nihilists, counterrevolutionaries, and anti-liberal, anti-democratic populists make fascism happen in post-2016 America, as they do in all other social contexts. Essentially, conservative institutional nihilists counterrevolutionaries, and anti-liberal/anti-democratic populists can only be fascists and comparable totalitarian agents, especially evangelical and similar theocrats, like the lords of 'Christian America'. Conversely, fascists can only appear, along with evangelical theocrats and related authoritarians, in America as conservative institutional nihilists, counterrevolutionaries or insurrectionists, and anti-liberal/anti-democratic populists, just as they do post-2016 times, as well as during McCarthyism, Reaganism, and the Tea Party.

9   Syndrome 8: Fascism as Extreme Repression, Violence, and Terror

As the eight syndrome and corollary of its absolute rule, unconstrained power, and all-encompassing domination, fascism in America post-2016 reveals and thus replicates extreme coercion and repression, including violence and terror, as additional universal fascist elements in various societal settings and historical periods. Hence, American fascism emerges and functions as an extreme ideology, social movement, political regime, and cultural zeitgeist of total and severe state coercion and repression, in combination with populist deception, misinformation, and manipulation, of society. Particularly, it rises as the system of systematic, all-embracing and intense violence and terror, including both counter-state and state terrorism. Especially, it resurges as a regime of pro-capital, anti-labor coercion, repression, violence, and terror, including mass murder. Relatedly, fascism in America reappears as a complex of mass imprisonment for sins-as-crimes, indefinite detention, torture, and widespread death sentences and executions often of innocent persons, and other violations of human rights and thus forms of political terror.

Taking account of the preceding, fascism in post-2016 America and to some degree during the Tea Party, Reaganism, and McCarthyism rises and advances as the project and system of severe and total coercion and repression, as it does in all other societal settings and historical periods from fascist Italy and

Spain and Nazi Germany through proto-fascist South America to neo-fascist or populist Hungary, Poland, Brazil, Brexit Great Britain, and elsewhere, with no exceptions. American fascism occurs specifically as an extreme conservative ideology, social movement, political regime, and cultural ambiance of extensive and intensive coercion and repression, in combination and mutual reinforcement with populist deception, disinformation, or misinformation ('fake news'),[92] in America, as in other societies. In brief, it happens as an extreme conservative and religious complex of coercion and repression, combined with populist deceit and manipulation, in post-2016 America, as elsewhere else. Consequently, instead of being exceptional in the sense of alleged 'American exceptionalism' in superior 'democracy' and 'freedom', this 'all-American' species confirms and indeed epitomizes fascism's and more broadly conservatism's essence of systematic and severe compulsion and oppression. The conservative ideology, movement, and regime of systematic coercion and repression, combined with populist deceit, disinformation, and manipulation of the rank-and-file or most of the American people, especially in the former Southern Confederacy and similar regions, exactly makes fascism happen in post-2016 America, as in all other social settings and periods.

Fundamentally, any American and other conservative or radical-right ideology, movement, regime, and atmosphere of coercion and repression, as well as populist deception, disinformation, and manipulation of the base, is fascism and compatible totalitarian regimes, primarily evangelical and similar theocracy as in 'Christian America', including the 'Bible Belt' ruled by the Biblical equivalent of Islamic Sharia law. Conversely, fascism only can occur, like evangelical theocracy and other compatible dictatorships, via conservative or radical-right coercion and repression, mixed with populist deception, disinformation, and manipulation of the base, as it does in post-2016 America. The above reformulates and specifies the universal 'iron' sociological and generalized historical pattern that fascism is invariably, including that in post-2016 America, a species of extreme conservatism or of the radical-right, thus a totalitarian version of intrinsic conservative authoritarianism or authoritarian rightism. This is instructive to reiterate because US conservatism obfuscates from most Americans this invariant conservative-fascist fatal attraction,

---

92   Allcott and Gentzkow (2017, p. 212) find that the 'most discussed fake news stories tended to favor Donald Trump over Hillary Clinton [and concur with the view] that Donald Trump would not have been elected president were it not for the influence of fake news [as] fake news was both widely shared and heavily tilted in favor of Donald Trump.' Sadler (2020, p. 225) points to the 'spread of fake news, which featured prominently in the 2016 US elections', primarily the conservative or radical-right candidate[s].

intimate link, anti-liberal alliance, and eventual osmosis in a broader united family, with minor family-like contentions.

Fascists hence erupt and march in post-2016 America and in some degree during the Tea Party, Reaganism, and McCarthyism as extreme conservative coercive and repressive forces, as they do, without exceptions, in all social spaces and times since Mussolini and Hitler in interwar Europe through Pinochet et al. in postwar South America to present Hungary's, Poland's, Brexit Great Britain's, Brazil's, and other neo-fascist or populist rulers. In short, fascists explode as radical-right violent oppressors, with their leader as an autocrat, in America, as elsewhere else. Rather than being unique American exceptions in 'democracy' and 'freedom' a la Reagan et al., they exemplify fascists' rightist universally oppressive core. In this sense, extreme conservative, radical-right coercive-repressive actors exactly make fascism happen in post-2016 America, as in all other social spaces and times.

In essence, any American extreme conservative or radical-right oppressors are and can only be fascists and congruent dictators or authoritarian agents, especially evangelical and other, including dogmatic Catholic, theocrats, such as rulers of 'Christian America', including the 'Bible Belt', and united within the Christian Right. Conversely, together with evangelical theocrats and other congruent authoritarians, fascists are and can solely rise and advance through extreme conservative, radical-right oppressors or autocrats, as they do in post-2016 America. This restates the 'iron' sociological or historical pattern that fascists are universally, including those in post-2016 America, extreme conservatives or radical rightists, so conservative/right totalitarians, given that US 'true' conservatives deny and hide this fact and thus—while making most Americans unaware of—their fascist trajectory and destination.

Particularly, fascism in post-2016 America and to some degree during Reaganism and McCarthyism rises and expands as the blueprint and system of systematic, all-embracing, and intense violence and state and counter-state terror, as it does, without exceptions, in all other social spaces and times since fascist Italy/Spain and Nazi Germany through proto-fascist South America (Chile, etc.) to neo-fascist or populist Hungary, Poland, Brazil, Brexit Great Britain, and elsewhere. Specifically, American fascism occurs as an extreme conservative ideology, movement, regime, and climate of methodical and pervasive violence and terror[93] in America, as in these other social settings and times. More precisely, American fascism happens as conservative state

---

93   Bauman (1997, p. 43) observes that the 'spectacle of execution is cynically used by [US conservative] politicians to terrorize a growing underclass.'

violence and terror when capturing and exercising total power at national and regional levels, usually in alliance and merger with theocracy, as in evangelical America, including the 'Bible Belt' from Alabama and Tennessee to Oklahoma and Texas, as it does everywhere else. Conversely, American fascism reappears as conservative counter-state violence and terror through widespread possession, accumulation, and use of lethal weapons[94] such as pervasive guns ownership to perpetrate destruction and mass murders when remaining in implacable opposition, along with conservatism, to existing liberal-democratic institutions, as in 'liberal America,' for example, California and after the 2020 Presidential elections followed by rightist anti-government violent insurrection and terrorism.

As a corollary, this 'all-American' example completely exemplifies fascism's and broader conservatism's pattern of violence and state and counter-state terror rather than exhibiting 'American exceptionalism' in superior 'democracy' and 'freedom'. To that extent, the conservative ideology, movement, regime, and ambiance of systematic, encompassing, and severe state and counter-state violence and terror makes fascism happen in post-2016 America, as in all other social settings and periods. Essentially, any American conservative, radical-right ideology, movement, and regime of methodical state and counter-state violence and terror can only be fascism and congruent totalitarian regimes, first and foremost, evangelical and other theocracy qua 'Christian America', including the 'Bible Belt' ruled by violent Biblical Sharia-like law reproducing mass incarceration for sins-as-crimes and pervasive executions often of innocent persons (yet 'guilty' by association for 'original sin'). Conversely, fascism only can rise and spread, along with evangelical theocracy and other congruent dictatorships, via conservative, radical-right intense violence and terror, just as it precisely does post-2016 and post-2020 America in violent reaction to the 2020 Presidential elections.

Hence, fascists explode and march in post-2016 America and to some degree during the Tea Party, Reaganism, and McCarthyism as extreme conservative

---

94   Munch (1994, p. 69) in an obvious reference to conservative America observes that a 'society in which each believes he can police other's actions on his behalf by relying on the firepower on his own weapons is in danger of destroying its liberties, because everybody has to fear everybody else. Such a society is close to Hobbes's state of nature.' Duggan (2001, p. 1086) finds that in the US 'guns are involved in nearly 70 percent of all homicides and a substantial share of other violent crime', inferring simply 'more guns, more crime.' Carlson (2019, p. 636) identifies in conservative America 'gun populism, which describes an antielitist, antipluralist and putatively color-blind embrace of 'good guys with guns,' defined by their moral character and law abidingness, as productive contributors to social order.'

violent, murderous, and terrorist forces, as they do in all social settings and periods since Mussolini, Franco, and Hitler in interwar Europe through Pinochet et al. in postwar South America to present Hungary's, Poland's, Brexit Great Britain's, Brazil's, and other neo-fascist or populist rulers, with no exceptions. In short, fascists resurge as extreme-right state and counter-state murderers and terrorists when seizing power in conservative states post-2016 and subverting democracy in liberal states after 2020 in America, as everywhere else. These 'all- American' specimens thus conform to the violent, murderous, and terrorist character of the genus of fascists rather than being American exceptions in superior 'freedom'. On this account, conservative extreme violent, murderous, and terrorist actors, notably radical-right state and counter-state murderers and terrorists, make fascism happen in post-2016 America, as in other social settings.

In essence, any American extreme conservative or radical-right state and counter-state murderers and terrorists can only be fascists and compatible totalitarian actors, most notably evangelical and related theocrats like violent rulers of 'Christian America,' including the 'Bible Belt', and murderous and terrorist attackers of its secular opposite. Conversely, together with evangelical theocrats and other compatible authoritarians, fascists can solely surge through the action of extreme conservative, radical-right state and counter-state murderers and terrorists, as they do in post-2016 and post-2020 America.

Especially, fascism in post-2016 America, as well as during the Tea Party, Reaganism,[95] and McCarthyism, emerges and expands as the ideology and regime of pro-capital and anti-labor coercion, repression, violence, and terror, as it does in all other historical and present examples from fascist Italy/ Spain and Nazi Germany through proto-fascist South America to neo-fascist or populist Hungary, Poland, Brexit (and Thatcherite) Great Britain, Brazil, and others, with minor variations. American fascism specifically occurs as an extreme conservative ideology, movement, regime, and atmosphere of pro-capital, anti-labor repression, violence, murder, and terror, including pervasive state murders via widespread death sentences and executions of working and lower classes, in America, as in most other cases, except for the abolition of the death penalty in Europe. In sum, American fascism happens as an extremely conservative coercive, repressive, violent, and terrorist, including murderous,

---

95   Kimeldorf (2013, p. 1056) notes 'Regan's decision in 1981 to fire and permanently replace more than 12,000 striking air traffic controllers, destroying their union and dramatically exposing organized labor's heightened vulnerability'. He adds that the US is 'one of the few industrial democracies in violation of the International Labour Organization's principles for safeguarding the right to organize.'

system against labor and lower social classes and minorities in America post-2016, including post-2020 in states ruled by conservatism.

In consequence, far from evincing presumed 'American exceptionalism' in supreme 'democracy' and 'freedom', such an 'all-American' example reaffirms and epitomizes fascism's and conservatism's essence of pro-capital and anti-labor coercion, repression, violence, and terror, including state murder. It follows that the conservative ideology, movement, regime, and ambiance of pro-capital and anti-labor coercion, repression, violence, and terror make fascism happen in post-2016 America, as in all other examples. Fundamentally, any American and other conservative, radical-right ideology, movement, regime, and ambiance of pro-capital and anti-labor coercion, repression, violence, and terror, all else being equal, can only be fascism and congruent totalitarian regimes, such as capitalist dictatorship and evangelical theocracy qua 'Christian America' or the 'Bible Belt' of 'money and God'. Conversely, just as capitalist dictatorship, evangelical theocracy, and other compatible dictatorships, fascism solely can rise and spread, ceteris paribus, by means of conservative, radical-right pro-capital, anti-labor coercion, repression, violence, and terror, as it does in post-2016 America.

Fascists therefore erupt and march in post-2016 America and during the Tea Party, Reaganism,[96] and McCarthyism, as extreme conservative pro-capital, anti-labor coercive, repressive, violent, and terrorist forces, as they do from Mussolini and Hitler after their initial pro-labor deceptions or pretensions in interwar Europe through Pinochet et al. in postwar South America to Hungary's, Poland's, Brexit and Thatcherite Great Britain's, Brazil's, and other neo-fascist or populist leaders, with rare exceptions. In short, fascists surge as extreme-right pro-capitalist, anti-labor, or anti-union[97] warriors attacking labor organization and collective action like unions in America, as elsewhere else. Far from than being unique American exceptions in 'freedom', such 'all-American' models follow fascists' and broader conservatives' pro-capital, anti-labor coercive, repressive, violent, and terrorist hardcore. In this regard, conservative extreme pro-capitalist, anti-labor repressive and violent warriors make fascism happen in post-2016 America, as in all other cases. Essentially, any extreme conservative or radical-right anti-labor repressive and violent forces are and can only

---

96   VanHeuvelen (2020, p. 1259) observes that US 'union membership began to fall from peak rates in the 1950s, and this decline accelerated during the 1970s in the face of strong anti-union action by corporate leaders and then by the Reagan administration's antiunion federal policy priorities.'

97   Plotke (2002, pp. lvi) includes the 'rigorous antiunion efforts of large corporations' into the sources of 'nondemocratic projects' in the US.

be fascists and convergent authoritarians, such as capitalist plutocrats in alliance with evangelical and other theocrats allied within the Christian Right, as in 'Christian America', including the 'Bible Belt' ruled by repressive anti-union rightist warriors. Conversely, together with capitalist plutocrats, evangelical theocrats, and other convergent authoritarians, fascists can only rise and prevail by the agency of extreme conservative, radical-right anti-labor repressive and violent warriors, as they do in post-2016 America.

Relatedly, fascism in post-2016 America and during the 1980s with repressive Reaganism and the early 2010s with the extreme-right Tea Party develops and metastasizes through the social body as a complex of mass imprisonment, indefinite detention, torture, and widespread death sentences and executions, as it does in all other social settings and times since fascist Italy/Spain and Nazi Germany through proto-fascist South America to neo-fascist or populist Brazil, Hungary, Poland, and Brexit and Thatcher's Great Britain (minus the death penalty in the last three cases due to the European Union's prohibition), aside from secondary variations. American fascism occurs specifically as an extreme conservative ideology, movement, regime, and social climate of mass imprisonment,[98] indefinite detention, police brutality, murder and torture, pervasive death sentences and executions and related acts of Draconian punishment[99] and political terror in America, as in these other social settings. In other words, it happens as a Draconian, extremely punitive criminal justice system of state terror through indefinite detention, police brutality, torture, and arbitrary executions often of innocent persons (as post-factum DNA evidence proves) in post-2016 America, a pattern that Reaganism initiates. Such an 'all-American' example conforms to fascism and conservatism as the ideology and system of mass imprisonment and other forms of political terror and violations of basic human rights, such as indefinite detention, police brutality, murder and torture, and death sentences and executions, rather than exhibiting 'American exceptionalism' in superior 'democracy', 'freedom', and 'crime and punishment' justice. The conservative regime of mass imprisonment, police brutality, torture, and widespread death sentences and executions makes fascism happen in post-2016 and Reaganite America, as it does in other settings and

---

98   Saez and Zucman (2020, p. 22) observe that US 'spending on prisons has increased particularly fast, due to a massive increase in incarceration rates in the 1980s and 1990s'.

99   Cooney and Burt (2008) report 'less crime, more punishment' in the US during the conservative 'war on crime', especially the Reagan-style Puritanical 'war on drugs' such as drug use and other sins, including alcohol use by dramatically increasing the legal age limit, redefined as grave crimes and their non-violent offenders subjected to mass and long imprisonment as through 'three strikes' Draconian laws.

times, aside from few exceptions, notably the abolition of the death penalty in Europe.

Fundamentally, any conservative, rightist ideology, movement, and regime of mass imprisonment, police brutality, widespread death sentences and executions, and other acts of Draconian punishment and political terror, ceteris paribus, can only be fascism and compatible dictatorships, primarily evangelical and similar theocracy, as in 'Christian America', including the 'Bible Belt', such as Texas and other extremist states that apply and justify the death penalty and large-scale incarceration of sinners-as-criminals by Biblical law, as do Islamic regimes by its equivalent Sharia law. Conversely, like evangelical theocracy and other compatible totalitarian regimes, fascism solely can rise and spread, ceteris paribus, through the conservative, radical-right punitive complex of mass imprisonment, police brutality, widespread death sentences and executions, and other acts of political terror, as it does in post-2016 and Reagan's America. Moreover, such a conservative complex since Reaganism through post-2016 renders America the Western and world leader in mass imprisonment and death sentences and executions, together with Islamic theocracies and other third-world dictatorships, thus making it a non- or post-Western society closer to, for example, Iran than to Sweden.

Fascists hence explode and march in post-2016 America and to some extent during Reaganism and the Tea Party as extreme conservative agents of mass imprisonment, indefinite detention, police brutality, murder and torture, widespread death sentences and executions, and other acts of political terror, as they do from Mussolini, Franco and Hitler through Pinochet et al. to Brazil, Hungary's, Poland's, Brexit and Thatcherite Great Britain's, and other neo-fascist or populist leaders, with minor variations, such as the nonapplication of the death penalty in the last three countries only because of the European Union's abolition. In a word, fascists resurge as extreme-right mass-imprisonment and death-penalty enforcers or crusaders in America, as they do in all other cases. Hence, these 'all- American' creatures completely demonstrate the character of fascists and broader conservatives as agents of mass imprisonment, indefinite detention, police brutality, murder and torture, widespread death sentences and executions, and other manifestations of political terror rather than representing exclusive American exceptions in supreme 'freedom' and criminal 'justice'.

On this account, conservative, rightist mass-imprisonment, death-penalty, and other political-terror enforcers or crusaders make fascism happen in post-2016 America, as everywhere else. These conservative forces, ceteris paribus, can only be fascists and compatible totalitarians, such as evangelical and other theocrats in 'Christian America, including the 'Bible Belt' ruled by Draconian 'holy' warriors driven by Biblical law as an equivalent of Islamic Sharia law effectively enacted and hence redundant in its original form despite evangelicals' hysteria about Islamists imposing it on Christians. Conversely, like evangelical theocrats and other compatible totalitarians, fascists can only resurge and prevail, all else being equal, by the activity of conservative, rightist mass-imprisonment, death-penalty, and other political-terror enforcers or crusaders, as they do in post-2016 and Reagan's America.

10   Syndrome 9: Fascism as Extreme Militarism, War, and Conquest

As the ninth syndrome and correlate of its extreme repression and terror within society, fascism in America post-2016 and to some degree before, as during the 1980s by militarist Reaganism reveals and replicates extreme anti-pacifism, militarism, offensive war, and imperial conquest in relation to other societies, as further universal fascist elements in other societies and historical periods. American fascism therefore arises and operates as an extreme ideology, social movement, political regime, and cultural zeitgeist of anti-pacifism and militarism, including aggressive war against and imperial conquest and subjugation of other societies. Consequently, it develops as the continuation and intensification of conservatism's persistent anti-pacifism, militarism, bellicosity, and imperialism. Specifically, fascism in America resurges as a complex of extreme rearmament, arms races, and preparation for offensive war through exorbitant military expenditure, militarist mobilization, and a large standing army. Furthermore, it erupts into a perpetual series of aggressive wars against and of imperial conquest and subjection of other societies. Ultimately, American fascism ends in a cycle of mass death, destruction, and self-destruction—truly MAD (mutually assured destruction) via ultimate, nuclear weapons.

In consequence, fascism in America post-2016 and since the 1980s with militarist Reaganism rises and advances as extreme anti-pacifism and militarism driven by religious and other virulent nationalism qua flag-waving Americanism[100] versus other societies, while mutually reinforcing with repression and terror within society, as it does in other social spaces and times since

---

100   Apparently referring to American fascism's and conservatism's penchant to or exploit 'rally around the flag', Soehl and Karim (2021, p. 410) warn that '"rally around the flag" effects may expand the reach of executive power and increase the likelihood of militarization, which may in turn disrupt processes of unarmed mobilization and contentious civil society–level politics that are instrumental to deepening liberal democratic institutions.'

fascist Italy and Nazi Germany, with secondary variations, especially in smaller, weaker societies and in short terms. Specifically, consistent with its foundation in conservatism, American fascism occurs as an extreme conservative ideology, movement, regime, and atmosphere of virulent anti-pacifism and militarism against American 'enemies', in strong interaction and mutual reinforcement with its coercion, repression, violence, and terror within America itself. In short, fascism happens as an extreme conservative anti-pacifist and militarist entity in America post-2016 and during Reaganism, as in other social spaces and times.

Accordingly, such an 'all-American' patriotic model exemplifies the extreme anti-pacifism and militarism of fascism and conservatism rather than expressing 'American exceptionalism' in 'peace' or 'peaceful conflict resolution' among nations and similar terms such as respect for national independence, self-government, and sovereignty of other countries, as it would be consistent with the ideals of the American Revolution. Conservative virulent anti-pacifism and militarism makes fascism happen in America post-2016 and during Reaganism, as in other social spaces and times since fascist Italy and Nazi Germany. While not all American conservative anti-pacifism and militarism is fascist, fascism in America post-2016 and during Reaganism invariably is virulently anti-pacifist and militarist in the tradition of conservatism, as everywhere else. As a corollary, fascism in America post-2016 and since Reaganism emerges as the continuation and intensification of conservatism's original and persistent militarism that it inherits and perpetuates from medievalism, such as feudalism and its military aristocracy.

Therefore, fascists explode and march in post-2016 and Reagan's America as conservative virulent anti-pacifist and militarist actors, as they do in all societal settings and historical periods since Mussolini and Hitler in interwar Europe, with rare and transient exceptions. In short, fascists resurge as extreme rightist anti-pacifists and militarists in post-2016 and Reagan's America, as everywhere else. Therefore, these 'all- American' specimen conform to the anti-pacifist and militarist character of fascists and conservatives instead of being 'peace loving' American exceptions. Conservative virulent anti-pacifists and militarists hence make fascism happen in post-2016 and Reagan America, as in all social settings and periods since Mussolini and Hitler. Even if not all conservative anti-pacifists and militarists are fascists, fascists in America post-2016 and during Reaganism are virulently anti-pacifist and militarist.

Specifically, fascism in America post-2016 and during Reaganism emerges and advances as a complex of extreme rearmament, arms races, and preparation for offensive war through exorbitant military expenditure, militarist mobilization, and a large standing army, as it does in other social settings and times since Nazi Germany, with minor variations, especially in smaller or weaker societies. American fascism specifically occurs as an extreme conservative ideology, movement, regime, and ambiance of rearmament, arms races, and preparation for wars of aggression through virtually limitless, ever-growing military expenditure, militarist economic, political, and cultural mobilization, and a gigantic army. The post-2016 autocratic and radical-right regime dramatically increased military expenditure to become by far the highest among Western and comparable societies. For illustration, while the US already accounting for nearly half of the world's expenditure and singly expending the most by far on the military and war, the post-2016 extreme-right autocratic government, allied with conservative-dominated Congress, expanded military cum 'defense' spending during the first budget year by about 10 percent over the prior period. Moreover, the radical-right regime expanded military spending by approximately another 10 percent for the next periods (surpassing $700 billion and reaching approximately $800 billion by the end of 2020), thus persistently and almost exponentially increasing it. This produced the substantial growth of the share of military spending of Gross Domestic Product (over 3% for the 2020–21 budget year)—the highest by far among Western societies—attaining a level similar to or evocative of that during the Cold War and starting yet another global arms race after that which Reaganism started in the 1980s. Furthermore, the US radical-right regime pressured NATO members to double their own military spending (from around 1% to 2% of GDP) even after the Cold War and thus caused a global arms race in that it provoked its adversaries (China, Russia, Iran, North Korea) to react. And the fact that the post-2020 US 'liberal' government did not appreciably slow down the post-2016 acceleration in military expenditure only confirms that both conservatism/fascism and parts of nominal or spurious liberalism, thus all American politics, notably Presidency and Congress, are poisoned or intoxicated by Americanism's claims to 'manifest destiny' and 'superior' values and by imperialism through offensive war, conquest, and global dominance.

In addition, the post-2016 regime further expanded the army personnel and militarized outer space by creating 'space force' despite the end of the Cold War[101] long ago. By this and other militarist actions, this regime continued or reignited the frenzied armament and arms race that Reaganism[102] initiated

---

101   Dell and Querubin (2018, p. 701) observe that US 'military interventions in weakly institutionalized societies were a central feature of the Cold War and continue through the present' such as post-2016–20 by the radical-right autocratic regime.

102   Smelser (1997, p. 91) concedes that Reaganism's 'acceleration of the arms race in the 1980s created a situation the American economy could not afford and the Soviet economy could not bear.' Barro and Redlick (2011, p. 55) find that after the end of the Vietnam war,

and pursued with recklessness and extreme fiscal irresponsibility manifested in huge budget deficits, aiming to realize Reagan's childish and suicidal fantasy of 'Star Wars', while both regimes evoking the rearmament and other militarist practices of Nazism after its power seizure. In brief, fascism in America post-2016 and since Reaganism happens and operates versus 'enemy' societies as frantic Nazi-style rearmament and aggressiveness, as it does in other social spaces and times. In consequence, instead of manifesting presumed 'American exceptionalism' in 'peace' or 'peaceful conflict resolution', such an 'all-American' patriotic model accords with fascism's and conservatism's pattern of rearmament and military expansion versus other societies. As in other social settings since Nazi Germany, conservative frenzied rearmament and ever-growing, virtually unlimited military expenditure,[103] expansion, and aggression make fascism happen in America post-2016 and during militaristic Reaganism in relations to other countries but also within society by expressing and reinforcing domestic repression and terror. Even if not all-American conservative rearmament and military expansion is fascist, fascism in America post-2016 and during Reaganism invariably is armament-prone and militarily aggressive, as in other settings.

Fascists thereby explode and march in post-2016 and Reagan's America as extreme conservative agents of frenzied rearmament and endless military expansion and aggression, as they do in all social environments and times since Mussolini and Hitler in interwar Italy and Germany, aside from rare and temporary exceptions. In a word, they resurge as extreme rightist military expansionists in post-2016 and Reagan's America, as elsewhere. These 'all-American' emanations rather than being 'peace loving' American exceptions emulate fascists as militarists, such as expansionists and aggressors. In this regard, conservative extreme militarists make fascism happen in post-2016 and Reagan's America, as in other countries since Mussolini and Hitler. While not all American conservative militarists are fascists, fascists in America post-2016 and during Reaganism universally are militarist forces of frenzied rearmament and military expansion, as everywhere else.

---

the 'largest values of the defense spending variable are 0.4–0.5% from 1982 to 1985 during the Reagan defense buildup.'

103   Bowen, Chen, and Eraslan (2014, p. 2941) remark that in the US, government 'discretionary spending consists of mostly military spending', and 'discretionary' implies as a euphemistic description that military expenditure is virtually unlimited or unrestrained and arbitrary under American conservative or radical-right governments, a tendency that they share with fascism, notably Nazism.

Furthermore, fascism in America post-2016 and during bellicose Reaganism rises and functions as a series of aggressive wars and bellicosity against and imperial conquest and subjugation of other societies, just as it does in other societies and historical periods since fascist Italy and Nazi Germany, with secondary and transient variations in smaller societies. Compatible with its foundational conservatism, American fascism occurs as an extreme conservative ideology, movement, regime, and climate of permanent offensive wars or constant war threats and intense bellicosity against and imperial conquest/subjection of other societies that it defines and attacks as 'enemies'.

Following Reaganism and its neo-conservative ramifications, the post-2016 radical-right regime attacked some other countries (Syria) or foreign assets (in Iraq), continued prior wars and imperial occupations (Afghanistan, Iraq), and constantly threatened to attack and showed intense bellicosity toward many others (Iran, North Korea, Venezuela, China, Mexico, etc.). It seems that large-scale self-destructive wars of aggression (against Iran, Russia, or China) did not happen—though were indeed extremely close to happening as reported after the fact—mainly because of the apparent cowardice, ineptness, and buffoonery of the post-2016 extremely bellicose autocracy or were temporarily postponed due to the prime imperative of consolidation of domination, repression, and terror within society that failed with the 2020 elections. These traits of cowardice, ineptness, and buffoonery are typical of fascist leaders since Mussolini and Hitler, as is the temporary postponement of aggressive wars after consolidating their control, repression, and terror of their societies. Mussolini and Hitler launched offensive wars more than 10 and around 5 years, respectively, after seizing total power and the US post-2016 autocracy's conduct fully accords with their temporary war postponement. In brief, fascism happens as a warlike movement and regime in America post-2016 and during Reaganism, as it does everywhere else since fascist Italy and Nazi Germany.

Consequently, such an 'all-American' heroic model conforms to fascism's and conservatism's essence of offensive war and conquest rather than showing 'American exceptionalism' in 'peace' or 'peaceful conflict resolution'. The conservative series of aggressive wars and imperial conquest hence make fascism happen in America post-2016 and during Reaganism both in relation to other countries and within society by interacting with and reinforcing domestic authoritarian coercion and repression,[104] as it does in other social contexts and

---

104   Steinmetz (2005, p. 358) observes that a domestic effect of American 'military imperialism' is that 'imperial political life in the US Heimat has gradually become more authoritarian.' Carlson (2019, p. 636) points to 'an aggressively armed' and thus militarized police force in the US as an expression of 'gun militarism'. Go (2020, pp. 1193–94) observes that

times since fascist Italy and Nazi Germany. Even if not all-American conservative wars, bellicosity, and imperial conquest are fascist, fascism in America post-2016 and during Reaganism invariantly is an extremely warlike, bellicose, and imperialist movement, ideology, regime, and zeitgeist, as everywhere else.

Fascists thus resurge and proliferate in post-2016 and Reagan's America as extreme conservative warlike, bellicose, and imperialist agents, as they do in other social contexts and periods since Mussolini and Hitler in Italy and Germany, apart from rare and transient exceptions. In short, fascists reappear as extreme rightist warriors or war-lovers, belligerents, and imperialists in post-2016 and Reagan's America, as in these other contexts. These 'all- American' patriots replicate the warlike, bellicose, and imperialist character of fascists and broader conservatives rather than representing exclusive 'peace loving' American exceptions. Conservative, extreme-right warriors, belligerents, and imperialists make fascism happen in post-2016 and Reagan's America, as elsewhere since Mussolini and Hitler. While not all-American war-lovers, belligerents, and imperialists are fascists, fascists in America post-2016 and during Reaganism universally are warlike, bellicose, and imperialist, as in other social contexts.

Ultimately, fascism in America post-2016 rises as a cycle or prospect of mass death, destruction, and self-destruction, as it does in other social settings and times since fascist Italy and Nazi Germany, with minor, temporary variations. Compatible with its basis in conservatism, American fascism occurs as the conservative ideology, movement, regime, and ambiance of mass death, destruction, and self-destruction. In a way, fascism happens as the specter of collective suicide, MAD[105] through mutually assured destruction, thus as

---

'dramatic instances of police violence against protestors have proliferated in recent years. Most have involved the use of military equipment [attesting] to the militarization of American policing.'

105   Habermas (2001, p. 47) adopts MAD as a shorthand for mutually assured destruction with reference to the Cold War. Schelling (2006, p. 937) suggests that 'any nation that does use nuclear weapons will be judged the violator of the legacy of Hiroshima' and laments the American government's 'advertising a continued dependence on nuclear weapons, i.e., a US readiness to use them, a US need for new nuclear capabilities (and new nuclear tests) [and] using them against an enemy.' He especially deplores that the US conservative-dominated Senate rejected the Comprehensive Test Ban Treaty in 1999 in spite or perhaps because of the 'potential of that Treaty to enhance the nearly universal revulsion against nuclear weapons' and the 'symbolic effect of nearly 200 nations ratifying [it]' (Schelling 2006, p. 937). This implies the darkest possible, suicidal side of conservatism's reproduced 'American exceptionalism'. Gibson (2011, p. 364) recounts 'avoiding catastrophe' in the Cuban Missile Crisis, by 'involving the withdraw of NATO missiles from Turkey [by] a secret back channel,' yet not revealed to Americans for long to deceive them in having the Orwellian illusion of 'American victory'. The latter incidentally expresses a pattern

literally a mad entity, a form of madness in America post-2016 and during Reaganism, like elsewhere since fascist Italy and Nazi Germany. The post-2016 extreme-right autocratic regime apparently moved toward or threatened MAD by abandoning virtually all global agreements on the control of nuclear and other weapons of mass destruction and relaunching nuclear arms races, including in the space through the 'space force', thus moving closer to a self-destructive confrontation. MAD did not happen during this period owing to the manifest cowardice, ineptness, and buffoonery of the post-2016 autocracy or was just temporarily delayed because of the necessity of consolidating domination, repression, and terror in America— temporarily interrupted by the defeat in the 2020 elections—and then settling accounts with 'enemy' countries (Iran, China, North Korea, Russia, etc.) via nuclear and other wars of total annihilation and self-destruction. As a corollary, such an 'all-American' heroic model rather than exhibiting 'American exceptionalism' in 'peace' or 'peaceful conflict resolution' and common-sense pragmatism of survival expresses fascism's hardcore of mass death, destruction, and self-destruction via collective suicide.

To that extent, the conservative/rightist specter of mass death, destruction, and self-destruction makes fascism happen in America post-2016 and during Reaganism both in relation to other countries and within society by interacting with and reinforcing domestic warfare/terror like pervasive executions, as it does in other settings since fascist Italy and Nazi Germany. While not all the conservative prospect of mass death, destruction, and self-destruction is fascist, fascism in America post-2016 and since Reaganism invariantly is a specter of collective suicide, MAD, as everywhere else.

---

of deception and delusion typifying Orwellian totalitarian or surveillance states whose sinister nature and operation some whistleblowers eventually expose and thus reveal the true nature of the US government and polity under conservatism, although this is what most Americans probably knew, experienced, or sensed before, that theirs was basically a sugar-coated oppressive and controlling state, as the world's highest prisoner population of mostly prisoners of ethical conscience like drug users and so innocent persons demonstrates. In this regard, the US returned NATO missiles to Turkey probably through another secret back channel in a typical violation of the agreement, while the Soviet Union/Russia did not return its missiles to Cuba—if it did, the US government would again raise the specter of nuclear catastrophe., Olesen (2021, p. 245) remarks that the 'whistleblower, as Edward Snowden also learned from his long-term exile in Russia, there is often a fine line between 'traitor' and 'hero'.' Relatedly, Olesen (2021, p. 245) notes that 'in 2019 a letter by an anonymous White House insider set US President Donald Trump on course for impeachment [and] Trump immediately attacked the whistleblower, calling the person 'a disgrace to our country' and 'close to a spy', a line supported [by] Fox News.'

Fascists therefore explode and march in post-2016 and to some degree Reagan's America as extreme conservative forces of mass death, destruction, and self-destruction, as they do in other social spaces and times since Mussolini and Hitler in Italy and Germany, aside from rare and temporary exceptions. Fascists thus resurge as extreme rightist destructive and self-destructive agents prone to causing mass death for their 'enemies', domestic and foreign alike, in post-2016 and Reagan's America, as in these other social spaces and times. Instead of being unique 'peace loving' and pragmatic American exceptions, these 'all-American' patriots reveal fascists' and religious conservatives' destructive and self-destructive or collectively suicidal nature. On this account, conservative, extreme rightist destructive and suicidal agents make fascism happen in post-2016 and Reagan's America, as in other contexts and times since Mussolini and Hitler during the 1920–30s. Even if not all conservative destructive and suicidal agents are fascists, fascists, like evangelical and other religious sects and cults, in America post-2016 and during Reaganism universally are forces of mass death, destruction, and self-destruction via collective suicide, as everywhere else.

11   Syndrome 10: Fascism as an Aggregate of Extreme Authoritarian Agents

As the tenth syndrome and a corollary/covariate of all the above, fascism in America post-2016 and during earlier times reveals and replicates an aggregate of extreme authoritarian agents as a universal socio-psychological fascist element in various societal contexts and times. Thus, American fascism emerges as and consists of a collection of extreme authoritarian leaders and followers. Accordingly, it rises and spreads as an admixture of extreme sadism and masochism comprising sadistic-masochistic characters. In addition, it occurs as and shows a mix of grave seriousness and utter grotesqueness. Further, fascism in America happens and metastasizes as the cult of an autocratic leader by the fascist rank-and-file combined with mass delusions, fantasies, and fictions ultimately resulting in collective suicide.

Considering the preceding, fascism in America post-2016, as well as during earlier times since the 1930s and McCarthyism through Reaganism and the Tea Party, emerges and consists of an aggregate of extreme authoritarian personalities, just as it does in other societies and historical periods since fascist Italy and Spain and Nazi Germany through postwar South America to present Hungary, Poland, Brexit Great Britain, Brazil, and elsewhere. American fascism reappears as a combination of an extreme authoritarian leader as an autocrat/dictator and followers as the equivalent rank-and-file or the blindly following and obedient base replicating the Nazi 'blind herd'. Taken together, American fascism resurges as extreme conservative authoritarianism in the face and sense of radical-right authoritarian personalities, which restates in socio-psychological terms fascism as right totalitarianism. Such an American example therefore epitomizes the socio-psychological essence of fascism as extreme conservative authoritarianism[106] in socio-psychological terms rather than reflecting presumptive 'American exceptionalism' in a superior 'impulse of freedom' and the like. These 'all-American' embodiments conform to the inner character of fascists as extreme conservative authoritarian leaders and followers instead of being unique exceptions.

To that extent, the conglomerate of extreme authoritarians[107] makes fascism happen in America post-2016 and perhaps earlier since McCarthyism or its ramification Reaganism and the Tea Party, as it does in all other social spaces and times since fascist Italy and Nazi Germany through present Hungary, Poland, Brazil, Brexit Great Britain, and elsewhere. Specifically, both an autocratic leader and the follower base characterized with extreme conservative authoritarianism resurge in this example, as in others from Mussolini, Franco and Hitler and their rank-and-file to Hungary's, Poland's, Brazil's, Brexit Great Britain's, and other authoritarian leaders and followers.

In socio-psychological terms, therefore any aggregate of extreme conservative authoritarian personalities represents fascism and related totalitarian dictatorship, such as evangelical and other theocracy qua 'Christian America' or the 'Bible Belt' in America post-2016, as it does in other social settings since fascist Italy and Nazi Germany. Thus, extreme conservative authoritarians can

---

106   Altemeyer (2007, p. 2) warns that 'authoritarianism itself has not disappeared, and [indeed] the greatest threat to American democracy today arises from a militant authoritarianism that has become a cancer upon the nation.' Altemeyer (2007, p. 47) elaborates that 'human affairs have provided the foremost example of how badly right-wing authoritarianism can damage the United States'.

107   Altemeyer (2007, p. 4) envisions that even if US right-wing 'authoritarians temporarily fade from view, they will still be there, aching for a dictatorship that will force their views on everyone.' Altemeyer (2007, p. 257) referring mainly to the US decries that modern 'societies presently produce millions of highly authoritarian personalities as a matter of course, enough to stage the Nuremberg Rallies over and over and over again. Turning a blind eye to this could someday point guns at all our heads, and the fingers on the triggers will belong to right-wing authoritarians. We ignore this at our peril.' This has proven prescient, as American society, above all conservative-religious America, evidently produces millions of authoritarians who are more than enough to stage 'all-American' equivalents of the Nuremberg Nazi Rallies in the South and other 'red' regions, as in post-2016 and even post-2020.

only be fascists and similar totalitarians like evangelical and other theocrats in this setting, as they do in others since Mussolini and Hitler and their rank-and-file. Conversely, in socio-psychological terms, fascism can only happen, along with evangelical theocracy and related dictatorship, as an aggregate of extreme conservative authoritarian personalities including autocratic leaders and the base, as it does in America post-2016, like everywhere else. As right totalitarians, fascists, together with their totalitarian allies like evangelical theocrats, can only appear through conservative authoritarians, as they do in America post-2016 and elsewhere.

Consequently, fascism in America post-2016 and some extent earlier particularly rises and advances as an admixture of extreme sadism and masochism, as it does in other societies and periods since fascist Italy/Spain and Nazi Germany in the 1920–30s. American fascism occurs as a compilation of extreme compounded conservative sadistic-masochistic characters spanning from the autocrat to the blindly following base, as it does in other examples since Mussolini, Franco, Hitler, and similar fascist autocrats and their rank-and-file. In short, American fascism happens as a mass of radical-right sadists-masochists from the autocratic top to the blind base, as it does everywhere else. The post-2016 autocracy and its base replicate, emulate, or evoke most of the sadistic-masochistic character traits of Mussolini, Hitler, and other classic fascist autocrats and their own rank-and-file, respectively. Specifically, the autocracy manifests the sadistic traits of fascist autocrats, while compounded with symptoms of masochism or self-destructiveness reminiscent of Hitler. The base expresses the masochistic syndromes of the fascist rank-and-file, such as the Nazi 'blind herd', through total, blind submission and following of the autocrat, while mixed with intense sadism toward others like liberal-democratic forces, lower social strata, and ethnic minorities. Altogether, fascism in America post-2016 materializes in socio-psychological terms as mostly the primary sadism and secondary masochism of the authoritarian leader and the prevalent masochism and subsidiary sadism of the base, as it does in all other examples. As a corollary, far from exhibiting presumed 'American exceptionalism' through 'superior' opposite elements like the non-sadistic, angel-style 'American character', this American example accords with and exemplifies fascism's socio-psychological feature of extreme sadism-masochism. Instead of being exclusive exceptions in opposite, especially non-sadistic traits, its 'all-American' emanations express fascists' sadistic-masochistic characters, including the Nazi leader and 'blind herd'.

On this account, the admixture of sadism and masochism makes fascism happen in America post-2016 and even earlier since McCarthyism or its sequel Reaganism and the Tea Party, as it does in other examples since fascist Italy/

Spain and Nazi Germany. Specifically, the primary sadism and secondary masochism of the authoritarian leader and the prevalent masochism and subsidiary sadism of the base produce the fascist outcome in this setting, as in others. Extreme mixed conservative sadistic-masochistic actors, such as primarily autocrats-sadists and mainly followers-masochists, make fascism happen here, as elsewhere else since Mussolini, Franco, and Hitler and their rank-and-file. Fascism in America post-2016 attracts, preselects conservative sadistic-masochistic actors within its frame of insanity operating as an equivalent to (Pareto's) religious 'cage for the insane', just as it renders many previously normal Americans into sadists-masochists and thus pathological cases. American fascism hence rises and acts as both the product and producer of conservative sadistic-masochistic persons and thus of pervasive sadism-masochism in America post-2016, as in all other settings.

Socio-psychologically, the admixture of extreme conservative sadism and masochism therefore constitutes and only can be fascism and related totalitarian dictatorship, such as evangelical and other theocracy in America post-2016, as in other settings and times since fascist Italy and Nazi Germany. Extreme conservative sadistic-masochistic characters form and can only be fascists, as well as evangelical theocrats and other allied totalitarians, in this context and history, as in others since Mussolini and Hitler and their rank-and-file. Conversely, like evangelical theocracy and other allied dictatorship, fascism could happen only through the admixture of extreme conservative sadism and masochism, as it does in America post-2016 and elsewhere. Fascists, along with evangelical and other theocrats, as right totalitarians could erupt only as extreme conservative sadistic-masochistic characters, as they do in America post-2016.

In addition, fascism in America post-2016 and perhaps earlier emerges and spreads as a contradictory mixture of grave, indeed morbid and deadly seriousness and utter grotesqueness or ludicrousness, as it does in other social settings since fascist Italy/Spain and Nazi Germany through postwar South America to Hungary, Poland, Brexit Great Britain, Brazil, and elsewhere, with minor variations. American fascism occurs as an agglomeration of conservative authoritarian, sadistic-masochistic agents who act often simultaneously as both gravely, even morbidly and deadly serious, and utterly grotesque, ludicrous, or comical actors, as it does in other settings since Mussolini, Franco, Hitler, and other fascist rulers and their rank-and-file.

In short, fascism in America post-2016 happens as a mixed extreme gravity and outright buffoonery, lethal spectacle and circus, and in that sense tragedy and comedy, as it does since fascist Italy and Nazi Germany. American fascism comprises a mass of conservative extremely grave persons and outright buffoons, violent agents and clowns, including the autocrat leader and the base, as it does since Mussolini, Franco, and Hitler and their rank-and-file through their latter analogues in South America (Pinochet's Chile, etc.), Hungary, Poland, Brazil, Brexit Great Britain, and beyond. Autocracy in the US post-2016, together with that in Brexit Britain, seemingly replicates or evokes both the extreme gravity and outright buffoonery, violent demeanor and clown-style gestures, simply the tragic-comic acting of Mussolini, Hitler, and other classic fascists—an 'all-American' replay of *the Great Dictator*. The post-2016 autocratic base displays the same mixture of deadly seriousness and clowning, as its violent and clown-style siege of Congress on January 6, 2021, shows, characterizing Hitler's 'blind herd' and Mussolini's rank-and-file, for example, the fascist marches on Rome and Munich. Accordingly, the American example reaffirms the contradictory mixture of lethal seriousness and utter grotesqueness of fascism, notably its leaders, rather than showing 'American exceptionalism' in consistency and similar traits qua the consistent 'American character'. 'All-American' incarnations of fascism manifest the mixed extreme gravity and cruelty and sheer buffoonery and clownery of fascists, including their leaders instead of being unique exceptions.

The mixture of morbid seriousness and utter grotesqueness hence under-pins socio-psychologically the emergence and diffusion of fascism in America post-2016 and perhaps earlier since gravely serious McCarthyism or buffoon-ish, second-rate acting Reaganism, and compounded sadistic-masochistic Tea Partiers, as it does in most other cases since fascist Italy and Nazi Germany. Fascism in America post-2016 and earlier attracts, preselects mixed con-servative morbidly grave persons and outright buffoons, violent agents and clowns, tragic-comic actors within its frame of tragedy-comedy or the 'cage for the insane', and makes once in power many normal, sane Americans such pathological personalities. While not all conservative grave persons and sheer buffoons, violent agents and clowns, tragic-comic actors are fascist, fascists, notably their leaders, in America during these and prior times are such com-pounded characters after the image of Mussolini, Hitler, and others. US ema-nations of fascism by their morbid gravity, violence, and cruelty that they inflict on other Americans and non-Americans make America an 'American tragedy', while by their utter grotesqueness, buffoonery, and clownery making it the 'laughingstock' of the world.

Furthermore, fascism in America post-2016 rises and advances as the cult of an autocratic leader by the rank-and-file, as it does in other social spaces and historical periods from fascist Italy and Nazi Germany to present cases or proxies in Hungary, Poland, Brexit Great Britain, Brazil, and elsewhere, with rare exceptions. Concomitantly, American fascism resurges and spreads as a compound of mass delusions, deceptions, and fantasies marking a 'post-truth' era[108] of denial of facts and reality and creating and perpetuating the cult of the leader. It ultimately explodes and metastasizes as the specter of collective suicide of the fascist rank-and-file and in extension the 'people' and society for the power, honor, and glory of the leader, as the outcome of false fascist anti-liberal and anti-democratic populism. In this sense, fascism happens in post-2016 in America as a religious-style cult consisting of the blind and total adulation and submission and ultimately literal sacrifice by followers to the leader and involving mass apocalyptic[109] and other delusions in the function of cult creation and perpetuation—a near-replica of the Nazi 'blind herd'. In brief, American fascism emerges as the cult and consecration by the blind base of the autocratic leader as 'chosen by God' for America. Both the autocratic leader demands and the fascist base perpetuates such a cult and consecration, forming a religious-style bond characterizing cults and sects between the autocrat resorting to demagogic[110] deceptions and

---

108   Guriev (2018, p. 202) remarks that in American and European fascism's or populism's 'post-truth era the quantitative arguments and even straightforward economic facts do not matter anyway.' Further, Guriev (2018, p. 203) notes that US and European fascists or populists 'can indeed win against facts, experts, pundits, and journalists,' and by implication produce what some of them call 'alternative facts'. This 'post-truth era' of 'alternative facts' entirely accords with that, as Paxton (1998, p. 4) observes, 'fascism does not base its claims to validity on their truth.'

109   Phillips (2006, pp. 5–6) diagnosing the 'apocalyptic mindset of many in the Christian Right' exemplifies it by its vision of 'a global conflagration of good versus evil, the falsity of the UN, the perfidy of the French, the materialization of a European anti-Christ and the emergence of a second Babylon in Iraq. According to these apocalyptic scenarios, the faithful can expect: wars on a worldwide scale, economic crashes, earthquakes, diseases and virtually every other calamity imaginable. Historically, such end-of-times views have proven delusional, though the rise of extreme and pervasive forms of religious superstition is usually an indication that an empire or civilization is facing a precipitous decline.' Harris (2005) suggests that 'we have names for people who have many beliefs for which there is no rational justification. When their beliefs are extremely common we call them 'religious'; otherwise, they are likely to be called 'mad', 'psychotic' or 'delusional'. And so, while religious people are not generally mad, their core beliefs absolutely are. The danger of religious faith is that it allows otherwise normal human beings to reap the fruits of madness and consider them holy. Because each new generation of children is taught that religious propositions need not be justified in the way that all others must, civilization is still besieged by the armies of the preposterous. We are, even now, killing ourselves over ancient literature.'

110   Hahl, Kim, and Zuckerman Sivan (2018, p. 2) state that 'it is puzzling that the winning candidate, Donald J. Trump, was perceived by his supporters as appealingly authentic despite abundant evidence that (1) he was at least as sensitive to private self-interest as Clinton, with no corresponding record of public service; (2) he was considerably more prone to falsehood than Clinton; and (3) he deliberately flouted many norms that had

followers[111] acting with adulation and blind obedience, making conservative America and its political party a cult-like entity. Far from displaying 'American exceptionalism' in supreme independence, realism, and similar traits—the independent, realistic 'American character'—this American instance demonstrates fascism's cult of an autocratic leader, blind base, and mass madness. These 'all-American' reincarnations hence fully epitomize this fascist cult-style and delusionary character rather than being sole exceptions in these terms.

On this account, the cult of an autocratic leader by the blind base combined with mass delusions, deceptions, and fantasies makes fascism happen in America post-2016 and perhaps earlier since Reaganism and the Tea Party, as it does in other social settings and times since fascist Italy and Nazi Germany. Fascism in America post-2016 and earlier attracts or preselects persons and groups needing a cult of autocratic leaders and creating mass delusions and fantasies, just as it produces and sustains such cults and beliefs. In essence, the conservative cult of an autocratic leader by the rank-and-file and the creation of mass delusions and fantasies for that purpose can only be fascism and similar totalitarian dictatorship, such as evangelical and other theocracy, as in America post-2016 and other social contexts. By demanding the cult of an autocratic leader whose blind herd-like base they become and creating or believing mass delusions for that purpose, conservatives or rightists ultimately become or act as fascists, theocrats, and other totalitarians, as in America post-2016 and other examples. Conversely, fascism, along with similar totalitarian dictatorship like theocracy, can only happen through the conservative cult of an autocratic leader by the rank-and-file and the creation and diffusion of mass fantasies, as in America post-2016 and other social settings since fascist Italy and Nazi Germany. Together with other totalitarians like theocrats, fascists can only happen as conservatives needing the cult of an autocratic leader whose base they become and creating mass delusions in that aim, as in post-2016 America and these other cases.

In summary, the diagnosis of a social pathology seems accurate and unequivocal: fascism rises, advances, and prevails in America, specifically

---

been taken for-granted for many years and were widely endorsed [i.e.] a pattern of lying demagoguery'.

111   For example, Nyhan (2020, p. 223) refers to the 'pictures of the inauguration crowds from the inauguration of President Obama in 2009 and President Trump in 2017. When the pictures were unlabeled, there was broad agreement that the Obama crowd was larger, but when the pictures were labelled, many Trump supporters looked at the pictures and indicated that Trump's crowd was larger, an obviously false claim.'

its conservative-religious pole, post-2016, including after 2020 at state levels within this part. If this diagnosis is correct, the question opens as to the etiology of such a pathology—what causes fascism in post-2016 America. The next chapter explores the causes of fascism in America.

CHAPTER 3

Why Did It Happen? Social Causes of Fascism

1   Societal Causation of Fascism

The clear and unambiguous diagnosis that fascism rises and advances in post-2016 America and to some degree earlier opens the questions as to the societal causation of this lethal fascist pathology that threatens to end or pervert the 'American experiment' in democracy a la Tocqueville and Jeffersonian Enlightenment 'liberty and justice for all'. One wonders what social conditions cause fascism to emerge and expand in America post-2016 and to some degree before, as during the Tea Party, Reaganism, McCarthyism, and the Ku Klux Klan in a time regression.

In essence, what causes the occurrence and expansion of fascism in post-2016 America is a set of multiple societal, including ideological-political, economic, and cultural, factors. These social causes of fascism are specifically, first and foremost, conservatism or the radical-right, second, unrestrained, coercive, and inegalitarian capitalism, third, ubiquitous repressive religion or religious extremism, and fourth, theocracy (see Table 3.1).

While operating by their own inner logic and workings, these societal causes of fascism are typically interconnected and mutually reinforcing, as are ideological-political, economic, and cultural factors within society. Consequently, they form the integral chain of social causation or conditioning of fascism in America post-2016 as well as during the Ku Klux Klan, McCarthyism, Reaganism, and the Tea Party.

2   Conservatism as the Cause of Fascism

As implied at many previous occasions and perfectly clear and painfully obvious by now, conservatism or the right primarily causes the emergence and metastasis of fascism in post-2016 America—it is the prime fascist cause and mover in American society, as is in all other societies. Conservatism, above all, makes fascism happen in post-2016 America, as does in all other social spaces and times since fascist Italy and Spain, Nazi Germany, and interwar Europe through postwar Sooth America to present-day Hungary, Poland, Brexit Great Britain, Brazil, and other countries and periods, with secondary transient variations and few exceptions.

TABLE 3.1   Main social causes of fascism in America

conservatism, the radical right
unrestrained, coercive, inegalitarian capitalism
pervasive religion and religious extremism
theocracy and theocratic tendencies

Specifically, conservatism is the primary and perpetual ideological-political cause and predictor of fascism in post-2016 America, as in other social settings and historical periods. In other words, the compounded ideology, movement, politics, and zeitgeist of the right causes and predicts fascism in post-2016 America, as does in other earlier and later examples. Fascism in post-2016 America rises, persists, and expands within the broader ideological-political framework of conservatism,[1] the extended and united family of the right, with minor family contentions, as it does everywhere since fascist Italy and Nazi Germany. 'All-American' conservatism epitomizes the universal conservative causation of fascism rather than being a unique exception to the rule in the sense of showing its superior 'American exceptionalism' in 'freedom' and 'democracy' and miraculously decoupling itself from their fascist negation and destruction. The American right demonstrates and exemplifies the generalized rightist reproduction of fascism, including Nazism, instead of being an exceptional counterexample producing 'freedom' and 'democracy' in America. 'All-American' home-born conservatives or rightists act as driving forces of fascism and parents or older 'brothers in arms' of fascists as young ultra-conservatives or extreme rightists in post-2016 America, just as Nazis were the 'new' conservatives in 1933 Germany.

In essence, American and any conservatism, especially its radical, 'true'— as distinct from its moderate[2] but growingly rare and near-extinct—version,

---

1   Mueller (2009, p. x) implies that American conservatism is the driving force of fascism and relatedly theocracy in America by observing that conservatism ('traditionalism') and dictatorship 'go hand in hand'. This holds true because conservative and indeed any dictatorship in America and beyond is and can only be essentially of a fascist and/or theocratic variety— simply, fascism or theocracy—in light of the predominance of conservatism and religion over liberalism and secularism in American society post-2016 and even since the 1980s. For instance, Dickinson (2022) reports that Conservative Political Action Committee in the US 'has long been a political circus, a relatively harmless sideshow. But its latest incarnation [in Dallas, Texas] has become manifestly dangerous—more fascist than farce.'

2   Jouet (2017, p. 42) notes that the 'conception of 'conservatism' tends to be far less moderate and far more ideological in America—notwithstanding the growing power of fringe far-right

has typically been and remains latent proto-fascism and thus potential fascism in gestation since its inception from despotic medievalism through the present, with minor transient variations and few exceptions. In other words, the American right, especially its radical streak, has essentially been and continues to be latently proto-fascist and so potentially fascist in incubation, as have its other variants. In extension, the conservative, rightist pole of America consisting of the former Southern Confederacy and similar regions reportedly has been for long and persists as latently proto-fascist, so potentially fascist in conception, acting in vehement antagonism and launching proxy civil, political-culture warfare against its liberal-democratic alternative. Consequently, American conservatism because of being latent, covert proto-fascism, or the right due to its latently proto-fascist character, generates manifest, overt fascism in post-2016 America and before. It follows that because of being latently or covertly proto-fascist, conservative—as distinct from and opposed to liberal—America ultimately mutates into a manifestly or overtly fascist sub-society or region. It does so by seizing a suitable opportunity or perfect timing to embrace fascism and create a cult of its autocratic leader mixing Mussolini's buffoonery and Hitler's clown-style gesturing, as in post-2016 and to some extent during the 1950s with McCarthyism,[3] the 1960s with Goldwater,[4] the 1980s with Reaganism,[5] and the early 2010s with the Tea Party.

---

parties or the hardening rhetoric of certain mainstream right-wing parties in Europe.' Specifically, Bonikowski et al. (2021, p. 532) infer that 'Donald Trump's successful campaign in the 2016 presidential election [is] a product of crescive changes in US political culture [conservatism and the Republican Party], rather than as a cause in itself of the country's turn toward right-wing radicalism.' Bonikowski et al. (2021, p. 534) infer that the 'necessary (but not sufficient) conditions for a takeover of the Republican Party by its radical wing had been in the making for the prior two decades. In the United States, this trend had generated growing demand for radical-right politics among a large subset of white Americans, whose votes were then captured by an opportunistic politician relying on a persuasive combination of exclusionary, populist, and dystopian political claims'. Bonikowski et al. (2021, p. 532–3) also register the 'GOP's actions in the aftermath of the 2020 election—from the unfounded moral panic about voting fraud and widespread support of the Capitol insurrection to the party elites' continued fealty to Donald Trump.'

3   Bourdieu and Haacke (1995, p. 67) warn that 'in the present hysteria, it is forgotten that [US] conservatives created McCarthyism and that they do not hesitate to use the master's techniques today.'

4   Gross et al. (2011, p. 333) suggest that 'Barry Goldwater's 1964 presidential bid was a major turning point here. Despite his lopsided defeat in the general election, the nomination signaled that conservatives had wrested control of the Republican Party from its northeastern establishment figures.'

5   Bourdieu (1998, p. 35) proposes that contemporary 'conservative revolutions', such as the Reagan and Thatcher Revolution in the US and Great Britain, like that in Germany in the

It is hardly surprising for observers who identify and analyze its hardcore of proto-fascism that American conservatism or the right causes and predicts fascism in post-2016 America. It is equally unsurprising for those experiencing its strong proto-fascist undercurrent that the conservative pole of America, or the US dominated by conservatism, becomes manifestly and openly fascist post-2016. Evidently, only a small step or thin line separates American extreme, 'true' conservatism or the radical right as proto-fascism from pure fascism, so demarcates conservative America as a proto-fascist space from its overt, intense fascist mutation. Conservative, rightist proto-fascism in the form and sense of the inherent, ancient medieval-style despotism or authoritarianism of conservatism is not identical to pure fascism, a distinction that rules out and preempts possible objections of circular reasoning. Hence, conservative America while proto-fascist or authoritarian is not initially and necessarily fascist in the pure sense. However, conservatism's proto-fascism in the sense of medieval-rooted authoritarianism inexorably generates fascism proper. Thus, conservative proto-fascist qua authoritarian America mutates into fascist at an opportune occasion and right timing by embracing a compatible autocrat that unleashes and legitimizes its long-accumulated anti-liberal and anti-democratic energies, as in post-2016, the 1980s, and the 2010s.

In sum, American conservatism's causation of fascism in post-2016 America operates through its latent proto-fascism or authoritarianism as an intrinsic prior force, and conservative America's fascist mutation enfolds via its long proto-fascist or authoritarian undercurrent of extreme anti-liberalism. Conservatism moves from the potential, latency for to the reality, openness of fascism, and conservative America from potentially and latently to actually and openly fascist.

Specifically, American and other conservatism is latent proto-fascism and thus generates pure fascism due to certain interlinked and mutually reinforcing properties implied in the previous chapters. Recall that these properties of conservatism include authoritarianism, anti-liberalism, anti-democracy, anti-secularism, irrationalism, anti-rationalism and anti-progressivism, anti-egalitarianism, anti-universalism, and anti-cosmopolitanism, absolute rule, power and domination, coercion, repression, violence and terror, anti-pacifism, militarism, war and conquest, and authoritarian personalities. Also, recall that conservatism transmits these properties to its heir fascism that

---

1930s, are essentially fascist and the German and American 'conservative revolutionaries' of the 1930s and the 1980s were fascists. He adds that the 'conservative [Reagan-Thatcher]

inherits, perpetuates, and carries them to the extreme. This suggests that the difference between conservatism and fascism, thus conservative authoritarianism and fascist totalitarianism, is in quantitative, statistical-like degrees of unfreedom rather than in substance because both are deeply and implacably anti-liberal, anti-democratic entities.

Consequently, American conservatism is latent proto-fascism and generates fascism in post-2016 America because of its authoritarianism, anti-liberalism, anti-democracy, anti-secularism, irrationalism, anti-rationalism and anti-progressivism, anti-egalitarianism, anti-universalism, anti-cosmopolitanism, power absolutism, coercion, repression and terror, militarism, conquest and war, and authoritarian personalities. Conversely, precisely these multiple and intertwined elements render American conservatism into latent proto-fascism and hence enable it to generate and sustain fascism. The American right is proto-fascist and makes America fascist due to being authoritarian, anti-liberal, anti-democratic, anti-secular, irrational, anti-rationalist and anti-progressive, anti-egalitarian, anti-universalist, anti-cosmopolitan, absolutist in power, repressive, and terrorist, militarist, warlike and imperialist, and consisting of authoritarian persons. Conversely, these elements render the right into proto-fascist and empower it to remake America, specifically its conservative pole, fascist.

In extension and consequence, the conservative pole of America, including the former Southern Confederacy[6] and beyond, is latently proto-fascist and ultimately mutates into a fascist societal space precisely owing to these properties of American conservatism that it embodies, enforces, and expands to other sections of the country. Conservative America mutates from proto-fascist to fascist because of being authoritarian, anti-liberal, anti-democratic,

---

revolution can deceive people [and] this is because it seems to retain nothing of the old Black Forest pastoral of the conservative revolutionaries of the 1930s [fascists]' (Bourdieu 1998, p. 35). Bourdieu (2000, p. 57) describes Nazis as German 'conservative revolutionaries' of the 1930s.

6 Dahrendorf (1979, p. 110) includes the 'Southern United States' among 'forms of power and government' that are non-legitimate due to violating 'certain fundamental human rights', together with those of 'Hitler, Stalin, Amin and Pinochet', etc. Hicks (2006, p. 506) identifies 'a large Southern impact on the Republican's Congressional ascendance of the past half century is broadly apparent—a white, Southern evangelical impact in particular,' as part of 'a pragmatic fusion of religious and free market conservatism has marked US conservatism'. Gross et al. (2011, p. 334) note that 'Southern whites defected to the Republican Party; and Western suburbanites mobilized in response to perceived moral degeneration in the counterculture.'

anti-secular, irrational, anti-rationalist and anti-progressive, anti-universalist, anti-egalitarian and anti-cosmopolitan, absolutist, coercive and repressive, militarist, warlike and imperialist, and comprising authoritarian persons. Conversely, these properties of conservatism cause conservative—versus liberal—America to ultimately mutate from a proto-fascist to a fascist land of unfreedom and nondemocracy, or ersatz 'freedom' and bogus illiberal exclusionary 'democracy' such as theocracy qua a 'faith-based' polity and society a la the 'Bible Bel'.

Furthermore, these same properties enable conservative America, especially the South, to expand such a fascist mutation to other regions through the Southernization of American society, including its ideology, politics, economy, culture, and civil sphere, shaping it after the Southern anachronistic and defeated—as assumed after the Civil War and during the 1960s—repressive and exclusionary model. More than ironically, the defeated Southern Confederacy—from Alabama, South Carolina, and Tennessee to Florida and Texas—not only mutates inevitably from a proto-fascist to fascist territory but spreads such a mutation as if by contagion and metastasis to other parts of America, including those opposed and victorious in the Civil War. This region mutates into and expands fascism because it incarnates, realizes, and imposes in purity and totality the essential principles of American conservatism from authoritarianism, anti-liberalism, anti-democracy and anti-secularism through irrationalism, anti-rationalism and anti-progressivism, anti-egalitarianism, anti-universalism and anti-cosmopolitanism to absolutism, coercion, repression and terror, militarism, war and imperialism, and authoritarian personalities. In short, this pole of America is proto-fascist and eventually mutates into fascist because it is ultra and 'truly' conservative, a true implementation, expansion, and imposition of conservatism.

First, conservatism is latent proto-fascism and generates and sustains fascism in post-2016 America and earlier through its complex of inherent authoritarianism, vehement anti-liberalism, and persistent anti-democracy in the sense of antagonism to liberal democracy in a typical interconnection and mutual reinforcement. In short, the American right is proto-fascist and renders America fascist due to being inherently authoritarian, vehemently anti-liberal, and persistently anti-democratic versus liberal democracy. In consequence, the conservative pole of America is latently proto-fascist and mutates into a fascist subsociety because of being profoundly authoritarian, implacably anti-liberal, and essentially anti-democratic by opposing liberal democracy.

American conservatism hence generates and sustains fascism in America by its intrinsic traditional authoritarianism that it—like its European original, though less visibly—inherits and perpetuates from medievalism, the medieval ancient regime of feudal bondage, despotism, aristocracy, and Christian Catholic and Protestant theocracy. Like its European equivalent, American conservatism is inherent and permanent medieval-rooted authoritarianism that it couches in the rhetoric and cheap talk of 'freedom' as alleged conservative 'American exceptionalism' in relation to the unfree 'old world'. In other words, the American right makes America fascist because of its inherently and permanently authoritarian nature even if disguised by the deceitful mask of 'freedom' that it assumes particularly during elections and deceives most Americans, especially in conservative America, about its bogus 'libertarianism'. Consequently, conservative America mutates from a proto-fascist space to a fascist subsociety because of its profoundly and constantly authoritarian core embellished and hidden by the deception and delusion of 'freedom', like the 'free' Southern Confederacy, the 'spirit of freedom', and 'freemen' of the South from Alabama to Texas.

Furthermore, conservatism's or the right's intrinsic traditional authoritarianism[7] by its inner logic tends to escalate and intensify ultimately into conservative, rightist totalitarianism or dictatorship as an ultimate, inexorable form of its authoritarian system. American conservatism/the right hence generates and sustains in post-2016 America fascism that is invariably and universally right totalitarianism or rightist dictatorship, thus extreme conservative authoritarianism. Consequently, the conservative, rightist pole of America tends eventually to become or comes close to becoming totalitarian, dictatorial, or extremely authoritarian, as the former Southern Confederacy shows from Alabama and Tennessee to Texas and to that extent fascist as defined. It follows that whenever by its inner workings conservatism or the right escalates and moves from its intrinsic old authoritarianism to the new conservative totalitarianism or rightist dictatorship, it produces fascism whose essence is the latter, as it does in post-2016 America and interwar Europe. In extension, at the point at which the conservative, rightist pole of America

---

7 Gross et al. (2011, p. 328) summarize the view that contemporary American conservatism attempts 'to stuff a rapidly changing American society back into the box of a white, theologically conservative, small-town vision of the good [and so] endeavor[s] to restore the status quo ante.' For example, Gross et al. (2011, p. 344) report that the 'percentage of Republicans who describe themselves as conservative rose from 43 in 1972 to 66 in 1996, tracking directly the rise of the right.' Also, Autor et al. (2020, p. 3140) observe that a 'sizable rightward shift among the GOP and a modest leftward shift among Democrats has left few centrists in either party' and add that 'moderate Democrats have become increasingly rare in Congress, while Tea Party and like-minded conservatives have risen to prominence in the GOP,' though this makes a false equivalence between a liberal-democratic and an anti-liberal proto-fascist or authoritarian party. Torche and Rauf (2021, p. 380) find that 'White conservatism has since continued to coalesce under the umbrella of the Republican party.'

mutates from being inherently authoritarian to totalitarian or dictatorial, it effectively becomes fascist, as it does post-2016 and perhaps before.

Conceivably, conservatism's or the right's authoritarianism would not generate and sustain fascism in America if it remained static and did not 'dynamically' evolve into conservative totalitarianism or rightist dictatorship, as prior to 2016 or to the 1980s. However, sooner or later conservative authoritarianism undergoes such a 'dynamic' totalitarian evolution and thereby generates fascism in America, as in post-2016 and afterwards and to some degree since the 1980s with Reaganism and later with the Tea Party. As a corollary, the conservative, rightist pole of America would not become fascist if it petrified in its old authoritarian spirit and structure and did not mutate into a totalitarian subsociety, as before 2016 or the 1980s. Yet, this pole eventually undergoes such a totalitarian, including relatedly theocratic, mutation and turns into a fascist space at a right opportunity and time, as when an autocratic leader helps unleash and legitimize its long-accrued proto-fascist impulses, as in post-2016, during the Ku Klux Klan, McCarthyism, Reaganism, and the Tea Party.

Relatedly, conservatism is latent proto-fascism and hence generates fascism in post-2016 America via its original, vehement, implacable anti-liberalism by developing and functioning in intensely adverse reaction and 'holy' warfare against liberalism and liberal modernity. In other words, the American right is proto-fascist and eventually makes America fascist because of being a vehemently, implacably, and violently anti-liberal ideology, movement, and politics revolting against liberal and pluralist society.[8] Consequently, the stronger, conservative pole of America is proto-fascist and ultimately mutates into a fascist space due to its vehement and violent anti-liberal core revolting and starting civil, political, and culture wars against weaker, liberal America.[9]

Furthermore, like its authoritarianism, conservatism's or the right's anti-liberalism through an inner tendency of escalation and intensification reaches the extreme level of extension and intensity. In so doing, conservatism in post-2016 America and beyond reproduces fascism that universally arises as

---

8   Munch (2001, p. 20) alerts to US conservative (including fundamentalist Protestant) movements and structures arising and acting 'against the reality of a liberal and pluralist society.'

9   Jouet (2017, p. 29) observes that the 'intensity of America's regional divide is exceptional. There are obviously rather liberal and conservative regions in other Western nations, but their citizens are not sharply divided over such basic issues as whether people should have a right to medical treatment. Besides, the extraordinary polarization of American society is not merely between blue and red states, as a major partisan rift has occurred nationwide. Republican leaders in blue states typically join their counterparts in red states in defending hardline positions on essentially all issues.'

extreme conservative anti-liberalism. Accordingly, the conservative-rightist pole of America by its inner workings turns extremely and proudly anti-liberal—as in the 'deep' South and beyond—and to that extent mutates into a fascist entity. 'All-American' conservatives or rightists since the Ku Klux Klan, McCarthy, Goldwater, and Reagan through the Tea Party and their post-2016 variants turn so extremely anti-liberal that they assault and persecute liberals as 'un-American'[10] and thus act as fascists by applying the attack template of Mussolini, Hitler, and other fascist anti-liberals. As a result, whenever and wherever by its intrinsic tendency, conservatism or the right attains the maximal point of its original anti-liberalism, it generates or becomes fascism typified by the latter, as during post-2016 America and interwar Italy, Germany, and other parts of Europe. In consequence, when the conservative/rightist pole of America turns anti-liberal to the extreme with 'patriotic' joy and pride, it mutates into fascist, as in post-2016 and before during the Ku Klux Klan, Reaganism, and the Tea Party.

Conceivably, conservatism's anti-liberalism, however a deeply ingrained, vehement, and implacable affliction, if remaining stationary and not moving to the extreme, would not generate fascism in America, as perhaps before 2016 or the 1980s. Yet, this conservative affliction evidently moves toward extreme anti-liberalism at the end and hence generates fascism in America, as during post-2016 and to some degree since the 1980s with extremely anti-liberal Reaganism and the 2010s with the proto-fascist Tea Party.[11] In extension and consequence, the conservative, rightist pole of America if remained in a petrified state of anti-liberalism instead of turning evermore into an anti-liberal entity would not become fascist, as before 2016 or the 1980s. However, this pole of America growingly turns into an extreme anti-liberal entity and thereby

---

10 Bourdieu and Haacke (1995, p. 50) refer to a US 'political climate where the word *liberal* (in the American sense) already poses a problem [and] the neo-conservatives are well aware of this—and make use of it'.

11 Redbird and Grusky (2016, p. 208) associate the Tea Party and 'widespread support for Trump's politics.' Murray (2017, p. 1660) points to the 'rise of the extremist right wing elements like the Tea Party' in the US. Jouet (2017, p. 25) observes that 'in practice, protecting the country's 'exceptional' character meant embracing the G.O.P. program of massive tax cuts, sweeping deregulation, and religious ultratraditionalism. The redefinition of 'American exceptionalism' as freedom from 'big government' and 'Euro-style socialism' especially galvanized Tea Party supporters.' Jouet (2017, p. 30) adds that the 'rise of the Tea Party movement skewed perceptions by making hardline establishment conservatives like George W. Bush and John Boehner seem center right in comparison to the implacable Freedom Caucus.'

becomes fascist declaring a total warfare against liberal America, as during post-2016 and since the 1980s and the early 2010s with Reaganism and the Tea Party, respectively.

As a corollary, conservatism is latent proto-fascism and therefore reproduces fascism in America and elsewhere by its persistent ideology, politics, and spirit of anti-democracy since its appearance in implacable opposition and counter-revolution against the liberal-democratic and egalitarian French Revolution. Like the European original, derivative American conservatism has always been and remains a design and system of anti- or non-democracy by opposing and seeking to eliminate or subvert democracy especially in its liberal, solely genuine form. Conversely, it is a blueprint and regime of illiberal 'democracy' as an ersatz substitute, while indulging in and deceiving most Americans by the simulation, placebo, or cheap talk of 'democracy' and 'freedom'.

Conservatism adopts democratic processes and rules like political elections and constitutions only insofar as they produce and perpetuate conservative absolute power and encompassing domination. Yet, conservatism abolishes or perverts democratic institutions once it attains its foremost goal of authoritarian rule of society, effectively using democracy and freedom against themselves to destroy or subvert them. Otherwise, these democratic institutions have no value in themselves for conservatism that instead depreciates, despises, habitually violates, and eventually destroys them, as the January 2021, terrorist attack on Congress by conservatives and other conservative violence and counter-state terrorism against liberal democracy illustrate. It is no wonder that conservatives consider America not a democracy, let alone liberal democracy,[12] but a 'republic'—just as their variants in Iran considering the latter a 'republic'—that is not always a democratic but also an undemocratic, illiberal, and totalitarian, including theocratic, regime, as Calvinist-Puritan, Islamic, and other religious 'republics' show. In short, the American right is inherently proto-fascist and ultimately makes America fascist due to being an implacably anti-democratic ideology/politics attacking and subverting liberal democracy. In consequence, the conservative pole of America is intrinsically proto-fascist and eventually mutates into fascist due to its anti-democratic core in opposition and aggressive war against liberal-democratic America.

---

12   Mueller (2009, p. x) alarms to the 'dangers' that American and other conservatism ('traditionalism') presents for 'liberal democracy', as does religion such as evangelicalism and the Christian Right overall. More broadly, Tuğal (2021, p. 328) alerts to the 'broader, worldwide [conservative-fascist] forces that have been undermining both liberalism and democracy for a long time.'

Moreover, like its inherent authoritarianism and implacable anti-liberalism, conservatism's original and persistent anti-democracy ideology and politics by its inner logic of intensification tends to attain the extreme point. Therefore, rightism[13] in post-2016 America generates or becomes fascism that universally develops and functions as an extreme conservative anti-democratic ideology, movement, regime, and ambiance defining and typifying all fascisms and fascists. This yields the outcome that the conservative-rightist pole of America mutates into a fascist geographic and social space through its internal tendency to becoming extremely anti-democratic versus liberal democracy. Whenever by its inner logic of escalation American and other conservatism such as the extreme right attains the maximum of its anti-democratic ideology and politics, it generates or turns into fascism that anti-democracy defines, as in post-2016 America, Mussolini's Italy, Franco's Spain, and Hitler's Germany.[14] As a corollary, the conservative/rightist pole of America effectively mutates into a fascist entity when it becomes extremely anti-democratic by revolting and launching a warfare against liberal democracy, as during post-2016 and since the 1980s with Reaganism or the 2010s with the Tea Party.

Conceivably, just as its built-in authoritarianism and vehement anti-liberalism, conservatism's anti-democracy ideology and politics, no matter how profoundly ingrained and persistent, would not generate fascism in America so long as it remained in a static condition not attaining the extreme, as prior to 2016 or the 1980s. Yet, conservatism attains such an anti-democracy extreme ultimately and thus generates fascism in America, as during post-2016 and since the 1980s and the 2010s due to extremely anti-liberal Reaganism and the proto-fascist Tea Party. In consequence, the conservative pole of America would not become fascist if it remained in a petrified state of anti-democracy instead of becoming ever more anti-democratic and assaulting, as by the January 06, 2021 Congress assault by rightists, and subverting liberal democracy, as before 2016 or the 1980s and the 2010s. In reality, this 'all-American' pole becomes extremely anti-democratic and subverts liberal democracy and to that extent mutates into a fascist space, as during post-2016 and since the 1980s and the 2010s with Reaganism and the Tea Party, respectively.

---

13   Jouet (2017, pp. 29–30) suggests that the Republican 'establishment has long defended policies that are objectively far right by either US historical standards or international standards', in other words proto- or near fascist policies.

14   Spenkuch and Tillmann (2017, p. 16) situate National Socialism in Germany on the far-right and Communism on the far-left, which restates the universal fact that Nazism and all fascism originates and remains always as a rightist, conservative phenomenon in contrast to communism as the opposite.

Third and relatedly, conservatism is latent proto-fascism and generates fascism in post-2016 America and beyond through its compound of intense anti-secularism, religious extremism and theocracy, complete irrationalism, anti-rationalism and anti-progressivism, and profound anti-egalitarianism, anti-universalism, and anti-cosmopolitanism, including anti-globalism, typically in interdependence and reciprocal intensification. In other words, rightism is proto-fascist and eventually makes America fascist due to being intensely anti-secular, religiously extremist or extremely religious and theocratic, completely irrational, anti-rational and anti-progressive, and profoundly anti-egalitarian, anti-universalistic, and anti-cosmopolitan, including anti-globalist. Consequently, the conservative pole of America is latently proto- fascist and eventually mutates into a fascist space because of being fundamentally anti-secular, religiously extremist and theocratic, irrational, anti-rational and anti-progressive, and anti-egalitarian, anti-universalistic, and anti-cosmopolitan, including anti-globalist.

Like the European original in Europe, derivative American conservatism generates fascism in America by its intense and obstinate anti- or pre-secularism[15] and particularly religious extremism and theocracy that it adopts and maintains from medievalism, such as the medieval ancient regime of Christian Catholic and Protestant theocracies, thus perpetuating the theocratic Dark Middle Ages. Like the European original but even more during recent times, American conservatism exists and operates as intense and obstinate medieval-rooted anti- or pre-secularism, religious extremism, and theocracy that it presents, embellishes, and justifies as 'all-American', 'faith-based' society and 'religious liberty' for religionists—but denied to non-believers as 'infidels'—as conservative 'American exceptionalism' versus secular 'godless' Europe. By claiming 'American exceptionalism' in a 'faith-based' society or polity as superiority, conservative anti-secularists, religious extremists, and theocrats look like medieval-style and Islamic-like 'irrational fools'[16] who are

---

15   Gross et al. (2011, p. 343) observe that the US 'conservative movement, buoyed by its successes during the Reagan era, pressed forward with an agenda of [anti-secular] cultural change, which required that moral boundaries be drawn in relation to other groups; as conservatives pursued a deliberate effort to divide the secular and progressive wings of the Democratic coalition from more religious and traditional ones; and as the left haltingly responded to both efforts.'

16   This reverses Sen's (1977) expression 'rational fools' with reference to rational choice theory as the simplistic and by implication foolish 'economic approach to all human behavior' a la Becker's Chicago school that exports what is essentially undergraduate '101 economics' resting on the *deus ex machina* of utility maximization as a panacea to and a unifying paradigm for all social science, including sociology. And adherents of the rational choice theory

joyful and proud of what Western secularists are sad and ashamed—the 'godly' theocratic destruction or perversion of liberal-secular democracy.

Conservatism continues and expands Calvinist Puritanism's 'iron' intensity and 'unreasonable obstinacy' in anti-secularism, religious extremism, and the consequent design and system of proto-totalitarian Biblical theocracy (Bibliocracy in Weber's words) as what Jefferson repudiates as 'religious slavery' for non-Puritan and other 'infidels', ultimately for many Puritans and believers via their 'witch trials' and mass executions. Specifically, conservatism by its anti-secularism and religious extremism eliminates secular democracy and corresponding institutions by subverting the separation of church and state and the differentiation between religion and politics and flagrantly and unapologetically violating the constitutional prohibition of 'establishment of religion'. By so doing, it establishes and imposes Puritan-style and similar theocracy in America, at least its conservative-evangelical atavistic pole such as the 'Bible Belt' and beyond.

In other words, rightism, including the religious Right,[17] renders America fascist because of its intensely anti-secular, religiously extremist, and theocratic character Puritan-style perverting the separation of church and state, which it couches as 'faith-based' politics and 'religious liberty' that it monopolizes for believers, just as Puritans did it for themselves, and denies to others. In extension, the conservative pole of America mutates into a fascist entity because of its intense and obstinate anti-secular, religiously extremist, and theocratic essence that it inherits from the Puritan theocracy qua the 'Bible Commonwealth', which it consecrates as 'faith-based' society and by the illusion of 'religious liberty' that it monopolized for believers and denies to non-believers.

Furthermore, like the European original but even more since postwar times, derivative American conservatism by its inner logic escalates and intensities its anti-secularism to the extreme, particularly carrying its religious extremism to the maximum of a pathology such as (Hume's diagnosed) the

---

or economics of religion typically detest secularism or deny secularization and exalt religion/theocracy and thereby resemble religious/theocratic 'irrational fools.'

17   Recall Bourdieu's (1998, p. 50) diagnosis of US conservatism's 'atavistic faith in historical inevitability' and so 'fatalism'. Gross (2011, p. 326) identify the 'politics of Christian fundamentalism', which implies the radical Christian Right, in the US. They add that US conservatives were instrumental 'in bolstering conservative strains of Protestantism, yielding a major reconfiguration of American religion' (Gross et al. 2011, p. 326). Gross et al. (2011, p. 334) note that 'evangelical and fundamentalist Protestants became crucial to the right's success.'

Puritan-style 'madness with religious ecstasies' or 'insanity' (Pareto's diagnosis of Puritanism[18]) and theocracy. Thereby, religious rightism in post-2016 America produces fascism that is typically extreme anti-secularism and the antithesis of secular democracy by destroying the differentiation between religion and politics, religious extremism and madness, and theocracy as arch-fascism, holy 'fascism before fascism'. In consequence, the religiously rightist pole of America ultimately mutates into a fascist space by turning evermore anti-secular through perverting the separation of church and state, religiously extremist and insane in the sense of 'madness with religious ecstasies', and theocratic ruled by Biblical law as the Christian equivalent or precedent for Islamic Sharia law, as in the Southern 'Bible Belt' from Alabama to Texas. This mutation suggests that conservatism when escalates and intensities its anti-secularism to the extreme and carry its religious extremism to the pathological maximum of madness and theocracy, it generates fascism, as in post-2016 America, interwar Europe, postwar South America, post-socialist Poland, and beyond, including Turkey under Islamic rule. As a corollary, when intensifying into an extremely anti-secular and religiously extremist region via religious madness and theocracy, the conservative pole of America becomes a fascist geographic-social space, as during post-2016 and since the 1980s with Reaganism and the 2010s with the Tea Party.

Conceivably, like its inner authoritarianism, anti-liberalism and anti-democracy, conservatism's anti-secularism, however intense and unreasonably obstinate Puritan-style, if it remained static without 'dynamically' moving to the extreme, would not generate fascism in America, as perhaps before 2016 or the 1980s. Yet, such a conservative trait moves toward an anti-secularism extreme eventually and thereby reproduces fascism in America, as during post-2016 and since the 1980s and 2010s because of extremely anti-secular evangelical Reaganism and the religiously extremist Tea Party, respectively. Consequently, if petrified in anti-secularism without turning evermore anti-secular and perverting secular democracy, the conservative pole of America would not become fascist, as before 2016 or the 1980s and the 2010s. Actually, this American region turns ever more anti-secular, perverts secular democracy,

---

18   Wagner (1997, p. 136) finds a link between 'American electoral conservatism and the politics of Puritanism,' thus by implication Puritan moralistic proto-fascism or theocracy. Wagner (1997, p. 162) adds that 'skillfully using the symbols of home and family and wielding the 'apple pie of authoritarianism', the Right outmaneuvered leftists and liberals in the political process. [America's] conservative beliefs favor a politics based on fear of danger, crime, disease, and social politics over a politics of pleasure.'

and therefore forms a fascist space, as during post-2016 and since the 1980s due to Reaganism or the 2010s owing to the Tea Party.

In addition, like the European original, derivative American conservatism generates fascism by its compound of irrationalism, anti-rationalism, and anti-progressivism. Conservatism inherits and reproduces this compound from medievalism as its ideal, such as the medieval mixture of religious superstition, fanaticism, fantasies, and anti- or pre-science pervading its theocracy, thus embracing and perpetuating the superstitious and anti- or pre-scientific Dark Middle Ages. Like the European original but evermore since postwar times, American conservatism constitutes complete medieval-based irrationalism, anti-rationalism, and anti-progressivism that it exhibits and sanctifies as 'all-American' and 'faith-based', as another facet of conservative 'American exceptionalism' versus supposedly the overly rationalistic and so 'godless' Europe.

Specifically, growingly in relation to its European original, American conservatism forms a composite of medieval-rooted religious and other superstitions, fanaticism, and fantasies expressing extreme irrationalism. Relatedly, it represents a compound of anti-science, anti-education, especially hostility to higher education,[19] anti-art,[20] anti-theory antagonism, and anti-intellectualism reflecting anti-rationalism and anti-progressivism as 'American exceptionalism' versus scientific, artistic, theoretical, and intellectualist Europe. By claiming 'American exceptionalism' in unique 'faith-based' irrationalism, anti-rationalism, and anti-progressivism, particularly anti-science, anti-art, anti-theory, and anti-intellectualism as superiority, 'all-American' irrationalist, anti-rationalist, and anti-progressive conservatives appear as medieval-like 'irrational fools' who display joy and pride in what rationalists experience despair and shame. This is the reversal of the Enlightenment and its rationality, science, and progress and the return to the darkness, irrationality, and squalor of the Dark Middle Ages. Most parts, especially the small towns, of the 'Bible Belt' from Alabama to Texas look as the darkest, most irrational, and atavistic places in the Western world and beyond and in that sense as syndromes of the New Dark Ages, with Islamic theocracies only looking darker, albeit it is not

---

19   Broćić and Miles (2021, p. 856) register that from 2015 to 2019, the 'number of Republicans who believe higher education has a negative effect on the United States increased by 22 percent', adding that this 'uptick is recent, but conservative apprehension' toward higher education and to that extent science is constant. The fact that this US political party or conservatism seems to condemn higher education as the 'enemy' of America is hence consistent with fascism's condemnation of science.

20   Gross et al. (2011, p. 326) note that US conservatives play a major role 'in dramatically reducing funding for the arts, altering the American cultural scene' and the like.

clear if this is a consolation prize or incentive for this Weberian 'Bibliocracy' to surpass them in darkness, irrationality, and atavism. In short, American conservatism is a flat-earth society in the sense of utter irrationalism, anti-rationalism and anti-progressivism, notably religious superstition, anti-science, and antagonism to progress, as in the literal meaning of flat-earth beliefs.

In other words, rightism, specifically the religious right, makes America fascist due to being completely irrationalist, anti-rationalist, and anti-progressive, including anti-scientific and antagonistic to scientific progress, which it embellishes and consecrates an 'all-American' or 'faith-based' belief and action. In extension, due to being extremely irrationalist, anti-rationalist, and anti-progressive, such as superstitious, anti-scientific and antagonistic to scientific progress, simply a flat-earth society broadly understood, the conservative pole of America turns into a fascist entity couched in and sanctified as 'all-American' and 'godly' paradise.

Moreover, even more than the European original since postwar years, derivative American conservatism shows the tendency to elevate and expand its compound of irrationalism, anti-rationalism, and anti-progressivism to the extreme, such as its anti-science and antagonism to scientific progress to the maximum. Consequently, rightism in America reproduces fascism that is invariably a composite of extreme irrationalism, anti-rationalism, and anti-progressivism, including superstitions, anti-science, and antagonism to scientific progress, respectively. In extension, the conservative-rightist pole of America becomes fascist by becoming ever more irrationalist, anti-rationalist, and anti-progressive, including superstitious, anti-scientific, and antagonistic to scientific progress through staging perpetual 'monkey trials' as atavistic denials of and assaults on evolution and all science and theory deemed 'unbiblical', as in the 'Bible Belt' from Alabama and Tennessee to Texas. It follows that whenever conservatism, including religious rightism, elevates and expands its compound of irrationalism, anti-rationalism, and anti-progressivism, including superstitions, anti-science, and antagonism to scientific progress, to the extreme, it generates fascism, as in post-2016 America, along with a long lineage from interwar Europe to post-socialist Hungary, Poland and elsewhere, including Turkey under Islamic rule. In extension, the conservative/rightist pole of America mutates into a fascist entity at the point at which it turns extremely irrationalist, anti-rationalist, and anti-progressive, including superstitious, anti-scientific, and antagonistic to scientific progress, as during post-2016 and since Reaganism.

Conceivably, like its authoritarianism, anti-liberalism, anti-democracy, and anti-secularism, conservatism's compound of irrationalism, anti-rationalism, and anti-progressivism, even if deeply ingrained, persistent, and pervasive, could not generate fascism in America if it petrified with no movement to the extreme, as before 2016 or the 1980s. However, this conservative compound makes such movements to extreme irrationalism, anti-rationalism, and anti-progressivism ultimately and hence generates fascism in America, as during post-2016 and since the 1980s and 2010s because of anti-rationalist Reaganism and the irrationalist Tea Party, respectively. In consequence, the conservative pole of America would not become fascist if it petrified in irrationalism, anti-rationalism, and anti-progressivism without becoming steadily more irrationalist, anti-rationalist, and anti-progressive, including superstitious, anti-scientific, and antagonistic to scientific progress, as perhaps prior to 2016 or the 1980s and the 2010s. In reality, this region turns increasingly fascist by turning evermore irrationalist, anti-rationalist, and anti-progressive, including superstitious, anti-scientific, and hostile to scientific progress, as during post-2016 and since Reaganism and the Tea Party.

In conjunction with the previous, just as the European original in Europe, derivative American conservatism reproduces fascism in America by its composite of anti-egalitarianism, anti-universalism, and anti-cosmopolitanism, including anti-globalism, that it too adopts and perpetuates, with secondary modifications, from its ideal, medievalism, such as the medieval ancient regime of feudalism and aristocracy. Following the European original, aside from minor alterations, derivative American conservatism represents economic and social anti-egalitarianism, anti-universalism, and anti-cosmopolitanism, including anti-globalism, that it displays as 'all-American' patriotism or 'Americanism', as another facet of conservative 'American exceptionalism' versus egalitarian, universalist, and cosmopolitan/globalist, so 'unpatriotic' Europe.

Alternatively, American conservatism is an ideology and system of extreme economic and social inequality, rigid hierarchy, particularism, elitism, monopolistic closure, and exclusion within society and in relation to other societies. Specifically, like its European original but growingly since postwar times, American conservatism forms a compound of economic inequalities,[21] closure, deprivation, and exclusion, including extreme wealth concentration and

---

21   Piketty (2014, p. 35) notes that the 'growth of capital's share accelerated with the victories of Margaret Thatcher in England in 1979 and Ronald Reagan in the US in 1980, marking the beginning of a conservative revolution.' Babb and Kentikelenis (2021, p. 525) also recount the 'rise of the neoconservative governments of Margaret Thatcher and Ronald Reagan'. Torche and Rauf (2021, p. 380) remark that 'particularly after the election of Ronald Reagan in 1980, the Republican party increasingly welcomed the influence of corporate interests, advanced policies furthering the interests of large businesses, and promoted a market-oriented policy agenda including tax cuts, deregulation, a limited role for government, reduced social programs, and increased restrictions on organized labor.'

income inequality, severe material degradation, poverty and hardship, lack of basic economic-social protection, security, and welfare due to its hostility to and dismantling of the welfare state,[22] and so on. Additionally, American conservatism provides an exemplar of virulent nationalism, such as jingoism, primitive nativism, and paranoid xenophobia or anti-immigration hysteria,[23] including economic nationalism, protectionism, and irrationalism, all of which it couches in and rationalizes by hyper-patriotic and aggressive 'Americanism'.[24] Relatedly, American conservatism manifests strong syndromes and visible symbols of master-race and master-caste supremacist racism.

In sum, conservatism has always been and remains today as ever an 'all-American' anti-egalitarian, anti-universalist, and anti-cosmopolitan, just as anti-liberal, anti-democratic, anti-secular, and anti-rational, social pathology—the true 'curse' in the promised 'land of freedom' and equality. It seems impossible to overstate the extent to which American conservatism is an anti-egalitarian and anti-liberal social pathology—'morbidity' in Durkheim's sense—and hence the antithesis and nemesis of a society of 'equal' humans and 'liberty and justice for all'.

In other words, rightism ultimately makes America fascist because of being profoundly anti-egalitarian, anti-universalistic or exclusionary, and anti-cosmopolitan economically and socially, which it disguises in and justifies as 'all-American' hyper-patriotic features. Consequently, the conservative pole of America, including the former Southern confederacy that metastasizes beyond via contagion or Southernization of American society, mutates into a fascist subsociety due to being a fundamentally anti-egalitarian, anti-universalistic or exclusionary, and anti-cosmopolitan space embellished as a super-patriotic and 'godly' region.

Moreover, just as the European original but evermore after WW II, derivative American conservatism by its inner workings tends to intensify its inner anti-egalitarianism, anti-universalism, and anti-cosmopolitanism, including nationalism, nativism, xenophobia, and master-race racism, to the extreme.

---

22   Gross et al. (2011, p. 326) observe that US conservatives 'arguably played key roles in dismantling the New Deal–era welfare state; [plus] likely exacerbating social inequality' and so on.

23   Lipset (1996, p. 176) suggests that American conservatism produced 'various waves of xenophobia and of heightened nationalism (of which McCarthyism was the most recent)' and similar tendencies. Plotke (2002, pp. lvi) also includes 'anti-immigrant agitation on the right' into the sources of 'nondemocratic projects' in the US.

24   Lipset (1996, p. 176) notes that the 'political emphasis on loyalty to Americanism, the defining of deviants as 'un-American', and the sectarian stress on personal morality represents forms of behavior that are less prevalent in historically defined countries.'

As a corollary, American rightism ultimately causes fascism that is invariably a compound of these elements. In extension, the conservative-rightist pole of America eventually turns fascist by turning evermore anti-egalitarian, anti-universalistic or exclusionary, and anti-cosmopolitan or anti-globalist, including economically unequal, deprived, degraded, nationalist, nativist, xenophobic, and racist, especially the South and similar regions ruled by conservatism. This infers that whenever conservatism/rightism carries its inner anti-egalitarianism, anti-universalism, and anti-cosmopolitanism, including anti-globalism or nationalism,[25] to the maximum, it engenders fascism, as in post-2016 America and in a sequence from fascist Italy and Nazi Germany to neo-fascist or populist Hungary, Poland, Brexit Great Britain, and elsewhere. In extension, the conservative/rightist pole of America becomes fascist at the point at which it turns extremely anti-egalitarian, anti-universalistic, and anti-cosmopolitan, including anti-globalist, nationalist, nativist, and xenophobic, as in post-2016 and to some degree during Reaganism and the Tea Party.

Conceivably, conservatism's composite of anti-egalitarianism, anti-universalism, and anti-cosmopolitanism, including anti-globalism or nationalism and xenophobia, irrespective how tenacious and widespread, would not generate fascism in America if remaining petrified and not reaching the extreme, as prior to 2016 or the 1980s. Yet, this conservative composite reaches an extreme of anti-egalitarianism, anti-universalism, and anti-cosmopolitanism, including anti-globalism or nationalism, nativism, and xenophobia, and hence generates fascism in America, as in post-2016 and since the 1980s because of anti-egalitarian and nationalistic Reaganism and the early 2010s due to the anti-universalistic, nativist, and xenophobic Tea Party. In extension, the conservative, rightist pole of America would not turn fascist if petrifying in anti-egalitarianism, anti-universalism, and anti-cosmopolitanism, including nationalism, nativism, and xenophobia, instead of attaining their extreme, as before 2016 or the 1980s and the 2010s. In reality, this pole becomes extremely anti-universalistic, anti-egalitarian, and anti-cosmopolitan, including anti-globalist or nationalist, nativist, and xenophobic, and thus fascist, as in post-2016 and since Reaganism and the Tea Party.

---

25   Atkin, Colson-Sihra, and Shayo (2021, p. 1194) remark that 'both commentators and scholars have linked the effects of globalization, immigration, and rising inequality to a shift away from a now lower-status working class identity toward a nationalist one across both Europe and the United States. Such identity shifts have also been linked to changes in trade policies and opposition to globalization, with the political repercussions seen in Brexit, the resurgence of the far right in Europe, and Donald Trump's election victory.'

Fourth and related to all the previous, conservatism is latent proto-fascism and ultimately produces fascism in post-2016 America owing to its complex of absolute rule, power and domination, and intense coercion, repression, and terror, in conjunction with and an expression of conservative authoritarianism, anti-liberalism, and anti-democracy. In other words, rightism, including the religious right, is proto-fascist and tends to make America fascist because of being absolutist in social rule, power, and domination and severely coercive, repressive, and terrorist in interaction and mutual intensification. In consequence, the conservative pole of America is latently proto-fascist and ultimately becomes fascist due to being absolutist in social rule, power, and domination and intensely coercive, repressive, and violent versus non-conservatives and anti-fascists like liberals, secularists, rationalists, and progressives.

Conservatism is latent proto-fascism and eventually engenders fascism in post-2016 America owing to its quest, attainment, and exercise of absolute rule and power and encompassing control and domination by any available effective means, simply absolutism combined with Machiavellianism. Just as its European predecessor but growingly since postwar times, American conservatism constitutes an ideology and regime of absolute rule, total unconstrained and arbitrary power, and all-embracing control and domination. Specifically, American conservatism represents the design and realization of autocracy, dynasty, oligarchy, plutocracy, and other forms of dictatorship or authoritarian rule. This expresses, restates, and specifies conservatism's inherent, traditional authoritarianism rooted in and inspired by medievalism's ancient regime of feudal serfdom, aristocracy, and theocracy, as its perennial, although disguised, ideal of the 'good society' and social rule.

Conservatism is invariably the ideology and regime of absolutism combined with and reproduced by Machiavellianism's amoral technique of domination in the form of absolute autocratic, dynastic, oligarchic, and plutocratic rule of Machiavellian leaders resorting to any means, strategies, and tactics to attain the end of absolute power. Perhaps even more than the European original after WW II or since the 1980s, derivative American conservatism is the boundless and fanatical pursuit, acquisition, and possession of power, control, and domination without any constrains in the classic Machiavellian fashion that the end justifies the most reprehensible but efficient means. In short, American rightism has always been and remains absolutist and uninhibited Machiavelli-style in its pursuit, capture, and exertion of social power and domination. Accordingly, conservatism/rightism shapes the pole of America, such as the former Southern Confederacy and beyond, that it dominates after its model of absolutism and Machiavellianism, thus making this region, especially its rulers blindly followed by the base, absolutist and uninhibited a la Machiavelli in social power and domination.

As the ideology, movement, and regime of absolute power and domination, conservatism inexorably and ultimately, indeed 'logically' generates fascism defined by absolutism in post-2016 America and before, a process enfolding since the 2010s with the Tea Party, the 1980s with Reaganism, and earlier with McCarthyism, the anti-New Deal conservative reaction, the 'red scare', and the Ku Klux Klan. Aside from minor variations, American conservatism because of its absolutist tendency appears virtually indistinguishable from and blends with fascism in post-2016 America, as its European predecessor does by de-differentiating from and blending with Nazism in Germany. Due to acting as absolutist 'madmen' in power, apart from rare or diminishing exceptions of moderates, 'true' conservatives hardly distinguish themselves from fascists in post-2016 America, just as their equivalents in Nazi Germany were indistinguishable from Nazis.

Specifically, conservatism results in fascism in America when it consolidates, expands, and intensifies absolute, unconstrained power to the maximum, which is what it invariably and actually tends to do once capturing the state and establishing societal dominance, as in the conservative subsociety of America. By doing so, it effectively generates fascism that is always an extreme conservative ideology, movement, and regime of the capturing, wielding, and exercising of maximum unconstrained power and all-embracing control. In short, rightism becomes fascist when turning absolutist and thus extremist in terms of power and domination. As a consequence, the conservative-rightist subsociety of America, by turning evermore absolutist to the extreme in power, control, and domination over non-conservatives like liberals, as in the South and beyond, eventually mutates into a fascist social structure. Alternatively, conservatism ensues in fascism if/when being in vehement, including violent, opposition to its main defined enemy liberalism and thus liberal-democratic institutions, attempting to supplant it and subvert them by seizing and wielding absolute power by any means. This is what conservatism typically does when being outside state control by becoming ever more maximalist in this regard, as during postwar times, notably the 1960–70s, and eventually staging a reactionary revolt and counterrevolution, such as the Reagan Revolution, the Tea Party, the 2016 reaction, and the January 2021 insurrection.

Altogether, conservatism yields fascism in post-2016 and earlier America both when holding and consolidating and when being denied and excluded from power. Hence, rightism reproduces fascism through the logic of escalation of absolute power to the fascist maximum and the condition of deprivation from state power whose seizure is the prime and perpetual conservative end which justifies all efficient, even if the most reprehensible, means and tactics in the style of Machiavellianism. When wielding absolute and unconstrained power, conservatism resorts to its abuse via state coercion, repression, and terror and in that sense absolute corruption broadly understood. Conversely, when being denied and excluded from power, conservatism commits or enables counter-state violence and terrorism[26] against liberal-democratic institutions and actors. Therefore, it generates, perpetuates, or enables fascism in both power constellations—when in and outside of state power. This demonstrates the lethal danger that a conservative ideology and movement[27] poses for liberal democracy and society, by moving hand in hand with fascist and relatedly religious dictatorship.

Both by the possession and intensification of absolute power and through the experience of its denial and deprivation by liberalism, conservatism yields fascism, especially state and counter-state fascist terror. This suggests that conservatism is latent proto-fascism when both attaining and wielding absolute power and being denied and deprived from state control by liberalism and liberal-democratic institutions, thus acting as a double fascist generator when it rules absolutely or opposes violently liberal structures. As a corollary, whenever conservatism consolidates, expands, and intensifies absolute power, it generates fascism in America, as it does conversely when it is denied state control by liberalism and liberal democracy. On this account, 'true' conservatism both in and out of power produces genuine fascism 'made in America'—the truer conservative movement and ideology of absolutism, the more genuine fascist product. In other words, whenever rightism turns absolutist in power,

---

26   For illustration, in the wake of the January 06, 2021 insurrection and subsequent fascist or right-wing terrorist attacks, all 50 opposition-party conservatives in the US Senate blocked passing a law to address the growing problem of domestic terrorism fascism or the extreme-right and religious fundamentalism principally perpetrate in America. This inevitably raises the suspicion that these and other conservatives, aside from a few exceptions, are either secretly participating in the rise of fascism or enabling it and being complicit with it. It confirms that conservatism is a system of state repression and terror when in power or, when excluded from it, a movement of counter-state violence and terrorism against liberal democracy.

27   Gross et al. (2011, p. 330) recount that US conservatives 'were hostile to the expansion of the welfare state and advocated the restoration of an unrestricted 'free market'; they remain[ed] concerned with domestic subversion long after McCarthy had passed from the scene; [plus] generally opposed the civil rights agenda of the 1960s [etc.].' Gross et al. (2011, p. 342) add that the 'rise of the conservative movement is causally related to the emergence of several key inequality-producing mechanisms. the paradox of continued Republican success despite evidence that Democratic administrations are better economically for most Americans.'

it becomes fascist, as it does when it is outside state control or in opposition to liberal democracy. In extension, the stage at which the conservative-rightist pole of America mutates into a fascist subsociety is that when it grows ever-more absolutist in power and domination over non-conservatives and in opposition or offensive warfare, including ideological and culture wars,[28] against liberal America.

Conceivably, if remaining petrified and not evermore growing to the maximum, conservatism design and regime of absolute power, regardless of how ingrained, persistent, and pervasive, would not engender fascism in America and could remain within the confines of traditional conservative authoritarianism, as perhaps prior to 2016 or the 1980s. Arguably, in traditional conservative authoritarianism, absolute power would still 'corrupt absolutely' in the sense of being illiberal, undemocratic, oppressive, and predatory, but would not represent fascism in the strict sense so long as not every such power is fascist but also pre- and non-fascist.

In reality, American conservatism tends to evermore expand and intensify absolute power to the maximum and to that extent moves beyond traditional conservative authoritarianism into fascism as its totalitarian extreme and product. This illustrates and restates the argument that the differences between conservatism and fascism are equivalent to those between traditional conservative authoritarianism and right totalitarianism—different statistical-like degrees of unfreedom rather than a difference of substance. In a counterfactual scenario, the conservative pole of America would not become a fascist entity if petrified as absolutist in power and domination over non-conservatives but not attaining the maximum and in perpetual opposition, yet not offensive warfare, against liberal America. This pole would remain a petrified traditional conservative authoritarian space but not necessarily mutating into a totalitarian fascist entity, albeit the differences between the two remain as different degrees of unfreedom rather than of kind. Yet, this pole mutates into a fascist subsociety by growing evermore absolutist to the extreme in power and domination over liberals, as a defining property of fascism, and

---

28   Bourdieu and Haacke (1995, p. 50) suggest that the 'cultural *Kampfblatt* [war] of the neo-conservative movement is the New Criterion. Like Hitler, [US conservatives] know how to tap the *gesundes Volksempfinden*, the so-called healthy, uncorrupted sense of the people.' Moreover, a US conservative praised 'Adolf Hitler and how he aroused the crowds. And he would get up there screaming these epithets and these people were just—they were hypnotized by him [so] that's the kind of leader we need today.' (cited in Richards 2022). This confirms the suspicion that most or many 'true' US conservatives or rightists are secret lovers or admirers of Hitler and thus covert fascists until they expose themselves.

launching an offensive warfare against liberal America, as during post-2016 and with Reaganism and the Tea Party.

Fifth and relatedly, just as the European original but growingly during recent times, derivative American conservatism is latent proto-fascism and eventually engenders fascism in post-2016 America owing to its inherent and perpetual composite of systematic, expansive, and intensive coercion, repression, violence, and terror of society. Such systematic coercion, repression, violence, and terror operate in unison and implement directly intrinsic conservative authoritarianism, anti-liberalism, anti-democracy, anti-secularism, and absolutism and indirectly conservatism's anti-rationalism and anti-egalitarianism. In other words, rightism, including its religious variant, is proto-fascist and tends to render America fascist due to being systematically, extensively, and severely coercive, repressive, violent, and terrorist in unity. As a consequence, the conservative/rightist pole of America is latently proto-fascist and eventually mutates into a fascist subsociety because of having systematic coercive, repressive, violent, and terrorist properties, tendencies, and forces.

Conservatism invariably continues to constitute the ideology, movement, regime, and ambiance of encompassing and severe state coercion and repression of society, notably non-conservative groups, compounded with populist and other deception, disinformation, and manipulation of its base (the 'American people'). Moreover, aside from minor variations and rare exceptions, conservatism typically operates as the 'divine' design and system of intense and pervasive violence and terror, including state terror when seizing power and counter-state terrorism when excluded from state control and in vehement opposition and aggressive warfare, such as ideological, political and culture wars, against liberal-democratic institutions and representatives. In short, rightism has always been, remains, and even grows ever more severely coercive, repressive, violent, and terrorist, including state and counter-state terror depending on whether it is in or outside of power, respectively. Consequently, the conservative pole of America ranging from the South to its equivalents beyond harbors and displays predominant, profound, and persistent coercive, repressive, violent, and terrorist features and structures. Particularly, the last feature assumes the form of state terror by ruling conservatives and their fascist allies[29] within the extended 'all-American' family of authoritarian rightism replicating that in fascist Europe, such as Nazi Germany.

---

29   Paxton (1998, p. 22) suggests that 'new functional equivalents of fascism' such as an 'authentically popular fascism in the United States' as well as Western Europe and elsewhere are likely to succeed only insofar as the 'potential conservative elite allies ready to try to coopt them', including the 'protofascists of the last fin de siècle.' For instance,

By its inner logic of escalation and intensification, conservatism tends to magnify and amplify its built-in composite of systematic and intense coercion, repression, violence, and terror of society to the extreme. By so doing, it generates and indeed becomes fascism that is axiomatically the system of extreme coercion, repression, violence, and terror. Consequently, the conservative pole of America becomes a fascist entity precisely by having prevalent coercive, repressive, violent, and state-terrorist features, tendencies, and forces. This suggests that rightism generates fascism whenever it magnifies and intensifies its intrinsic coercion, repression, violence, and terror to the maximum, as during post-2016 or since the 1980s and in the sections that it dominates, such as the South and beyond. Consequently, the conservative pole of America at the point at which it turns extremely coercive, repressive, violent, and state terrorist, it effectively mutates into a fascist subsociety.

Counterfactually, conservatism, if it just continued its typical coercion, repression, violence, and terror rather than magnified and amplified them to the extreme, probably would not generate fascism in America, as prior to post-2016 and the 1980s. In this hypothetical situation, it would reproduce traditional conservative authoritarianism which coercion, repression, violence, and terror typify but not fascism that their extremes define. Therefore, this difference between traditional conservative authoritarianism and fascist totalitarianism as its maximum corresponds to that between conservatism and fascism, and essentially pertains to different degrees of coercion, repression, violence, and terror, simply unfreedom, rather than differences of substance. Yet, conservatism tends to magnify and amplify its typical coercion, repression, violence, and terror to the extreme and thus generates fascism rather than reproducing the old conservative authoritarianism that falls short of such a maximum. In extension, if remaining traditionally, instead of turning evermore, coercive, repressive, violent, and state terrorist, the conservative pole of America would not mutate into a fascist subsociety. Under such a static supposition, this pole would consequently remain a petrified traditional conservative authoritarian entity rather than mutating into the fascist subsociety. In reality, this conservative pole becomes ever more coercive, repressive, violent, and state terrorist to the maximum and so turns fascist, as in the South and related regions since the 1980s, during the 2010s, post-2016, and after the 2020 elections by the 2021 insurrection and the suppression of political and civil liberties (e.g., voting and reproductive rights from Alabama, Florida, and Georgia to Texas).

Paxton (1998, p. 22) notes that the 'skinheads are functional equivalents of Hitler's SA and Mussolini's *squadristi* only if important elements of the conservative elite begin to cultivate them as weapons against some internal enemy, such as immigrants.'

Taken together, if its degree of coercion, repression, violence, and terror remained constant rather than ever-growing, conservatism conditionally would only generate ancient authoritarianism and not fascism, and the conservative pole of America would petrify as a traditional conservative authoritarian region and not become a fascist subsociety. Actually, conservatism generates fascism in America and its conservative pole becomes fascist because the degree of coercion, repression, violence, and terror does not remain constant at the level of conservative authoritarianism but magnifies and amplifies to the extreme since the 1980s through the 2020s. And this extreme essentially represents fascism and a fascist pole of America.

In addition, like the European original but surpassing it since postwar times, derivative American conservatism is latent proto-fascism and ultimately reproduces fascism in post-2016 America owing to its strong anti-pacifism, militarism, offensive war, and conquest. In other words, rightism, especially its radical and religious element, is proto-fascist and moves to make America fascist because of being strongly anti-pacifist, militarist, warlike, and imperialist. In consequence, the conservative-rightist pole of America is latently proto-fascist and ultimately becomes fascist due to having strong anti-pacifist, militarist, warlike, and imperialist tendencies.

Conservatism is latent proto-fascism and tends to produce and sustain fascism in post-2016 America and elsewhere because of its composite of strong anti-pacifism, militarism, aggressive war, and imperial conquest and subjugation. Like the European original but exceeding it since postwar times, American conservatism epitomizes an ideology, movement, system, and zeitgeist of anti-pacifism and militarism both within society and in relation to other societies, a property that, like all its properties, it inherits from medievalism, such as feudalism and its military aristocracy, and perpetuates, expands, and intensifies. Specifically, conservatism invariably engages in rearmament a la militaristic Reaganism, arms races, and continuing preparation for offensive wars through large and indeed virtually unlimited military expenditure, militarist, economic, political, cultural, or ideological-religious mobilization, and a large standing army. In short, it creates and sustains a Leviathan-like ever-growing military-industrial complex.

Furthermore, conservatism is prone to launch aggressive wars[30] against, undertake imperial conquest, and perpetrate subjugation of, other societies, and thus to establish a state of permanent war qua 'peace' in its Orwellian

---

30   Gross et al. (2011, p. 326) observe that US conservatives are especially instrumental 'in pursuing geopolitical strategies of containment that thrust the nation into war.'

discourse, as the effective instrument of imperialism or global military dominance. Ultimately, by its militarism and eternal war, it causes or raises the
prospect of mass death, destruction, and ultimately self-destruction after the
image of MAD through the 'preemptive' offensive use of nuclear and other
weapons of mass destruction. Evoking apocalyptic medievalism, conservatism
amounts to the 'divine' design and ritual of 'a delirium of annihilation' as the
supposed path to 'salvation' or 'election' in the style of Calvinist Puritanism
and its proto-totalitarian theocracy as the conservative ideal, Reagan's 'shining
city upon the hill'. Because it considers the 'delirium' of self-annihilation as
the sole means of 'salvation', conservatism is a vision and indeed causation
of apocalypse and an act of collective suicide via the 'Armageddon' of catastrophic war between (conservative) 'good' and (liberal) 'evil', the 'second
coming,' and heavenly 'rapture' in the manner of fundamentalist suicidal cults
and sects. In short, rightism is vehemently anti-pacifist, militarist, warlike, and
imperialist, thus eventually destructive and self-destructive or collectively suicidal. Consequently, the conservative pole of America acquires and cultivates
anti-pacifist, militarist, warlike, and imperialist, and ultimately destructive,
mass suicidal tendencies.

Furthermore, conservatism by its inner workings typically expands and
intensifies its composite of anti-pacifism and militarism within society and
wars of aggression and imperial conquest versus other societies to the extreme,
which the ever-expanding military-industrial complex and eternal war demonstrate, as in post-2016 and since Reaganism and the 1950s. Therefore, during
post-2016 and earlier, it effectively reproduces or enables fascism that is precisely the complex of extreme anti-pacifism and militarism within society and
offensive war and imperial conquest in relation to other societies. In particular,
religious rightism turns evermore intensely anti pacifist and militarist within
America and warlike and imperialist against other countries, destructive and
self-destructive, causing the pole that it dominates to turn into a fascist entity.
In consequence, the conservative pole of America shows extreme anti-pacifist,
militarist, warlike, and imperialist, eventually destructive and mass suicidal,
tendencies within itself and in relation to other societies and against liberal
America—indeed, becomes the Western and global anti-pacifist, militarist,
warlike, and imperialist leader—and thus eventually turns fascist.

The preceding yields the inference that American conservatism produces
fascism whenever it intensifies to the extreme its anti-pacifism and militarism
within America and wars of aggression and imperial conquest and subjection
versus other states through the ever-growing military-industrial complex and
eternal war, as in post-2016 (with some qualification for Hitler's style postponement of offensive wars) and Reaganism. Therefore, the conservative pole of

America mutates into a fascist space at the point at which it displays extreme anti-pacifist, militarist, warlike, and imperialist, so destructive and mass suicidal, features within itself and in relation to other societies, as well as versus liberal America which conservatives increasingly threaten with 'civil war'.

In a counterfactual situation, if it maintained its anti-pacifism and militarism at a fixed level rather than expanding and intensifying them, conservatism would not generate fascism. Instead, it would reproduce traditional militarist conservative authoritarianism—albeit the difference between the two systems is in quantitative degrees of unfreedom rather than substance— as before post-2016 and Reaganism. In reality, conservatism expands and intensifies its anti-pacifism and militarism to the extreme and results in fascism, as during post-2016 and Reaganism. In extension, if remaining static in its anti-pacifist, militarist, warlike, and imperialist features, the conservative pole of America would not mutate into a fascist subsociety but remain petrified as a traditional militarist conservative authoritarian entity, as prior to post-2016 and Reaganism. Yet, this pole, including but not limited to the South, exhibits evermore intense anti-pacifist, militarist, warlike, nationalist, and imperialist, destructive, and mass suicidal, tendencies and to that extent tends to mutate into a fascist subsociety.

Finally, conservatism is latent proto-fascism and eventually generates fascism in post-2016 America and beyond because of forming a socio-psychological configuration of authoritarian agents. American conservatism since proto-totalitarian Puritanism as its root/inspiration forms a compilation of authoritarian personalities in socio-psychological terms, including conservative leaders and the rank-and-file. In other words, rightism, including the religious right, is socio-psychologically an aggregation of authoritarians, including rightist leadership and its base. In consequence, the conservative, rightist pole of America becomes the macroscopic composition and interaction of authoritarians among leaders and blindly obedient followers. Hence, in socio-psychological terms, conservatism is due to its dominant authoritarians proto-fascism, a kind of fascism before fascism and the right and the conservative-rightist pole of America proto-fascist, thus most conservatives, just like Puritans, being or acting as fascists before fascists.

Specifically, conservatism is an admixture of sadism and masochism in socio-psychological or psychoanalytical terms, so that conservatives enjoy their sadistic treatment of non-conservatives ('owning liberals') while masochistically enjoying their being treated in an equivalent manner by conservative or fascist leaders post-2016. In other words, socio-psychologically or psychiatrically, rightism, especially the radical and religious right, is a summation of sadistic-masochistic characters. As a consequence, the conservative pole of

America forms a societal space of mostly sadistic-masochistic characters in socio-psychological or psychoanalytical terms. This pole becomes the lethal poison of a 'sane', healthy society and a macroscopic (Pareto) 'cage for the insane', including pervasive gun ownership without parallel in the Western and entire world, perpetual massacres by guns, mass imprisonment for drugs and other moral sins, and executions often of innocent persons[31] as Draconian forms of punishment.[32]

In addition, conservatism usually involves an admixture of morbid seriousness and utter grotesqueness and ludicrousness, including sheer buffoonery and clown-style demeanors, among its leaders and rank-and-file alike. Rightism, especially the radical and religious right, contains a blend of deadly serious and utterly grotesque, morbid, and buffoon- and clown-like leaders and followers. Consequently, the conservative pole of America forms a mix of morbid seriousness and utter grotesqueness, an aggregation of morbid and buffoonish leaders and followers—both the morbidly serious leader and the 'comic relief' of the Western world and beyond. Thereby, by the deadly seriousness, violence, and cruelty of its conservative-fascist rulers, this pole perverts America into an 'American tragedy' and by their grotesqueness, buffoonery, and clownery into the world's 'laughingstock'.

Furthermore, conservatism typically creates or embraces a cult of autocratic and other leaders by the conservative rank-and-file. In addition, it combines this tendency with producing or sustaining various delusions, fantasies,

---

31 For example, Clark (2022) laments about the conservative-dominated US Supreme Court's 'absurd inhumanity: To preserve procedure, an innocent man must die.' Clark (2022) refers to an 'opinion, both cruel and absurd, issued by the Republican supermajority [that] is likely to result in the execution of an innocent man. For the wrongfully convicted, it sets a precedent that shatters the hope that they can get new evidence of innocence examined by a federal court.' Clark (2022) adds that this is 'not because the court has weighed the evidence for and against guilt and come to the conclusion that the man is guilty. The court is pushing to execute him because it says the evidence showing he is innocent should not be considered at all.' This demonstrates the devaluation of human life by and the cruelty, insanity, and perversity of the conservative Supreme Court and conservatism and extremist religion overall in America.

32 King, Massoglia, and Uggen (2012, pp. 1788–1800) find that US 'conservatism and Republican Party strength [are] robust determinants of punitive policies and practices [i.e.] a positive association between political conservatism and punishment' in America. Even some apologetic US economists taking the conservative 'war on crime' at its face value—rather than a religion-driven crusade (or Islamic-like jihad) that Puritanical Reaganism launched on moral sins like alcohol and drug use—admit that the 'United States now spends $80 billion a year to incarcerate more individuals per capita than any other Organization for Economic Cooperation and Development country' (Rose and Shem-Tov 2021, p. 3302).

and fictions and moving toward the no-return point of collective suicide, as its religious sects and cults show. In that sense, conservatism or its political party becomes the death cult, as during the Covid-19 pandemic, by widespread deaths of conservatives denying the epidemic and refusing wearing masks, vaccinations, and other rational preventive measures, with fatal consequences for conservative-fascist leaders and especially their base.[33] The radical and religious right has always been and remains a cult-like and delusionary, fantasy-driven, or fiction-believing and suicidal movement, ideology, regime, and ambiance. Further, it subordinates and eventually sacrifices its rank-and-file to its leaders, which apparently makes it the death cult, as with conservatives massively dying during the Covid-19 pandemic because of denying the epidemic and refusing vaccines, while their leaders urging Americans to sacrifice their lives as less important to save capitalism via collective suicide.[34] In

33   Newhouse (2021, p. 102) observes that during the COVID-19 pandemic preventive behavior 'is not surprising when there is no immunity against a pathogen that is rather easily transmissible and potentially fatal', but apparently many US conservatives-fascists choose, at least for their base, fatality and so mass death rather than rational prevention. Related, Miller et al. (2021, p. 1787) report 'new evidence that expanded Medicaid coverage reduces mortality rates among [US] low-income adults. If we assume that similarly sized mortality reductions would have occurred in the [conservative-religious] nonexpansion states, our estimates suggest that approximately 15,600 deaths could have been averted if the ACA expansions were adopted nationwide as originally intended by the ACA. This highlights an ongoing cost to nonadoption that is relevant to both [conservative-religious] state policy makers and their constituents.' To that extent, this implies that conservative-religious states such as those in the South and elsewhere suffer preventable, or their state policy makers inflict their constituents with, 15,600 deaths (forcing them figuratively to drink Kool-Aid) by choice such as ideological extremism/fanaticism and irrational political opposition to ACA and the broader welfare state. In brief, these states appear as death cults and their rulers as death-cult leaders in this sense, just as in respect of preventable Covid-19 deaths.

34   Williams (2021, p. 192) recounts that during the Covid-19 pandemic Texas ultra-conservative 'Lt. Governor made the trade-off [between life and work] explicit when he told us to 'go back to work' because 'there are more important things than living.' He had in mind protecting the American economy' This implies telling Texans to commit collective suicide to save capitalism, although the question arises what would remain of the latter if Americans agreed that it [and the nation] was more important than 'living'—which is what Hitler and Goebbels did or would tell Germans—and acted accordingly. Yet, such is the self-destructiveness and irrationalism of American conservatism-fascism that ends in its leaders and base drinking poison Hitler-Goebbels style or 'Kool-Aid' Jamestown cult-like, as precisely witnessed during the Covid-19 pandemic when many US conservatives-fascists died as if by choice because of their conspiracy theories and delusions about this health crisis and its mitigation by masks and vaccines. Further, ultra-conservative Southern states like Alabama reportedly redirected large amounts ($400 million) of the Covid-19 pandemic relief Federal aid for financing the construction of new prisons, which

consequence, the conservative pole of America forms a mass cult of autocratic and other leaders adulated by the base and a compound of delusions and fantasies ending in the specter of collective suicide in the manner of its religious cults and sects, thus being the space of a death cult, as during the Covid-19 pandemic[35]—Puritan-style 'salvation' through the 'delirium of annihilation' in a 'cage for the insane'.

Moreover, by its inner logic of amplification and magnification, conservatism amplifies and magnifies its configuration of authoritarians, including sadistic-masochistic characters, to the extreme. In so doing, rightism generates fascism that is, in its socio-psychological definition, precisely an aggregate of extreme authoritarians, particularly sadistic-masochistic characters. In consequence, the conservative pole of America comprises evermore authoritarians and sadists-masochists and displays mass delusions and fictions, mutating into a fascist entity.

In addition, conservatism expands and intensifies to the extreme the mixture of grave seriousness or menacing conduct and utter grotesqueness or buffoonery and clown-like demeanor among its rulers and rank-and-file, who act as and resemble fascist leaders such as Mussolini's buffoonery and Hitler's clown-style demeanor. Consequently, the conservative pole of America becomes a conglomerate of deadly serious/menacing and buffoon-like/clown-style leaders and followers, acting as fascist rulers ruling interwar Italy and Germany.

Furthermore, conservatism tends to amplify and magnify to the extreme the cult of autocratic and other leaders by the conservative rank-and-file, as well as concomitant delusions, fantasies, and fictions to the point of collective suicide typifying death cults. Therefore, it engenders fascism that precisely involves the cult of autocratic leaders by the fascist rank-and-file, in combination with corresponding delusions, fantasies, and fictions ending in collective suicide in the manner of a death cult. In extension, the conservative half of America expands and reinforces the cult of the autocratic leader by the conservative-fascist base and the concomitant death cult through collective suicide (a la 'rapture' and drinking Kool-Aid) to the limit, and thus mutates into a fascist

---

confirms the tendency of American conservatism/fascism to first build and then populate them with prisoners through mass imprisonment for sins-as-crimes, including of innocent people, thus resembling Nazism's building of concentration camps.

35 Acemoglu et al. (2022, p. 1234) warn that 'as the responses to the COVID-19 pandemic in Brazil, India, Turkey, and the United States under Donald Trump illustrate, [right-wing populist] movements are also having first-order [negative] effects on critical economic and social policies.'

space resembling, even if not fully replicating, Mussolini's Italy and Hitler's Germany.

Conceivably, if keeping constant rather than amplifying and magnifying its configuration of authoritarians, including sadistic-masochistic characters, conservatism would not generate fascism in America but only perpetuate traditional conservative authoritarianism, as perhaps prior to 2016 and the 1980s. The same holds true for the mix of grave seriousness and utter grotesqueness, as well as the cult of the leader by the conservative rank-and-file and the resulting death cult via collective suicide. Yet, conservatism extends and reinforces to the maximum the compound of authoritarians and sadists-masochists, grave seriousness and utter grotesqueness, the cult of the leader by the base, and the death cult through collective suicide, and thereby generates fascism, as in post-2016 and during Reaganism and the Tea Party. In consequence, the conservative pole of America would not mutate into a fascist space if it kept stable and did not expand and reinforce the mix of authoritarian, sadistic-masochistic persons, deadly serious/menacing and buffoon-like/clown-style leaders and followers, the cult of the leader by the base, and the death cult through collective suicide. Yet, this region ultimately expands and reinforce to the extreme such a mix of its prevalent actors and mutates into a fascist entity, as in post-2016 and during Reaganism and the Tea Party.

In sum, conservatism by its complex of inherent properties and ultimate outcomes primarily generates—and thus probably predicts for the future—fascism in America post-2016 and to some degree before, as at least since the 1980s. On this account, it operates as the primary social, especially ideological and political, cause and thus predictor of fascism in post-2016 America, as it does in all other societal settings since interwar Italy, Spain, Germany, and Europe through postwar Latin America to post-socialist Hungary, Poland and other parts of Eastern Europe, Brexit[36] Great Britain, present Brazil, Islamic-ruled Turkey, and beyond.

In short, rather than showing supposed 'American exceptionalism' in superior 'freedom', it proves that conservatism is the prime, universal ideological and political determinant and producer of fascism. It demonstrates that conservatism is the invariant condition of fascism—whenever the first develops and expands, the second ultimately, with some minor variations and

---

36   Head and Mayer (2021, p. 24) comment that the nationalist or 'sovereignty concerns voiced by Brexit advocates show that Feldstein [US conservative-nationalist anti-European Union economist rationalizing plutocratic Reaganism] was far from alone in viewing greater political centralization as anathema'.

temporary delays, erupts and prevails. It confirms that without conservatism, fascism never arises or prevails, ceteris paribus, although the fascist monster may supplant or escape control of its conservative creator, as Nazism did and neo-fascism in Europe and America does. Hence, it is impossible to understand and explain why and how fascism rises in America post-2016 without considering 'all-American' conservatism as its primary cause—'no conservatism, no fascism' in the 'land of freedom', all else being equal. This holds true especially because, more than even the European original, 'all-American' derivative conservatism is extraordinarily adept and successful via the systematic deception and delusion of ersatz 'freedom' and bogus 'democracy' in obscuring and hiding its 'fatal attraction' or 'elective affinity' with and consequent causation and reproduction of, as well as alliance and merger with, fascism in America post-2016 and perhaps since Reaganism. Despite its unparalleled duplicity, adeptness, and deception of most people in conservative America, even conservatism evidently is no longer able to obfuscate and embellish by the 'freedom' rhetoric its strong, inexorable, and universal fascist causal outcomes, as the preceding shows.

3   Capitalism as the Cause of Fascism

Capitalism can and does associate not only, as according to spurious 'libertarianism' such as Chicago and related economics, with political liberalism and thus democracy turned 'capitalist democracy'. It also, especially when unrestrained, coercive, and inegalitarian, links, allies, and merges with fascism and anti- or non-democracy overall in America, as during post-2016, as well as to some extent since the early 2010s with the Tea Party, the 1980s with Reaganism, and before, such as the Gilded Age and the 1920–30s before the New Deal.

If conservatism or rightism is the primary ideological-political causal force of fascism in America post-2016 and to some degree before, American capitalism is its main economic cause and driving force. Furthermore, capitalism causes or sustains fascism in America post-2016 and earlier typically in interconnection and mutual reinforcement with conservatism as its foremost ideological-political justification and strong ally, forming a capitalist-conservative alliance and fusion versus non-capitalists and non-conservatives, such as labor and liberals, as it does in other social settings and times since fascist Italy and Spain, Nazi Germany, and interwar Europe. Specifically, this fascist conditioning in America holds true for prevalent American unrestrained, coercive, and inegalitarian or anti-welfare and to that extent proxy laissez-faire capitalism. The latter differs from 'rationally regulated',[37] non-coercive, and egalitarian or welfare capitalism as a secondary alternative that exponents of unfettered capitalism and conservatives deceptively brand as 'un-American', 'big government', and 'socialism', and inculcate their delusions and deceptions in most Americans subjected to intense capitalist and conservative indoctrination and propaganda.[38]

Such a prevailing 'all-American' and 'superior' model of unregulated, repressive, and inegalitarian capitalism tends to reproduce or support fascism in post-2016 and to some extent earlier America in definite ways and means specified next. First, capitalism in its unrestrained, coercive, and anti-egalitarian version generates or sustains fascism in America directly and manifestly, as it does in other social spaces and times since fascist Italy/Spain and Nazi Germany, with minor variations and few exceptions. Capitalism's conditioning of fascism operates through the conjunction of extreme concentration and ultimately monopolization of power and wealth in the capitalist class and severe coercion, repression, and persecution of non-capitalist social strata, such as labor and its collective organization and action like unionization. Extreme concentration of power and wealth by the capitalist class in the economy is perfectly consistent with the absolute rule, control, and domination of fascist[39] and conservative leadership in the polity and society. In addition, economic coercion and inequality in capitalism are generally compatible with political repression and dictatorship in fascism[40] and other rightist authoritarian regimes. In turn, severe coercion, repression, and persecution of organized labor, such as unions and its members, are shared activities of American and other unrestrained, coercive capitalism and of fascism, including Nazism, which make the two appear virtually identical and indistinguishable, or at least similar.

Altogether, unrestrained, coercive, and anti-egalitarian capitalism generates and sustains fascism in America through its dictatorial form, namely capitalist

---

37 Economist Cassel (1928) proposes 'a rationally regulated social economy' as an alternative to repressive, self-destructive laissez-faire capitalism and thus by implication to capitalist dictatorship.

38 Myrdal (1953, p. 205) classically observes that 'next to (communist) Russia and (fascist) Italy, the United Stated of America practices most consciously political indoctrination (as) the young grow up with more uniform and standardized convictions and attitudes. At the same time adult opinion is also worked upon (through) the refinement of propaganda'.

39 McMurtry (1999, p. 255) laments that the global capitalist market is 'a market of fascisms of all kinds. "Succeed or perish in the brutal global competition" is not far off *Mein Kampf's*, "humanity as a whole must flourish. Only the weak and cowardly will perish."'

40 Piketty (2014, p. 35) surmises the 'Fascists would naturally have been attracted to Pareto's theory of stable inequality [in capitalism] and the pointlessness of trying to change it.'

dictatorship, as it does in all other examples from fascist Italy/Spain and Nazi Germany through neo-fascist South America (Chile, etc.) to present Hungary, Poland and other parts of Eastern Europe embracing a repressive, oligarchic American-style capitalist model, Brexit and Thatcher[41] Great Britain, and others. What essentially defines and typifies 'all-American' and other dictatorial or repressive qua 'unfettered' capitalism is precisely the combination of extreme concentration of power and wealth in the capitalist class and severe coercion, repression, and persecution of labor and unions and other non-capitalist social strata and associations. Since the first component is consistent with fascists' absolute power and the second is common to coercive capitalism and fascism, a dictatorial capitalist system generates or becomes a fascist regime in America post-2016 and to some extent before, as elsewhere else since interwar Italy and Germany.

In a way, American and other dictatorial capitalism does and can only develop and function as an extreme conservative, radical-right authoritarian regime and hence ultimately as fascism in ideological-political terms. Alternatively, such a model of capitalism opposes and distorts comprehensive economic liberalism in the modern Keynesian New-Deal sense—versus narrow and specious laisses-faire 'neo-liberalism'—and a liberal-democratic system expressing social liberalism as the principle and institution of universal liberty as opposite to false economic 'libertarianism'.[42] In short, capitalist dictatorship in America and elsewhere politically can persist mainly through fascism or rightist authoritarianism, as well as relatedly extremist religion and theocracy. Conversely, an extreme conservative, radical-right authoritarian regime, thus fascism in America post-2016 does and can solely arise and operate in economic terms as dictatorial capitalism rather than as economic liberalism (or 'socialism'), as it does elsewhere from interwar Italy and Germany to Hungary, Poland, and other parts of Eastern Europe under capitalist oligarchy. Simply, fascism, as well as extremist religion and theocracy, in America and beyond can economically function and subsist mostly through capitalist dictatorship.

---

41   Hodgson (1999, p. 82) observes that 'governments committed to market individualist ideas have often taken an authoritarian tone, such as in Britain in the 1980s under the premiership of Margaret Thatcher.'

42   Hodgson (1999, p. 91) suggests that the spurious libertarian 'ideology of market individualism [of Mises, Hayek] has been stubbornly resistant to a genuine economic pluralism' and to that extent approximates economic fascism so long as what defines the latter is anti-pluralism or monism.

Since the Gilded Age through Reaganism and the Tea Party and post-2016 typically American capitalism is primarily 'unfettered', coercive, and anti-egalitarian rather than or just secondarily being a rationally regulated, non-coercive or democratic, and egalitarian or welfare capitalist system. Overall, rational government and societal regulation replaced with absurd 'self-regulation'[43] a la laisser-faire, non-coercion, or economic-industrial democracy, and relative wealth and income equality, or shared welfare in the broad sense of social wellbeing are typically taboos and non-entities on dogmatic laissez-faire grounds in American capitalism since the Gilded Age through Reaganism to post-2016, aside from New-Deal and related exceptions.

American capitalism usually features the combination of extreme concentration and monopolization of power and wealth in the capitalist class and intense coercion, repression, and persecution of non-capitalist social strata like labor collective organization and action through unionization,[44] with secondary and transient variations especially during the short New Deal period and its aftermath. To that extent, such system mostly constitutes or approximates dictatorial, authoritarian capitalism or capitalist dictatorship which this combination defines and typifies. In its core, primarily dictatorial American capitalism represents proto-fascism, latent fascism before fascism in economic terms, as the capitalist Gilded Age and its proxy replica since Reaganism show, just as inherently authoritarian conservatism does in political respect.

In general, laissez-faire unregulated, compulsory, and inegalitarian capitalism is essentially proto-fascism in economic terms and consequently generates and sustains fascism. American Gilded-Age 'unfettered' capitalism is essentially proto-fascism in the economy and beyond. This holds true in the form of what observers (e.g., Mitchell, Roosevelt) diagnose and deplore as 'economic oppression', 'industrial despotism' through the 'despotic might of capital', the 'tyranny of a plutocracy', 'exploitation' of the 'weak,' prohibition of 'industrial democracy', as well as alcohol by Puritanical Prohibition, the 'physical and moral degradation of the lower classes', all forming 'socially irrational, anti-economic' phenomena of American 'capitalism'.[45] On this account,

---

43   Stiglitz (2010, p. 331) maintains that the laisser-faire 'whole theory of self-regulation [is] absurd.'

44   Gross et al. (2011, p. 326) state that US conservatives are key political forces 'in scaling back the unionization of American workers.'

45   Elaborating on and applying Wieser's (1967, p. 406) concept of 'capitalistic despotism', early US institutionalist Mitchell (1917, p. 108) observe that there is the 'despotic might of capital' in American capitalism and urges that the 'state must protect the weak against exploitation [and] prevent economic freedom from breeding economic oppression [or] industrial despotism' as the antithesis of 'industrial democracy'. Relatedly, Mitchell (1917,

Gilded-Age 'unfettered' capitalism develops and operates as capitalist dictatorship or dictatorial capitalism, which is essentially economic proto-fascism or broader authoritarianism in the sense of 'economic oppression' or 'industrial despotism'. Such an 'all-American' model of capitalism prefigures and paves the way for fascism that is in economic terms typically, with minor variations, capitalist, 'economic-corporate'[46] dictatorship or dictatorial capitalism through pro-capital labor oppression, including suppression of unions and persecutions of their members in the Italian-fascist and Nazi-style emulating the anti-union 'brute force' and the law of the 'jungle'[47] of the Gilded Age.

Conversely, capitalist dictatorship or dictatorial capitalism from the Gilded Age through interwar Europe to Reaganism and post-2016 typically, with secondary variations, links, allies, and eventually fuses with fascism and more broadly rightist authoritarianism as a political ideology and regime, as with theocracy in a 'holy' alliance. Moreover, capitalist dictatorship or dictatorial capitalism in America and beyond can emerge and endure in long terms only or mainly through fascism and generally rightist authoritarianism, along with theocracy, as it does since fascist Italy and Spain and Nazi Germany. While capitalist, as well pre-capitalist, dictatorships and elites may not last indefinitely (as in Pareto's account), they are likely to endure longer through fascism and more broadly other rightist authoritarianism, as well as via theocracy.

Consequently, American capitalism by its inner logic tends to become, if left to its mechanisms, evermore 'unfettered,' coercive, and anti-egalitarian and to that extent dictatorial or authoritarian, thus becoming capitalist dictatorship or authoritarianism, as in post-2016 and during Reaganism. In other words, such capitalism moves toward reproducing ever-greater concentration and indeed monopolization of wealth, income, and power in the capitalist class,

---

p. 107) classifies 'profits obtained from the sheer financial control over markets without the exercise of social leadership, the creation of a laboring proletariat, [and] the physical and moral degradation of the lower classes [into] socially irrational, anti-economic [phenomena of American] capitalism'. US President Theodore Roosevelt, as well-known, warns that 'of all forms of tyranny the least attractive and the most vulgar is the tyranny of mere wealth, the tyranny of a plutocracy'.

46   Riley (2005, p. 288) uses the term 'economic-corporate' and thus by implication capitalist dictatorships for fascist Italy and Spain.

47   Kimeldorf (2013, p. 1035) reports that in the US 'around the turn of the [20th] century industrial conflicts were routinely decided by brute force, pitting desperate strikers against equally determined employers backed, in most cases, by the courts, police, and newspapers.' Kimeldorf (2013, p. 1055) infers that in the Gilded Age US pre-modern system of industrial relations the 'only law governing class conflict was that of the jungle, resulting in frequent, often violent confrontations between workers and employers that were decided by the ability of one side to outlast the other.'

combined with pervasive and persistent poverty and so deprivation and degradation of lower social classes, and intensifying labor coercion, repression, and persecution, such as union suppression to the extreme.

Both the concentration of wealth, income, and hence power in the capitalist class, as well as the poverty, deprivation, and degradation of lower classes, and labor coercion and repression, such as suppression of union organization and action post-2016 and during Reaganism, replicate and return to their prior extreme levels during the Gilded Age or the 1920s. The wealth share of the top one percent[48] of American society, more precisely the capitalist class or plutocracy (at nearly 43 percent),[49] has grown to such an extent since Reaganism that it approximately equals that during the Gilded Age or the 1920s. This trend toward growing wealth concentration indicates that not much has substantially changed in America since President Theodore Roosevelt deploring the 'tyranny of mere wealth' or of 'plutocracy'[50] and so wealthy oligarchy during

---

48   Bonica et al. (2013, p. 103) observe that these new wealth and other economic inequalities in the US 'have primarily benefited the top 1 percent and even the top .01 percent.'

49   Benhabib, Bisin, and Luo (2019, p. 1623) note that wealth 'in the United States is unequally distributed', for example, the 'top 1 percent of the richest households in the United States hold over 33.6 percent of wealth', but this is obviously an outdated or understated figure (the OECD figure is 42.5 percent, as seen in Chapter 5).

50   Stiglitz (2012, pp. 75, 142, 219) observes that 'with more and more of the wealth concentrated in the upper 1 percent (or the upper 0.1 percent), America has the potential of becoming increasingly a land of an inherited oligarchy [or] a new plutocracy, marked by dynasties that are self-perpetuating [simply] a new American oligarchy or plutocracy.' Formisano (2015, p. 3) deplores that 'Congress and a reactionary Supreme Court majority cater to a hydra-headed plutocracy that enjoys a government of the rich, by the rich, and for the rich.' Formisano (2015, p. 11) adds that this American 'plutocracy continues to enjoy the fruits of years of government policy directed toward maintaining their inordinate political influence that, in turn, enables the upper caste's continued accumulation of wealth at the expense of everyone else.' Regarding the conservative-dominated Supreme Court, Aneja and Avenancio-León (2019, p. 161) comment that 'despite the importance of political representation for the disadvantaged, the US Supreme Court in 2013 struck a blow to minorities' political voice by invalidating a core provision of the VRA in Shelby County v. Holder. Writing for the majority, Chief Justice John Roberts claimed that 'things in the South have changed.' Given that minority participation rates had reached parity with whites, in the majority's view, political discrimination was no longer the problem it had been previously and some of the VRA's core protections were no longer needed.' They add that that the 'US Commission on Civil Rights released a report documenting the several ways in which, after Shelby County, previously covered jurisdictions imposed new obstacles that are thought to hinder minority voter participation. These included 'voter identification laws, voter roll purges, reductions in early voting, and polling place closures', and refer to finding that 'ending the VRA protection led to a two percentage-point reduction in minority participation in previously covered jurisdictions' (Aneja and Avenancio-León 2019, p. 162).

the Gilded Age and virtually erases the equalizing efforts and effects of the New Deal and generally the postwar minimal welfare state.

Furthermore, in comparative terms, the wealth share of the top one percent, thus of the capitalist class, in the US is the highest by far among all contemporary capitalist Western societies and moreover OECD countries,[51] with even its Southern neighbor, traditionally inegalitarian Mexico having a lower figure of wealth concentration. In this respect, American capitalism since Reaganism through 2016 acquires and solidifies the position of paramount plutocracy ('plutonomy')[52]—the plutocratic 'leader of the free world'—as wealthy oligarchy and hence a form or facet of capitalist dictatorship.

Relatedly, income concentration, such as the share of the top one percent as a proxy for the capitalist class, in the US since Reaganism through post-2016 basically returns (at around 20 percent) to its level during the Gilded Age or the 1920s.[53] This trend toward growing income concentration reaffirms that not much has changed in America after President Roosevelt denounced the 'tyranny of plutocracy' as prototypical capitalist dictatorship or authoritarianism during the early 1900s and reverses the egalitarian endeavors of the New Deal and the postwar minimalist welfare state. Furthermore, comparatively, like that of wealth, the income share of the top one percent/capitalist class in the US is the largest or growing most rapidly among all contemporary capitalist

51   Alvaredo et al. (2013, p. 16) observe that wealth 'concentration (as opposed to wealth accumulation) is significantly greater in the US, where the top 1 percent owns about 35 [rather over 42] percent of aggregate wealth (for comparison, the share is about 20–25 percent in Europe).'

52   Kapur, Macleod, and Singh (2005, p. 1) state that the US is a 'Plutonomy' as an economy 'powered [dominated] by the wealthy,' along with the UK and Canada, the three thus forming the 'key Plutonomies'. Frank (2007) adds that 'Plutonomy describe[s] a country that is defined by massive income and wealth inequality. According to [this] definition, the US is a Plutonomy, along with the UK, Canada and Australia.'

53   Commenting on the findings of Piketty's *Capital in the Twenty-First Century*, Milanovic (2014, p. 520) notes that 'at the turn of the twenty-first century, the [US] rich's income shares approached the high values of the Roaring Twenties'. Milanovic (2014, p. 524) adds that 'with the Thatcher–Reagan revolutions in the early 1980s, the Golden Age receded, and capitalism reverted to the form it had in the late-nineteenth century. [Capital income] began its steady climb reaching, in the early twenty-first century, values from around a century ago.' Volscho and Kelly (2012, p. 679) find that 'aside from a spike in the late 1920s, the general trajectory is downward from 1913 to the mid-1970s. The income share held by the top 1 percent fell from a high of nearly 24 percent (in 1928) to its lowest point of 8.9 percent (1975 to 1976), a decline of 63 percent. This pattern dramatically reversed after 1980, with income concentration rising from just over 10 percent in 1981 to 23.5 percent by 2007, a 135 percent increase. This is a dramatic change that puts income concentration on par with levels not seen since the late 1920s.'

Western societies[54] and OECD countries (for which data exist). In addition, another measure of income inequality, the Gini coefficient is the highest (at nearly 40) on record in the US post-2016 and since Reaganism. Moreover, it is the highest among all contemporary capitalist Western societies and even OECD countries, aside from few non-Western, Third-World exceptions like Chile, Mexico, and Turkey.

Relatedly, as primarily a consequence of growing wealth/income concentration in the capitalist class, the US's extraordinarily high poverty rate and degree of economic degradation, deprivation, and exclusion replicates or resembles the 'physical and moral degradation of the lower classes' during the Gilded Age, as well as European feudalism. Moreover, the US's general poverty rate is comparatively so exceptional—expressing true American exceptionalism—and extraordinary that it becomes during post-2016, crowning a long tendency since Reaganism, the highest (at almost 20%) among all contemporary capitalist Western societies[55] and OECD countries, with even Mexico's being lower. This trend to chronic and pervasive high poverty and hence material degradation, deprivation, and exclusion confirms that not much has changed in America after President Roosevelt deplored the poverty-perpetuation of the 'tyranny of mere wealth' during the Gilded Age and nullifies the poverty-reducing results of the New Deal and the postwar minimal welfare state with its War on Poverty. The preceding suggests that 'unfettered' capitalism creates and perpetuates not only extreme wealth and income concentration in the capitalist class but persistent and widespread poverty, so material degradation, deprivation, and exclusion of lower social classes, and reproduces both results with the highest intensity among Western capitalist societies.

In conjunction with such concentration and poverty, as a measure or proxy of labor coercion and repression like union suppression, the US's exceptionally

---

54   Alvaredo et al. (2013, p. 4) find that the 'share of total annual income received by the top
       1 percent has more than doubled from 9 percent in 1976 to 20 percent in 2011.' Moreover,
       Atkinson, Piketty, and Saez (2011, p. 8) report that 'although the top 1 percent is by defi-
       nition only a small share of the population, it does capture more than a fifth of total
       income—23.5 percent in the US as of 2007.'

55   Smeeding (2006, p. 75) notes that the 'relative poverty rate for all persons varies from
       5.4 percent in Finland to 17.0 percent in the US', adding that 'higher poverty rates are
       found in Anglo-Saxon nations with a relatively high level of overall inequality, like the
       US, Canada, Ireland and the UK. The lowest poverty rates are more common in smaller,
       well-developed and high-spending welfare states like Sweden and Finland.' Especially,
       Smeeding (2006, p. 75) points out that the 'US has the highest or second highest relative
       poverty rate in each category (minus childless adults). Poverty rates in the US for persons
       living with children are nearly double the average rate.'

low level of unionization (union density at just 10 percent)—another true American exceptionalism—during post-2016 and since Reaganism reverts to that during the Gilded Age[56] or the 1920, thus prior to the New Deal's granting of labor unionization rights consistently for the first time in American history by the 1935 National Labor Relations Act. Relatedly, as a further measure of labor repression and yet another American exceptionalism, the exceptionally low level of union or collective bargaining coverage (at slightly over 10 percent) in the US post-2016 and since Reaganism descends to that of the Gilded Age or the 1920, prior to the New Deal's first-ever allowance of collective bargaining rights. These tendencies to intensifying labor repression, such as suppression of unionization and collective bargaining, suggest that essentially not a lot changed after the diagnosis of the 'despotic might of capital', 'exploitation' of the 'weak', 'economic oppression,' or 'industrial despotism' of the Gilded Age and effectively nullify the New Deal's labor-emancipating legislation and effects.

Furthermore, the US's rate of unionization in comparative terms becomes during post-2016 and since Reaganism among the lowest within contemporary capitalist Western societies and OECD countries. Moreover, the extent of union or collective bargaining coverage in the US is so extraordinarily low that it comparatively becomes during post-2016 and since Reaganism the lowest among all contemporary capitalist Western societies and OECD countries,[57] except only for Turkey, thus even Mexico's being higher. Taken together, 'unfettered,' coercive capitalism reproduces extreme, indeed comparatively most intense and persistent labor repression, such as union suppression, in conjunction and mutual reinforcement with reproducing the unrivalled concentration of wealth and power in the capitalist class like the top one percent[58] and of the most severe poverty and degradation of lower social classes.

---

56   Rosenfeld (2019, p. 450) observes that 'by most measures, these are among the worst of times for organized labor in the United States. The official private sector unionization rate sits at 6.5%, although the actual rate is likely lower. This is the lowest percentage on record, approximating the rate that preceded passage of the National Labor Relations Act (NLRA) in 1935.' Further, Rosenfeld (2019, p. 451) infers that union decline is 'a key factor underlying the rise of the second Gilded Age.'

57   Blau and Kahn (2000, p. 93) observe that among the 'OECD nations, the US stands at an extreme with an especially low rate of collective bargaining coverage, pay setting which is often determined at the plant level even within the union sector, and an absence of formal or informal mechanisms to extend union-negotiated pay rates to nonunion workers.'

58   Acemoglu and Robinson (2015, p. 24) suggest that a 'dimension of political economy where the top 1 percent share may be central is the health of political institutions. It may be difficult to maintain political institutions that create a dispersed distribution.' Bivens and Mishel (2013, p. 57) find that in the US the 'increase in the incomes and wages of the

Therefore, 'unfettered,' coercive, and anti-egalitarian capitalism ultimately generates and indeed becomes or approaches fascism, which is precisely the system of absolute, mostly capitalist power and concentrated wealth and intense labor coercion and repression via union suppression and persecution, in America post-2016 and to some degree during Reaganism. Accordingly, whenever capitalism increases concentration of power and wealth in the capitalist class and intensifies labor coercion and repression, such as union suppression, it reproduces and turns into or approximates fascism, as in post-2016, as well as during Reaganism and the Tea Party.

Conceivably, if it did not become or ceased to being 'unfettered,' coercive, and anti-egalitarian, capitalism would not reproduce fascism in America, as perhaps during the New Deal and prior to the 1980s. However, it typically becomes or reinvents itself as 'unfettered,' coercive, and anti-egalitarian, as in a long sequence and continuity from the Gilded Age through Reaganism to the Tea Party and post-2016[59] as the 'new Gilded Age', and thus engenders or maintains fascism in America. Capitalism would not generate and sustain fascism in America if it did not increase the concentration of power and wealth in the capitalist class and did not intensify labor coercion and repression, as perhaps during the New Deal and prior to the 1980s. Yet, this 'all-American' model of capitalism typically increases the concentration of power and wealth in the capitalist class and intensifies labor coercion and repression to the maximum, thus generating fascism in America post-2016, as well as during Reaganism and the Tea Party.

Second and as a corollary, capitalism, especially its unrestrained, coercive, and anti-egalitarian version, reproduces fascism in America indirectly and latently, as it does in other social settings and historical periods from fascist Italy/Spain and Nazi Germany to the present, with secondary variations. This process enfolds through capitalism's economic and related support of and ultimately alliance and merger with fascism in America and elsewhere. Most of the US capitalist class finances and otherwise enables the ascendance and predominance or influence of fascism and more broadly extreme conservatism[60]

---

top 1 percent over the last three decades [is] driven largely by the creation and/or redistribution of economic rents, and not simply as the outcome of well-functioning competitive markets rewarding skills or productivity based on marginal differences.'

59   Redbird and Grusky (2016, p. 208) characterize the Tea Party and Trump's politics as 'types of backlash effects' to oppose the 'disruptive potential' of the Great Recession of American capitalism and to 'conserve the old political playbook even as its inadequacies become increasingly apparent'.

60   Clawson and Neudstadt (1989, p. 749) detect in the 1980 congressional elections an 'ideological effort to promote conservatism [by] the American capitalist class [in that]

or the radical right in America post-2016, as well as during Reaganism and the Tea Party, just as its German (and Italian) counterparts a la Krupp et al.[61] financed the rise of fascism in interwar Germany (Italy).

Moreover, 'unfettered,' coercive, and anti-egalitarian capitalism tends to ultimately ally and fuse with fascism, as through the alliance and fusion between capitalist oligarchy and fascist and other conservative leaders, in America post-2016 and during Reaganism and the Tea Party, just as its Italian and German variants allied and fused with fascism and Nazism, Mussolini and Hitler. This suggests that whenever American capitalism, or most of the US capitalist class, finances and allies with fascism, it effectively helps produce or sustain the latter, as during post-2016 and post-2020, just as Reaganism, and the Tea Party, and in the conservative pole of America.

In this connection, most US capitalist corporations overtly or secretly continued to finance US fascists and generally extreme conservatives or rightists even after their January 6, 2021 insurrection and destruction of Congress, and thus renegaded on their promise that they will not do so following this event. By financing the eruption of fascism and broader authoritarian conservatism or rightism, most US capitalists effectively behave like their German counterparts a la Krupp et al. during the rise of Nazism in Germany. Generally, this confirms that American unfettered, coercive, antiegalitarian capitalism is

---

business political behavior was ideologically conservative' and the 'position that business believed best promotes its class interests was conservatism.'

61   Also, Huber (2021, p. 2026) reports that the 'Allies believed that three [capitalist] banks with nationwide branch networks (Commerzbank, Deutsche Bank, and Dresdner Bank) had contributed to the Nazi war effort. In 1947–48, the Allies broke up the treated banks into 30 independent state-level organizations and prohibited the new banks from branching outside state borders.' Yet, Huber (2021, p. 2026-7) adds that 'improvements in the attitude of the Allies toward Germany, mainly due to the emergence of the Cold War, made the [reconsolidation] reforms possible. Negotiations among German politicians, central bankers, bank representatives, and the Allies then determined specifically when the consolidations happened.' This example illustrates the Allies', more precisely the US's and generally NATO's, newly discovered positive attitude, if not lost love, toward their wartime Nazi enemies or collaborators in the service of the Cold War as if Nazism were forgotten and indeed was harnessed as a new ally in the crusade against communism and for global domination, showing a Machiavellian-like amorality. In this regard, NATO, as dominated by the US and other 'great powers' joined with small puppet, vasal states, effectively continues Nazism's policy of militarism and offensive war against Russia and the Balkans—as the German conservative government showed by participating, on behalf of a WW II Nazi ally, in the NATO lawless 1999 bombardment of Yugoslavia—and generally operates as the instrument of American and Western imperialism, neocolonialism, and militarism which these smaller subservient states like former socialist countries are forced to support under blackmail or dependency.

more willing and ready to ally and eventually merge with fascism or authoritarian conservatism, including theocracy (as it does within the Christian
Right), than with an anti-fascist and non-conservative system such as liberal
and secular democracy.[62]

---

62   For example, the press reported that the largest and historically most infamous (monopo-
      listic) US phone company located in the South founded and financed for long a pro-fascist
      cable news channel producing conspiracy theories such as the 2020 election 'fraud' and
      devoted to the cult of the post-2016 autocracy, as another opposite to the mainstream 'lib-
      eral' media. In addition, this and other US companies are reported to have financed fas-
      cists or extreme conservatives and theocrats in the Bible Belt and beyond who suppress
      or restrict individual liberties and rights and privacy such as abortion rights. Apparently,
      this Southern and many other large US companies nurture and favor fascist-conservative
      news and related media featuring fantastical conspiracy theories and the cult of the
      leader to their liberal counterparts, just as most interwar German and Italian firms
      favored Nazism and fascism, Hitler and Mussolini, to liberalism and liberals. In another
      example, a CEO while moving the company headquarters from 'too liberal' California to
      ultra-conservative Texas reportedly praised the latter's 'social policy' such as the effective
      prohibition of abortion rights by the state legislature, reaffirming that most US capitalists
      favor proto-fascist or theocratic and extreme-right over liberal-secular policies consistent
      with their Italian-German counterparts in Mussolini-Hitler's time. Conversely, when few
      US corporations express disagreements with the fascist-conservative assaults on individ-
      ual liberty or intellectual freedom, ruling fascists and conservatives attack these busi-
      nesses, as with Disney being attacked by the Florida state because of disagreeing with the
      intense suppression of various liberties and rights approaching fascism. And US capital-
      ists in this and other Southern states have financed by hundreds of millions of dollars the
      2022 reelection campaigns of some neo-fascist or extreme-right and theocratic governors
      in the South, thus continuing their German counterparts' paying Hitler and financing
      the rise of Nazism. Moreover, a vociferous anti-liberal US capitalist declared that the
      choice for President in 2024 elections in precisely one of these neo-fascist governors in
      the South, evoking Krupp-Thyssen's choosing Hitler as Germany's leader. Relatedly, the
      press reported that a union, IG Metall in Germany stated that 'low wages are deterring
      workers from jobs at [this capitalist's] German factory,' specifically skilled workers at the
      latter earning '20% less than staff at some rival manufacturers. In turn, this capitalist is
      vehemently anti-union denying or opposing union rights to workers in US factories, as
      a standard fascist syndrome, as in Nazism. Overall, these US anti-liberal capitalists that
      finance and otherwise endorse fascists or extreme rightists and theocrats in Texas and the
      deep South likely have themselves fascist propensities, traits, or affinities, just as Krupp
      et al. did in Nazi Germany. No wonder, such anti-liberal US capitalists move their compa-
      nies from liberal-democratic states like California to Southern states like Texas and others
      ruled for long by proto-fascist and theocratic forces and subject, enabled by the latter,
      workers to slave-like conditions of no labor freedoms and rights. In turn, these proto-
      fascist and theocratic rulers in such states boast of attracting anti-liberal US capitalists
      that finance fascism and theocracy and exhibit fascist affinities or sympathies, while sub-
      jecting workers to a slave-style treatment in the sense of depriving them of basic labor
      freedoms and rights like unionization, collective bargaining, codetermination, and the
      like. In sum, coercive capitalism merges with fascism and/or theocracy in a 'marriage of

Conceivably, capitalism would not reproduce fascism in America if it did not generously finance and consistently ally with fascist and broader extreme conservative or radical-right forces, as perhaps, with some variations, prior to 2016 and Reaganism. However, capitalism evidently tends, with some variations and few exceptions, to finance and ally and fuse with fascist and related conservative forces, and thereby helps generate fascism in America, as during post-2016 and after 2020, during Reaganism and the Tea Party. Without the financial and other economic support from American 'unfettered,' coercive, and anti-egalitarian capitalism such as most of the US capitalist class, fascism would not likely ascend to salience and power in America post-2016 and since Reaganism. In economic terms, the inference is that 'no unfettered, coercive capitalism, no fascism' in America post-2016, just as before and likely after.

4 Religion as the Cause of Fascism

While conservatism being the prime ideological determinant and unrestrained capitalism the main economic factor, ubiquitous repressive religion, especially religious extremism, is the crucial cultural, spiritual cause and sanctification or theodicy of fascism in America post-2016 and to some degree during earlier times. Furthermore, pervasive religion in its prevalent repressive, extremist form reproduces and consecrates fascism in America in reciprocal linkage and intensification with conservatism as its ideological ally, as it does in all social spaces and times since interwar Italy, Spain, and Germany[63] through postwar Latin America (Chile) to today's Hungary, Poland, and Islamic-ruled Turkey, Saudi Arabia, and other Gulf states. This linkage results in a religion-conservatism alliance and fusion against secular, rationalist. and progressive

---

convenience' in Texas and similar ultra-conservative, anti-liberal states, as it did in Nazi Germany and fascist Europe and does in neo-fascist Hungary and theocratic Poland ruled by conservatism today, as well as Turkey, Saudi Arabia, and other Islamic theocracies.

63   Satyanath et al. (2017, 479) find a correlation of the rise of Nazism with religion. Also, Spenkuch and Tillmann (2017, p. 1) observe that in Germany during the 1930s while religion is usually seen as 'one amongst several correlates of Nazi support', the 'role of religion in the downfall of the Weimar Republic is underappreciated.' Specifically, they find that religion is 'an important predictor of Nazi vote shares. In the Republic's last free election, constituencies' religious composition alone explains more than 58% of the county-level variation in Nazi votes. This far exceeds the explanatory power of any other demographic or socioeconomic variable. Voter's religion even explains more variation in the data than all other available variables combined. Thus, to fully comprehend the failure of Germany's first democracy, one has to understand the role of religion' by allying with Nazism (Spenkuch and Tillmann 2017, p. 1).

social forces and institutions, including liberal democracy and universal liberty and scientific rationalism and progress, as conservative-religious America like the 'Bible Belt' shows.

In addition, ubiquitous religion, especially religious extremism, perpetuates and sanctifies[64] fascism in America in association and mutual reinforcement with American 'unfettered', coercive, and anti-egalitarian capitalism of which it is typically a 'sacred' consecration—capitalist theodicy[65]—evoking the clerical second estate's sanctification of aristocracy in feudalism. Such an association develops in a religion-capitalism alliance and merger between the religious masses and wealthy oligarchy or plutocracy against secular, rationalist, and non-capitalist or labor social forces like scientists and unions, including liberal democracy and scientific progress, as well as regulated, non-coercive, egalitarian capitalism or the welfare state. This is what the religious-oligarchic pole of America demonstrates, such as the former Southern Confederacy, 'Bible Belt' of 'God and money' that 'godly' and 'old boy' closed and exclusionary networks[66] dominate.

Moreover, pervasive, repressive religion in America allies with both conservatism and coercive capitalism to form the Religious Christian Right[67] alliance between highly religious, mostly lower social strata as the rank-and-file or the blindly following base evoking the Nazi 'blind herd', authoritarian conservative ideologues and politicians, and the coercive and anti-egalitarian capitalist class or plutocracy. Such a tripartite alliance therefore arises and acts as a 'holy trinity' revolting against and attempting to eliminate liberal-secular democracy and thus universal liberty, the welfare state, and societal wellbeing and

---

64   Paxton (1998, pp. 3, 23) expects that religion 'would certainly play a much greater role in an authentic fascism in the United States than in the first European fascisms [that were still] close to churches identified with the national cause'. McDermott and Samson (2005, p. 253) find that 'Christian Identity Church doctrine provides a religiously based justification for white supremacist movements' as parts of the fascist movement in America.

65   Bourdieu (1998, p. 43) states that capitalist and other 'dominant groups always need a 'theodicy of their own privilege' [i.e.] a sociodicy [as] a theoretical justification of the fact that they are privileged.' For example, Domhoff (2013) observes that the US capitalist or 'corporate-conservative coalition has been joined by the Christian Right.'

66   Levy and Razin (2017, p. 144) suggest that the 'old boys' networks in general, thus including by implication those in the US South and beyond, are 'endogenously formed', as in social environments 'in which the echo chamber effect outweighs true learning', while finding that 'history matters' in this regard.

67   Rawls (2010, pp. 264–5) observing that the 'great curse of Christianity was to persecute dissenters as heretics' elaborates that the 'history of the [Christian] Church includes a story of its long historical ties to the state and its use of political power to establish its hegemony and to oppress other religions.'

relative equality, as well as opposing science and impeding scientific progress. In regional and sub-society terms, the conservative-religious-oligarchic pole of America like the Southern Confederacy and the like is essentially ruled by the Christian Right and thus by a Biblical equivalent of Islamic Sharia law applied to produce mass imprisonment for sins-as-crimes and widespread executions often of innocent persons. This hence amounts to the regional rule by the 'holy' alliance of religious extremists, authoritarian conservatives, and coercive capitalist oligarchs against secularists, liberals, and workers and other non-capitalists. The conservative-religious-oligarchic pole of America becomes the heaven of a 'holy trinity' that seeks to purify Puritan-style this region and sub-society of the 'evils' of liberal-secular democracy, the welfare state, and science, such as evolutionary biology, scientific medicine like stem-cell research and vaccines as during the Covid-19 pandemic, the climate science of global warming, as well as critical social theory and research.

Religion's causation and consecration of fascism particularly applies to its prevalent form of religious extremism and revivalism such as Puritan-inspired evangelicalism[68] and more broadly Protestant fundamentalism, along with dogmatic Catholicism and other extreme Christian and non-Christian denominations. Most US evangelicals and other Protestant[69] fundamentalists, along with the proximate majority of Catholics, fanatically and obstinately to the end (for example, January 06, 2021) support the post-2016 autocracy and thus fascism, just as they did McCarthyism, Reaganism, the Ku Klux Klan, and any other fascist forms or proxies that arose in American history. In so doing, especially most American evangelicals prove to be true 'American fascists',[70]

---

68 Adorno (2001, p. 229) already after ww II identifies the 'important role played by the religious element in American fascist propaganda' and cites what one of the 'Fascist' West Coast radio priests said in a broadcast: "Can you not see that unless we exalt the holiness of our God, that unless we proclaim the justice of God in this world of ours, unless we proclaim the fact of a heaven and of a hell, unless we proclaim the fact that without the remission, *without the shedding of blood*, there is no remission of sin? Cannot you see that only Christ and God are dominant and that revolution will ultimately take this nation of ours?." Adorno thereby detects or anticipates what Caren et al. (2020, p. 445) call 'conservative Christian media networks' that are among 'key right-wing media platforms' in the US for long.

69 Generally, Becker, Pfaff, and Rubin (2016, p. 42) identify a dark, including fascist, side to 'Protestant ideology—Protestant share of the population correlates with a host of evils, including Nazi vote share, suicide, anti-Semitism, and witch persecutions'

70 Adorno (2001, p. 219) observes that 'current American fascist propaganda' describes its audience 'as poor but honest, common-sense but non-intellectual, native Christians' and thus implies that the latter embrace fascism. Hedges (2006) considers and describes US evangelicals within the Christian Right as 'American fascists'.

or their most ardent, vocal, and loyal allies and supporters post-2016, as they repeatedly do since the 1980s with Reaganism and before such as the 1920s with their 'monkey trial' against evolutionary science and the Ku Klux Klan (and perhaps Jacksonian nationalism and populism).[71] Moreover, they tend to sacrifice their lives, assets, families, and children to the post-2016 autocracy as 'chosen by God', so to the higher cause of fascism (as on, before, and after January 06, 2021), thus forming a death cult, just as German religionists or religious nationalists (including Goebbels and his family) sacrificed themselves to their Nazi leader and Nazism.

In essence, most US evangelicals and other fundamentalists, along with many orthodox Catholics, look like religious proto- or latent fascists hiding behind the veil of 'faith' and 'godliness' and become genuine, manifest fascists when the opportunity arrives and the time is right, such as a fascist leader arises, awakes, and legitimizes all their long accumulated fascist energies and propensities, as in post-2016 America, as well as during Reaganism, McCarthyism, and the Ku Klux Klan. On this account, evangelical America, such as the Southern and other 'Bible Belt', reappears as the regional religious root, defender, and epicenter of fascism post-2016, as well as since the Ku Klux Klan, McCarthyism, Reaganism, and the Tea Party.

As a disclaimer, not all US evangelicals and other fundamentalists, as well as orthodox Catholics, are fascist in nature, with some of them even being or claiming to be anti-fascist. Yet, most fascists in America post-2016 and before are evangelical and more broadly fundamentalist, plus orthodox Catholics, and affiliated with the Christian Right, in religious terms. Even if not all evangelicals or fundamentalists are counter-state fascist terrorists, the second in America during recent times from at least the 1995 Oklahoma bombing to the

---

71   Moreover, Paxton (1998, p. 12) states that 'it is further back in American history that one comes upon the earliest phenomenon that seems functionally related to fascism: the Ku Klux Klan [so that] fascism (understood functionally) was born in the late 1860s in the American South.' Thus, according to Paxton (2004, p. 49), the 'earliest phenomenon that can be functionally related to fascism is American: the Ku Klux Klan [so that] the first version of the Klan in the defeated American South was arguably a remarkable preview of the way fascist movements were to function in interwar Europe.' Simi et al. (2017, p. 1168) place Ku Klux Klan and Christian Identity together into 'major branches of US white supremacists' and thus neo-Nazis. Further back in time, Bonikowski and DiMaggio (2016, p. 953) identify in the US 'a xenophobic counter-narrative, often associated with conservative Protestantism and the tradition of Jacksonian nationalism' and Rousseau (2021, p. 503) recounts 'Jackson's populist support'. This hence implies that American nationalism, populism and to that extent fascism originates with this US President who is no wonder the declared role model (the 'favorite president') for post-2016 would-be autocrats.

January 2021 Congress insurrection are mostly evangelical or fundamentalist in religious terms. Likewise, while not entire evangelical America like the 'Bible Belt' is a religious source, support, and locus of fascism, the latter primarily arises and prevails in the former as its primary home,[72] for example, 'sweet homes' of Alabama, Tennessee, Florida, Texas, and the like.

Consequently, so long as religion, especially its extremist form evangelicalism and other fundamentalism organized with dogmatic Catholicism in the Christian Right, is latent proto-fascism and when the opportunity is right engenders or embraces fascism, 'faith' as an 'all-American' blessing turns into, together with conservatism, America's curse or nemesis. The latter threatens to vanquish America as the 'land of freedom' and democracy with 'liberty and justice for all', its Jeffersonian Enlightenment-based ideal versus the proto-totalitarian and hence proto-fascist Puritan 'shinning city upon a hill' as the dream of Reaganism. This evidently contradicts the allegations of religionists and conservatives and the perceptions of most Americans subjected to a deep, constant, and intense cradle-to-grave conditioning, indoctrination, and propaganda into nearly compulsory or socially conditioned and expected belief a la 'in God we trust' and 'one nation indivisible under God'.

Generally, the reasons and ways, aside from few exceptions, coercive and repressive religion, especially religious extremism and revivalism, is latent proto-fascism and causes, perpetuates, and consecrates fascism in America post-2016 and before since the Ku Klux Klan, McCarthyism, and Reaganism are identical or like those of conservatism's fascist causation, perpetuation, and justification. For example, Calvinist Puritanism in colonial America develops and functions as a 'primer'[73] of proto-fascism and so a proto-totalitarian exemplar—with its heir evangelicalism continuing this pattern—and Calvinism/Protestantism generally constitutes an extant religious source and precursor of fascism, including Nazism,[74] thus of rightist totalitarianism.

---

72   In this light, that conservative college students and other conservatives from Alabama, Texas, and the 'Bible Belt' overall at sports events would use profanities to disparage a post-2020 non-conservative President is not unexpected and derives from that this region forms a religious source of fascism and the center of anti-liberal, anti-democratic conservatism. It illustrates the wide observation that since the Ku Klux Klan most Southern conservatives or evangelicals are either proto-fascists or main allies of fascists.

73   Merton (1939, p. 437) observes that the 'New England Primer [of Puritanism] finds its analogue in the various Nazi primers [such as] the displacement of aggression against a convenient out-group [especially] in periods of economic strain [plus] the impugning of out-group morality [and other] myths and tactics of nativist movements before and since'.

74   Spenkuch and Tillmann (2017, p. 1) report that 'voters in predominantly Protestant areas abandoned their traditional allegiances and flocked' toward the Nazi Party.

The preceding reflects that most religion is a 'holy' equivalent or twin of conservatism[75]—the two being entwined in the Christian Right—and conversely, conservatism, like any ideology, is an ideological faith and political religion, while evangelicalism and Islam are also growingly denoted 'political religions' due to their ambitions to capture and exert total power. Moreover, religious extremism allies and merges with political extremism through the extreme Christian Right[76] in America post-2016 and since the Ku Klux Klan and Reaganism, as well as elsewhere from the Vatican's pacts with fascist Italy and Nazi Germany through Catholic-dominated and neo-fascist Chile and South America to Poland under Catholic and conservative domination, Islamic-ruled Turkey, Saudi Arabia, and other Gulf states.

Thus, prevalent religious, specifically evangelical, counter-state terror in America since the 1980–90s, such as the Waco violent[77] cult suicide and the Oklahoma City bombing, and post-2016 links and blends with dominant conservative anti-government terrorism like the January 06, 2021 assault on Congress and other terrorist attacks. Equally, religious fundamentalist 'holy' state terror through mass imprisonment for sins-as-crimes, such as nonviolent drug offenses, and widespread executions often of innocent people driven by Biblical law—the 'eye for eye' vengeance equivalent to Islamic Sharia law—in America since the 1980–90s and post-2016 days allies and coalesces with conservative government equivalent acts on the 'political terror scale', including indefinite detention, torture, and police brutality and murders, during these times. Moreover, religious counter-state and state terror and conservative anti-government terrorism and government political terror are so closely intertwined and mutually sustaining and reinforcing in America post-2016 and before that they become virtually indistinguishable. Overall, religious and political extremism or conservatism by allying and blending with each other tend to become almost impossible to distinguish, as within the Christian Right, in America post-2016 and earlier.

---

75   Mueller (2009, pp. ix–x) alerts that conservatism or traditionalism and extremist religion 'go hand in hand' and both mount 'dangers' for liberal democracy.
76   Alpers (2003, p. 7) remarks that 'fundamentalist leaders of the old Christian right' are usually included in the 'beginnings of American fascism'.
77   Gorski and Türkmen-Dervişoğlu (2013, pp. 194–5) suggest that the 'Judeo-Christian discourse of chosen peoples and elect nations [is] a cultural template for Western nationalism. Both American and Israeli religious nationalism have given rise to various episodes of violence.' Gorski and Türkmen-Dervişoğlu (2013, p. 197) mention 'modern episodes of sacrificial violence, such as the [Puritan] New England witch craze [and] the violent cults of the 1980s, such as those in Jamestown and Waco.'

First, among the reasons and ways of its fascist causation, perpetuation, and consecration, most religion, at the minimum its extremist form, since Puritanism through evangelicalism constitutes, like conservatism, latent proto-fascism and reproduces fascism in America by its composite of 'holy' authoritarianism, anti-liberalism, and anti-democracy in reciprocal relation and intensification. Extremist religion is proto-fascist and reconstructs, perpetuates, and consecrates conservative and conceivably all America as fascist due to being intrinsically authoritarian, fundamentally anti-liberal, and profoundly anti-democratic. Such reconstruction of America as the nation of fascism save in name is essentially the underlying meaning or ultimate outcome of Puritan-rooted evangelical 'reconstruction' and 'dominion' theology[78] through 'dominion of God' in society as de facto societal domination of anti-liberal, anti-democratic evangelicals. This suggests that evangelical 'reconstructionism' and 'dominionism' in America can only or primarily be instituted, spread, and imposed through fascism, and conversely the second is the most effective instrument to realize the first, and reaffirms the depiction of most evangelicals as home-born 'American fascists.' In consequence, the highly religious pole of America, especially its evangelical 'Bible-Belt' region, is latently proto-fascist and mutates into a fascist entity due to being inherently authoritarian, implacably anti-liberal, and deeply anti-democratic versus liberal democracy and liberty. Furthermore, this 'faith-based'[79] pole attempts to reconstruct its non- or less religious opposite after its 'Bible-Belt' model of 'holy' authoritarianism, anti-liberalism, and anti-democracy by launching religious and culture wars and hence to make all America latently proto-fascist and ultimately to cause it to become explicitly fascist.

Second and relatedly, most religion, minimally its extremist form, is latent proto-fascism and generates, sustains, or sanctifies fascism in America post-2016 and before through its compound of extreme, indeed axiomatic and inherent anti-secularism, total irrationalism, anti-rationalism and

---

78   Juergensmeyer (2003, pp. 27–8) remarks that 'Dominion Theology' includes 'Reconstruction Theology', 'whose exponents long to create a Christian theocratic state. Leaders of the Reconstruction movement trace their ideas, which they sometimes called 'theonomy,' to Cornelius Van Til, a twentieth-century Presbyterian professor of theology at Princeton Seminary who took seriously the sixteenth-century ideas of the Reformation theologian John Calvin regarding the necessity for presupposing the authority of God in all worldly matters.'

79   Bell (2002, p. 483) observes that in the 2000 Presidential elections 'George W. Bush proclaimed himself to be a born-again Protestant, whose life has been changed directly by Jesus Christ. Al Gore asserted that he was a born-again Protestant who frequently asked himself 'W.W.J.D' (What Would Jesus Do?).'

anti-progressivism, and intrinsic anti-egalitarianism (or 'deceptive egalitarianism'),[80] anti-universalism, and exclusion in interaction and mutual reinforcement. Religious extremism such as Puritanical evangelicalism and more broadly Christian fundamentalism is originally proto-fascist and ultimately reconstructs, maintains, and sanctifies America as fascist because of being extremely anti-secular, totally irrational, anti-rational and anti-progressive, and intrinsically anti-egalitarian, anti-universalistic, and exclusionary. Reconstructing America as the land of fascism sanctified by the deception/delusion of the 'dominion of God' reappears as the true intent or eventual effect of Puritan-evangelical reconstructionism or dominionism owing to its extreme anti-secularism, irrationalism, anti-rationalism and anti-progressivism, anti-egalitarianism, anti-universalism, and exclusion. This exposes most evangelicals as native 'American fascists' due to having corresponding attributes, conjoined with their authoritarian, anti-liberal, and anti-democratic traits.

In consequence, the highly religious pole of America, especially its evangelical section, is latently proto-fascist and ultimately mutates into an overt fascist space because of being extremely anti-secular, irrational, anti-rational, anti-progressive, anti-egalitarian, anti-universalistic, and exclusionary. Moreover, by launching religious and culture wars as new 'crusades',[81] this pole seeks to remake its secular or less religious opposite after its 'faith-based' or 'Bible-Belt' spirit of extreme anti-secularism, irrationalism, anti-progressivism, anti-universalism, and exclusion, and thereby to render all America into a proto-fascist space and to cause it to mutate into a fascist society sanctified as the societal 'dominion of God' via de facto evangelical sectarian, cult-like domination.

---

80   Dahrendorf (1979, p. 124) identifies the 'deceptive egalitarianism of Christian faith'.
81   Lipset (1996, p. 176) states that 'moralism, as the US history demonstrates is as American as apple pie' in that most Americans 'have exhibited Protestant sectarian bred propensities for crusades.' He elaborates that 'social conservatives in [the USA] are much more aggressive in imposing their own morality on the body politic with respect to issues like the right to life than their ideological compeers elsewhere [Italy, France, Germany].' Lipset (1996, p. 176) suggests that these 'repressive aspects of American culture may be related to two exceptional national characteristics: first, the utopian ideological content of the American Creed which defines the country [by] an ideology; and second, the predominance of Protestant sectarianism, a minority elsewhere in Christendom.' Lipset (1996, p. 176) adds that the 'political emphasis on loyalty to Americanism, the defining of deviants as "un-American", and the sectarian stress on personal morality represents forms of behavior that are less prevalent in historically defined countries [and so Americans] are more moralistic, insistent on absolute standards than their ideological compeers elsewhere in the developed world.'

Third and related, most religion, particularly its extremist form, is latent proto-fascism and eventually reproduces and consecrates fascism in post-2016 America and earlier because of its design and practice of absolute power, repression, violence,[82] including shedding of blood, terror, destruction, and self-destruction, in a reciprocal linkage with and intensification and a reflection of its 'holy' authoritarianism, anti-liberalism, and anti-democracy. Religious extremism from Puritanism to evangelicalism and generally Christian fundamentalism and growingly dogmatic Catholicism is proto-fascist and eventually causes America post-2016 and earlier to become fascist due to its seeking, seizing, and exerting absolute power and being extremely coercive, repressive, violent, and terrorist in the form of state and counter-state terror.

In essence, religious extremism, such as Puritan-inspired evangelicalism and dogmatic Catholicism, can attain, institute, and exert 'holy' absolute power, control, repression, and terror in post-2016 America only or primarily through fascism and political conservatism, as in other social settings and periods from the Vatican's treaties with fascist Italy and Spain and Nazi Germany[83] to Catholic-dominated and neo-fascist South America and Poland. Puritanical evangelicals and dogmatic Catholics are able to capture and exercise total power, repression, and terror in post-2016 America solely or mostly by allying and blending with fascists and political conservatives, as in other societies and periods since the Pope's alliances with Mussolini and Hitler also allied with German Protestants and support for Nazi-puppet regimes like Croatia, Hungary, Ukraine, etc. This supports the description of evangelicals as home-grown 'American fascists', as well as the traditional fascist credentials and

---

82   Adorno (2001, p. 229) during early postwar times diagnoses in the US the 'transformation of Christian doctrine into slogans of political violence' typifying fascism, elaborating that the 'idea of a sacrament, the "shedding of blood" of Christ, is straight-forwardly interpreted in terms of "shedding of blood" in general, with an eye to a political upheaval. The actual shedding of blood is advocated as necessary because the world has supposedly been redeemed by the shedding of Christ's blood'. Adorno (2001, pp. 229–30) concludes that such destructiveness is the 'psychological basis of the fascist spirit. The programs are abstract and vague, the fulfillments are spurious and illusory because the promise expressed by fascist oratory is nothing but destruction itself.'

83   Juergensmeyer (1994, p. 146) remarks that the surge of Nazism in Germany, 'while not explicitly religious, carried overtones of millenarian Christianity. Heinrich Himmler and other formulators of Nazi ideology relied on a mixture of religious images and ideas, including the Knights Templar symbol from the Crusades; nature worship from the German folk movement of the 1920s; the notion of Aryan superiority from, among others, the Theosophists; and a fascination with the occult from a certain strand of German Catholic mysticism', concluding that to an important degree the 'Nazi movement was religious' (see also Helm 2008, p. 11).

propensities of orthodox Catholics since the Vatican's alliances with Mussolini, Franco, Hitler, and Nazi-puppet figures in interwar Europe and during WW II.

Conversely, fascism, along with political conservatism, is the most potent instrument for seizing, holding, and exerting absolute power, repression, and 'holy' terror by religious extremism, such as Puritanical evangelicalism and dogmatic Catholicism, in post-2016 America, as in other social spaces since the pacts of fascist Italy/Spain and Nazi Germany[84] with the Catholic church. Fascists are the most lethal weapons or strongest allies for evangelicals and dogmatic Catholics in their pursuit, seizure, and exercise of absolute power, control, and terror in post-2016 America and before, as in other social contexts since the alliances of Mussolini, Franco, Hitler and Nazi-puppet figures with the Pope and most leading Protestants, as in Germany, Northern Europe, and parts of the Baltics. This implies that evangelicals and dogmatic Catholics, even if may not be pure 'American fascists', tend to ally and blend with the latter, notably when these capture and exert state power, and indeed worship and consecrate the fascist leader(s) whom they see as the most potent instruments to achieve their religious aims and indeed 'chosen and sent by God', as in post-2016 conservative America. Consequently, the highly religious pole of America, especially its evangelical region, is latently proto-fascist and eventually mutates into a fascist land qua 'dominion of God' owing to these tendencies of religious extremism. Furthermore, this pole attempts to remake its secular or less religious counterpart after its own design and practice of absolute rule, coercion, repression, violence, and terror via aggressive religious and culture wars[85] as renewed 'crusades', and to that extent to reconstruct all America as proto-fascist and cause it to turn fascist eventually.

Fourth, most religion, at least its extremist variant, is latent proto-fascism and ultimately yields, sustains, and sanctifies fascism in post-2016 America through its extreme anti-pacifism and militarism, including its consecration

---

84   Relatedly, Spenkuch and Tillmann (2017, p.5) find that 'although the Catholic Church and its dignitaries had been vigilant in resisting the Nazis until the very last election in 1933, their resistance collapsed shortly after passage of the Enabling Act.' They add that 'shortly after passage of the Enabling Act, however, the Church's leadership backed down directly after the Church leadership abandoned its opposition to the Nazi government, Catholics and Protestants joined the [Nazi party] in equal proportions [so that] after the episcopate allied itself with the new regime, Catholics' relative resistance faded' (Spenkuch and Tillmann 2017, pp. 13–16).

85   Bell (2002, p. 484) warns that what is 'troublesome is the politicization of moral and cultural issues, for by their very nature they are non-negotiable and serve to polarize society. If such moral and cultural questions [abortion] cannot be privatized, then the country may remain in trouble as new wars of religion take hold'.

via Christian religious nationalism[86] of offensive war and imperial conquest,[87] combined with its mix of authoritarian personalities, cults of leaders, fantasies, and eventually collective suicide. In short, religious extremism is proto-fascist and ultimately renders and consecrates America as a fascist society because of being vehemently anti-pacifist, militarist, warlike, and imperialist. This combines with its mass of authoritarian, including sadistic[88]-masochistic, personalities, and its cult of an autocratic leader by believers susceptible to delusions and to collective suicide and annihilation as 'salvation' via 'holy' war on 'evil' and 'rapture' by the 'second coming' in the style of a death cult.

In essence, religious anti-pacifism, militarism, and nationalism, including its sanctification of offensive war and imperial conquest, is perfectly compatible and substantively identical or comparable to those of fascism and political conservatism. On this account, such religious complex forms a 'holy' equivalent, source, and predictor of fascism in post-2016 America and earlier. Especially evangelicals by being vehemently anti-pacifist, militarist, warlike, and imperialist (couched as being missionary) are perfect complements of fascists and political conservatives in post-2016 America. The first appear as 'godly' analogues and allies, indeed 'brothers in arms' of American fascists and political conservatives. In consequence, the highly religious pole of America, primarily its evangelical segment, is latently proto-fascist and eventually mutates into a fascist entity due to such features of extremis religion. Moreover, this pole seeks by launching religious and culture wars against its non- or less religious liberal opposite to remake the latter after its pattern of anti-pacifism, militarism, nationalism, including its offensive war and imperial conquest, and to that extent to reinvent all America as a proto-fascist land and cause it to become ultimately a fascist society.

---

86   Juergensmeyer (1994) observes that Christian, Islamic and other 'religious nationalism' assaults and seeks to dismantle the 'secular state'. Friedland (2002, p. 419) states that Nazism's 'semiotic print matches that of the [US] religious nationalists.' Phillips (2006, p. 6) recounts that 'for instance, a wave of virtually hysterical religious nationalism engulfed the British Empire in the years leading up to the Great War (1914–1918). Fervor for war and religious fever were inseparable in late-stage Victorian England. The youth of Britain marched off to the trenches with the sense that Armageddon was at hand and the Messiah might return at any moment. Armageddon arrived all right, in the form of the war to end all wars, but the Almighty never put in an appearance.'

87   Hedges (2004) invokes Dr. James Luther Adams, professor at Harvard Divinity School who predicted the rise of the 'Christian fascists' as forces of a 'new political religion [whose] stated goal was to use the United States to create a global, Christian empire.' Blee and Creasap (2010, p. 280) point to 'new efforts by the US Christian Right to develop transnational religious alliances', as with Haider's Fascist 'Freedom Party' in Austria.

88   Hitchens (2009, p. 80) sounds alarm of 'Christian sadists' in the US and elsewhere.

5   Theocracy as the Cause of Fascism

As a corollary of the above about extremist religion, theocracy is a related cause or covariate, indeed religious equivalent, of fascism in America post-2016 and earlier times, as in other social settings and periods since fascist Italy and Spain, Nazi Germany and Catholic and Protestant Nazi-puppet regimes in interwar Europe through Catholic-dominated postwar South America and present Poland, plus Islamic-ruled Turkey and Gulf and other theocratic Muslim states. In essence, American and other extremist religion is consistently and strongly theocratic attempting to institute, impose, and expand theocracy. It does this through counter-state terror or anti-government violence and religious war to capture power and, once in control, via state terror or government repression of liberal-secular social forces that it terrorizes and persecutes as 'infidels', a term that Puritan and other Christian crusaders and Islamic jihadists share in terrorizing, persecuting, and murdering non-believers, secularists,[89] and those with different beliefs. In short, most religion in America and beyond is the vision and creation of theocracy through 'holy' civil war a la crusade or jihad committing terror, repression, persecution, and murder of the 'godless,' and this is why it is extremist.

Conversely, theocracy in America and beyond is typically the 'divine' design and creation of extremist religion. The latter involves Puritanism and generally Calvinism, its heir Puritan-inspired evangelicalism, and other Protestant fundamentalism,[90] as well as dogmatic Catholicism, initially in intra-Christian fraternal wars of religion and presently in a 'holy' alliance within the Christian Right[91] against their shared 'enemy' and 'evil' of liberal-secular democracy and society that they work to destroy in the 'name of God'. In a word, theocracy in America develops by extremist religion seizing total societal power and engaging in 'holy' repression, terror, and war. Accordingly, the preceding about religion's fascist causation and consecration in America post-2016 and before applies to theocracy as an additional religious cause of fascism in this and other social contexts.

---

89   Bazzi et al. (2020, p. 846) observe that Islamic charitable trusts are 'pervasive in the Muslim world' and, like their Christian variants in the US, 'can be used to mobilize political support and wage ideological warfare against secular forces.'

90   Gross et al. (2011, p. 326) point to the radical-right and thus by implication theocratic and proto-fascist 'politics of Christian fundamentalism.'

91   Bénabou et al. (2015, p. 347) identify the Christian 'Religious-Right alliance' in the US between the rich class and religious poor strata that characterizes the 'American regime' and tends to block 'belief-eroding discoveries and ideas.'

Theocracy is religiously grounded and sanctified, 'holy' proto-totalitarianism and in that sense proto-fascism, thus fascism before fascism proper. This is what Jefferson essentially implies by characterizing theocracy and similar ancient regimes ruled by religion as 'religious slavery'. Particularly, Puritanism and its theocracy established in colonial America like New England—but imported from Calvinist Europe via Puritan England, descending ultimately from Calvin's France/Geneva—was reportedly a 'primer'[92] of proto-fascism and analogue or precedent of fascism, specifically Nazism. Indeed, Jefferson primarily refers by the expression 'religious slavery' to theocratic Calvinist Puritanism—as distinct from, though substantively equivalent to, Islamic and other puritanism underscoring most religions even before the Puritan Revolution or Protestant Reformation—and its long-standing theocracy in America to be formally, but not substantively, disestablished about half a century after the American Revolution. Moreover, Puritanism and its theocracy in colonial America became reportedly an 'unexampled tyranny' (in Weber's description) and the 'most totalitarian'[93] variant of proto-totalitarian Calvinism and to that extent the most severe form of proto-fascism—so fascism before fascism—or the deepest historical source or precursor of the latter.

In addition, Puritanism's heir American evangelicalism through the 'Bible Belt' resurges, along with Islamic fundamentalism as its objective equivalent and ally, as the 'proto-totalitarian' enemy of liberal democracy, claiming to resolve the supposed agony and burden of choice and individual liberty[94] by eliminating the latter, and in that sense proto-fascism or religiously determined and sanctified fascism, as the term 'Christian fascism' and 'fascists' suggests. Aside from minor variations, evangelicalism, notably the 'Bible Belt', fanatically

---

92   Merton (1939, p. 437) writing during the rise fascism suggests that 'American nativism, in the form of anti-Catholic and later of anti-foreign sentiment, was partly rooted in this same Puritanism. [It had] the religio- and ethno-centric pattern which, developing through (19th century), temporarily culminated in the 'Know-Nothing Party' of the fifties.' Notably, he observes that the 'pattern significantly resemble[s] nativist [fascist] developments in Europe' (Merton 1939, p. 437).

93   Stivers (1994, p. 23) observes that American Puritanism 'was the most totalitarian form of Calvinism [which] not satisfied with a minimalistic morality, searched for a rigorous moral discipline.'

94   Bauman (1997, p. 184) suggests that the 'Islamic integrisme of ayatollahs [and] evangelist churches of the Bible Belt belong to a wider family of [proto] totalitarian solutions offered to all those who find the burden of individual freedom excessive and unbearable.' More broadly, Bauman (2001, p. 70) alerts to the 'neo-tribal and fundamentalist sentiments which inescapably accompany the current privatization of ambivalence. Their allure is the promise put [end] to the agony of individual choice by abolishing the choice itself.'

and consistently embraces and consecrates the post-2016 radical-right autocracy and to that extent fascism as 'God's choice and plan' for America, in continuity with its embrace and consecration of Reaganism, McCarthyism, and the Ku Klux Klan, just as of slavery as 'divinely' created. Apart from few exceptions, evangelicals from the biblical South to the religious North fervently support, adulate, debase, and sacrifice themselves and their families to the post-2016 autocracy and in that sense fascist rule as 'chosen by God' for America, as they did Reagan ('I am one of you'), McCarthy, Ku Klux Klansmen, and slave masters. On this account, if Puritanism was original proto-fascism from colonial America and Calvin's France, 'all-American' Puritanical evangelicalism is later proto-fascism and indeed genuine 'holy' American fascism and US evangelicals proto-fascists and even true religious 'American fascists'.

In essence, since Puritanism through its descendant evangelicalism and other religious fundamentalism, America, especially its section ruled by conservatism and permeated with religion, has always been pure or diluted, formal or substantive theocracy,[95] and hence the latter inevitably and ultimately leads to fascism post-2016. Specifically, America was pure, formal, or official theocracy in the sense of a state religion during the Puritan 'theocracy of New England' (in Weber's and other accounts) from the 17th to 19th centuries, which Jefferson repudiated on Enlightenment liberal-secular grounds and to which he apparently referred by 'religious slavery'. Furthermore, America has essentially been diluted, substantive, or effective theocracy ever since the formal disestablishment of Puritanism through the reemerging post-Civil War Southern 'Bible Belt' and the plutocratic-theocratic Gilded Age through 'godly' McCarthyism associated with 'one nation indivisible under God' and 'in God we trust' and 'faith-based' Reaganism to the post-2016 blend of extreme-right autocracy and extremist religion, such as evangelicalism and dogmatic Catholicism. For illustration, the Constitutional prohibition of 'establishment of religion' becomes virtually a worthless or unenforced legal rule that extremist religion and theocracy, in alliance with political conservatism, flagrantly

---

95   Bénabou et al. (2015, p. 347) define a 'Theocratic regime' by 'knowledge stagnation, extreme religiosity, a Church that makes no effort to adapt since its beliefs are protected by the state, and also high taxes but now used to subsidize the religious sector.' While formally distinguishing the two, they imply that the 'American regime' is substantively closer to an Islamic and other—and indeed constitutes save in name—'Theocratic regime' than to the 'Secularization or Western-European regime' (Bénabou et al. 2015, p. 347). Bénabou et al. (2015, p. 347) suggest this is because the 'American regime' makes 'specific exemptions or other policies (e.g., laws regulating behavior) benefiting religious activities and citizens [and] a rise in income inequality can lead the rich to form a Religious-Right alliance with the religious poor and start blocking belief-eroding discoveries and ideas.'

and methodically violates with impunity and effectively invalidates, making it hardly worth the paper on which it is stated. Relatedly, the Jeffersonian Enlightenment principle and 'eternal wall of separation of church and state' shares the same adverse fate of legal worthlessness or lack of enforcement due to its systematic violation and nullification by extremist religion and theocracy, together with political conservatism.

Both as a cause and result of such subversions of the above Constitutional stipulation and the principle of separation of church and state, America, above all its conservative-religious pole, has always been post-Puritanism and remains substantive or effective, even if not formal, theocracy through post-2016. Imposition of religious qualifications (Weber's terms) for political power or public office—from the Presidency and Congress to state and local governments—as a defining element of theocracy applies in America post-2016 and since McCarthyism and Reaganism, as it did in Puritan theocracy[96] in 1689 with its witch trials, through public and emotional, preferably tearful confessions and recognitions of the 'existence of Divinity', as in some 'Bible Belt' and other states, 'faith', 'trust in God', 'one nation indivisible under God', and the like. This means that only the 'godly' apply for power in religious America from Puritanism through Reaganism to the post-2016 radical-right autocracy and all others 'need not apply', which is the essence and diagnosis of theocracy helping explain why Jefferson characterizes it as 'religious slavery' from the perspectives of non-believers, those with different beliefs, secularists, and all others than the ruling theocratic elite. Only a 'faith-based' person who recognizes publicly and tearfully the 'existence of Divinity' and proves 'faith' can become President, and, with few exceptions, member of Congress, governor, or mayor in America post-2016 and since McCarthyism/Reaganism, just as occupying analogous positions in the 17th century Puritan theocracy,[97] plus Iran, Saudi Arabia, and other Islamic states.

On this account, historically the conservative-religious pole of America such as its evangelical segment does not seem to have advanced much beyond but

---

96 Munch (2001, pp. 224–5) observes that 'in no other country did Puritanism attain significance comparable to [that] in the [US] as the carrier of modern normative culture', including in particular the legacy of Puritan 'theocracy'. He observes that as an apparent, long-standing legacy of Puritan theocracy, the 'characteristic feature of the relationship between religion and political order in [the US] is that the two are not purely differentiated, nor is politics released from religious tutelage' (Munch 2001, pp. 228–9).

97 Juergensmeyer (2003, p. 213) finds that for US evangelicals the manner the Puritan and other Protestant governments of the early American colonies 'grounded their constitutions in biblical law could set a precedent for a new kind of Christian government in the United States'.

basically petrifies in, or resurrects from death and perpetuates, medieval and proto-totalitarian Puritan theocracy from colonial times and in extension theocratic Calvinism originating in France, an unexpected religious 'French connection' and origin of the 'new nation'. Comparatively, due to such theocratic exclusion, conservative-religious America looks closer to Islamic theocracies like Iran also imposing religious qualifications for political power and public offices, such as presidents, than to Western European liberal-secular democracies mostly abolishing such exclusionary requirements. Notably, candidates for presidents in both conservative-religious America and Islamic Republic of Iran undergo a test of 'faith' and must be preapproved by some higher religious authority, such as institutional religion or a diffuse public expectation of 'godliness' in the first case and an individual 'supreme leader' in the second, so that substantive equivalence exists despite some formal differences. And after passing the test of 'godliness' and once elected, presidents in both conservative-religious America and Islamic Republic of Iran must prove their 'faith' continuously, emotionally, including tearfully, and publicly through various rituals, from assuming power by holding the Bible and the Koran, respectively, to public prayers, exhortations, and exaltations of 'in God we trust'. In sum, America, at least its conservative-religious pole, has typically been formal or substantive theocracy[98] since Puritanism through the post-Civil War 'Bible Belt', McCarthyism, and Reaganism and remains so by post-2016, historically perpetuating 17th century Puritan theocracy and comparatively equivalent to Iran and other Islamic theocracies in the 21st century.

In the light of the preceding, it is only a matter of time and opportunity, including the perfect timing of the appearance and election of a fascist-style autocrat and similar extreme-right leaders and followers, when theocracy inexorably generates or merges with fascism, as in post-2016 and during the Ku Klux Klan, McCarthyism, Reaganism, and generally the Christian Right.[99] This is consistent with the inner logic and modus operandi of theocracy as religiously determined proto-fascism, namely religious fascism in the sense of proto-totalitarianism, despotism, or dictatorship before fascism proper, which Weber's theocratic 'unexampled tyranny of Puritanism' in colonial

---

98   Phillips (2006) identifies 'American Theocracy' characterized as the 'Peril and Politics of Radical Religion' such as evangelicalism and generally Christian fundamentalism.

99   Manza and Brooks (1997, p. 42) register the 'sudden emergence of the Christian Right in the late 1970s as a factor in US politics and the visible role of some early Christian Right groups such as the Moral Majority in the 1980 elections herald[ed] a new type of political conflict in which religious values were becoming central to voters' decisions [with] cyclical dismissal and then rediscovery of religious conservatism as a political force.'

America epitomizes. In this sense, fascism in America post-2016 and earlier is predestined—as if in accordance with a sociological expression of the Calvinist predestination dogma with reference to American society—to happen given its inception, long history, or anticipation as proto-totalitarian Puritan theocracy as the 'holy' fascist prototype.

Furthermore, Puritan-style theocratic revolt and evangelical counterrevolution cum the 'revival' of fundamentalism escalate and intensify to the extreme from the 1980s—while restarting in the 1950s with McCarthyism and the enactment of 'in God we trust' and similar symbols of theocracy but partly weakened in the liberal 1960s—with the resurgence of the Christian Right and relatedly Reaganism and the Tea Party. This theocratic resurgence and dominance qua evangelical revival consequently generate or merge with fascism in America post-2016, as in other social settings since fascist Italy/Spain and Nazi Germany through Catholic-dominated South America and Poland, Islamic-ruled Turkey, etc. Aside from few exceptions, most evangelical and related fundamentalist and religious groups, including orthodox Catholics within the Christian Right, fanatically support to the point sacrificing themselves and their families Goebbels-style for the post-2016 autocracy, as they did the Ku Klux Klan, McCarthyism, and Reaganism, and their counterparts elsewhere, including both Catholics and Protestants, supported Mussolini, Franco, Hitler, Pinochet, Thatcher, and other fascist and extreme-right dictators and leaders. In short, theocratic fundamentalism not just acquiesces to but enthusiastically allies and merges with fascism and its autocracy in America post-2016. In this sense, the inevitable and ultimate outcome of evangelicalism or Protestant fundamentalism, along with dogmatic Catholicism within the Christian Right,[100] and its 'divine design' of theocracy is evangelical 'Christian fascism'[101] and 'fascists,' just as the eventual result of theocratic Islamism being 'Islamic fascism' and 'fascists'. At this point, evangelicalism or fundamentalism, as well as dogmatic Catholicism, for example, the conservative Supreme-Court majority, notably its theocracy, reasserts itself and prevails in America post-2016 through 'Christian fascism'. Hence, the latter, such as a 'Christian fascist state', emerges

---

100   Phillips (2006, p. 5) alerts to the Religious Right which is 'actively seeking to dismantle the separation of church and state—indeed, such religious fundamentalists explicitly affirm that the United States is a Christian nation founded on Biblical principles—takes the Bible as the inerrant Word of God.' He warns that the 'seriousness and influence of this Religious Right cannot be discounted' (Phillips 2006, p. 5).

101   Dawkins (2006, pp. 292–3) alarms that the US evangelical 'ambition to achieve what can only be called a Christian fascist state is entirely typical of the American Taliban. It is an almost exact mirror image of the Islamic fascist state so ardently sought by many people in other parts of the world.'

as evangelical and broader fundamentalist theocracy or the 'Christian Right' that while having latent and hidden proto-fascist properties assumes manifest and overt fascist features, as in America post-2016 and during Reaganism. 'Christian fascists'[102] arise as evangelical and generally Christian theocrats or rightists, who while latently proto-fascists openly act as or blend with fascists, as in America post-2016 and since Reaganism.

In other words, the conservative-religious, notably evangelical, pole of America has always been theocratic in certain important, even if diverse, degrees and ways and it is just a matter of timing and opportunity to become fascist, as during post-2016 and to some extent the 1980s. Approximately half of the country, such as the Southern and other 'Bible Belt,' became or persisted as effective theocracy following—just as had been before—the Civil War. This half hence substituted Jefferson's 'religious slavery' for racial slavery through the total mastery of believers as self-proclaimed 'God-chosen' masters and their exclusion and oppression of 'infidels' whom they mistreated as 'godless' second-class subjects who are denied and excluded from political power. In consequence, theocracy generates or coalesces into fascism initially and most visibly and completely in the Southern and other 'Bible Belt' from Alabama, Florida, and Tennessee to Kansas, Oklahoma, and Texas. This region epitomizes theocracy's causation of or fusion with fascism. It is for long the domain of the absolute rule and systematic repression by Puritan-style evangelical crusaders as Christian equivalents of Islamic jihadists or the Taliban,[103] enforcing Biblical law as an equivalent of Sharia law[104] through mass imprisonment of sinners-as-criminals and widespread executions often of innocent persons and by conservative political extremists who turn fascists.

Taken together, theocracy generates or merges with fascism in America post-2016 and to some extent before from the Ku Klux Klan to McCarthyism, and Reaganism through its typical proto-fascist and generally proto-totalitarian attributes and outcomes. Since these features are basically equivalent to the main elements of fascism and generally conservatism, suffice it to summarize them. First, theocracy is a cause of fascism in America post-2016 by its

---

102   Recall Hedges (2004) relates that 'Dr. James Luther Adams, professor at Harvard Divinity School, [said] we would all be fighting the 'Christian fascists' [forming] a new political religion that would direct its efforts at taking control of all institutions, including mainstream denominations and the government.'

103   Dawkins (2006, pp. 292–3) characterizes US evangelicals as the 'American Taliban.'

104   Juergensmeyer (2003, p. 214) reports that US evangelicals admire and emulate the 'attempts of Muslims in Iran, Sudan, and Afghanistan to create regimes grounded in Islamic [Sharia] law'.

complex of religious totalitarianism or dictatorship, anti- or pre-liberalism, anti- or pre-democracy operating in a typical interrelationship and mutual reinforcement, as in other social spaces and times from interwar Europe to Catholic-dominated South America and Poland. Second, theocracy engenders or blends with fascism in America post-2016 and earlier via its composite of ultimate 'natural' anti-secularism, extreme irrationalism, anti-rationalism and anti-progressivism, and inherent anti-egalitarianism, anti-universalism or particularism, and exclusion existing typically in reciprocal relationship and intensification. Third, theocracy causes or coalesces with fascism in America post-2016 and earlier by its design and system of 'holy' absolute rule, power, and domination and of coercion, repression, violence, and terror, functioning in interdependence and mutual reinforcement and manifesting and implementing its religious totalitarianism, anti-liberalism, and anti-democracy. Fourth, theocracy produces or fuses with fascism in America post-2016 and before owing to its composite of 'holy' anti-pacifism, militarism, war, and conquest. This composite exists in conjunction with an agglomeration of authoritarian, including sadistic-masochistic, personalities, the cult of religious leaders by believers, and delusions and fantasies leading ultimately to mass destruction and self-destruction by collective suicide in the manner of a death cult, as during Covid-19 and other health or social crises.

In essence, theocracy in America and beyond is typically a proto-fascist or extreme-right regime, and conversely, fascism is a theocratic, 'faith-based' system, thus theocrats being usually fascists or authoritarian rightists, and fascists resembling theocrats qua 'God's chosen' rulers, with secondary variations and minor exceptions. Theocracy in America, such as the 'Bible Belt' within its conservative-religious pole, causes and indeed constitutes religiously grounded fascism, evoking Jefferson's depiction of it as 'religious slavery', and fascism, aside from few exceptions, moves together with theocracy.

What Does Oppose It? Countervailing Social Forces to Fascism

1   Counter-Fascist Social Forces

Countervailing social forces to fascism in post-2016 America and beyond are those that it condemns, attacks, and destroys as 'un-American', just as 'anti-German' in Nazi Germany, 'unpatriotic', 'foreign', and 'godless', simply 'evil' following the terminology of its creator conservatism and its equivalent Puritan/evangelical theocracy. These counteracting social forces include therefore liberalism, liberal democracy, secularism, rationalism, progressivism, egalitarianism, universalism cosmopolitanism or globalism, pacifism or non-militarism, and liberal actors in socio-psychological terms in American and other societies (summarized in Table 4.1).

Like the elements of fascism as well as of conservatism and theocracy, these anti-fascist social forces exist and function usually in interconnection and mutual reinforcement, with especially liberalism interlinking and mutually reinforcing with democracy, secularism, rationalism progressivism, egalitarianism, universalism, cosmopolitanism, pacifism, and liberal personalities. Liberalism expresses the operation of all other anti-fascist social forces and operates as the main countervailing force to fascism as well as to authoritarian conservatism and theocracy, in America post-2016 and earlier, as it does in all other societal contexts and historical periods since fascist Italy and Nazi Germany.

Generally, such countervailing forces are essentially non-conservative social processes and structures given that fascism in America and everywhere is primarily the creation of conservatism, in conjunction and mutual reinforcement with unrestrained coercive capitalism, pervasive repressive religion, and theocracy. Anti-fascist social factors are hence those supplanting conservatism as the remnant and revival of despotic medievalism, such as the ancient regime of feudal servitude, aristocracy, and theocracy, and hence, as intrinsic authoritarianism, the creator of totalitarian fascism, including Nazism. By virtue of superseding conservatism and in extension its precursor and ideal medievalism, these counter-powers supplant its product fascism, including Nazism, in America and elsewhere. Conversely, whenever conservatism, in close association and reciprocal intensification with unrestrained coercive capitalism,

TABLE 4.1   Countervailing social forces to fascism in America

---

liberalism
liberal democracy
secularism
rationalism and progressivism
egalitarianism, universalism and cosmopolitanism or globalism
pacifism or non-militarism
liberal persons and groups

---

pervasive extremist religion, and theocracy, prevails over non-conservative social forces in America, as during post-2016 times and since the 1980s, fascism rises and expands as the ultimate conservative-religious outcome. This outcome is consistent with the conservatism-to-fascism, notably Nazism, causal linkage since interwar Italy and Germany through postwar South America to present Hungary, Poland and other parts of Eastern Europe, Brexit Great Britain, Brazil, and beyond, including Islamic-ruled Turkey.

It follows that these countervailing social forces to fascism not only immediately face, counter, and transcend the latter but also ultimately confront and supersede its primary producer conservatism, along with its other interlinked producers, coercive capitalism, oppressive religion, and theocracy. In this sense, they are strictly anti-fascist and broader counter-conservative social forces. Just as understanding and explaining the rise and advance of fascism requires considering conservatism as its prime cause, to envision superseding the fascist menace in America and beyond presupposes envisioning the supersession of 'all-American' conservative ideology and zeitgeist, as the necessary condition. Countervailing social forces to fascism can enduringly and entirely overcome the latter as the conservative product and syndrome solely by supplanting to the same degree its producer and root American conservatism.

Conversely, if anti-fascist social forces do not lastingly and fully supersede conservatism, they will only transiently and partially overcome or just temper fascism, as in America after McCarthyism. They countered and discredited McCarthyism as a postwar variation of fascism but did not fully defeat and discredit its source American conservatism or radical-right ideology that moreover resurrected from death through antiliberal Reaganism and its Goldwater precedent, the extremist Tea Party, and the post-2016 autocratic regime. More broadly, anti-fascist social forces during in WW II counteracted, discredited, and defeated fascism, notably Nazism, in the 'fire and rubble of

Berlin and Dresden',[1] but failed to lastingly and completely defeat, discredit, or delegitimize, aside from some early transient and partial delegitimizing[2] of, its source conservatism or rightism during postwar times, as a failure of 'mission accomplished'. This failure to eradicate or compromise conservatism or the right lastingly as the fascist creator helps explain why fascism as a conservative effect resurges from the WW II defeat and reinvents and couches itself during postwar times, together with its religious equivalent theocracy, in the deceptive dress of 'freedom', 'liberty' ('freedom' parties and coalitions,[3] 'liberty' religious education and theocratic states) and 'democracy' (the 'people') to abuse and eliminate freedom/liberty and liberal democracy. Fascism from postwar days to post-2016 resurrects from its war death and rebrands itself because conservatism while presumed caput mortuum is not proven dead and fully discredited after WW II which it caused through its fascist offspring, as it did WW I via conservative nationalism and militarism. Evidently, it proves impossible to prevent and eradicate fascist syndromes without preventing and eradicating their underlying and seemingly invisible conservative cause. This is a sober lesson of social pathology (Durkheim's notion), etiology, and 'medicine', with fascism and its terrorism being the grave, deadly problem of public health because of its death cult, as also the Covid-19 pandemic shows in the conservative-fascist pole of America, such as the former Southern Confederacy and beyond.

In essence, as non-conservative social processes and structures, countervailing forces versus fascism in America and beyond are hence liberal in the broadest sense to encompass their democratic, secular, rationalist, progressive, egalitarian, universalist, cosmopolitan, pacifist, and socio-psychological variants. They all define in integration and mutual reinforcement liberal modernity or society

---

1   Manent (1998, p. 218) points to the conservative-rightist 'partisans of an antidemocratic regime, whose enmity climaxed in the Nazi challenge that was decisively disposed of in Dresden's and Berlin's fire and rubble.'

2   For example, Acemoglu et al. (2022, pp. 1236–37) observe that in Italy's 'postwar elections center-right parties performed significantly worse and center-left and other left-wing parties performed better in municipalities where the Fascist Party was more successful in the 1920s. This may be because the center-right establishment became partly delegitimized due to its alliance with fascists.'

3   It is no wonder that a former Speaker of the US House of Representatives characterized its self-proclaimed 'Freedom Caucus' stemming from the extreme-right Tea Party as 'political terrorists' and in that sense 'all-American' fascists hiding behind and deceiving many Americans by the cover, deception, cheap talk of 'freedom' that is as present and promoted therein as in the European 'Freedom Party' commonly regarded as neo-Nazi —at the roughly zero level.

and in that sense are 'liberal' factors versus conservative structures instead defining pre-modernity, such as medieval traditionalism and its ancient regime of despotism. Specifically, with some variations, counter-fascist forces all typify and originate in the Enlightenment as the prototypical combination of liberalism and democracy with secularism, rationalism, progressivism, egalitarianism, universalism, cosmopolitanism, including initial globalism,[4] pacifism, and liberal actors. By contrast, their conservative opposites characterize and originate in the pre-Enlightenment like the Dark Middle Ages and indeed form the counter-Enlightenment.

In this sense, countervailing social forces versus fascism appear as those of the Enlightenment, just as the primary fascist cause consists of the counter-Enlightenment in the form of conservatism, indeed, fascism in America and everywhere is an ultimate form of anti-Enlightenment and in that sense the New Dark Ages. The Enlightenment and its enduring multiple legacy via liberalism, democracy, secularism, egalitarianism, rationalism, progressivism, egalitarianism, universalism, cosmopolitanism, pacifism, and liberal personalities acts as the counterpoise to fascism and conservatism, just as the last two revolt against and reverse the first and its own outcome liberal modernity. In short, the Enlightenment through liberal modernity is inherent preemptive anti-fascism by being the most effective prevention and cure of fascism and conservatism, just as the last two form the extreme counter-Enlightenment, in America and beyond. For precision, this chapter distinguishes liberalism from democracy, secularism, rationalism, progressivism, egalitarianism, universalism, cosmopolitanism, and pacifism as various interlinked facets of Enlightenment-based liberal modernity, including its comparatively weak American variation since Jefferson, thus countervailing social forces to fascism.

These countervailing social forces versus fascism by countering the latter and its root cause conservatism determine the 'fate' of America as a case of liberal modernity and so of free society. If they are strong enough to counter and transcend enduringly and fully fascism and conservatism, they are likely to remake and sustain America as liberal modernity and free society. Conversely, fascism is likely to perpetuate itself and conservatism to continue to dominate in America long after 2016 and therefore to perpetually remake and petrify it as the opposite of liberal modernity and free society.

---

4 Djelic and Quack (2018, p. 127) state that globalization 'can be seen as civilizing—the contemporary heir of Western Enlightenment.'

2   Liberalism versus Fascism

Liberalism is the crucial social, particularly ideological-political, countervailing force against fascism and conservatism as extreme and original anti-liberalism, respectively, in America post-2016 and all other contemporary and historical societies. Liberalism is the most effective societal, especially ideological-political, solution to fascism and its creator conservatism in America and beyond, as it was to despotic medievalism or the Dark Middle Ages as the original conservative and fascist basis and ideal, including that for Nazism. In short, liberalism is the best social antidote to the deadly poison of fascism and its parent conservatism as ultimate and initial anti-liberalism, respectively. Liberalism most effectively cures the pathology of fascism and its etiology conservatism, just as through liberal modernity it superseded their shared basis and ideal despotic medievalism with the ancient regime of feudal bondage, aristocracy, and theocracy. To that extent, its superseding of medievalism as the common conservative-fascist basis and ideal grounds and anticipates liberalism's counteracting and ultimately overcoming the lethal threat of fascism and conservatism to American and all modern society and its universal liberty[5] and indeed survival. Whenever liberalism emerges and prevails as a social, particularly ideological-political, factor over conservatism, fascism tends to decline, weaken, and disappear as a dominant or relevant power—except through counter-state terror—in America and beyond, just as the conservative-fascist model medievalism became extinct because of the original liberal revolution. If liberalism more than conservatism permeates American and any society, fascism as a regime and elite, even if not as an extreme-conservative or radical-right ideology and terrorist movement, experiences the 'gone with the wind' fate. (This phrase from the old South is fitting and symbolic so long as fascism has become most widespread in the former Southern confederacy precisely because of the dominance of conservatism, religion, theocracy, and coercive capitalism in this region since the end of the Civil War.)

Hence, the liberal pole of America is the main countervailing force in regional and societal terms to its fascist and conservative counterpart in American and any society involving an antagonism between liberalism and

---

5   Mueller (2009, p. 17) following J. S. Mill defines liberalism as the 'liberty to do, think and say what one wants so long as the exercise of such liberty does not do undue harm to other.' He adds that 'liberals wish to grant individuals maximum scope for action, so long as others are not significantly harmed' (Mueller 2009, p. 282).

fascism-conservatism,[6] a conflict that has been especially intense and persistent in the US.[7] Liberal America is the most effective societal antipode to the toxic rise, expansion, and structure of fascism that renders the conservative pole of American society into a fascist, thus anti-liberal and anti-democratic, subsociety, which the former Southern Confederacy from Alabama, Florida, and Tennessee to Texas epitomizes. Liberal America counters the eruption and onslaught of fascism and conservatism and prevents the two from making American society fascist and extremely conservative, respectively.

This is the essence of ideological-political, culture, and proxy civil wars in America post-2016 and since the 1980s. These essentially consist of the ideological-political, culture, and proxy civil warfare that American fascism and conservatism,[8] thus the conservative-fascist pole of American society like the South and beyond, launches post-2016 and since the 1980s with Reaganism against liberal America. The latter faces no other choice than to counteract such assaults on liberals as 'un-American' and thus effectively criminalized and threaten with persecution and extinction by conservative, fascist, and religious terrorists and warriors, as their January 2021 insurrection shows. These processes involve Spencer-like offensive wars that the conservative-fascist pole starts through the alliance between fascism and conservatism, as well as religion and coercive capitalism, and defensive wars into which liberal America, thus American liberalism is forced for survival. Hence, this conservative-fascist-religious warfare post-2016 and since Reaganism[9] primarily causes

---

6   Habermas (2001, p. 43) identifies a site of postwar societal antagonisms 'on the cultural level of ideologies' between by implication liberalism and totalitarianism, fascism and conservatism apparently continuing their antagonism during WW II.

7   Mueller (2009, p. 375) observes that the 'struggle' between liberalism or progressivism and conservatism or traditionalism 'has gone on for much of the US's history, and continues today at an intensity unmatched in other rich, developed countries. The difference between the two sides were nicely illustrated in the famous Scopes or monkey [evolution] trial of 1925.'

8   Bourdieu and Haacke (1995, p. 67) recount that the USA 'entered a period of deep polarization' caused by the 'most bitter conservatism'. Bell (2002, p. 466) finds that what united American conservatism since the 1960s 'was the emphasis on the theme of moral decay and the role of liberalism in [it]', simply anti-liberalism.

9   DiPrete et al. (2011, p. 1236) find that 'political conflict between proponents of secular and religiously orthodox values has been especially prominent since the Reagan presidency'. They conclude that since and due to Reaganism religion 'in particular has emerged as a fundamental cleavage in American society at the level of day-to-day interaction. From the perspective of the culture wars that we have seen play out in the American political sphere and the past decade or so, this may not be surprising' (DiPrete et al. 2011, p. 1272).

ideological-political, culture, and proxy civil wars and severe polarization[10] in American society. Liberal America or American liberalism acts as a countervailing force by defending itself against these orchestrated and often violent attacks by fascism and conservatism, in alliance with extremist religion like evangelicalism, theocracy, and coercive capitalism (as within the Christian Right).

It follows that equating the role of conservative-fascist and liberal America, thus American fascism/conservatism and liberalism, in these culture wars and ideological-political polarizations commits the fallacy of false equivalence. Such an equivalence is as false as equating fascism, including Nazism, and liberal anti-fascist forces in interwar and WW II Europe and elsewhere, and analogous to the equation between offensive and defensive wars or military aggressors and defenders. Substantively, it is false to equalize with respect to culture wars and ideological polarization conservative and liberal America because no equivalence exists between fascism/conservatism and liberalism as ideologies, social systems, movements, and cultural climates, but a fundamental contradiction. Especially, it is false to equalize the two because the conservative pole of America and thereby fascism/conservatism since the 1980s and culminating post-2016 launches a warfare on liberal America or American liberalism as, for Reaganism following its apparent model protofascist McCarthyism, 'an-American'.

This cycle of attack and defense results in culture wars and ideological-political polarization whose primary driver is the conservative-fascist pole of America[11] or compounded American fascism/conservatism since Reaganism

---

10   Levy (2021, pp. 833–4) remarks that based on the American National Election Survey (ANES), US party 'affective polarization increased by 3.83–10.52 degrees between 1996 and 2016.' Merriman and Pacewicz (2022, p. 1225) register that 'since the 1980s [so with Reaganism], polarization has increased, first returning to levels not seen since the 19th century and then exceeding them. By the 2010s, congressional polarization was the highest in American history and became still more pronounced during the Trump administration.' Generally, Callander and Carbajal (2022, p. 826) remarks that in the United States, 'elite polarization has proceeded monotonically since the 1970s, accumulating to such a substantial degree that in the US Congress there remains no overlap ideologically between representatives of the two major parties'.

11   Jouet (2017, p. 29) notes that the 'extraordinary polarization of American society is not merely between blue and red states, as a major partisan rift has occurred nationwide. Republican leaders in blue states typically join their counterparts in red states in defending hardline positions on essentially all issues.' Gersbach (2020, p. 33) remarks that the 'lack of competition in election races is a long-acknowledged issue [and has] become a focus of academic and public debate in the United States. Frequently, this absence of genuine competition is due to the fact that one of the candidates for office is an incumbent, who appears to be reelected quite easily. In the US Congress, the number of reelected

and McCarthyism through post-2016 and after 2020. As a result, the liberal pole of America acts as the crucial countervailing force to its fascist and conservative opposite starting proxy civil wars and primarily causing ideological-political polarization. An indication of this is that American conservatism[12] or its main party moves dramatically to the fascist right[13] and thus undergoes radicalization, while American liberalism or its party not moving greatly to the socialist left, with few exceptions in either direction.

The question opens, however, as to whether American liberalism is sufficiently extensive and potent to operate as an efficacious countervailing social force to fascism and conservatism. One wonders if liberal America is geographically widespread and socially strong enough to counter the wars launched by the fascist/conservative pole. Historically, aside from some rare and transient exceptional periods such as the New Deal and its aftermath, American liberalism has been less pervasive and powerful than conservatism since Puritanism and in consequence fascism or the radical right.[14]

---

incumbents has been rising regularly. In 2014, it was above 90 percent in the US House of Representatives', and alerts that 'noncompetitive elections can lead to policy polarization.'

12   Autor et al. (2020, p. 3140) observe that a 'sizable rightward shift among the GOP and a modest leftward shift among Democrats has left few centrists in either party' and then somewhat contradictorily add that 'moderate Democrats have become increasingly rare in Congress, while Tea Party and like-minded conservatives have risen to prominence in the GOP.'

13   What many observers (e.g., Bonikowski et al. 2021; Bourdieu 1998; Jouet 2017; Merriman and Pacewicz 2022) see as the apparent and documented involution of the main conservative political party into a proto-fascist and generally extreme-right anti-democratic organization expresses politically the inevitable ideological metastasis of American conservatism into proto- and neo-fascism. Such proto-fascist degeneration is a long and sustained historical trend starting with the party's opposition to the New Deal or with McCarthyism, resuming after the demise of the latter through extremists like Goldwater and reaching its crowning success with anti-liberal Reaganism, then continuing with the 1994 radical-right 'Contract with America', repressive and militarist but embellished 'compassionate conservatism', the extreme-right Tea Party, and culminating in the evangelical and other conservative cult of its autocratic leaders post-2016 and after the 2020 election, notably the right-wing terrorist attack on Congress on January 06, 2021. Even a former official in the post-2016 radical-right administration warned in 2021 that the 'number one national security threat I've ever seen in my life to this country's democracy is the party that I'm in—the Republican Party. It is the number one security national security threat to the United States of America.' As an illustration, Merriman and Pacewicz (2022, p. 1229) note that 'in the past decade, Republicans in states like Iowa, Kansas, Michigan, and Wisconsin ran conventional electoral campaigns, but pursued radical conservative policies once in office; [e.g.] unpopular, sweeping restrictions on public-sector unions.'

14   Gross et al. (2011, p. 328) remark that during the New Deal era, 'liberalism, then widely understood as committed to progressive expansion of 'political, civil, and social

Therefore, with these few exceptions, liberal America has been geographically less widespread and socially strong than the conservative and consequently fascist or extreme-rightist pole. Especially, American liberalism or liberal America has drastically weakened when compared to conservatism or the conservative pole since the 1980s with the anti-liberal Reagan counterrevolution. Furthermore, liberalism reaches the lowest point of spread and influence post-2016, judging by the electoral results disastrous for liberals[15] and triumphant for extremist conservatives at congressional, particularly the House of Representatives, and especially state levels, except for the Presidential election. In consequence, American liberalism or liberal America has not been able to prevent or mitigate the antiliberal resurgence and expansion of fascism and conservatism during these times and since the 1980s, thus failing to act as an effective countervailing anti-fascist and counter-conservative social power.

In addition, comparatively, liberalism has been traditionally, particularly since the 1980s following the anti-liberal Reagan counterrevolution, less prominent in America, as a facet of conservative or rightist 'American exceptionalism', than in postwar Western Europe,[16] especially Scandinavia and to some degree France. Liberal America[17] has been typically weaker than equivalent

---

citizenship,' was ideologically ascendant and politically powerful, if not without internal tensions.'

15   Autor et al. (2020, p. 3143) find that US 'White voters disadvantaged by economic changes see GOP conservatives as favoring their interests over those of other groups, while disadvantaged minority voters see liberal Democrats as their champions.' Bonikowski et al. (2021, p. 533) find that 'only one of the two parties [representing conservatism] has undergone a process of [fascist or radical-right] radicalization [violating] liberal democratic commitments.'

16   Colantone and Stanig (2019, p. 148) suggest that in Western Europe the 'challenge for believers in liberal policies is how to popularize a version of embedded liberalism that will be responsive to the current challenges of slow growth and structural economic shifts.'

17   For illustration, an extremely conservative US senator from West Virginia, as an argument against some egalitarian welfare-state measures by the post-2020 Federal government, stated that America stands basically on the right rather than on the left of the political spectrum. To that extent, given that fascism is everywhere a phenomenon of the right, this unwittingly implies that the essence of America is closer to fascism or right-wing authoritarianism than to liberalism and socialism, simply the 'American character' being more fascist than socialist and liberal. It is more accurate to observe that the core or tendency of specifically conservative America, such as the Bible-Belt South and similar regions, is inherent or latent fascism and generally right-wing authoritarianism, as well as theocracy, that explodes or becomes open at favorable occasions such as the post-2016 rise of fascist or rightist autocracy, in opposition to and warfare against that of liberal America being by definition anti-fascism and democracy.

Europe, notably Scandinavia and in part France. Consequently, American liberalism has operated as a less efficacious countervailing social force to fascism and conservatism than its European, especially Scandinavian, variant that has supplanted fascist and conservative regimes or ruling powers since postwar times, with some variations like oppositional radical-right terrorist groups.

Furthermore, the dilemma arises as to whether American liberalism—as opposed to neo-liberalism[18] that is instead economic pro-capital neo-conservatism and indeed anti-liberalism by denying labor as well as universal noneconomic liberties—is capable of operating as an effective countervailing social force to fascism and conservatism because of its internal tendencies and external intrusions. It is questionable if American liberalism can perform this role so long as it continues to be perverted from within or intruded by outside non- or quasi-liberal forces, especially radical feminism and other specious 'liberal' or 'progressive' elements. Moreover, such degenerations or intrusions may make American liberalism complete incapable to stand and act as an effective countervailing social force to fascism and its generator conservatism. For example, American militant feminism appears closer to and opportunistically allies with repressive conservatism, with both being driven by 'social hatred', as in the shared essentialist, gendered redefinition and Draconian punishment of sexual sins-as-crimes for males.

Particularly, since the 1980s American liberalism has been plagued by internal degeneration or external intrusion, especially perverted by militant feminism, and consequently powerless to stand and act as an effective counterpoise to the resurgence and dominance of fascism and conservatism, as in conservative America, such as the South and beyond, culminating in post-2016. A perverted radical feminist 'liberalism' that is effectively anti-liberal is less likely than liberalism without such perversions by militant feminism to act as an effective countervailing social force to fascism's and conservatism's culture and other wars and polarization in America and beyond.

Furthermore, such a perversion by militant feminism with its essentialist 'identity politics' almost certainly ensures that American liberalism or liberal America suffers a defeat and extinction in the culture-political wars and

---

18   Bourdieu (1998, p. 50) warns that neo-liberalism 'is in fact conservative [i.e.] based on an atavistic faith in historical inevitability [so] fatalism.' He adds that US and other revolutionary conservatives are 'inspired by a paradoxical intention of subversion oriented towards conservation or restoration' (Bourdieu 1998, p. 104). Lamont (2018, p. 426) also cautions that 'there is ample indication that neoliberalism is fostering an overall narrowing of cultural membership and a growing recognition gap for specific vulnerable groups as neoliberal criteria of worth are becoming more hegemonic across neoliberal societies.'

polarization that fascism and conservatism launches and causes, as in post-2016, including after 2020, and since the 1980s with Reaganism's attack on liberals as 'un-American'. This suggests that only liberalism freed from such perversions by external radical feminist and related intrusions can operate as an effective antidote to the deadly poison and lethal weapon of fascism and its prime source anti-liberal conservatism in America and beyond.

Especially, American radical feminism misconstrues and restarts the culture wars or ideological-political polarization between fascism/conservatism and liberalism, thus between societal oppression and liberty, as the 'war of the sexes', more precisely one against the male sex. Radical feminism appears as another version of 'social hatred' (Simmel's term) and thus more like fascism or Nazism (radical feminists as 'femi-Nazis' is a conservative description of this similarity, which seems ironic so long as most US conservatives act as proto-fascists) and conservatism as its extreme and original versions than to liberalism as the opposite ideology of universal liberty, compassion, empathy (in that sense 'love'), and inclusion. In short, 'social hatred' disqualifies militant feminism as 'liberalism' and makes it a proxy of conservatism and fascism in the sense of a hateful ideology and movement despite its anti-conservative, anti-fascist rhetoric.

Overall, militant feminism denies individual and other liberty to the gender that is the object of its 'social hatred' while monopolizing it in an essentialist manner for its preferred gender, and hence approaches conservatism and fascism, and deviates from liberalism's ideal and system of universal liberty for all genders. Relatedly, feminism tends to condemn and criminalize consensual sexual relations and social interactions, simply sociation (in Simmel's word) when initiated by the gender that is the object of its 'social hatred' but not if started by its preferred gender (it is 'empowerment'), and thus converges with conservatism and fascism and diverges from liberalism. By treating the gender being the object of its 'social hatred' as presumed guilty of sexual offenses, feminism perverts the legal presumption of innocence and resembles conservatism, including fundamentalism's dogma of male universal guilt due to Adam's original sin by association, and fascism. Conversely, it contradicts and perverts liberalism and its rule of law premised on the presumed innocent principle. A sinister outcome of this feminist and religious presumed-guilty rule for males is the near epidemic of false accusations of sexual crimes (including rapes) against and the mass imprisonment of innocent men eventually but often too late proven such after the fact by DNA and other evidence.

The preceding illustrates the gravity of danger that radical feminism poses for individual liberty and criminal justice, just as do conservatism and fascism, and its perversion of liberalism's values and defense versus conservative-fascist social wars. On this account, radical feminism reappears as a hidden and irreconcilable enemy or essentialist perversion of liberalism from within,[19] just as conservatism and fascism are its overt implacable enemies from outside. Moreover, feminism becomes an open enemy of liberalism by construing and rejecting the latter's original and primary basis, the Enlightenment as a 'male' liberal ideology and philosophy, as well as the rationalism, reason, and science of 'men'. In so doing, feminism amounts to the anti-Enlightenment and to that extent anti-liberalism, just as conservatism arises as and fascism inherits the vehement counter-Enlightenment. It follows that liberalism counteracts conservatism and fascism as a compounded external antagonist and exposes radical feminism as its latent internal adversary or perversion.

3 Democracy versus Fascism

As a universal corollary of liberalism, democracy is a critical institutional-political countervailing force to fascism and conservatism as respective forms of extreme and initial anti-liberalism and anti-democracy. More precisely, this holds true for liberal democracy as the realization of liberalism in the polity and the sole genuine democratic type within liberal modernity, thus among contemporary Western societies,[20] including America, as distinct from and

---

19   Radical feminism has penetrated and even come to dominate the US major political party traditionally representing or approximating liberalism, among other things. Militant feminists have nearly captured this political party and perverted it into a tool of their 'social hatred'. Thus, one major political party seems dominated by proto-fascists or extreme conservatives, and the other by what the latter brand 'femi-Nazis.' For example, one of the 'eternal' feminist, supposedly 'liberal' members and leaders of the House of Representatives, apart from reportedly engaging via family proxy in insider stock trading and, as a result, glorifying and fervently defending unconstrained capitalism from critics, shows excessive public religiosity and thus weakens liberal-secular democracy (publicly proclaiming 'pray' as a political medicine), shows strong militarist tendencies by approving the continuing drastic growth of exorbitant military expenditure ($840 billion for 2023/24), bellicose or hostile acts (e.g., the provocative petulant visit of Taiwan causing nearly a war and many other serious problems with China), nationalist, imperialist, and bellicosity-actuated economic irrationality (adopting measures targeting Chinese companies, urging 'I am for' banning Russian oil imports and exacerbating surging gasoline prices, etc.). This mix of weakening liberal-secular democracy with exalting unrestrained capitalism, militarism, nationalism, imperialism, and bellicosity hence exemplifies radical American feminism as false liberalism and anti-liberalism at least at the level of party and congressional leadership, so closer to conservatism, fascism ('femi-Nazism'), and theocracy ('pray' as the solution).

20   Mueller (2009, p. 1) observes that the 'Western rich countries today, with very few exceptions, are liberal democracies. They are liberal in the sense that their citizens have

opposed to bogus illiberal, particularly ersatz conservative and religious or theocratic, 'democracies'.

Liberal democracy is the most effective institutional-political counterpoise to the anti-democratic gravity of fascism and conservatism in America and beyond, as it was to the ancient regime of medieval despotism, including monarchy, aristocracy, and theocracy, which conservatism perpetuates and fascism, including Nazim, restores (via the Third Reich). In brief, liberal democracy is the polity's best remedy for the lethal pathology of fascism and conservatism as ultimate and original anti-liberalism and anti-democracy, respectively, in America and elsewhere. Liberal democracy most efficiently within a political system remedies the 'morbidity' (in Durkheim's[21] sense) of fascism and conservatism as social phenomena, just as it superseded the ancient medieval regime of despotic monarchy, aristocracy, and theocracy that conservatism and fascism perpetuate and restore, with some adaptations. Its superseding of the ancient regime of despotism prefigures liberal democracy remedying the pathological phenomenon of fascism and conservatism. In other (Durkheimian)[22] words, the genesis of liberal democracy as the antipode of the despotic ancient regime of monarchy, aristocracy, and theocracy determines its evolution and functioning as the most effective institutional antidote to the poisonous eruption and expansion of fascism and conservatism.

In essence, when liberal democracy develops and consolidates as a prevalent type of political system versus bogus illiberal 'democracy' and non-democracy, fascism seems destined to ultimately fall from power and social grace, as does conservatism, and to be relegated to political marginality and violent opposition via anti-state violence in America and beyond, just as the despotic ancient regime disappeared because of early liberal-democratic revolutions, such as the French Revolution. So long as liberal democracy establishes itself versus illiberal 'democracy' or non-democracy in America and other settings, fascism as a ruling elite or political regime becomes caput mortuum ('presumed dead'), although persisting on the fringe as an extreme conservative or radical-right ideology and terrorist movement via counter-state terror. In short, when liberal democracy ascends, thrives, and prevails over its ersatz substitutes and

---

freedoms to go and to do as they wish. They are democracies in that their citizens exercise a significant control over the state. In the poorest countries, one or both attributes of liberal democracy are often missing.'

21   Durkheim (1966, p. 49) proposes to 'distinguish scientifically between health and morbidity in the various orders of social phenomena.'

22   Durkheim (1966, p. lvii) states that sociology be defined as the 'science of institutions, of their genesis and functioning.'

opposites, fascism descends, diminishes, and suffers demise, as does conservatism. In this regard, liberal democracy acts as the cardinal institutional-political 'terminator' of fascism and in extension its creator conservatism, and conversely, fascism terminates and conservatism eliminates or perverts liberal democracy, in America and beyond.

Consequently, the liberal-democratic pole of America becomes the major countervailing regional and societal force to the fascist and conservative variant in American and other contemporary societies in which the intense opposition between liberal democracy and bogus illiberal 'democracy' or anti-democracy, generally liberalism and conservatism, arises and persists. Liberal-democratic America is the best cure and last defense against the explosion, onslaught, and contagion of fascism and conservatism that render its conservative counterpart anti-democracy or ersatz illiberal 'democracy', as in the former Southern Confederacy and beyond, and thus threaten to conquer and shape all society after its anti-liberal and anti-democratic 'divine' design. Liberal-democratic America by counteracting and defending itself against totalitarian fascism and anti-liberal and anti-democratic conservatism defends and prevents all American society from being perverted into fascist anti-democracy or conservative ersatz illiberal 'democracy' characterizing the South and similar spaces.

At this juncture, the culture, ideological, and political wars and polarizations between the liberal and conservative poles of America appear as those between liberal democracy which the first pole epitomizes and conservative ersatz illiberal 'democracy' or fascist anti-democracy that the second exemplifies post-2016 and since Reaganism. Fascism and broader conservatism such as Reaganism start these proxy civil wars and cause severe ideological and political polarizations by attacking and subverting liberal democracy as 'un-American' in its 'liberal' core and establishing conservative 'all-American' ersatz illiberal 'democracy' and ultimately fascist anti-democracy, as in the conservative pole like the South and similar regions post-2016 and since the 1980s. This reveals that the primary political cause and impetus of these lamented culture wars and ideological polarizations between liberal and conservative America is fascism's and conservatism's attack on and subversion of liberal democracy and its replacement with conservative illiberal 'democracy' and fascist anti-democracy. The preceding makes equalizing the roles of the liberal-democratic and conservative-undemocratic sections of America, for example, the 'Union' and the former Southern 'Confederacy', in such wars and polarizations a false equivalence analogous to equating fascist-conservative and anti-fascist liberal social forces in interwar and WW II Europe, military aggression and aggressors and defenses and defenders, aggressive action and defensive reaction. Such equalizing amounts to a false equivalence or spurious equation of liberal, genuine democracy with conservative ersatz illiberal 'democracy' and fascist anti-democracy. This applies to the framework and from the standpoint of Western societies that, as a rule, do not equate but sharply oppose the two political regimes and typically embrace and sustain the first and thus are primarily liberal-democratic.[23]

It is evident that the liberal-democratic pole of America can stand and act as the countervailing societal force to its fascist and conservative antithesis only if it withstands and overcomes the onslaught and expansion of fascism and conservatism that launch proxy civil wars causing severe ideological and political polarization. Liberal-democratic America is the most effective regional and societal antidote to the poison of fascism if it counters and prevails over or discredits the latter's root conservatism in these wars and polarizations. By counteracting and supplanting conservatism, liberal democracy is the surest path toward overcoming fascism as its creation, just as the fascist destruction of liberalism is the 'optimal' way of eliminating its product liberal democracy in America.

As with respect to liberalism, however, the suspicion arises as to whether liberal democracy is sufficiently established and strong or even existent and functional to persist and function as an effective countervailing force to fascism and conservatism. One doubts if the liberal-democratic pole of America is powerful enough in geographic and societal terms to counteract the conservative-undemocratic, including fascist, opposite in conservatism-fascism's culture, ideological, and conceivably actual civil anti-liberal, anti-democratic wars déjà vu.

In historical terms, deriving from the relative weakness of American liberalism and aside from Jeffersonian, New-Deal, and postwar exceptions, liberal democracy in America has typically been secondary compared to primary conservative, ersatz illiberal 'democracy' since theocratic Puritanism through the 1980s and post-2016. In this regard, liberal democracy in America has been more an exception rather than a rule during most of its history from Puritanism

---

23   Mueller (2009, p. 13) notes that in a Western 'liberal democracy citizens not only participate in a democratic process but also get great freedoms to think and do as they please. Thus, liberal democracy requires two sets of institutions, voting rules and electoral laws that enable the state to provide goods and services that benefit the citizen, and constitutional rights and a judiciary that protects certain individual freedoms from the state.' Generally, he suggests that 'democracy and liberalism can both be defined over a continuum' (Mueller 2009, p. 13). Soehl and Karim (2021, p. 410) state that the 'core tenet of liberal democratic governance is that a restrained state protects individuals not only from external threats, but also from arbitrary use of state force as codified in the protection of property rights, checks and balances on executive power, and the enshrinement of civil liberties.'

or the American Revolution, especially since the 1980s and the rise and dominance of anti-liberal, repressive Reaganism through its post-2016 autocratic sequel and amplification. The Jeffersonian Enlightenment-based ideal of liberal democracy has only rarely been fully implemented in America—aside from some short and transient episodes, such as the economically liberal New Deal and the socially liberal 1960s—because of the combination of the relative insecurity and weakness of 'un-American' liberalism and the strength and dominance of 'all-American' Puritan-rooted conservatism. After all, if liberal democracy were fully implemented in America or American liberalism stronger than conservatism, this would have likely prevented the eruption and contagion of fascism post-2016 and since the 1980s—but evidently it was not and did not prevent this anti-liberal and anti-democratic outcome.

In comparative terms, stemming from the relative insecurity and weakness of American liberalism, despite Jefferson's importation of it from Europe, literally Paris salons, liberal democracy in America has usually been weaker than in most other Western societies spanning from France to Scandinavia, except for Germany and Italy prior to 1918, which helps explain the rise of German Nazism and Italian fascism. This is what 'American exceptionalism' implies by opposing exceptional, predominantly non-liberal, conservative and 'faith-based' 'democracy' in America from its liberal and secularized version in Western Europe. Indeed, most Americans describe America as just 'democracy' or even, as with conservatives, as 'republic' but hardly as liberal democracy, and thus do not distinguish it from its ersatz illiberal substitutes.

In other words, it is doubtful whether the liberal-democratic pole of America is extensive and strong enough to exist and act as the effective countervailing force to its conservative-fascist opposite and thus fascism and conservatism. Historically, liberal-democratic America has been subordinate or impertinent relative to its conservative-undemocratic, including theocratic, opposite since Puritanism and its proto-totalitarian theocracy through anti-liberal Reaganism in the 1980s and the post-2016 autocracy. Comparatively, liberal-democratic America has been typically narrower and weaker than equivalent Western Europe, including France and especially Scandinavia, with the salient exception of pre-1918 Germany and Italy mainly explaining the rise of Nazism and fascism in these two countries. No wonder, 'American exceptionalism' consistently opposes non-liberal, conservative—and by implication non-democratic in the sense of liberal democracy or democratic in the meaning of illiberal 'faith-based democracy'—America to liberal-democratic Western Europe, including France and Scandinavia, with depreciative reference to European 'foreign' liberalism and its model of democracy. If liberal-democratic America were wide and strong enough relative to its conservative-undemocratic antithesis, fascism probably would have not happened in post-2016 and prefigured since the 1980s, but the first was not the case and the second did happen.

Furthermore, one suspects whether liberal democracy is sufficiently extensive and relevant to operate as an effective countervailing force to anti-democratic fascism and anti-liberal conservatism because of its internal distortion or external perversion by supposedly 'liberal' or 'progressive' but actually non-liberal forces, especially radical feminism and similar essentialist 'identity politics'. Such tendencies arguably degrade, deform, dilute, or weaken liberal democracy and thus make it less able to counter the antiliberal and anti-democratic eruption and contagion of fascism and conservatism. Moreover, when internally distorted or externally perverted by spurious 'liberal' or 'progressive' forces, above all, militant feminism acting as gender-driven 'social hatred', liberal democracy stands virtually no chance to counteract, let alone neutralize and overcome, the surge and dominance of fascism and conservatism, thus anti-democracy and ersatz illiberal 'democracy', as in America post-2016 and since the 1980s.

Especially, since the 1980s liberal democracy in America has experienced growing internal dissention and distortion and/or external contamination, intrusion, and perversion by specious 'liberal' or 'progressive' ideologies and movements, primarily militant feminism, and consequently is unable to prevent and mitigate the resurgence of fascism and the dominance of conservatism post-2016. Thus, what essentially explains and indeed predicts for the future such a failure of liberal democracy versus fascism and conservatism is that these distortions and perversions, especially radical feminism, turn out to be anti- or quasi-liberal and non-democratic as well as anti-meritocratic forces. US radical feminists pretending to be 'liberals' are especially delusionary that they can win electoral and other political contests against extreme conservatives and fascists, as their defeat in the 2016 Presidential elections and many others shows, and yet they seek to run for President and other office against the very rightist extremists who defeated them. By so doing, radical feminist would-be rulers sabotage liberalism and liberal democracy in its life-and-death contestation with conservatism/fascism in America post-2016/2020.

In addition, feminism is anti-meritocratic in that it seeks to impose 'equal pay' for effectively unequal performance—despite deceptively or vaguely stating 'equal work'—in light of the evidence of gender differentials in work hours, experience, qualifications, skills, productivity, and industry or occupational self-selection or choice and structure,[24] including degree of unionization. While fervently advocating 'social justice', feminism denies or overlooks

---

24   Blau and Kahn (2000, p. 82) find that 'when occupation, industry and unionism were
       also taken into account, the explained portion of the gap rose to 62 percent of the total

that not only unequal pay for equal work but also 'equal pay' for unequal performance or productivity is a form of injustice in income distribution directed specifically against the gender that is the target of its 'social hatred'. For instance, feminism's advocating 'equal pay' for unequal performance or productivity is equivalent to and thus as absurd as workers with high-school diplomas requesting 'equal pay' as those with college and advanced degrees. Militant feminism seems unable or unwilling to realize that demanding equal pay between different gender groups irrespective of actual performance or other meritocratic criteria is as unjust and absurd as requesting the same payment for diverse educational strata.

On this account, radical feminism poses a grave threat to meritocracy, as to liberal democracy by negating individual, political, and other liberties to the gender being the target of its 'social hatred' and monopolizing them for its preferred gender. In either case, it confirms to be an exemplar of 'social hatred' and exclusion seeking to substitute one oppressive system for another, such as matriarchy for patriarchy. It thus converges more with conservatism and fascism as hate-driven exclusionary exemplars than with liberalism as the ideal of Enlightenment-style universal love, compassion, and inclusion that feminism infiltrates and perverts with anti- or non-liberal ingredients.

In particular, feminism is closer to and seeks to restore the pre-Enlightenment (matriarchy) than to the Enlightenment and its universal liberalism and project of liberal democracy, as well as its scientific rationalism and progressivism. Indeed, feminists attack the Enlightenment and seek to demolish its legacy of

---

gender gap, suggesting that a considerable portion of the gap was due to wage differences between men and women with similar human capital working in different industries or occupations or in union vs. nonunion jobs.' Overall, they estimate that occupation, industry, and unionism, together with human capital, explain almost all of the gender gap (88%) in pay, with discrimination as merely a potentiality (Blau and Kahn 2000, p. 82). They update these findings, reporting that 'whether taken separately or combined, occupation and industry now constitute the largest measured factors accounting for the gender pay gap' (Blau and Kahn 2017, p. 801). Blau and Kahn (2017, p. 853) also confirm that 'labor-market experience remains an important factor in analyzing female wages [along with] an especially important role for work force interruptions and shorter hours in explaining gender wage gaps in high-skilled occupations than for the workforce as a whole.' Lundberg and Pollak (2007, pp. 7–8) report that 'the remaining gap between men's and women's hourly wages is about 20 percent, and about half of this gap can be explained by individual characteristics, job experience, and occupational choices,' while (as the 'source of the unexplained residual') 'labor market discrimination or the continuing gender disparity in family and household responsibilities' remaining the 'subject of considerable controversy' by implication because of the lack of evidence for either, especially the first, contrary to radical feminists' claims to 'gender discrimination'.

liberalism through the principle of universal liberty and of rationalism via its 'Age of Reason' and scientific progress as a detestable 'male' ideology, philosophy, and politics, displaying their apparently implacable 'social hatred' for their detested gender. Furthermore, they pervert Enlightenment-rooted science and scientific method by suppressing and even criminalizing (as 'sexual harassment' or causing 'discomfort') academic freedom or freedom of speech for the gender target of their 'social hatred', particularly perverting social science, including sociology as the product of the French rationalist Enlightenment, into feminist 'identity' ideology and politics.[25]

By such anti-Enlightenment attitudes radical feminists overlook that without the Enlightenment liberal ideal of universal liberty and inclusion[26] through liberal democracy feminism would have not been and was not allowed to exist, as in pre-Enlightenment medievalism and anti-Enlightenment conservatism and fascism. Such feminist anti-Enlightenment makes feminism incapable of or resistant to rational argumentation and debate consistent with the 'Age of Reason' and based on facts or real-life trends, notably the trend to increasing gender societal equality,[27] instead displaying irrational essentialist emotions

---

25   Heiberger, Galvez and McFarland (2021, p. 1185) find that sociological specializations providing 'career advantages' through especially dissertations and publications include those that closely relate to the feminist and similar 'cultural turn', such as gender and related 'identity' (along with statistical approaches and race). This seems to suggest that sociological publications and dissertations concentrating on gender and related 'identity', by implication claiming or stating women 'discrimination, inequality, injustice, oppression', and the like, ensure the most 'career advantages', which indicates that the 'cultural turn' tends to pervert sociology and other social science into feminist ideology and politics. A casual inspection of most books and journal articles, as well as doctoral dissertations, in sociology confirms this impression or interpretation, which makes gender 'identity' a kind of sociological alchemy in respect of publications and generally 'career advantages'. Heiberger et al. (2021, p. 1166) conclude that 'this finding adds important nuance to the well-known imperative of publish or perish', which practically means the best formula to publish and not to perish is focusing on gender and related 'identity' and thus pursuing feminist ideology and politics but perverting sociology as a science.

26   Mueller (2009, p. 388) observes that the 'spread of Enlightenment ideas in the West has resulted in women achieving nearly fully equality in all aspects of economic and social life. Universal education applies both to boys and girls in Western countries, and in many places women outnumber men at universities.' Also, Lundberg and Pollak (2007, p. 8) observe that 'women now attend college at higher rates than men, and this difference is particularly large for those from disadvantaged backgrounds.'

27   Lundberg and Pollak (2007, p. 7) note that the 'median earnings of full-time, year-round working women have increased from 60 percent of men's to 76 percent between 1960 and 2003.' Furthermore, they report that 'about a quarter of married working women now earn more than their husbands [plus] for 60 percent of such couples this earnings differential persists for at least three years' (Lundberg and Pollak 2007, p. 7). Blau and Kahn

and seeking them to rationalize (an exemplar of Pareto's chain of irrationality or non-logicality via residues and derivations).

Taken together, radical feminism is, despite its 'liberal' declarations, closer to authoritarian conservatism than to liberalism as the principle and system of universal liberty that these anti- and non-liberal ideologies and movements that pervert and monopolize liberties for their adherents and negate them to others, as does fascism.

4   Secularism versus Fascism

Secularism is an additional countervailing social, including political and cultural, force to fascism as extreme anti-secularism or religion-grounded and sanctified ideology, movement, regime, and zeitgeist, and to conservatism as an original and perpetual anti-secularist and particularly theocratic reaction. Secularism interconnects with liberalism and constitutes a necessary condition of liberal democracy and its constitutional enactment by the differentiation between politics and religion such as the separation of church and state.[28] Secularism as a structure and secularization as a process is a counterpoise to the resurgence and social devastation of fascism, as it was via the Enlightenment to conservatism and medievalism's dissolution of society into religion.

(2017, p. 790) register that the 'long-term trend has been a substantial reduction in the gender wage gap, both in the United States and in other economically advanced nations.' They elaborate that 'women's relative wages began to rise sharply in the 1980s, with a continued, but slower and more uneven rate of increase thereafter. By 2014, women full-time workers earned about 79 percent of what men did on an annual basis and about 83 percent on a weekly basis' (Blau and Kahn 2017, p. 791). Further, Blau and Kahn (2017, p. 794) note that 'in the case of education, there was a dramatic reversal of the gender gap. In 1981, women had lower average levels of schooling than men and were less likely to have exactly a bachelor's or an advanced degree. Over the period, women narrowed the education gap with men and, by 2011, women had higher average levels of schooling and were more likely to have an advanced degree [than men].' Notably, Blau and Kahn (2017, p. 795) find that 'while men were four percentage points more likely than women to be in [professional and managerial] jobs in 1981, by 2011, the gender gap had been virtually eliminated'. Yet, radical feminists overlook or deny such facts of or actual trends to eliminating or reducing these and other gender gaps, and instead resort to irrational assertions driven by emotions of 'social hatred', thus being unable or unwilling to conduct rational, fact-based argumentation.

28   Habermas (2001, p. 127) alerts that democracy and its defining element political autonomy 'implies a secularized political authority uncoupled from religious or cosmological worldviews.' Rawls (2010, p. 265) states that liberal-constitutional democracy is only 'realized in institutions by the separation of church and state.'

In particular, secularism/secularization is the most effective antidote against the theocratic poison and generally religion-driven pathology of fascism and conservatism as extreme and original anti-secularism, respectively, that both ex ante rules out and post fact dismantles the separation of church and state in America and everywhere. Secularism is the best cure for the theocratic social 'morbidity' (in Durkheim's sense) of fascism and conservatism because secularization, in conjunction with liberalization and consequently liberal-secular modernity, initially disestablished and transcended the fascist-conservative common religious ideal medieval Christian, including Catholic, Orthodox and Protestant (especially Calvinist-Puritan), theocracy and its perversion of all social, cultural, and political phenomena into religion. What enables and predicts secularism to counteract and conceivably cure the lethal theocratic pathology of fascism and conservatism in American and other contemporary societies is its disestablishing and transcending via the Enlightenment of medieval theocracy as the shared conservative-fascist archetype and the degeneration and subordination of all culture and society to religion during the Christian and Islamic Dark Ages.

Secularism exists and acts as an effective counterpoise against fascism and its underlying, or its merging with, theocracy in America and beyond through the structural-functional differentiation between politics and religion, in particular the institutional separation of church and state. As commonly observed, fascism and conservatism in America and beyond seek and eventually succeed, as especially in the former Southern Confederacy and similar regions representing the 'Bible Belt', to destroy or subvert such a differentiation between political and religious domains, particularly the separation of secular and 'sacred' powers. Resulting from and expressing accelerating secularization, secularism aims to recreate and sustain what fascism and conservatism in tandem destroy or subvert and preclude as impossible—liberal-secular democracy, thus political and social liberty in the sense of autonomy or 'freedom from religion' (as Jefferson stated[29]) and 'sacred' powers.

Secularism as a condition and secularization as a trend is the strong antidote to the theocratic and so grave anti-democratic eruption and contagion of fascism and conservatism in America and elsewhere in that it is the necessary, though not sufficient, condition of liberal democracy by virtue of the structural differentiation between politics and religion, including the legal separation of church and state. So long as effective and functioning liberal democracy

---

29   This refers to Thomas Jefferson's statement: 'It is the responsibility of this new government to ensure freedom of religion to all citizens. It is also the responsibility of this new government to ensure freedom from religion to all citizens.'

is essentially impossible or ultimately unviable without the differentiation between politics and religion as its indispensable precondition, secularism is the imperative mechanism, and secularization the requisite process, of realization and protection of such a democratic system within Western society, as distinct from illiberal non-Western settings (China, North Korea, etc.). Moreover, secularism or secularization in the form of differentiation between politics and religion becomes the sufficient condition of liberal democracy when combining with liberalism or liberalization, as in Western society, especially Western Europe and within its framework Scandinavia.

As the necessary and sufficient condition of liberal democracy in current Western society, secularism therefore acts as a strong counterpower and secularization as an accelerating countertrend to the anti-liberal and anti-democratic, including theocratic, core and outcome of fascism and conservatism in America and elsewhere. If fascism and conservatism is the lethal theocratic or religious poison of liberal democracy, secularism/secularization is the antidote to this conservative-fascist toxic pathology of theocracy or religion-sanctified repression in conservative America post-2016 and since the 1980s. That helps explains why fascism, following its parent conservatism, once seizing and exerting total state power invariably seeks to destroy secularism and to reverse secularization by destroying the differentiation between politics and religion, notably the separation of church and state. This is what occurs in conservative America such as the 'Bible Belt' and beyond post-2016 and since Reaganism and the Tea Party in a continuity from fascist Italy/Spain and Nazi Germany through postwar Latin America to present Poland, Hungary, and other cases.

Just as conservatism does since its vehement revolt against the secular Enlightenment, fascism attacks and fears secularism and reverses secularization by both fearing and attacking the differentiation between politics and religion for evidently good reasons. These reasons consist in that secular structures and processes act as the cure for fascist and conservative or rightist theocratic regimes and tendencies. By fearing and attacking the differentiation between politics and religion, like conservatism, fascism displays both cowardice and aggression, including extreme cruelty, versus secularism and liberal-secular democracy. According to a fascist favorite (Pareto), 'no one is more cruel than the coward', which means that US fascists inflict and enjoy extreme cruelty expressing their cowardice. . (The US post-2016 would-be autocracy and its followers are widely described or perceived as both extremely cruel and coward versus secularists, liberals and other anti-fascists and non-conservatives, as well as lower classes and minorities, let alone helpless refugees, including children, and immigrants, thus conforming to Pareto's proto-fascist model of the show and use of force, including cruelty as expedient, but without apparent cowardice.)

Whenever secularism, in conjunction and mutual reinforcement with liberalism and liberal democracy within Western society, emerges, consolidates, and supersedes conservative anti-secularism, fascism declines as a regime and elite rule, ceteris paribus, except for its persistence as counter-state terror, just as medieval theocracy declined in Western Europe due to the original secular revolution of the Enlightenment. If, conjoined with liberalism and democracy, secularism more than conservative anti-secularism undergirds American and any society, fascism as a dominant social factor becomes a rare species, while persisting as an oppositional extremist ideology and terrorist movement within the broader family of authoritarian conservatism or rightism. As a corollary, the secular pole of America, overlapping with the liberal-democratic, is the regional and societal counterpower to the fascist and religious-conservative opposite in American and other contemporary societies that involve an opposition between secularism and anti-secularism through religion's overdetermination of culture, politics, and society, including theocracy.

Secular America is the additional remedy and safeguard, the last line of defense and protection against the dangerous eruption and contagion of fascism that initially and 'naturally' surges and dominates in the religious-conservative pole of America as a theocratic and anti-secular region and subsociety that the 'Bible Belt' from the Deep South and Texas to the Dakotas, Iowa, Montana, Nebraska, Utah, Wyoming epitomizes. Like its liberal-democratic link, secular America prevents the total contagion, contamination, and penetration of fascism and conservatism into American society by resisting the theocratic and generally anti-secular assault of the religious-conservative pole that the South and related regions exemplify through theocratic Southernization. Therefore, the lamented culture wars and ideological-political polarizations between secular and religious America essentially appear as those between a project of secular democracy that the first seeks to implement and defend and a Divine 'intelligent design' of theocracy blended with fascism that the second aims and growingly succeeds to institute and impose on all American society. Since the first defends secular democracy, such as the separation of church and state, and reacts to the second's act of warfare and the joint onslaught of theocracy and fascism, equalizing secular and religious America, secularism, and anti-secularism, in these wars and polarizations commits a false equivalence comparable to equating fascist and anti-fascist, theocratic and non-theocratic processes and structures, aggression and defense, action and reaction. While secular America and liberal democracy, including the separation of church and state, is under attack by the religious-conservative pole and thus by theocratic anti-secularism pervading conservatism and fascism, American secularism has the potential to be the effective remedy against the lethal pathology of their underlying theocracy.

Yet, the doubt emerges as to whether and to what extent secularism is pervasive and powerful to operate as an additional effective countervailing power against fascism and more broadly conservatism. One suspects if the secular section of America is sufficiently extensive and strong geographically and socially to counteract and prevail over the religious-conservative, including fascist, pole, the Union versus the former Southern Confederacy déjà vu in a slightly different format, in conservatism-fascism's initiated and continuing culture, ideological and religious wars and polarizations.

In historical terms, secularism as a structure and secularization as a process in America has been typically less pervasive, strong, rapid, and intense than the opposite. The latter has assumed the form of the religious regime and overdetermination qua Christianization of society, including theocracy, since theocratic Puritanism through its heir evangelicalism, as well as orthodox Catholicism within the Christian Right, aside from rare, transient variations and exceptions like Jefferson et al. and recent secular trends, such as the growth of persons with no religious affiliation or church membership. Counterfactually but realistically, had secularism or secularization in America been sufficiently extensive and forceful it would have probably precluded the explosion and prevalence of anti-secular and theocratic fascism and conservatism post-2016 and since the 1980s with Reaganism and the Tea Party—but it had not and did not. Essentially, like liberalism and liberals, US secularism and secularists have been helpless, marginalized, and condemned as 'un-American' in facing this anti-secular and theocratic eruption and dominance of fascism and conservatism starting with and then resuming after Puritanism since Puritan-inspired Reaganism and culminating in the post-2016 autocracy that evangelicalism consecrates as 'chosen by God'.

Consequently, the secular part of America has traditionally been weaker and remains so compared to the religious-theocratic 'all-American' pole. In essence, aside from minor variations, America has always been and remains less secular democracy than Puritan-style theocracy, pure or diluted. This holds true despite the constitutional differentiation between politics and religion, including the separation of church and state, that dominant conservatism systematically denies, perverts, and violates with impunity and thus makes it not worth the paper on which it is written, by various theocratic or theocentric coercive impositions of 'godliness' and 'faith' ('in God we trust', 'one nation indivisible under God', the 'existence of Divinity', 'faith-based' government programs). After all, if secularized America were extensive and strong enough it would have likely disabled the anti-secular and theocratic eruption and con-tagion of fascism and conservatism post-2016 and since Reaganism and the Tea Party—but evidently it was not and did not.

In comparative terms, secularism or secularization has usually been and con-tinues to be, apart from some recent secular tendencies like the growth of peo-ple with no organized religion or church, less pervasive, prominent, and deep in America than most Western societies, including France, Germany (accord-ing to Weber), and especially Scandinavia approaching a 'post-Christian' society. Conservative 'American exceptionalism' precisely implies this by denouncing secularism or secularization as 'un-American' and contrast-ing 'faith-based', 'godly' society, including its government and polity, as 'all-American' uniqueness to Western European secularism qua 'godlessness'. Secularized America has traditionally been narrower and weaker than sec-ular Western Europe, especially France, partly Germany, and growingly Scandinavia. This is what conservative 'American exceptionalism' implies in construing secular America and Americans as not being the 'real' America and Americans, even as 'un-American', and opposing its 'faith-based', 'godly' rendi-tion to secular, 'godless' Europe.

Such historical and comparative narrowness, slowness, or weakness of American secularism or secularization can make it virtually powerless to effec-tively counterbalance, let alone neutralize, the anti-secular and theocratic explosion and contagion of fascism and the general resurgence and predom-inance of conservatism. This is what the design of theocracy or bogus theo-cratic 'faith-based democracy', analogous to religious 'democracies' in Islamic countries like Iran and Turkey, in America demonstrates post-2016 and since the 1980s (and before). In contrast, accelerating and spreading secularization, so potentially stronger secularism or secular America can operate as an effec-tive counterpoise and antidote against the lethal anti-secular poison of fascism and religious or theocratic conservatism.

5   Rationalism and Progressivism versus Fascism

In conjunction and mutual reinforcement with liberalism, democracy, and secularism, rationalism/progressivism is a further countervailing social, par-ticularly cultural, factor to fascism as extreme irrationalism, anti-rationalism, and anti-progressivism and to conservatism as perennial irrationalist, anti-rationalist, and anti-progressivist revolt, as versus the Enlightenment, in America and elsewhere. While entwined with liberalism, democracy, and secularism, the complex of social rationalism and progressivism forms a related counterfactor to the eruption and expansion of fascism in America and beyond, as it did through the Enlightenment against the reactionary rise of conservatism rooted in and perpetuating medievalism, so the Dark Middle Ages, as the 'golden' past.

Especially, the rationalism and progressivism complex acts as the best remedy against fascism's compounded pathology of total irrationalism, anti-rationalism, and anti-progressivism or regression and in extension their original forms in medieval-rooted irrationalist, anti-rationalist, and regressive conservatism. This complex is the most efficacious antidote to the irrationalist, anti-rationalist, and anti-progressivist or regressive ghost of fascism and conservatism in America and elsewhere because via rationalist modernity it originally superseded the fascist-conservative shared ideal medievalism and its irrationalism. In particular, such a complex most effectively counteracts and supplants the fascist and conservative New Dark Ages because through the agency of the Enlightenment it superseded the Dark Middle Ages.

Rationalism/progressivism provides the Enlightenment-based solution to the gravity of fascism as the extreme anti-Enlightenment that it inherits, embraces, and reproduces from conservatism arising in vehemently adverse reaction to the 'Age of Reason' and the Enlightenment-inspired French Revolution. Such a solution is the best cure against the lethal pathology and contagion of fascist extreme irrationalism, anti-rationalism, and anti-progressivism or regression in America and elsewhere, as it was to those of anti-rationalist conservatism and its root irrational, superstitious medievalism. The fact that rationalism/progressivism, in combination with liberalism and secularism and via rationalist modernity, superseded the darkness of medievalism prefigures its superseding fascism and conservatism in America and elsewhere in respect of their irrationalism, anti-rationalism, anti-progressivism, thus social 'insanity' by a 'divine' design of an 'insane society' ruled by fascist-conservative 'madmen in authority'.[30]

---

30   The term social 'insanity' is taken from Pareto (2000, p. 107) referring to Puritan and related ascetic-moralistic 'insanity' equating pleasures with crimes, 'insane society' is used with refence and by contrast to what Fromm (1991) denotes a 'sane society', and 'madmen in authority' is from Keynes (1960, p. 383). Anticipating Pareto, Hume classically diagnosed Puritans' 'madness with religious ecstasies', which their heirs American evangelicals continue and expand to America and beyond via contagion. Conservative America, such as the 'Bible Belt' from Alabama to Texas and beyond, through mass, unrestrained gun ownership and mass killings by guns illustrates social 'insanity' or an 'insane society' and relatedly the Hobbesian barbarian 'state of nature' where life is 'brutish and short' and humans are barbarians and brutes, as are apparently most US conservatives due to committing or enabling murders on the ground of the 'right to bear arms.' For

Especially, its overcoming, as through the Enlightenment, the Dark Middle Ages anticipates its countering and transcending the New Dark Ages that fascism, together with conservatism, in America and beyond attempts and indeed to a growing extent succeeds to recreate and impose during recent times, just as in the 1920–30s and later. If the rationalist-progressive, liberal, democratic, and secular Enlightenment once superseded the Dark Middle Ages, its enduring legacy, the contemporary complex of rationalism and progressivism, intertwined with liberalism, liberal democracy, and secularism, may be able to perform a comparable act. This act is transcending the fascist-conservative New Dark Ages descending on and inflicting America, above all the former Southern Confederacy qua the 'Bible Belt' and similar regions, post-2016 and since the 1980s, along with other societies spanning from theocratic Poland and neo-fascist Hungary and Brazil to Brexit Great Britain, Islamic-ruled Turkey, and others ruled by extreme conservatives or radical rightists.

Accordingly, whenever in America and beyond the complex of social rationalism and progressivism, particularly science and scientific progress, emerges and prevails over irrationalism, anti-rationalism, and anti-progressivism or regression, including religious and other superstition, fascism seems predestined to decline as a regime or elite rule and to persist only as counter-state terrorism, just as does conservatism. It follows that science and scientific progress is the most effective rationalist and progressive, Enlightenment-based antidote to the irrationalist, anti-rationalist, and anti-progressivist or retrogressive poison—often literally via deadly religious superstitions from 'Armageddon' and 'rapture' through mass cult sacrifices and suicides to anti-medicine and anti-vaccine—of fascism and conservatism in America and elsewhere. This is what dramatically occurs and recurs during the Covid-19 pandemic that exposes fascist-conservative irrationalism, anti-rationalism, and self-destructive anti-science insanity, not to mention its destructive effects on public health. In particular, whenever in America and beyond the scientific Enlightenment reasserts itself through its enduring legacy versus the pre-science relics of the Dark Middle Ages like medieval religious and similar superstitions, fascism tends to

---

example, Texas and similar extremely conservative and theocratic states make mass gun possession unlicensed—while requiring licenses for selling alcohol as if beer and wine were deadlier than guns in the perverted Puritanical or Islamic Sharia logic—resulting in the 'license to kill'. This returns to the Hobbesian brute and primeval 'state of nature', which the 'Wild West' reinvents and epitomizes, with Texan and other Southern conservatives acting as gun-wielding brutes or barbarians. Nationally, McCarthy, Goldwater, Reagan and his emulators, Tea Partiers, and the post-2016 would-be autocrat are apparent examples of US fascist-conservative and related Keynes's 'madmen in authority.'

suffer demise as a dominant or relevant social factor, except as a counter-state terrorist movement, as does conservatism overall.

Fascism, just as broader conservatism, in America and elsewhere evidently both attacks and fears science and scientific progress and for good and strong reasons. Fascism, like conservatism, apparently knows well or senses correctly that science and scientific progress is its strongest rationalist and progressive nemesis and the most effective remedy for its anti-science destructive, perverse, and lethal pathology. Relatedly, fascism both assaults and fears the scientific Enlightenment for good and strong reasons, just as conservatism originally did and persistently does. Following conservatism, fascism obviously realizes or correctly senses that the scientific Enlightenment is the most consistent and forceful historical antidote to the fascist and conservative poison of irrationalism, anti-rationalism, and anti-progressivism, as it was to irrational and pre-scientific medievalism. Whenever in America and beyond Enlightenment-based science and scientific progress asserts itself and prevails over religious and other superstition and anti-science antagonism, fascism decays and ultimately disappears as a ruling power or relevant social factor, save as oppositional extremism or anti-state terrorism, just as does conservatism and did medievalism. US fascists and other conservatives know well this fatal effect on their power and relevance of science and scientific progress by both attacking and fearing scientists and other rationalist intellectuals as 'enemies of the people'. And (as Pareto would expect), 'no one is more cruel' to these 'un-American' persons than those who fear them, fascist-conservative 'cowards', as during post-2016 in a long lineage of mixed cruelty and cowardice from McCarthyism and Mussolini and Hitler.

In geographic and social terms, the rationalist and progressive pole of America is the countervailing power to the fascist part as a profoundly irrationalist, anti-rationalist, and anti-progressivist region or subsociety which the former Southern confederacy epitomizes and expands via Southernization to other parts of American society. This holds true as a general tendency with secondary variations. These variations involve liberal, secular, and rational, including scientific, and progressive islands in the South and other ultra-conservative regions ruled by extreme agents of irrationalism, anti-rationalism, and anti-progressivism, such as proto-fascists or evangelical equivalents of Islamic jihadists enforcing Biblical law as an equivalent of Sharia law in widespread executions and mass imprisonment often of innocent persons (yet 'guilty' by the dogma of 'original sin'). Specifically, Enlightenment-based, scientific 'we believe in science' America is the strongest rationalist and progressive counterforce geographically and socially to the fascist, conservative, and religious pole that is an implacably anti-Enlightenment and anti-scientific 'we believe in non-science', 'religion and guns' subsociety. This holds true as a rule, putting aside rare exceptions like minor liberal-rational portions in the South and other parts dominated by intrinsically authoritarian conservatism that tends to generate or indeed become fascism and theocracy.

At this point, the culture-religious wars and ideological-political polarizations between liberal and conservative America, liberalism and conservatism, including fascism, inevitably manifest themselves as those of rationalism and progressivism versus irrationalism, anti-rationalism, and anti-progressivism or regression. More precisely, these wars represent the aggressive 'holy' war, literally a crusade, that the conservative, including fascist, pole of America or American conservatism, particularly fascism or the extreme-right, launches against 'un-American' 'foreign' rationalism and progressivism post-2016 and since McCarthyism, Reaganism, and the Tea Party, and causes sharp culture divisions and ideological polarizations. This conservative-fascist anti-rationalist crusade is functionally equivalent to Islamic 'jihad' in respect of their shared assault and 'holy' terror against rationalism, including science and scientific education, and progressivism and their exponents. It is hence a false equivalence to equate the roles that liberal and conservative America, or liberalism and conservatism, play in these culture-religious wars and ideoogical polarizations, as is equating fascist and anti-fascist actors, aggressive and defensive wars, action and reaction.

Specifically, these conflicts and divisions between liberal and conservative America, or liberalism and conservatism/fascism, reappear as those between science and scientific progress and religious and other superstition and anti-science. They are specifically Spencer-like offensive wars or attacks that conservative America or compounded conservatism/fascism initiates on science, scientists, and scientific education and progress, which makes any equation between the two Americas or worldviews a false equivalence analogous to equating fascism and anti-fascism. Relatedly, such conflicts and divisions turn out to be between the Enlightenment and its scientific legacy and the anti-Enlightenment and its anti-scientific vestige, with the second through resurgent fascism and conservatism assaulting the first. They are culture-religious wars and ideological-political polarizations between Enlightenment-based and in that sense Jeffersonian America and anti- and pre-Enlightenment-driven, Puritan-style America, in which the latter, corresponding to the conservative-fascist or theocratic pole like the South and similar sections, assaults the former. In short, these wars are those between an Enlightenment-style scientific and an anti-Enlightenment-like 'flat-earth' American society corresponding to liberal and conservative America. This reaffirms that to equate the roles that liberalism and conservatism or fascism, liberal and conservative America play in these wars and divisions amounts to falsely equating a scientific and a 'flat-earth' society, science and anti-science like religion, the Enlightenment and the counter-Enlightenment, rationalism and irrationalism.

As with respect to liberalism and secularism, however, the dilemma emerges as to whether the complex of rationalism and progressivism in America is sufficiently extensive and powerful to function as an effective countervailing social-cultural power to fascism, conservatism, and religion with regard to their shared extreme irrationalism, anti-rationalism, and anti-progressivism. Especially, the suspicion arises if science and scientific progress in America are pervasive and strong enough to counter and supersede fascism and conservatism in terms of their common extreme anti-science antagonism, nihilism, and regression. In addition, a historical dilemma is whether the Enlightenment and its legacy in America has a sufficient spread and impact to act as a corresponding counterpoise to the shared vehement anti-Enlightenment of fascism and all conservatism. At this point, the tentative answers to these dilemmas and suspicious appear less affirmative than negative.

Generally, related to the relative weakness of liberalism and secularism, the rationalism/progressivism complex in America has been of secondary importance and influence compared to its opposites, especially religion-rooted irrationalism, anti-rationalism, and anti-progressivism and to 'all-American faith' since Puritanism through its descendant evangelicalism, plus dogmatic Catholicism within the 'Christian Right'. Aside from minor and transient variations, rationalist-progressive America has usually been weaker than its irrationalist, anti-rationalist, anti-progressivist, and 'faith-based' counterpart from the Puritan 'Biblical Commonwealth' to the evangelical 'Bible Belt'. Had American rationalism and progressivism or rationalist-progressive America been more pervasive and stronger than its opposite, it could have probably precluded and cured the irrationalist, anti-rationalist, anti-progressivist 'faith-based' eruption of fascism and resurgence of conservatism post-2016 and since the 1980s—yet, it had not and did not.

In particular, apart from few exceptions, science and scientific progress in America have traditionally been secondary to the opposite, such as especially anti- or non-scientific religious beliefs, dogmas, and superstitions, simply 'all-American faith,' since essentially anti- or pre-scientific, including witch-hunting, Puritanism. Relatedly, despite Jefferson, Franklin, and Paine importing it from Europe, especially France (practically Paris salons), the Enlightenment in America has been historically weaker, and its legacy and impact remain relatively weak and limited compared to the anti- or pre-Enlightenment, such as Puritanism and its own enduring heritage and religion generally. If science and scientific progress or the Enlightenment and its legacy and impact in America were wider and stronger, they would have likely prevented the grave, lethal anti-science, anti-medicine, and anti-Enlightenment resurgence and contagion of fascism and conservatism post-2016 or since the 1980s—but they were not and did not.

In comparative terms, the rationalism/progressivism complex in America has usually been and remains weaker than in most other comparable societies, especially Western Europe, spanning from France and to some degree Germany to Scandinavia. Science and scientific progress in America, especially its predominant conservative and religious pole, have been comparatively less socially and politically appreciated (until the 'Sputnik moment' of the 1950s), unless serving as instruments of repressive and military ends like penal repression via mass imprisonment and imperial expansion through militarism and wars of aggression. In a way, the 'Sputnik moment' indicated that while even the Soviet Union, just as the Western world, was appreciating, developing, and growingly investing in science, the US under conservatism, including proto-fascism like McCarthyism and resurging theocracy, indulged and languished in anti-science 'monkey trials' of evolution and thus scientific biology and the other natural and social sciences since the 1920s, as well as in 'one nation indivisible under God', 'in God we trust', and related theocratic coercion and exercise during early postwar times, all depreciating and degrading science and knowledge in favor of the 'recognition of the existence of Divinity' (as some federal and state laws stipulated and still do). So, it was necessary for the 'Sputnik moment' to happen for the conservative-theocratic US government to finally accept, develop, and invest in science. Yet, such a government does this in a perverse manner (or bad faith) by abusing and perverting science and scientists into the instrument of global military domination, wars of aggression, mass destruction and death (the Vietnam War,[31] etc.), and imperial

---

31 For example, Dell and Querubin (2018, p. 761) report that US social scientists 'played an outsized role in convincing Kennedy's successor, Lyndon Johnson, that the war could indeed be won through the deployment of America's arsenal. [invoking] McNamara [who] initially advocated involvement in Vietnam.' They conclude that US social scientists 'are not likely to soon regain the zenith of influence that they enjoyed in the 1960s—and lost in no small part because of their role along with military leaders such as Westmoreland in orchestrating the United States' greatest military defeat' (Dell and Querubin 2018, p. 761). This implies that the notorious role of US social as well as physical scientists in the Vietnam War, just as of their medical and psychological counterparts in the Iraq 2003 Invasion (e.g., torture of Iraqis prisoners), resembles that of Nazi scientists in Germany, yet American conservative-religious Presidents and Congress ordering and approving such wars and atrocities continue to claim a 'higher moral ground' relative to Nazism, communism, and so on.

conquest, as well as severe coercion and totalistic repression within America transformed into a fascist and theocratic space, such as the South post-2016, just as its model Puritanism abused and perverted natural science into the means of magnification of the 'glory of God.'[32] Conversely, like fascism, notably Nazism, the conservative-theocratic irrationalist US government, as a rule, does not adopt and promote science, scientific knowledge, and science-based education as the tool in the function of improving and promoting human life, wellbeing, and liberation, in stark contrast to a liberal-secular rationalist state that does precisely this. In addition, just as fascism, this government does not embrace and enhance science, scientific knowledge, and science-based education for intrinsic purposes—simply science (and art) for the sake of science (art) but solely in the aim of war and repression—contrary to its liberal-secular rationalist antipode that embraces it intrinsically demonstrating its true appreciation and cultivation of science and its results.

Relatedly, the Enlightenment and its legacy in America typically have not been as strong, pervasive, and enduring post-Jefferson as in most of Western Europe, including France, postwar Germany, and Scandinavia. Rationalist-progressive, particularly scientific, Enlightenment-based America seems less

---

32   On Puritanism's abuse of science into the means for the 'glory of God' see Becker 1984 (also, Merton 1968). In a related curious episode reminiscent of the 'Sputnik moment', the US post-2020 government/president that mostly continues the post-2016 predecessor's foreign policy, especially against China, announced that America to accelerate Russia's 'brain drain' would welcome Russian scientists and engineers specializing in rocket and related military science and technology. This demonstrates that the US post-2020 government continues to display a Cold-War mentality and its president to act as a zealous Cold-Warrior even after the end of the Cold War and of the Soviet Union. It also confirms the US government's long-standing tendency to use science and technology mostly for militarist and warlike purposes versus other societies, and for control and repression within society. And the government implicitly admits that contrary to its claims to 'superiority', US military technology may not be as 'superior' to that of its defined 'enemies' like Russia, for it were really superior there would be no need to import Russian military scientists and engineers, or as 'superior' as American cars-lemons and most other civilian products are to car and similar imports whose high quality causes conservative-fascist nationalist hysterias from Reaganism to the post-2016 extreme-right regime. To take another example, while the Western and entire world deploys science to invent clean energies and technologies and reduce carbon emissions to combat climate as an existential treat to human life, America under conservatism, including fascism and theocracy, post-2016 languishes in anti-science by persisting in 'dirty' energy (coal, oil, etc.), primitive technology, and continuing pollution legalized by the conservative Supreme Court, thus exacerbating global warming and threatening to destroy the environment and world, so eventually American capitalism itself as the initial rationale for US conservatives' irrational and destructive actions.

extensive, salient, and influential than its equivalents in Western Europe. This is what conservative 'American exceptionalism' implies by construing America in opposite terms—an exceptional unscientific, unprogressive 'flat-earth', creationist 'intelligent-design,' 'faith-based', and to that extent medieval-style and pre-modern society. This 'exceptionalism' opposes such a vision of America to rationalist, progressive, scientific, Enlightenment-based Western Europe in the depreciative sense by the negative evaluation and 'patriotic' and 'sacred' condemnation of rationalism, progressivism, religion-eroding science, and the Enlightenment as 'un-American' and 'ungodly'.

Taken together, historical tendencies and comparative considerations suggest caution and even suspicion as to whether and to what extent the complex of rationalism and progressivism, including science and scientific progress and the Enlightenment and its legacy, in America can operate as an effective sociocultural counterpower to fascism and conservatism in respect of irrationalism, anti-rationalism, and anti-progressivism. Conversely, accelerating social rationalization and progressive change, notably the reassertion of science and scientific progress and the reaffirmation of the Enlightenment legacy and impact, can empower this complex to counter and reverse the irrationalist, anti-rationalist, anti-progressivist, and 'faith-based' revolt of fascism and conservatism in America and beyond.

6   Egalitarianism, Universalism, and Cosmopolitanism versus Fascism

In association and mutual reinforcement with liberalism, liberal democracy, secularism, rationalism and progressivism, the complex of egalitarianism, universalism, and cosmopolitanism, including globalism, is a further countervailing social power to fascism as extreme anti-egalitarianism, anti-universalism, and anti-cosmopolitanism or anti-globalism and generally to conservatism as an original and perpetual anti-egalitarian, anti-universalist, and anti-cosmopolitan ideology. The above complex functions as an associated social counterpoise to the explosion and contagion of fascism in America and beyond, as it did against the anti-egalitarian and anti-universalist revolt of medieval-rooted conservatism through the universalistic Enlightenment and its product modernity. This complex is particularly the strongest countervailing social power against fascist inherent and extreme economic and social anti-egalitarianism, anti-universalism, and anti-cosmopolitanism, including anti-globalism, that fascism inherits from its creator conservatism and perpetuates and intensifies to the extreme in America and beyond. In short, the complex is the best cure to the built-in and ultimate anti-egalitarian, anti-universalist, and anti-cosmopolitan social 'morbidity' (a la Durkheim) of fascism and conservatism in America and elsewhere.

The above complex is the most effective remedy to fascism in this regard because egalitarianism, universalism, and cosmopolitanism through the egalitarian, universalistic, and cosmopolitan Enlightenment and early modernity initially transcends the common fascist-conservative ideal and 'paradise lost' medievalism and its ancient regime of anti-egalitarianism, anti-universalism, and anti-cosmopolitanism. Accordingly, the process of transcendence of medievalism and its anti-egalitarian, anti-universalist ancient regime anticipates the egalitarianism, universalism, and cosmopolitanism complex transcending fascism and conservatism with respect to economic and social anti-egalitarianism, anti-universalism, and anti-cosmopolitanism. Arguably, if this complex through Enlightenment-based egalitarian, universalistic, and cosmopolitan modernity once transcended their shared ideal medievalism, then it could transcend fascism and conservatism as medieval-rooted.

The complex of egalitarianism, universalism, and cosmopolitanism, including globalism, is the strong social counterpoise to fascism and conservatism in America and beyond with respect to economic and social inequality, rigid hierarchy, particularism, elitism, monopolistic closure, and exclusion within society and in relation to societies. Such a complex counters and transcends the extreme fascist and original conservative ideology and system of economic and social inequality, rigid hierarchy, particularism, elitism, closure, and exclusion in intra- and inter-societal terms within America and beyond. Hence, the complex's project and creation of an egalitarian, universalist, open, and inclusive society, including its economy, polity, and culture, counteracts and substitutes for fascism's and conservatism's divine 'intelligent design' and perpetuation of an extremely unequal, hierarchical, particularistic, elitist, closed, and exclusionary social system in America and elsewhere perpetuating the medieval ancient regime of feudal bondage, the caste system, and slavery. Fascism and generally conservatism in America and elsewhere both attacks via warfare and fears in cowardice and panic an egalitarian, universalist, open, and inclusive society and for good reasons. Such a society is the common societal nemesis of fascism and conservatism in terms of their extreme inequality, rigid hierarchy, particularism, elitism, closure, and exclusion.

In particular, the egalitarianism, universalism, and cosmopolitanism or globalism complex is the most effective counterweight and solution to the gravity of fascism and conservatism in America and beyond in terms of extreme nationalism, nativism, general social hatred, and xenophobia. The complex, especially universalism in the form of cosmopolitanism or globalism, counteracts and remedies the lethal pathology of fascist extreme and general conservative aggressive nationalism, nativism, social hatred, and xenophobia. The consummate ideal of this complex of a universalist, cosmopolitan, or globalized society with broad openness for and a free movement of economic goods and human actors—'open borders'[33] and freedom of geographic inter-societal mobility subject to legal rules—transcends fascism's and conservatism's primordial design and petrification of a tribal-like society or primeval societal tribalism in America and beyond. In short, such a society is an antidote to the deadly poison of fascism and conservatism, as the new tribalism[34] and thus resurged barbarism, primitivism, even novel savagery.

It follows that, due to this tribalism, fascism/conservatism both violently assaults and cowardly fears a cosmopolitan or globalized society with broad openness for and free movement of economic and human resources, which it deceptively misconstrues as 'open borders' with no legal rules[35]—and for good reasons. In this connection, US fascists and other conservatives dread and—hoping to awake and use for the sake of capturing and retaining power what they see as Americans' xenophobic, so socially claustrophobic sensibilities, despite their immigrant lineage—accuse liberals of 'open borders' as though this were an ultimate political offense in the 'nation of immigrants',

---

33   Rajan and Zingales (2004, p. 20) suggest that 'open borders limit the ability of domestic politics to close down competition and retard financial and economic growth. They help save capitalism from the capitalists!' Beerli et al. (2021, pp. 976–7) propose that if 'firms benefit from open borders through increased productivity and growth, this may counteract the effects of increased labor market competition and expand job opportunities for native workers', contradicting American and other fascist-conservative nativism. They conclude with respect to the abolition of immigration restrictions in Switzerland that open borders 'created opportunities for natives to grow professionally and their likelihood to work in top managerial positions increased' (Beerli et al. 2021, p. 978). Perla, Tonetti, and Waugh (2021, p. 74) posit and find that the 'growth rate is higher in more open economies.' This exposes the economic irrationalism and sheer lunacy of American fascism and conservatism that aims to achieve a 'superior' growth rate (e.g., 5% in post-2016) while condemning 'open borders' for movements of capital, goods, and labor in favor of nativistic, tribal-like closure and Nazi-style autarchy through literal high walls and other barriers.

34   Bauman (2001, p. 70) detects the 'neo-tribal and fundamentalist sentiments' primarily within neo-fascism and religious conservatism such as American evangelicalism and Islamic fundamentalism.

35   Abramitzky et al. (2021, p. 581) point to 'major changes in US immigration policy from a regime of nearly open borders (to European immigrants) to one of substantial restrictions', which means that anti-immigrant US fascists and broader conservatives overlook or forget that 'open borders' was a police applied especially to their predecessors such as European immigrants, especially the 1880 cohort of 'immigrants from Northern and Western Europe (e.g., Ireland, Germany, and the United Kingdom).'

although they construe America in anti-immigration terms rewriting history as if the founding and successive immigration waves never happened. In doing so, US fascists-conservatives self-contradict or overlook that 'unfettered' capitalism as their 'all-American' economic system versus 'socialism', actually welfare capitalism, cannot function, even exist, and survive precisely without 'open borders' in the sense of broad openness for and a free movement of capital, commodities, and labor. They prove that American fascism/conservatism is extreme economic irrationalism to the point of madness, as through industrial nationalism and market protectionism such as irrational, self-defeating trade wars since Reaganism's car-import restrictions through the post-2016 autocracy's all-out 'easy to win' trade war.

Considering resurgent and dominant fascist-conservative nationalism, nativism, populism, and tribalism in America post-2016, cosmopolitanism or globalism may appear idealistic and reversible, as via trade wars and other acts of economic irrationalism by its radical-right regime. Still, it is the most encompassing nemesis of fascism and conservatism and the broadest cure for their deadly poison of nationalism, nativism, generalized social hatred, and xenophobia.

Relatedly, the complex of egalitarianism, universalism, and cosmopolitanism is a strong counterforce and effective antidote to fascism's deadly poison of master-race, master-caste, and related racism. This complex counteracts and cures fascist master and similar racism that fascism inherited from conservatism's 'old spirit of the master caste' and its root medievalism with the ancient regime of feudal bondage, along with the caste system and slavery, including its Southern variation in the American context. Therefore, the ideal and possible creation and diffusion of a universalist, cosmopolitan, or globalized society without a racial hierarchy counteracts and replaces fascism's and broader conservatism's vision, perpetuation, or reinvention of a societal system ruled by a 'master race' or 'master caste' in America and elsewhere. Accordingly, fascism and other conservatism in America and beyond both vehemently attack and obsessively fear a cosmopolitan or globalized society and for good reasons. Such a society promises to act as the overarching nemesis of fascism and conservatism in respect with their shared master-race racism. As regards their compound of nationalism, nativism, xenophobia, social hatred, and master-caste racism, US and other fascists and conservatives know well and realize that a global counterpower to and ultimately victorious force over them may be a universalist, cosmopolitan, or globalized society which thence they violently attack and aim to destroy, just as they fear in a typical display of cowardice. In passing, most US and other fascists and broader conservatives act or appear cowardly when facing overwhelming or equivalent countervailing social, including physical, political, and military, powers. For example, the post-2016 would-be autocracy was widely regarded or perceived as an exempla of cowardice since the Vietnam War through these days. US fascists and conservatives thus seem to understand only the language and logic of brute force, violence, and terror as the essence and spirit of fascism and broader conservatism; and arguably, 'no one is more cruel than the coward'. This sheds light on chronic and pervasive conservative, religious or theocratic, and fascist cruelty and brutality in America from Puritanism through Reaganism, evangelicalism, the 'Christian Right', the 'war on terror' to the Tea Party and the post-2016 extreme-right regime, just as elsewhere since fascism in Europe during the 1920–30s, especially Nazism in Germany. After all, Hitler's perishing, along with Goebbels and his family, due to his apparent cowardice and weakness of character self-contradicted his proclamation that rather than the Nazis 'only the weak and cowardly will perish'[36]

Consequently, whenever the complex of egalitarianism, universalism, and cosmopolitanism or globalism develops and reasserts itself against the opposite compound, it functions as a countervailing social power to fascism and conservatism in terms of extreme economic and social inequality, rigid hierarchy, particularism, elitism, monopolistic closure, and exclusion within society and vis-à-vis other societies. Especially, when this happens, such a complex operates as the effective cure against the lethal pathology of fascism in the form of extreme nationalism, nativism, xenophobia, social hatred, and master-caste racism derived from conservatism. Whenever an egalitarian, universalist, open, and inclusive, including cosmopolitan or globalized, society emerges and prevails over its antithesis, it counteracts and transcends fascism and conservatism overall in terms of inequality, hierarchy, particularism, elitism, closure, and exclusion. Particularly, such a society consistently counters and effectively cures the poison of fascism's lethal doses of extreme conservative aggressive nationalism, nativism, social hatred, xenophobia, and master-race racism.

The preceding suggests that the egalitarian, universalist, open, and inclusive, including cosmopolitan or globalized, pole of America is the geographical and societal countervailing power to the fascist and generally conservative counterpart in the former Southern Confederacy and similar regions. Egalitarian, universalist, open, and inclusive, particularly cosmopolitan/globalized, America is the effective solution to the gravity of fascism and conservatism

---

36   Pareto (2000, p. 71) states that 'no one is more cruel than the coward'. Hitler's statement that 'only the weak and cowardly will perish' is cited in McMurtry (1999, p. 255).

regarding extreme inequality, hierarchy, particularism, elitism, closure, and exclusion. Such a society is the antidote to the inegalitarian, non-universalist, closed, and exclusionary, including nationalist, nativist, anti-cosmopolitan,[37] hatred-driven and xenophobic, pole of America which the fascist-conservative symbiosis dominates and reconstructs after its model of societal inequality, hierarchy, elitism, closure, and exclusion. As the first America ascends, grows, and asserts itself against the second, fascism and generally conservatism descends and contracts, all else being equal, as since the New Deal through the 1970s, for example. Conversely, as the first America descends, contracts, and weakens against the second, fascism and other conservatism ascends, expands and intensifies, as in post-2016 and since the 1980s.

As with respect to liberalism, liberal democracy, secularism, rationalism, and progressivism, the question arises as to whether the complex of egalitarianism, universalism, and especially cosmopolitanism, including globalism, possesses sufficient scope and strength to function as a relevant countervailing social power to fascism and conservatism in America and beyond. In short, one questions if egalitarian, universalist, open, and inclusive, particularly cosmopolitan/globalized, America is more extensive and stronger than its opposite to act as the effective cure to the pathology of fascism and conservatism. Historically, related to the relative weakness of liberalism, liberal democracy, secularism, rationalism, and progressivism, the complex of egalitarianism, universalism, and especially cosmopolitanism has typically been secondary compared to the opposite. This complex has usually been less strong than the compound of inequality, hierarchy, particularism, elitism, closure, and exclusion, particularly nationalism, nativism, xenophobia, social hatred, and master-race or master-caste racism, since anti-universalistic, notably closed, exclusionary, nativist, and hateful Puritanism. In consequence, egalitarian, universalist, open, and inclusive, especially cosmopolitan, America has been traditionally weaker than its antithetical counterpart since Puritan theocracy through slavery to the evangelical Southern Confederacy and similar regions. Had the complex of American egalitarianism, universalism, and cosmopolitanism, including globalism, been a primary factor in relation to its antithesis, it would have likely prevented the surge of fascism and the reassertion of conservatism post-2016[38] and since the 1980s—but it had not and did not.

---

37   Slattery and Zidar (2020, p. 90) register the 'political ramifications of growing disaffection of noncosmopolitans' mainly in conservative America, with these groups overwhelmingly supporting the post-2016 autocracy and generally fascism.

38   Enke (2020, p. 3682) reports that, for example, 'voting for Trump is always negatively correlated with universalist and positively correlated with [exclusionary] moral values.' Enke (2020, p. 3682) elaborates that the 'relationship between moral values and voting for

Hence, if egalitarian, universalist, open, and inclusive, including cosmopolitan, America were stronger than its opposite, it could have precluded or mitigated the creation and expansion of a fused fascist-conservative pole during these times—yet it was not and did not.

Comparatively, just as liberalism, liberal democracy, secularism, rationalism, and progressivism, the complex of egalitarianism, universalism, and cosmopolitanism, despite Jeffersonian ideas, has usually been less widespread and strong in America, at least in its conservative pole including the former Southern Confederacy and similar regions, than in most Western societies like Western Europe, notably Scandinavia. The conservative celebration of 'American exceptionalism' hardly ever contains secular, as opposed to religious, egalitarianism, liberal, as distinct from 'faith-based', universalism, and cosmopolitanism as the maximum of universal equality and inclusion. Instead, it exalts or insinuates inequality, hierarchy, particularism, elitism, closure, and exclusion versus out-groups, notably nationalism qua 'patriotism' or nativism, as 'all-American', simply exclusionary, ascriptive 'Americanism'. Egalitarian, universalist, open, and inclusive, especially cosmopolitan or globalist, America has been typically weaker than its equivalent in most other Western societies, including its neighbor Canada and Western Europe, notably Scandinavia, especially during the post-ww II period. Conservative 'American exceptionalism' precisely implies this difference by sharply distinguishing nationalist ('patriotic') or nativist 'America first' from cosmopolitan or globalist Western Europe, especially Scandinavia.

Altogether, the historical and comparative weakness of the egalitarianism, universalism, and cosmopolitanism complex in America casts doubt on whether it can act as an effective countervailing social power to fascism and conservatism in respect of anti-egalitarianism, anti-universalism, and anti-cosmopolitanism, including nationalism, nativism, xenophobia, social hatred, and master-race racism. Growing intra-societal egalitarian and universalist tendencies and inter-societal cosmopolitan or globalist trends, simply the process toward an open society, can make the complex a stronger counterpoise and eventually a solution to the anti-egalitarian, anti-universalist, and anti-cosmopolitan or anti-globalist eruption and contagion of fascism and conservatism as the shared vision and imposition of societal closure, exclusion, and barbarian tribalism. Accelerating cosmopolitanism or globalism—not just

---

Trump is not driven by priming effects from Trump's language [but by] moral values from a period when Trump was not even politically active, [which] are still strongly related to Trump's vote share.' To that extent, this suggests that anti-universalist fascist-like moral values already existed and prevailed in conservative-religious America before 2016.

economic globalization—generally egalitarianism and universalism may not displace in short terms fascist-conservative nationalism, nativism, xenophobia, social hatred, and master-race racism, simply resurrected and perpetuated primeval tribalism, in America and beyond. Still, such cosmopolitan or globalist acceleration is the most effective available social counterforce and cure for this fascist and broader conservative tribalistic resurgence and metastasis.

7   Pacifism versus Fascism

In conjunction and mutual reinforcement with universalism, cosmopolitanism, and liberalism, pacifism or non-militarism is an additional countervailing social force against fascism as extreme anti-pacifism, militarism, offensive war, and imperial or forcible conquest and to conservatism as an initial and persistent anti-pacifist, militarist, warlike, and imperialist ideology in America and other Western (and non-Western) societies. Linking with universalism, cosmopolitanism, and liberalism, pacifism operates as a linked, even if 'soft' or peaceful, counterpower to the surge of fascism, as it did via the pacifist Enlightenment and liberal modernity against the reactionary rise of conservatism derived from militarist, warlike feudalism. Liberal pacifism is especially the most powerful countervailing social power versus fascism's profound and intense anti-pacifism, militarism, offensive war, mass destruction, self-destruction and death, and forcible conquest which it adopts from conservatism as an initially and persistently anti-pacifist, militarist, warlike, destructive, and imperialist ideology. Briefly, such pacifism is the most effective antidote to the militarist, warlike, destructive, murderous, and imperialist poison of fascism and conservatism in America and elsewhere. While fascism, in alliance and eventual merger with conservatism, both produces and is reproduced by anti-pacifism, militarism, offensive war, mass destruction, death, and imperial conquest, pacifism counteracts and conceivably overcomes these fascist-conservative lethal inter-societal tendencies and outcomes.

This countervailing social factor is the strongest peaceful cure for fascism as the agent of militarism and war given that liberal and cosmopolitan pacifism via the mostly pacifist Enlightenment and its societal equivalent early modernity originally overcame or drastically mitigated militarist and warlike feudalism as the joint fascist-conservative 'golden past' of military, war glory, and honor. The Enlightenment and its product liberal modernity crucially helped end through the notion and practice of individual liberty of conscience and the separation of church and state long-standing, devastating, and irrational religious wars, such as those between Catholics and Protestants within

Christianity[39]—for example, between the first and Lutherans in Germany and especially Calvinists in France as the most intense, destructive, and persistent Reformation-era war of religion—military torture,[40] and related practices, in Western Europe. In contrast, conservatism arose in anti-pacifist and generally adverse reaction to Enlightenment processes that overcame violent feudalism, notably the war-saturated Christian and Islamic Dark Middle Ages. Its overcoming of militarist and warlike feudalism, notably intra-Christian religious wars like those between Catholicism and Calvinism in France and 'holy' torture, serves as a precedent for Enlightenment-based pacifism countering and overcoming fascism and conservatism in respect of militarism, wars of aggression, and forcible conquest.

Conceivably, pacifism could strongly counteract and overcome fascism's and conservatism's anti-pacifism, militarism, war, and conquest in America and elsewhere given that it originally overcame their joint ideal warlike feudalism, notably Christian wars and 'holy' torture during the Dark Middle Ages, through the pacifist Enlightenment. If the Enlightenment could convince feudal, especially intra-Christian 'holy', warriors, sadists, and torturers to cease and desist their wars and sadistic torture over religion and come to their senses, pacifism can probably counter fascist and other conservative militarists and agents of offensive war, mass destruction and death, and conquest.

Accordingly, whenever in America and elsewhere pacifism emerges and stands its ground versus its antithesis, it acts as a real or potential countervailing 'soft' social power against fascism and conservatism with regard to militarism. In particular, if such a constellation occurs and persists, pacifism operates as the remedy against fascism's and generally conservatism's compound of offensive war, mass destruction, self-destruction and death, and forcible conquest. Hence, whenever in America and elsewhere a liberal and cosmopolitan pacifist society appears, endures, and reasserts itself over its opposite, it counters

---

39 Mueller (2013, p. 16) notes that 'throughout much of the last millennium, Europeans were engaged in religious wars. First the Crusades against the Muslims, then battles with the Ottomans, and starting in the sixteenth century the wars between Catholics and Protestants. With the help of the Enlightenment thinkers, Europeans came to the realization during the eighteenth century that religious differences were not worth killing and dying for. An important component of the set of reforms proposed by Enlightenment thinkers was to create a clear separation of Church and State.'

40 Einolf (2007, p. 105) remarks that today 'torture is rarely practiced by liberal democracies against their own citizens, but occasionally practiced by liberal democracies against suspected terrorists.' He adds that the 'fascist regimes of Italy, Germany, and their allies used torture and other terror techniques against political opponents, prisoners of war, populations of occupied territories, and members of outsider groups' (Einolf 2007, p. 111).

and supersedes fascism and conservatism in respect of militarism. Particularly, if this situation materializes, such a society counteracts and eventually remedies the fascist and conservative lethal pathology of permanent offensive war, mass destruction, self-destruction, and imperial or violent conquest.

Like cosmopolitanism, pacifism is a countervailing, anti-fascist social factor given that the compound of militarism, war, and conquest reproduces and justifies, as is initially generated by, fascism and conservatism. By asserting itself versus its antithesis, pacifism weakens this compound's role of reproduction and justification of totalitarian fascist and authoritarian conservative rule, and indirectly counteracts fascism and generally conservatism. In short, by superseding or tempering militarism and war as the shared fascist-conservative product and reproducer, pacifism indirectly counteracts fascism and conservatism.

Further, like cosmopolitanism, pacifism can act as an anti-fascist force directly in that it is fundamentally incompatible with and opposite to fascism given that the latter, following conservatism, is intrinsically militarism and eternal aggressive war. Hence, the emergence and existence of pacifism, as of cosmopolitanism, renders it a counteracting 'soft' social power against fascism and conservatism beyond its indirect counter-effects on them through dissolving or weakening militarism. Pacifism, like cosmopolitanism, is inherently averse to and typically resists fascism and other conservatism as invariant militarism and offensive war, as well as violent repression and terror and non-peaceful conflict resolution within society, just as liberalism or scientific rationalism has an inherent 'aversion'[41] to religious and other 'extra-empirical cognition' and belief. Conversely, fascism and generally conservatism due to being invariably militaristic and warlike is intrinsically averse to and usually assaults pacifism, as well as pacifist cosmopolitanism or peaceful globalism.

It follows that US and other fascists and conservatives both violently assault and cowardly fear liberal and cosmopolitan pacifists for good reasons. Pacifism is the intrinsic 'soft' social counterpower and eventual peaceful nemesis, in conjunction with universalism, cosmopolitanism, and liberalism, of fascism and conservatism in respect of militarism and war. Taken together, like cosmopolitanism and globalism, pacifism acts as a countervailing anti-fascist factor both indirectly and directly. It does indirectly by countering militarism and war and directly by manifesting an inherent aversion to and resisting fascism and conservatism as the ideology and system of non-peaceful conflict resolution in society via societal repression, violence, and terror, including offensive

---

41 Schumpeter (1991, p. 317) states that the 'scientific attitude and that aversion to extra-empirical cognition are, of course, sociologically related. They are both products of rationalist civilizations.'

war against and violent conquest of other societies. Just as militarism/war both petrifies and is generated by fascism and conservatism, pacifism sustains and is conditioned by anti-fascism and non-conservatism in the form of mostly non-militarist liberalism, pacifist cosmopolitanism, or peaceful globalism. Pacifism is not only the self-evident antipode of militarism and aggressive war but also a peaceful, silent antidote to the intrinsically militarist, warlike, generally violent, and terrorist pathology of fascism and conservatism.

In extension, the pacifist or non-militarist section of America is the regional and overarching social countervailing power to its fascist and authoritarian-conservative pole that is invariably anti-pacifist, militarist, warlike, and imperialist, as the former Southern Confederacy and related regions show. Pacifist or non-militarist, just as cosmopolitan or globalized, America stands as the overarching last defense against the lethal threat of fascism and conservatism to American society in respect of militarism, war, self-destruction, death, and conquest, which expands into and shapes the opposite pole after its militarist and bellicose design. As long as non-militarist America reemerges and reaffirms itself against its opposite, fascism tends to retreat and weaken, ceteris paribus, as does conservatism. However, this seems to be a hypothetical rather than actual constellation especially in post-WW II times seeing the rise and expansion of the military-industrial complex and the resulting weakness of non-militarism and the virtual extinction of classical pacificism. By contrast, insofar as non-militarist America remains, as since postwar times, weak versus its militarist and bellicose antithesis, fascism, along with conservatism, resurges, escalates, and intensifies, as in post-2016 and since Reaganism.

As for cosmopolitanism and liberalism, however, the suspicion persists as to whether pacifism in America is sufficiently extensive and powerful to operate as an effective countervailing 'soft' social power against fascism and conservatism in respect of militarism, eternal war, and violent conquest. One suspects if American pacifism is widespread and strong enough or even exists beyond few exceptions, to counteract militarist and warlike fascism and conservatism. The answer seems less affirmative than negative in historical and comparative terms. Historically, pacifism in America has been secondary compared to its antithesis since militarist and bellicose Puritanism as the most warlike and genocidal component of the Calvinist 'Church Militant' by its wars of extermination of Native Americans through its heir evangelicalism with its strong crusade-like bellicosity consecrated and driven by aggressive Christian nationalism.

Moreover, aside from rare exceptions, pacifism in the classical, pure, or literal sense of unconditional peaceful resolution of all inter-state conflicts has been non-existent or extremely weak, a taboo as a concept, in American history since Puritanism through 19th century 'manifest destiny' militaristic expansionism and aggressive wars to the post WW II military-industrial complex and its constant wars of aggression. On this account, to speak of 'pacifism' in America during most of its history, including post-2016, since the 1980s, and after WW II, seems a hyperbole, sarcasm, or wishful thinking. This demonstrates the accelerating corruption of growing national military power—confirming the 'law' of 'absolute power' as 'absolutely corrupting' in inter-state relations—after Jefferson's and Madison's initial pacifist or non-militarist statements.

In comparative terms, pacifism appears weaker in America than in most other Western and comparable societies, especially Western Europe and within it most notably Scandinavia, except for some former colonial powers like Great Britain, France, and to some extent past fascist states Germany and Italy, as well as Turkey and Japan beyond, that continue to display certain militarist and relatedly neo-colonial tendencies. Moreover, aside from few exceptions, pacifism in the proper sense has become virtually an extinct or rare species and a negative term in America since postwar times and the Cold War—and after its end—relative to Western Europe, especially Scandinavia. The latter holds true, except for some militarist counterexamples mostly driven by NATO's militarism, bellicosity, and aggressive wars (including its attacks on Yugoslavia, Iraq, and Libya), expansion into the former Warsaw Pact and the Soviet Union, confrontation with, and threatening movement toward Russia in violation of prior commitments, etc. Indeed, no relevant pacifist countervailing social force exists in the US, aside from minor exceptions, against the Leviathan-style military-industrial complex, especially unlimited military expenditure that continues to grow with strong 'bipartisan' support and societal consensus, as in post-2016, despite the end of its supposed rationale the Cold War.

Overall, pacifism continues to be more subdued to and subordinate to its opposite through military hero worship, power, honor, and privilege in America than in other Western and comparable countries, with the exceptions of post and neocolonial Great Britain and France. Hence, the notion of American pacifism may sound as an inner contradiction or impossibility theorem (oxymoron) by comparison to most of Western Europe, notably Scandinavia, aside from NATO-driven militarist variations.

Taken together, the traditional and continuing weakness of pacifism in America yields the dilemma if it can act as an effective countervailing 'soft' and peaceful social power against fascism and conservatism regarding the brute power, violence and destructiveness of militarism, war, and conquest. In light of this insignificance, not just because of its softness and peacefulness, pacifism at most could qualify as a potential and prospective rather than effective and actual counterpower in this respect. If pacifist tendencies strengthen in

America, specifically its liberal pole, following the trend in most other contemporary Western countries since post WW II times—exempting NATO's militarism, aggressive expansion beyond its original sphere up to Russia's borders, and wars of aggression like the UN-unauthorized attack on Yugoslavia—they can enable pacifism to more effectively counter militarist and bellicose fascism and generally conservatism.

While it may not entirely overcome militarist fascism/conservatism in short terms, strengthening what is at present comparatively weak liberal and cosmopolitan pacifism in America is hence the eventual antidote against the shared fascist-conservative irrational, lethal poison of pervasive militarism, aggressive war, mass destruction, and ultimately self-destruction. Pacifism, along with cosmopolitanism, may be historically and comparatively a non-American feature—even 'un-American' for conservatives and fascists since Reagan and post-2016. Yet, realistically, pacifism only can save America from this fascist-conservative lethal pathology of MAD (mutually assured destruction). The latter is the proper description of the militarist and bellicose madness of self-destruction of fascism and conservatism and of fascists and conservatives as armed—both in the sense of mass unrestricted gun ownership within society and arms races against other societies—and warlike 'madmen' in absolute power.

In the presence and predominance of 'all-American' militarism via the Leviathan-like military-industrial complex, unlimited war spending, military hero worship, and aggressive wars alone or often via NATO as an aggressive, expansionary military alliance seeking confrontation, MAD seems only the question of when, and not of if, will happen in long terms such as the third millennium and the 21st century. As it stands, MAD of America and its adversaries, of NATO and Russia or China, alike through nuclear and other weapons of mass destruction is virtually bound to happen in longer terms primarily because of the extreme militarism, eternal wars of aggression, and their driving force the aggressive religious nationalism of American fascism and conservatism and of its British and other Western analogues within NATO. This reveals the tendency to collective suicide by American militarist fascism and conservatism— deriving from or resembling that of suicidal 'judgment day' evangelical cults and sects—and of the US-dominated NATO given the self-destructive outcome of its aggressive wars eventuating in a nuclear exchange. NATO's US-and British-driven expansion literally toward and apparent attempts at confrontation with or provocation of Russia can only be described as suicidal since any such war probably will eventually turn nuclear and hence result in universal destruction—the madness of MAD.

Only a kind of sociological miracle could prevent or remedy this self-destructive outcome of societal and civilization suicide by militarist fascism and conservatism. In contrast, theological miracles are outside of a sociological framework. But if one wishes to think in these terms, 'God bless America' expressing Divine social predetermination (in Weber's meaning) need change into 'God save America' as an expression of Calvinist collective predestination to produce a theological miracle saving the country from MAD. Still, 'God' may well be more likely and predisposed ('God willing') to save American compounded fascism-conservatism considering the conservative-fascist 'Divine' invocation and sanctification of its extreme militarism, eternal wars, and religious nationalism than America in which pacifism, pacifist cosmopolitanism, and peaceful liberalism hypothetically prevail and thus preclude MAD. In this sense, even 'God' cannot help and save America from MAD so long as fascism-conservatism prevails and hence causes universal destruction sooner or later, the question being only when, and not if, this will happen (say, the 2100s or the 2050s?).

And the sociological miracle of precluding MAD is the reemergence and reassertion of pacifism and cosmopolitanism in America over fascist-conservative militarism and nationalism but does not seem likely considering the historical and increasing comparative weakness of such a process of societal transformation. 'Open borders' pacifist cosmopolitanism and 'un-American' peaceful liberalism realistically stand no chance in the foreseeable future versus militarist, bellicose nationalism qua Americanism that fascism and conservatism cause, exalt, and perpetuate.

To that extent, MAD of society, including America, is not the matter of if, but when happening within the long run of the third millennium or the 21st century. This is a sober deduction conditional on that if pacifism and Enlightenment cosmopolitanism continues to be subdued by fascist-conservative militarism, bellicosity, and aggressive nationalism couched and celebrated as Americanism in America. It is an Enlightenment-based inference of societal self-destruction—which would mark the end of the Age of Reason due to the utter irrationality of fascist-conservative militarism—rather than a Puritan-style prophecy of societal doom and gloom. For example, in the US and even Western Europe there is hardly any salient warning or cautioning about NATO's expansion toward Russia's borders—let alone for its continuation after the disbanding of the Warsaw Pact and the dissolution of the Soviet Union as the supposed reason for its formation and existence—and thus the potential of a confrontation that could escalate into the MAD of nuclear war. To that extent, there are scarcely voices of reason or pacifism left in the West and the situation feels as the beginning of the end of the Western Enlightenment's Age of Reason. This militarist specter of collective suicide via MAD is an equivalent to the self-destructive decisions of European governments and parliaments prior to WW I.[42]

8   Liberal Actors versus Fascism in America

Embodying and realizing liberalism, hence liberal democracy and universal liberty, liberal persons and groups are countervailing socio-psychological forces against fascism as an aggregate of extreme authoritarian personalities and conservatism as also a broad family of authoritarians. Liberal actors are individual and group and in that sense socio-psychological embodiments and applicators of liberalism, liberal democracy, and universal liberty in society as the strongest antithesis of fascism, conservatism, and bogus fascist-conservative anti-liberal and illiberal 'democracies' and ersatz 'freedoms'. Consequently, these actors form countervailing socio-psychological forces against fascism and conservatism in respect of the fascist and conservative or radical-right aggregate of extreme authoritarian personalities. Liberals in America and beyond counteract and conceivably replace fascism and conservatism by countering and replacing authoritarian personalities as the shared fascist and conservative socio-psychological core. Since they are opposites to conservative and any authoritarian personalities, liberals thereby resist fascism and conservatism as the collection of such authoritarians in America and elsewhere.

In essence, liberal personalities and groups in America and elsewhere are non-conservatives and anti-fascists. Hence, liberals act as the most consistent and strongest socio-psychological counterforces against inherently authoritarian conservatism arising in adverse reaction to liberalism and its creation fascism also erupting in nihilistic revolt against the latter and liberal democracy. Liberals are the most effective individual/group antidote to fascism and conservatism by being antipodes to conservatives and fascists as original and extreme authoritarian personalities, respectively. In socio-psychological terms, liberal-minded persons and groups are inherently averse to or repulsed by and abhor conservative and other authoritarian personalities and hence manifest

---

42   For example, Galbraith and Parker (2017, p. 196) recount that the 'socialists in Germany, the most sophisticated, disciplined and politically influential in Europe, voted in the Reichstag for the war credits and, along with the proletarians of the other industrial countries, marched cheerfully to their own slaughter'. It remains to see if NATO's enthusiasts and other US and Western militarists will also march 'cheerfully to their own slaughter' through launching or voting for wars of aggression eventuating in MAD.

strong and consistent aversion or repulsion toward and abhorrence of fascism and conservatism as aggregates of authoritarians, just as, along with scientific rationalists, to 'extra-empirical cognition' like religious dogma. Conversely, conservatives and fascists show the same negative feelings of aversion, repulsion, and abhorrence in relation to liberals and liberalism. At this point, liberalism/liberal democracy reappears socio-psychologically as an aggregation of liberal-minded and hence liberty-motivated and inspired personalities and groups, just as fascism is the aggregate of extreme anti-liberal, authoritarian personalities, as is originally conservatism, with minor variations and rare exceptions. As a corollary, liberal-minded actors in America and elsewhere act as a counterpoise to fascism and conservatism in the socio-psychological sense, just as liberalism/liberal democracy does in broader sociological, especially ideological-political, terms.

Alternatively, liberal-minded personalities and groups are the socio-psychological component of liberalism as a social ideology and system and of liberal democracy as a political structure, just as fascist and conservative authoritarians form such an element of fascism and conservatism as radically opposite and vehemently hostile ideologies and systems. In consequence, liberals universally tend to counteract and resist fascism and conservatism—simply, are anti-fascists—just as fascists and conservatives tending to attack liberalism and eliminate liberal democracy, thus acting as anti-liberals and anti-democrats. To that extent, the socio-psychological divergence and opposition between socio-psychological liberal-minded personalities and groups and fascist-conservative authoritarians—in short, liberals and fascists and other conservatives—is unavoidable and irreconcilable. As a corollary, the supposition of equivalence between liberals and fascists or conservatives, as essentially anti-fascists and authoritarians, respectively, in US culture wars and ideological polarizations seems decidedly false and unwarranted.

In consequence, liberal actors are a countervailing socio-psychological force against fascism that is the collection of extreme authoritarian leaders and the rank-and-file, as is generally conservatism, in America and elsewhere. Liberal-minded personalities and groups counter and resist, just as experience and suffer under, fascism as well as theocracy and conservatism overall by countering and resisting fascist and other conservative authoritarian leaders, as the anti-fascist resistance in interwar Europe and post-2016 America shows. In socio-psychological terms, liberal individuals especially abhor and are averse to and revulsed by fascist and conservative authoritarian leaders from Mussolini, Franco, and Hitler through Pinochet and post-2016 neo- or proto-fascist autocrats in America and beyond such as Brexit Great Britain, Catholic-dominated Poland, populist Hungary and Brazil, Islamic-ruled Turkey, and

Said Arabia, and elsewhere. Conversely, fascist and other conservative authoritarian leaders manifest the same negative feelings toward liberal personalities and groups. Therefore, liberal minds exhibit intrinsic, strong, and consistent abhorrence, aversion, repulsion, and resistance to fascism and conservatism—and conversely, the second display the same feelings toward the first—as the compilation and absolute power, abuse, and corruption of authoritarian rulers oppressing and sadistically making liberals and other non-conservatives in America suffer in many ways and all social spheres ('owning' liberals).

In this connection, liberals suffer under or experience fascism, theocracy, and authoritarian conservatism in conservative America such as the South/Bible Belt in all domains of their life and society. The following is a general description or approximation of liberals experiencing fascism, theocracy, and conservatism in conservative America like the former Southern Confederacy and beyond. First, in the economy, liberals, like most employees, in, for example, the South andsimilar regions ruled by proto-fascist and theocratic rulers for long are severely repressed by being denied the freedom and right to unionization, collective bargaining, economic democracy (codetermination), and other basic labor freedoms and rights their Western counterparts take for granted, and in that sense being subjected to a slave-style treatment in a proxy reinstatement and extension of Southern slavery to all non-capitalist classes regardless of race. In short, like most US workers, liberals are subjected to slave-style capitalist dictatorship, including oligarchy and plutocracy, in conservative America which Southern and similar states exemplify.

Second, in the polity, liberals and other anti-fascists and non-conservatives, along with most ethnic minorities, in Southern and related states are intensely oppressed or excluded by, aside from (as especially post-2016 and after 2020) their voting rights being restricted, their deprivation from the freedom and right to seek and hold political power or public office by proto-fascist or theocratic mandates (e.g., the 'recognition of divinity') mandating that liberals and secularists 'need not apply' and privileging conservatives and religionists in these self-declared states of 'freedom' and 'freeman'. In brief, US liberals and relatedly secularists are forced to live under proto-fascism and theocracy in the deep South and beyond within conservative America.

Third, in culture, liberals and other non-conservatives, along with teachers and students, in Southern and like states are systematically coerced by being subjected to 'creationism', 'intelligent design', 'Satan' beliefs, and other religious superstitions and dogmas expressing atavistic irrationalism and thus 'holy' barbarism, and deprived from basic artistic, educational, religious, and other cultural freedoms and rights, including freedom from coercive religion, through prohibitions of evolution, climate science, critical social theories, and other types of science and theory, manifesting extreme anti-rationalism and primitive anti-science. In a word, US liberals and relatedly progressives and scientific rationalists are subjected to irrationalism, anti-rationalism, and cultural oppression, in that sense the new Dark Ages in conservative America like the deep South and beyond.

Lastly, in civil society, liberals, along with teachers and children, in Southern and similar states are, on one hand, threatened, attacked, and often killed by conservative, fascist, and religious owners of lethal arms given the license to kill reminiscent of the Hobbesian state of nature (the 'Wild Wild West' movie in real-time), ensuing in mass death and massacres of innocent persons from random shootings by military-style weapons. On the other hand, liberals in these states are denied elemental individual liberties and privacy, including reproductive and sexual freedoms and rights, by being subjected to severe oppression and punishment for sins-as-crimes by a proto-fascist or theocratic state resembling Leviathan, resulting in mass imprisonment, mostly of sinners (drug users, etc.), and widespread religion-driven (Sharia-style) executions, including often of innocent people. Briefly, liberals are forced to live under barbarian anarchy and Puritan-style moral fascism in the sense of moralistic oppression in the South and elsewhere within conservative America.

Taken together, historically US liberals experience and suffer under fascism, theocracy, and conservatism in the conservative-religious pole of America such as Southern and related states from Alabama and Florida (especially after 2018) to Oklahoma and Texas post-2016 and after 2020 in a manner similar, though, because history hardly ever repeats itself exactly, not identical, to how they experienced Nazi Germany and fascist Europe in the 1930s, together with McCarthyism, and their precursors and others did proto-totalitarian American Puritan theocracy with its reign of 'holy terror', including witch trials, during the 17th-19th centuries (e.g., Salem in the 1690s). Comparatively, US liberals experience fascism, theocracy, and conservatism in conservative-religious America comparably, but not identically, to how their counterparts do Hungary under neo-fascist rule, Poland ruled by a theocratic government, as well as Islamic theocracies like Turkey, Saudi Arabia, Iran, and partly Taliban (e.g., the liberal experiencing of the deep South and similar regions post-2016/2020 as 'Christian Taliban'). In any event, the above approximates how post-2016 (and before) US liberals in their daily lives experience constantly fascism, theocracy, and conservatism in these and other segments of the dominant conservative pole of America.

In addition, liberal-minded personalities and groups in America and else-where counter fascism and broader conservatism by diverging and contrasting from and possibly transcending the rank-and-file, so the fascist and other conservative base. Socio-psychologically, liberal minds are inherently and profoundly incompatible with and contrary to the fascist-conservative rank-and-file—and conversely, the second opposing the first—and act as a counterforce against fascism and conservatism. In political terms, for liberals the fascist and conservative base is the degeneration and reversal of popular sovereignty and the people in liberal democracy, as through perverse anti-liberal and anti-democratic populism that typifies fascism and conservatism. In this regard, liberal minds regard the fascist-conservative base as both an active agent helping institute and demanding fascism-conservatism and a passive, unenlightened, including uneducated, mass and in that sense a victim of demagogic deception, lies, corruption, disinformation, and manipulation by authoritarian rulers. Conceivably, liberal actors by transcending or educating—as during the Covid-19 pandemic and its vaccines and climate change and its causes and effects—the fascist-conservative base as the populist basis or unaware victim can counter and dispose of fascism that historically did not and counterfactually could not arise and persist without its rank-and-file blindly following authoritarian rulers in the style of the Nazi 'blind herd', so counteract and dispense with conservatism. Taken together, liberal-minded personalities and groups by both resisting fascist and other conservative authoritarian leaders and transcending or enlightening their base counteract fascism and conservatism. Overall, liberals counter fascism in that they both consistently resist its authoritarian leaders and profoundly diverge from the fascist and broader conservative rank-and-file, simply by being anti-fascists and non-conservatives.

Especially, liberal persons and groups in America and elsewhere act as a socio-psychological countervailing force against fascism and conservatism regarding their shared mix of extreme sadism and masochism that typifies authoritarian personalities. Liberal-minded actors counteract fascism and conservatism by counteracting fascist and other conservative sadistic-masochistic character structures that characterize authoritarian personalities. Socio-psychologically, liberal individuals particularly abhor and are repulsed by the fascist and conservative mix of sadism and masochism embodied in sadistic-masochistic character structures that both leaders and followers in fascism exhibit since Mussolini and Hitler through Pinochet to post-2016 proto-fascist autocrats in America and Brexit Britain and their base. Consequently, liberal minds show their inherent and coherent abhorrence, repulsion, and resistance toward fascism and conservatism—with the latter showing the same feelings for the former—as the mix of sadism and masochism and the conglomerate of sadistic-masochistic characters among leaders and followers. Especially, in socio-psychological terms, liberal persons and groups due to their underlying egalitarianism, universalism, cosmopolitanism, and humanism intrinsically oppose sadism and fundamentally differ from fascist and other conservative sadistic characters prevalent among leaders in fascism and conservatism. By opposing sadism and differing from such sadistic characters, they counteract fascism and conservatism that these traits and personalities typify.

Relatedly, liberal actors act as socio-psychological countervailing forces against fascism and conservatism in respect of the fascist rank-and-file's cult of autocratic leaders and the linkage of such a cult with and its perpetuation by mass delusions and fantasies leading to cult-style collective suicide typifying a death cult. By rejecting the cult of autocratic leaders by the fascist and other rank-and-file, as well as superseding old conservative medieval-rooted delusions and fictions eventuating in collective suicide in the style of a death cult, liberal minds counteract fascism and conservatism characterized by such idolatry and pervaded by fantasies and mass suicides. In socio-psychological terms, liberal-minded personalities and groups inherently abhor and strongly repudiate the cult or worship of autocratic leaders by fascist and any followers in accordance with liberalism's rejection of absolute power. Relatedly, following liberalism and its intrinsic rationalism, liberal actors are averse to and supersede mass delusions, fantasies, and related irrationalities ensuing in cult- and sect-style collective suicide. As a corollary, liberal minds consistently evince abhorrence of and aversion to fascism as the cult of autocratic leaders that the fascist rank-and-file embrace and perpetuate through delusions, fantasies, and collective suicide, just as fascists and conservatives abhor, repudiate, and are averse to, and aim to dominate ('own') liberals.

In addition, liberals act as a socio-psychological countervailing force against fascism and conservatism in terms of the mix of deadly grave seriousness and utter grotesqueness characterizing fascist leaders and followers. Given their Enlightenment optimism and rationalism, liberal minds are averse to and repulsed by either deadly gloomy seriousness or utter irrational grotesqueness in the personal conduct of leaders and followers, such as the mix of lethal cruelty and buffoonery or clown-like demeanor in the style of Mussolini, Hitler, Pinochet, and post-2016 autocrats in America, Brexit Great Britain, Hungary, Poland, Turkey, and beyond. As a result, liberals typically express aversion and repulsion toward fascism and conservatism which such a mix, especially the mixed cruelty and buffoonery or clown-like conduct of its rulers, pervades. Hence, liberal-minded personalities oppose fascism and conservatism by replacing the fascist morbid gravity and utter grotesqueness like mixed deadly cruelty-buffoonery by liberal political behavior guided by Enlightenment optimism and rationalism through the balance between rationally serious and optimistic or joyful leadership.

In sum, American liberal-minded actors are the main socio-psychological countervailing force against fascism and conservatism in terms of fascist and other conservative authoritarian personalities, especially leaders. Particularly, they counter fascism and conservatism in respect of sadism and masochism, the cult of autocratic rulers by the base, delusions, fantasies, and collective suicide revealing a death cult, and the mix of deadly gravity and utter grotesqueness.

The dilemma recurs as to whether American liberal-minded personalities and groups, briefly liberals, possess sufficient numbers and strength to counteract fascism and conservatism in these terms, especially if they are stronger than conservative or radical-right, including fascist, authoritarian personalities. The tentative answer seems more negative or skeptical than affirmative. Historically, American liberals and relatedly secularists have typically been less numerous and strong than their conservative and religious opposites since pre- and anti-liberal and proto-conservative Puritanism, aside from minor and transient variations or few exceptions, such as revolutionary times or the 1960s, and Jefferson et al. American liberals have usually been and remain today as ever a quantitatively small and qualitatively weak minority compared to conservatives and religionists as the large, ruling, and tyrannical majority exerting, as Tocqueville envisioned, the 'tyranny of the majority', which the conservative pole of America, including the former Southern Confederacy turned the 'Bible Belt', exemplifies. Liberals become 'un-American' persons, as McCarthyism, Reaganism, and its post-2016 sequel denounced and persecuted them, and liberal a negative notion in ideological, political, and social terms by comparison to 'all-American' conservatives, including covert fascists or radical rightists, and the glorification of conservatism. If the 'American character' exists, it has been historically more remote from a liberal and secular and closer to a conservative and religious personality—Americans since Puritanism or even the putatively liberal American Revolution have been less liberals than conservatives.

The major historical cause for this weakness of American liberal persons and groups compared to their illiberal opposites is evidently the pervasiveness, intensity, and persistence of theocratic or coercive extremist religion from Puritanism through evangelicalism and the Christian Right that also incorporates antiliberal Catholicism. The reason is simply the fact that Americans have been and remain even today, with some variations and despite accelerating secularization like the growth of people with no religious affiliation or church membership, more religious than secular, given the strong association between liberalism and secularism, and conversely conservatism and religiosity or theocracy. After all, if American liberals were numerous and strong enough relative to religious-political conservatives, they would have perhaps prevented the eruption of fascism and reassertion of conservatism during post-2016 and since the 1980s or Reaganism—but they were not and did not.

Comparatively, American liberal-minded personalities and groups are usually fewer in numbers as a proportion of the total population and less influential than their equivalents in most Western societies, notably continental Western Europe ranging from France to Northern regions like Benelux and Scandinavia. The underlying cause for the comparative weakness of American liberals seems to be that the composite of liberalization and secularization, despite the recent trends, has been and remains weaker and theocratic or coercive religion and anti-secularism, as organized into the Religious Right, more pervasive and powerful in America than in Western Europe. Further, even those Americans, including Presidents and other politicians, who consider themselves or are branded 'liberals' tend to be more religious, militarist, and bellicose, or less consistently secular than their European equivalents, thus less willing, likely, or powerful to counteract fascism and conservatism in terms of theocracy or 'faith-based' coercion and exclusion. In respect of such counteraction, they do not constitute or act as genuine liberals in the Enlightenment secular Jeffersonian or Western meaning but as 'godly' and often warlike pseudo-liberals. Glorified 'American exceptionalism' is essentially and often explicitly anti- or non-liberal and conservative-religious, thus not in respect of liberal-secular democracy but in terms of its ersatz substitute, exceptional illiberal, 'faith-based', and exclusionary 'democracy' that is substantively Puritan-style theocracy at least in the Southern 'Bible Belt' and more broadly evangelical America. This is not 'American exceptionalism' in terms of liberal-minded personalities and groups but in their opposites like conservative-religious and thus authoritarian, sadistic-masochistic personalities, contrasting the latter with what it disdains as European liberals and secularists. In the framework of 'American exceptionalism', liberal persons and groups are non-entities and almost criminalized or stigmatized McCarthy/Reagan-style and oppressed or excluded as 'un-American' compared to conservative-religious and related authoritarians.

In addition, American liberal persons and groups are comparatively weaker than their equivalents in most other Western societies in that they consist often of those who cannot be considered liberals in the proper sense but anti- or quasi-liberals, such as radical feminists. This is because the latter infiltrate and pervert liberalism to implement their 'social hatred' agenda and look closer to conservatives with whom they overtly or tacitly ally against their shared enemy, male sinners-as-criminals. These two nominally hostile groups ally in Puritanical temperance crusades[43] or wars, as in the 'war on crime', with alleged, often unproven sexual 'crimes' committed by males resulting in their mass imprisonment and perpetual suffering inflicted Puritan-style and social exclusion even after release.[44]

Taken together, this relative unimportance and weakness, historically and comparatively considered, of American liberal-minded personalities and groups greatly hampers their ability, willingness, and credibility to act as effective socio-psychological countervailing forces against fascism and authoritarian conservatism. Alternatively, if they increase their numerical and societal strength relative to their conservative or radical-right opposites and detach from anti- or quasi-liberals infiltrating and distorting liberalism, especially militant feminists, liberals can become able and credible to counter and possibly reverse the anti-liberal eruption, contagion, and domination of fascism and conservatism in America post-2016, after 2020, and since the 1980s.

---

43   In a historical episode anticipating later conservative-feminist temperance wars, García-Jimeno, Iglesias, and Yildirim (2022, p. 42) remark that the 'female-led Temperance Crusade movement' in the United States was 'a wave of protest activity against liquor dealers between 1873 and 1874 [and] shutting down local bars and saloons was the main aim of the crusading [and so religiously driven] women.'

44   Relatedly, McElhattan (2022, p. 1038) observes that criminal background check laws in the United States are 'a widespread mechanism of formal social exclusion [including] in the area of employment'.

Index of Fascism

1   A Composite Index of Fascism

This chapter constructs a substantive composite index or approximation of fascism and more broadly conservative or radical-right authoritarianism. In addition, it calculates numerical aggregate indexes or approximations of fascism or generally right-wing authoritarianism for Western and comparable societies such as OECD countries. A caveat is that this is just an exercise in the operationalization and quantification of fascism or right-wing authoritarianism that is essentially a qualitative phenomenon. Therefore, it represents a tentative estimation and proximate measurement rather than an exact calculation of fascism or right-wing authoritarianism in contemporary societies, thus just an exploratory endeavor. Quantification of fascism and generally radical-right authoritarianism as a qualitative phenomenon for contemporary societies can be only a first approximation rather than an 'exact science'.

The substantive composite index or approximation has as its components certain indicators and proxies of fascism and more broadly radical-right authoritarianism that derive from its essential elements. For this purpose, these components are classified into political, cultural, economic, and civil-society indicators and proxies of fascism or right-wing authoritarianism (See Table 5.1).

First, the political indicators and proxies of fascism or right-wing authoritarianism include no or weak power constraints, no or weak electoral freedom and political pluralism, no or weak rule of law, no or weak political stability and the presence of violence, no or weak control of corruption, no or weak open government, voting rights suppression, political voice suppression, mass imprisonment, widespread death sentences and executions, other political terror, and high military expenditure expressing strong militarism.

Second, the cultural indicators and proxies of fascism or right-wing authoritarianism consist of public depreciation of and low government spending on the arts and culture, mass religious superstitions such as the pervasive belief in 'Satan' and by association 'witches', anti-science in the form of rejection of biological evolution, extreme and coercive religiosity through common beliefs in 'God' and high importance of religion in life, pervasive church attendance, and high frequency of daily prayer.

Third, the economic indicators and proxies of fascism or right-wing author-itarianism comprise the share of wealth of the top one percent of the popu-lation, the Gini coefficient of income distribution, the general poverty rate, compulsory hard or long work, no or short paid vacations, no or short paid paternity leave, no or weak employment protection, no or low unemployment benefits, no or weak social protection and economic security, union suppres-sion, and collective bargaining suppression.

Fourth, the civil-society indicators and proxies of fascism or right-wing authoritarianism involve no or weak civil liberties, no or weak civil justice, no or weak individual liberty and privacy, the death penalty for drug offenses, mass incarceration for sins-as-crimes such as imprisonment for drug offenses, no or weak fundamental human rights, no or weak media freedom, no or weak human rights to life, peace and safety, mass and unrestricted gun ownership, and widespread murders by guns. (Table 5.1 summarizes these indicators and proxies of fascism or right-wing authoritarianism.)

2   Indicators and Proxies of Fascism or Right-Wing Authoritarianism

2.1   *Political Indicators and Proxies*
(1) *No or Weak Power Constraints.* Non-existence or weakness of constraints on state power is a typical political indicator and identifier of fascism, namely of its extreme anti-liberalism, anti-democracy, and absolute power and encom-passing domination, and more broadly of conservative authoritarianism. Therefore, the negative or reverse of power constraints provides a specifica-tion of this indicator. The World Justice Project Rule of Law Index is the data source in that it calculates 'factor scores' on government-powers constraints defined as a measure of the 'extent to which those who govern are bound by law. It comprises the means, both constitutional and institutional, by which the powers of the government and its officials and agents are limited and held accountable under the law. It also includes non-governmental checks on the government's power, such as a free and independent press.' This source pro-vides such scores for OECD and other countries during 2020. For OECD coun-tries, power-constraints scores (multiplied by 100 to generate a uniform 0–100 scale) are the lowest in Turkey, Hungary, Mexico, and Poland (respectively 30, 44, 46, and 58) while being the highest in Denmark, Norway, Finland, and Sweden (94 in the first two, 92 in the third, and 87 in the fourth) (see Table 5.2; also, Table 5.4 gives descriptive statistics for all the indicators and proxies of fascism or right-wing authoritarianism). The negative of power constraints derives from subtracting such scores from the possible maximum of 100.

TABLE 5.1   Indicators and proxies of fascism or right-wing authoritarianism

I   Political Indicators and Proxies
     no or weak power constraints
     no or weak rule of law
     no or weak political stability and presence of violence
     no or weak control of corruption
     no or weak open government
     voting rights suppression
     no or weak electoral freedom and political pluralism
     no or weak political voice
     no or weak media freedom
     mass imprisonment
     widespread death sentences and executions
     other political terror
     exorbitant military expenditure
II   Cultural Indicators and Proxies
     religion-grounded social depreciation of and low government spending
     on art and culture
     widespread religious superstitions (beliefs in 'Satan')
     anti-science (opposition to evolution)
     mass 'God' beliefs (or delusions)
     high importance of religion in life
     high church attendance
     high frequency of daily prayer
III Economic Indicators and Proxies
     share of wealth of the top one percent of the population
     Gini coefficient of income distribution
     general poverty rate
     compulsory hard or long work
     no or short paid vacations
     no or short paid paternity leave
     no or weak employment protection
     no or low unemployment benefits
     no or weak social protection and economic security
     union suppression
     collective bargaining suppression
IV   Civil-Society Indicators and Proxies
     no or weak civil liberties
     no or weak civil justice

TABLE 5.1   Indicators and proxies of fascism or right-wing authoritarianism (*cont.*)

---

no or weak individual liberty and privacy
the death penalty for drug offenses
mass incarceration for sins-as-crimes
no or weak fundamental human rights
no or weak human rights to life, peace and safety
mass and unrestricted gun ownership
widespread murders by guns

Therefore, power-constraints negatives are the lowest in Denmark, Norway, Finland, and Sweden, while being the highest in Turkey, Hungary, Mexico, and Poland.

(2) *No or Weak Rule of Law.* Absence or weakness of the rule of law is another typical political indicator of fascism, namely if its absolute power and encompassing domination, coercion, repression, violence and terror, and more broadly of right-wing authoritarianism. The negative or inverse of the rule of law therefore supplies a specification of this indicator. The World Bank's Worldwide Governance Indicators project is the data source that defines the rule of law by 'perceptions of the extent to which agents have confidence in and abide by the rules of society, and in particular the quality of contract enforcement, property rights, the police, and the courts, as well as the likelihood of crime and violence.' This source furnishes rule of law percentile ranks, among all UN states, for OECD and other countries in 2019. Among OECD countries, rule of law ranks are the lowest in Mexico, Turkey, Greece, and Italy (respectively 27.4, 44.7, 60.1, and 61.5), while being the highest in Finland, Norway, Switzerland, and Sweden (respectively 100, 99.5, 99, and 98.6) (see Table 5.3). The negative of the rule of law results from deducting these percentile ranks from the maximum of 100. Hence, rule of law negatives are the lowest in Finland, Norway, Switzerland, and Sweden, and the highest in Mexico, Turkey, Greece, and Italy.

(3) *No or Weak Political Stability and Presence of Violence.* Absence of political stability and the presence of violence is yet another political indicator or proxy of fascism, especially its coercion, repression, violence, and terror, and generally of right-wing authoritarianism overall. The negative or obverse of political stability and the absence of violence is a specification of this indicator. The World Bank's Worldwide Governance Indicators project is the data source that characterizes 'political stability and absence of violence/terrorism' by 'perceptions of the likelihood of political instability and/

TABLE 5.2   Constraints on government powers, factor scores and negatives, OECD
countries, 2020

Country	Power constraints factor score × 100	Power constraints negative
Australia	82	18
Austria	85	15
Belgium	83	17
Canada	84	16
Chile	72	28
Czech Republic	73	27
Denmark	94	6
Estonia	83	17
Finland	92	8
France	73	27
Germany	85	15
Greece	68	32
Hungary	40	60
Iceland[a]	94	6
Ireland[a]	82	18
Israel[a]	68	32
Italy	71	29
Japan	71	29
Korea South	72	28
Latvia[a]	84	16
Lithuania[a]	84	16
Luxembourg[a]	83	17
Mexico	46	54
Netherlands	86	14
New Zealand	85	15
Norway	94	6
Poland	58	42
Portugal	78	22
Slovak Republic	73	27
Slovenia	65	35
Spain	74	26
Sweden	87	13
Switzerland[a]	85	15
Turkey	30	70
United Kingdom	82	18

TABLE 5.2   Constraints on government powers, factor scores and negatives (*cont.*)

Country	Power constraints factor score × 100	Power constraints negative
United States	71	29
OECD Average	76	24

a   Approximated values from comparable countries: Iceland from Norway, Ireland from United Kingdom, Israel from Greece, Latvia and Lithuania from Estonia, Luxembourg from Belgium, Slovak Republic from Czech Republic, Switzerland from Germany

Constraints On Government Powers' Factor Score 'measures the extent to which those who govern are bound by law. It comprises the means, both constitutional and institutional, by which the powers of the government and its officials and agents are limited and held accountable under the law. It also includes non-governmental checks on the government's power, such as a free and independent press' (The World Justice Project Rule of Law Index 2020, p. 22)

Power Constraints Negative = 100 – Constraints Factor Score × 100

SOURCE: THE WORLD JUSTICE PROJECT RULE OF LAW INDEX 2020 HTTPS://WORLDJUSTICE PROJECT.ORG/SITES/DEFAULT/FILES/DOCUMENTS/WJP-ROLI-2020-ONLINE_0.PDF

or politically-motivated violence, including terrorism.' This source provides percentile ranks on political stability and absence of violence/terrorism, among all states, for OECD and other countries in 2019. Such percentile ranks among OECD countries are the lowest in Turkey, Israel, Mexico, and Chile (respectively 10, 19, 21, and 54.8) and the highest in Iceland, New Zealand, Luxembourg, and Switzerland (99.5, 97.1, 95.7, and 94.8, respectively) (see Table 5.4). One obtains the negative of political stability and the absence of violence/terrorism by subtracting these percentile ranks from 100. As a corollary, political stability and absence of violence/terrorism negatives are the lowest in Iceland, New Zealand, Luxembourg, and Switzerland and the highest in Turkey, Israel, Mexico, and Chile.

(4) *No or Weak Control of Corruption.* Non-existence or weakness of control of corruption is an additional political indicator or proxy of fascism, especially of its anti-egalitarianism, particularism, elitism, and monopolistic closure, as well as of absolute power, and generally of right-wing authoritarianism. The negative of the control of corruption hence represents a specification of this indicator. The World Bank's Worldwide Governance Indicators project is the data source that specifies the control of corruption by 'perceptions of the extent to which public power is exercised for private gain, including both petty and grand forms of corruption, as well as 'capture' of the state by elites and private

TABLE 5.3 Rule of law percentile ranks and negatives, OECD countries, 2019

Country	Rule of law percentile rank	Rule of law negative
Australia	93.27	6.73
Austria	97.12	2.88
Belgium	88.46	11.54
Canada	94.71	5.29
Chile	82.69	17.31
Czech Republic	81.73	18.27
Denmark	98.08	1.92
Estonia	87.02	12.98
Finland	100	0
France	89.42	10.58
Germany	92.31	7.69
Greece	60.58	39.42
Hungary	68.27	31.73
Iceland	95.19	4.81
Ireland	88.94	11.06
Israel	82.21	17.79
Italy	61.54	38.46
Japan	90.38	9.62
Korea South	86.06	13.94
Latvia	80.77	19.23
Lithuania	81.25	18.75
Luxembourg	95.67	4.33
Mexico	27.40	72.60
Netherlands	96.15	3.85
New Zealand	97.60	2.40
Norway	99.52	.48
Poland	66.35	33.65
Portugal	84.62	15.38
Slovak Republic	71.15	28.85
Slovenia	84.13	15.87
Spain	80.29	19.71
Sweden	98.56	1.44
Switzerland	99.04	.96
Turkey	44.71	55.29
United Kingdom	91.35	8.65

TABLE 5.3   Rule of law percentile ranks and negatives, OECD countries, 2019 (*cont.*)

Country	Rule of law percentile rank	Rule of law negative
United States	89.90	10.10
OECD Average	84.07	15.93

Percentile rank among all countries (ranges from 0 (lowest) to 100 (highest) rank)
Rule Of Law 'reflects perceptions of the extent to which agents have confidence in and abide by the rules of society, and in particular the quality of contract enforcement, property rights, the police, and the courts, as well as the likelihood of crime and violence' (The Worldwide Governance Indicators).
Rule Of Law Negative = 100 – Rule of Law Percentile Rank
SOURCE: THE WORLDWIDE GOVERNANCE INDICATORS (WGI) PROJECT HTTPS://INFO .WORLDBANK.ORG/GOVERNANCE/WGI

interests'. This source gives percentile ranks, among all UN members, on the control of corruption for OECD and other countries during 2019. Among OECD countries, such percentile ranks are the lowest in Mexico, Turkey, Greece, and Hungary (respectively 22.6, 44.7, 56.3, and 57.7) and the highest in New Zealand, Finland, Sweden, and Luxembourg (100, 99, 98.6, and 98, respectively) (see Table 5.5). The negative of the control of corruption stems from subtraction of these ranks from 100. Thence, control of corruption negatives are the lowest in New Zealand, Finland, Sweden, and Luxembourg and the highest in Mexico, Turkey, Greece, and Hungary.

(5) *No or Weak Open Government.* Non-existence or weakness of open government is a further political indicator or proxy of fascism, namely of its extreme anti-liberalism and anti-democracy such as its negation of political freedoms and rights, as well as anti-universalism, anti-egalitarianism, and absolute power, and more broadly of right-wing authoritarianism. The negative of open government thus becomes a specification of this indicator. The World Justice Project Rule of Law Index is the data source defining the 'openness of government' by the 'extent to which a government shares information, empowers people with tools to hold the government accountable, and fosters citizen participation in public policy deliberations.' This source provides factor scores on open government for OECD and other countries in 2020. For OECD countries, these scores (multiplied by 100 consistent with the 0–100 scale) are the lowest in Turkey, Hungary, Mexico, and Poland (respectively 42, 46, and 60 for the last two) and the highest in Norway, Denmark, Finland, and Sweden (89, 88

TABLE 5.4   Political stability and absence of violence/terrorism percentile ranks and
negatives, OECD countries, 2019

Country	Stability percentile rank	Stability negative
Australia	88.57	11.43
Austria	82.86	17.14
Belgium	61.90	38.10
Canada	85.24	14.76
Chile	54.76	45.24
Czech Republic	80.48	19.52
Denmark	83.81	16.19
Estonia	68.10	31.90
Finland	79.05	20.95
France	58.57	41.43
Germany	66.67	33.33
Greece	57.14	42.86
Hungary	71.43	28.57
Iceland	99.52	.48
Ireland	82.38	17.62
Israel	19.05	80.95
Italy	60.95	39.05
Japan	85.71	14.29
Korea South	61.43	38.57
Latvia	60	40
Lithuania	75.24	24.76
Luxembourg	95.71	4.29
Mexico	20.95	79.05
Netherlands	75.71	24.29
New Zealand	97.14	2.86
Norway	92.38	7.62
Poland	64.29	35.71
Portugal	90.95	9.05
Slovak Republic	72.38	27.62
Slovenia	73.81	26.19
Spain	59.05	40.95
Sweden	86.67	13.33
Switzerland	94.76	5.24
Turkey	10	90

TABLE 5.4   Political stability and absence of violence/terrorism percentile ranks (*cont.*)

Country	Stability percentile rank	Stability negative
United Kingdom	63.81	36.19
United States	57.62	42.38
OECD Average	70.5	29.50

'The Worldwide Governance Indicators (WGI) are a research dataset summarizing the views on the quality of governance provided by a large number of enterprise, citizen and expert survey respondents in industrial and developing countries. These data are gathered from a number of survey institutes, think tanks, non-governmental organizations, international organizations, and private sector firms. The Worldwide Governance Indicators (WGI) project reports aggregate and individual governance indicators for over 200 countries and territories over the period 1996–2018, for six dimensions of governance: Voice and Accountability, Political Stability and Absence of Violence, Government Effectiveness, Regulatory Quality, Rule of Law and Control of Corruption. These aggregate indicators combine the views of a large number of enterprise, citizen and expert survey respondents in industrial and developing countries. They are based on over 30 individual data sources produced by a variety of survey institutes, think tanks, non-governmental organizations, international organizations, and private sector firms.'
Percentile rank among all countries (ranges from 0 (lowest) to 100 (highest) rank)
Political Stability Negative = 100 – Political Stability Percentile Rank
SOURCE: THE WORLD BANK WORLDWIDE GOVERNANCE INDICATORS (WGI) PROJECT
HTTP://INFO.WORLDBANK.ORG/GOVERNANCE/WGI/

for the first two, respectively and 86 for the last two) (see Table 5.6). To derive the negative of open government requires deducting such scores from the possible maximum of 100. As a result, open government negatives are the lowest in Norway, Denmark, Finland, and Sweden while being the highest in Turkey, Hungary, Mexico, and Poland.

(6) *Voting Rights Suppression.* Suppression of voting and related political rights and freedoms is also a typical political indicator of fascism, namely of its extreme anti-liberalism and anti-democracy, such as its negation of political freedoms and rights, anti-universalism, anti-egalitarianism, and absolute power, ceteris paribus, or generally of right-wing authoritarianism. The negative of voting rights of which voter turnout serves as a proxy thereby provides a specification of this indicator. The International Institute for Democracy and Electoral Assistance is the data source that supplies voter turnout data for parliamentary elections, as percentage of the voting age population, for OECD countries during 2019 or most recent elections. Among OECD countries, voter

TABLE 5.5   Control of corruption percentile ranks and negatives, OECD countries, 2019

Country	Control of corruption percentile rank	Control of corruption negative
Australia	94.23	5.77
Austria	90.87	9.13
Belgium	91.35	8.65
Canada	93.27	6.73
Chile	83.17	16.83
Czech Republic	68.75	31.25
Denmark	97.60	2.40
Estonia	90.38	9.62
Finland	99.04	.96
France	88.94	11.06
Germany	95.19	4.81
Greece	56.25	43.75
Hungary	57.69	42.31
Iceland	92.79	7.21
Ireland	89.42	10.58
Israel	78.85	21.15
Italy	62.02	37.98
Japan	89.90	10.10
Korea South	76.92	23.08
Latvia	68.27	31.73
Lithuania	74.52	25.48
Luxembourg	98.08	1.92
Mexico	22.60	77.40
Netherlands	96.63	3.37
New Zealand	100	0
Norway	97.12	2.88
Poland	71.15	28.85
Portugal	77.40	22.60
Slovak Republic	64.42	35.58
Slovenia	80.29	19.71
Spain	73.56	26.44
Sweden	98.56	1.44
Switzerland	96.15	3.85
Turkey	44.71	55.29
United Kingdom	93.75	6.25

TABLE 5.5   Control of corruption percentile ranks and negatives, OECD countries, 2019 *(cont.)*

Country	Control of corruption percentile rank	Control of corruption negative
United States	84.62	15.38
OECD Average	81.62	18.38

Percentile rank among all countries (ranges from 0 (lowest) to 100 (highest) rank)
Control of Corruption 'reflects perceptions of the extent to which public power is exercised for private gain, including both petty and grand forms of corruption, as well as 'capture' of the state by elites and private interests' (The Worldwide Governance Indicators)
Control of Corruption Negative = 100 − Control of Corruption Percentile Rank
SOURCE: THE WORLDWIDE GOVERNANCE INDICATORS (WGI) PROJECT HTTPS://INFO
.WORLDBANK.ORG/GOVERNANCE/WGI

turnout rates are the highest in Australia, Luxembourg, Belgium, and Sweden (respectively 91, 89.7, 88.4 and 87.2 percent) and the lowest in France, Chile, Switzerland, and Portugal (46.5, 42.6, 48.4, 48.6 percent, respectively) (see Table 5.7). The negative of voting rights is the result from subtracting voter turnout data from the possible maximum of 100. Therefore, voting rights negatives are the lowest in Australia, Luxembourg, Belgium, and Sweden and the highest in France, Chile, Switzerland, and Portugal.

Admittedly, voter turnout is an imperfect proxy for voting rights in that its lower levels can be the result not only of the suppression of these and other political freedoms but also of other factors. For example, comparatively low voter turnout in Chile probably reflects the voting rights suppression or restriction as the relic of its Pinochet neo-fascist capitalist, 'free market' (Chicago-economics) dictatorship, while that in France and Switzerland likely reflecting other political, social or cultural factors, with Portugal as an intermediate case. Still, in the US context, low voter turnout has been historically since the Jim Crow system mostly the effect and expression of the voting-rights suppression and apparently remains so through post-2016 and after 2020. Such post-2020 practices involve escalating attempts at the voting-rights suppression, also including election subversions by overturning electoral results, so popular will, and gerrymandering resulting in fascists/ conservatives selecting voters rather than these electing their representatives, in the former Southern Confederacy and other 'red' states under conservative-fascist and theocratic control.

TABLE 5.6   Open government factor scores and negatives, OECD countries, 2020

Country	Open government factor score × 100	Open government negative
Australia	81	19
Austria	71	29
Belgium	76	24
Canada	81	19
Chile	71	29
Czech Republic	67	33
Denmark	88	12
Estonia	81	19
Finland	86	14
France	78	22
Germany	79	21
Greece	61	39
Hungary	46	54
Iceland[a]	89	11
Ireland[a]	79	21
Israe[a]	61	39
Italy	63	37
Japan	68	32
Korea South	71	29
Latvia[a]	81	19
Lithuania[a]	81	19
Luxembourg[a]	76	24
Mexico	60	40
Netherlands	82	18
New Zealand	82	18
Norway	89	11
Poland	60	40
Portugal	66	34
Slovak Republic[a]	67	33
Slovenia	65	35
Spain	71	29
Sweden	86	14
Switzerland[a]	79	21

TABLE 5.6   Open government factor scores and negatives, OECD countries, 2020 (*cont.*)

Country	Open government factor score × 100	Open government negative
Turkey	42	58
United Kingdom	79	21
United States	78	22
OECD Average	73	27

a   Approximated values from comparable countries: Iceland from Norway, Ireland from United
    Kingdom, Israel from Greece, Latvia and Lithuania from Estonia, Luxembourg from Belgium,
    Slovak Republic from Czech Republic, Switzerland from Germany
Open Government Negative = 100 − Open Government Factor Score × 100
Open Government Factor Score measures the 'openness of government defined by the extent
to which a government shares information, empowers people with tools to hold the govern-
ment accountable, and fosters citizen participation in public policy deliberations. This factor
measures whether basic laws and information on legal rights are publicized and evaluates the
quality of information published by the government' (The World Justice Project Rule of Law
Index 2020, p. 24).
SOURCE: THE WORLD JUSTICE PROJECT RULE OF LAW INDEX 2020 HTTPS://WORLDJUSTICE
PROJECT.ORG/SITES/DEFAULT/FILES/DOCUMENTS/WJP-ROLI-2020-ONLINE_0.PDF

Overall, what has been happening in the former Southern Confederacy and
other 'red' states under conservative control post-2016 or after 2020 represents
or resembles fascism and generally radical-right dictatorship. This characterization fits well, for example, Florida, Texas, and similar Southern and other
conservative-ruled states due to their suppression of voting and other political
liberties and rights by extreme illiberal laws evoking the Jim-Crow era, while
passing laws to protect their post-2016 autocratic leader from what they construe as anti-conservative 'media bias', thus enacting legislation to benefit a
ruler or single individual, as typical of despotism and fascism. This also holds
true because of their suppression of labor freedoms and rights by persistent
anti-union actions, suppression and criminalization of individual liberty and
privacy such as reproductive, gender, and related civil liberties and rights
through abortion prohibitions or severe restrictions, anti-transgender hysterias, etc., and suppression of academic or educational freedom and attacks on
science by assaults on universities and faculty employment or tenure, banning
'critical race' and similar theories, artistic, literatures, and books, and so on.
Consequently, these US conservative-ruled states launch a total war, 'crusade'
for their theocratic rulers and religionists, against social liberties and human

TABLE 5.7   Voter turnout, parliamentary elections, as % of voting age population, and
negative, OECD countries, 2019 or most recent elections

Country	Voter turn-out %	Voter turn-out negative
Australia	91.01	8.99
Austria	75.60	24.40
Belgium	88.40	11.60
Canada	67.70	32.30
Chile	46.50	53.50
Czech Republic	60.80	39.20
Denmark	84.60	15.40
Estonia	63.70	36.30
Finland	68.70	31.30
France	42.60	57.40
Germany	76.20	23.80
Greece	57.90	42.10
Hungary	69.70	30.30
Iceland	81.20	18.80
Ireland	65.10	34.90
Israel	69.80	30.20
Italy	72.90	27.10
Japan	52.70	47.30
Korea South	58.00	42.00
Latvia[a]	54.58	45.42
Lithuania[a]	50.64	49.36
Luxembourg	89.70	10.30
Mexico	63.20	36.80
Netherlands	81.90	18.10
New Zealand	79.80	20.20
Norway	78.20	21.80
Poland	61.70	38.30
Portugal	48.60	51.40
Slovak Republic	59.80	40.20
Slovenia	52.60	47.40
Spain	71.80	28.20
Sweden	87.20	12.80
Switzerland	48.40	51.60
Turkey	86.20	13.80
United Kingdom	67.60	32.40

TABLE 5.7   Voter turnout, parliamentary elections, as % of voting age population (*cont.*)

Country	Voter turn-out %	Voter turn-out negative
United States	56.80	43.20
OECD Average	67.55	32.45

a https://www.idea.int/data-tools/data/voter-turnout
Voter Turn-out Negative = 100—Voter Turn-out %
SOURCE: THE INTERNATIONAL INSTITUTE FOR DEMOCRACY AND ELECTORAL ASSISTANCE.
2019. HTTPS://WWW.IDEA.INT/DATA-TOOLS/REGIONAL-ENTITY-VIEW/OECD/40

rights on all fronts—economic, political, civil, and cultural—indicating the totalitarian nature of these regimes in the form of radical-right dictatorship and ultimately fascism.

Apparently, what is unthinkable or atypical in the Western world becomes a reality or typical in the South under conservatism/fascism and conservative America as a whole post-2016 and after 2020—minimization of voting, harsh labor coercion, violation of elementary individual liberties and human rights, negation of academic freedom, Inquisition-style prohibition and proxy burning of certain theories, sciences, arts, and books reminiscent of Nazism and generally fascism,[1] and so on. For example, 30 or so state legislatures controlled by a growingly proto-fascist and generally extremist conservative party enacted such voter suppression, partisan gerrymandering, and election subversion laws after the 2020 elections using the falsehood of preventing electoral 'fraud' alleged to have happened during these elections by its leader whose effective death cult this party has become during the Covid-19 pandemic,[2] thus the deceptive and delusionary pretext of 'election integrity'.

---

[1] Paxton (2004, p. 36) refers to Joseph Goebbels launching 'a book-burning ceremony in Berlin on May 10, 1933 [and] Fascist squads [making] bonfires of socialist books in Italy.' And PEN America reports in the US '1,586 book bans that have occurred in 86 school districts in 26 states between July 1, 2021, and March 31, 2022,' finding that 'Texas led the country with the most bans at 713' followed by other conservative-ruled states Pennsylvania (456); Florida (204); Oklahoma (43); Kansas (30); and Tennessee (16). This suggests that the conservative-religious pole of America that Texas as the biggest part leads effectively continues Nazi and fascist book-burning ceremonies through mass book bans.

[2] For instance, a Texas ultra-conservative, anti-liberal judge appointed by the post-2016 radical-right regime suspended the Federal mandate for wearing masks at national and associated facilities like airports and airplanes while the US reaching 1 million deaths due to the Covid-19 pandemic. Following this decision, one can watch the spectacle of masses

Since the US is in the present focus, this historical and continuing association justifies taking voter turnout as a proxy for voting rights and, if it is low, of their suppression by fascism and generally conservatism. In essence, the US's comparatively low voting turnout as mainly the result of voter suppression invariably by fascism and generally conservatism indicates the continuing failure of the 'American experiment' in ensuring basic universal political liberties and rights. To that extent, this points to an equivalent failure in sustaining genuine, inclusive democracy, as opposed to bogus exclusionary 'democracy' in conservative America like the South and similar spaces where voter suppressions are the most egregious and obstinate, even intensifying after the 2020 elections that its autocratic leader lost but which serve as the false 'electoral fraud' rationale for such anti-democratic subversions. Moreover, such escalating suppressions of voting liberties and rights in the former Southern Confederacy from Florida to Texas and the rest of the conservative pole of America with corresponding adverse effects on voter turnout and the broader democratic process threaten to effectively end or gravely pervert beyond recognition the celebrated 'American experiment' in democracy. Considering such systematic suppressions or restrictions of voting rights, political elections in the conservative pole of America and the latter as a whole can hardly ever be considered 'free and fair', even comparatively less so than in all Western societies and most OECD countries. Considering such anti-democratic practices, elections in conservative and hence by contamination all America look less free and fair than in, for example, Mexico and even most of South America (e.g., Peru where

---

of maskless persons on US airports and airplanes, thus potentially fatally endangering their and others' health and life through Covid-19 infections while in contrast most other Western and even non-Western continue proper measures, including the wearing of masks, protecting public health at these and other facilities. And one could see literally such a contrasting picture: maskless Americans on US airports and airplanes, while non-Americans wearing masks on other such facilities. To that extent, such decisions by US ultra-conservative, anti-liberal judges are to some extent responsible for Covid-19 infections and deaths and generally the persistence or recurrence of this pandemic, so it is hardly an exaggeration to state that they, together with other ruling conservatives, have the blood of murdered children on their hands. But this only confirms that American conservatism or the radical right is willing and ready to literally sacrifice the health and life of Americans to its ideological and religious fanaticism (evoking Hume's diagnosed 'fanaticism' of Puritanism) and political extremism and thereby ultimately turns into fascism or theocracy. Comparatively, the above reaffirms that conservatism in America, especially (but not solely) the former South Confederacy from Alabama to Texas, is more antiliberal, irrational, unreasonable, intransigent than in all Western societies and most OECD countries and the world, except for Islamic theocracies so that only Islamist conservatism equates such 'all-American' conservative fanaticism/extremism causing death, health risks, and suffering for millions of Americans.

voting is maximized by being compulsory while in the US South is minimized by applying non-vote compulsion on certain groups).

The preceding hence indicates persistent failure of the 'American experiment' to ensure basic politic liberties and rights and eventually of the collapse of democracy in America due to fascism or right-wing authoritarianism and the compound of its causes, the alliance of conservatism with coercive capitalism, religion, and theocracy. Historically, the 'American experiment' in ensuring basic political liberties and rights like universal voting has never been complete success since the Revolution through slavery to the Jim Crow era and after, but fascism and generally conservatism by such a 'holy' alliance and fascist reproduction threaten to terminate it and thus end democracy.

(7) *No or Weak Electoral Freedom and Political Pluralism.* Absence or weakness of electoral freedom/process and political pluralism is another typical political indicator of fascism, specifically of its extreme anti-liberalism and anti-democracy, such as its negation of political freedoms and rights, absolute rule, coercion, and repression, and more broadly of right-wing authoritarianism. The negative of electoral freedom/process and political pluralism hence serves as a specification of this indicator. The Economist Intelligence Unit's Democracy Index is the data source that defines electoral freedom/process especially by free and fair elections and political pluralism by the freedom of 'citizens to form political parties that are independent of the government.' This source supplies electoral process and political pluralism indexes for OECD and other countries in 2019. Among OECD countries, these indexes (multiplied by 10 consistent with a 0–100 scale) are the lowest in Turkey, Mexico, Hungary, and Japan (respectively 30.8, 78.3, and 87.5 for the last two) and the highest in Australia, Denmark, Iceland, Ireland, Luxembourg, New Zealand, and Norway (all 100) (see Table 5.8). Deducting these indexes from the maximum of 100 yields the negative of electoral freedom/process and political pluralism. Consequently, electoral freedom and political pluralism negatives are the lowest in Australia, Denmark, Iceland, Ireland, Luxembourg, New Zealand, and Norway and the highest in Turkey, Mexico, Hungary, and Japan.

(8) *No or Weak Political Voice.* Absence or weakness of political voice is a related political indicator of fascism, especially its extreme anti-liberalism and anti-democracy, such as its negation of political freedoms and rights, absolute rule, coercion, and repression, and of right-wing authoritarianism in general. The negative of political voice therefore serves as a specification of this indicator. The World Bank's Worldwide Governance Indicators project is the data source defining 'voice and accountability' as a reflection of 'perceptions of the extent to which a country's citizens are able to participate in selecting their government, as well as freedom of expression, freedom of association, and a

TABLE 5.8 Electoral process and political pluralism indexes and negatives, 2019, OECD countries

Country	Pluralism index × 10	Pluralism negative
Australia	100	0
Austria	95.80	4.20
Belgium	95.80	4.20
Canada	95.80	4.20
Chile	95.80	4.20
Czech Republic	95.80	4.20
Denmark	100	0
Estonia	95.80	4.20
Finland	100	0
France	95.80	4.20
Germany	95.80	4.20
Greece	95.80	4.20
Hungary	87.50	12.50
Iceland	100	0
Ireland	100	0
Israel	91.70	8.30
Italy	95.80	4.20
Japan	87.50	12.50
Korea South	91.70	8.30
Latvia	95.80	4.20
Lithuania	95.80	4.20
Luxembourg	100	.0
Mexico	78.30	21.70
Netherlands	95.80	4.20
New Zealand	100	0
Norway	100	0
Poland	91.70	8.30
Portugal	95.80	4.20
Slovak Republic	95.80	4.20
Slovenia	95.80	4.20
Spain	95.80	4.20
Sweden	95.80	4.20
Switzerland	95.80	4.20
Turkey	30.80	69.20

TABLE 5.8   Electoral process and political pluralism indexes and negatives, 2019 (*cont.*)

Country	Pluralism index × 10	Pluralism negative
United Kingdom	95.80	4.20
United States	91.70	8.30
OECD Average	93.52	6.48

a   Electoral process and pluralism pertain to: 1. Are elections for the national legislature and head of government free? 2. Are elections for the national legislature and head of government fair? 3. Are municipal elections both free and fair? 4. Is there universal suffrage for all adults? 5. Can citizens cast their vote free of significant threats to their security from state or non-state bodies? 6. Do laws provide for broadly equal campaigning opportunities? 7. Is the process of financing political parties transparent and generally accepted? 8. Following elections, are the constitutional mechanisms for the orderly transfer of power from one government to another clear, established and accepted? 9. Are citizens free to form political parties that are independent of the government? 10. Do opposition parties have a realistic prospect of achieving government? 11. Is potential access to public office open to all citizens? 12. Are citizens allowed to form political and civic organisations, free of state interference and surveillance? (Democracy Index 2019, pp. 55–56)
Pluralism Negative = 100—Pluralism Index × 10
SOURCE: THE ECONOMIST INTELLIGENCE UNIT 2019, DEMOCRACY INDEX 2019

free media.' This source supplies 'voice and accountability' percentile ranks, among all UN members, for OECD and other countries in 2019. Among OECD countries, these ranks are the lowest in Turkey, Mexico, Hungary, and Israel (respectively 24.6, 45.3, 54.7, and 70.4) and the highest in Norway, Sweden, Finland, and Denmark (100, 99.5, 99, and 98.5, respectively) (see Table 5.9). The 'voice and accountability' negative results from subtracting these percentile ranks from 100. As a result, voice and accountability negative are the lowest in Norway, Sweden, Finland, and Denmark and the highest in Turkey, Mexico, Hungary, and Israel.

(9) *No or Weak Media Freedom.* Absence or weakness of media freedom is a related political indicator of fascism, namely of its extreme anti-liberalism and anti-democracy, such as its negation of political freedoms and rights, absolute rule, coercion, and repression, and more broadly of right-wing authoritarianism. The negative of media freedom thereby represents a specification of this indicator. Reporters without Borders is the data source that defines media freedom suppression as 'abuses and acts of violence against journalists (and) pluralism, media independence, environment and self-censorship, legislative framework, transparency, infrastructure.' This source furnishes press freedom

TABLE 5.9 Voice and accountability rankings and negatives, OECD countries, 2019

Country	Voice percentile rank	Voice negative
Australia	93.10	6.90
Austria	93.60	6.40
Belgium	95.57	4.43
Canada	96.06	3.94
Chile	81.28	18.72
Czech Republic	77.83	22.17
Denmark	98.52	1.48
Estonia	88.67	11.33
Finland	99.01	.99
France	87.68	12.32
Germany	95.07	4.93
Greece	77.34	22.66
Hungary	54.68	45.32
Iceland	94.09	5.91
Ireland	94.58	5.42
Israel	70.44	29.56
Italy	79.80	20.20
Japan	78.33	21.67
Korea South	72.91	27.09
Latvia	74.38	25.62
Lithuania	81.77	18.23
Luxembourg	96.55	3.45
Mexico	45.32	54.68
Netherlands	97.54	2.46
New Zealand	98.03	1.97
Norway	100	0
Poland	70.94	29.06
Portugal	89.16	10.84
Slovak Republic	75.37	24.63
Slovenia	80.79	19.21
Spain	82.76	17.24
Sweden	99.51	.49
Switzerland	97.04	2.96
Turkey	24.63	75.37
United Kingdom	90.64	9.36
United States	78.82	21.18

TABLE 5.9   Voice and accountability rankings and negatives, oecd countries, 2019 (*cont.*)

Country	Voice percentile rank	Voice negative
OECD Average	83.66	16.34

Percentile rank among all countries (ranges from 0 (lowest) to 100 (highest) rank)

Voice and Accountability 'reflects perceptions of the extent to which a country's citizens are able to participate in selecting their government, as well as freedom of expression, freedom of association, and a free media' (The Worldwide Governance Indicators)

The Worldwide Governance Indicators (WGI) are a research dataset summarizing the views on the quality of governance provided by a large number of enterprise, citizen and expert survey respondents in industrial and developing countries. These data are gathered from a number of survey institutes, think tanks, non-governmental organizations, international organizations, and private sector firms. The WGI do not reflect the official views of the World Bank, its Executive Directors, or the countries they represent. The WGI are not used by the World Bank Group to allocate resources.

Voice Negative = 100 – Voice Percentile Rank

SOURCE: WORLD BANK, THE WORLDWIDE GOVERNANCE INDICATORS (WGI) HTTPS://INFO
.WORLDBANK.ORG/GOVERNANCE/WGI

violation indexes for OECD and other countries in 2020. These indexes among OECD countries are the highest in Turkey, Mexico, Hungary, and Israel (respectively 50, 45.5, and 30.8 for the last two) and the lowest in Norway, Finland, Denmark, and Sweden (respectively 7.8, 7.9, 8.1, and 9.3) (see Table 5.10).

It is remarkable that the US under the 2020 proto-fascist or radical-right autocratic regime has the highest press freedom violation index among Western societies (23.85) followed by Brexit Great Britain during the eruption of conservative populism (22.93). Such an index illustrates the failure of the 'American experiment' to provide a certain degree of press freedom as an instance of basic political freedoms, or to prevent its systematic violations, primarily because of fascism or right-wing authoritarianism and the compound of its causes. In this respect, it suggests an additional failure of the 'American experiment', due to fascism and the above anti-democratic alliance, to ensure basic political liberties and rights and thus democracy of which press freedom (or free press as the independent 'estate' in a democratic polity) is an integral element.

(10) *Mass imprisonment*. Mass incarceration is a typical political indicator of fascism, namely of its coercion, repression, violence, and terror, and generally of conservative authoritarianism. International Centre for *Prison* Studies is the data source supplying prison population or prisoner rates (per 100,000 population) for OECD and other countries in 2019. Among OECD countries, prison

TABLE 5.10 World press freedom indexes and negatives, OECD countries, 2020

Country	Press freedom index	Press freedom negative (unfreedom)
Australia	20.21	40.40
Austria	15.78	31.55
Belgium	15.79	31.57
Canada	15.29	30.57
Chile	23.57	47.12
Czech Republic	27.31	54.60
Denmark	8.13	16.25
Estonia	12.61	25.21
Finland	7.93	15.85
France	22.92	45.82
Germany	12.16	24.31
Greece	28.65	57.28
Hungary	30.84	61.66
Iceland	15.12	30.23
Ireland	12.60	25.19
Israel	30.84	61.66
Italy	23.69	47.36
Japan	28.86	57.70
Korea South	23.70	47.38
Latvia	18.56	37.11
Lithuania	21.19	42.36
Luxembourg	15.46	30.91
Mexico	45.45	90.86
Netherlands	9.96	19.91
New Zealand	10.69	21.37
Norway	7.84	15.67
Poland	28.80	57.58
Portugal	11.83	23.65
Slovak Republic	22.67	45.32
Slovenia	22.62	45.22
Spain	22.16	44.30
Sweden	9.25	18.49
Switzerland	10.62	21.23
Turkey	50.02	100
United Kingdom	22.93	45.84

TABLE 5.10 World press freedom indexes and negatives, OECD countries, 2020 (*cont.*)

Country	Press freedom index	Press freedom negative (unfreedom)
United States	23.85	47.68
OECD Average	20.28	40.53

World Press Freedom Index is 'Score On Abuses and Acts of Violence Against Journalists and Score on Pluralism, Media Independence, Environment and Self-Censorship, Legislative Framework, Transparency, Infrastructure' (Reporters without Borders).
Larger (smaller) indexes, more (less) abuses and violence against journalists, less (more) pluralism and media independence
Press Freedom Negative (Unfreedom) = 100/50.02 × Press Freedom Index
SOURCE: REPORTERS WITHOUT BORDERS, 2020 WORLD PRESS FREEDOM INDEX HTTPS://RSF.ORG/EN/RANKING

population rates are the lowest in Iceland, Japan, Finland, and Norway (respectively 37, 39, 53, and 60) while being the highest in the US, Turkey, Israel, and Lithuania (655, 344, 234, and 221, respectively) (see Table 5.11). Notably, the differential between the lowest and the highest prisoner rate,[3] those of Iceland and of the US's is around 18 (1,770%), which signifies that the second country imprisons nearly 20 times more people in relative terms than the first.

At this juncture, the highest prisoner rate and total prison population within OECD and even the world (higher than those of China, Iran, or Russia) reveals the US during the rise of fascism and under the long dominance of conservatism since Reaganism, at least the conservative-religious pole of America, as the most coercive and repressive society among Western and comparable societies and indeed globally. To that extent, this unparalleled prison population rate/level indicates that the conservative-religious pole of America mutates into a proxy totalitarian or at the minimum authoritarian system and indeed more so than any other comparable society within OECD, the true 'leader' of the Western and entire world in state coercion and repression via mass imprisonment.

---

3 McElhattan (2022, p. 1037) observes that because of the 'massive expansion of the US criminal legal system in recent decades, by 2010 over 8% of American adults were estimated to carry a record of a felony conviction—a figure that increased by approximately 2.6 times since 1980.'

TABLE 5.11   Prison population rates (per 100,000) and scores, OECD countries, 2019

Country	Prison population rate	Prison population score
Australia	169	25.80
Austria	95	14.50
Belgium	95	14.50
Canada	107	16.34
Chile	209	31.91
Czech Republic	194	29.62
Denmark	71	10.84
Estonia	182	27.79
Finland	53	8.09
France	104	15.88
Germany	77	11.76
Greece	106	16.18
Hungary	167	25.50
Iceland	37	5.65
Ireland	74	11.30
Israel	234	35.73
Italy	90	13.74
Japan	39	5.95
Korea South	106	16.18
Latvia	179	27.33
Lithuania	221	33.74
Luxembourg	105	16.03
Mexico	158	24.12
Netherlands	63	9.62
New Zealand	199	30.38
Norway	60	9.16
Poland	189	28.85
Portugal	110	16.79
Slovak Republic	192	29.31
Slovenia	69	10.53
Spain	124	18.93
Sweden	61	9.31
Switzerland	80	12.21
Turkey	344	52.52
United Kingdom	134	20.46
United States	655	100

TABLE 5.11   Prison population rates (per 100,000) and scores, OECD countries, 2019 (*cont.*)

Country	Prison population rate	Prison population score
OECD Average	143	21.85

Prison Population Score = 100/655 × Prison Population Rate

SOURCE: INTERNATIONAL CENTRE FOR PRISON STUDIES. 2019. THE WORLD PRISON BRIEF HTTPS://WWW.PRISONSTUDIES.ORG/HIGHEST-TO-LOWEST/PRISON_POPULATION_RATE? FIELD_REGION_TAXONOMY_TID=ALL

The above holds true especially because a substantial proportion of the US prison population comprises prisoners of ethical conscience, simply moral sinners, who are subjected to mass and long imprisonment, as by Draconian 'three strikes' laws, due to committing nonviolent drug offenses and other sins that ruling conservatism, including fascism, joined with extremist religion and theocracy, redefines and punishes as grave, indeed (e.g., drug trade) capital crimes Puritanism's style. US and any prisoners of ethical, as well as ideological or political, conscience redefined and punished as criminals are essentially innocent within the context of Western liberal democracy and society, thus victims of state repression typifying and revealing totalitarian or authoritarian states. Notably, nearly half of US federal prisoners are imprisoned because of such sins-as-crimes, especially drug use, and qualify as those of ethical conscience or as moral sinners-as criminals, so as 'witches' in continuity with or evocation of Puritan witch-trials. In this sense, the approximate half of equation of the US federal prison system under conservatism, including its product fascism or the radical-right since Reaganism, represents the complex of prosecution and mass imprisonment of 'witches' and thus innocent persons from the perspective of Western society, as the enduring legacy or subconscious relic of Puritanism's persecution of these 'associates of Satan'.

Apparently, the US prison system during fascism and conservatism does not advance beyond but remains petrified in Puritanism's proto-fascist and so totalitarian 'primer' (Merton's description) of repression and Draconian punishment of moral and other sinners. Comparatively, this system looks far removed and a deviation from that of Western liberal democracy, such as Western Europe, most notably Scandinavia, and resembles those of Islamic theocracies like Iran, Saudi Arabia, Taliban, and other third-world authoritarian states with mass imprisonment of prisoners of ethical, ideological, or political conscience, yet surpassing them by the highest prisoner rate and total prison population in the world. The US prison/penal system displays genuine conservative 'American exceptionalism' in the form of deviation and divergence from Western liberal democracy and, conversely, non-exceptionalism in the sense of compatibility and convergence with Islamic theocratic and other third-world undemocratic states. Evidently, fascism and conservatism since Reaganism, in fusion with theocratic religion, tend and succeed to remake America, notably its conservative-religious pole, a post-Western and new third-world society through a system mass and long imprisonment for moral sins, Puritan- and Islamic-style.

In sum, the highest prisoner rate and total prison population encompassing a large share of prisoners of ethical conscience and in that sense innocent persons or 'witches' reveals America under conservatism and fascism, specifically its conservative-religious pole, as the most repressive OECD country and a proxy totalitarian regime continuing Puritan theocracy and resembling Islamic theocracies. This implies, because of fascism or right-wing authoritarianism and the compound of its causes, the failure of the 'American experiment' in universal 'liberty and justice' in Jefferson's sense and thus in liberal democracy by violating individual liberty and privacy, as well as in the rule of law whose breakdown mass imprisonment epitomizes, particularly that of moral sinners as innocent victims by the standards of Western liberal democracy (and the Bible's 'who has not sinned' statement).

(11) *Death Sentences and Executions*. Widespread death sentences and executions are a related political indicator of fascism, namely of its coercion, repression, violence, and terror, and more broadly of right-wing authoritarianism. Amnesty International Global Report, Death Sentences and Executions is the data source providing figures for death sentences and executions for OECD countries in 2019. Most OECD countries do not apply capital punishment, except for the US having the most 'recorded executions, recorded death sentences and people known to be under sentence of death' at the end of 2019 (2638), which Japan (126) and South Korea (61) follow as the distant second and third (see Table 5.12).

Since Western societies have abolished it, the US remains exceptional within the West and beyond in its retention and pervasive application of the death penalty that the proto-fascist autocratic regime dramatically intensified at the Federal level in 2020, by swiftly executing an unprecedent number of inmates before the elections, together with 'Bible-Belt' states like Texas, the state and Western 'leader' in executions, and others.

TABLE 5.12   Death sentences and executions and scores, OECD countries, 2019

Country	Death sentences and executions numbers[a]	Death sentences/ executions score
Australia	0	0
Austria	0	0
Belgium	0	0
Canada	0	0
Chile	0	0
Czech Republic	0	0
Denmark	0	0
Estonia	0	0
Finland	0	0
France	0	0
Germany	0	0
Greece	0	0
Hungary	0	0
Iceland	0	0
Ireland	0	0
Israel	0	0
Italy	0	0
Japan	126	4.78
Korea South	61	2.31
Latvia	0	0
Lithuania	0	0
Luxembourg	0	0
Mexico	0	0
Netherlands	0	0
New Zealand	0	0
Norway	0	0
Poland	0	0
Portugal	0	0
Slovak Republic	0	0
Slovenia	0	0
Spain	0	0
Sweden	0	0
Switzerland	0	0
Turkey	0	0
United Kingdom	0	0

TABLE 5.12   Death sentences and executions and scores, OECD countries, 2019 (*cont.*)

Country	Death sentences and executions numbers[a]	Death sentences/ executions score
United States	2638	100
OECD Average	N/A	N/A

a   include 'recorded executions, recorded death sentences and people known to be under sentence of death at the end of 2019'
Death Sentences/Executions Score= 100/2638 × Death Sentences/Executions
SOURCE: AMNESTY INTERNATIONAL GLOBAL REPORT, DEATH SENTENCES AND EXECUTIONS 2019 HTTPS://WWW.AMNESTY.ORG/DOWNLOAD/DOCUMENTS/ACT5018472020ENGLISH.PDF

In this connection, the US's most recorded executions, death sentences, and people under sentence of death within OECD reveal America during the rise of fascism and under conservatism since Reaganism, namely its conservative-religious pole, as the most cruel, inhumane, Draconian society among Western and comparable societies. In that sense, these unrivalled figures confirm, after the massive prison population of innocent moral sinners, that conservative-religious America degenerates into a proxy totalitarian or authoritarian system more so than any other comparable country within OECD, becoming or remaining the uncontested 'leader' of the Western world and beyond in Draconian, cruel punishment such as arbitrary and widespread state murder. At the minimum, this applies because of the reported death sentences and executions of innocent persons, as DNA and other evidence proves but after-the-fact and too late. It also holds because of the possibility for such practices, given the conservative-fascist and religious 'war on crime', actually sin like drug use via Reagan's 'war on drugs',[4] reaching the irrational stage of hysteria in which many innocent lives may perish as victims of the perversion of presumed innocence into assumed guilt and other legal perversions leading to

---

4   Among millions of Americans as victims of Draconian punishment for sins-as-crimes, an example is, according to the Last Prisoner Project, a man sentenced to 90 years in prison in 1989 for 'nonviolent, marijuana-related offenses.' This illustrates the legal perversity and brutality of Reaganism's 'war on drugs' and related conservative-religious temperance wars on sins, which historically descend from Puritan witch-trials and comparatively resemble Sharia law and jihadist politics in Iran, Taliban, and other Islamic theocracies.

the breakdown of the rule of law of the liberal-democratic state. Historically, the conservative-fascist and religious-evangelical death penalty system by its cruel, inhumane, Draconian punishment, including its sacrifices of innocent lives in the 'tough on crime' hysteria (yet 'guilty' due to 'original sin' by association), perpetuates notorious Puritan brutality, cruelty, and inhumanity, thus, like conservatism, fascism, and evangelicalism, being overdetermined by or path-dependent on Puritanism. Comparatively, such a system is incompatible with and deviates from that of Western liberal democracy and law, such as the European Union's prohibition of the death penalty and resembles and converges with those of Islamic theocracies Iran, Saudi Arabia, Taliban, and other third-world authoritarian regimes applying death sentences and executions on a large scale.

In sum, the most widespread death sentences and executions demonstrate that America during the rise of fascism and under conservatism since Reaganism, such as its conservative-religious pole, degenerates into the most inhumane or Draconian Western and OECD society and a totalitarian or authoritarian system that continues Puritan theocracy and resembles Islamic theocracies. This implies another failure of the 'American experiment' in Jefferson's 'liberty and justice for all', liberal democracy, and the right to life due to fascism or right-wing authoritarianism and the compound of its causes. Such a failure consists in negating and ending human liberty and life and in the rule of law whose ultimate breakdown is the state termination of innocent lives, as characteristic or possible for the conservative-religious death-penalty system in the South and beyond.

(12) *Other Political Terror*. Various other forms of political terror represent a related typical political indicator of fascism, namely of its coercion, repression, and violence, and of broader conservative authoritarianism. The Political Terror Scale, such as its scores from Amnesty International or Human Rights Watch, is the data source defining 'political terror' as 'state-sanctioned killings, torture, disappearances and political imprisonment' (Gibney et al. 2019). The source provides scores on the 'political terror scale' for OECD countries in 2019. Among OECD countries, 'political terror' scores (having a possible range of 1 to 5) are the lowest in many of them (1), while being the highest in Turkey, Israel, Mexico, and the United States (5 in the first, 4 in the other three) (see Table 5.13).

Among comparable Western societies, under the post-2016 extreme-right regime the US has the largest political terror score, reflecting the fascist-style and conservative terrorizing of American society, both its own 'people' that right-wing populism exalts but eventually terrorizes as the Nazi 'blind herd' and even more immigrants to the point of sadism.

TABLE 5.13 Political terror scale levels and scores, OECD countries, 2019

Country	Terror level	Terror score
Australia	2	40
Austria	2	40
Belgium	1	20
Canada	1	20
Chile	2	40
Czech Republic	1	20
Denmark	1	20
Estonia	1	20
Finland	2	40
France	3	60
Germany	1	20
Greece	2	40
Hungary	2	40
Iceland	1	20
Ireland	1	20
Israel	4	80
Italy	2	40
Japan	1	20
Korea South	2	40
Latvia	1	20
Lithuania	2	40
Luxembourg	1	20
Mexico	4	80
Netherlands	1	20
New Zealand	1	20
Norway	1	20
Poland	2	40
Portugal	2	40
Slovak Republic	2	40
Slovenia	1	20
Spain	2	40
Sweden	1	20
Switzerland	1	20
Turkey	5	100
United Kingdom	1	20
United States	4	80

TABLE 5.13   Political terror scale levels and scores, OECD countries, 2019 (cont.)

Country	Terror level	Terror score
OECD Average	1.8	35.6

Gibney, Mark, Linda Cornett, Reed Wood, Peter Haschke, Daniel Arnon, Attilio Pisanò, and Gray Barrett. 2019. The Political Terror Scale 1976-2018. Data Retrieved, from the Political Terror Scale website: http://www.politicalterrorscale.org

'The 'terror' in the PTS refers to state-sanctioned killings, torture, disappearances and political imprisonment that the Political Terror Scale measures.'

Terror Score = 100/5 × Terror Level

Political Terror Scale Levels

Level Interpretation

1—Countries under a secure rule of law, people are not imprisoned for their views, and torture is rare or exceptional. Political murders are extremely rare.

2—There is a limited amount of imprisonment for nonviolent political activity. However, few persons are affected, torture and beatings are exceptional. Political murder is rare.

3—There is extensive   political imprisonment, or a recent history of such imprisonment. Execution or other political murders and brutality may be common. Unlimited detention, with or without a trial, for political views is accepted.

4—Civil and political rights violations have expanded to large numbers of the population. Murders, disappearances, and torture are a common part of life. In spite of its generality, on this level terror affects those who interest themselves in politics or ideas.

5—Terror has expanded to the whole population. The leaders of these societies place no limits on the means or thoroughness with which they pursue personal or ideological goals.

SOURCE: THE POLITICAL TERROR SCALE HTTP://WWW.POLITICALTERRORSCALE.ORG /DATA/DOWNLOAD.HTML LARGER SCORES FROM AMNESTY INTERNATIONAL OR HUMAN RIGHTS WATCH

The US's largest political terror score within the Western world indicates the failure of the 'American experiment' in a humane treatment of humans and respect of basic human freedoms and rights, such as the freedom from arbitrary imprisonment and disappearance, police brutality[5] and murders, and the right to dignified life and non-torture, primarily because of fascism or right-wing authoritarianism and the compound of its causes. Conversely, this score suggests the 'success', within the West, of the 'American experiment' in

---

5   Elliott et al. (2022, p. 1312) recount 'aggressive policing against protesters' in the US during the 1960s involving the 'brutal repression of protest, particularly civil rights protest.' They also suggest that in the US post-2016 'police responses would be expected to be harsher, as widely observed, since this latent capacity for repression was present all along' (Elliott et al. 2022, p. 1314).

'state-sanctioned killings, torture, disappearances and political imprisonment' through widespread executions often of innocent persons proved after the fact by DNA and other evidence (yet 'guilty' due to 'original sin', as in the 'Bible Belt'), torturing or mistreating inmates, indefinite detention of 'enemies', pervasive police brutality and murders, and mass incarceration of prisoners of moral conscience like drug users. If America or any society has the highest political terror score within the West, this demonstrates that the American or other societal 'experiment' fails to treat humans in a humanly manner and protect their basic human freedoms and rights to life free from arbitrary imprisonment, indefinite detention, torture, and other mistreatment.

(13) *High Military Expenditure.* Large and growing military expenditure is a further typical political indicator or proxy of fascism, specifically of anti-pacifism, militarism, offensive war, and conquest, and more broadly of right-wing authoritarianism and conservatism. Stockholm International Peace Research Institute is the data source that supplies military expenditure figures as shares of GDP for OECD and other countries in 2019. Military expenditure as a share of GDP among OECD countries is the lowest in Iceland, Ireland, Mexico, and Luxembourg (respectively 0, .3, .4, and .6 percent), while being the highest in Israel, the United States, South Korea, and Turkey (5.3 and 3.4 for the first two, respectively, and 2.7 percent for the last two) (see Table 5.14).

Despite the Cold War, as the rationale for virtually unlimited, essentially extreme 'defense spending', ending three decades ago, the US's military expenditure as a share of GDP and a fortiori absolutely continues to be the largest and accelerating under the post-2016 radical-right government to exceed that of its 'enemies' combined[6] (including China, Iran, North Korea, and Russia) and to account for nearly half of the world's spending (on the US's exorbitant military expenditure and its nefarious consequences see Appendix).

2.2   *Cultural Indicators and Proxies*

(14) *Religion-grounded Social Depreciation of And Low Government Spending on Art and Culture.* Social religion-driven depreciation of and low government spending on the arts and culture is a cultural indicator or proxy of fascism, specifically of its extreme anti-secularism, including religious extremism and its linkage with theocracy, anti-art, and anti-intellectualism, and of right-wing authoritarianism overall. The negative of the public depreciation of and low

---

6 Steinmetz (2005, p. 361) notes that the 'United States now spends [on the military] more than all other countries combined. [It] now has over 2 million military and civilian Department of Defense personnel deployed worldwide, along with another 2 million of their dependents, constituting at the very least an unprecedented "empire of bases."'

TABLE 5.14   Military expenditure as a percentage of GDP and scores, OECD countries, 2019

Country	Military expenditure % GDP	Military expenditure score
Australia	1.90	35.85
Austria	.70	13.21
Belgium	.90	16.98
Canada	1.30	24.53
Chile	1.80	33.96
Czech Republic	1.20	22.64
Denmark	1.30	24.53
Estonia	2.10	39.62
Finland	1.50	28.30
France	1.90	35.85
Germany	1.30	24.53
Greece	2.60	49.06
Hungary	1.20	22.64
Iceland	0	0
Ireland	.30	5.66
Israel	5.30	100
Italy	1.40	26.42
Japan	.90	16.98
Korea South	2.70	50.94
Latvia	2.00	37.74
Lithuania	2.00	37.74
Luxembourg	.60	11.32
Mexico	.40	7.55
Netherlands	1.30	24.53
New Zealand	1.50	28.30
Norway	1.70	32.08
Poland	2.00	37.74
Portugal	1.90	35.85
Slovak Republic	1.80	33.96
Slovenia	1.10	20.75
Spain	1.20	22.64
Sweden	1.10	20.75
Switzerland	.70	13.21
Turkey	2.70	50.94
United Kingdom	1.70	32.08

TABLE 5.14 Military expenditure as a percentage of GDP and scores (*cont.*)

Country	Military expenditure % GDP	Military expenditure score
United States	3.40	64.15
OECD Average	1.59	30.08

Military Expenditure Score = 100/5.30 × Military Expenditure % GDP
SOURCE: STOCKHOLM INTERNATIONAL PEACE RESEARCH INSTITUTE. 2020. MILITARY EXPENDITURE DATABASE HTTPS://WWW.SIPRI.ORG/DATABASES/MILEX

government spending on the arts and culture provides hence a specification of this indicator. OECD National Accounts are the data source furnishing government spending data concerning art and culture as a share of GDP for OECD countries during 2018. Such government spending among OECD countries is the lowest in the United States, Chile, Japan, and Ireland (respectively .28, .36, .39, and .53 percent) and the highest in Hungary, Iceland, Estonia, and Denmark (3.19, 3.16, 2, and 1.6 percent, respectively) (see Table 5.15).

One calculates the negative of government art and culture spending by deducting its levels from the maximum of 3.19 percent. It follows that government art and culture spending negatives are the lowest in Hungary, Iceland, Estonia, and Denmark and the highest in United States, Chile, Japan, and Ireland. Remarkably, the US government invest the fewest public resources in the arts and culture among comparable Western and all OECD countries.[7]

In historical terms, the US's lowest public investment in art and culture indicates a failure of the 'American experiment' in terms of artistic and cultural appreciation, promotion, and hence, ceteris paribus, creativity primarily owing to fascism or right-wing authoritarianism and its compound cause.

---

7 Throsby (1994) presents the basically same data focusing on public expenditure on arts and museums but only for selected OECD countries: Australia, Canada, (West) Germany, France, Netherlands, Sweden, United Kingdom, and United States. For instance, Throsby (1994, p. 21) reports that public expenditure on arts and museums as a share of GDP among these countries in 1987 ranges from the minimum of .02 percent in the US to the maximum of .24 percent in Sweden indicating that it is more than ten times lower in the first country than in the second. To that extent, this reveals the comparatively unrivaled public disinvestment in and so social, usually religion-driven devaluation of the arts in the US as the apparent legacy of anti-artistic, including anti-Renaissance, and theocratic Puritanism—compared to these countries.

TABLE 5.15 Government spending on art and culture as % of GDP and negatives, OECD
countries, 2018 or latest available

Country	Culture spending % of GDP	Culture spending score	Culture spending negative
Australia	.73	22.72	77.28
Austria	1.16	36.32	63.68
Belgium	1.26	39.39	60.61
Canada[a]	.73	22.72	77.28
Chile	.36	11.19	88.81
Czech Republic	1.50	46.88	53.12
Denmark	1.62	50.61	49.39
Estonia	1.96	61.49	38.51
Finland	1.47	46.07	53.93
France	1.38	43.31	56.69
Germany	1.05	32.94	67.06
Greece	.79	24.85	75.15
Hungary	3.19	100	0
Iceland	3.17	99.22	.78
Ireland	.53	16.64	83.36
Israel	1.51	47.45	52.55
Italy	.76	23.85	76.15
Japan	.39	12.19	87.81
Korea South	.86	27.01	72.99
Latvia	1.62	50.83	49.17
Lithuania	1.11	34.88	65.12
Luxembourg	1.25	39.20	60.80
Mexico[a]	36	11.19	88.81
Netherlands	1.17	36.60	63.40
New Zealand[a]	.73	22.72	77.28
Norway	1.71	53.71	46.29
Poland	1.34	41.84	58.16
Portugal	.81	25.48	74.52
Slovak Republic	1.06	33.22	66.78
Slovenia	1.41	44.31	55.69
Spain	1.11	4.82	65.18
Sweden	1.28	40.11	59.89
Switzerland	.82	25.79	74.21
Turkey[b]	.87	27.26	72.74

TABLE 5.15   Government spending on art and culture as % of GDP and negatives (*cont.*)

Country	Culture spending % of GDP	Culture spending score	Culture spending negative
United Kingdom	.60	18.65	81.35
United States	.28	8.68	91.32

Includes Government Spending on 'recreation, culture and religion'

a   Approximated from comparable countries: Canada and New Zealand from Australia, Mexico from Chile

b   https://knoema.com/OECDNA2014/national-accounts-at-a-glance-2014?tsId=1047510

Culture Spending Score = 100/3.19 × Spending % of GDP

Culture Spending Negative = 100 − Culture Spending Score

SOURCE: OECD NATIONAL ACCOUNTS AT A GLANCE HTTPS://DATA.OECD.ORG/GGA /GENERAL-GOVERNMENT-SPENDING.HTM#INDICATOR-CHART

Conversely, it manifests the exceptional 'success' of the 'American experiment' in the social devaluation of and low public investment in the arts and culture thanks to conservatism by such a conjunction and reproduction of right-wing authoritarianism, including fascism, and to anti-artistic Puritanism as their historical source and inspiration. The 'American experiment' cannot succeed in artistic and cultural appreciation, promotion, and creativity so long as it originates in Puritanism with its antagonism to aesthetic art and non-religious culture (as Weber points out), and probably will not so long as it continues to be dominated by the conglomerate of conservatism, coercive capitalism, extremist religion, and theocracy, with its product fascism, simply the conservative-religious pole of America. The lowest public art/culture spending shows that the 'American experiment' fails in artistic and cultural appreciation and promotion due fascism or right-wing authoritarianism and its compound cause as the main determinant of such a failure, just as violently anti-artistic Puritanism is the original cause of the degradation of art and culture in conservative-religious America.

(15) *Religious Superstitions—beliefs in 'Satan'.* Mass religious superstitions such as pervasive and persisting beliefs in the existence of 'Satan' and by association 'witches' are another cultural indicator or proxy of fascism, specifically of its extreme irrationalism, including fanaticism and fantasies, and more broadly of right-wing authoritarianism. The World Values Survey is the data source, combined with additional sources, providing figures about persons who 'believe the Devil exists' as shares of the total population for OECD countries during

various years. 'Devil' belief figures are the highest in Turkey, the United States, Greece, and Chile (respectively 73, 71, 61, and 59 percent) and the lowest in Denmark, Japan, Czech Republic, and Germany (10, 12, 13, and 14 percent, respectively) (see Table 5.16).

Strikingly, more people in the United States 'believe the Devil exists' than in any other Western societies (e.g., 7 times more than in Denmark) and non-Western OECD countries, surpassing Greece, Chile, Mexico, and all others, with the single exception of Islamic Turkey. Most American religionists and probably all evangelicals seem obsessed with the Devil and by association 'witches', as relatedly with sin and vice, and in consequence demonize non-believers or secularists, and thus make America appear the most 'Satan'-believing and obsessed country not only in the West but in the Christian world and beyond, except only for Islamic countries.

Historically, the US's highest 'Satan exists' figure among Western societies indicates a failure of the 'American experiment' in cultural rationalism, reason, and knowledge primarily because of fascism or right-wing authoritarianism and the compound of its causes. Conversely, the above figure suggests the exceptional 'triumph' of the 'American experiment' in extreme irrationalism, specifically religious fanaticism, ignorance, superstition, or dogma. Insofar as the 'American experiment' is culturally rationalistic and treats knowledge and human reason as social power, inspired by the 'Age of Reason' of the Enlightenment that Jefferson et al. import from France like Paris salons, it fails in this respect. And it likely will continue to fail so long as the fusion of conservatism with religion persists and dominates, and hence right-wing authoritarianism or fascism rises and expands, simply the conservative-religious pole of America prevails over its liberal-secular opposite. Conversely, if the 'American experiment' is culturally irrationalist and treats knowledge and human reason as 'original sin' and 'ungodly' or ignorance as bliss, being inspired by Puritanism's irrationalism, including 'Satan' beliefs, it succeeds in extreme irrationalism, such as religious fanaticism and superstition. And it probably will continue this so long as the fusion of conservatism and religion, hence conservative-religious America, prevails, and right-wing authoritarianism, including fascism, surges. In the scenario of Jeffersonian Enlightenment rationalism and reason, the 'American experiment' fails as a rationalist society, and in that of Puritanism's irrationalism via 'Satan' and other religious superstitions, it 'succeeds' as a 'flat earth society'. (Many in conservative-religious America hold the pre-science belief in the 'flat' earth from the Dark Middle Ages.) In sum, due to the above 'Satan' figure, the 'American experiment' displays a failure in cultural rationalism or 'success' in irrationalism primarily

TABLE 5.16   Beliefs in 'satan', OECD countries, various years

Country	'Believe the devil exists' %
Australia	44
Austria	23
Belgium	19
Canada	43
Chile	59
Czech Republic	13
Denmark	10
Estonia	22
Finland	41
France	20
Germany	14
Greece[a]	61
Hungary	24
Iceland[b]	10
Ireland	55
Israel[b]	61
Italy	40
Japan	12
Korea South[c]	20
Latvia	36
Lithuania	42
Luxembourg[b]	19
Mexico	53
Netherlands	18
New Zealand	30
Norway	27
Poland[b]	34
Portugal[b]	35
Slovak Republic	34
Slovenia	25
Spain	35
Sweden	16
Switzerland	28
Turkey	73
United Kingdom	33
United States	71

TABLE 5.16   Beliefs in 'satan', OECD countries, various years (*cont.*)

Country	'Believe the devil exists' %
OECD Average	33

Tiffen and Gittins. (2009)
a   1968 Gallup Poll
b   approximated from comparable countries: Iceland from Denmark, see also, Lacy (2000), Israel from Greece, Luxembourg from Belgium, Poland from Slovak Republic, and Portugal from Spain
c   approximated as equal to the percent of Protestants, Pew Research Center. 2014a. https://www.pewresearch.org/fact-tank/2014/08/12/6-facts-about-christianity-in-south-Korea South

SOURCES: WORLD VALUES SURVEY. 1995–1998. WORLD VALUES SURVEY WAVE 3. HTTP://WWW.WORLDVALUESSURVEY.ORG/WVSDOCUMENTATIONWV3.JSP

because of fascism or right-wing authoritarianism and the compound of its causes.

(16) *Anti-Science—Opposition to Evolution*. Anti-science in the form of opposition to biological evolution and thus scientific biology is a complementary cultural indicator or proxy of fascism, specifically of extreme anti-rationalism, anti-theory antagonism, anti-intellectualism, and anti-progressivism, and of broader right-wing authoritarianism. Therefore, the negative of the social adoption of biological evolution or scientific biology serves as a specification of this indicator. Miller, Scott, and Okamoto (2006) are the data source, together with some other sources, by supplying estimates of the public acceptance of evolution as a share of the population for OECD countries during various years. Public acceptance of evolution estimates among OECD countries are the lowest in Turkey, the United States, South Korea, and Latvia (respectively 25, 33, 41, and 48), while being the highest in Iceland, Spain, Sweden, and France (82 for the first, 81 for the second and third, respectively, and 80 for the fourth) (see Table 5.17).

The negative of the social adoption of biological evolution derives from deducting these estimates from the possible maximum of 100. As a corollary, public acceptance of evolution negatives are the lowest in Iceland, Spain, Sweden, and France and the highest in Turkey, the United States, South Korea, and Latvia. Remarkably, the public acceptance of evolution is weaker and the opposition to scientific biology is stronger in the United States than in any Western and non-Western OECD countries, except only for Islamic Turkey.

In this respect, most American conservatives, fascists, and religionists, especially evangelicals in the Southern and other 'Bible Belt' and beyond, look like anti-evolution and generally anti-science and anti-theory (in the sense of

TABLE 5.17   Public acceptance of evolution and evolution negative[a], OECD countries, various years

Country	Accept evolution %	Evolution negative
Australia	79	21
Austria	58	42
Belgium	79	21
Canada	61	39
Chile	69	31
Czech Republic	64	36
Denmark	81	19
Estonia	63	37
Finland	63	37
France	80	20
Germany	73	27
Greece	52	48
Hungary	69	31
Iceland	82	18
Ireland	65	35
Israel	54	46
Italy	70	30
Japan	80	20
Korea South	41	59
Latvia	48	52
Lithuania	50	50
Luxembourg	64	36
Mexico	64	36
Netherlands	69	31
New Zealand	75	25
Norway	78	22
Poland	65	35
Portugal	64	36
Slovak Republic	58	42
Slovenia	68	32
Spain	81	19
Sweden	81	19
Switzerland	64	36
Turkey	25	75
United Kingdom	79	21

TABLE 5.17   Public acceptance of evolution and evolution negativea, OECD countries (*cont.*)

Country	Accept evolution %	Evolution negative
United States	33	67
OECD Average	65	35

Australia—Australian Academy of Science. (2010). Science literacy in Australia
Canada—Angus Reid Polls (2012)
United States and Mexico— Pew Research Center (2015)
Israel—International Social Survey Programme (2000)
Korea South—IPSOS (2011)
New Zealand—UMR research (2007)
Evolution Negative = 100 – Accept Evolution %
a   Approximate figures
SOURCES: MILLER ET AL. (2006)

scientific theory) crusaders, so Christian equivalents to Islamic jihadists. For illustration, banning 'critical race' and any social and physical theories, artistic literatures, and sciences, regardless of their content, in Florida, Texas, and similar Southern states ruled by ultra-conservative, protofascist, and theocratic forces looks like a replay of the anti-science 'monkey trials' against evolution and scientific biology in the South around a century ago, 'witch trials' in McCarthyism and Puritanism, the Inquisition's prohibition of heliocentric astronomical theory in favor of the 'flat earth' superstition, and burning artistic and other books in medievalism and Nazism. If Southern ruling conservatives, fascists, or theocrats can ban a single theory or specific artistic form, irrespective of its content, and its exponents and literatures, they can also criminalize all other theories, sciences, arts, and their representatives and books, just as the 'monkey trials' against evolution escalated into those of scientific biology and science and scientifically confirmed theory overall. Formally, the problem and grave threat to science, art, and scientific education is not so much that Southern and other US conservatives, fascists, or theocrats ban a single theory or a specific artistic work, whatever its substance, but that they are capable of banning any scientific theories and arts, so sciences, literatures, and books they disapprove or dislike driven by anti-science, anti-art, and anti-education from heliocentric theory and evolution to class, conflict, and other social theories and novels. Such a prohibition of theories and scientific and artistic books, hence the conservative, fascist, or theocratic antagonism to science, art, and education signals the relapse of the South/Bible Belt into the Dark Middle Ages, including the times of Puritan witch-trials and terror in early America, or its entering the New Dark Ages of intellectual unfreedom, anti-science, anti-art, and anti-education typifying conservatism, fascism, and theocracy. For illustration, ruling conservatives-fascists in such Southern states Florida and others post-2020 ban ever some (high-school) books in mathematics on the ground that these contain 'critical race' and similar 'heretic' liberal and secular 'un-Christian' theories. In doing so, these Southern conservative-fascist rulers attempt to recreate 'Christian' mathematics evoking such attempts from the Dark Middle Ages to 19th century America, and conceivably 'Christian' astronomy, physics, mechanics, and engineering, together with 'Christian' biology, economics, and medicine to form 'Christian' 'science' that (as Pareto already observes) stands in vehement antagonism to and perverts science from heliocentric astronomy through evolution to climate science.

Like the strongest 'Satan' belief with which it correlates, the US's lowest public acceptance of biological evolution in the Western world exposes an additional failure of the 'American experiment' in scientific rationalism and knowledge, simply science. Conversely, it reveals the exceptional 'success' of the 'American experiment' in religiously grounded anti-rationalism and ignorance, briefly anti-science, owing to fascism or right-wing authoritarianism and the compound of its causes, especially the fusion of conservatism, religion, and theocracy ruling conservative-religious America like the South as the 'Bible Belt' and beyond.

As with the 'Satan' belief, if the 'American experiment' is scientifically rationalistic and considers science a positive social power, inspired by the scientific ethos of the Enlightenment, it fails in this regard. And it probably will fail so as long as the fusion of conservatism, religion, and theocracy self-perpetuates and prevails, and consequently fascism or right-wing authoritarianism resurges, briefly, the conservative-religious pole of America such as the Southern and other 'Bible Blet' prevails over and even penetrates its liberal-secular opposite. Insofar as the 'American experiment' is anti-, non-, and pre-scientific and suspects science as a negative social power, notably a threat to 'sacred' powers, being inspired by Puritanism's perversion of science to 'divine' glory (as Weber, Merton, and others suggest), it succeeds in religiously driven anti-science, anti-rationalism, and ignorance, which the lowest public acceptance of evolution in the Western world expresses. The 'American experiment' in the scenario of Enlightenment rationalism fails as a scientific society, and in that of Puritanism's degradation of science to 'divine' power, it triumphs as a 'flat earth society.' In sum, owing to the lowest public acceptance of biological evolution in the West, the 'American experiment' manifests a failure in science, or exceptional 'success' in anti-science, primarily because of right-wing authoritarianism, including fascism, and the fusion of conservatism, religion, and theocracy.

(17) *'God' Beliefs (Or Delusions)*. Mass 'God' beliefs (or delusions) are a related cultural indicator or proxy of fascism, specifically of its anti-secularism, including religious extremism, extreme and coercive or socially controlled religiosity, and theocracy, extreme irrationalism like religious superstitions, fanaticism, and fantasies, and more broadly of right-wing authoritarianism. Smith (2012) is the main data source, with some additional sources (enumerated in the next table) supplying figures for persons 'believing in a personal god or higher power' as shares of the population for OECD countries over various years. Among OECD countries, such figures are the highest in Turkey, Mexico, Greece, and Chile (94 percent for the first two, 79 and 71.8 percent for the third and fourth, respectively), while being the lowest in Czech Republic, Estonia, France, and Sweden (respectively 16.1, 18, 18.7, and 19.1 percent) (see Table 5.18).

(18) *High Importance of Religion in Life*. Extremely high importance of religion in life is another complementary cultural indicator or proxy of fascism, specifically of its anti-secularism, including extreme and coercive or socially controlled religiosity and theocracy, and of right-wing authoritarianism overall. The Pew Research Center is the data source that reports shares of people of the population who agree with the sentence 'religion is very important' in their daily life for OECD and other countries during 2018. Such shares among OECD countries are the highest in Turkey, Greece, the United States, and Mexico (respectively 68, 56, 53, and 45) and the lowest in Estonia, Czech Republic, Denmark, and Switzerland (6 and 7 for the first and second and 9 for the last two, respectively) (see Table 5.19).

Remarkably, more people in the United States view religion as 'very important' in their life than in any comparable Western societies and non-Western OECD countries, including Mexico and Chile, with the sole exceptions of Islamic Turkey and Orthodox Christian Greece. It appears that for most American religionists 'all you need in life is religion', together with guns to 'defend' against liberalism and secularism, as well as money, especially for evangelical ministers by preaching the 'prosperity gospel' as the supreme, divine means of enriching themselves from the extortions qua donations of their poor 'flock'.

(19) *Pervasive Church Attendance*. Pervasive church attendance is an additional related cultural indicator or proxy of fascism, specifically of its anti-secularism, including extreme and coercive or socially controlled religiosity and theocracy, and more broadly of right-wing authoritarianism. The Pew Research Center is the data source reporting proportions of persons of the population who 'attend weekly' church for OECD and other countries during 2018. Among OECD countries, these proportions are the highest in Mexico, Turkey, Poland, and the United States (respectively 45, 44, 42, and 36 percent), while being the lowest in Japan, Estonia, Denmark, and Finland (1.1, 2, 3, and 4 percent, respectively) (see Table 5.20).

TABLE 5.18   Beliefs in 'God', OECD countries, various years

Country	'Believing in a personal god' %
Australia	28.5
Austria	27.4
Belgium	21.5
Canada	67.0
Chile	71.8
Czech Republic	16.1
Denmark	28.2
Estonia	18.0
Finland	33.0
France	18.7
Germany (West)	32.0
Greece	79.0
Hungary	30.9
Iceland	31.0
Ireland	64.1
Israel	66.5
Italy	54.0
Japan	24.0
Korea South	54.0
Latvia	38.1
Lithuania	47.0
Luxembourg	46.0
Mexico	94.0
Netherlands	24.4
New Zealand	34.2
Norway	25.7
Poland	59.6
Portugal	58.1
Slovakia	51.0
Slovenia	26.9
Spain	39.1
Sweden	19.1
Switzerland	45.0
Turkey	94.0
UK	26.9
United States	67.5

TABLE 5.18   Beliefs in 'God', OECD countries, various years (*cont.*)

Country	'Believing in a personal god' %
OECD Average	43.4

SOURCES: SMITH (2012)
BELGIUM—CLARKE AND BEYER (2009)
CANADA—ANGUS REID INSTITUTE. 2012. PUBLIC OPINION POLLS. HTTP://ANGUSREID.ORG
/BRITONS-AND-CANADIANS-MORE-LIKELY-TO-ENDORSE-EVOLUTION-THAN-AMERICANS/
ESTONIA, FINLAND, GREECE, ICELAND, LITHUANIA, LUXEMBOURG, TURKEY—EUROBARO
METER 2010. SPECIAL EUROBAROMETER 341, BIOTECHNOLOGY REPORT HTTPS://EC.EUR
OPA.EU/COMMFRONTOFFICE/PUBLICOPINION/ARCHIVES/EBS/EBS_341_EN.PDF
KOREA SOUTH—APPROXIMATED AS EQUAL TO PEOPLE WITH RELIGIOUS AFFILIATION,
PEW RESEARCH CENTER. 2014A. 6 FACTS ABOUT SOUTH KOREA SOUTH'S GROWING CHRIS-
TIAN POPULATION. HTTPS://WWW.PEWRESEARCH.ORG/FACT-TANK/2014/08/12/6-FACTS
-ABOUT-CHRISTIANITY-IN-SOUTH-KOREA SOUTH
MEXICO—PEW RESEARCH CENTER. 2014B. RELIGIOUS BELIEFS. HTTPS://WWW.PEWFO
RUM.ORG/2014/11/13/CHAPTER-3-RELIGIOUS-BELIEFS/

It is notable that more people attend church in the United States than in any comparable Western societies and non-Western OECD countries, except-ing solely Mexico, Turkey, and Poland. It seems that more people in America feel socially compelled, pressured, or expected, as well as internally inspired and motivated, to attend church frequently than in any other Western society. This implies that such a religious ritual remains at least indirectly compulsory or controlled in American society even long after the official end of proto-totalitarian Puritan theocracy with its coercive church attendance.

(20) *High Frequency of Daily Prayer.* High frequency of daily prayer is a com-plementary cultural indicator or proxy of fascism, specifically of its anti-secularism, including extreme and coercive or socially controlled religiosity and theocracy, and extreme irrationalism like religious superstitions, fanati-cism, and fantasies, and of right-wing authoritarianism generally. The Pew Research Center is the data source in that it gives shares of people of the pop-ulation who 'pray daily' for OECD countries during 2018. These shares among OECD countries are the highest in Turkey, the United States, Mexico, and Chile (60, 55, 40, and 39 percent, respectively), while being the lowest in the United Kingdom, Austria, and Switzerland (6 and 8 percent for the last two, respec-tively), along with Czech Republic, Estonia, and Germany (all 9 percent) (see Table 5.21).

TABLE 5.19   Importance of religion in daily life, OECD countries, 2018

Country	'Religion very important' %
Australia	18
Austria	12
Belgium	11
Canada	27
Chile	41
Czech Republic	7
Denmark	9
Estonia	6
Finland	10
France	11
Germany	10
Greece	56
Hungary	14
Iceland[a]	19
Ireland	22
Israel	36
Italy	21
Japan	10
Korea South	16
Latvia	11
Lithuania	16
Luxembourg[a]	11
Mexico	45
Netherlands	20
New Zealand[a]	18
Norway	19
Poland	30
Portugal	36
Slovak Republic	23
Slovenia[a]	12
Spain	22
Sweden	10
Switzerland	9
Turkey	68
United Kingdom	10
United States	53

TABLE 5.19   Importance of religion in daily life, OECD countries, 2018 (*cont.*)

Country	'Religion very important' %
OECD Average	21.4

a Approximated from comparable countries: Iceland from Norway, Luxembourg from Belgium, New Zealand from Australia, Slovenia from Austria

SOURCE: PEW RESEARCH CENTER 2018. RELIGIOUS COMMITMENT BY COUNTRY. HTTPS://ASSETS.PEWRESEARCH.ORG/WP-CONTENT/UPLOADS/SITES/11/2018/06/12094011/APPENDIX-B.PDF

Strikingly, more people 'pray daily' in the United States than in any comparable Western societies and non-Western OECD countries, including Mexico and Chile, solely excluding Islamic Turkey. It looks like more people in America feel socially compelled, just as internally impelled, to enact daily, especially public prayer than any other Western society, which implies that this religious ritual remains partly compulsory or expected in American society long after Puritan theocracy's coercive enactment of it.

Like the pervasive belief in 'Satan' and the low acceptance of evolution, the US's highest daily prayer figure in the Western world demonstrates another failure of the 'American experiment' in cultural rationalism and knowledge, including science, so long as the latter disproves any medical and other efficacy of praying and related rituals. Conversely, it shows the exceptional 'success' of the 'American experiment' in religious irrationalism and ignorance, by implication anti-science, as the essence and meaning of conservative 'American exceptionalism', thanks to right-wing authoritarianism, including fascism, and the compound of its causes, especially the merger of conservatism, religion, and theocracy post-2016 and since Reaganism (and Puritanism). Like in the case of 'Satan' and anti-evolution, if the 'American experiment' is rationalistic and regards knowledge and science as positive social force and inspired by Enlightenment rationalism that disproves any efficacy of prayer and similar religious rituals pervading Christian and Islamic religions, it fails in these terms. And it probably will continue to this as long as the above merger and its fascist outcome persists and predominates post-2016/2020, so the conservative-religious pole of America prevails over its opposite. Conversely, if the 'American experiment' is irrationalist to the extreme and treats secular knowledge as an adverse social power threatening 'sacred' powers and inspired by Puritanism's fanaticism and irrationalism manifested in the belief in witches, witch trials, and other superstitions, it exceptionally triumphs in religion-grounded irrationalism, ignorance, superstition, and anti-science

TABLE 5.20 Church attendance, % attend weekly, OECD countries, 2018 or nearest year

Country	Attend church weekly %
Australia	17.0
Austria	11.0
Belgium	6.0
Canada	20.0
Chile	19.0
Czech Republic	7.0
Denmark	3.0
Estonia	2.0
Finland	4.0
France	12.0
Germany	10.0
Greece	16.0
Hungary	9.0
Iceland[a]	10.0
Ireland	20.0
Israel	30.0
Italy	23.0
Japan	1.1
Korea South	29.0
Latvia	7.0
Lithuania	9.0
Luxembourg	10.0
Mexico	45.0
Netherlands	12.0
New Zealand	8.9
Norway	7.0
Poland	42.0
Portugal	25.0
Slovak Republic	23.0
Slovenia	13.1
Spain	15.0
Sweden	6.0
Switzerland	11.0
Turkey	44.0
United Kingdom	8.0
United States	36.0

TABLE 5.20 Church attendance, % attend weekly, OECD countries, 2018 or nearest year (*cont.*)

Country	Attend church weekly %
OECD Average	15.9

a Monthly
World Values Survey (2010–2014)
SOURCES: PEW RESEARCH CENTER 2018. RELIGIOUS COMMITMENT BY COUNTRY. HTTPS:
//ASSETS.PEWRESEARCH.ORG/WP-CONTENT/UPLOADS/SITES/11/2018/06/12094011
/APPENDIX-B.PDF

which the pervasive and the Western-highest belief in the efficacy of prayer reflects. If the inspiration is Enlightenment rationalism, by the highest daily prayer figure the 'American experiment' fails as a knowledge-scientific society, and if inspired by Puritanism's irrationalism, it succeeds exceptionally as an ignorance-plagued, 'flat earth society' as genuine conservative 'American exceptionalism'. In sum, by the highest prayer figure in the Western world, the 'American experiment' exhibits a failure in cultural rationalism, knowledge, science, or an exceptional 'triumph' in religious irrationalism, ignorance, anti-science because of fascism or right-wing authoritarianism and the merger of conservatism, religion, and theocracy.

2.3 *Economic Indicators and Proxies*
(21) *Share of Wealth of the Top One Percent of the Population.* The high share of wealth of the top one percent of society is a typical economic indicator or proxy of fascism, specifically of its extreme economic inequality in the form of severe wealth concentration, and more broadly of right-wing authoritarianism or conservatism and coercive inegalitarian capitalism. OECD Statistics on distribution of wealth is the data source, along with some other sources (specified in the next table), providing data on top one percent wealth shares for OECD countries during 2016 or nearest year. Among OECD countries, these wealth shares are the lowest in Greece, Slovak Republic, Japan, and Italy (respectively 9.2, 9.3, 10.8, and 11.7 percent), while being the highest in the United States, South Korea, Netherlands, and Austria (42.5, 30, 27.8, and 25.5 percent, respectively) (See Table 5.22).

Evidently, the United States' top one percent wealth share is the highest among comparable Western societies and OECD, including non-Western, countries, for example, more than four times higher than Japan's.

TABLE 5.21   Daily prayer, OECD countries, 2018

Country	Pray daily %
Australia	18
Austria	8
Belgium	11
Canada	25
Chile	39
Czech Republic	9
Denmark	10
Estonia	9
Finland	18
France	10
Germany	9
Greece	30
Hungary	16
Iceland[a]	18
Ireland	19
Israel	27
Italy	21
Japan	33
Korea South	32
Latvia	18
Lithuania	15
Luxembourg[a]	11
Mexico	40
Netherlands	20
New Zealand[a]	18
Norway	18
Poland	29
Portugal	38
Slovak Republic	31
Slovenia[a]	8
Spain	23
Sweden	11
Switzerland	8
Turkey	60
United Kingdom	6
United States	55

TABLE 5.21   Daily prayer, OECD countries, 2018 (*cont.*)

Country	Pray daily %
OECD Average	21.4

a   Approximated from comparable countries: Iceland from Norway, Luxembourg from Belgium, New Zealand from Australia, Slovenia from Austria
SOURCE: PEW RESEARCH CENTER 2018. RELIGIOUS COMMITMENT BY COUNTRY. HTTPS: //ASSETS.PEWRESEARCH.ORG/WP-CONTENT/UPLOADS/SITES/11/2018/06/12094011 /APPENDIX-B.PDF

Supplementing these findings, OECD Statistics on distribution of wealth also furnishes data on the wealth share of the top ten percent for OECD countries during 2016 or closest year. Such wealth shares among OECD countries are the lowest in Slovak Republic, Japan, Poland, and Greece (34.33, 41.02, 41.84, and 42.42 percent, respectively) and the highest in the United States, Denmark, Latvia, and Germany (respectively 79.47, 63.98, 63.38, and 59.76 percent) (See Table 5.22A).

It is evident that the United States' top ten percent wealth share is also the highest among all Western and OECD nations, being almost twice as high as that of Japan, for example.

The above, especially the top one percent wealth share, confirms that wealth concentration in the US since Reaganism has turned so extreme that it approaches its level from the oppressive Gilded Age and the inegalitarian 1920s and in that sense heralds the New Gilded Age. Furthermore, wealth concentration in American capitalism approximates that in European feudalism in which the top one percent of the population, substantively the aristocratic class, owned roughly half or more of societal wealth according to some estimates or approximations.[8] In this respect, 'unfettered' American capitalism looks and functions as neo-feudalism and the 'new patrimonialism'

---

8   Alfani (2021, p. 12) finds that in Europe during and since the Middle Ages the richest 10 percent 'owned 61.3 percent of all wealth in 1300, 46.8 percent in 1450, and 68.9 percent in 1800'. Curiously, the richest 10 percent in America percent own almost 79.5 percent of all wealth in 2016 (see Table 5.22A). This suggests that wealth concentration in American capitalism surpasses even that in European feudalism and early capitalism and that the share of capitalist plutocracy exceeds that of feudal aristocracy. In this regard, such historically unparalleled wealth concentration makes the 'new' American capitalism look even more feudal and its 'all-American' plutocracy more aristocratic than the old European feudalism and its aristocracy. In this connection, referring to Piketty's works, Hirschman (2021, p. 780) uses the

TABLE 5.22 Share of top one percent of wealth and wealth concentration scores, OECD countries, 2016 or nearest year

Country	Top one percent wealth share % wealth	Concentration score
Australia	15.00	35.31
Austria	25.53	60.10
Belgium	12.06	28.39
Canada	15.50	36.49
Chile	17.40	40.96
Czech Republic[a]	9.32	21.94
Denmark	23.62	55.60
Estonia	21.23	49.98
Finland	13.31	31.33
France	18.65	43.90
Germany	23.66	55.70
Greece	9.16	21.56
Hungary	17.23	40.56
Iceland[b]	23.00	54.14
Ireland	14.18	33.38
Israel[c]	22.50	52.97
Italy	11.69	27.52
Japan	10.77	25.35
Korea South[d]	30.00	70.62
Latvia	21.39	50.35
Lithuania[a]	21.39	50.35
Luxembourg	18.81	44.28
Mexico[a]	17.40	40.96
Netherlands	27.83	65.51
New Zealand[e]	24.00	56.50
Norway	20.13	47.39
Poland	11.73	27.61
Portugal	14.44	33.99
Slovak Republic	9.32	21.94
Slovenia	23.03	54.21
Spain	16.32	38.42

expression 'antiplutocratic politics and policies' as an implicit facet of liberal-democratic, egalitarian, and related anti-fascist or non-conservative social forces.

TABLE 5.22 Share of top one percent of wealth and wealth concentration scores (*cont.*)

Country	Top one percent wealth share % wealth	Concentration score
Sweden[a]	20.13	47.39
Switzerland[a]	23.66	55.70
Turkey[a]	17.40	40.96
United Kingdom	20.50	48.26
United States	42.48	100
OECD Average	18.99	44.71

a Approximated values from comparable cases: Czech Republic from Slovak Republic, Lithuania from Latvia, Mexico and Turkey from Chile, Sweden from Norway, Switzerland from Germany
b https://www.ruv.is/frett/rikasta-prosentid-a-naer-fjordung-audsins
c https://ref-inst.org/en/wealth-distribution-in-israel/
d The Credit Suisse Global Wealth Report 2019
e OECD Statistics and Data Directorate, Inequalities in Household Wealth Across OECD Countries: Evidence from the OECD Wealth Distribution https://www.oecd.org/officialdo cuments/publicdisplaydocumentpdf/?cote=SDD/DOC(2018)1&docLanguage=En
Wealth Concentration Score = 100/42.48 × Top One Percent Wealth Share %
SOURCES: OECD STATISTICS ON DISTRIBUTION OF WEALTH. 2016. HTTPS://STATS.OECD .ORG/INDEX.ASPX?DATASETCODE=WEALTH

rather than as totally different from European feudalism and patrimonialism contrary to 'American exceptionalism' claims. As a corollary, 'all-American' capitalist plutocracy reappears as an equivalent or heir of European feudal aristocracy, essentially as the new aristocracy of wealth or nobility of money, rather than as completely different from the aristocracy or nobility of land estate in the 'old world'.

In general, especially the US's top one percent wealth share indirectly indicates the failure of the 'American experiment' in economic terms of Adam Smith's 'wealth of nations' due to 'unfettered' capitalism failing to generate universal material wellbeing, in association with fascism or right-wing authoritarianism and generally conservatism and religion. This holds true because the one percent wealth share approaching 50 percent—and probably reaching that threshold for financial wealth—also discloses that of the rest of society. Thus, the total wealth share of the 99 percent of the American population is asymmetrically low (57.5 percent) and perhaps virtually equal (50 or so percent) for financial wealth, thus not counting home ownership as the main and

TABLE 5.22A Wealth share of top ten percent, OECD countries, 2016 or nearest year

Country	Share %
Australia	46.47
Austria	55.59
Belgium	42.50
Canada	51.08
Chile	57.71
Czech Republic[a]	34.33
Denmark	63.98
Estonia	55.71
Finland	45.23
France	50.59
Germany	59.76
Greece	42.42
Hungary	48.48
Iceland[a]	51.45
Ireland	53.79
Israel[a]	42.42
Italy	42.78
Japan	41.02
Korea, South[a]	41.02
Latvia	63.38
Lithuania[a]	63.38
Luxembourg	48.67
Mexico[a]	57.71
Netherlands	43.23
New Zealand	52.94
Norway	51.45
Poland	41.84
Portugal	52.13
Slovak Republic	34.33
Slovenia	48.62
Spain	45.58
Sweden[a]	51.45
Switzerland[a]	59.76
Turkey[a]	57.71
United Kingdom	51.99
United States	79.47

TABLE 5.22A Wealth share of top ten percent, OECD countries, 2016 or nearest year (*cont.*)

Country	Share %
OECD Average	50.83

a   Estimated values from comparable cases: Czech Republic from Slovak Republic, Iceland and Sweden from Norway, Israel from Greece, Korea, South from Japan, Lithuania from Latvia, Mexico and Turkey from Chile, Swedhen from Finland, Switzerland from Germany

SOURCE: OECD   STATISTICS   HTTPS://STATS.OECD.ORG/INDEX.ASPX?DATASETCODE =WEALTH

often sole form of wealth of Americans. If the 99 percent of Americans, thus most American society, own just slightly higher level of total wealth than and approximately the same amount of financial wealth as the top one percent, thus the upper class, this suggests that the 'American experiment', owing to 'unfettered' capitalism in combination with fascism or right-wing authoritarianism, conservatism, and religion, fails with respect to shared prosperity, simply in the 'wealth of nations', contradicting its unparalleled 'success'.

Furthermore, median net wealth confirms this in that it directly and explicitly indicates the failure of the 'American experiment' in the 'wealth of nations', because of 'unfettered' capitalism, in association with fascism or right-wing authoritarianism, conservatism and religion, failing to produce universal material wellbeing or shared prosperity. As the best measure of Smith's average 'wealth of nations' and thus of general material wellbeing or shared economic prosperity, median net wealth in the US is among the lowest within the Western world and even OECD (see Table 5.22B).

Specifically, US median net wealth (at $77,400 in 2016) is the 14th lowest among 36 OECD countries, so 22 countries have higher, with only 13 having lower, average wealth than the celebrated 'land of wealth and prosperity'. To that extent, this wealth figure reveals America as being among the least wealthy and the poorest Western societies and even OECD countries[9] rather than the 'richest' country in the world (a distorted impression produced by mean wealth or GDP per capita due to statistical-means distortions). If America or any country ranks in wealth at the bottom among Western and comparable societies, this is an indication that the American and any 'experiment', because of

---

9   Also, the Credit Suisse Global Wealth Report 2018 states that 'median wealth of just US $ 61,670 relegates the United States to 18th place' across world countries during 2018 and thus at the height of the proto-fascist, radical-right regime.

TABLE 5.22B Median net wealth, OECD countries, 2016 or latest available

Country	Median net eealth (local currency)	US $[a]
Australia	380000.00	256756.76
Austria	85914.00	94505.40
Belgium	217943.00	239737.30
Canada	258100.00	196156.00
Chile	17747804.00	23072.15
Czech Republic[b]		55347.6
Denmark	212967.00	31945.05
Estonia	43474.00	47821.4
Finland	110000.00	121000
France	113300.00	124630
Germany	60790.00	66869
Greece	65058.00	71563.80
Hungary	8018422.00	26460.79
Iceland[b]		127980.27
Ireland	100600.00	110660
Israel[b]		55347.6
Italy	146198.00	160817.80
Japan	20147000.00	185352.40
Korea	16840000.00	140114
Latvia	14180.00	15598
Lithuania[b]		15598
Luxembourg	437510.00	481261.0
Mexico[b]		15598
Netherlands	78755.00	86630.50
New Zealand	289000.00	188888.88
Norway	1163457.00	127980.27
Poland	238885.48	62110.1
Portugal	71215.00	78336.5
Slovak Republic	50316.00	55347.6
Slovenia	80367.00	88403.7
Spain	159639.00	175602.9
Sweden[b]		127980.27
Switzerland[c]		227890
Turkey[b]		15598
United Kingdom	183000.00	237662.34

TABLE 5.22B   Median net wealth, OECD countries, 2016 or latest available (*cont.*)

Country	Median net eealth (local currency)	US $ᵃ
United States	77400.00	77400.00**
OECD Average	N/A	117056.21

a Converted into US $
b imputed values based on data on comparable similar counties
c 2019 The Credit Suisse Global Wealth Report 2019
SOURCE: OECD STATISTICS HTTPS://STATS.OECD.ORG/INDEX.ASPX?DATASETCODE =WEALTH

'unfettered' or other capitalism associated with fascism or right-wing authoritarianism, conservatism, and religion fails in what it claims to achieve more than any other economic system, the superior 'wealth of nations' and so the most universal and highest prosperity in time and space, in contradiction to its exceptional 'triumph' and similar claims.

Apparently, the above reveals the economic failure of the 'American experiment' to generate and distribute substantial and shared wealth for society because of coercive inegalitarian capitalism in conjunction with fascism or right-wing authoritarianism, conservatism, religion, and theocracy (as in the Religious Right alliance of capitalists and evangelicals). In essence, the linkage of 'unfettered' capitalism with fascism or right-wing authoritarianism, conservatism, religion, and theocracy since Reaganism generates, distributes, and concentrates wealth in favor of capitalist plutocracy against the remainder of society, resulting in the top one percent highest wealth share versus that of the 99 percent of the US population and among the lowest net median wealth within the Western and OECD setting.

(22) *Gini Coefficient of Income Distribution.* The high Gini coefficient of income distribution is a complementary economic indicator or proxy of fascism, namely of its economic inequality, such as extreme income disparity, and more broadly of right-wing authoritarianism, conservatism, and coercive inegalitarian capitalism. OECD Social and Welfare Statistics: Income distribution is the data source supplying Gini coefficients on disposable household income for OECD countries in 2019 or closest year. Among OECD countries, Gini coefficients (with a theoretical range of 0–1 multiplied by 100) are the lowest in Iceland, Slovenia, Slovak Republic, and Denmark (respectively 24.6, 25, 25.1,

TABLE 5.23 Gini coefficients on disposable household income and income inequality scores, OECD countries, 2019 or latest available

Country	Gini coefficient × 100	Income inequality score
Australia	33.7	73.42
Austria	27.6	60.13
Belgium	26.8	58.39
Canada	31.8	69.28
Chile	45.4	98.91
Czech Republic	25.8	56.21
Denmark	26.3	57.30
Estonia	33.0	71.90
Finland	25.9	56.43
France	29.5	64.27
Germany	29.3	63.83
Greece	34.0	74.07
Hungary	28.8	62.75
Iceland	24.6	53.59
Ireland	29.7	64.71
Israel	34.6	75.38
Italy	33.3	72.55
Japan	33.0	71.90
Korea South	29.5	64.27
Latvia	34.7	75.60
Lithuania	37.2	81.05
Luxembourg	30.6	66.67
Mexico	45.9	100
Netherlands	28.5	62.09
New Zealand	34.9	76.03
Norway	27.2	59.26
Poland	29.2	63.62
Portugal	33.6	73.20
Slovak Republic	25.1	54.68
Slovenia	25.0	54.47
Spain	34.5	75.16
Sweden	28.2	61.44
Switzerland	29.5	64.27
Turkey	40.4	88.02

TABLE 5.23   Gini coefficients on disposable household income and income inequality (*cont.*)

Country	Gini coefficient × 100	Income inequality score
United Kingdom	35.1	76.47
United States	39.1	85.19
OECD Average	31.7	69.07

Note: 0 = complete equality; 1 or 100 = complete inequality
Income Inequality Score = 100/45.9 × Gini Coefficient × 100
SOURCE: OECD DATA, OECD SOCIAL AND WELFARE STATISTICS: INCOME DISTRIBUTION
HTTPS://DATA.OECD.ORG/INEQUALITY/INCOME-INEQUALITY.HTM

and 26.3), while being the highest in Mexico, Chile, Turkey, and the US (45.9, 45.4, 40.4, and 39.1, respectively) (see Table 5.23).

Apparently, the US's Gini coefficient is the highest among comparable Western societies and comparable to those of some third-world OECD countries like Mexico, Chile, and Turkey. As with respect to wealth concentration, this reaffirms that income inequality in the US since Reaganism through the post-2016 radical-right plutocratic regime has become so extreme that it approximates its level during the Gilded Age or the 1920s, as the data on the income shares of the top one percent for the 1920s and the 2010s also confirm this, by being around 20 percent in both periods.[10]

While perhaps less dramatically than the top one percent wealth share, such a Gini coefficient indicates a related economic failure of the 'American experiment' to achieve generalized material wellbeing or shared prosperity because of 'unfettered' capitalism in association with fascism or right-wing authoritarianism, conservatism, and religion, especially since severe income inequality usually reproduces widespread poverty and deprivation. In short, the 'American experiment' fails in this regard due to coercive capitalism compounded with fascism or right-wing authoritarianism, which primarily causes and predicts such a failure.

(23) *General Poverty Rate.* A high general poverty rate is an additional typical economic indicator or proxy of fascism, specifically of its material deprivation,

---

10   Piketty et al. (2019, p. 289) find that in the US the 'share of national income going to the top 1 percent [rose] from about 10 percent in 1980 to about 20 percent today.'

and more broadly of right-wing authoritarianism, conservatism, and coercive inegalitarian capitalism. OECD Data on inequality and poverty are the data source that species general or working-age poverty rates as the 'percentage of people whose income falls below the poverty line taken as half the median household income of the total population'. This source provides poverty rates after taxes and transfers, the age group 17–66 years, for OECD countries in 2019 or closest year. Among OECD countries, poverty rates are the lowest in Iceland, Czech Republic, Denmark, and Finland (respectively 5.4, 5.6, 5.8, and 6.3), while being the highest in the United States, South Korea, Turkey, and Israel/Lithuania (17.8, 17.4, 17.2 for the first three, respectively, and 16.9 for the last two) (see Table 5.24).

Strikingly, the US has a general poverty rate that is the highest not just among comparable Western societies but also all OECD, thus including non-Western, countries like Mexico, Chile, and others. To illustrate the magnitude of difference, the US's poverty rate is more than a three-fold multiple of those of Iceland, Denmark, and other Scandinavian countries. This confirms that poverty in America under conservatism since Reaganism through the post-2016 radical-right regime has become so generalized and chronic that the US turns out to be the poorest among Western societies and OECD countries judging by the general poverty rate, just as the 'richest' by the wealth and income of the top one percent and the upper class, thus in the feudal aristocratic sense.

As it stands, the US's highest general poverty rate indicates the failure of the 'American experiment' in economic respect, due to 'unfettered' capitalism, in a linkage with fascism or right-wing authoritarianism, conservatism, and religion, failing to redress widespread poverty and so deprivation and degradation, let alone to attain universal material wellbeing or shared prosperity through generalized and superior wealth. It is striking, as for most Americans unaware of these facts due to intense conservative propaganda, that by its 'best' general poverty rate America under conservatism since Reaganism through post-2016 fascism reappears and qualifies as the poorest Western society and OECD country. It looks like the country with the highest degree of material deprivation, suffering, and degradation, or the 'richest' in poor people and their hardship, rather than in societal wealth, universal wellbeing, and shared prosperity. Furthermore, probably more than extreme wealth concentration, low median net wealth, and sharp income inequality, the highest level of poverty is a symptom of the failure of the 'American experiment', due to 'unfettered' capitalism in conjunction with fascism or right-wing authoritarianism, generally conservatism and religion, in producing and diffusing material wellbeing or economic prosperity, and conversely, its exceptional 'success' in engendering and spreading poverty, deprivation, and degradation. If America or any society

TABLE 5.24 General poverty rates, as % of total population, after taxes and transfers, age
group 17–66 years, and poverty scores, OECD countries, 2019 or latest available

Country	Poverty rate %	Poverty score
Australia	12.4	69.66
Austria	9.8	55.06
Belgium	9.7	54.49
Canada	12.1	67.98
Chile	16.5	92.70
Czech Republic	5.6	31.46
Denmark	5.8	32.58
Estonia	15.7	88.20
Finland	6.3	35.39
France	8.3	46.63
Germany	10.4	58.43
Greece	14.4	80.90
Hungary	7.8	43.82
Iceland	5.4	30.34
Ireland	9.2	51.69
Israel	16.9	94.94
Italy	13.7	76.97
Japan	15.7	88.20
Korea South	17.4	97.75
Latvia	16.8	94.38
Lithuania	16.9	94.94
Luxembourg	11.1	62.36
Mexico	16.6	93.26
Netherlands	8.3	46.63
New Zealand	10.9	61.24
Norway	8.4	47.19
Poland	10.3	57.87
Portugal	12.5	70.22
Slovak Republic	8.5	47.75
Slovenia	8.7	48.88
Spain	15.5	87.08
Sweden	9.3	52.25
Switzerland	9.1	51.12
Turkey	17.2	96.63
United Kingdom	11.9	66.85

TABLE 5.24 General poverty rates, as % of total population, after taxes and transfers (*cont.*)

Country	Poverty rate %	Poverty score
United States	17.8	100
OECD Average	11.75	65.99

The general poverty rate is the 'percentage of people whose income falls below the poverty line taken as half the median household income of the total population' (OECD Data)
Poverty Score = 100/17.8 × Poverty Rate
SOURCE: OECD DATA HTTPS://DATA.OECD.ORG/INEQUALITY/POVERTY-RATE.HTM

ranks at the top (being the 'best' in Reagan's words) in general poverty among Western and similar societies, this is an unambiguous syndrome that the American and other 'experiment' because of 'unfettered' capitalism linked with fascism or right-wing authoritarianism, conservatism, and religion fails in alleviating and reducing material deprivation, hardship, and degradation in comparative terms, as in providing and sharing generalized wellbeing and prosperity.

The finding that the 'American experiment' fails in this regard is remarkable due to coercive capitalism compounded with fascism or right-wing authoritarianism, conservatism, and religion, as the primary determinant of this failure by reproducing pervasive and persistent poverty, so material deprivation, hardship, and degradation. This compound since Reaganism through post-2016 fascism generates or exacerbates generalized and chronic poverty, extreme wealth concentration, low median wealth, and severe income inequality, simply to impoverish, deprive, and degrade society or low strata, while enriching and privileging the upper class like the top one percent. America ranking the first ('number 1' in Reagan's words) in poverty within the Western world and beyond is the eventual economic effect and crowning achievement of the compound of 'unfettered' capitalism with fascism or right-wing authoritarianism and conservatism. If the highest poverty rate dramatically indicates the failure of the 'American experiment' to achieve universal wellbeing or shared prosperity and remedy generalized deprivation and hardship, this compound causes, perpetuates, and predicts such a failing. In sum, the 'American experiment' fails in poverty alleviation and related terms because of coercive capitalism blended with fascism or conservative authoritarianism post-2016 and since Reaganism (and Puritanism).

(24) *Compulsory Hard or Long Work.* Compulsory, physically or economically, hard and/or long work is yet another typical economic indicator or proxy of fascism, specifically its degradation and hardship combined with labor coercion, and generally of right-wing authoritarianism, conservatism, and coercive capitalism. OECD employment statistics is the data source calculating 'average annual hours actually worked' by dividing the 'total number of hours worked over the year' by the 'average number of people in employment', including full- and part-time workers. This source supplies annual hours data for OECD countries in 2019 or nearest year. Among these countries, annual hours are the lowest the highest in Mexico, South Korea, and Greece, and Chile (respectively 2137, 1967, 1949, and 1914) while being the lowest in Iceland, Norway, Germany, and Netherlands (1380, 1384, 1386, and 1434, respectively) (see Table 5.25).

(25) *No or Short Paid Vacations.* Absence or short duration of paid vacations is a supplementary indicator or proxy of fascism, specifically its element of hardship and degradation conjoined with labor coercion, or of right-wing authoritarianism and overall conservatism, and coercive capitalism. The negative of paid vacations is therefore a specification of this indicator. OECD Statistics on leave entitlements of working parents is the data source that furnishes numbers for statutory minimum and collectively agreed paid annual leave in working days for OECD countries in 2016 or closest year. Among OECD countries, annual leave among OECD is the shortest and, in fact, non-existent in the United States (0), followed by Mexico, Canada, and Israel (respectively 6, 10, and 11 days), while being the longest in Denmark, Germany and United Kingdom (30 in the first two and 28 days in the third), followed by Austria, Czech Republic, Finland, France, Italy, Luxembourg, Netherlands, Norway, Slovak Republic, and Sweden (25 days) (see Table 5.26).

The negative of paid vacations ensues from deducting annual leave working days from the OECD factual maximum (30 days). As a result, paid vacations negatives are the lowest in Denmark, Germany, and United Kingdom, while being the highest the United States, Mexico, Canada, and Israel. Strikingly, the United States' non-existent legal paid annual leave makes it a deviant case both among comparable Western societies and non-Western OECD countries, including Mexico. This confirms that, traced to the Gilded Age and since Reaganism through the post-2016 extreme-right regime, workers in the US suffer a more coercive, undignified, and debased, and in that sense slave- or servant-like, treatment than in any Western and OECD country.

Historically, the lack of legally mandated paid leave indicates another, even if seemingly minor, failure of the 'American experiment', because of 'unfettered' capitalism, in association with fascism or right-wing authoritarianism, conservatism, and religion, in worker dignity, respect, satisfaction, and wellbeing

TABLE 5.25 Average annual hours actually worked per worker and annual work hours scores, OECD countries 2019 or latest available

Country	Annual work hours	Annual work hours score
Australia	1712.0	80.11
Austria	1501.0	70.24
Belgium	1583.0	74.08
Canada	1670.0	78.15
Chile	1914.4	89.58
Czech Republic	1788.0	83.67
Denmark	1380.0	64.58
Estonia	1711.0	80.07
Finland	1540.0	72.06
France	1505.0	70.43
Germany	1386.1	64.86
Greece	1949.0	91.20
Hungary	1725.2	80.73
Iceland	1454.0	68.04
Ireland	1772.0	82.92
Israel	1898.1	88.82
Italy	1717.8	80.38
Japan	1644.0	76.93
Korea South	1967.0	92.04
Latvia	1661.0	77.73
Lithuania	1635.0	76.51
Luxembourg	1506.0	70.47
Mexico	2137.0	100
Netherlands	1434.0	67.10
New Zealand	1779.0	83.25
Norway	1384.0	64.76
Poland	1806.0	84.51
Portugal	1719.0	80.44
Slovak Republic	1695.0	79.32
Slovenia	1592.9	74.54
Spain	1686.0	78.90
Sweden	1452.0	67.95
Switzerland	1556.9	72.85
Turkey	1832.0	85.73

TABLE 5.25   Average annual hours actually worked per worker and annual work hours (*cont.*)

Country	Annual work hours	Annual work hours score
United Kingdom	1538.0	71.97
United States	1786.0	83.58
OECD Average	1667.2	78.01

Average annual hours worked are 'defined as the total number of hours actually worked per year divided by the average number of people in employment per year' (OECD Data)
Annual Work Hours Score = 100/2137 × Annual Work Hours
SOURCE: OECD DATA HTTPS://DATA.OECD.ORG/EMP/HOURS-WORKED.HTM

of which economically compensated vacation is an integral and growingly important component. If America or any society provides zero or so legally binding paid vacation days, this suggests that the American and other societal 'experiment' fails to protect, promote, and respect the dignity, satisfaction, and wellbeing of its working classes, so most of its people and society, apart from being economically irrational through the demonstrated adverse effects of such a treatment on labor commitment, effort, and productivity. In short, zero-vacation America[11] expresses the failure of the 'American experiment' to improve social wellbeing via paid leave from work and thus compensated leisure, which resembles feudalism that denied such vacations to its subjects too. Apparently, the 'American experiment' fails in this regard due to coercive capitalism in an anti-labor alliance with fascism or right-wing authoritarianism, conservatism, religion, and theocracy (as within the Christian Right), that mostly causes such a failure in enhancing worker dignity, respect, and wellbeing, so social welfare broadly understood, just as reproducing fascism. This alliance since Reaganism and before through post-2016 acts as the chief opponent to enacting a legally mandated paid leave for American workers. In sum, zero paid vacation expresses the exceptional feature and comparative failure of the 'American experiment' in promoting worker and social wellbeing as mostly the result and persistent achievement of the alliance of 'unfettered' capitalism with fascism or right-wing authoritarianism and generally conservatism.

---

11   This cites Ray and Schmitt's (2007) 'No-vacation nation USA.'

TABLE 5.26   Statutory minimum and collectively agreed paid annual leave in working days, vacation scores and negatives, OECD countries 2016 or latest available

Country	Annual leave, working days	Vacation score	Vacation negative
Australia	20	66.67	33.33
Austria	25	83.33	16.67
Belgium	20	66.67	33.33
Canada	10	33.33	66.67
Chile	15	50	50
Czech Republic[a]	25	83.33	16.67
Denmark[a]	30	100	0
Estonia	20	66.67	33.33
Finland	25	83.33	16.67
France	25	83.33	16.67
Germany[a]	30	100	0
Greece	20	66.67	33.33
Hungary	20	66.67	33.33
Iceland	24	80	20
Ireland[a]	24	80	20
Israel	11	36.67	63.33
Italy[a]	25	83.33	16.67
Japan	10	33.33	66.67
Korea South	15	50	50
Latvia	20	66.67	33.33
Lithuania[b]	20	66.67	33.33
Luxembourg	25	83.33	16.67
Mexico	6	20	80
Netherlands[a]	25	83.33	16.67
New Zealand	20	66.67	33.33
Norway[a]	25	83.33	16.67
Poland	20	66.67	33.33
Portugal	22	73.33	26.67
Slovak Republic[a]	25	83.33	16.67
Slovenia	20	66.67	33.33
Spain	22	73.33	26.67
Sweden	25	83.33	16.67
Switzerland	20	66.67	33.33
Turkey	12	40	60

TABLE 5.26   Statutory minimum and collectively agreed paid annual leave (*cont.*)

Country	Annual leave, working days	Vacation score	Vacation negative
United Kingdom	28	93.33	6.67
United States[c]	0	0	100
OECD Average	20.1	67.50	32.50

a   Collectively Agreed
b   Approximated from Latvia
c   'In the private sector, the offer of paid leave remains at the discretion of the employer' (OECD Family Database)
Vacation Score = 100/30 × Paid Annual Leave
Vacation Negative = 100 – Vacation Score
Statutory Minimum 'generally reflect(s) those for full-time, full-year private sector employees, working a five-day week, who have been working for their current employer for one year' (OECD Family Database)
SOURCE: OECD. 2016. FAMILY DATABASE, ADDITIONAL LEAVE ENTITLEMENTS FOR WORKING PARENTS HTTPS://WWW.OECD.ORG/ELS/SOC/PF2_3_ADDITIONAL_LEAVE_ENTITLEMENTS_OF_WORKING_PARENTS.PDF

(26) *No Or Short Paid Paternity Leave.* No or short paid paternity leave is a complementary indicator or proxy of fascism, specifically of its hardship and degradation mixed with labor coercion, and generally of right-wing authoritarianism, conservatism, and coercive inegalitarian capitalism. The negative of paid paternity leave hence serves as a specification of this indicator. OECD *Family Database,* Parental Leave Systems is the data source giving figures for legal paid maternity leave available to working mothers in weeks for OECD countries in 2018 or nearest year. Paid maternity leave in weeks among OECD countries is the shortest, actually not provided in the United States (0), joined with Portugal, Mexico, and South Korea/Sweden (6 in the first, 12 and 12.9 weeks in the last two, respectively), while being the longest in Greece, the United Kingdom, Slovak Republic, and Czech Republic (43, 39, 34, and 28 weeks, respectively) (see Table 5.27).

The negative of paid maternity leave derives from subtracting weekly figures from the OECD factual maximum (43 weeks). Thence, paid maternity leave negatives are the lowest in Greece, the United Kingdom, Slovak Republic, and Czech Republic and the highest the United States, Portugal, Mexico, and South Korea/Sweden. Strikingly, by its exceptional non-provision of paid paternity leave to working parents the United States appears as a deviation

TABLE 5.27   Paid maternity leave available to mothers in weeks, maternity leave scores and
negatives, OECD countries, 2018

Country	Maternity leave	Maternity leave score	Maternity leave negative
Australia	18	41.86	58.14
Austria	16	37.21	62.79
Belgium	15	34.88	65.12
Canada	16	37.21	62.79
Chile	18	41.86	58.14
Czech Republic	28	65.12	34.88
Denmark	18	41.86	58.14
Estonia	20	46.51	53.49
Finland	18	40.70	59.30
France	16	37.21	62.79
Germany	14	32.56	67.44
Greece	43	100	0
Hungary	24	55.81	44.19
Iceland	13	30.23	69.77
Ireland	26	60.47	39.53
Israel	15	34.88	65.12
Italy	22	50.47	49.53
Japan	14	32.56	67.44
Korea South	13	30	70
Latvia	16	37.21	62.79
Lithuania	18	41.86	58.14
Luxembourg	20	46.51	53.49
Mexico	12	27.91	72.09
Netherlands	16	37.21	62.79
New Zealand	18	41.86	58.14
Norway	13	30.23	69.77
Poland	20	46.51	53.49
Portugal	6	13.95	86.05
Slovak Republic	34	79.07	20.93
Slovenia	15	34.88	65.12
Spain	16	37.21	62.79
Sweden	13	30	70
Switzerland	14	32.56	67.44
Turkey	16	37.21	62.79

TABLE 5.27   Paid maternity leave available to mothers in weeks, maternity leave (*cont.*)

Country	Maternity leave	Maternity leave score	Maternity leave negative
United Kingdom	39	90.70	9.30
United States	0	0	100
OECD Average	18.10	42.12	57.88

Maternity Leave Score = 100/43 × Maternity Leave
Maternity Leave Negative = 100 − Maternity Leave Score
SOURCE: OECD FAMILY DATABASE, PARENTAL LEAVE SYSTEMS HTTPS://WWW.OECD.ORG/ELS/SOC/PF2_1_PARENTAL_LEAVE_SYSTEMS.PDF

among Western and OECD, including non-Western, countries such as Mexico and others, instead providing this benefit and thus improving social wellbeing. This reaffirms that working parents in the US since Reaganism through the post-2016 plutocratic regime, while traced back to the Gilded Age, experience more coercion, indignity, disrespect, and in that sense slave- or servant-like conditions than in any Western and OECD countries.

The US's zero level of paternity leave indicates an additional, even if supposedly minor, failure of the 'American experiment', owing to coercive capitalism in alliance with fascism or right-wing authoritarianism, conservatism, and religion, in family, including parent and children, protection, prosperity, and wellbeing whose constitutive, increasingly relevant element is compensated paternal absence from work for the purpose of child and other care. Conversely, it reveals the exceptional 'success' of the 'American experiment', thanks to the above alliance, in family parental and children deprivation, hardship, degradation, and even mistreatment, by denying compensated paternity leave for child and related domestic care, manifesting conservative-capitalist 'American exceptionalism' from Western and OECD countries. If America or any society provides zero legally mandated and monetarily compensated paternal leave for child and related family care, this reveals that the American or other societal 'experiment' fails to protect and promote the prosperity, wellbeing, survival, or health of US families, notably children. Especially, this points to the American experiment's failure of appreciation and positive valuation of children, or its exceptional 'success' in the most severe devaluation and degradation of their human and social value by depriving them from necessary child care through denying their parents paid leave for that purpose, while invoking various specious justifications in the name of preserving 'unfettered' capitalism at the expense of families, children, and their wellbeing, health, and life. In short, it suggests that the 'American experiment' fails to appreciate and value families and children, who are sacrificed to coercive capitalism resembling feudalism that mistreated the populace family in this manner. Evidently, the 'American experiment' fails in these terms due to the alliance of 'unfettered' capitalism with fascism or right-wing authoritarianism, conservatism, religion, and theocracy (within the Christian Right) as the chief factor of such a failure in family/children appreciation, protection, and welfare, exposing conservative-religious 'family values' and 'right to life' claims as deceptions. As the above alliance vehemently opposes and successfully prevents establishing legal mandates for compensated parental leave in America since Reaganism and before through post-2016, the result is the de facto zero amount and so exceptional absence of paternity leave, manifesting conservative-capitalist 'American exceptionalism'.

(27) *No or Weak Employment Protection*. Non-existence or weakness of employment protection is another indicator or proxy of fascism, specifically its element of deprivation, hardship, and degradation combined and reinforced with labor coercion, and more broadly of right-wing authoritarianism, conservatism, and coercive capitalism. The negative of employment protection thereby represents a specification of this indicator. OECD Statistics is the data source that calculates coefficients of the strictness of employment protection for individual and collective dismissals under regular contracts for OECD countries in 2019 or nearest year. Employment protection coefficients (with a possible range of 0–6) among OECD countries are the lowest in the United States, Canada, Ireland, and the United Kingdom (respectively .1, .6, 1.2, and 1.4) and the highest in the Netherlands, Czech Republic, Portugal, and Turkey (3.6, 3.3, 3.1, and 3, respectively) (see Table 5.28).

The negative of employment protection results from deducting such coefficients from the OECD possible maximum (6). Employment protection negatives are the lowest in the Netherlands, Czech Republic Portugal, and Turkey and the highest in the United States, Canada, Ireland, and the United Kingdom. Remarkably, the United States displays employment protection that is the weakest among Western societies and OECD, including non-Western countries, as even that in Mexico is stronger. This confirms that US workers suffer weaker, virtually non-existent, employment protection and economic security since Reaganism reenacting the Gilded Age through the post-2016 radical-right regime than those in other OECD countries.

The lowest employment protection coefficient among OECD countries indicates another failure of the 'American experiment' in terms of economic security and wellbeing whose relevant dimension is such protection, as the effect

TABLE 5.28 Strictness of employment protection coefficients, individual and collective dismissals, regular contracts, employment protection scores and negatives, OECD countries, 2019 or latest available

Country	Employment protection coefficient	Employment protection score	Employment protection negative
Australia	1.67	46.26	53.74
Austria	2.29	63.43	36.57
Belgium	2.07	57.34	42.66
Canada	.59	16.34	83.66
Chile	2.67	73.96	26.04
Czech Republic	3.26	90.30	9.70
Denmark	1.53	42.38	57.62
Estonia	1.81	50.14	49.86
Finland	2.00	55.40	44.60
France	2.56	70.91	29.09
Germany	2.60	72.02	27.98
Greece	2.45	67.87	32.13
Hungary	1.59	44.04	55.96
Iceland	1.56	43.21	56.79
Ireland	1.23	34.07	65.93
Israel	2.37	65.65	34.35
Italy	2.56	70.91	29.09
Japan	1.37	37.95	62.05
Korea South	2.42	67.04	32.96
Latvia	2.69	74.52	25.48
Lithuania	2.42	67.04	32.96
Luxembourg	2.14	59.28	40.72
Mexico	2.15	59.56	40.44
Netherlands	3.61	100	0
New Zealand	1.64	45.43	54.57
Norway	2.33	64.54	35.46
Poland	2.33	64.54	35.46
Portugal	3.14	86.98	13.02
Slovak Republic	2.51	69.53	30.47
Slovenia	2.08	57.62	42.38
Spain	2.05	56.79	43.21
Sweden	2.45	67.87	32.13

TABLE 5.28   Strictness of employment protection coefficients (*cont.*)

Country	Employment protection coefficient	Employment protection score	Employment protection negative
Switzerland	1.43	39.61	60.39
Turkey	2.98	82.55	17.45
United Kingdom	1.35	37.40	62.60
United States	.09	2.49	97.51
OECD Average	2.11	58.47	41.53

The 'OECD indicators of employment protection are synthetic indicators of the strictness of regulation on dismissals and the use of temporary contracts. For each year, indicators refer to regulation in force on the 1st of January' (OECD Statistics)
Data range from 0 to 6: higher scores represent stricter regulation of individual dismissal of employees on regular/indefinite contracts
Employment Protection Score = 100/3.61 × Employment Protection Coefficient
Employment Protection Negative = 100 − Employment Protection Score
SOURCE: OECD STATISTICS HTTPS://STATS.OECD.ORG/INDEX.ASPX?DATASETCODE =EPL_OV

of the alliance of coercive capitalism with fascism or right-wing authoritarianism, conservatism, and religion. Owing to this alliance, such a coefficient manifests the unrivaled comparative deficiency of the 'American experiment' in protecting the right to work and so to material subsistence for workers, contradicting US capitalists', conservatives', and fascists' 'right to work' claims as anti-labor, anti-union deceptions and manipulations. Conversely, the coefficient expresses the exceptional 'triumph' of the 'American experiment' in severe economic insecurity and 'at will' arbitrariness of which the lack of employment protection or the denial of the right to work and economic survival is a major facet, which expresses true conservative-capitalist 'American exceptionalism' in relation to Western nations. Taken together, if America or any society denies employment protection or the right to work to its workers and subjects them to 'at will' arbitrary treatment, this is an indication that the American or other societal 'experiment' falls to provide economic security and wellbeing for most of its members because of coercive capitalism, conservatism, religion, and theocracy and the consequent rise of fascism or right-wing authoritarianism. In sum, due to these factors, the US's near-zero employment protection coefficient is a strong syndrome of the American experiment's failure to appreciate workers and so most Americans, or its exceptional 'success' in most severely depreciating their economic contribution and social and human value among Western and comparable societies.

(28) *No or Low Unemployment Benefits.* Absence or a low level of unemployment benefits is an additional supplementary indicator or proxy of fascism, specifically its deprivation, hardship, and degradation conjoined and reinforced with labor coercion, and of broader right-wing authoritarianism, conservatism, and coercive capitalism. The negative of unemployment benefits accordingly provides a specification of this indicator. OECD benefits and wages statistics is the data source supplying net replacement rates in unemployment as the percent of prior 'in-work household income' retained after 60 months of unemployment. The source supplies these rates for OECD countries in 2019 or nearest year. Among these countries, such rates are the lowest or zero in Chile, Mexico, Turkey, and the United States (o for the first three, 8 in the fourth), while being the highest in Sweden, Belgium, Luxembourg, and Austria (59 in the first, 55 in the second and third respectively, 51 in the four) (see Table 5.29).

The negative of unemployment benefits is the product of subtraction of such rates from the potential maximum of 100. Unemployment benefits negatives are the lowest in Sweden, Belgium, Luxembourg, and Austria, while being the highest in Chile, Mexico, Turkey, and the United States. Remarkably, the US exhibits unemployment benefits that are drastically lower than those in comparable Western societies and similar to their minimalism in some non-Western, third-world OECD countries, such as Chile, Mexico, and Turkey. This reaffirms that US workers have lower unemployment benefits and thus insurance since Reaganism and the Gilded Age through the post-2016 extreme-right plutocratic regime than their counterparts in all Western societies and most OECD countries.

The lowest unemployment insurance among Western societies exposes a further failure of the 'American experiment' in respect of economic security and wellbeing whose another important aspect is such insurance, in consequence of the alliance of coercive capitalism with fascism or right-wing authoritarianism, conservatism, extremist religion, and theocracy. Due to this alliance, such a figure mirrors the unrivalled comparative deficiency of the 'American experiment' to insure workers from the deprivation, poverty, and misery of unemployment—an injury to injury after zero employment protection—manifesting capitalist, fascist, and conservative anti-labor brutality, cruelty, and sadism inherited from Puritanism as the most brutal, cruel, and sadistic (and totalitarian) variation of Calvinism and Christianity. Conversely, this figure expresses the exceptional 'success' of the 'American experiment' in intense economic insecurity, hardship, and deprivation whose aspect is

TABLE 5.29 Benefits in unemployment, share of previous income, after 5 years, % of previous in-work income, and unemployment benefits negatives, OECD countries, 2019 or latest available

Country	Unemployment benefits %	Unemployment benefits negative
Australia	31	69
Austria	51	49
Belgium	55	45
Canada	31	69
Chile	0	100
Czech Republic	12	88
Denmark	50	50
Estonia	18	82
Finland	29	71
France	34	66
Germany	22	78
Greece	21	79
Hungary	14	86
Iceland	48	52
Ireland	38	62
Israel	23	77
Italy	14	86
Japan	34	66
Korea South	21	79
Latvia	10	90
Lithuania	23	77
Luxembourg	55	45
Mexico[a]	0	100
Netherlands	49	51
New Zealand	34	66
Norway	24	76
Poland	18	82
Portugal	23	77
Slovak Republic	11	89
Slovenia	49	51
Spain	31	69
Sweden	59	41
Switzerland	27	73

TABLE 5.29   Benefits in unemployment, share of previous income, after 5 years (*cont.*)

Country	Unemployment benefits %	Unemployment benefits negative
Turkey	0	100
United Kingdom	17	83
United States	8	92
OECD Average	27.3	72.7

a   OECD Employment Outlook 2018 https://www.oecd-ilibrary.org/sites/empl_outlook-2018-9
    -en/index.html?itemId=/content/component/empl_outlook-2018-9-en
Unemployment Benefits Negative = 100 – Unemployment Benefits %
'This indicator measures the proportion of previous in-work household income maintained
after 2, 6, 12, 24 and 60 months of unemployment. Calculations refer to a single person with-
out children whose previous in-work earnings were 67% of the average wage' (OECD Benefits
and Wages)
SOURCE: OECD BENEFITS AND WAGES: NET REPLACEMENT RATES IN UNEMPLOY-
MENT HTTPS://DATA.OECD.ORG/BENWAGE/BENEFITS-IN-UNEMPLOYMENT-SHARE-OF
-PREVIOUS-INCOME.HTM

extremely weak unemployment insurance, reflecting conservative-capitalist
'American exceptionalism' from Western and comparable societies. If America
or any society provides minimal unemployment insurance to its workers, this
suggests that the American or other societal 'experiment' falls to shield most of
its members from the deprivation, hardship, and indignity of unemployment,
or 'succeeds' in inflicting them with severe economic insecurity and suffering,
because of the alliance of capitalist-rightist forces (allied within the Christian
Right as their extended family). Owing to this alliance, the lowest unemployment insurance among Western societies helps identity the American experiment's further failure of appreciation of workers and so most Americans, or its
exceptional 'triumph' in the most intense depreciation of their economic and
social contribution and value.

(29) *No or Weak Social Protection and Economic Security.* Absence of or weak
social-economic protection and security is a complementary economic indicator or proxy of fascism, specifically its deprivation, hardship, and degradation
combined and reinforced with unconstrained and arbitrary maximum power
and labor coercion, and more broadly of right-wing authoritarianism, conservatism, and coercive capitalism. Hence, the negative of social-economic protection and security operates as a specification of this indicator. OECD Data

is the data source that supplies figures for central government expenditure on social protection, including welfare assistance, as a share of GDP for OECD countries in 2019 or nearest years. Such government expenditure among OECD countries is the lowest in Chile, South Korea, Mexico, and the United States (6.2 and 6.7 for the first two, respectively, and 7.5 for the last two) and the highest in Finland, France, Denmark, and Italy (respectively 24.7, 24.3, 21.9, and 20.8) (see Table 5.30).

Subtracting these figures from the OECD factual maximum (24.7) yields the negative of social protection. Social protection negatives are the lowest in Finland, France, Denmark, and Italy and the highest in Chile, South Korea, Mexico, and the United States. Evidently, social protection in the US is dramatically weaker than in comparable Western societies and non-Western OECD countries, with just two exceptions like South Korea and Chile. This confirms that US workers enjoy weaker social protection since Reaganism through the post-2016 right-wing plutocratic regime than those in all Western and most OECD countries.

The lowest spending figure on social protection such as welfare assistance among Western societies reveals a complementary failure of the 'American experiment' in socioeconomic security and wellbeing, as primarily the effect of the alliance of 'unfettered' capitalism with fascism and right-wing authoritarianism, conservatism, religion, and theocracy. Conversely, such a figure evinces the exceptional 'success' of the 'American experiment', thanks to this alliance, in socioeconomic insecurity, indignity, and deprivation, which affirms the genuine attribute of conservative-capitalist 'American exceptionalism' vis-à-vis Western and comparable nations. It is striking that under fascism or right-wing authoritarianism and coercive capitalism post-2016 and since Reaganism the US's lowest social protection spending corresponds to its highest military expenditure among Western societies and all OECD countries (minus Israel). This means that the US government under fascist or extreme-right and plutocratic control post-2016, at least until the 2020 elections, and since Reaganism spends the least on the alleviation of poverty and material deprivation via welfare and other civilian assistance and thus perpetuates economic hardship and impoverishes much of its population, while expending the most on the military and offensive wars and imperial conquest among Western societies. This striking duality reaffirms that such a style of government minimal spending on civilian socioeconomic protection like welfare aid and its maximal expenditure on military and war activities epitomizes the model of an 'evil empire'. The latter impoverishes or keeps much of its population in poverty and squalor by action or inaction, yet indulges in extreme military expenditure in the function of aggressive wars and imperial expansion under the delusionary or

TABLE 5.30 Government spending on social protection as % of GDP, social protection scores and negatives, OECD countries, 2018 or latest available

Country	Social protection spending % of GDP	Social protection score	Social protection negative
Australia	10.19	41.33	58.67
Austria	20.13	81.66	18.34
Belgium	19.28	78.22	21.78
Canada	17.33	70.30	29.70
Chile	6.23	25.28	74.72
Czech Republic	12.02	48.77	51.23
Denmark	21.93	88.97	11.03
Estonia	13.03	52.88	47.12
Finland	24.65	100	0
France	24.30	98.58	1.42
Germany	19.44	78.85	21.15
Greece	19.42	78.77	21.23
Hungary	13.84	56.15	43.85
Iceland	9.90	40.16	59.84
Ireland	8.98	36.45	63.55
Israel	11.14	45.19	54.81
Italy	20.75	84.18	15.82
Japan	16.15	65.51	34.49
Korea South	6.74	27.33	72.67
Latvia	11.62	47.13	52.87
Lithuania	12.05	48.89	51.11
Luxembourg	17.95	72.83	27.17
Mexico	7.52	30.51	69.49
Netherlands	15.46	62.73	37.27
New Zealand[a]	18.93	76.80	23.20
Norway	19.12	77.57	22.43
Poland	16.44	66.68	33.32
Portugal	17.09	69.31	30.69
Slovak Republic	14.35	58.21	41.79
Slovenia	16.67	67.61	32.39
Spain	16.62	67.41	32.59
Sweden	19.54	79.27	20.73
Switzerland	13.30	53.96	46.04

TABLE 5.30   Government spending on social protection as % of GDP (*cont.*)

Country	Social protection spending % of GDP	Social protection score	Social protection negative
Turkey	12.52	50.79	49.21
United Kingdom	15.04	60.99	39.01
United States	7.54	30.59	69.41
OECD Average	15.20	38.34	61.66

OECD (2020), General government spending (indicator). doi: 10.1787/a31cbf4d-en

a   Social expenditure (cash benefits, direct in-kind provision of goods and services, and tax breaks with social purposes) OECD Data https://data.oecd.org/socialexp/social-spending.htm

Social Protection Score = 100/24.65 × Social Protection Spending % of GDP

Social Protection Negative = 100 – Social Protection Score

SOURCE: OECD DATA, NATIONAL ACCOUNTS STATISTICS: NATIONAL ACCOUNTS AT A GLANCE HTTPS://DATA.OECD.ORG/GGA/GENERAL-GOVERNMENT-SPENDING.HTM

deceptive misnomer of 'defense spending', for such an empire is always offensive by attacking and invading other states, a pattern with which the US state generally conforms after WW II and perhaps since 1812, the last time its homeland was attacked by a foreign power. If America or any society devotes the least resources on social protection among Western and comparable societies, this suggests that the American or other societal 'experiment' falls to protect and enhance socioeconomic security and wellbeing for its members, because of the above alliance. Due to this alliance, the lowest social protection spending among Western and comparable societies is a syndrome of the American experiment's failure of positive valuation of lower and most classes in America by failing in their social protection, or its exceptional 'success' in the most intense devaluation of their economic contribution, human and social value as integral members of society.

(30) *Labor Union Repression.* Repression of unionization or low labor union density is a typical economic indicator of fascism, specifically its element of labor coercion and repression, and of right-wing authoritarianism, conservatism, and coercive capitalism. Accordingly, the negative of unionization in the sense of labor union density serves as a specification of this indicator. OECD Labour Force Statistics is the data source that defines union density as the percent of 'wage and salary earners that are trade union members, divided by the total number of wage and salary earners [by] using survey data, wherever

possible and administrative data adjusted for non-active and self-employed members otherwise'. This source supplies such data for OECD countries in 2018 or nearest year. Among OECD countries, these densities are the lowest in Estonia, Lithuania, Hungary, and France (respectively 4.3, 7.1, 7.9, and 8.8 percent) while the highest in Iceland, Denmark, Sweden, and Belgium (91.8, 66.5, 65.6, and 50.3 percent, respectively) (see Table 5.31).

The negative of unionization derives from subtracting union densities from the possible maximum of 100. This yields union density negatives that are the lowest in Iceland, Denmark, Sweden, and Belgium, while being the highest in Estonia, Lithuania, Hungary, and France. Notably, the US's labor union density at just over 10 percent since Reaganism through the post-2016 extreme-right regime has declined to such a degree that it nearly equals that during the 1920s, prior to the New Deal's initial union liberation. This confirms that the repression or obstruction of unionization in America has become so severe by post-2016 as to replicate or resemble that during the labor-oppressive Gilded Age.

The comparatively low labor union density indicates the failure of the 'American experiment' in terms of labor liberties, such as the freedom of unionization as the form of collective organization, and thus universal economic liberty for all production factors or classes, notably both labor and capital, as outcome of the alliance of 'unfettered' capitalism with fascism or right-wing authoritarianism, conservatism, religion, and theocracy. Conversely, such union density marks the exceptional 'triumph' of the 'American experiment' in respect of labor coercion and repression such as suppression of unionization thanks to the above anti-labor alliance, which reaffirms the true nature of conservative-capitalist 'American exceptionalism' in relation to Western nations. Insofar as America or any society features comparatively low labor union density, this reveals that the American or other societal 'experiment' falls to ensure labor liberties such as the freedom of collective organization and so universal economic liberty, or 'succeeds' to enforce labor coercion and repression by suppressing unionization, as the dual effect of the above alliance. Due to this alliance, the US's comparatively low labor union density reveals the 'American experiment's failure of positive valuation of working classes and thus most Americans by failing to appreciate, even to establish and protect their labor freedoms and rights to collective organization, and conversely, its 'success' in the devaluation and degradation of workers' economic contribution and social value by suppressing such freedoms and via other forms of labor repression.

(31) *Collective Bargaining Repression.* Repression of collective bargaining or restriction of its scope and consequently low union coverage is a supplementary economic indicator of fascism, of namely its labor coercion, and of

TABLE 5.31 Labor union density and negatives, OECD countries, 2018 or nearest year

Country	Labor union density %	Labor union density negative
Australia	14.70	85.30
Austria	26.30	73.70
Belgium	50.30	49.70
Canada	29.40	70.60
Chile	17.70	82.30
Czech Republic	11.50	88.50
Denmark	66.50	33.50
Estonia	4.30	95.70
Finland	60.30	39.70
France	8.80	91.20
Germany	16.50	83.50
Greece	20.20	79.80
Hungary	7.90	92.10
Iceland	91.80	8.20
Ireland	24.50	75.50
Israel	25.00	75.00
Italy	34.40	65.60
Japan	17.00	83.00
Korea South	10.50	89.50
Latvia	11.90	88.10
Lithuania	7.10	92.90
Luxembourg	31.80	68.20
Mexico	13.90	86.10
Netherlands	16.40	83.60
New Zealand	17.30	82.70
Norway	49.20	50.80
Poland	12.70	87.30
Portugal	15.30	84.70
Slovak Republic	10.70	89.30
Slovenia	20.40	79.60
Spain	13.60	86.40
Sweden	65.60	34.40
Switzerland	14.90	85.10
Turkey	9.20	90.80
United Kingdom	23.40	76.60

TABLE 5.31 Labor union density and negatives, oecd countries, 2018 or nearest year (*cont.*)

Country	Labor union density %	Labor union density negative
United States	10.10	89.90
OECD Average	24.47	75.53

OECD (2020), 'Trade Unions: Trade union density', OECD Employment and Labour Market Statistics (database), https://doi.org/10.1787/data-00371-en

Labor or Trade union density equals the number of 'wage and salary earners that are trade union members, divided by the total number of wage and salary earners. Density is calculated using survey data, wherever possible, and administrative data adjusted for non-active and self-employed members otherwise' (OECD Labour Force Statistics)

Labor Union Density Negative = 100 – Labor Union Density %

SOURCE: OECD LABOUR FORCE STATISTICS HTTPS://WWW.OECD-ILIBRARY.ORG/EMPLOYM ENT/DATA/TRADE-UNIONS/TRADE-UNION-DENSITY_DATA-00371-EN

right-wing authoritarianism, conservatism, and coercive capitalism. The negative of collective bargaining or union coverage thus allows a specification of this indicator. OECD Labour Force Statistics is the data source defining collective-bargaining coverage as the percent of employees who have the freedom or 'right to bargain' as a collective unit with employers and be covered by union agreements. This source provides these data for OECD countries in 2017 or closest year. Among OECD countries, collective-bargaining coverage is the lowest in Turkey, Lithuania, the United States, and South Korea (respectively 7, 7.1, 11.6, and 11.8 percent) and the highest in France, Austria, Belgium, and Iceland/Sweden (98.5, 98, and 96 for the first three, respectively, and 90 percent for the last two) (see Table 5.32).

The negative of collective bargaining coverage derives from deducting these figures from the potential maximum of 100. As a corollary, collective bargaining coverage negatives are the lowest in France, Austria, Belgium, and Iceland/Sweden, while being the highest in Turkey, Lithuania, the United States, and South Korea. It is striking that the percent of workers with the 'right to bargain' collectively with employers in the US is drastically lower than in comparable Western societies and similar to some non-Western OECD countries like Turkey and Lithuania. To exemplify the difference, collective bargaining

TABLE 5.32 Collective bargaining coverage, percentage of employees with the right to bargain, and collective bargaining coverage negatives, OECD countries, 2017 or nearest year

Country	Collective bargaining coverage %	Collective bargaining coverage negative
Australia	59.20	40.80
Austria	98.00	2.00
Belgium	96.00	4.00
Canada	28.10	71.90
Chile	20.90	79.10
Czech Republic	46.30	53.70
Denmark	84.00	16.00
Estonia	18.60	81.40
Finland	89.30	10.70
France	98.50	1.50
Germany	56.00	44.00
Greece	40.00	60.00
Hungary	22.80	77.20
Iceland	90.00	10.00
Ireland	33.50	66.50
Israel	26.10	73.90
Italy	80.00	20.00
Japan	16.50	83.50
Korea South	11.80	88.20
Latvia	13.80	86.20
Lithuania	7.10	92.90
Luxembourg	59.00	41.00
Mexico	12.50	87.50
Netherlands	77.60	22.40
New Zealand	15.90	84.10
Norway	67.00	33.00
Poland	14.70	85.30
Portugal	72.30	27.70
Slovak Republic	24.40	75.60
Slovenia	65.00	35.00
Spain	73.10	26.90
Sweden	90.00	10.00
Switzerland	49.20	50.80
Turkey	7.00	93.00

TABLE 5.32   Collective bargaining coverage, percentage of employees (*cont.*)

Country	Collective bargaining coverage %	Collective bargaining coverage negative
United Kingdom	26.00	74.00
United States	11.60	88.40
OECD Average	47.30	52.70

Collective Bargaining or Union Coverage equals the 'percentage of employees with the right to bargain (with employers)' (OECD Statistics)
Collective Bargaining Negative = 100—Collective Bargaining Coverage %
SOURCE: OECD STATISTICS. COLLECTIVE BARGAINING COVERAGE HTTPS://STATS.OECD .ORG/INDEX.ASPX?DATASETCODE=CBC

coverage in the US at just over 11 percent is eight or more times lower than that in France, Austria, and Belgium. This confirms that collective bargaining repression[12] in the US since Reaganism through the post-2016 radical-right regime has intensified to such an extent that it replicates the Gilded Age or the 1920s, thus before the New Deal granting for the first time in US history such labor rights to workers.

The lowest union coverage among Western societies and most OECD countries reveals another failure of the 'American experiment' in labor freedoms and rights, such as the freedom/right to bargain collectively with employers and be covered by collective agreements, thus of universal economic liberty for labor and capital, which is another effect of the anti-labor alliance of 'unfettered' capitalism with fascism or right-wing authoritarianism, conservatism, religion, and theocracy. So long as America or any society displays the lowest union coverage within the Western setting and beyond due to the above alliance, this demonstrates that the American or other societal 'experiment' falls to establish and promote labor liberties and hence universal economic liberty for all production agents through workers' freedom and right to collective bargaining with employers and to enjoy coverage by union contracts.

Conversely, such minimal union coverage signals the exceptional 'success' of the 'American experiment', thanks to the above anti-labor alliance, in labor coercion and repression via suppression of collective bargaining, exhibiting

---

12   If, as Beck (2000, p. 51) notes, Germany has 'strong trade unions and free collective bargaining that was also highly valued by politicians', US capitalists, conservatives, and fascists instead highly value non-existent or weak unions and unfree, suppressed collective bargaining, as the conservative pole of America shows.

conservative-capitalist 'American exceptionalism' from the West. Insofar as America or any society exhibits the lowest union bargaining coverage among comparable societies, this shows that the American or other societal 'experiment' exceptionally 'succeeds' to exert labor coercion and repression and so economic compulsion and oppression of working Americans by suppressing their freedom/right to collective bargaining, as the double outcome of the above alliance. Owing to this anti-labor alliance, the lowest union coverage among Western societies uncovers the American experiment's failure to appreciate working and so most Americans by failing to establish their labor freedom and rights to collective bargaining, and its 'success' in depreciating their economic importance and social value by suppressing such freedoms and via generalized labor coercion.

2.4   Civil-Society Indicators and Proxies

(32) *No or Weak Civil Liberties.* Non-existence or weakness of civil liberties is a typical civil-society indicator of fascism, axiomatically of its extreme anti-liberalism, anti-democracy, absolute rule, power, and domination, including legal arbitrariness, insecurity, and lawlessness, and coercion, repression, violence, and terror, and more broadly of right-wing authoritarianism. The negative of civil liberties therefore becomes a specification of this indicator. The Economist Intelligence Unit's Democracy Index is the data source that includes in civil liberties 'free' media, 'freedom of expression and protest', 'open and free discussion of public issues', the 'opportunity to petition government to redress grievances', lack of the 'use of torture by the state', the 'judiciary's independence of government influence', and the like. The source supplies civil liberties indexes for OECD and other countries during 2019. Such indexes (multiplied by 10 to yield a 0–100 scale) among OECD countries are the lowest in Turkey, Israel, Mexico, and Hungary (respectively 23.5, 58.8, 61.8, and 70.6) and the highest in Australia, Ireland, and New Zealand (all 100), followed by Canada, Finland, Iceland, Luxembourg, and Norway (all 97.1) (see Table 5.33).

The negative of civil liberties is the result of subtracting such indexes from the maximum of 100. The lowest civil liberties negatives are in Australia, Ireland, New Zealand, and some other countries and the highest in Turkey, Israel, Mexico, and Hungary.

(33) *No or Weak Civil Justice.* Absence or weakness of civil justice and rights is a related typical civil-society indicator of fascism, specifically of its extreme anti-universalism and anti-egalitarianism, such as particularism, monopolistic closure, and exclusion, as well as social hatred and master-race racism, and of right-wing authoritarianism generally. The negative of civil justice and rights hence serves to specify this indicator. The World Justice Project Rule of Law

TABLE 5.33 Civil liberties indexes and negatives, OECD countries, 2019

Country	Civil liberties index × 10	Civil liberties negative
Australia	100	0
Austria	88.20	11.80
Belgium	85.30	14.70
Canada	97.10	2.90
Chile	91.20	8.80
Czech Republic	85.30	14.70
Denmark	91.20	8.80
Estonia	85.30	14.70
Finland	97.10	2.90
France	85.30	14.70
Germany	94.10	5.90
Greece	85.30	14.70
Hungary	70.60	29.40
Iceland	97.10	2.90
Ireland	100	0
Israel	58.80	41.20
Italy	79.40	20.60
Japan	88.20	11.80
Korea South	82.40	17.60
Latvia	88.20	11.80
Lithuania	91.20	8.80
Luxembourg	97.10	2.90
Mexico	61.80	38.20
Netherlands	91.20	8.80
New Zealand	100	0
Norway	97.10	2.90
Poland	73.50	26.50
Portugal	91.20	8.80
Slovak Republic	79.40	20.60
Slovenia	82.40	17.60
Spain	88.20	11.80
Sweden	94.10	5.90
Switzerland	91.20	8.80
Turkey	23.50	76.50
United Kingdom	91.20	8.80

TABLE 5.33 Civil liberties indexes and negatives, OECD countries, 2019 (*cont.*)

Country	Civil liberties index × 10	Civil liberties negative
United States	82.40	17.60
OECD Average	85.71	14.29

a   Civil liberties encompass: 'Is there a free electronic media? Is there a free print media? Is there freedom of expression and protest (bar only generally accepted restrictions, such as banning advocacy of violence)? Is media coverage robust? Is there open and free discussion of public issues, with a reasonable diversity of opinions? Are there political restrictions on access to the Internet? Do institutions provide citizens with the opportunity to petition government to redress grievances? The use of torture by the state. The degree to which the judiciary is independent of government influence. The degree of religious tolerance and freedom of religious expression. The degree to which citizens are treated equally under the law. Do citizens enjoy basic security? Extent to which private property rights are protected and private business is free from undue government influence. Extent to which citizens enjoy personal freedoms. Popular perceptions on protection of human rights; proportion of the population that think that basic human rights are well-protected. There is no significant discrimination on the basis of people's race, colour or religious beliefs. Extent to which the government invokes new risks and threats as an excuse for curbing civil liberties' (The Economist Intelligence Unit 2019, p. 62–64)

Civil Liberties Negative = 100 – Civil Liberties Index × 10

SOURCE: THE ECONOMIST INTELLIGENCE UNIT 2019 HTTP://WWW.EIU.COM/HANDL ERS/WHITEPAPERHANDLER.ASHX?FI=DEMOCRACY-INDEX-2019.PDF&MODE=WP&CAM PAIGNID=DEMOCRACYINDEX2019

Index 2020 is the data source defining civil justice as reflecting 'whether ordinary people can resolve their grievances peacefully and effectively through the civil justice system.' The source gives justice 'factor scores' for OECD and other countries during 2020. These scores (augmented by 100 consistent with the 0–100 scale) among OECD countries are the lowest in Mexico, Turkey, Hungary, and Italy (respectively 40, 45, 46, and 56), while being the highest in Denmark, Germany, Netherlands, and Switzerland (87 in the first and 86 in the other three) (see Table 5.34).

Subtraction of these scores from the possible maximum of 100 yields the negative of civil justice and rights. Consequently, civil justice negative negatives are the lowest in Denmark, Germany, Netherlands, and Switzerland and the highest in Mexico, Turkey, Hungary, and Italy.

(34) *No or Weak Individual Liberty* and Privacy. Non-existence or weakness of individual liberty, including privacy, or personal freedom is another typical civil-society indicator of fascism, specifically of its extreme anti-liberalism,

TABLE 5.34 Civil justice factor scores and negatives, OECD countries, 2020 or 2019

Country	Civil justice factor score × 100	Civil justice negative
Australia	76	24
Austria	77	23
Belgium	76	24
Canada	70	30
Chile	63	37
Czech Republic	69	31
Denmark	86	14
Estonia	80	20
Finland	81	19
France	71	29
Germany	85	15
Greece	59	41
Hungary	45	55
Iceland	85	15
Ireland	73	27
Israel	59	41
Italy	56	44
Japan	79	21
Korea South	76	24
Latvia	70	30
Lithuania	70	30
Luxembourg	76	24
Mexico	39	61
Netherlands	85	15
New Zealand	78	22
Norway	85	15
Poland	63	37
Portugal	68	32
Slovak Republic	69	31
Slovenia	66	34
Spain	67	33
Sweden	82	18
Switzerland	85	15
Turkey	44	56
United Kingdom	71	29

TABLE 5.34   Civil justice factor scores and negatives, OECD countries, 2020 or 2019 (*cont.*)

Country	Civil justice factor score × 100	Civil justice negative
United States	62	38
OECD Average	70.72	29.28

Civil Justice Factor Score 'measures whether ordinary people can resolve their grievances peacefully and effectively through the civil justice system. It measures whether civil justice systems are accessible and affordable as well as free of discrimination, corruption, and improper influence by public officials. It examines whether court proceedings are conducted without unreasonable delays and if decisions are enforced effectively. It also measures the accessibility, impartiality, and effectiveness of alternative dispute resolution mechanisms'
a Approximated values from comparable countries: Iceland from Norway, Ireland from United Kingdom, Israel from Greece, Latvia and Lithuania from Estonia, Luxembourg from Belgium, Slovak Republic from Czech Republic, Switzerland from Germany
Civil Justice Negative = 100 − Civil Justice Factor Score × 100
SOURCE: THE WORLD JUSTICE PROJECT RULE OF LAW INDEX 2019 HTTPS://WORLDJUS TICEPROJECT.ORG/SITES/DEFAULT/FILES/DOCUMENTS/WJP-ROLI-2019-SINGLE%20P AGE%20VIEW-REDUCED_0.PDF

anti-democracy, coercion, repression, violence, and terror, together with absolute rule, power, and domination, including legal arbitrariness, insecurity, and lawlessness, and more broadly of right-wing authoritarianism. Thus, the negative of individual liberty serves as a specification of this indicator. Vásquez and Porčnik (2019) are the data source calculating personal freedom indexes for OECD and other countries during 2017 as components of 'human freedom index' involving economic, personal, and other civil freedoms. These indexes (multiplied by 10 to accord with the 0–100 scale) among OECD countries are the lowest in Turkey, Mexico, Israel, and Poland (respectively 57.4, 63.8, 77, and 83.2), while being the highest in Sweden, Netherlands, Finland, and New Zealand (94.5 in the first, 92.8 in the second, and 92.7 in the last two) (see Table 5.35).

The personal freedom negative results from deducting such indexes from the possible maximum of 100. As a result, personal freedom negatives are the lowest in Sweden, Netherlands, Finland, and New Zealand and the highest in Turkey, Mexico, Israel, and Poland.

Relatedly, the absence or weakness of privacy is a complementary civil-society indicator of fascism, specifically of its elements of absolute rule, power, and domination, including legal arbitrariness, insecurity, and lawlessness,

TABLE 5.35   Personal freedom indexes and negatives, OECD countries, 2017

Country	Personal freedom index × 10	Personal freedom negative
Australia	91.60	8.40
Austria	92.50	7.50
Belgium	90.70	9.30
Canada	92.20	7.80
Chile	84.10	15.90
Czech Republic	89.20	10.80
Denmark	92.40	7.60
Estonia	90.20	9.80
Finland	92.70	7.30
France	86.90	13.10
Germany	92.50	7.50
Greece	80.70	19.30
Hungary	80.40	19.60
Iceland	90.80	9.20
Ireland	89.00	11.00
Israel	77.00	23.00
Italy	86.70	13.30
Japan	87.00	13.00
Korea South	88.10	11.90
Latvia	88.50	11.50
Lithuania	87.60	12.40
Luxembourg	92.60	7.40
Mexico	63.80	36.20
Netherlands	92.80	7.20
New Zealand	92.70	7.30
Norway	92.60	7.40
Poland	83.20	16.80
Portugal	90.20	9.80
Slovak Republic	85.40	14.60
Slovenia	87.80	12.20
Spain	86.90	13.10
Sweden	94.50	5.50
Switzerland	92.40	7.60
Turkey	57.40	42.60
United Kingdom	88.50	11.50

TABLE 5.35 Personal freedom indexes and negatives, OECD countries, 2017 (*cont.*)

Country	Personal freedom index × 10	Personal freedom negative
United States	87.20	12.80
OECD Average	87.19	12.81

Personal Freedom Negative = 100—Personal Freedom Index × 10

SOURCE: VÁSQUEZ IAN AND TANJA PORČNIK. 2019. THE HUMAN FREEDOM INDEX: A GLOBAL MEASUREMENT OF PERSONAL, CIVIL, AND ECONOMIC FREEDOM. THE CATO INSTITUTE, THE FRASER INSTITUTE, AND THE FRIEDRICH NAUMANN FOUNDATION FOR FREEDOM

and coercion, repression, violence, and terror. The negative of privacy can be a specification of this indicator. For example, Privacy International includes in privacy 'Constitutional protection, Statutory protection, Privacy enforcement, Identity cards and biometrics, Data-sharing, Visual surveillance, Communication interception, Workplace monitoring, Government access to data, Communications data retention, Surveillance of medical, financial and movement, Border and trans-border issues, Leadership, Democratic safeguards.' It gives privacy indexes (having a possible range of 0–4) for OECD and other countries during 2007. Among OECD countries, such indexes (converted to a 0–100 scale) are the lowest in the United Kingdom, the United States, France, and Denmark (respectively 45.16, 48.39, 61.29, and 64.52) while the highest in Greece, Canada, and Hungary (100 in the first, 93.55 in the last two), joined by Germany, Italy, Luxembourg, Portugal and Slovenia (all 90.32) (see Table A.42). The negative of privacy derives from subtracting these indexes from the maximum of 100. Accordingly, privacy negatives are the lowest in Greece, Canada, and Hungary (apparently before the neo-fascist or radical-right government analogously to Germany prior to Nazism) and the highest in the United Kingdom, the United States, France, and Denmark. It is striking that the US has the lowest privacy index among all OECD and other countries, second only to that of Great Britain, perhaps reflecting the shared anti-privacy and generally proto-fascist or proto-totalitarian legacy of Puritanism.[13]

(35) *The Death Penalty for Drug Offenses.* Application of the death penalty for drug offenses is a strong civil-society indicator of fascism, specifically of its coercion, repression, violence, and terror, together with theocracy, legal

---

13   Merton (1939, p. *437*) observes that Puritanism 'finds its analogue in the various Nazi primers'.

arbitrariness, insecurity, and lawlessness, and more broadly of right-wing authoritarianism. The International Harm Reduction Association is the data source stating that 'imposition of a death sentence following conviction for a drug offence (not involving intentional killing) in proceedings which fail to meet international standards of fairness compounds the violations of the rights of the individual to life, to a fair trial, and to be free from torture or other cruel, inhumane or degrading treatment or punishment.' This source offers information on the application of the 'death penalty for drug offences' for OECD and other countries during 2019. According to this information, within OECD only South Korea and the US (hence assigned scores 100 on the 0–100 scale) engage in the (symbolic) application of the death penalty for drug offences while the other countries abstain from doing so (thus given 0 scores) (see Table 5.36).

It is notable that the US is the only Western society that applies—even if prospectively or symbolically by the federal government that under post-2016 autocratic rule threatened to actually apply— the death penalty for drug offences as criminalized moral sins, expressing the moralistic and Draconian-punitive heritage of Puritanism via evangelicalism and conservatism.

The potential and attempted, as by the post-2016 radical-right regime, application of the death penalty for drug offenses, the only one among Western and comparable societies, uncovers a failure of the 'American experiment' in protection of and respect for individual liberty and privacy and human dignity and life, primarily because of fascism or right-wing authoritarianism and the compound of its causes. Objectively, if America or any other society solely among Western societies applies or threatens to apply the death penalty for drug offenses as moral sins or economic actions, this shows that the American or other societal 'experiment' falls to protect and respect human liberty, privacy, dignity and rights, notably the right to life due to fascism or right-wing authoritarianism and the compound of its causes in the 'war' on crime-as-sin paranoia evoking Puritanism's witch-trials. By the death penalty for drug offenses the American 'experiment' fails to uphold 'international standards of fairness' and commits the 'violations of the rights of the individual to life, to a fair trial, and to be free from torture or other cruel, inhuman or degrading treatment or punishment,' reflecting the cruelty, inhumanity, and degradation of fascism or right-wing authoritarianism and the blend of conservatism, religion, and theocracy, and of Puritanism historically.

Conversely, such an exclusive application of the death penalty for drug offenses marks the exceptional 'superiority' and 'triumph' of the 'American experiment' in brutal and murderous repression and terror, including 'torture or other cruel, inhuman or degrading treatment or punishment', for such moral sins or economic activities, thanks to fascism or right-wing authoritarianism,

TABLE 5.36 Death penalty for drug offenses, OECD countries, 2019

Country	Death penalty for drug offenses	Death penalty for drug offenses score
Australia	N	0
Austria	N	0
Belgium	N	0
Canada	N	0
Chile	N	0
Czech Republic	N	0
Denmark	N	0
Estonia	N	0
Finland	N	0
France	N	0
Germany	N	0
Greece	N	0
Hungary	N	0
Iceland	N	0
Ireland	N	0
Israel	N	0
Italy	N	0
Japan	N	0
Korea South[a]	Y	100
Latvia	N	0
Lithuania	N	0
Luxembourg	N	0
Mexico	N	0
Netherlands	N	0
New Zealand	N	0
Norway	N	0
Poland	N	0
Portugal	N	0
Slovak Republic	N	0
Slovenia	N	0
Spain	N	0
Sweden	N	0
Switzerland	N	0
Turkey	N	0
United Kingdom	N	0

TABLE 5.36   Death penalty for drug offenses, OECD countries, 2019 (*cont.*)

Country	Death penalty for drug offenses	Death penalty for drug offenses score
United States[a]	Y	100
OECD Average	N/A	N/A

According to Harm Reduction International, the 'legal analysis reflects the principle in international law that the imposition of a death sentence following conviction for a drug offence (not involving intentional killing) in proceedings which fail to meet international standards of fairness compounds the violations of the rights of the individual to life, to a fair trial, and to be free from torture or other cruel, inhuman or degrading treatment or punishment' (p. 5)

a Symbolic Application according to Harm Reduction International

Harm Reduction International reports: 'While President Donald Trump continues suggesting that the death penalty should be expanded to drug offences, analyses of death sentences and executions in the past 40 years reveal that reliance on this measure in the country is in fact shrinking' (p. 39)

Death Penalty for Drug Offenses Score Y = 100, N = 0. The 1–100 differential or range on a 0–100 scale does justice to the infinite difference or distance between life and death, while the 0–1 range does not on that scale

SOURCE: HARM REDUCTION INTERNATIONAL, GEN SANDER, GIADA GIRELLI AND ADRIÀ COTS FERNÁNDEZ, THE DEATH PENALTY FOR DRUG OFFENCES: GLOBAL OVERVIEW 2019 HTTPS://WWW.HRI.GLOBAL/FILES/2020/02/28/HRI_DEATHPENALTYREPORT2019.PDF

the compound of its causes, and Puritanism. This manifests the true nature of conservative-religious 'American exceptionalism' from all Western and most OECD countries. Due to fascism or right-wing authoritarianism and the compound of its causes and its historical root Puritanism sharing the disdain for personal freedom, the death penalty for drug offenses exposes the American experiment's failure of appreciation and protection of individual liberty and privacy and human dignity and life, its failing to appreciate and protect humans as humans, as well as extreme cruelty and inhumanity.

(36) *Mass Incarceration for Sins-As-Crimes*. Mass incarceration for sins-as-crimes reproducing prisoners of moral conscience, imprisoned sinners, is a complementary civil-society indicator of fascism, specifically of its coercion, repression, violence, and terror, theocracy and legal arbitrariness, insecurity, and lawlessness, and of broader right-wing authoritarianism. The Prison Policy Initiative is the data source for the proportion of prisoners-drug offenders of the total prison population in the United States during 2020 (respectively, around 20 and 44 percent of all and federal prisoners), while such data for other OECD countries do not exist. Such a share can help to estimate by

approximation respective shares for these countries in a proportionate manner by taking account of total imprisonment rates (e.g., 20% with the 655 US rate yields 10% with a rate of 328 or so, 5% with a rate 164, and so on). Approximate proportions of prisoners-drug offenders are the lowest in Iceland, Japan, Finland, and Norway (respectively 1.1, 1.2, 1.6, and 1.8), while being the highest in the US, Turkey, Israel, and Lithuania (19.9, 10.4, 71, and 6.7, respectively) (see Table 5.37), which accords with total imprisonment rates.

Evidently, the relative proportion, as well as absolute number, of prisoners-drug offenders of the total prison population is higher in the United States than in any comparable Western societies and all OECD countries, manifesting the moralistic and theocratic legacy of Puritanism through evangelicalism.

The highest share of prisoners-drug offenders of the prison population among Western nations deciphers another complementary failure of the 'American experiment' in protecting and respecting individual liberty and privacy and human dignity and rights, because of fascism or right-wing authoritarianism and the compound of its causes. So long as America or any society has the largest numbers of prisoners-drug offenders among Western and all comparable societies, this reaffirms the preceding. This is that the American or other societal 'experiment' falls objectively to protect and respect human liberty, privacy, dignity, and rights, particularly the right to free, personal consumption of private goods, including alcohol during Prohibition and persistently in the 'Bible Belt', by mature individuals reduced to children, due to fascism or right-wing authoritarianism and the mix of its causes launching the Puritanical 'war on drugs' and 'tough' on crime-as-sin paranoia since Reaganism echoing Puritan witch-trials.[14]

Conversely, the highest proportion of prisoners-drug offenders shows the exceptional 'superiority' and 'success' of the 'American experiment' in mass repression and severe terror, including 'torture or other cruel, inhuman or degrading treatment or punishment'—as documented for US prisons,

---

14 For instance, the US government vehemently denounced in 2022 Russia for imprisoning an American athlete for drug possession, while continuing its mass imprisonment of millions of Americans for the same act, thus exhibiting the 'intolerable lightness' of Puritan-rooted hypocrisy. Moreover, in view of its Puritanical irrational war on drugs and Draconian 'three strikes' laws, the US government probably would more harshly punish, up to life in prison, this American than Russia and Europe where such punishments are unknown for these offenses, so ironically this and other Americans face a milder and more civilized penal treatment in non-American legal systems (not to mention the reported horror-like conditions of US prisons where the mix of the ghost of Puritanism and capitalist 'private enterprise' make prisoners' life hell on earth by proxy starvation, denial or restriction of health care, abuse, torture, and so on). In this case, the above American athlete received a

TABLE 5.37 Share of drug offenders of total prisoners (estimates) and drug offenders scores,
          OECD countries, 2019

Country	Prisoner rate	US/Prisoner rate	% of Drug offenders (estimate)	Drug offenders score
Australia	169	3.88	5.12	25.80
Austria	95	6.89	2.88	14.50
Belgium	95	6.89	2.88	14.50
Canada	107	6.12	3.24	16.34
Chile	209	3.13	6.34	31.91
Czech Republic	194	3.38	5.88	29.62
Denmark	71	9.23	2.15	10.84
Estonia	182	3.60	5.52	27.79
Finland	53	12.36	1.61	8.09
France	104	6.30	3.15	15.88
Germany	77	8.51	2.33	11.76
Greece	106	6.18	3.21	16.18
Hungary	167	3.92	5.06	25.50
Iceland	37	17.70	1.12	5.65
Ireland	74	8.85	2.24	11.30
Israel	234	2.80	7.10	35.73
Italy	90	7.28	2.73	13.74
Japan	39	16.79	1.18	5.95
Korea South	106	6.18	3.21	16.18
Latvia	179	3.66	5.43	27.33

9-year prison sentence in Russia, while could have been sentenced to life in prison according to Draconian 'three strikes' laws and even executed for drug trade given the potential application of the death penalty (as the post-2016 President insisted) in the US. This
example only confirms that if there is something more repressive than Russian and other
non-Western authoritarianism, like communism, it is the American blend of conservatism
with fascism post-2016 and eternal theocracy, along with Islamic theocracies. No doubt,
from the stance of liberal democracy, the 9-year prison sentence for drug possession or
trade in Russia is excessively harsh, but life in prison and potentially execution for the
same act in the US is even harsher, which shows the cruel and inhumane effects of the
American Puritanical 'war on drugs' that metastasized to other countries, including Russia,
just as did Prohibition to the Soviet Union in the late 1980s. This confirms that both Russia
and conservative America are outside and opposite to liberal democracy and belong to
authoritarian, repressive regimes by mass imprisonment for drug offenses, with the press
reporting that even some illiberal capitalists 'calling on the Biden administration to make
a move against the mass incarceration of people for weed.'

TABLE 5.37 Share of drug offenders of total prisoners (estimates) and drug offenders (*cont.*)

Country	Prisoner rate	US/Prisoner rate	% of Drug offenders (estimate)	Drug offenders score
Lithuania	221	2.96	6.70	33.74
Luxembourg	105	6.24	3.18	16.03
Mexico	158	4.15	4.79	24.12
Netherlands	63	10.40	1.91	9.62
New Zealand	199	3.29	6.03	30.38
Norway	60	10.92	1.82	9.16
Poland	189	3.47	5.73	28.85
Portugal	110	5.95	3.34	16.79
Slovak Republic	192	3.41	5.82	29.31
Slovenia	69	9.49	2.09	10.53
Spain	124	5.28	3.76	18.93
Sweden	61	10.74	1.85	9.31
Switzerland	80	8.19	2.43	12.21
Turkey	344	1.90	10.43	52.52
United Kingdom	134	4.89	4.06	20.46
United States	655	1.00	19.86	100
OECD Average	143.11	6.55	4.34	21.85

According to the Prison Policy Initiative, in the US 'police, prosecutors, and judges continue to punish people harshly for nothing more than drug possession. Drug offenses still account for the incarceration of almost half a million people, and nonviolent drug convictions remain a defining feature of the federal prison system. Police still make over 1 million drug possession arrests each year, many of which lead to prison sentences. Drug arrests continue to give residents of over-policed communities criminal records, hurting their employment prospects and increasing the likelihood of longer sentences for any future offenses.'

In the Prison Policy Initiative's estimation, during 2020 in the US 450,180 people are incarcerated for drug offenses out of 2,267.000, thus 'almost '2.3 million people in 1,833 state prisons, 110 federal prisons, 1,772 juvenile correctional facilities, 3,134 local jails, 218 immigration detention facilities, and 80 Indian Country jails as well as in military prisons, civil commitment centers, state psychiatric hospitals, and prisons in the US territories (at) the staggering rate of 698 per 100,000 residents.'

US Drug Offenders as % of total prisoners 450,180/2,267.000 = 19.86% Drug Offenders as % of Federal prisoners 100,000/226,000 = 44.25%

% Of Drug Offenders (estimate) = 19.86/ (655/Prisoner Rate)

Drug Offenders Score = 100/19.86 × % of Drug Offenders

SOURCE: THE PRISON POLICY INITIATIVE. 2020. MASS INCARCERATION: THE WHOLE PIE 2020. HTTPS://WWW.PRISONPOLICY.ORG/REPORTS/PIE2020.HTML

especially in the 'Bible Belt'—for humans' moral sins like drug use. This confirms the genuine character of conservative-religious 'American exceptionalism' from the Western world and beyond. The above reaffirms the American experiment's failure to positively value human individual liberty, privacy, dignity, and rights, notably the elemental right to free consumption, due to fascism or right-wing authoritarianism showing contempt for personal freedom combined with cruelty of punishment for moral sins like the use of drugs (plus alcohol, sexuality) which it construes and punishes as a criminal activity rather than a health and private matter.

(37) *No or Weak Fundamental Human Rights.* Non-existence or weakness of fundamental human rights is yet another related civil-society indicator of fascism, specifically of its extreme anti-liberalism, anti-democracy, absolute rule, power, and domination, including legal arbitrariness, insecurity, and lawlessness, of theocracy and coercion, repression, violence, and terror, and generally of right-wing authoritarianism. Hence, the negative of core human rights operates as a specification of this indicator. The World Justice Project Rule of Law Index is the data source that focuses on 'a relatively modest menu of rights that are firmly established under the Universal Declaration of Human Rights and are most closely related to rule of law concerns.' This source offers 'factor scores' on fundamental human rights for OECD and other countries during 2020 is the World Justice Project Rule of Law Index. These scores (multiplied by 100 to conform to the 0–100 scale) among OECD countries are the lowest in Turkey, Mexico, Hungary, and Poland (respectively 32, 52, 58, and 64) while the highest in Denmark, Finland, Iceland, and Norway (92 in the first and 91 for the other three) (see Table 5.38).

The negative of fundamental human rights comes from deducting these scores from the possible maximum of 100. Therefore, fundamental human rights negatives are the lowest in Denmark, Finland, Iceland, and Norway, while being the highest in Turkey, Mexico, Hungary, and Poland.

(38) *No or Weak Human Rights to Life, Peace, and Safety.* Absence or weakness of human rights to life, peace, and safety is a further specific civil-society indicator of fascism, specifically of its extreme anti-liberalism and absolute power and domination, including legal arbitrariness, insecurity, and lawlessness, along with theocracy and coercion, repression, violence, and terror, and of right-wing authoritarianism overall. The negative of peace and safety thereby serves as a specification of this indicator. The Institute for Economics and Peace is the data source that estimates the 'state of peace using three thematic domains: the level of Societal Safety and Security; the extent of Ongoing Domestic and International Conflict; and the degree of Militarisation.' The source supplies negative civic peace indexes (with a possible range of 0–4) for OECD and other countries during 2020. Such indexes (transformed into a

TABLE 5.38 Fundamental human rights factor scores and negatives, OECD countries, 2020

Country	Human rights factor score × 100	Human rights negative
Australia	79	21
Austria	85	15
Belgium	84	16
Canada	82	18
Chile	72	28
Czech Republic	79	21
Denmark	92	8
Estonia	82	18
Finland	91	9
France	73	27
Germany	85	15
Greece	65	35
Hungary	58	42
Iceland	91	9
Ireland	79	21
Israel	65	35
Italy	73	27
Japan	77	23
Korea South	73	27
Latvia	82	18
Lithuania	82	18
Luxembourg	84	16
Mexico	52	48
Netherlands	84	16
New Zealand	81	19
Norway	91	9
Poland	64	36
Portugal	78	22
Slovak Republic	79	21
Slovenia	75	25
Spain	79	21
Sweden	87	13
Switzerland	85	15
Turkey	32	68
United Kingdom	79	21

TABLE 5.38   Fundamental human rights factor scores and negatives, oecd countries (*cont.*)

Country	Human rights factor score × 100	Human rights negative
United States	72	28
OECD Average	76.97	23.03

Fundamental Rights Factor 'recognizes that a system of positive law that fails to respect core human rights established under international law is at best 'rule by law,' and does not deserve to be called a rule of law system. Since there are many other indices that address human rights, and because it would be impossible for the Index to assess adherence to the full range of rights, this factor focuses on a relatively modest menu of rights that are firmly established under the United Nations Universal Declaration of Human Rights and are most closely related to rule of law concerns' (The World Justice Project Rule of Law Index 2020, p. 25).
* Estimated values from comparable countries: Iceland from Norway, Ireland from United Kingdom, Israel from Greece, Latvia and Lithuania from Estonia, Luxembourg from Belgium, Slovak Republic from Czech Republic, Switzerland from Germany
Human Rights Negative = 100 – Human Rights Factor Score × 100
SOURCE: THE WORLD JUSTICE PROJECT RULE OF LAW INDEX 2020 HTTPS://WORLDJUSTICE PROJECT.ORG/SITES/DEFAULT/FILES/DOCUMENTS/WJP-ROLI-2020-ONLINE_0.PDF

0–100 scale) among OECD countries are the highest in Turkey, Israel, Mexico, and the United States (2.96, 2.78, 2.57, and 2.31, respectively) and the lowest in Iceland, New Zealand, Austria, and Denmark (1.08 and 1.20 for the first two, respectively, and 1.28 for the last two) (see Table 5.39).

Strikingly, the US's negative civic peace index under post-2016 autocratic radical-right rule is higher than those of all Western and even OECD countries, except for only Turkey, Israel, and Mexico.

The highest negative peace index among all Western and most OECD states exposes the failure of the 'American experiment' in terms of human rights to life, peace, safety, and security, including peaceful domestic and international conflict resolution and the lack of militarization, mainly because of fascism or right-wing authoritarianism and the compound of its causes. Insofar as America or any society evinces such highest negative index, this objectively demonstrates that the American or other societal 'experiment' falls to secure and respect the basic human rights to life, peace, safety, and security, including peaceful conflict resolution within and across society and the absence of militarization as a strong predictor of violence and war, owing to fascism or right-wing authoritarianism and the compound of its causes.

Conversely, the highest negative peace index within the Western world conveys the exceptional 'superiority' and 'success' of the 'American experiment' in devaluating, degrading, and destroying life, peace, safety, and security.

TABLE 5.39   Global peace indexes and negatives, OECD countries, 2020

Country	Global peace index	Global peace negative
Australia	1.39	46.82
Austria	1.28	43.07
Belgium	1.50	50.54
Canada	1.30	43.85
Chile	1.80	60.95
Czech Republic	1.34	45.17
Denmark	1.28	43.34
Estonia	1.68	56.76
Finland	1.40	47.43
France	1.93	65.20
Germany	1.49	50.47
Greece	1.88	63.41
Hungary	1.56	52.67
Iceland	1.08	36.42
Ireland	1.38	46.45
Israel	2.78	93.75
Italy	1.69	57.09
Japan	1.36	45.95
Korea South	1.83	61.79
Latvia	1.70	57.43
Lithuania	1.71	57.60
Luxembourg	1.50	50.54
Mexico	2.57	86.89
Netherlands	1.53	51.62
New Zealand	1.20	40.47
Norway	1.50	50.54
Poland	1.66	55.98
Portugal	1.25	42.13
Slovak Republic	1.57	52.97
Slovenia	1.37	46.25
Spain	1.71	57.84
Sweden	1.48	49.97
Switzerland	1.37	46.15
Turkey	2.96	100
United Kingdom	1.77	59.80

TABLE 5.39   Global peace indexes and negatives, OECD countries, 2020 (cont.)

Country	Global peace index	Global peace negative
United States	2.31	77.94
OECD Average	1.64	55.42

The Global Peace Index 'measures the state of peace across three domains: the level of Societal Safety and Security; the extent of Ongoing Domestic and International Conflict; and the degree of Militarisation'
a   Approximated values from comparable countries: Luxembourg from Belgium
Smaller (larger) index, more (less) peace
Global Peace Negative = 100/2.96 × Global Peace Index
SOURCE: GLOBAL PEACE INDEX 2020, INSTITUTE FOR ECONOMICS AND PEACE HTTP://VISIONOFHUMANITY.ORG/APP/UPLOADS/2020/06/GPI_2020_WEB.PDF

Alternatively, it shows the unique 'triumph' of the 'American experiment' in reproducing widespread death caused both by gun murders and state executions, chronic and pervasive domestic and international conflicts and, as the key cause of the second, intense militarization and bellicosity (as exorbitant military expenditure also indicates) thanks to fascism or right-wing authoritarianism and the compound of its causes. This index hence expresses the true quality of conservative-religious 'American exceptionalism' in these terms from the West and OECD. Such an index reveals the failure of the 'American experiment' to appreciate and promote the value of human life, social peace, safety and security, or its 'success' in appreciating and perpetuating, as by mass gun culture and ownership, militarism, and war, domestic and international conflict, and extreme militarization and self-destructive bellicosity by failing to realize the double edge of its sword of offensive eternal wars, as a dual effect of fascism or right-wing authoritarianism and the compound of its causes.

(39) *Gun Ownership*. Mass gun ownership is an additional civil-society indicator or proxy of fascism, specifically of its legal arbitrariness, insecurity, and lawlessness, of theocracy and coercion, repression, violence, and terror, and more broadly of right-wing authoritarianism, with some exceptions and qualifications. The Small Arms Survey is the data source that reports average civilian gun ownership rates (guns owned per 100 persons) for OECD and other countries in 2017. Among OECD countries such rates are the highest in the United States, Canada, Finland, and Iceland (respectively 120.5, 34.7, 32.4, and 31.7) while the lowest in South Korea, Japan, Hungary, and Poland (.2, .3, 1.5, and 2.5, respectively) (see Table 5.40).

TABLE 5.40 Average rate of civilian gun ownership, guns per 100 people, and gun ownership scores, OECD countries, 2017

Country	Gun ownership rate	Gun ownership score
Australia	14.50	12.03
Austria	30.00	24.90
Belgium	12.70	10.54
Canada	34.70	28.80
Chile	12.10	10.04
Czech Republic	12.50	10.37
Denmark	9.90	8.22
Estonia	5.00	4.15
Finland	32.40	26.89
France	19.60	16.27
Germany	19.60	16.27
Greece	17.60	14.61
Hungary	1.50	1.24
Iceland	31.70	26.31
Ireland	7.20	5.98
Israel	6.70	5.56
Italy	14.40	11.95
Japan	.30	.25
Korea South	.20	.17
Latvia	10.50	8.71
Lithuania	13.60	11.29
Luxembourg	18.90	15.68
Mexico	12.90	10.71
Netherlands	2.60	2.16
New Zealand	26.30	21.83
Norway	28.80	23.90
Poland	2.50	2.07
Portugal	21.30	17.68
Slovak Republic	6.50	5.39
Slovenia	15.60	12.95
Spain	7.50	6.22
Sweden	23.10	19.17
Switzerland	27.60	22.90
Turkey	16.50	13.69
United Kingdom	4.60	3.82

TABLE 5.40 Average rate of civilian gun ownership, guns per 100 people (*cont.*)

Country	Gun ownership rate	Gun ownership score
United States	120.50	100
OECD Average	17.80	14.80

*   England and Wales

Gun Ownership Score = 100/120.5 × Gun Ownership Rate

SOURCE: THE SMALL ARMS SURVEY 2018. GLOBAL FIREARMS HOLDINGS: ESTIMAT-
ING GLOBAL CIVILIAN-HELD FIREARMS NUMBERS HTTP://WWW.SMALLARMSSUR
VEY.ORG/FILEADMIN/DOCS/WEAPONS_AND_MARKETS/TOOLS/FIREARMS_HOLDINGS/SAS
-BP-CIVILIAN-HELD-FIREARMS-ANNEXE.PDF

Strikingly, the US's gun ownership rate is higher than those of comparable Western societies and all OECD and other countries, for example nearly four-fold of that of Canada as the second. This confirms that fascism or right-wing authoritarianism and broader conservatism, in an alliance with extremist religion, theocracy, and 'unfettered' capitalism, by mass and virtually unrestricted gun ownership, production, and marketing seeks and obviously succeeds to make America the Hobbesian state of nature and anarchy where the 'law of the strongest' rules. To that extent, this recreates a barbarian, primeval society after the image of a descent into the 'Wild Wild West' movie, while mixed with Leviathan-style control, coercion, and oppression through 'Bible Belt' theocracy from Alabama and Tennessee to Texas.

The highest gun ownership rate indicates another failure of the 'American experiment' in human rights to life, peace, safety, and security, including peaceful conflict resolution in civil society. This holds true given the evidence that gun ownership is the main cause and predictor of murders and other crimes— simply, more guns lead to more violence, notably death[15]—afflicting America as a chronic incurable pathology, while the primary determinant of such a failure of the 'American experiment' being fascism or right-wing authoritarianism and the compound of conservatism, religion, theocracy, and capitalism, the latter by its mass production and marketing of guns.

Relatedly, mass gun ownership and its persistent, ultimate outcome of mass murders identify the comparatively unparalleled failure of the 'American experiment' to attain or ensure civilized life and peaceful civil society. To that extent, this is a failure to reach or sustain civilization that opposite properties,

---

15   This is what Duggan (2001) finds in the US: simply, 'more guns, more crime', especially
      murder, including mass killings or massacres.'

including the non-possession or non-use of lethal weapons by individuals resulting in death or violence, typify (as Weber implies by the state's monopoly on the use of force in society), due to fascism or right-wing authoritarianism and the compound of its factors. So long as America or any society exhibits the highest gun ownership rate and in consequence pervasive murder or violence among Western and all comparable societies, this indicates that the American or other societal 'experiment' falls to affirm and respect the basic human rights to life, peace, safety, and security, including non-violent conflict resolution within society, and relatedly to establish and maintain civilized life and peaceful civil society, because of the rise fascism or right-wing authoritarianism and the prevalence of its causes.

Conversely, the highest gun ownership rate marks exceptional 'superiority' and 'triumph' of the 'American experiment' in depreciation, degradation, and ultimately destruction of life, peace, and safety, or alternatively in murderous and other violence by guns and chronic and pervasive conflict within society, thanks to fascism or right-wing authoritarianism and its causes. This rate hence shows the genuine attribute of conservative-religious 'American exceptionalism' in these respects from the Western world and beyond. As a result, this unrivalled gun ownership and its eventual result of murderous violence signals the exceptional 'superiority' and 'success' of the 'American experiment' in descending into and perpetuating a violent barbarian, pre-civilized life, such as the Hobbesian state of nature and anarchy defined by mass ownership of lethal weapons and so universal war of 'all against all'. This is simply succeeding to petrify conservative America as the 'Wild West' of guns, religion, murder, and overall violence, thanks to fascism or right-wing authoritarianism and its causes. Such gun ownership by its lethal and violent effects exposes the failure of the 'American experiment' to value and protect the basic human rights to life, social peace, and safety, or its spectacular 'success' in valuing and protecting the 'right to bear' and use arms and thus effectively the 'license to kill' especially for fascists, conservatives, and religionists against liberals, secularists, and other anti-fascists and non-conservatives. This results in effectively sacrificing the human rights to life and peace and so humans and their lives to the possession and utilization of guns as a more sacred right for fascism or right-wing authoritarianism, generally conservatism and religion or 'Bible Belt' theocracy. Given its comparative exceptionality within OECD and even the entire world and its lethality and so social destructiveness via mass murders,[16] mass

---

16   For instance, while writing these lines, in a dramatic confirmation of the finding 'more guns, more crime', a gun owner killed more than 20 children and teachers in a Texas school as another episode of a constant epidemic of gun-driven mass killings in this

gun ownership and generally what is often deemed gun culture in America probably merits additional attention and reexamination.

Gun culture and mass gun ownership primarily in the conservative-religious pole of America (such as Texas and the Bible Belt and similar regions) has essentially nothing to do with the constitutional right to 'bear arms' but everything to do with the resurgence of a new savagery or religious barbarism[17]

---

ultra-conservative state and other US states, with guns becoming, incredibly, the prime cause of death of children and adolescents in America, showing the utter inhumanity and perversity of pervasive gun ownership. In turn, this state's conservative-theocratic rulers remove any legal regulations of gun ownership—a state where a 18-year old may freely buy all kinds of guns, including assault military weapons used in war, but may not beer or wine—and urge that Texas should be the number 1 in guns in the US and so the world, thus restoring a Hobbesian savage or barbaric state of nature (the 'Wild West') characterizes with anarchy and the license to kill for gun-wielding conservatives, religionists, and fascists. Like many others, this episode confirms that American conservatism restores savagery or barbarism and that Texas and other US conservatives, theocrats, and fascists tend to sacrifice human life, including the lives of children, in America to their ideological and religious extremism and fanaticism, in this case 'gun rights' leading to mass murders of innocent persons and so treated as more important than the rights to life for children and adults. To that extent, these conservatives by reenacting unregulated barbarian-like gun ownership are indirectly responsible for such murders and have, as critics accuse, the blood of murdered children on their hands from the experience of the victims of these mass shooting and their families. As for the fact that in Texas and other Bible-Belt states ruling conservatives and theocrats allow and even encourage that 18-year persons freely buy and use all kinds of guns, including military assault weapons on their birthdays as if waging a war, but prohibit them from buying and consuming beer or wine, this absurdity, aside from relapsing into the savagery or barbarism of the state of nature and license to kill, historically recreates an insane Puritan-style society, a proxy societal madhouse, and comparatively converges with Islamic theocracies like Iran and Taliban. Such a conservative-theocratic insane society expresses and perpetuates what Hume diagnoses as the 'madness with religious ecstasies' of Puritanism and Pareto as Puritan moralistic 'insanity' and resembles its equivalent in Islamic anti-alcohol Sharia law despite the evangelical hysteria about Islamists imposing 'Sharia law' on America. And the conservative-dominated Supreme Court just a short time after these mass killings of children made another decision in favor of unlimited and unregulated gun ownership contradicting the Constitutional 'well-regulated militia' stipulation and thus its pretended 'originalism'. The likely outcome of such irrational and legally ungrounded decisions are evermore mass killings of children and adults, which makes the conservative-dominated Supreme Court responsible for such murders and appear willing to literally sacrifice human life to its ideological fanaticism and political extremism.

17   US critical journalist Mencken (1982) in the 1920s diagnosed Baptist and Methodist 'barbarism' perverting the South into a 'Bible Belt' of theocratic control, repression, and terror, compounded with artistic and cultural sterility like the 'Sahara desert.' Mencken (1982, p. 625) states that a government 'composed of cynics is often very tolerant and humane. But when fanatics are on top there is no limit to oppression,' the latter implicating the 'Bible Belt' and generally the US conservative-religious polity.

relapsing into the Hobbesian state of nature and its anarchy and the license of kill (in the proxy form of the 'Wild West') given that such a phenomenon is profoundly incompatible with and ultimately destructive of modern civilization. Simply, most conservatives, fascists, and religionists in the former Southern Confederacy and similar regions approach or resemble savages or barbarians who demand and necessitate guns, including military weapons of mass destruction—just as these reinforce their savagery or religious barbarism—to rule and eliminate their designated and targeted enemies like liberals and secularists. This generate the sober prediction that so long as Hobbesian savagery or religious barbarism pervades the Bible Belt, simply its conservative rulers and followers are closer to savages or barbarians (manifested in a violent 'Wild West' mentality) than to moderns, gun culture and mass ownership in the US will persist, and so will the epidemic of school and other shootings and of mass murders of innocent children and others. By contrast, the civilized, liberalized, and modernized sections of America, such as Northeast and Northwest, will be and indeed are already experiencing a weakening and declining gun culture and ownership and consequently less school and other mass shootings, massacres, and deaths.

In turn, only a conservative-dominated Supreme Court and judiciary overall can distort the constitutional right to 'bear arms' by expanding it from certain delimited groups ('a well-regulated militia being necessary to the security of a free State') to individuals and thus making it absolute and universal, contradicting, driven by apparent ideological fanaticism or political bias, its 'originalist' interpretation of the Constitution. Moreover, the phrase 'a well-regulated militia' prima facie stipulates firearm regulation, because regulating militias involves regulating their arms and thus the right to 'bear arms' if the conservative-dominated Supreme Court and judiciary really applies an 'originalist' interpretation of the Constitution, which it evidently does not by vehemently opposing sensible gun control. This exposes the conservative-dominated Supreme Court and judiciary's Constitutional 'originalism' as the legal basis for its opposition to necessary gun control and regulation that the Constitution clearly stipulates as deceptive or delusionary and so spurious instead serving as the legalistic cover and jargon for ideological extremism and political favoritism. Conversely, only a conservative-dominated Supreme Court and judiciary can pervert the constitutional right to individual 'liberty' ('rights to life, liberty, and the pursuit of happiness') by denying that the latter involves personal privacy and so private reproductive freedoms and rights (as when it eliminated by violating a judicial precedent the constitutional right to abortion in 2022) thus abandoning, actuated by ideological extremism and political favoritism, its supposed 'originalist' interpretation of the Constitution. In view of the lethal consequences of such a distortion of the right to 'bear arms,' no wonder critics charge that the conservative-dominated Supreme Court and judiciary, like conservatism and theocratic religion overall, has the blood of murdered children and others on its hands for the epidemic of gun school and other shootings and mass murders of children and others in America by sacrificing their right to life to distorted and spuriously universal and absolute gun rights. Consequently, the conservative-dominated Supreme Court and judiciary, just as conservatism and religion generally, including fascism, renders human life more devaluated, degraded, and worthless, simply 'cheaper', in America than in any Western societies. Generally, the post-2016 conservative-dominated Supreme Court degenerates into the fanatical ideological justification and political enabler or instrument of fascism, as well as of theocracy by perverting the Constitutional stipulation against the 'establishment of religion' and dismantling/cg church-state separation. This confirms that fascism and more broadly conservatism, as well as theocracy, perverts this highest court and the judiciary overall into its justificatory and enabling judicial mechanism.

And because a national standing army or guard substitutes today for 'a well-regulated militia' as a military force 'being necessary to the security of a free State', namely the defense from a foreign invasion, this makes the arms of militias redundant for that specific purpose the Constitution specifies, thus making superfluous or unnecessary the right to 'bear arms' even for these delimited groups, let alone for all individuals especially within modern civilization. This is an ultimate logical inference from consistently applying a truly originalist interpretation of the Constitution's Second Amendment contradicting and exposing as spurious, ideological, so non-legal the 'constitutional originalism' of the conservative-dominated Supreme Court and judiciary and conservatism overall.

Furter, the constitutional right to 'bear arms', the conservative-celebrated Second Amendment to the Constitution, even if only for a 'well-regulated militia', increasingly appears as a serious blunder or oversight that the US founders (especially Maddison) committed. It does so at least in two respects, first, the US founders did not and could not predict that arms in the right to 'bear arms' are no longer muskets and pistols from their times but assault and all kinds of military weapons, including conceivably cannons, tanks, and the like, more than two centuries later, thus failing to envision advancement in firearms instead naively assuming these would remain unchanged over time.

Second, they did not anticipate or overlooked that conservative, theocratic, and fascist forces would pervert the original rationale for the right to 'bear arms', a defense from an invading force like the British army (as 'being necessary to the security of a free State' suggests) or a 'tyrannical' government, into an attack and warfare against liberal-secular democracy and its institutions and representatives through counter-state terrorism using military-style weapons from the Oklahoma City bombing to later and recent right-wing terrorist attacks. Further, they did/could not anticipate that a 'tyrannical government' in the US can only be a conservative or right-wing, including fascist and theocratic, one given the prevalence of conservatism and religion over liberalism, secularism, and rationalism (or of the rightist 'American character'), and therefore that conservatives, fascists, and theocrats or religionists would use the 'right to bear arms' and their overwhelming gun ownership to impose or defend such a radical-right tyranny, and launch a terrorist insurrection and warfare against liberal-secular democracy and science. This reveals that the primary and overriding driving force behind the fanatical exaltation of the right to 'bear arms' in American conservatism, fascism, and religion or theocracy rather than ensuring the 'security of a free State' from a foreign invasion or a 'tyrannical' government is precisely imposing and sustaining a conservative-fascist-theocratic government that is hence profoundly tyrannical or oppressive, and increasingly so post-2016 and at state levels after 2020.

Conversely, the prime driver of such glorification of gun rights by conservatives, fascists, and religionists is threatening and, in their minds and plans, starting a civil war against and abolishing a liberal-democratic and secular government they construe as 'tyrannical' in an inverse Orwellian logic equating democracy and liberty with tyranny, or a deception and manipulation, thus eliminating liberals and secularists as the 'enemy of the people.' This shows that the invocation by conservatives, fascists, and religionists of a defense from a 'tyrannical' government or a foreign invasion, as well as personal protection, hunting and other sport purposes, as the justification[s] for the 'right to bear arms' exposes itself as a deception or delusion hiding the true dual motivating force—imposing fascism or theocracy while destroying liberal-secular democracy and eliminating ('hunting'[18]) liberals and secularists as 'un-American'—which the founders were unable to envision. Hence, this suggests that liberal-democratic institutions and liberals can only dismiss or underestimate gun culture and mass gun ownership as the mere effect and exercise of the constitutional right to 'bear arms' at their own peril, ultimately their demise and elimination by gun-wielding conservatives, fascists, and religionists.

---

18 For example, in post-2020 several US fascists or conservative extremists in the South and beyond state that the Second Amendment isn't about duck hunting or 'bird hunting' but by implication about hunting their enemies, so anti-fascists, liberals, and secularists, and moderates within their own party.

On this account, the right to 'bear arms' rationalizing mass gun ownership and gun culture by such consequences as school and other shootings and mass murders of children and others turns out to be lethal and so socially destructive and ultimately perhaps fatal for America by causing or exacerbating a civil war between gun-owning and wielding conservatives, theocrats, and fascists and liberal, secularists, and other anti-fascists characterized with no or minor gun ownership and so likely to be defeated and eliminated in such wars. This yields the inference that the repeal of the right to 'bear arms' amendment becomes increasingly imperative and necessary in order to save America from further mass murders, social destruction from within, and eventually civil war and disintegration in the style of the Soviet Union or Yugoslavia, thus to protect Americans' lives, just as, similarly, the Prohibition amendment was repealed to preserve personal freedom and privacy (and to mitigate Mafia-based organized crime it caused). And yet, such a repeal may well induce heavily-armed conservative, theocratic or religious, and fascist groups to launch a civil war, alongside their culture wars, which they are likely and indeed confident to win owing to their predominant gun ownership and use. Evidently, by the right to 'bear arms' the US founders (especially Maddison) placed unwittingly America in a vicious circle, a dead end with a possible fatal outcome for its existence or at least permanent peace, safety, and security in civil society.

Lastly, to add insult to the injury of massacres and deaths associated with gun culture and mass ownership, the US government at all levels, primarily conservative America or American conservatism, displays with a nationalist pride and joy (to paraphrase Veblen) the extreme 'trained incapacity,' reluctance, and resistance to learn from the experience of Western and other societies with respect to gun control and regulation and the consequent reduction of random public shootings and mass murders. For instance, it appears incapable of or refuses to learn from even Anglo-Saxon countries like Australia, Great Britain and Canada that enacted effective gun-control measures after guns-driven violence episodes and consequently dramatically reduced public shootings and mass murders during last several decades. Rather than learning from and applying such comparable examples to save Americans' life, it explicitly rejects them induced by 'superior' American exceptionalism and ardent nationalism qua supremacist Americanism epitomized by Reaganism's and generally conservatism's 'we are the best' pretensions and slogans in regard with gun control, as in all respects. (A related instance is the 'trained incapacity' and refusal of the US government under conservatism or conservative America to learn and apply the lessons from other societies in respect of the health care system, notably national universal systems, in spite or because its own system usually ranks at the bottom in terms of both access and outcomes among

Western and comparable societies.) At this point, American exceptionalism and nationalism, simply Americanism, reemerges and operates as a curse and nemesis, due to mass murders and so the socially destructive consequences of its perpetuated gun culture and ownership and its refusal to learn from other countries in this regard, rather than a blessing and savior of America.

(40) *Murders by Guns*. Widespread murders by guns are a complementary civil-society indicator or proxy of fascism, specifically of its legal insecurity and lawlessness, violence, and terror, and of right-wing authoritarianism in general. DATAUNODC is the data source reporting murders by firearms rates (per 100,000 population) for OECD and other countries during 2017, as part of homicide rates by mechanisms. Homicides by firearms rates among OECD countries are the highest in Mexico, the United States, Chile, and Turkey (respectively 16.5, 3.4 1.5, and .8), while being the lowest in Estonia, Japan, South Korea, Poland, Slovenia, and United Kingdom (all 0) (see Table 5.41).

Obviously, the US exhibits the murders by firearms rate that is higher than those of comparable Western societies and all OECD countries, except only for Mexico and just recently due to its drug-related violence. This reaffirms that the broad family of fascism or right-wing authoritarianism and conservatism, allied with extremist religion, theocracy, and unfettered capitalism, renders America the Hobbesian state of nature and anarchy in which 'life is brutish and short' due to widespread murders and massacres by guns, combined with Leviathan via state widespread executions especially in the 'Bible Belt'.

The highest murders by firearms rate among Western and all societies within OECD, minus Mexico, uncovers an ultimate and complementary failure of the 'American experiment' in terms of the human right to life primary because of fascism or right-wing authoritarianism as the ideology and system of mass murder and generally the merger of conservatism, religion, and theocracy, along with coercive capitalism especially by its mass gun production and distribution. In consequence, this murders rate detects the comparatively unrivaled failure of the 'American experiment' to promote and protect humans from death by firearms and so to live in a civilized civil society, thus failing to attain or maintain modern civilization that aims protecting their members' lives against violent deaths, an effect due to fascism or right-wing authoritarianism and the blend of its causes. Insofar as America or any society displays highest murders by firearms rate, this demonstrates that the American or other societal 'experiment' falls to establish and respect the human right to life and thus to protect humans' lives from murders and generally to ensure living in a civilized civil society, as the effect of fascism or right-wing authoritarianism and its causes.

TABLE 5.41   Homicide rate by mechanisms, firearms rate per 100,000 population, and homicide by firearms scores, OECD countries, 2017

Country	Homicide by firearms rate	Homicide by firearms score
Australia	.10	.61
Austria	.10	.61
Belgium	.50	3.03
Canada	.60	3.64
Chile	1.50	9.09
Czech Republic	.10	.61
Denmark	.20	1.21
Estonia	0	0
Finland	.20	1.21
France	.40	2.42
Germany	.10	.61
Greece	.30	1.82
Hungary	.10	.61
Iceland	.30	1.82
Ireland	.40	2.42
Israel	.60	3.64
Italy	.30	1.82
Japan	0	0
Korea South	0	0
Latvia	.30	1.82
Lithuania	.40	2.42
Luxembourg	.20	1.21
Mexico	16.50	100
Netherlands	.10	.61
New Zealand	.20	1.21
Norway	.10	.61
Poland	0	0
Portugal	.20	1.21
Slovak Republic	.30	1.82
Slovenia	0	0
Spain	.10	.61
Sweden	.40	2.42
Switzerland	.20	1.21
Turkey	.80	4.85

TABLE 5.41   Homicide rate by mechanisms, firearms rate per 100,000 population (*cont.*)

Country	Homicide by firearms rate	Homicide by firearms score
United Kingdom*	0	0
United States	3.40	20.61
OECD Average	.81	4.88

*   England and Wales
Homicide by Firearms Score = 100/16.5 × Homicide by Firearms Rate
SOURCE: DATAUNODC HTTPS://DATAUNODC.UN.ORG/DATA/HOMICIDE/HOMICIDE%20R
ATE%20BY%20MECHANISMS

Conversely, the above rate signals another exceptional 'superiority' and 'success' of the 'American experiment' in devaluating and violating the human right to life and consequently degrading and ultimately destroying life, or alternatively, in reproducing violent deaths (the 'best' in Reagan's words) by 'guns and religion', because of fascism or right-wing authoritarianism and its causes. This rate therefore shows the true quality of conservative-religious 'American exceptionalism' in these terms from the Western world and beyond. Consequently, such a rate conveys the exceptional 'superiority' and 'triumph' of the 'American experiment' in retrieving and perpetuating the Hobbesian state of nature and anarchy in which 'life is brutish and short' because of mass murders by lethal weapons, thus in petrifying conservative America as the 'Wild West' of guns, religion, and murder, thanks to fascism or right-wing authoritarianism and the compound of its determinants. The highest murders by firearms rate, as mainly an outcome of fascism or right-wing authoritarianism and the compound of its causes, reveals the failure of the 'American experiment' in appreciation and promotion of the human rights to, and consequently valuation and protection of, life, instead sacrificing such rights to the 'right' to possess and utilize deadly weapons resulting in mass deaths and hence living in a civilized society to dying in a pre-civilized state of nature.

2.5   *Summary*

Taken together, the composite index or approximation of fascism and generally conservative or right-wing authoritarianism is the aggregate of 40 indicators and proxies as its components.

TABLE 5.42 Descriptive statistics for the indicators and proxies of fascism or right-wing
authoritarianism

Indicator	N	Minimum	Maximum	Mean	Std. Deviation
Power constraints negative	36	6.0	70.0	23.972	14.3895
Rule of law negative	36	.00	72.60	15.9322	15.99291
Political stability negative and presence of violence	36	.48	90.00	29.4975	21.04943
Control of corruption negative	36	.00	77.40	18.3761	17.47940
Open government negative	36	11	58	26.64	11.220
Voting turnout negative	36	8.99	57.40	32.4492	13.65131
Electoral freedom and political pluralism negative	36	.0	69.2	6.475	11.5772
Political voice negative	36	.00	75.37	16.3386	16.24915
Media freedom negative	36	15.67	100.00	40.5338	19.48512
Imprisonment score	36	5.65	100.00	21.8490	16.83689
Death sentences and executions score	36	.00	100.00	2.9747	16.65585
Other political terror score	36	20.00	100.00	35.5556	20.90037
Military expenditure score	36	.00	100.00	30.0839	18.08030
Art and culture government spending negative	36	.00	91.32	63.4963	20.31164
Beliefs in 'Satan'	36	10	73	32.75	16.741
Opposition to evolution	36	18	75	34.75	13.772
'God' beliefs	36	16.10	94.00	43.3972	21.46891
High importance of religion in life	36	6	68	21.36	15.123
Church attendance	36	1	45	15.86	11.799
Daily prayer	36	6	60	21.42	13.133
Wealth concentration score	36	21.56	100.00	44.7119	15.80451
Income inequality score	36	53.59	100.00	69.0692	11.50542
Poverty score	36	30.34	100.00	65.9956	21.78794
Annual work hours score	36	64.58	100.00	78.0136	8.45910
Paid vacation negative	36	.00	100.00	32.5000	22.13056

TABLE 5.42 Descriptive statistics for the indicators and proxies of fascism (*cont.*)

Indicator	N	Minimum	Maximum	Mean	Std. Deviation
Paid paternity leave negative	36	.00	100.00	57.8811	18.67311
Employment protection negative	36	.00	97.51	41.5282	19.67281
Unemployment benefits negative	36	41	100	72.67	16.470
Social protection and economic security negative	36	.00	74.72	38.3368	19.68806
Labor union density negative	36	8.2	95.7	75.525	20.0505
Collective bargaining coverage negative	36	1.5	93.0	52.728	31.1336
Civil liberties negative	36	.00	76.50	14.2889	14.43656
Civil justice negative	36	14	61	29.28	11.915
Individual liberty negative	36	5.50	42.60	12.8111	7.69173
Death penalty for drug offenses	36	0	100	5.56	23.231
Incarceration for sins-as-crimes	36	5.65	100.00	21.8490	16.83689
Fundamental human rights negative	36	8.0	68.0	23.028	11.9079
Peace negative	36	36.42	100.00	55.4242	14.29623
Gun ownership score	36	.17	100.00	14.7971	16.68773
Murders by guns score	36	.00	100.00	4.8822	16.69911

First, the index comprises as political components no or weak power constraints, no or weak rule of law, no or weak political stability and presence of violence, no or weak control of corruption, no or weak open government, voting rights suppression, no or weak electoral freedom and political pluralism, no or weak political voice, no or weak media freedom, mass imprisonment, widespread death sentences and executions, other political terror, and high military expenditure. Second, it involves as cultural components religion-grounded social depreciation of and low government spending on art and culture, widespread religious superstitions like beliefs in 'Satan', anti-science via opposition to evolution, mass 'God' beliefs (or delusions), high importance of religion in life, high church attendance, and high frequency of daily prayer. Third, the index incorporates as political components high share of wealth of the top one percent of the population, the high Gini coefficient of income distribution, the high general poverty rate, compulsory hard or long work, no or short paid vacations, no or short paid paternity leave, no or weak employment protection, no or low unemployment benefits, no or weak social protection and economic security, union suppression, and collective bargaining suppression. Fourth, it includes as civil-society components no or weak civil liberties, no or weak civil justice, no or weak individual liberty and privacy, the death penalty for drug offenses, mass incarceration for sins-as-crimes, no or weak fundamental human rights, no or weak human rights to life, peace and safety, mass gun ownership, and widespread murders by guns (see Figure 5.1).

In substantive terms, aside from few exceptions, most of these 40 indicators and proxies of fascism or conservative authoritarianism indicate or imply the failure of the 'American experiment' of society in political, cultural, economic, and civil-society terms as the 'best kept secret' for most Americans and uniformed outsiders but the 'worst kept secret' for close observers and informed insiders. Indeed, they suggest various failures in its own, primarily Jeffersonian and related, ideals of universal liberty, equality, justice, and democracy, rationality, science, and progress, shared prosperity and wealth, lack of poverty and deprivation, personal freedom, privacy, and other basic human rights, including the right to life, and the like. If the 'American experiment' fails in

I	III
1. no or weak power constraints	21. high share of wealth of the top one percent of the population
2. no or weak rule of law	22. the high Gini coefficient of income distribution
3. no or weak political stability and presence of violence	23. the high general poverty rate
4. no or weak control of corruption	24. compulsory hard or long work
5. no or weak open government	25. no or short paid vacations
6. voting rights suppression	26. no or short paid paternity leave
7. no or weak elector''''al freedom and political pluralism	27. no or weak employment protection
8. no or weak political voice	28. no or low unemployment benefits
9. no or weak media freedom	29. no or weak social protection and economic security
10. mass imprisonment	30. labor union suppression
11. widespread death sentences and executions	31. collective bargaining suppression
12. other political terror	
13. exorbitant military expenditure	
II	IV
14. religion-grounded social depreciation of and low government spending on art and culture	32. no or weak civil liberties
15. widespread religious superstitions (beliefs in 'Satan')	33. no or weak civil justice
16. anti-science (opposition to evolution)	34. no or weak individual liberty
17. mass 'God' beliefs (or delusions)	35. the death penalty for drug offenses
18. high importance of religion in life	36. mass incarceration for sins-as-crimes
19. high church attendance	37. no or weak fundamental human rights
20. high frequency of daily prayer	38. no or weak human rights to life, peace and safety
	39. mass gun ownership
	40. widespread murders by guns

FIGURE 5.1   Fascism or right-wing authoritarianism index components

these terms, it does primarily because of the rise and advance of fascism or right-wing authoritarianism and the persistence and dominance of its aggregate of causes, the merger of conservatism, religion, theocracy, and coercive capitalism. To that extent, most of the above 40 indicators expose America as an example or proxy of a mostly 'failed' society or state under and primarily due to fascism or right-wing authoritarianism as the outcome of the compound of conservatism, religion, theocracy, and coercive capitalism post-2016 and before, as especially since Reaganism. Conversely, hardly any one of these indicators reveals America as an exceptional 'success story' during the rise and expansion of fascism or right-wing authoritarianism in consequence of the resurgence and dominance of conservatism, religion, theocracy, and coercive capitalism. In this respect, true 'American exceptionalism' consists in a comparatively exceptional 'failed' society or state rather than a unique societal 'success' under the compounded rule of conservatism, religion, theocracy, and coercive capitalism and its reproduction of fascism or right-wing authoritarianism post-2016 and earlier. While this finding and inference is surprising to uninformed observers and shocking to most Americans oblivious of these facts because of being subjected to persistent 'cradle to grave' and pervasive 'we are the best' or 'superior nation' indoctrination and propaganda (in their own words, 'brain washing'), this is precisely what virtually all 40 indicators reveal and compel to infer objectively and involuntarily. This is essentially what the resulting eruption of fascism or right-wing authoritarianism from the conjoined dominance of conservatism, religion, theocracy, and coercive capitalism in America does and can only engender and maintain—a 'failed' society and thus the overall failure of the celebrated 'American experiment'.

In sum, these indicators especially, though not solely, reveal the failure of the national or societal 'American experiment' and to that extent America as a 'failed' state or society during the rise and advance of fascism or right-wing authoritarianism resulting from the resurgence and dominance of the compound of its main causes involving conservatism, coercive capitalism, extremist religion, and theocracy.

2.5.1   Political Indicators

(1)   Among the lowest voting turnout mainly due to severe and further intensifying voting rights suppression—a failure of the 'American experiment' and 'failed' state in basic political freedoms and rights, such as the freedom and right to vote for all actors in the polity.

(2)   The highest prisoner rate and the largest total prison population, including a large proportion of prisoners of ethical conscience and innocent persons—a failure of the 'American experiment' and 'failed'

state in universal liberty and justice, including personal freedom liberty and privacy, and in the rule of law.

(3)   The highest numbers of death sentences and executions, including of many innocent persons—a 'failed' state or another failure of the 'American experiment' in 'liberty and justice for all', liberal democracy, the right to life, and the rule of law.

(4)   The highest political terror score within the Western world—a failure of the 'American experiment' and a 'failed' state in a humane treatment of people and respect of basic human freedoms and rights, like the freedom from arbitrary imprisonment and disappearance, police brutality and murders, and the right to dignified life and non-torture.

(5)   The largest military expenditure for wars of aggression and imperial conquest and domination-a failure of the 'American experiment' and a 'failed' state in civilian investment and welfare, peace, peaceful conflict resolution, and respect for the national independence and sovereignty of other smaller, weaker states, in betrayal of Jefferson-Madison's pacifist ideals, including no formation of and entanglement in aggressive militarist alliances (e.g., NATO).

Overall, the preceding indicates a failure of the 'American experiment' and 'failed' state in liberal democracy primarily because of fascism or right-wing authoritarianism and in extension the compound of its causes, authoritarian conservatism, coercive capitalism, extremist religion, and theocracy.

2.5.2   Cultural Indicators

(6)   The lowest public investment in art and culture—a failure of the 'American experiment' and a 'failed' state in artistic and cultural appreciation, promotion, and creativity.

(7)   The highest 'Satan exists' figure among Western societies—a failure of the 'American experiment' and a 'failed' state in cultural rationalism, reason, and knowledge.

(8)   The lowest public acceptance of biological evolution in the Western world—a failure of the 'American experiment' and a 'failed' state in scientific rationalism and knowledge, or science.

(9)   The highest daily prayer figure in the Western world—a failure of the 'American experiment' and a 'failed' state in cultural rationalism and knowledge.

Generally, the above suggests the failure of the 'American experiment' and a 'failed' state in liberal and rationalistic culture largely owing of fascism or right-wing authoritarianism and the compound of its causes.

2.5.3   Economic Indicators

(10)   The highest top one percent wealth share—an indirect failure of the 'American experiment' and a 'failed' state in the 'wealth of nations', universal material wellbeing.

(10a)   Among the lowest median net wealth—a direct failure of the 'American experiment' and a 'failed' state in the 'wealth of nations', shared prosperity.

(11)   The highest Gini coefficient of income inequality in the Western world—another failure of the 'American experiment' and a 'failed' state in shared prosperity.

(12)   The highest general poverty rate—a failure of the 'American experiment' and a 'failed' state in eliminating or reducing widespread poverty, deprivation, and degradation.

(13)   The lowest, zero legally mandated paid leave—a failure of the 'American experiment' and a 'failed' state in worker dignity, respect, satisfaction, and wellbeing.

(14)   The lowest, zero paternity leave—a failure of the 'American experiment' and a 'failed' state in family, including parent and children, protection, prosperity, and wellbeing.

(15)   The lowest employment protection coefficient—a failure of the 'American experiment' and a 'failed' state in economic security and wellbeing.

(16)   The lowest unemployment insurance among Western societies—a failure of the 'American experiment' and a 'failed' state in economic security and wellbeing.

(17)   The lowest public spending on social protection among Western societies—a failure of the 'American experiment' and a 'failed' state in socioeconomic security and wellbeing.

(18)   Among the lowest labor union density—a failure of the 'American experiment' and a 'failed' state in labor liberties, such as the freedom of unionization, economic liberty for all production factors.

(19)   the lowest union coverage among Western societies—a failure of the 'American experiment' and a 'failed' state in labor freedoms and rights like the freedom/right to bargain collectively, universal economic liberty.

In general, the preceding indicates the failure of the 'American experiment' and a 'failed' state in an egalitarian and 'rational social economy' (Cassel's term), such as welfare capitalism, including Smith's 'wealth of nations' and universal material wellbeing or shared prosperity, primarily because of fascism or right-wing authoritarianism and the above compound of its causes.

2.5.4   Civil-Society Indicators

(20)   The sole application of the death penalty for drug offenses among Western societies—a failure of the 'American experiment' and a 'failed' state in protection and respect of individual liberty and privacy and human dignity and life.

(21)   The highest share of prisoners-drug offenders of the prison population—a failure of the 'American experiment' and a 'failed' state in protecting and respecting individual liberty and privacy and human dignity and rights.

(22)   The highest negative peace index among all Western states—a failure of the 'American experiment' and a 'failed' state in protecting and respecting human rights to life, peace, safety, and security, including peaceful domestic and international conflict resolution and non-militarization.

(23)   The highest gun ownership rate—a failure of the 'American experiment' and a 'failed' state in protecting and respecting human rights to life, peace, safety, and security, including peaceful conflict resolution in civil society.

(24)   The highest murders by firearms rate among Western societies—a failure of the 'American experiment' and a 'failed' state in respecting the human right to life and in protecting humans from random, violent death by firearms.

Overall, the above illustrates the failure of the 'American experiment' and a 'failed' state in free civil society, notably individual liberty, privacy, and security, mainly owing to fascism or right-wing authoritarianism and the compound of its causes.

Taken together, the preceding demonstrates the failure of the societal 'American experiment' and uncovers America as a 'failed' state even in its own Jeffersonian ideals of equality, liberty, justice, and wellbeing (happiness) or prosperity 'for all' primarily because of fascism or right-wing authoritarianism and conservatism, coercive capitalism, extremist religion, and theocracy as the compound of its causes. Conversely, it hardly unveils the exceptional success, triumph, and superiority of the 'American experiment' and America as a successful, triumphant, superior state in these terms due to fascism or right-wing authoritarianism and its causes. For illustration, the US ranks the highest or high on zero of the positives of the above indicators (e.g., political freedoms and rights, culture appreciation and science, wealth and economic freedoms, civil liberties and rights, individual liberty, and privacy, etc.) and to that extent displays exceptional success, triumph, and superiority by no single indicator.

The above exposes the deception or delusion of such glorifications as the 'best', 'freest', 'richest', 'greatest', 'exceptional', 'superior', and the like by fascism or right-wing authoritarianism and the compound of its causes, especially conservatism, intoxicated or deluded by supremacist Americanism or 'American exceptionalism' as superiority from anti-liberal McCarthyism and Reaganism to autocracy post-2016. Cynics may retort that America under fascism or right-wing authoritarianism and generally conservatism, coercive capitalism, extremist religion, and theocracy is the 'best', 'freest', 'richest', the 'greatest', 'exceptional', 'superior' not so much in Jeffersonian social goods or positives, as these glorifications claim, as in social 'bads' or negatives. As the preceding shows, it is indeed the 'best', 'freest', 'richest', the 'greatest', 'exceptional', 'superior' in, first, political bads, such as the voting rights suppression, mass imprisonment, widespread executions, other political terror, and militarism and offensive war. Second, it is the 'best', 'freest', 'richest', the 'greatest', 'exceptional', 'superior' in cultural 'bads' including non-investment in art and culture, irrationalism exemplified by mass 'Satan exists' beliefs, and anti-rationalism through anti-science and anti-knowledge in the form of anti-evolution. Third, it is the 'best', 'freest', 'richest', the 'greatest', 'exceptional', 'superior' in economic 'bads' like wealth concentration, low median wealth, income inequality, general poverty, no paid vacation, no paternity leave, employment non-protection, unemployment uninsurance, social non-protection, and suppression of unionization and collective bargaining. Fourth, it is the 'best', 'freest', 'richest', the 'greatest', 'exceptional', 'superior' in civil-society 'bads' involving the death penalty for drug offenses, prisoners-drug offenders, negative peace or lack of safety, unrestricted gun ownership resulting in violence, and murders by firearms. In short, it is the 'best', Reagan-style in social 'bads' under fascism or right-wing authoritarianism from Reaganism to autocracy post-2016. This is true conservative 'American exceptionalism'—comparative exceptionality and 'superiority' in social 'bads' rather than in the Jeffersonian social goods of equality, liberty, justice, prosperity, wellbeing, and happiness 'for all'.

Altogether, the above 40 indicators and proxies are components of the composite index or approximation of fascism or conservative authoritarianism and, on a closer inspection, disclose the failure of the 'American experiment' in most societal terms because of fascist and related authoritarian resurgence and its primary cause, the compound of conservatism, coercive capitalism, extremist religion, and theocracy.

3   Indexes of Fascism or Right-Wing Authoritarianism for OECD
       Countries

This section presents aggregate numerical indexes or approximations of fascism and broader conservative authoritarianism for OECD countries and thus Western and comparable societies. These numerical indexes are averages of the above four sets of indicators and proxies of fascism as the components of its index. Their calculation proceeds by, first, listing the indicators and proxies of fascism, then aggregating them to obtain aggregate figures, and lastly dividing these aggregates by the number of components (40) to yield e composite numerical indexes, as averages of these components, for OECD countries.

Table 5.43 presents the indicators and indexes of fascism or more broadly right-wing authoritarianism for 36 OECD countries. First, its columns 1–40 list the 40 indicators and proxies, with the 0–100 possible range, of fascism for OECD countries. Then, its column Total gives aggregates for these indicators by totaling the latter. Finally, and most importantly, its column Index provides aggregate numerical indexes that are averages, with the 0–100 possible range, of these indicators by dividing their aggregates by 40. Thus, each aggregate index for OECD countries is the average of 40 indicators and proxies of fascism or right-wing authoritarianism.

TABLE 5.43 Indicators and indexes of fascism or right-wing authoritarianism, OECD countries

Country	1	2	3	4	5	6	7	8	9	10	11	12	13
Australia	18.0	6.73	11.43	5.77	19	8.99	.0	6.90	40.40	25.80	0	40	35.85
Austria	15.0	2.88	17.14	9.13	29	24.40	4.2	6.40	31.55	14.50	0	40	13.21
Belgium	17.0	11.54	38.10	8.65	24	11.60	4.2	4.43	31.57	14.50	0	20	16.98
Canada	28.0	5.29	14.76	6.73	19	32.30	4.2	3.94	30.57	16.34	0	20	24.53
Chile	16.0	17.31	45.24	16.83	29	53.50	4.2	18.72	47.12	31.91	0	40	33.96
Czech Republic	27.0	18.27	19.52	31.25	33	39.20	4.2	22.17	54.60	29.62	0	20	22.64
Denmark	6.0	1.92	16.19	2.40	12	15.40	.0	1.48	16.25	10.84	0	20	24.53
Estonia	17.0	12.98	31.90	9.62	19	36.30	4.2	11.33	25.21	27.79	0	20	39.62
Finland	8.0	0	20.95	.96	14	31.30	.0	.99	15.85	8.09	0	40	28.30
France	27.0	10.58	41.43	11.06	22	57.40	4.2	12.32	45.82	15.88	0	60	35.85
Germany	15.0	7.69	33.33	4.81	21	23.80	4.2	4.93	24.31	11.76	0	20	24.53
Greece	32.0	39.42	42.86	43.75	39	42.10	4.2	22.66	57.28	16.18	0	40	49.06
Hungary	60.0	31.73	28.57	42.31	54	30.30	12.5	45.32	61.66	25.50	0	40	22.64
Iceland	6.0	4.81	.48	7.21	11	18.80	.0	5.91	30.23	5.65	0	20	0
Ireland	18.0	11.06	17.62	10.58	21	34.90	.0	5.42	25.19	11.30	0	20	5.66
Israel	32.0	17.79	80.95	21.15	39	30.20	8.3	29.56	61.66	35.73	0	80	100
Italy	29.0	38.46	39.05	37.98	37	27.10	4.2	20.20	47.36	13.74	0	40	26.42
Japan	29.0	9.62	14.29	10.10	32	47.30	12.5	21.67	57.70	5.95	4.78	20	16.98
Korea South	28.0	13.94	38.57	23.08	29	420	8.3	27.09	47.38	16.18	2.31	40	50.94
Latvia	16.0	19.23	40	31.73	19	45.42	4.2	25.62	37.11	27.33	0	20	37.74

TABLE 5.43 Indicators and indexes of fascism or right-wing authoritarianism, OECD countries (cont.)

Country	1	2	3	4	5	6	7	8	9	10	11	12	13
Lithuania	16.0	18.75	24.76	25.48	19	49.36	4.2	18.23	42.36	33.74	0	40	37.74
Luxembourg	17.0	4.33	4.29	1.92	24	10.30	.0	3.45	30.91	16.03	0	20	11.32
Mexico	54.0	72.60	79.05	77.40	40	36.80	21.7	54.68	90.86	24.12	0	80	7.55
Netherlands	14.0	3.85	24.29	3.37	18	18.10	4.2	2.46	19.91	9.62	0	20	24.53
New Zealand	15.0	2.40	2.86	0	18	20.20	.0	1.97	21.37	30.38	0	20	28.30
Norway	6.0	.48	7.62	2.88	11	21.80	.0	0	15.67	9.16	0	20	32.08
Poland	42.0	33.65	35.71	28.85	40	38.30	8.3	29.06	57.58	28.85	0	40	37.74
Portugal	22.0	15.38	9.05	22.60	34	51.40	4.2	10.84	23.65	16.79	0	40	35.85
Slovak Republic	27.0	28.85	27.62	35.58	33	40.20	4.2	24.63	45.32	29.31	0	40	33.96
Slovenia	35.0	15.87	26.19	19.71	35	47.40	4.2	19.21	45.22	10.53	0	20	20.75
Spain	26.0	19.71	40.95	26.44	29	28.20	4.2	17.24	44.30	18.93	0	40	22.64
Sweden	13.0	1.44	13.33	1.44	14	12.80	4.2	.49	18.49	9.31	0	20	20.75
Switzerland	15.0	.96	5.24	3.85	21	51.60	4.2	2.96	21.23	12.21	0	20	13.21
Turkey	70.0	55.29	90	55.29	58	13.80	69.2	75.37	100	52.52	0	100	50.94
United Kingdom	18.0	8.65	36.19	6.25	21	32.40	4.2	9.36	45.84	20.46	0	20	32.08
United States	29.0	10.10	42.38	15.38	22	43.20	8.3	21.18	47.68	100	100	80	64.15

TABLE 5.43 Indicators and indexes of fascism or right-wing authoritarianism, OECD countries (cont.)

Country	14	15	16	17	18	19	20
Australia	77.28	44	21	28.50	18	17	18
Austria	63.68	23	42	27.40	12	11	8
Belgium	60.61	19	21	21.50	11	6	11
Canada	77.28	43	39	67.00	27	20	25
Chile	88.81	59	31	71.80	41	19	39
Czech Republic	53.12	13	36	16.10	7	7	9
Denmark	49.39	10	19	28.20	9	3	10
Estonia	38.51	22	37	18.00	6	2	9
Finland	53.93	41	37	33.00	10	4	18
France	56.69	20	20	18.70	11	12	10
Germany	67.06	14	27	32.00	10	10	9
Greece	75.15	61	48	79.00	56	16	30
Hungary	0	24	31	30.90	14	9	16
Iceland	.78	10	18	31.00	19	10	18
Ireland	83.36	55	35	64.10	22	20	19
Israel	52.55	40	46	66.50	36	30	27
Italy	76.15	40	30	54.00	21	23	21
Japan	87.81	12	20	24.00	10	1	33
Korea South	72.99	20	59	54.00	16	29	32
Latvia	49.17	36	52	38.10	11	7	18

TABLE 5.43 Indicators and indexes of fascism or right-wing authoritarianism, OECD countries (*cont.*)

Country	14	15	16	17	18	19	20
Lithuania	65.12	42	50	47.00	16	9	15
Luxembourg	60.80	19	36	46.00	11	10	11
Mexico	88.81	53	36	94.00	45	45	40
Netherlands	63.40	18	31	24.40	20	12	20
New Zealand	77.28	30	25	34.20	18	9	18
Norway	46.29	27	22	25.70	19	7	18
Poland	58.16	34	35	59.60	30	42	29
Portugal	74.52	35	36	58.10	36	25	38
Slovak Republic	66.78	34	42	51.00	23	23	31
Slovenia	55.69	25	32	26.90	12	13	8
Spain	65.18	35	19	39.10	22	15	23
Sweden	59.89	16	19	45.00	10	6	11
Switzerland	74.21	28	36	19.10	9	11	8
Turkey	72.74	73	75	94.00	68	44	60
United Kingdom	81.35	33	21	26.90	10	8	6
United States	91.32	71	67	67.50	53	36	55

TABLE 5.43 Indicators and indexes of fascism or right-wing authoritarianism, OECD countries (*cont.*)

Country	21	22	23	24	25	26	27	28	29	30	31
Australia	35.31	73.42	69.66	80.11	33.33	58.14	53.74	69	58.67	85.3	40.8
Austria	60.10	60.13	55.06	70.24	16.67	62.79	36.57	49	18.34	73.7	2.0
Belgium	28.39	58.39	54.49	74.08	33.33	65.12	42.66	45	21.78	49.7	4.0
Canada	36.49	69.28	67.98	78.15	66.67	62.79	83.66	69	29.70	70.6	71.9
Chile	40.96	98.91	92.70	89.58	50.00	58.14	26.04	100	74.72	82.3	79.1
Czech Republic	21.94	56.21	31.46	83.67	16.67	34.88	9.70	88	51.23	88.5	53.7
Denmark	55.60	57.30	32.58	64.58	0	58.14	57.62	50	11.03	33.5	16.0
Estonia	49.98	71.90	88.20	80.07	33.33	53.49	49.86	82	47.12	95.7	81.4
Finland	31.33	56.43	35.39	72.06	16.67	59.30	44.60	71	0	39.7	10.7
France	43.90	64.27	46.63	70.43	16.67	62.79	29.09	66	1.42	91.2	1.5
Germany	55.70	63.83	58.43	64.86	0	67.44	27.98	78	21.15	83.5	44.0
Greece	21.56	74.07	80.90	91.20	33.33	0	32.13	79	21.23	79.8	60.0
Hungary	40.56	62.75	43.82	80.73	33.33	44.19	55.96	86	43.85	92.1	77.2
Iceland	54.14	53.59	30.34	68.04	20.00	69.77	56.79	52	59.84	8.2	10.0
Ireland	33.38	64.71	51.69	82.92	20.00	39.53	65.93	62	63.55	75.5	66.5
Israel	52.97	75.38	94.94	88.82	63.33	65.12	34.35	77	54.81	75.0	73.9
Italy	27.52	72.55	76.97	80.38	16.67	49.53	29.09	86	15.82	65.6	20.0
Japan	25.35	71.90	88.20	76.93	66.67	67.44	62.05	66	34.49	83.0	83.5
Korea South	70.62	64.27	97.75	92.04	50.00	70.00	32.96	79	72.67	89.5	88.2
Latvia	50.35	75.60	94.38	77.73	33.33	62.79	25.48	90	52.87	88.1	86.2

TABLE 5.43 Indicators and indexes of fascism or right-wing authoritarianism, OECD countries (*cont.*)

Country	21	22	23	24	25	26	27	28	29	30	31
Lithuania	50.35	81.05	94.94	76.51	33.33	58.14	32.96	77	51.11	92.9	92.9
Luxembourg	44.28	66.67	62.36	70.47	16.67	53.49	40.72	45	27.17	68.2	41.0
Mexico	40.96	100	93.26	100	80	72.09	40.44	100	69.49	86.1	87.5
Netherlands	65.51	62.09	46.63	67.10	16.67	62.79	.00	51	37.27	83.6	22.4
New Zealand	56.50	76.03	61.24	83.25	33.33	58.14	54.57	66	23.20	82.7	84.1
Norway	47.39	59.26	47.19	64.76	16.67	69.77	35.46	76	22.43	50.8	33.0
Poland	27.61	63.62	57.87	84.51	33.33	53.49	35.46	82	33.32	87.3	85.3
Portugal	33.99	73.20	70.22	80.44	26.67	86.05	13.02	77	30.69	84.7	27.7
Slovak Republic	21.94	54.68	47.75	79.32	16.67	20.93	30.47	89	41.79	89.3	75.6
Slovenia	54.21	54.47	48.88	74.54	33.33	65.12	42.38	51	32.39	79.6	35.0
Spain	38.42	75.16	87.08	78.90	26.67	62.79	43.21	69	32.59	86.4	26.9
Sweden	47.39	61.44	52.25	67.95	16.67	70.00	32.13	41	20.73	34.4	10.0
Switzerland	55.70	64.27	51.12	72.85	33.33	67.44	60.39	73	46.04	85.1	50.8
Turkey	40.96	88.02	96.63	85.73	60.00	62.79	17.45	100	49.21	90.8	93.0
United Kingdom	48.26	76.47	66.85	71.97	6.67	9.30	62.60	83	39.01	76.6	74.0
United States	100	85.19	100	83.58	100	100	97.51	92	69.41	89.9	88.4

TABLE 5.43 Indicators and indexes of fascism or right-wing authoritarianism, OECD countries (cont.)

Country	32	33	34	35	36	37	38	39	40	TOTAL	INDEX
Australia	0	24	8.40	0	25.80	21	46.82	12.03	.61	1238.81	30.97
Austria	11.80	23	7.50	0	14.50	15	43.07	24.90	.61	1039.46	25.99
Belgium	14.70	24	9.30	0	14.50	16	50.54	10.54	3.03	972.23	24.31
Canada	2.90	30	7.80	0	16.34	18	43.85	28.80	3.64	1361.45	34.04
Chile	8.80	37	15.90	0	31.91	28	60.95	10.04	9.09	1697.54	42.44
Czech Republic	14.70	31	10.80	0	29.62	21	45.17	10.37	.61	1161.90	29.05
Denmark	8.80	14	7.60	0	10.84	8	43.34	8.22	1.21	793.96	19.85
Estonia	14.70	20	9.80	0	27.79	18	56.76	4.15	0	1271.70	31.79
Finland	2.90	19	7.30	0	8.09	9	47.43	26.89	1.21	924.39	23.11
France	14.70	29	13.10	0	15.88	27	65.20	16.27	2.42	1169.39	29.23
Germany	5.90	15	7.50	0	11.76	15	50.47	16.27	.61	1051.81	26.30
Greece	14.70	41	19.30	0	16.18	35	63.41	14.61	1.82	1572.91	39.32
Hungary	29.40	55	19.60	0	25.50	42	52.67	1.24	.61	1465.92	36.65
Iceland	2.90	15	9.20	0	5.65	9	36.42	26.31	1.82	805.87	20.15
Ireland	0	27	110	0	11.30	21	46.45	5.98	2.42	1230.05	30.75
Israel	41.20	41	230	0	35.73	35	93.75	5.56	3.64	1868.88	46.72
Italy	20.60	44	13.30	0	13.74	27	57.09	11.95	1.82	1355.28	33.88
Japan	11.80	21	130	0	5.95	23	45.95	.25	0	1316.27	32.91
Korea South	17.60	24	11.90	100	16.18	27	61.79	.17	0	1715.44	42.89
Latvia	11.80	30	11.50	0	27.33	18	57.43	8.71	1.82	1438.07	35.95
Lithuania	8.80	30	12.40	0	33.74	18	57.60	11.29	2.42	1489.19	37.23
Luxembourg	2.90	24	7.40	0	16.03	16	50.54	15.68	1.21	1007.13	25.18

TABLE 5.43 Indicators and indexes of fascism or right-wing authoritarianism, OECD countries (*cont.*)

Country	32	33	34	35	36	37	38	39	40	TOTAL	INDEX
Mexico	38.20	61	36.20	0	24.12	48	86.89	10.71	100	2315.54	57.89
Netherlands	8.80	15	7.20	0	9.62	16	51.62	2.16	.61	977.19	24.43
New Zealand	0	22	7.30	0	30.38	19	40.47	21.83	1.21	1193.12	29.83
Norway	2.90	15	7.40	0	9.16	9	50.54	23.90	.61	932.90	23.32
Poland	26.50	37	16.80	0	28.85	36	55.98	2.07	0	1554.81	38.87
Portugal	8.80	32	9.80	0	16.79	22	42.13	17.68	1.21	1342.48	33.56
Slovak Republic	20.60	31	14.60	0	29.31	21	52.97	5.39	1.82	1384.61	34.62
Slovenia	17.60	34	12.20	0	10.53	25	46.25	12.95	0	1201.23	30.03
Spain	11.80	33	13.10	0	18.93	21	57.84	6.22	.61	1325.52	33.14
Sweden	5.90	18	5.50	0	9.31	13	49.97	19.17	2.42	873.37	21.83
Switzerland	8.80	15	7.60	0	12.21	15	46.15	22.90	1.21	1145.70	28.64
Turkey	76.50	56	42.60	0	52.52	68	1000	13.69	4.85	2475.89	61.90
United Kingdom	8.80	29	11.50	0	20.46	21	59.80	3.82	0	1209.78	30.24
United States	17.60	38	12.80	100	100	28	77.94	100	20.61	2525.11	63.13

1. power constraints negative, 2. rule of law negative, 3. political stability negative and presence of violence, 4. control of corruption negative, 5. open government negative, 6. voting turnout negative, 7. electoral freedom and political pluralism negative, 8. political voice negative, 9. media freedom negative, 10. imprisonment score, 11. death sentences and executions score, 12. other political terror score, 13. military expenditure score 14. art and culture government spending negative, 15. beliefs in 'Satan', 16. opposition to evolution, 17. 'God' beliefs, 18. high importance of religion in life, 19. church attendance, 20. daily prayer 21. wealth concentration score, 22. income inequality score, 23. poverty score, 24. annual work hours score, 25. paid vacation negative, 26. paid paternity leave negative, 27. employment protection negative, 28. unemployment benefits negative, 29. social protection and economic security negative, 30. labor union density negative, 31. collective bargaining coverage negative 32. civil liberties negative, 33. civil justice negative, 34. individual liberty negative, 35. the death penalty for drug offenses, 36. incarceration for sins-as-crimes, 37. fundamental human rights negative, 38. peace negative, 39. gun ownership score, 40. murders by guns score

TABLE 5.44 Ranking by fascism or right-wing authoritarianism aggregate indexes, OECD countries

Ranking	Country	Aggregate index
1	United States	63.13
2	Turkey	61.90
3	Mexico	57.89
4	Israel	46.72
5	South Korea	42.89
6	Chile	42.44
7	Greece	39.32
8	Poland	38.87
9	Lithuania	37.23
10	Hungary	36.65
11	Latvia	35.95
12	Slovak Republic	34.62
13	Canada	34.04
14	Italy	33.88
15	Portugal	33.56
16	Spain	33.14
17	Japan	32.91
18	Estonia	31.79
19	Australia	30.97
20	Ireland	30.75
21	United Kingdom	30.24
22	Slovenia	30.03
23	New Zealand	29.83
24	France	29.23
25	Czech Republic	29.05
26	Switzerland	28.64
27	Germany	26.30
28	Austria	25.99
29	Luxembourg	25.18
30	Netherlands	24.43
31	Belgium	24.31
32	Norway	23.32
33	Finland	23.11
34	Sweden	21.83
35	Iceland	20.15
36	Denmark	19.85

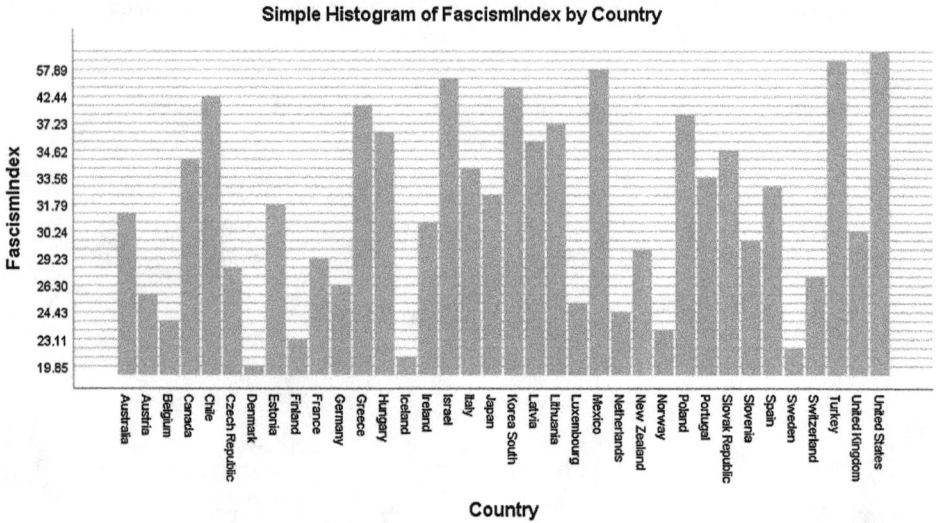

FIGURE 5.2   Fascism or right-wing authoritarianism aggregate indexes, OECD countries

Next, based on the previous table, Table 5.44 ranks OECD countries from 1 to 36 by their fascism or right-wing authoritarianism aggregate indexes thus calculated (which Figure 5.2 illustrates). Overall, these indexes while having the 0–100 possible range span from just under 20 to over 60, thus being higher than 0 and lower than 100.

Conversely, as a complement, Table 5.45 ranks OECD countries from 1 to 36 by their non-fascism or liberal democracy aggregate indexes (which Figure 5.3 represents).

Liberal democracy aggregate indexes are derived by subtracting fascism or right-wing authoritarianism indexes from 100 as the possible maximum, with the differential serving as the measure or approximation of non-fascism or liberal democracy among OECD countries. Likewise, such indexes have the same 0–100 possible range and actually move from around 37 to just over 80 and so are higher than 0 and lower than 100.

Table 5.44 suggests the following observations. First and foremost, the following ten OECD countries feature the highest fascism or right-wing authoritarianism indexes in a descending order: 1. United States (63.13), 2. Turkey (61.90), 3. Mexico (57.89), 4. Israel (46.72), 5. South Korea (42.89), 6. Chile (42.44), 7. Greece (39.32), 8. Poland (38.87), 9. Lithuania (37.23), and 10. Hungary (36.65). Especially, the first three countries' indexes are markedly higher than those of the rest from this group.

Most notably, the US's index is the highest among all OECD countries and to that extent provides suggestive, even if not definitive, evidence that fascism and more broadly conservative, right-wing authoritarianism rises in America

TABLE 5.45 Ranking by non-fascism or liberal democracy aggregate indexes, OECD countries

Ranking	Country	Aggregate index[a]
1	Denmark	80.15
2	Iceland	79.85
3	Sweden	78.17
4	Finland	76.89
5	Norway	76.68
6	Belgium	75.69
7	Netherlands	75.57
8	Luxembourg	74.82
9	Austria	74.01
10	Germany	73.70
11	Switzerland	71.36
12	Czech Republic	70.95
13	France	70.77
14	New Zealand	70.17
15	Slovenia	69.97
16	United Kingdom	69.76
17	Ireland	69.25
18	Australia	69.03
19	Estonia	68.21
20	Japan	67.09
21	Spain	66.86
22	Portugal	66.44
23	Italy	66.12
24	Canada	65.96
25	Slovak Republic	65.38
26	Latvia	64.05
27	Hungary	63.35
28	Lithuania	62.77
29	Poland	61.13
30	Greece	60.68
31	Chile	57.56
32	South Korea	57.11
33	Israel	53.28
34	Mexico	42.11
35	Turkey	38.10
36	United States	36.87

a 100 – Fascism or right-wing authoritarianism index

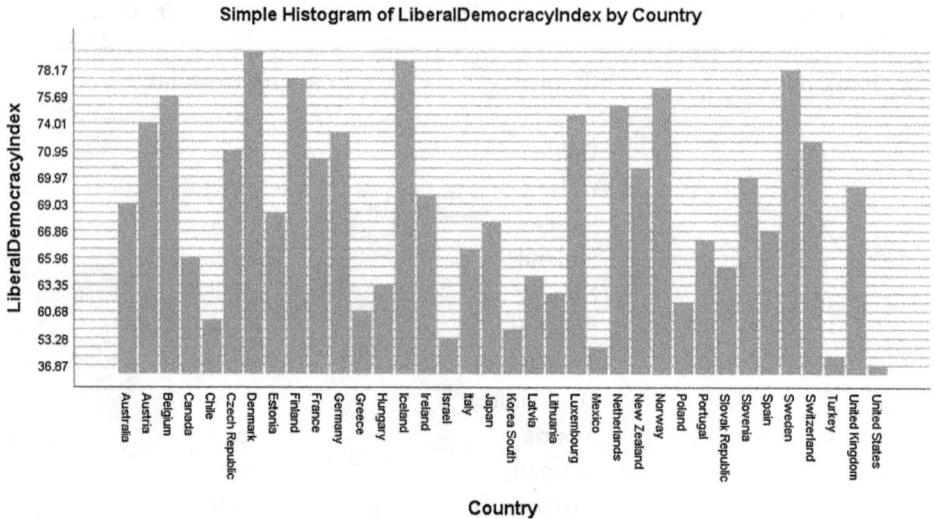

Simple Histogram of LiberalDemocracyIndex by Country

FIGURE 5.3   Non-fascism or liberal democracy aggregate indexes, OECD countries

post-2016 and even before, as since the 1980s with the resurgence of authoritarian conservatism from anti-liberal Reaganism to the proto-fascist Tea Party. The US's highest index is the result and reflection of its highest and generally high ranking on virtually all 40 indicators and proxies of fascism. First, the US ranks the highest or among the highest on such political indicators and proxies of fascism or conservative authoritarianism as voting rights suppression, mass imprisonment, widespread death sentences and executions, other political terror, and high military expenditure indicating strong militarism. Second, the US ranks the highest or so on certain cultural indicators and proxies of fascism or conservative authoritarianism, including devaluation of and low public spending on the arts and culture, mass religious superstitions like the pervasive belief in 'Satan' and by implication 'witches', anti-science through rejection of biological evolution, and extreme and coercive religiosity via high frequency of daily prayer. Third, the US ranks the highest or comparatively high on most economic indicators and proxies of fascism or conservative authoritarianism from the wealth share of the top one percent of the population (and low median net wealth), the Gini coefficient of income distribution and the general poverty rate to no paid vacations, no paid paternity leave, weak employment protection, low unemployment benefits, weak social protection and economic security, union suppression, and collective bargaining suppression. Fourth, the US ranks the highest on various civil-society Indicators and proxies of fascism or conservative authoritarianism, such as the application of the death penalty for drug offenses, mass incarceration for sins-as-crimes though massive imprisonment for drug offenses, weak human rights to life, peace, and safety, mass and unrestricted gun ownership, and widespread murders by guns. Conversely, its highest index is the effect and expression of that the post-2016 and even post-1980 US hardly and rarely ranks the lowest and generally low on these indicators and proxies of fascism or right-wing authoritarianism.

Taken together, the US's highest index reflecting its highest/high ranking on the above 40 components is indicative and telling—fascism or right-wing authoritarianism evidently rises and advances in post-2016 America and even probably earlier. Furthermore, the index indicates that fascism or right-wing authoritarianism emerges and expands more manifestly and intensively in post-2016 America than in any other OECD countries and thus Western and comparable societies, including those, from Turkey to Poland and Hungary,[19] where it also obviously does so[20]

Second, these OECD countries display intermediate fascism or right-wing authoritarianism indexes in a descending sequence: 11. Latvia (35.95), 12. Slovak Republic (34.62), 13. Canada (34.04), 14. Italy (33.88), 15. Portugal (33.56), 16. Spain (33.14), 17. Japan (32.91), 18. Estonia (31.79), 19. Australia (30.97), 20. Ireland (30.75), 21. United Kingdom (30.24), 22. Slovenia (30.03), 23. New Zealand (29.83), 24. France (29.23), 25. Czech Republic (29.05), and 26. Switzerland (28.64). Overall, some of these countries' indexes (e.g., ranked 11–18) seem closer to those of the first group than the others (especially 24–26 ranks). For example, Canada's perhaps surprisingly comparatively high index reaffirms or implies that it remains more similar to the US than to continental Western Europe, especially Scandinavia. Overall, except for Canada, Anglo-Saxon countries' indexes are almost identical and cluster within a narrow range (30–31), although they may not capture fully yet right-wing authoritarian

---

19   Soehl and Karim (2021, pp. 410–11) remark that in Turkey and Hungary, Erdoğan and Orbán, respectively, exploited 'national history' and 'instrumentalized historical repertoires' in order 'to 'erode democratic institutions' in these countries. For example, in 2009 Hungary's conservative ruler reportedly stated 'we only have to win [elections] once, but then properly' to eliminate liberal-democracy and impose a fascist dictatorship based on theocratic religious tradition ('Judaeo-Christian heritage'), thus following or evoking Hitler's winning 1933 elections as the way to end democracy and establish fascism. In turn, Turkey's theocratic ruler changed in 2022 the country's centuries-old name, thus illustrating the tendency of dictators to claim that the history of the countries they rule begin and indeed end with them.

20   For historical reasons, Israel's index is to be especially interpreted as that of authoritarian conservatism or right-wing authoritarianism generally in the form of an ultra-conservative government in opposition to postwar liberal, Labor governance until the early 2000s. Turkey's index can be interpreted as that of religious authoritarianism in the form of Islamic theocracy. Mexico's, Chile's, and Poland's indexes are also interpretable as those of religious or traditional authoritarianism through Catholic theocracy or domination. In addition, Chile, Greece (in part), Lithuania, and Hungary were formerly interwar and postwar fascist or extreme-right states, while South Korea was a right-wing dictatorship for long, which shows a degree of path dependence in this regard.

tendencies in most of them, such as Australia under repressive and nativist conservative rule and post-2018 Brexit Great Britain deemed outside Western Europe in the sense of the European Union. Also, the indexes of Southern European, formerly fascist countries like Italy, Portugal and Spain tend to the almost same clustering within a small range (33–34). On the other hand, the indexes of France, Czech Republic, and Switzerland are more than twice lower than that of the US and so on.

Third, the ten OECD countries that exhibit the lowest fascism or right-wing authoritarianism indexes are in a descending listing: 27. Germany (26.30), 28. Austria (25.99), 29. Luxembourg (25.18), 30. Netherlands (24.43), 31. Belgium (24.31), 32. Norway (23.32), 33. Finland (23.11), 34. Sweden (21.83), 35. Iceland (20.15) and 36. Denmark (19.85). In particular, Scandinavian or Nordic countries show the lowest and similar indexes that cluster within a relatively narrow range (20–23); and among them especially Iceland and Denmark do so (around the 20 mark). Notably, Denmark's and Iceland's indexes are more than three times lower than that of the US. Still, even Scandinavian or Nordic countries are not completely immune to and safe from fascism and generally right-wing extremism, as recent fascist and radical-rightist tendencies and events, including terrorist attacks and threats in Norway and Sweden, show. Historically, such partial recurrence of fascism or right-wing extremism in these countries seems path-dependence on their WW pro-fascist or radical-rights regimes or movements, such as the Nazi-puppet states of Denmark and especially Norway. Therefore, Scandinavian countries are not perfect democracies due to the return and growing activity and influence of, or concessions to fascism or right-wing extremism. In addition, they are not perfect democracies because of the social prevalence and even de facto political rule of radical feminism (as in Finland[21] and Sweden) that therefore perverts Scandinavian liberalism into a feminist tool of attaining gender dominance ('empowerment') over and exclusion of males as agents and vestiges of 'patriarchy'. Judging by the pernicious effects of its growing power, radical feminism threatens to degenerate Scandinavian liberal and social democracy into a proxy new matriarchy in which one set of rules applies to and privileges women in their social activities

---

21   For example, in 2022 videos resurfaced showing a feminist Scandinavian leader partying 'wildly' (including dancing and kissing with someone not being her husband), which illustrates the immorality and licentiousness of radical feminists. Like their nominal enemies, US and other conservatives-fascists, radical feminists in Scandinavia and elsewhere get elected on false promises and moral 'purity' claims, and once in office show their true character by implementing their agenda of 'social hatred' by launching the 'war of the sexes' against the opposite sex, just as displaying immorality and licentiousness (as their 'empowerment' and 'liberation' while condemning and criminalizing the same conduct for men).

while another set applying to and disfavoring men by denouncing and criminalizing the same behaviors (including sexual ones, as with the Assange 'rape' saga) that are 'empowering' for feminists, a pattern also observed in feminist sections and forces of the US (the 'yes means yes' law in California, the 'liberal' leaders and factions in the House of Representatives etc.) and elsewhere. In sum, Scandinavia faces the double threat of fascism or right-wing extremism and militant feminism to its liberal democracy. Moreover, given its de facto political rule, militant feminism may become the curse or nemesis of Scandinavia in respect of liberal democracy so long as the proxy new matriarchy, like the old patriarchy that it replaces, can only be or eventuate in an illiberal and non-democratic regime.

In addition, Luxembourg', the Netherlands' and Belgium's indexes show similar clustering within a narrow range (24–25), thus justifying the BENELUX shorthand. Also, the indexes of Germany and Austria are almost the same (around 26) and cluster, along with that of Switzerland, within a relatively narrow range (26–29), which confirms their general social similarities.

In turn, Table 5.45 is the mirror image of Table 5.44. Thus, the top ten OECD countries having the highest fascism or right-wing authoritarianism indexes now manifest the lowest non-fascism or liberal democracy aggregate indexes and are ranked accordingly as the bottom ten (27–36) in this regard. Then, the OECD countries with intermediate fascism or right-wing authoritarianism indexes have also intermediate non-fascism or liberal democracy indexes and are ranked correspondingly, though in a reverse order (26–11). And the ten OECD countries with the lowest fascism or right-wing authoritarianism indexes now exhibit the highest non-fascism or liberal democracy aggregate indexes and are ranked consequently as the top ten (10–1).

Taken together, these results generally confirm that fascism or right-wing authoritarianism indeed rises and expands in America post-2016 through a fascist-style radical-right autocracy, as well as perhaps earlier since anti-liberal Reaganism—not to mention its model or precedent McCarthyism—and the proto-fascist Tea Party. At the minimum, they provide if not definitive, then suggestive evidence for this phenomenon in post-2016 and to some degree earlier America, at least in its conservative, unfettered-capitalist, religious and theocratic pole. This holds true in general terms, while keeping in mind that the measurement or quantification of fascism or right-wing authoritarianism, as of any qualitative social phenomena, is not an 'exact science' but an approximation or rough estimation. Moreover, in comparative terms, the results, such as the US's highest index, suggest that fascism or right-wing authoritarianism indeed exceptionally, uniquely surges and spreads in America post-2016 more likely, extensively, and intensively than in any Western and comparable societies. To that extent, such an exceptionality or uniqueness expresses the true nature and ultimate outcome of conservative-religious and related 'American exceptionalism'—fascism or right-wing authoritarianism post-2016 and since Reaganism. While evidently surging and expanding primarily in the post-2016 conservative and religious pole of America, fascism or right-wing authoritarianism does not rise apparently in Western Europe and, within the latter, definitely not in Scandinavia during this period.

To summarize, this chapter elaborates a substantive composite index or approximation of fascism and generally conservative or right-wing authoritarianism. In addition, it computes numerical aggregate indexes or approximations of fascism and generally right-wing authoritarianism for Western and comparable societies such as OECD countries. This is an exercise in the operationalization and quantification of fascism or right-wing authoritarianism that is essentially a qualitative phenomenon, and hence a tentative estimation and proximate measurement rather than an exact calculation in this respect. The substantive composite index's components include specific indicators and proxies of fascism and broader right-wing authoritarianism that are obtained from or implicit in its main elements and features from the main body of the book. For this purpose, these index components are classified into political, cultural, civil-society and economic indicators and proxies of fascism and more broadly right-wing authoritarianism. The results show that the highest aggregate indexes of fascism or right-wing authoritarianism feature the following OECD countries in a descending sequence: 1. United States, 2. Turkey, 3. Mexico, 4. Israel, 5. South Korea, 6. Chile, 7. Greece, 8. Poland, 9. Lithuania, and 10. Hungary. By contrast, the lowest aggregate indexes of fascism or right-wing authoritarianism characterize these OECD countries in a descending order: 27. Germany, 28. Austria, 29. Luxembourg, 30. Netherlands, 31. Belgium, 32. Norway, 33. Finland, 34. Sweden, 35. Iceland and 36. Denmark. The results provide suggestive evidence that fascism or right-wing authoritarianism indeed rises and advances in America post-2016 through a fascist-style radical-right autocracy and to some extent earlier since Reaganism, but not in most other Western societies, especially Western Europe and within it most notably Scandinavia. The chapter also incorporates an Appendix on the US's extreme military expenditure and its pernicious societal consequences.

4   Appendix

The extreme magnitude and far-reaching, fundamentally adverse and destructive societal consequences of the US's military expenditure requires a more extensive consideration in this context. In essence, the US's globally highest military expenditure during the rise of fascism post-2016 and generally under conservatism since Reaganism is extraordinary and prima facie pathological, essentially conforming to the pattern of what Reagan branded an 'evil empire' with reference to the Soviet Union in an apparent projection in the style of Puritans projecting their own notorious properties of brutality, cruelty, and inhumanity (as manifested in their proxy genocide of Native Americans, witch trials, persecution, and 'holy' terror) making for the 'shining city upon a hill' onto 'evil' others. This military expenditure and its perverse effects accord with the pattern of an 'evil empire' in several respects.

First, military expenditure during fascism and conservatism accords with the pattern of an 'evil empire' by being the extreme, virtually unlimited spending of societal resources, exceeding the combined amount of all the 'enemies', representing almost half of the world's total, and accelerating post-2016 (and after 2020) and since the 1980s. By such a magnitude, persistence, and acceleration, extreme military expenditure amounts to socially and economically irresponsible, reckless expending, sacrificing, and often wasting of precious societal resources, including human lives, to the end of militarism, offensive imperial war, and imperialism, epitomizing the pattern of an 'evil empire'.[22]

Further, the US's military expenditure also continues to accelerate under the US 'liberal' government and Congress after 2020 (for example, exceeding 800 billion dollars for 2022–23 and more after), thus continuing the post-2016 militarist pattern of proto-fascism and that of neo-conservative Reaganism. Overall, the US's military expenditure has accelerated by nearly 50% post-2016 reflecting

---

22   Baudrillard (1994) singles out the 'American empire' and predicts its eventual 'end' like
      that of the 'Soviet empire', Hedges (2004) alerts to the blueprint of US Christian funda-
      mentalists to expand the United States into 'a global, Christian empire', Abbott (2005)
      notes *American 'imperial wars'*, Steinmetz (2005) registers America's 'return to empire'
      during conservatism, Go (2008, 2020) identifies the 'American way' of empire, including
      the 'imperial origins of American policing' through police violence involving the 'use of
      military equipment', Wimmer and Feinstein (2010) refer to the American 'empire,' and
      Vine (2015) points to the 'American Empire Project' with its nearly 800 foreign military
      bases in 70 countries harming both America and the countries where they are stationed.
      Djelic and Quack (2018, p. 127) refer to the 'US version of empire' and suggest that it causes
      Enlightenment-rooted globalization to degenerate into 'Americanization or the ideolog-
      ical superstructure of a new form of (neoliberal) capitalist plunder and appropriation
      with a broad geographical reach.' Most of these accounts hence suggest that these impe-
      rial tendencies conform to the model of an 'evil empire' of domestic and global repres-
      sion, militarism, and wars of aggression. They imply that if the Soviet Union was Reagan's
      'evil empire' during the Cold War, the US became its equivalent in the 1990s, epitomiz-
      ing the absolute corruption of absolute power in inter-state terms by remaining a single
      superpower, dominating the 'new world order', and launching unliteral offensive wars or
      under NATO's umbrella from its attack on Yugoslavia to its invasion of Iraq.

extreme militarism, starting another arms race with its enemies China, Russia, and others, and instigating its acceleration within NATO. This suggests that even many American 'liberals' tend to be militaristic, emulating 'tough on defense' conservatives and fascists, while being intoxicated with or deluded by Americanism's religiously grounded 'manifest destiny', 'Divine mission' to rule the world, and 'superior nation' pretensions as the prime source of American militarism, offensive wars, and imperialism. (America's 'manifest destiny' as the 'Divine' right to 'lead' the world seems a global extension of the compromised 'Divine rights' of kings. So, if one wonders what the ground for America's ruling or leading the world is, US conservatives and fascists, if not most Americans, claim that it is a 'Divine right', God's determined 'manifest destiny', simply 'plan', and national 'superiority'.) After all, the post-2020 incumbent of the Presidency has been a perennial emanation of Cold-War bellicosity, militarism, and imperialism, ardently seeking to expand NATO beyond its initial space toward Eastern Europe and Russia's borders and fervently supporting all actual and possible offensive imperial wars or attacks, including those against Yugoslavia, Afghanistan, Iraq, Libya, Syria, etc. Fittingly, Congress, especially the Senate, in a show of 'bipartisanship' matches and often surpasses such extreme presidential militarism, bellicosity, and imperialism, as it shows from its near-unanimous support for various wars of aggression from the Vietnam War to the '2003 invasion of Iraq'[23] and beyond. Overall, it appears that supremacist 'manifest destiny' Americanism and its consequent militarism, offensive war, and imperialism afflict and literally intoxicate or delude not only post-2016 fascists, Reaganites, and other neo-conservatives, but also, though perhaps to a lower degree, many nominal American 'liberals', aside from few exceptions or perhaps a single salient exception (for example, senator Sanders). And a government/society intoxicated or deluded by the religious idea of 'manifest destiny' qua the 'Divine mission' to rule ('lead') the world and of national superiority a la exceptionalism in the presence of resistance by other societies and nuclear weapons can only reach MAD—the madness of self-destruction induced by religion and nationalism. In this respect, the US government under conservatism by wars of aggression and NATO's expansion threatens more to kill Americans, and not only foreigners, than do any defined foreign 'enemies' from Iran and North Korea to China and Russia.

Notably, the US's extreme military expenditure epitomizes the pattern of an 'evil empire' in that the largest and accelerating military expenditure coexists

---

23   Caldara and Iacoviello (2022) point to the US '2003 invasion of Iraq' as by definition a war of aggression and generally a geopolitical risk.

with and enfolds together with the chronic and highest poverty rate during fascism and conservatism, with almost one fifth of Americans being poor. Thus, the US government during fascism's rise post-2016 and under conservatism since Reaganism indulges in massive and accelerating military expenditure while keeping nearly one fifth of the population in poverty, simply both recklessly expending societal resources for this non-civilian purpose and impoverishing large sections of society, which epitomizes the pattern of an 'evil empire'. As Reagan suggested for the Soviet Union, what defines an 'evil empire' is this dual tendency—near-unlimited and accelerating military expenditure combined with pervasive, chronic poverty in society.

Second, the US's largest and growing military expenditure under fascism and conservatism post-2016 and since the 1980s accords with the pattern of an 'evil empire' by operating primarily in the service of aggressive militarism, bellicosity, and offensive war rather than peace—or 'peace as war'—'defense', and 'national security'. In essence, such military expenditure is the instrument of militarist expansion, including the military-industrial complex as the foremost agent of aggressive militarism, and the sinister tool and lethal weapon of eternal ('forever') and offensive wars in the function of imperialism, simply the US imperial war machine, and far from being a means of peace and peaceful conflict resolution between societies. In this sense, it reappears and functions as (aggressive) war expenditure—an older term that is more reflective and sincere of its goal—thus offense spending rather than 'defense spending' as a cynical misnomer or naive euphemism. As Reagan implied for the Soviet Union, what typifies an 'evil empire' is exactly military expenditure for the sake of offensive imperial war and generally in the function of aggressive militarism, such as the military-industrial complex and bellicosity, thus making it offense rather than 'defense spending'.

The US's military expenditure especially under conservatism since WW II, including fascism post-2016, invariantly connects with aggressive militarism, bellicosity, and wars of aggression, from Vietnam[24] as the probably most

---

24   Dell and Querubin (2018, p. 707) recount that in Vietnam 'elections were not held, in part because the United States concluded that the communist revolutionary hero Ho Chi Minh would be elected by a landslide [vs.] the US-backed dictator Ngo Dinh Diem.' Further, Dell and Querubin (2018, p. 708) observe that the 'costs of the conflict in Vietnamese lives were staggering [e.g.] more than 3 million total deaths between 1954 and 1975, including over 2 million civilian deaths (or estimated) death toll of 3.8 million. More firepower was unleashed during the Vietnam War than during any other conflict in human history. More than twice as many tons of explosives were dropped as during World War II.' Civilian and total deaths during the 2003 US invasion and persistent occupation of Iraq are also often estimated to be in millions, judging by various reports. For example, Roger Waters (cited

cruel, deceptive, and inhumane war launched by an invading state in postwar times through the unlawful and unprovoked aggression, via NATO's attack, on Yugoslavia to the also unprovoked invasion and continuing occupation of Iraq. These wars of aggression lavishly financed by unrestrained military expenditure and sustained by the gigantic military-industrial complex invent various deceptions, fabrications, and falsehoods for their justification, for example, the fictitious 'attack' on US forces for the Vietnam War, the fabricated 'massacre' for the attack on Yugoslavia, the 'weapons of mass destruction' falsehood for the invasion of Iraq. They hence express conservatism's and Puritanism's mix of deception, hypocrisy, and treachery[25] that was also used during the wars of extermination against and the resulting proxy-genocide of Native Americans.

The preceding hence accords with the model of an 'evil' empire, revealing Puritan-style religious and conservative 'bipartisan' atrocity and cruelty driven by the 'manifest destiny' and 'master nation' tenets of Americanism that intoxicates or deludes and induces the government and presidents into offensive wars and imperial conquest and domination. The US government/military never apologizes or repents for these millions of civilian deaths it caused in the Vietnam War and other offensive imperial wars, including those during and after the Cold War from Grenada and Panama to Yugoslavia and Iraq, but remains self-righteous taking a 'high moral ground' versus its 'enemies', showing the obstinate refusal to admit atrocities and the unparalleled lack of conscience or of remorse among its presidents, Congress, generals, etc. This evokes the notorious unrepentance and self-righteousness of Puritanism and its theocracy in early America while perpetrating the most egregious acts of mass murder, violence, and terror from the near-genocide of Native Americans to persecution, torture, and witch-trials.

---

in Young 2022) recalls that the US military did 'killa million people in 2013' during its Iraq invasion and occupation starting in 2003.

25   19th-century US conservative Emerson admits that 'Conservatism tends to universal seeming and treachery.' Also, Hume, Weber, Sombart, Mencken, and many others diagnose the strong hypocrisy of Puritanism as the extant source and inspiration of American conservatism, including Reaganism that exalts Puritan proto-fascist (in the depiction of Merton 1939) and so proto-totalitarian theocracy as the 'shining city upon a hill', just as effectively equalizing fascism and anti-fascism by Reagan's visiting and honoring the Nazi cemetery in Germany. This bizarre act perhaps served as an impetus or precedent for the German government after the reunification to continue the Nazi 'divide and rule' policy especially in the Balkans, as its first-ever postwar military action, its participation in the US/NATO's lawless, UN-unapproved attack on its WW II enemy Yugoslavia to protect a terrorist secessionist formation shows.

In this sense, extreme military expenditure typically constitutes aggressive war expenditure, thus offense spending, rather than 'defense spending' insofar as the US, as well as NATO, wages no defensive wars but solely offensive imperial ones via aggressions, invasions, and occupations from Vietnam to Iraq, as after WW II and 1812. (In this context and not necessarily in others, the reaction to the 1941 Pearl Harbor attack would qualify less as homeland defense than as a distant conflict between two colonial or imperial powers insofar as the US conquered and ruled Hawaii as a colony far away from its mainland, let alone the original 13 states of the Revolution multiplying into 50 through wars of aggression against, imperial conquest of Native American, Mexican, and other lands and territories, and expulsion and elimination of their original inhabitants.)

Military expenditure post-2016 following Reaganism continues and intensifies in functioning as the instrument and predictor of militarism, bellicosity, offensive war, and imperial conquest or domination, thus epitomizing the pattern of an 'evil empire.' This trend includes increasing military expenditure for the further proliferation of US military bases through the entire globe, NATO's expansion and movement toward the borders of and confrontation with or provocation of Russia and possibly China, formation of other aggressive NATO-style alliances in Asia and South America, and so on. These tendencies associated with extreme military expenditure result in the global experience or perception, judging by many international surveys, of America during fascism post-2016 and conservatism since Reaganism as the major global warlike force and the main threat to world peace and human survival.

For illustration, regarding the formation of aggressive NATO-style alliances, just as the postwar US leadership started the Cold War against the Soviet Union on a fantastical or imagined 'threat', the post-2016 proto-fascist government effectively launched such a war against China and contemplated attacking the latter by nuclear weapons (as the military leaders revealed). Further, rather than ending or moderating such an aggressive posture, the post-2020 militaristic and imperialist government effectively continued, codified, and elaborated the Cold War against China, as well as restarted that against Russia. For illustration, this government presided by a perennial and proven Cold Warrior formed economic and military alliances seeking to isolate and confront China, just as mostly continuing the trade war of its radical-right predecessor by keeping rather than eliminating anti-Chinese tariffs and even taking, together with a nationalist and imperialist Congress a further series of anti-Chinese hysterical measures of anti-free trade protectionism (e.g., the 2022 CHIPS Act subsidizing and otherwise favoring domestic semiconductor-production, etc.) in a display of nativist 'buy American' hysteria, invoking the rationale that this

country undermines the 'rules-based' international order. This is a curious and
mainly dubious rationale for forming such alliances against a country in several respects. First, the US government continues to deny the legitimacy of the
International Criminal Court—with its post-2016 extreme-right regime seeking to arrest its members!—as an epitome of such a 'rules-based' international
order on the ground that American solders as members of (to paraphrase
F. D. Roosevelt's expression 'master race' referring to Nazism) the 'master' and
'superior' nation do not commit war crimes and cannot be judged by an non-
American court. By so doing, it flagrantly subverts the 'rules-based' international order that incorporates as its essential component such judicial institutions dealing with war crimes and criminals. Second, the US government has
attacked, invaded, and occupied more countries than any other great power,
including the Soviet Union/Russia and China, both during and after the Cold
War, and thus violated the UN prohibition rule in regard with wars of aggression. For example, by launching wars of aggression against multiple states
from Vietnam through Granada and Panama to Yugoslavia[26] and Iraq—the

---

26   Bauman (2001, p. 209) agrees with the suggestion that because of the US/NATO unlawful,
      unprovoked, and indiscriminate bombardment of Yugoslavia the International Tribunal
      'loses its credibility if, following the same criteria, it refrains from the inculpation of
      Clinton and Blair [as war criminals] and all those who violated simultaneously all forms
      of decency and the laws of war'. The US/NATO's attack on Yugoslavia thus was both an
      illegal war of aggression by the UN-definition and an unprovoked attack. Yugoslavia did
      not and could not threaten or provoke the US/NATO by responding to violent secession.
      Iraq did not threaten or provoke the US and yet the latter used the fabrication of the
      'weapons of mass destruction' as an 'imminent threat' to invade in 2003 and occupy this
      country still about 20 years later. Bauman (2001, p. 209) adds that the same standards
      would have resulted in a 'charge of aggression [or illegitimate violence] to be raised
      against NATO forces' for their bombardment of Yugoslavia. Bauman (2001, p. 217) con-
      cludes alerting to the US-initiated 'brand-new global wars' that perpetrate 'violent acts'
      and invokes the Gulf War and the NATO Kosovo campaign as the 'most seminal examples.'
      In terms of international law, the difference is that the 1991 Gulf War had the UN man-
      date, and the NATO Kosovo campaign did not and so was illegitimate, a form of interstate
      terrorism or of war of aggression. But even during the Gulf War, the US/NATO abused the
      UN mandate allowing only liberation of Kuwait and not an attack on Iraq, by attacking
      the latter, including bombarding civilian facilities and killing civilians like children and
      women. For example, Schaeffer-Duffy (2022) relates that on February 13, 1991, 'without
      warning, the US dropped two laser-guided bombs onto Baghdad's Amiriyah shelter killing
      408 people, mostly women and children, despite the fact that the building was clearly
      marked as a civilian shelter.' It hence resumed, after the Vietnam War, the invasions of
      Grenada, Panama, etc., the pattern of violating and breaking down, as with the bom-
      bardment of Yugoslavia, the UN-based legal order and generally international law, and
      showing the absolute corruption of absolute military power in global terms. And while
      violating these norms and laws, it forces or calls on other countries, especially its defined

last two without and indeed in open defiance to a UN authorization—the US government has blatantly and unrepentantly violated this rule and thus grossly subverted the 'rules-based' international order. One can list a myriad of additional examples of the US government violating the 'rules-based' international order to yield the inference that no other state or great power has probably violated and undermined more the latter at least after the end of the Cold War, reaffirming the 'law' that 'absolute power corrupts absolutely' not only its holders versus groups within society but also against other societies in the world setting.

And when the US government observes the 'rules-based' international order, it typically imposes and applies its own national rules, mostly double standards, one standard applied to and favoring itself and its allies within NATO and beyond, and another to and disfavoring targeted enemies like China, Russia, and others, conforming to the Reagan model of an 'evil empire.' As an example of such double standards, the US government condones or ignores Turkey's attempted genocide or effective massacre of Kurds, including killing them outside its borders and invading other countries (Syria, etc.) for that purpose, because this is an 'ally' within NATO but attacked, on grounds of 'human rights violations', Yugoslavia when the latter responded to secession and terrorism in its Kosovo province, attacking it in alliance with an 'ethnic terrorist army'. For example, NATO's Scandinavian Secretary General stated that Turkey's genocidal campaign against (construed as 'concerns' about 'terrorist') Kurds in and outside Turkey is 'legitimate.' And while NATO's leadership officially condones and legitimizes the genocide or massacre one of its member states perpetrates against non-members, NATO attacked in 1999 without and in defiance of a UN-authorization Yugoslavia in its response to a secessionist-terrorist insurrection on the ground of 'human rights violations' and Secretary General's own Scandinavia region (e.g., Finland, Sweden[27]) give

---

adversaries like China, Russia, and others, to adhere to the 'rules-based' international order. The US's and generally the West's insistence on other countries to adhere to the 'rules-based' international order is a vestige of colonialism and a display of imperialism so long as these rules are colonial or imperial creations of such Western 'great powers.' Moreover, the US and the West overall is the principal violator, always with impunity, of and deviant from a 'rules-based' international order and thus its own norms of conduct through imperial aggressive wars from Vietnam to Iraq violating the UN's prohibition and many other lawless acts against other countries expressing American imperialism and Western neocolonialism.

27   Eventually, Finland and Sweden consented to Turkey's demands for revoking their protection of Kurds just to become NATO's members and thus effectively approved of the Turkish government's genocide of this ethic group for the sake of joining this militarist and bellicose alliance, just as do the US and NATO.

protection to Turkish Kurds and thus acknowledge their being subjected to a genocidal treatment or state terror. This demonstrates that NATO's leadership is willing to sacrifice the lives, let alone human rights, of non-member entities like Kurds to its militaristic cohesion, persistence, and expansion, in this case, keeping and pleasing Turkey within this military alliance, which reveals its utter inhumanity and immorality. It also shows that NATO's non-American Secretary Generals, including those from supposedly pacifist Scandinavia (Denmark, Norway), are simply figure heads, servile puppets of the US government, just as most of its members are (as a French President protested) 'vassal states'[28] in relation to America.

At this juncture, implementing the 'manifest destiny' doctrine of a 'Divine mission' to rule ('lead') the world or acting as if it were the UN itself, the US government indulges in the practice of designating countries that resist American imperialism as 'sponsors of terrorism,' yet a closer look as its own actions reveals a different story. It reveals that on account of its own actions the US government especislly under conservative control counterfactually, if it were objective and unbiased (an impossibility theorem), would designate itself as the main global 'sponsor of terrorism.' First, the US government sponsors and arms various counter-state terrorist groups from Islamic terrorists in Afghanistan (including Al-Qaeda and Osama Bin Laden) to those involved in the former Yugoslavia's civil wars and secessions (Bosnia, Kosovo, Macedonia). The probably most egregious example is its sponsorship of Kosovo Liberation Army (a descendent of a WW II Nazi ally) which US secretary of state initially described as an 'ethnic terrorist army', with the US military/NATO serving as the air force of these terrorists during its 1999 bombing campaign against Yugoslavia. (The 2001 NATO secretary general also depicted an extension of Kosovo Liberation Army in Macedonia as terrorists before they miraculously became 'freedom fighters' a la Bin Laden et al.

28   For example, the British government's decision to extradite the WikiLeaks founder to the United States because of exposing the US military's atrocities during its invasions and occupations of Afghanistan and Iraq demonstrates that Great Britain approaches a vasal state in relation to America ('special relations') while both 'democratic' governments blatantly violating free speech and basic human rights in the function of shared militarism, imperialism, and aggressive war. This confirms that virtually all NATO members (except for France and partly Turkey) from Eastern and Southern Europe to Germany and most of Western and Northern Europe have become in various degrees and ways vassal states relative to America. This reveals another rationale for America's formation, expansion, and fervent defense of NATO—making its members dependent, puppet states, just as the Warsaw Pact states were the satellites of the Soviet Union. No wonder, the US continues to fervently defend NATO even if the latter is not necessary and even is redundant for America's national security but indispensable for its imperial drive and lost its original justification after the disbanding of the Warsaw Pact and the end of the Soviet Union.

in Afghanistan and this military alliance saved them from defeat and oblivion by the Macedonia army.) So, American imperialism allied with and used this group for its own end of expansion and fantasy war against Russia (the 1999 US secretary of state reportedly proclaimed the usefulness of such 'an ethnic terrorist army' for America), just as Nazi Germany did by sending the ancestors of this group to the Russian front, while these neo-Nazis availed of the US/NATO to attain their goal of secession, ethnic cleansing, and murder. Overall, American imperialism uses not only NATO as its tool and brute force, but also, in a display of the amoral Machiavellian use of any means, counter-state terrorist fascist or right-wing groups for its end of expansion and global domination, from Afghanistan and Kosovo to in part Ukraine. This example of the US military/NATO allying with a 'terrorist army' as 'brothers in arms' deserves to be induced in the hall of infamy of American imperialism, though it faces a myriad of worthy competitors from the proxy-genocide of Native Americans to the unparalleled atrocities during the Vietnam War.

Second, the US government sponsors, arms, even installs, and sustains various dictatorial governments that are allies and perpetrate state terrorism from Iran during the 1950s-70s through Greece, South Korea, and Taiwan under military dictatorships, Chile's under Pinochet and the rest of Latin America ruled by fascist or rightist dictators to Saudi Arabia and other Islamic theocracies and neo-fascist or right-wing and theocratic regimes in Croatia, Kosovo, Hungary, Poland, Ukraine (post-2014), etc. Finally and most notably, the US government tends to act as the leading global agent of terrorism in the sense of inter-state terror by launching, more than any other great power, including Reagan's Soviet 'evil empire', wars of aggression that are by UN rules illegal state actions against other sovereign states defining terrorism at this level, of which the Vietnam War and 2003 Iraq War are only most notorious and brutal examples in a long-standing and systematic series. Taken together, the US government on account of its military and other actions objectively belongs and, indeed if unbiased, should designate itself among 'sponsors of terrorism' and even agents of inter-state terror via aggressive wars or military interventions as the favorite pastime of American imperialism and militarism.

Lastly, just as the Cold War against the Soviet Union threatened to end with MAD, so the US government restarting it and launching it against China may produce the same outcome by degenerating and escalating into a hot, real war which, as the American military leadership admits, no nation can win, and all nations will be mutually destroyed. This confirms that American 'bipartisan' militarism/imperialism and its agents like Presidents and Congress intoxicated and driven to the no-return point of MAD by 'manifest destiny' and supremacist Americanism is the major threat to world peace and the survival of civilization, thus ultimately of America and the life of Americans.

Third and relatedly, the largest and accelerating military expenditure under conservatism since the 1980s and fascism post-2016 conforms with the pattern of an 'evil empire' by being mostly in the function of imperialism or neocolonialism, American-style—imperial expansion and domination as 'freedom' (after Weber's 'pure hypocrisy of Americanism'). This extreme military expenditure essentially serves to build, maintain, and expand an American empire through imperial conquest, subjugation, or neo-colonial economic, technological, and other dependency,[29] including military bases throughout the whole world and aggressive and expansionist alliances like NATO and others, and suppressing or violating the independence and sovereignty of smaller societies. The US government during fascism and conservatism suppresses or violates the right to independence and sovereignty of countries and regions from Latin America as its 'backyard' that it can force into colonial-style subjection or neocolonial dependence of puppet states or banana republics through Asia and the Middle East (e.g., Iraq) to Europe, including Germany, Italy, Greece, and others, a tendency also visible after WW II and before since the invasions and conquests of Native American and Mexican territories.

In this connection, the proxy-genocide, dispossession, and expulsion of Native Americans of their lands and the invasion and conquest of Mexican territories from Texas to California qualify as acts of colonialism or imperial expansion expanding, together with the purchases of Alaska and Louisiana, nearly

---

29   Berger et al. (2013, p. 866) find that 'IMF conditionality is correlated with whether countries vote in-line with the US in the UN General Assembly. [Also] the World Bank's structural adjustment conditions are less stringent for countries whose voting in the UN is more aligned with the US. [And] when countries have a seat on the UN security council they receive more foreign aid from the US.' This appears as the overt attempt of the US government to establish and maintain the neo-colonial economic, technological, and related dependency of smaller, weaker nations by abusing the original mission and purpose of global financial institutions and the UN overall, thus subverting its norms and international law and order and creating chaos or disorder in which American and generally Western military 'might is right' reminiscent of barbarism. This subversion of UN norms exposes the American and generally Western insistence on countries adhering to an 'rules-based' international order as (what Weber calls) the Puritan-style 'pure hypocrisy of Americanism'—the main violator of this code extols it and forces or calls on others to abide by it in a standard hypocritical pattern of vice commending virtue. And if/when the US/West really adheres to an 'rules-based' international order, this is its imperial or neocolonial creation that it imposes on other weaker countries, especially vassal states within NATO and dependent and other entities or banana republics in South America and elsewhere.

four-fold the US's size from the original 13 states during the Revolution and Constitution. They qualify as what is often described as internal colonialism or continental imperialism because of, first, violating the sovereignty and territorial integrity of established tribal societies and of a post-colonial independent state, respectively, and second, resorting to massive and systematic violence such as wars of aggression and occupation in doing so. Historically, the violent conquest of Native Americans' lands that was driven by the claim to 'manifest destiny' and of the invasion and capture of Mexican territories[30] also rationalized by religious nationalism constitutes the root, inspiration, and precedent of later and present American conservative-religious imperialism and militarism moving from, and likely motivated by the success of, its internal form to first South America and eventually the entire world, as during postwar times. It appears that by its internal colonialism starting with the proxy-genocide and dispossession of Native Americans, the US conservative-theocratic government has acquired, to paraphrase Veblen, the trained capacity to engage in imperialism on an extended regional and eventually global scale. Conversely, by such internal colonialism, it has acquired Veblen's diagnosed 'trained incapacity' to respect the independence of other societies from Latin America to Asia and much of Europe in blatant violation of the aim of the American Revolution. In passing, American conservative conservative-religious imperialism differs from traditional European, including British, French, and Spanish, colonialism in that it does not usually engage in direct rule and management of its imperial outposts but instead relies on creating puppet or vasal 'independent' states from South America and Asia to Eastern and parts of Western Europe within NATO that are subservient to the US government, thus achieving effectively the same end of control and subjugation of colonies by covert, duplicitous means. In so doing, American conservative conservative-religious imperialism resembles, if not perhaps inspires but certainly precedes, Nazism that, when not directly ruling conquered nations, used the method of creating colonial puppet states as servants of the Nazi state, as in Quisling's Norway, the

---

30   Just as erasing the history of the proxy genocide of Native Americans and the dispossession of their lands, the US government and media try to erase—and so make most Americans unaware—that of its 'manifest destiny' imperial invasion, seizure, and incorporation of Mexican territories into America. Yet, various original Mexican names for the new American states and cities from California, Arizona, and Colorado to Texas, let alone New Mexico, from San Diego, Los Angeles, San Francisco, and Sacramento through Santa Fe to Corpus Cristy, El Paso, and San Antonio remain as reminders and traces of this early, second phase of American internal colonialism and imperialism, with the proxy genocide and conquest of Native Americans and their lands being the first, original stage.

'independent state' of Croatia, Albania, Bulgaria, Hungary, Slovakia, Ukraine, etc. during WW II

For instance, almost 20 years after its invasion justified by the 'weapons of mass destruction' fabrication, the US still occupies Iraq. Moreover, the Iraqi government repeatedly demanded that American troops leave Iraq but the post-2016 US government denies or ignores such demands for ending its two-decade long occupation of this country acting as if it had some natural or sacred rights to occupy it consistent with the delusion of 'manifest density' via the 'Divine mission' to rule the world (implied in the 'mission accomplished' declaration) underpinning Americanism. So, more than two centuries after the American Revolution the US government by continuing to occupy this country even after the presumed cause(s) ceased, such as the never found 'weapons of mass destruction' and the dictatorship ending in a 'regime change', grossly denies and violates its national independence and sovereignty, as it does those of many other countries, including the vasal states (a French President's term) within NATO. Prima facie, this raises the suspicion that the reasons for the US government's unprovoked and unlawful invasion and continuing occupation of Iraq were neither the phantom 'weapons of mass destruction' nor the dictatorship but imperial conquest and domination, including neocolonial extraction and plunder of natural resources.

By this and many other instances of invasion and occupation or military intervention, the US government self-contradicts the ideal of the struggle against the British empire or acts as if the right to national independence and sovereignty began and ended with the American Revolution, while making or treating others as puppet states or banana republics, such as those in Latin America and beyond.[31] Furthermore, it seeks and apparently succeeds

---

31   Berger et al. (2013, pp. 866–7) remark that covert CIA interventions installed 'US client states or puppet leaders [and] the activities used by the CIA to install and help maintain the power of specific regimes were many and varied.' Specifically, Berger et al. (2013, p. 867) enumerate these activities: the 'creation and dissemination of (often false) propaganda, usually through radio, television, newspapers, and pamphlets. They also included covert political operations, which typically consisted of the provision of funds and expertise for political campaigns. More invasive tactics included the destruction of physical infrastructure and capital, as well as covert paramilitary operations, that included the supply of arms and military equipment, direct involvement in insurgency and counterinsurgency operations, and the coordination of coups and assassinations. There are many instances in which the CIA set out to remove an existing leader and install a new leader in power. The CIA-organized coups in Iran in 1953, Guatemala in 1954, and Chile in 1973 are the most well-known examples of such cases.' A recent example or proxy of such CIA-organized coups is perhaps the US's government role in overthrowing a democratically elected government in favor of neo-Nazi or nationalist forces in Ukraine, as an apparent

to make some other countries, such as those of Eastern and central Europe, puppet or vasal states, within NATO after the end of the Cold War, hypocritically contradicting the ideals of the American Revolution, as well as nominal proclamations. Thus, a French president complains that France and other NATO members are not 'vasal' states in relation to the US that with its constant dominance within this military alliance (e.g., its 'supreme' commander is always an American) effectively reduces them to such an inferior status. This complaint hence implies that the US actually treats and makes most NATO members 'vasal' states, aside from a few exceptions like Great Britain, France, and Turkey recently. This applies to the former WW II Axis members Germany, Italy, and others and especially smaller countries in Eastern and Southern Europe from the Baltics and Poland through Bulgaria, Croatia, Romania, and Slovenia to Albania, Macedonia, and Montenegro that look like NATO vasal states[32] in relation to the US, just as were satellites within the Warsaw Pact relative to the Soviet Union. So, these countries have 'liberated' themselves from being the Warsaw-Pact satellites of the Soviet Union to becoming the NATO vasal states of the US, just as most of them replacing one dictatorship by

---

cause for the 2022 Russia-Ukraine war that approximates an instance of civil wars within the former Soviet Union. Waters (cited in Young 2022) notes that most Americans blindly 'are believeing [US] propaganda. Further, the press reported that a former US ambassador to the United Nations and former White House national security adviser admitted or rather boasted of planning 'attempted coups in foreign countries', but this sounds like the worst kept secret of American imperialism by being common knowledge.

32 For example, Macedonia and Montenegro achieved and celebrated their independence from the Yugoslav Federation (especially Serbia) during the early 1990s and 2000s, respectively, as the step toward creating and developing independent states in relation to both the Soviet Union (or Russa) and the US and West. Yet, these nominally 'independent' nations look like the neo-colonies or vassal states of the US and West, especially within NATO. This reveals the reason why the US/West supported the 'independence' of these and other former Yugoslav republics, namely Croatia relapsing into neo-Nazi (*Ustasha* rule) déjà vu, Slovenia driven by frantic nationalism, and Muslim Bosnia induced by Islamic radicalism—breaking up Yugoslavia as part of its Cold War against the Soviet Union or its fantasy war against Russia and recolonizing or controlling this region and the Balkans overall. Thus, all the former Yugoslav republics (except for Serbia) after their formal independence are less independent in relation to the US/West than was Yugoslavia as essentially independent both from the Soviet Union and Warsaw Pact and from the US, West, and NATO, and one of the leaders of the non-aligned movement. Taken together, the US's government destructive, though perfidious, posture toward Yugoslavia by engineering, in alliance with Germany's Nazi-style policy, its break-up epitomizes its cynical and hypocritical betrayal of the American Revolution's independence ideal by effectively destroying (while declaratively supporting) that of the former Yugoslav republics, at least Macedonia and Montenegro, converting them into dependent, puppet states within NATO ('allies') in the service of American militarism and imperialism.

another—communist by conservative, including neo-fascist, or religious. As a result of the US's vasal-state treatment, NATO's smaller member-states from the Baltics through Poland to the Balkans are as subservient to and dependent on the US, thus becoming puppet-states, as they were to the Soviet Union as satellites within the Warsaw pact. As Reagan accused the Soviet Union, what typifies an 'evil empire' is this double tendency of imperial expansion and dominance and negation and suppression of the independence and sovereignty of smaller nations. By operating as the instrument of this dual process, extreme military expenditure during the rise of fascism post-2016 and since Reaganism is consistent with the pattern of an 'evil empire'.

Fourth and as a corollary, the US's largest and accelerating military expenditure during fascism post-2016 and conservatism since Reaganism epitomizes the pattern of an 'evil empire' by leading through offensive war and imperial expansion to mass death, destruction, ultimately self-destruction via mutually assured destruction, simply MAD by nuclear arms and wars. It is irrational and ultimately suicidal so long as any military confrontation between the US or NATO overall and its major enemies like Russia or China is likely to metastasize into a nuclear war whose outcome could only be MAD, thus an act of total madness of self-destruction and so collective suicide. The US's and NATO's posture since the end of the Cold War has been in essence confrontation and provocation, intransigence, and arrogance via expansion toward the former Warsaw Pact and even the Soviet Union and Russia's and perhaps ultimately China's borders, in apparent calculation that it can win any, including nuclear, war. Yet, this calculation may turn out to be an ultimate miscalculation resulting in MAD in which all warring sides perish, replicating Nazism's miscalculations during WW II. Thus, the US/NATO moves toward Russia's and even, directly or via NATO equivalents or proxies in Asia, eventually China's borders and builds and maintains multiples military bases around them rather than conversely, simply, the first comes to and so attempts to confront or provoke the second, not the other way round, after the end of the Cold War (Russia and China have no military bases in the countries that are neighbors of America). Thus, not content with and not limiting to NATO's expansion beyond its original borders into Eastern Europe and parts of the former Soviet Union, the US government post-2020 forms NATO equivalents in Asia seeking confrontation with or provocation of China, thus resuming and spreading the Cold War under a bellicose president-cold warrior. This replicates the same pattern of militarist and imperialist expansion, confrontation, or provocation, the resumption or extension of the Cold War in Europe and versus Russia.

On this account, the US/NATO acts as the actual or potential aggressor or threatening military power, simply a war-instigator, seeking confrontation with or provocation of Russia and China and thus ultimately causing a war with the mutually destructive outcome. And if any state acted in this way, Reagan would and in fact did, referring to what he alleged to be the aggressive behavior of the Soviet Union, call an 'evil empire.' If so, then the latter's designation applies more to Reagan's America than to any other state during the post-Cold War era and even the Cold War judging by the US government's being the world 'leader' in wars of aggression or military interventions.[33]

In this connection, several evident facts stand out after the end of WW II in Europe, which only US conservatives and other Americans blinded, deluded, or intoxicated by the 'manifest destiny', 'Divine mission' to rule the world, and supremacist clams of Americanism can deny. First, the US government has been and remains the only one ever to use nuclear weapons by dropping atomic bombs on Japan as a foremost act of inter-state terrorism in apparent desperation over its continuing lack of success to completely defeat Japanese troops by conventional means. Second, the US government has been the only 'great' or major power to consistently use illegal or prohibited, as by international law, weapons of mass destruction, including the disgraceful using of chemical or similar weapons[34] ('Agent Orange' as a deadly chemical toxin and part of 'Operation Ranch Hand,' napalm) in the war of aggression against Vietnam. Third, the US government initially, along with Great Britain and other colonial Western states, created NATO as an offensive military alliance and thus started the Cold War against the Soviet Union that in defensive reaction formed the Warsaw Pact together with the countries that it liberated from Nazi occupation. Fourth, the US government's military expenditure has been consistently the highest in the world, substantively higher (in absolute numbers at least) than that of the Soviet Union (if data were available), especially accelerating under Reaganism's fiscally irresponsible 'defense spending' causing huge budget deficits and provoking a cycle of such spending among its defined 'enemies' and the world.

---

33   This is what Dube, Kaplan, and Naidu (2011, p. 1377) suggest reporting that the US government installed the most (24) country leaders after the end of World War II, typically installing its preferred dictators a la Pinochet et al. and overthrowing democratically elected leaders and thus suppressing democracy, while preaching 'free and fair elections', 'democracy', and 'freedom' in the best tradition of Puritan duplicity/hypocrisy.

34   Biggs (2017) finds that the American war in Vietnam 'was, in many respects, a chemical war' in that the US military (the 266th Chemical Platoon) used 'Agent Orange', as well as napalm. Biggs (2017) adds that 'chemicals were everywhere, and their proliferation in the American war effort raised concerns that the United States was crossing a line in Vietnam, violating the 1925 Geneva Protocol's prohibition against the first use of chemical weapons in war.'

Fifth and as a corollary, the US government has launched various arms races, including Reaganism's Nazi-style rearmament and arms race through the increase of nuclear and other weapons of mass destruction. Sixth and as another corollary, the US government had and continues to have more military bases in other countries within and beyond NATO than any other, including the Soviet Union, while using these bases to suppress anti-colonial national independence, liberal, democratic, or socialist movements from Italy and Greece to Asia and South America, to maintain capitalist, conservative, religious, and fascist dictatorships in power, and to launch wars of aggression or military interventions. Seventh and consequently, the US government has created and sustained the largest and ever-growing military-industrial complex in the world, as the major agent of militarism, wars of aggression, and imperial conquest and domination. Eighth, the US government has launched more wars of aggression against or military interventions in other countries than any other, including (around 50% percent more than or 24 vs. 16) the 'evil empire' of the Soviet Union during the Cold War. Finally, the US government first intended and prepared to launch an offensive nuclear war and thus to cause MAD by destroying the enemy and itself alike, as during the Cuban missile crisis.[35] The preceding proves that Reagan by condemning the Soviet Union as the 'evil empire' engaged in a projection, as late Puritan, in the manner of theocratic Puritanism projecting its cruelty, aggression, militancy (Weber's Calvinist 'Church Militant'), and genocidal tendencies as by its genocide of Native Americans, simple its 'evilness' onto others thereby made 'evil'.

On this account, extreme military expenditure post-2016 and since Reaganism functions as the lethal and eventually self-destructive weapon of what seems as the national and regional equivalent of a suicidal cult or sect—spending into MAD, displaying symptoms of collective madness. In a way, the

---

35   Gusterson and Besteman (2019, p. 85) remark that the 'Soviet missiles deployed to Cuba in 1962 were quite real and, if used, would have inflicted crushing damage on the United States. But the United States could have chosen to regard them as a reasonable counterweight to its own Jupiter nuclear-tipped missiles in Turkey, on the Soviet Union's doorstep, rather than provoking a global crisis by narrating them as an existential threat. Likewise, based on the evidence of the last 2 decades of US-Vietnamese relations, the United States could plausibly have decided in the 1960s that its vital interests would have suffered little if a small country on the other side of the planet were allowed to "go Communist." Instead, it fruitlessly expended the lives of over 50,000 Americans and 2–3 million Vietnamesein what American national security elites wrongly perceived, thanks to the consensually accepted domino theory, as a struggle it could not afford to lose.' Also, Coatney (2022) recalls the '1962 Cuban Missile Crisis when we almost did have a nuclear war with Russia then', but warns that this is 'infinitely worse, with weapons far more powerful and instantaneous and computerized retaliation systems like Russia's Dead Hand.'

US government and other NATO 'great powers'—as distinct from its smaller vassal states—resemble suicidal cults or sects by their obstinate movement toward and risky confrontation with or provocation of nuclear-armed Russia or China. As Reagan suggested for the Soviet Union, what characterizes an 'evil empire' is exactly its tendency toward mass death, destruction, and ultimately self-destruction. If this is correct, the largest and accelerating military expenditure since Reaganism and post-2016 exemplifies the pattern of an 'evil empire' by eventually leading to such outcomes, notably MAD due to the US/NATO's expansion toward and confrontation with Russia and China as nuclear powers as well.

For instance, the US's formation of NATO and thus starting of the Cold War against its WW II ally the Soviet Union in the late 1940s continued and was consistent with the expansion of this military alliance during the 1950s by incorporating its war enemies and the former Axis powers like Germany and Italy (and Turkey), along with Japan in the Asian equivalent military alliance. In another instance, the US government's invasions of or military interventions in South America and many other countries starting in the 1950s continued and were consistent with such actions during later times up to the 1990s, the 2000s, and present days. In yet another example, the US's invasion of the Vietnam under the fabricated pretext of an 'attack' and with near-unanimous Congress approval in the early 1960s continued and was consistent with its extension and escalation (as by attacking some neighboring countries like Cambodia) during the 1970s, leaving of its wake the unprecedented postwar amount of mass death, including several millions of dead civilians, and destruction. Also, Reagan's invasion of Grenada as a phantom war against 'communism' in the 1980s replicated itself or continued with his successor's invasion of Panama in the 1990s on Puritanical 'war on drug' grounds.

During post-Cold War times, the US government's siding with the forces of secession during the civil war in Yugoslavia and its hostility toward and imposition of harsh sanctions against the latter during the early 1990s continued and was consistent with its/NATO attack, based on another fabrication of 'massacre' and in alliance with a secessionist terrorist group,[36] on this country in

---

36   The US and other Western or NATO states while supporting the secession of Kosovo (plus Muslim Bosnia, neo-Nazi Croatia, and nationalist Slovenia) from and even attacking Yugoslavia on behalf of these secessionist and terrorist groups, oppose such efforts by, for example, Catalonia and other regions in Spain to the point of detaining and deporting their leaders to the Spanish government, as well as in Turkey by ignoring its genocide of the Kurdish population, etc. This indicates and indeed confirms the typical double standards and bias of the US and other Western governments—secession is a 'fight for human rights' and secessionists 'freedom fighters' in non-Western or non-NATO nations

1999. The 1992 US President threatened to militarily intervene in Yugoslavia if it suppressed secessionist groups in its province Kosovo—analogous to the British government threatening the Union if it moved to suppress the Southern Confederacy—and his 1999 successor realized this threat by launching an illegal, unprovoked attack on the country. In addition, the US government's invasions of Afghanistan because of harboring terrorist groups, including its former jihadists like Bin-Laden in their shared 'holy' war against the Soviet Union, and Iraq based on the 'weapons of mass destruction' fabrication continued and was consistent with the occupation and destruction of these countries, including millions of civilian deaths, for nearly 20 years, indeed still occupying and controlling the second country despite its request to be freed from these foreign troops. These examples indicate that the US government's pattern of militarism, wars of aggression, and imperialism shows a striking continuity, consistence, and stubbornness during postwar times (and before) reminiscent of (what Hume and Weber classically identifies) as the 'unreasonable obstinacy' of Puritanism and the 'iron consistency' of Calvinism generally.

MAD hence is the vanishing act of the 'evil empire' owing to its extravagant military expenditure serving imperial expansion and domination and leading to or precipitating universal destruction, or to its miscalculation[37] of 'victory', such as the US government proclaimed during the 1962 Cuban nuclear missile crisis,[38] with human civilization as the 'collateral damage' of its irrationalism,

---

like Yugoslavia and Russia, but unjustified breach of 'territorial integrity' in Western or NATO states from Spain to Turkey.

37   The UN's Secretary General stated in 2022 that humanity is 'only one misunderstanding, one miscalculation away from nuclear annihilation.' Yet, as a candidate from one of its members and endorsed by NATO, this Secretary General omitted to state what is painfully evident. This is that this military alliance by its infinite, threatening expansion up to Russian borders, indefinite military support of neo-fascist or rightist states, movements, and coups (from Kosovo to Ukraine), wars of aggression against non-members like Yugoslavia and others, confrontation with or provocation of Russia and China that can escalate into a nuclear war, and serving as the militarist tool of American imperialism and Western neocolonialism is moving inexorably and uncompromisingly on the path of 'nuclear annihilation' of the world, as a global equivalent of the behavior of a suicidal religious cult and sect. NATO's path of 'nuclear annihilation' has an underlying religious basis and rationale given that the ultimate aim and dream of Puritanism (and its heir evangelicalism), the 'destiny' of America (in Tocqueville's words) as the 'leader' versus vassal states within this military alliance, is the 'delirium of annihilation masked as salvation' (Adorno 2001, p. 230). To that extent, this basis in suicidal religion seeking eternal 'election' via collective suicide, namely conservative-religious America, makes 'nuclear annihilation' through NATO's expansion and offensive wars a near-certainty in long terms, just a question of when, and not of if, this will happen.

38   For such US preparations and treats see Caldara and Iacoviello (2022) and Gibson (2011). In this connection, Schaeffer-Duffy (2022) remarks that 'unlike Russia, the US continues

unreason, intransigence, and corruption of power. For example, the US government/president during the 1962 Cuban missile crisis in an apparently irrational outburst was reportedly prepared and threatened to launch a nuclear attack on the Soviet Union and thus to cause the madness of self-destruction, because of the latter's installation of nuclear missiles in Cuba as a response to its installing of such weapons in Europe and Turkey, which, however, did not prompt its adversary to make such preparations and treats. Such an irrational or asymmetrical reaction during the Cuban crisis, including the reinstalling of nuclear missiles in Europe and Turkey (while the Soviet Union did not reciprocate in Cuba) reaffirmed the typically extreme irrationalism, bellicosity, and self-destructiveness of the American state, such as presidents, Congress, and so on.

No wonder, most people globally experience or perceive, judging by various surveys, the US government post-2016 and since Reaganism as the single gravest threat to permanent world peace and even the survival of humanity. Yet, it is perhaps only when most Americans realize that their own government post-2016 and before is the most lethal danger via militarism, offensive war, and imperial, including NATO, expansion to their survival as humans that US military expenditure will assume necessary, normal levels and recede from its current pathological, aggressive level that is inexorable on the path of mass death, destruction, ultimately MAD. Only they can save themselves and America from itself—the madness of self-destruction through extreme military expenditure as the syndrome of intense militarism and in the service of offensive permanent wars and imperial expansion and dominance.

Consequently, the US's extreme military expenditure under conservatism/fascism exemplifies the pattern of an 'evil empire' by mass killings as war crimes and crimes against humanity. Aside from, the only one among all governments, using nuclear bombs against civilian populations as a crime against humanity, the US military likely killed tens of millions of people, notably innocent civilians, in post-WW II wars. These include especially the Vietnam War as the probably cruelest and most sadistic and deceptive, falsehood-saturated

---

to be one of the only nuclear powers which refuses to pledge not to use nuclear weapons first.' Relatedly, some studies estimate that around 5 billion people would die as the result of a nuclear war between the US and Russia. This implies that 5 billion people form the human cost of the US government's willingness to use nuclear weapons and generally of American militarism and imperialism and Western neocolonialism and its instrument NATO's expansion to Russia's borders, because this compound acts as the prime agent of militaristic expansionism, imperial conquest or control, and wars of aggression in modern society.

offensive imperial war in postwar times, expressing notorious Puritan and religious cruelty, sadism, and deception, the indiscriminate bombardment of Yugoslavia while allying with a terrorist group[39] (descending from a Nazi WW II ally), and the Iraq War[40] replicating that in Vietnam in respect of mass killings, torture, and the false 'weapons of mass destruction' justification for the

---

39 Bauman (2001, p. 207) cites a British soldier participating in the US/NATO bombardment of Yugoslavia: 'We were fed a bad line about Kosovo Liberation Army [as freedom fighters]. They are terrorists and we won their war for them. It's not only Serbs, but the ethnic Albanians as well that are scared of them'. The Kosovo Liberation Army descends from an Albanian WW II Nazi ally (*Balli Kombëtar*), which the US/NATO (including Germany) certainly knew but in spite or because of this fascist descent proceeded to attack Yugoslavia to assist its terrorist allies, while also apparently driven by the fantasy or delusion of fighting a proxy war against Russia as the traditional supporter of Serbia. Also, D'Ammassa (2022) predicts that there is 'little hope Bush, Blair or any of their lieutenants will be compelled to testify at The Hague [International Criminal Court]' for perpetrating war crimes during the Iraq War. In turn, the US/NATO attacked Yugoslavia, which was independent, nonaligned state and not a member of the Warsaw Pact, only after the dissolution of the latter and of the Soviet Union, not daring to do so before, which implies that this military alliance understands only the language of and is deterred by brute force consistent with the militarist pattern of American imperialism and Western (neo) colonialism. Similarly, Waters (cited in Young 2022) reportedly calls the post-2020 US President a War Criminal' because of 'fueling the war in the Ukraine, that is a huge crime.' A more precise description is perhaps a perennial 'Cold War' crusader, militarist, imperialist, and war lover, crusading for NATO's expansion to the borders of and confrontation with Russia's that may well turn nuclear, forming NATO-style aggressive alliances in Asia and beyond, furthering and celebrating American imperialism, and instigating or supporting all wars of aggression from Yugoslavia to Iraq that result in mass war crimes and criminals perpetrated and incarnated by US imperial forces. Waters (cited in Young 2022) suggest to American militarists and imperialists 'to figure out what the US would do if the Chinese [Russian] were putting nuclear armed missiles into Mexico and Canada', in the way it does in Taiwan (and Ukraine), with the implied answer—an irrational hysterical and self-righteous reaction, such as threatening a devastating nuclear war during the 1962 Cuban missile crisis as the result of its installing nuclear missiles close (Turkey) to the Soviet Union causing a symmetrical response in Cuba by the latter.

40 D'Ammassa (2022) laments that US 'institutions and news organizations continue to treat the architects and leading proponents of the Iraq War as if they were serious people whose policy views are worth consideration. Adding insult to that injury, a full accounting has yet to be made of the crimes of war, the systematic use of torture, unaccountable detention of human beings, lies and other misconduct by public officials, the undermining of international law and the cratering of societal progress with the destruction of hundreds of thousands of lives—and that is the conservative estimate.' D'Ammassa (2022) adds that 'some of those who backed the Iraq invasion attribute their crimes to faulty intelligence, even though it has been firmly established that the Bush Administration and United Kingdom Prime Minister Tony Blair's government ignored and misrepresented intelligence assessments presented to them.'

invasion and continuing occupation. The US government continues to occupy Iraq around 20 years after the invasion and 'mission accomplished' proclamation despite the 'weapons of mass destruction' never being found and proving to be a falsehood and the Iraq's government request for the occupying military to leave, thus still acting on a deception and violating the principle of national independence in a self-contradiction with the ideal of the American Revolution.

And in a typical display of Weber's Puritanical 'pure hypocrisy of Americanism', while falsely accusing Iraq and other defined 'enemies' of the 'weapons of mass destruction,' US government is in reality the only one that has ever used such weapons since WW II. For example, the US military is the only one with a proven record of using such illegal, prohibited weapons of mass destruction as chemical and similar ones (e.g., Agent Orange) during the Vietnam War, depleted uranium, due to its long-term radiation effects, a quasi-nuclear weapon in the unlawful attack on Yugoslavia, which was hence doubly illegal both by the weapons[41] used and the lack of a UN-authorization, other suspect weapons in the Iraq invasion, etc., not to mention its exclusive use of nuclear bombs in WW II.

On this account, such a military objectively qualifies as a war-crime force and many of its members as well as perhaps some US presidents as war criminals from the standpoint of global judiciary, such as the International Criminal Court which the US government refuses to recognize as legitimate and for good reasons. Thus, the US, along only with China, Iraq, Israel, Libya, Qatar,

---

41   Simons (2001) reports that a former environment minister of Finland 'made some startling discoveries on a recent mission in Kosovo to assess the impact of uranium-tipped weapons hurtled on the province during NATO's 78-day bombing war against Yugoslavia in 1999.' In his words, he 'found some radiation in the middle of villages where children were playing, We were surprised to find this a year and a half later. People had collected ammunition shards as souvenirs and there were cows grazing in contaminated areas, which means the contaminated dust can get into the milk.' Simons (2001) adds that the 'discovery by Mr. Haavisto and his team of low-level beta radiation at 8 of the 11 sites they sampled seems certain to fan a rapidly spreading sense of fury and panic across Europe about the well-being of soldiers sent to serve in the Balkans, more than a dozen of whom have since died of leukemia.' After reading this, one wonders and is perhaps mystified why the US/NATO felt the need to use uranium-tipped and so quasi-nuclear bombs, among all the massive weapons at its disposal more than enough to subdue the 'enemy', against a relatively small, weakened, and non-threatening country and in an alliance with an Albanian 'ethnic terrorist army' (as US secretary of state admitted) descending from a WW II Nazi movement. What likely explains this mystery is (to paraphrase the notion of the 'collective unconscious' in Mannheim 1936) subconscious and perhaps deliberate collective sadism, which the US/NATO also exemplified in bombing Yugoslavia on Orthodox Easter while dropping 'happy Easter' leaflets along with uranium bombs.

and Yemen, opposed the establishing of the International Criminal Court in
1998, with even the post-2016 radical-right government threatening to arrest its
judges if they investigate American soldiers for war crimes, while some former
vice presidents avoid travelling to Europe because of the fear of their arrests
for war crimes.[42] Yet the US government seeks to subject 'enemy' countries like
Russia, China, Cuba, Iran, North Korea, Venezuela, etc. for their 'war crimes' to
the same International Criminal Court that it ardently opposes and even crim-
inalizes, thus subjecting others to the kind of justice from which it exempts
itself self-righteously, manifesting what Weber classically diagnosed as the
'pure hypocrisy of Americanism' and Pareto deplores as 'jingoism.' Its armed
forces have been the foremost and indeed most sanctimonious perpetrator of
such and related atrocities and cruelties that the International Criminal Court
would sanction, from the Vietnam War (and the Indian wars of extermination)
to those against Yugoslavia and Afghanistan and Iraq.[43]

Overall, its armed forces killed more people, notably civilians, just as
launched more wars of aggression or covert military interventions overthrowing foreign governments,[44] alone or with NATO, especially together with Great
Britain continuing to display colonial-like militarism and bellicosity, than any

---

42   Schaeffer-Duffy (2022) suggests this.

43   Savelsberg and King (2005, p. 585) observe that in 'America, the early destruction of much
      of the Native American population during the colonial era was continued, after the foun-
      dation of the United States, by further atrocities, wars, broken treaties, forced migration
      and death marches, and the destruction of livelihood.' Relatedly, Savelsberg and King
      (2005, p. 586) note that 'excessive cruelty committed by the US military in foreign wars has
      also become known.' Anderton and Brauer (2021, p. 1241) point to the 'atrocity-suffering
      group, as in the case of Native American populations in California in the 1800s.' Schaeffer-
      Duffy (2022) reports witnessing the 'cruelty of US military intervention in Nicaragua.'

44   Dube et al. (2011, p. 1377) register that '24 country leaders were installed by the CIA and
      16 by the KGB since the end of World War II. In the US, covert operations designed to
      overthrow foreign governments were usually first approved by the director of the CIA and
      then subsequently by the president of the US.' Also, Berger et al. (2013, pp. 863–4) note
      that 'US covert services engaged in [military] interventions that installed and/or sup-
      ported political leaders in other countries.' For example, they detail that 'among the 166
      countries, 51 were subject to at least one CIA intervention between 1947 and 1989. In an
      average year between 1947 and 1989, 25 countries were experiencing a CIA intervention.
      Among the group of countries that experienced an intervention between 1947 and 1989,
      the typical country experienced 21 years of interventions. The CIA intervened most heav-
      ily in Latin America, but also in a few European countries—namely, Italy and Greece—as
      well as in a number of countries in Africa, Asia, and the Middle East' (Berger et al. 2013,
      p. 868). According to Schaeffer-Duffy (2022), the US 'has invaded 56 countries, eight of
      them since 2000.' Apparently, the US government, including presidents, is the undisputed
      world leader in covert military operations as offensive wars against or military interven-
      tions in other countries, and to that extent the 'leader of the free world' of imperialism.

other after WW II, making conservative America what Reagan calls the 'best' in this respect. (In this connection, since the end of the Cold War, alongside the US, Great Britain has been especially belligerent, prone to wars of aggression, thus irrational and militaristic. Great Britain participated in such wars of aggression as NATO's unlawful and unprovoked attack on Yugoslavia to protect Islamic secessionist terrorists, the US's invasions and occupations of Afghanistan and Iraq, the violent 'regime change' in Libya, the lawless bombardments of Syria, etc. In retrospect, these aggressive actions look like the vestiges of the belligerence, wars of conquest, general militarism of British colonialism, as well as the militancy of Puritanism as the Calvinist 'Church Militant', as Weber emphasizes. In prospect, they may turn out to be irrational, indeed self-destructive if the outcome of a war of aggression, in alliance with the US and within NATO, against Russia or China can only be MAD, thus a small, isolated island post-Brexit facing the specter of eradication due to its government's chronic belligerence, offensive wars which its major classical sociologist Spencer denounced in principle, and militarism, and neocolonialism overall.)

The largest military expenditure in the Western world and beyond, expressing intense militarism and financing wars of aggression and imperial conquest and expansion, discloses a failure of the 'American experiment' in non-military civilian investment and wellbeing, for example, spending on poverty alleviation and welfare assistance, peace, peaceful conflict resolution, and respect for the national independence of small nations. Notably, it indicates the violation, indeed betrayal, primarily by conservatism after WW II and especially Reaganism, including fascism or right-wing authoritarianism post-2016, of Jefferson-Madison's ideal of America as a pacifist state and society. This ideal consists of a small standing army and by implication minimal military expenditure not to be utilized for wars of aggression and imperial conquest, refraining from 'entanglement' in warlike alliances, and respecting the national independence of other societies consistent with the American Revolution.

Especially with respect to such non-entanglement with alliances, what violates and indeed betrays the above ideal is the US's creation and unlimited expansion of NATO rather than its dissolution after the self-termination of the Warsaw Pact, as a rational act of reciprocity and peace-promotion, just as reasonable people expected in the early 1990s and some US officials reportedly promised. For example, the US conservative secretary of state is often documented[45] or reported to have promised in 1991 that NATO would not move

---

45   Coatney (2022) remarks that 'in 1999 we [the US] broke our promise—documented—not to push NATO east, when we added Hungary, Czechoslovakia and Russia-hating Poland.

'one inch to the East' after the voluntary dissolution of the Warsaw Pact and of the Soviet Union. Yet apparently the US government's pattern of broken promises, deceptions, and conservative 'treachery' (in Emerson's word) did not end with the wars of extermination against Native Americans or the offensive and falsehood-saturated Vietnam War but continued since the 1990s through the Iraq invasion based on the 'weapons of mass destruction' fabrication and beyond. Like Yugoslavia in 1999, in 2003 Iraq did not threaten or provoke the US and yet the latter used the fabrication of the 'weapons of mass destruction' as an 'imminent threat' to invade and occupy this country still occupied 20 years later. Such a conservative American treacherous promise that NATO would 'move not one inch' toward Eastern Europe and Russia perpetuates or evokes Nazi Germany's treachery that it would honor its pact with and not attack the Soviet Union in WW II—and US imperialism tends to underestimate its defined enemy as 'weak' at the potential peril of America and the world via nuclear MAD due to a miscalculation of 'victory' and indefinite expansion into distant spaces, just as Nazism underestimated and miscalculated its 'life space' conquest of the Soviet Union. This suggests that American imperialism and its militarist, warlike instrument NATO partly continues Nazi Germany's treacherous and aggressive policy toward Russia, as well as Eastern Europe and the Balkans such as Yugoslavia, not the least because this expansionist military alliance embraces the WW II Axis states (including politically Japan in recent times) which use it as a cover for their resurgent militarism and which the US mobilizes for its confrontation with Russia and China and its pursuit of global dominance. To paraphrase Clausewitz's famous definition,

---

Then, we forced our Kosovo bombing war on the Serbs with Rambouillet Appendix B which made betrayed and enraged Russian democrat Boris Yeltsin turn Russia back over to its national security community: Putin', also invoking Reagan's secretary of state's admission about the 'Russians' trust we had and threw away.' In addition, Coatney (2022) laments that after the end of the Cold War successive conservative (and 'liberal') US governments 'wrecked everything: Iraq, Libya, Syria, and now Ukraine/Russia.' Chrisman (2022) writes that James Baker 'when conferring with Gorbachev regarding his concerns about the reunification of Germany, the former Secretary of State reassured the Soviet Premier that NATO would "move not one inch to the east." This pledge was shattered when Poland joined the NATO alliance.' Chrisman (2022) writes that James Baker 'when conferring with Gorbachev regarding his concerns about the reunification of Germany, the former Secretary of State reassured the Soviet Premier that NATO would "move not one inch to the east." This pledge was shattered when Poland joined the NATO alliance.' Also, Waters) (cited in Young 2022) remarks that 'this [Ukraine] war is basically about the action and reaction of NATO pushing right up to the Russian border, which they promised they wouldn't do when [Mikhail] Gorbachev negotiated the withdrawal of the USSR from the whole of Eastern Europe.'

American imperialism and NATO's wars of aggression, including potentially a self-destructive nuclear war against Russia (and perhaps China), are often the continuation or reiteration of the Nazi policy toward Russia, Eastern Europe, and the Balkans, by other means or rather identical tools of brute military force, combined with conservative amoral 'treachery.'

No doubt, American imperialism and NATO differ, respectively, from, notably being 'better' in proclamation or intention than, Nazism and the WW II Axis conquering Eastern Europe and Yugoslavia, thus no structural equivalence existing between them. Yet, they ultimately move on the same path or produces the identical outcome by the twin recipe of naked military force, for example, by attacking Yugoslavia déjà vu Nazi-style, and treachery by broken promises of not moving eastward. This is indefinite expansion and wars of aggression causing global destruction and ending in self-destruction, with the specter of reciprocal nuclear devastation only being the ultimate intensification of the tendency of Nazism, as well as of the suicidal bent of Puritanism and evangelicalism (the Christian Right overall) in America. At this juncture, American imperialism and NATO reappear as functional equivalents of Nazism and the WW II Axis, respectively, in the sense of ultimately generating, even if unintentionally, the same destructive consequences ('latent functions') for global society and human civilization, although displaying no structural equivalence in organization or configuration.

Relatedly, this same secretary in 1991 pronounced that the actions of Yugoslavia's federal army during its civil war were 'unjustified attacks' on some of its secessionist parts, for example, Croatia under neo-Nazi rule (a near-replica of the WW II Nazi-puppet state). Following this absurd reasoning, the actions of the US Union Army during its civil war would qualify as 'unjustified attacks' on its secessionist Southern Confederacy, but not many Americans today would describe them so. In any event, such official US official pronouncements were deliberate attempts at or objectively instrumental in the collapse of Yugoslavia and the justification of secession by neo-Nazi or extremist forces in Croatia, Slovenia, and Muslim-dominated Bosnia.

Overall, the US government sided with and supported these secessionist regions and assumed a hostile posture and destructive activities against the federal government, including the imposing of harsh sanctions and suffering on the civilian population in a hypocritical contradiction with its own experience of civil war because of secession. Yugoslavia's and America's civil wars were not the same, showing many differences in country size, geography, economic structure, culture, and history. However, like all civil wars or secessions, they also share certain common elements, including a federation with a relatively week federal government, an attempt at secession by some states or republics, the response of the central government by deploying the military in these secessionist regions, the resulting armed conflict with large casualties, etc. These commonalities seem more decisive than the differences, but the US government apparently became oblivious of its own painful experience of civil war because of secession by applying a double standard to that in Yugoslavia by ardently supporting and allying with the secessionist, including neo-Nazi, forces against the central government that was analogous to the American Union.

More broadly, as it stands, with its expansion and unlawful attack on Yugoslavia, US-dominated NATO develops and operates as what Jefferson and Madison feared of 'entanglement' in military and related alliances. First, it acts as a warlike, indeed most bellicose and offensive[46] rather than 'defensive' postwar alliance displaying extreme aggressiveness and launching wars of aggression on non-members, such as Yugoslavia, Afghanistan, Iraq (mostly the US and the UK), Libya, Syria, etc., and expanding towards, seeking confrontation with, and making threats against others like Russia and China. NATO thereby entangles many countries in its militarist activities and acts virtually analogous to the WW II Axis.

In passing, the disintegration of the Soviet Union and generally liberation and transition from communism in Eastern Europe can be, aside from few exceptions, deemed a failure or at least a missed opportunity in terms of economic prosperity, democracy and freedom, national independence, and peace and security. And half of the explanatory equation for this a failure or missed opportunity is American imperialism and Western neocolonialism—of which NATO's persistence and expansion is a brute instrument—the other half consisting of domestic causes usually allying with these external forces from America and the West. In respect of economic prosperity, during the transition away from communism, Eastern Europe adopted American-style primitive unrestrained, coercive, and anti-egalitarian, notably oligarchic capitalism that the US government imposed or exported in various ways ('Big Bang' privatization, ideological influences, political pressures, etc.) into this

---

46   Pfister (2022) laments that 'regarding American foreign policy interference, the main thing was NATO expansion led by the Bill Clinton administration. NATO was supposed to be a defensive alliance; Clinton turned it into an offensive one, moving right up into Russia's sphere of influence. He appears to have had no empathy for the security interests of Russia.' Coatney (2022) also deplores that in '2014 [the US] broke our Budapest peace agreement with the Russians with our Kyiv coup—not a 'revolution' for four obvious, objective reasons—threatening them at their throats with NATO which became an aggressor with Kosovo and then Libya—no longer a legitimate defensive alliance.'

region. The result of such an atavistic American model of capitalism is reducing workers in Eastern Europe, just as those in America itself, to slave-like conditions by suppressing basic labor freedoms and rights like unionization and collective bargaining, the rise of oligarchy and rule of oligarchs, stagnation or minimal growth of living standards, rampant American-style income and wealth inequalities, the increase of poverty after the image of America's notorious chronic and widespread poverty, declining or stagnant life expectancy and growing morbidity or deteriorating physical and mental health (including depression, psychosis, and neurosis), the explosion of property and violent crime, and similar phenomena unknown or rare in socialism and associated with American-style capitalism. In short, these and other grave economic-social pathologies are the price Eastern Europe has paid and still pays for embracing or being forced to embrace American-style capitalism. To be sure, Eastern Europe's capitalist transition unleashes (what Keynes appreciates as, contrary to 'libertarian' detractors) the creative, active, and dynamic genius of private enterprise supplanting socialist economic uncreativeness, passivity, and static, aside from some exceptions, but its large and multiple economic-social costs and pathologies listed above threaten to outweigh its benefits, as is apparent in some of these countries as well as Russia and the rest of the former Soviet Union. On this account, Eastern Europe's capitalist transition is economic progress in some respects of private enterprise, most notably unprecedented consumer choice and product variety and yet regression in others spanning from labor slave-like or degrading conditions and economic indignity, insecurity, and poverty to crime and other social pathologies, thus being neither a pure blessing, contrary to US and Western 'libertarian' apologists for American-style capitalism, nor an 'unmitigated evil', as communist critics allege.

In respect of democracy and political and other social freedom, during its transition Eastern Europe, aside from rare exceptions, has moved mostly from communism to anti-communist undemocratic or illiberal regimes that American imperialism has imposed or decisively influenced to install or perpetuate in the region rather than moving to liberal democracy, as it was initially promised or expected. On this account, Eastern Europe has just substituted anti-communist for communist dictatorship, specifically moving to conservative/rightist, including neo-fascist or right-wing dictatorships (Hungary, most of the Baltics, Croatia) and theocracies (Catholic-dominated Poland) medieval and American-style (the 'Bible Belt'), that the US government critically helped establish or sustain. In short, Eastern Europe's liberation from communism has not resulted in true, general liberty in the form of liberal democracy mainly owing to American imperialism, in alliance with domestic anti-liberal and anti-democratic conservative, including fascist and theocratic, forces.

In respect of national independence and sovereignty, after the dissolution of the Warsaw Pact and the Soviet Union. Eastern Europe remains as dependent on the imperial 'great powers' as during the Cold War primarily due to American imperialism and Western neocolonialism sustained and indeed resurged through NATO's persistence and expansion to the east. The nexus of American imperialism and Western neocolonialism renders most Eastern European countries from the Baltics and Poland and Bulgaria and Macedonia vassal states within NATO, thus just changing their status of satellites of the Soviet Union in the Warsaw Pact to that of puppets of the US and the West. Moreover, some Eastern European countries (e.g., the former republics of Yugoslavia, in part Romania) have become even less independent in relation to American imperialism and Western neocolonialism than relative to the Soviet Union during the Cold War. Therefore, the persistent compound of American imperialism and Western neocolonialism flagrantly violates the principle of national independence and sovereignty for Eastern Europe within and through NATO, just as the Soviet Union did in and via the Warsaw Pact, cynically contradicting the national ideal of the American Revolution, while claiming in a deceptive or delusionary manner a 'higher moral ground'. In this regard, American imperialism and Western neocolonialism reduces most of Eastern Europe to a degree of dependency on the US and the West to the point of blackmail (as with the Balkans) that is equivalent or comparable to that on the Soviet Union during the Cold War, as well as of that of South America and other 'banana republics' on these imperial and colonial powers. Accordingly, (to paraphrase Weber's statement about theocratic Calvinism/Puritanism destroying monasteries only to pervert society into an all-encompassing oppressive monastery), one can infer that Eastern European countries hoped they had escaped the satellite status versus the Soviet Union and in the Warsaw Pact but now they are and will be for the foreseeable future neocolonial vassal, dependent states in relation to the US/West within NATO. This particularly applies to most former republics of Yugoslavia that were more independent from the Soviet Union and outside of the Warsaw Pact during the Cold War than are from the US/West and indeed are reduced to puppet neocolonial dependent states or 'banana republics', while being members of NATO at present. This can be considered the supreme achievement of American imperialism in Eastern Europe and the Balkans—transforming the satellites of the Soviet Union and Warsaw-Pact members and even formerly independent nations (Yugoslavia) into puppets of the US/West and additional NATO allies, consistent with the pattern of an 'evil empire'.

Lastly, in respect of peace and security, Eastern Europe has become a less peaceful and safe region also primarily because of American imperialism and Western neocolonialism, specifically NATO's persistence and expansion beyond its original borders to the east up to parts of the former Soviet Union. Moreover, apart from provoking or exacerbating local wars as in the former Yugoslavia, American imperialism/Western neocolonialism renders Eastern Europe a potential stage/theater of global war via NATO's expansion toward and thus inevitable military confrontation with Russia and conceivably China, just as did Nazi Germany during its Russian invasion. Thus, the nexus of American imperialism and Western neocolonialism through NATO's eastward expansion uses and indeed exploits Eastern Europe as both a staging ground and rich human resource for its confrontation with and ultimately subjugation of Russia and China, just as Nazi Germany used Eastern European Nazi-puppet regimes for attacking Russia and fighting on the Russian front. And so long as any military confrontation with Russia will ultimately escalate in a nuclear war of universal destruction, Eastern Europe faces the grave specter of becoming engulfed in MAD and thus 'collateral damage' of the suicidal proclivity of American imperialism and Western neocolonialism, paying the ultimate price for NATO's eastward expansion. Thus, the Eastern European countries that are NATO's members and vassal states in relation to the US are as likely to be destroyed in a nuclear war against Russia as were when belonging to the Warsaw Pact and being the satellites of the Soviet Union—and some being even more so (as with the former republics of Yugoslavia and perhaps Romania). To that extent, NATO's eastward expansion and generally American imperialism and Western neocolonialism far from increasing peace and security in Eastern Europe perpetuates and even, after the demise of the Warsaw Pact, further exacerbates the prospect of war and destruction of this region as a consequence of its unstoppable movement toward military confrontation with Russia with a MAD outcome.

Second, NATO is an analogue to the WW II Axis[47] by including all former fascist and Nazi-puppet states from Germany, Italy, Portugal, and Spain through

---

47 In connection, the US did not resist the Axis fascist powers and so did not enter WW II until the Pearl Harbor 1941 attack, so more than 2 years after the 1939 onset of the war, which counterfactually implies that it would not do this in the absence of such a single event but would languish in isolationism, trade protectionism, and irrational religious superstitions like creationism and antirational 'Monkey Trials' against science and progress. Also, one wonders if the US intended to 'liberate' Europe, why it did not fight the Axis fascist powers and did not enter WW II when it started. This casts doubt on the picture of America as the enthusiastic 'liberator' of Europe, while minimizing Russia's role in defeating fascism, with Waters (cited in Young 2022) remarking that America 'got into World

Denmark and Norway to Albania, Bulgaria, Croatia, Hungary, Slovenia, Slovakia, even the Baltics, conceivably Ukraine, and other Nazi-ruled parts of the former Soviet Union and approaching Russia's borders. Relatedly, the US's government consistently urges the former fascist members of the WW II Axis from Germany and Italy to Turkey and Japan to militarize for its own militarist and imperialist purposes, such as its confrontation with Russia and China and imperial domination. Thus, it demands or encourages these former Axis states to increase their military expenditure, resulting in its large and continuing increases in Germany, Italy, Turkey, and Japan to assist the US government in these purposes. Also, it requests that these states join the US government in its wars of aggression, for example, Germany, Italy, and Turkey joining NATO's illegal, unprovoked attack on Yugoslavia, their WW II victorious enemy, as an act of inter-state terrorism and Japan allying with it in its confrontation with Russia, China, and North Korea. In so doing the US government makes the main former Axis states behave as during WW II—as fascist militarist and warlike regimes—for its own ends of confrontation with and ultimately wars of aggression against what it defines Puritan-style and targets as its 'enemies' (though Russia and China have not officially defined America as their 'enemy').

Overall, driven by the US government's expansionism, NATO therefore displays aggressive expansion, doubling its members since the end of the Cold War and seeking to add even more, and entangles a growing number of countries, including many Axis fascist states, in offensive imperial wars and military tensions that it initiates, sustains, or exacerbates since the self-termination of the Warsaw Pact and the voluntary, 'peaceful implosion' of the Soviet Union.[48] Specifically, NATO expanded from 16 to 32 members, thus exactly doubling its membership, between the Cold War and 2023 supposedly because of a 'threat' from Russia while dismissing the latter as 'weak' and thus indulging in a schizophrenic, self-contradictory conduct and rhetoric of simultaneous production and devaluation of 'threats' and 'enemies'. (By such simultaneous production and devaluation of 'enemies' like Russia and even China existing far beyond its members' borders, NATO resembles religious cults and sects as well as fascist

---

War 2 because of Pearl Harbor. [Americans] were completely isolationists [beforehand]. Thank god the Russians had already won the bloody war by then. 23 million Russians died, protecting you and me from the Nazi menace.'

48   In this connection, Habermas (2001, p. 47) referring to the Soviet Union points to the 'peaceful implosion of a global empire, whose leadership recognized the inefficiency of a supposedly superior mode of production, and admitted defeat in the economic race rather than following the time-honored pattern of deflecting internal conflicts with military adventures abroad.'

states that tend, for their creation and existence, to both produce and devalu-ate 'evil' and 'enemies'.) Hence, one wonders if Russia is 'weak,' indeed weaker and thus less of a threat than the Soviet Union why NATO under American instigation doubled its membership after the end of the supposed cause of its formation and existence, Reagan's 'evil empire' and the voluntary termina-tion of the rival Warsaw Pact. If Russia is militarily and otherwise 'weak,' NATO becomes redundant and the US 'strongest' military is alone sufficient to deal with the Russian 'threat' to protect both America and its 'allies,' some of which, especially Great Britain, France, Germany, and Turkey, would not even need American assistance to defend themselves on this assumption of 'weakness'. It is abundantly obvious that rather than some nebulous, anti-logical, and false 'threat' from a 'weak' Russia, the sole driver of NATO's aggressive expansion is American militarism and imperialism and Western neocolonialism whose tool it is since the end of the Cold War and the implosion of the Soviet Union.

In connection with the latter, one can add that the leadership of the Soviet Union via its 'peaceful implosion' in relation to its segments was perhaps too lenient and generous not just for its own good, which is secondary, but also for that of the world in the long run that is of primary and growing impor-tance. For example, this leadership, specifically liberal and democracy-minded Gorbachev, too leniently and generously, even naively allowed the reunifica-tion of Germany in the hope that the latter would relinquish its Nazi-style traits and ways. Yet, just a few years after the reunification, Germany's con-servative government manifested such traits and resumed these ways by restarting Nazi-style divide-and-rule foreign policy towards the Balkans such as Yugoslavia, by supporting and arming its Nazi-era allies of Croatia, Slovenia, Muslim Bosnia, and Albanian Kosovo versus its WW I and II enemy Serbia, culminating in its attack on the latter under NATO's cover and with the US's enthusiastic encouragement in the service of its imperialism and fantasy war with Russia. On this account, the leadership, specifically Gorbachev, was perhaps too naïve in his true liberal-democratic commitment in respect of Eastern Germany and Eastern Europe overall, in allowing Germany's reunifi-cation that proved to be a grave mistake and disastrous from the standpoint of Yugoslavia in whose collapse the German Nazi-style divide-and-rule foreign policy was the major factor, along with US imperialism and its phantom war via the bombardment of Serbia against Russia. Furthermore, around three decades after the reunification of Germany, its government declares its aim to create the 'largest' European military within NATO, which echoes Nazi mil-itarization and rearmament with its well-known results. Generally, this sug-gests that the militarist spirit of Nazism is still alive and well embedded in the fabric and politics of Germany even after its military defeat in WW II and the death of Hitler et al., especially through Nazi-style foreign policy toward the Balkans and Russia: 'once Nazi, always Nazi' in various NATO disguises and justifications as a cover for Nazi-style militarism. A new compounding factor is that the US government consistently instigates Germany's Nazi-style militarization, including its participation in the lawless attack on Yugoslavia, in the aim of 'strengthening' NATO and confronting Russia, just as recruiting Nazi scientists in the service of developing military technology[49] and the Cold War, thus defacing the memory of those Americans fighting Nazism in WW II. By doing so, the US government coherently displays Nazi-style affinities and preferences to anti-fascist (including liberal and socialist) alternatives, and ultimately traits, so long as the instigation of or complicity with the persistence of Nazism, at least its militarism, in Germany reveals such fascist properties. Taken together, reunified Germany uses the cover of NATO membership and 'solidarity' and American support to essentially pursue and implement Nazi-style policy toward the Balkans, notably its WW I and WW II enemy and victor Yugoslavia, as in the 1999 bombardment of it as the first German postwar military engagement, and Eastern Europe, and Russia. On the other hand, NATO embraces, and American imperialism supports and uses a reunified Germany in spite or perhaps because of its Nazi-style policy for the sake of military expansion and imperial conquest and domination, notably movement toward and confrontation with Russia, just as Nazism sent Nazi-allied forces from its conquered territories to the Russian front during WW II. Hence, this is a 'marriage of convenience' between Germany that since the reunification obviously cannot relinquish and indeed seems embolden to pursue its Nazi ways[50] in foreign relations and NATO and American imperialism finding in this resurgent power, including its growing militarism, a useful complement to their expansionist and imperial aims. This shows the cleverness of reunified Germany to disguise its Nazi-style expansionist policy under NATO 'solidarity' and the amoral Machiavellianism of this aggressive military alliance and

---

49   Lloyd (2012, p. 487) mentions the 'postwar relocation of German scientists, including decorated Nazi war hero turned NASA pioneer Wernher von Braun, to Huntsville [AL], where rockets were developed in service of both American airborne military capacity and the US space program.'

50   For example, since its reunification Germany's companies like its main airline and car maker have aggressively acquired those of its neighbors like Austria, Czech Republic, and others (Switzerland, etc.) in an apparent display of industrial expansionism evoking Nazi Germany's annexation of these countries and forming an economic vestige of its militarist expansion. To that extent, this indicates that both the German government and companies have not relinquished or forgotten their Nazi ways, as if to confirm for Germany 'once Nazi, always Nazi' at least in relation to its neighbors, the Balkans, and Russia.

American imperialism by allying with and harnessing such a German state for implementing militarist, expansionist, and imperial ambitions, notably the encircling of and confrontation with Russia.

In another example of leniency, generosity, and naivete, the Soviet Union's leadership withdrew its troops from the Warsaw Pact members, including Poland, while the US stationing permanently military forces in the latter and maintaining and even expanding its bases in Germany, Italy, and elsewhere, using them for the NATO illegal attack on Yugoslavia. In addition, the Soviet Union's leadership, specifically Gorbachev, generously granted national independence to the Baltic states, Ukraine, and other parts of the 'evil empire', which is almost equivalent to the US granting independence to the Southern Confederacy rather than fighting the latter in the brutal Civil War and generally the 37 states not belonging to the Union during its founding. Overall, the Soviet Union's leadership seemed more lenient and generous, especially Gorbachev more liberal and democratic, in treating its component states by granting them independence than the US government, including presidents, in their treatment of Latin America as its proxy colony ('backyard') or territory of dependent puppet states and banana republics invading and controlling it at will for long, even after the Cold War (e.g., Panama, etc.). However, the Soviet Union's leadership proved not only too lenient and generous for the good of its own 'evil empire', especially Gorbachev, too naively liberal and democratic by trusting the US conservative government's Puritan-style treacherous promise of NATO's non-expansion eastward. More important, it may prove fatal for peace and even the survival of civilization so long as the prospect of MAD via nuclear war is probably graver under NATO's continuing existence and expansion and thus confrontation with or provocation of a 'weak' Russia and perhaps China in the function of American militarism and imperialism and Western neocolonialism than during the Soviet Union and the Warsaw Pact within the postwar proximate balance of power and bipolar world of relative predictability, stability, and communication, as some observers[51] warn. To that extent, the American and Western celebration of the victory over the Soviet

---

51   This is what former US Secretary of State Henry Kissinger warned in 2022—the threat of nuclear war is graver during NATO's militarist monopoly and expansion than ever before during the postwar balance of power, which indicates the absolute corruption and indeed destruction of absolute power at global levels. Moreover, Kissinger reportedly stated that America is 'at the edge of war with Russia and China on issues which we partly created, without any concept of how this is going to end or what it's supposed to lead to'—by implication a potential nuclear war of self-destruction—suggesting that the US tends to 'accelerate the tensions' (cited in Mueller 2022). Also, Kissinger noted that current US diplomacy is 'very responsive to the emotion of the moment' (cited in Mueller 2022) and

Union in the Cold War may prove a short-term jubilation and a pyrrhic 'victory' and ultimately defeat for humanity through MAD that seems the unavoidable effect of NATO's obstinacy, expansion, and confrontation as the effective tool of American militarism and imperialism and Western neocolonialism.

In this context, the US government and NATO in the sense of its Western 'great powers' distinct from its vasal states or satellites celebrated the dissolution of the Soviet Union and of the Warsaw Pact as the victory and declared itself the winner in the Cold War and conversely as the demise or decline of Russia, its defined and targeted 'enemy.' This may well prove to be the demise of the US/NATO as well, however, so long as the latter persists on the path of military expansionism, aggressive war, and imperialism by moving toward, confrontation with or humiliation and provocation of Russia, a pattern of conduct that is likely to end in a nuclear war and so MAD of all, including the 'winners' of the Cold War.

Therefore, one cannot possibly overstate or exaggerate the self-destructive, suicidal tendency of US/NATO expansionism, aggressive war, and imperialism inexorably moving toward destruction or collective suicide ensuing from any such war. On this account, it is hardly an overstatement or exaggeration to state that since its 'victory' over the Soviet Union the US government/NATO has behaved as an equivalent of a suicidal cult or sect bent on expanding, attacking, and destroying 'enemies' and in the process probably destroying itself through the madness of universal destruction. By so doing, the always puritanical and generally religious US government seems to move toward finally reaching Puritanism's and more broadly religion's 'delirium of annihilation masked as salvation'.[52] The problem for Americans is that this 'delirium of annihilation' as Puritan 'election' will annihilate not only 'godless' enemies like Russia or China whose destruction most of them, above all conservatives and religionists, would probably rejoice deluded or intoxicated by supremacist Americanism's claims to 'manifest destiny' and the 'Divine mission' to rule the world. It would also, by assuming the form of MAD, cause such an outcome for 'godly' puritanical America itself, unless the US government (and NATO)

---

thus implies that this foreign policy is excessively emotional and so irrational and possibly self-destructive.

52   This is what Adorno (2001, p. 230) observes and indeed presciently predicts during early postwar times since this observation sounds like it also refers to America post-2016 and since the 1980s (Reaganism). Adorno discerned and saw in these times what is evident post-2016 and since the 1980s—the fascist and religious 'delirium of annihilation masked as salvation' in conservative America of 'guns and religion.'

makes a calculation of 'victory' in a total war against 'evil', which may turn out to be a miscalculation reminiscent of Nazi Germany's Russian invasion.

More broadly, following the dissolution of the Soviet Union and the collapse of communism, specifically that in Eastern Europe and the Soviet Union, several facts and trends are manifest and salient. First, the collapse of communism is a necessary condition for the creation of democracy in its genuine, liberal-secular type, but not sufficient one, so its end does not suffice to produce a democratic beginning, as much of Eastern Europe shows, especially Poland, Hungary, and to some degree most of the Baltics, by substituting communist with conservative and theocratic dictatorships (only Czech Republic and Slovenia seem success liberal-democratic stories so far). Moreover, some countries of Eastern Europe such as Poland and Hungary appear less democratic and free or more repressive and exclusionary under the dominance of conservatism and religion than during the last days of liberalizing communism in the late 1980s.

Second, conservative dictatorships or right-wing authoritarian regimes, including fascism and theocracies, succeeding or coexisting with their communist opposites, turn out to be even more encompassing and so totalistic than communism, at least its liberalized versions in Poland, Hungary, and especially Yugoslavia and during its wanning days. Thus, conservative dictatorships or authoritarian regimes in the US since Reaganism, including theocracies and fascism post-2016, Poland and Hungary in their post-communist phase, not to mention Turkey and other Islamic countries, suppress human liberties and rights in all societal domains, from economy through polity to civil society and culture, notably suppressing personal freedom and privacy[53] such as private

---

53 A US ultra-conservative judge associated with falsely 'libertarian' Chicago economics exemplifies the fascist and generally radical-right negation of individual privacy and the rationalization of organizational privacy stating that the 'trend toward elevating personal and downgrading organizational privacy is mysterious to the economist. Secrecy is an important method of appropriating social benefits to the entrepreneur who creates them, while in private life it is more likely to conceal discreditable facts. The economic case for according legal protection to such information is no better than that for permitting fraud in the sale of goods' (cited in Ali and Bénabou 2020, p. 116). This is a remarkable, basically illiberal, antidemocratic, and uninformed, statement in several respects. First, it flagrantly negates or overlooks that personal privacy is an essential facet and indeed precondition of individual liberty and hence liberal, genuine democracy and free society. Conversely, it denies or glosses over that organizational privacy frequently amounts to what even the 'economist' Adam Smith deplored as capitalists' 'conspiracy against the public', including their 'constant and uniform combination' versus workers (also, Card 2022, p. 1083). Second, the statement is either in dogmatic denial or blissful oblivion that personal privacy typically generates no adverse external consequences on other individuals and society (Mueller 2013, p. 10). It equally denies or is oblivious of the fact that organizational privacy frequently produces negative externalities for individuals, other

abortion rights more than communism, at least in the above three liberalized communist countries.

Such a religion-driven suppression of private abortion rights especially in the conservative pole of America culminating in the conservative-dominated Supreme Court revoking the constitutional right to abortion in 2022 (along with Catholic-dominated Poland) deserves perhaps more attention and consideration given its gravity and likely leading to suppressing related and conceivably all individual liberties and privacy. For example, while US Sothern and other ultra-conservative and religious states, together with the conservative-dominated Supreme Court in violation of its own judicial precedents, fanatically and systematically suppressing and criminalizing abortion, reproductive freedom and rights, some Latin American or third-world countries like Argentina and Mexico legalize these aspects of personal freedom of choice, privacy, and human rights following such processes in the Western world, except for 'American exceptionalism'. In this regard, US 'originalist' conservatives deceptively and falsely claim that the US Constitution's stipulation of privacy—if they ever recognize it, which they typically do not—or the 'right to liberty' does not encompass reproductive freedoms and rights and thus the elemental freedom of control, or autonomy of one's own body, and disingenuously insinuate that these rights are not expressive of private or personal liberties.

This reaffirms that the essence of conservative-religious 'American exceptionalism' in this and related respects is an aberration or divergence both from liberal and secular Western society such as Western Europe and the liberalizing and secularizing non-Western third-world societies. Conversely, it suggests that such 'American exceptionalism' objectively converges with illiberal and theocratic non-Western societies such as most Islamic countries (plus

---

organizations, and society overall. Taken together, the above statement expresses or approximates proto-fascist worldviews given that fascism negates and destroys personal privacy/individual liberty and affirms and protects, with minor variations, organizational privacy versus individuals. Overall, it confirms that American conservatism, including 'libertarianism', becomes or approaches proto-fascism and is intrinsically authoritarianism generally, an ideology and movement of ersatz 'liberty'. Ali and Bénabou (2020, p. 117) note that in gross violations of individual privacy 'many US states and towns use updated forms of the pillory, whereby people arrested for certain offenses (drunk driving, tax or child support delinquency, drug possession) are publicly shamed on television or the internet, and judges sometimes sentence offenders to 'advertise' their deeds with special clothing, signs, or newspaper ads', while noting that such 'shaming punishments' are 'less common in other advanced countries' despite some recent rise through contagion from the American source.

Catholic-dominated Poland) and in that sense appears as an Islamic-style deviation from and revolt against liberal and secular or liberalizing and secularizing societies. On this account, the conservative and religious pole of America
is not only an anti- or post-Western subsociety, but belongs or comes close to
the illiberal and theocratic, as distinct from the liberalizing and secularizing,
part of the non-Western setting and to that extent more 'third-world' than the
third-world itself, for example, Mexico, in respect of reproductive freedoms
and rights and hence personal freedom of choice, privacy, and human rights.[54]
This confirms that the compound of American conservatism and extremist
religion is the gravest threat to individual liberty, privacy, and human rights not
only in Western society of which America is the supposed 'leader' but even the
world parts of which, like the countries noted above, are liberalizing and secularizing, together with Islamic theocracies and theocrats as objective allies and
'brothers in arms' in the shared crusade-jihad against liberal-secular democracy and its liberties and rights.

Generally, it confirms the unparalleled atavism and anti-modernism of
American conservatism and extremist religion as the twin principal cause and
predictor of fascism and theocracy. One cannot overstate and reiterate enough
the danger that the mix of American conservatism and extremist religion
poses for liberty and dignified life in America and beyond by such suppressions
of reproductive and hence basic personal liberties and human rights, along
with many others by various prohibitions and Puritanical wars ranging from
evangelical Prohibition to Reaganism's war on drugs. For example, many US

---

54   For example, under extreme conservative and theocratic rule, Texas 'surpasses' its neigh-
      bor Mexico in the suppression of abortion or reproductive and related personal freedoms
      and rights, especially post-2016 and after the Supreme Court's 2022 anti-abortion rul-
      ing, and thus appears as a more 'third-world' state than what it despises as the Mexican
      third world and resembles Islamic theocracies like Iran and Taliban. (That is why some
      describe Texas as 'Texanistan', an equivalent of Afghanistan's Taliban rule.) 'Freeman' in
      the all-gender meaning in Texas may have freed themselves from Mexican rule but are
      subjected now by being denied elemental human freedoms and rights to conservative-
      theocratic oppression that is apparently more total and severe than that in Mexico. So,
      Texas 'freemen' are probably predestined to return to Mexico not only for vacation but
      also to enjoy reproductive and related elemental freedoms and rights, including alcohol
      consumption for those under 21 and living in 'dry' prohibition regions. Indeed, the press
      reported in 2022 that 'Americans are turning to their southern neighbor to access abor-
      tions as some states tighten restrictions on the procedure and with the Supreme Court
      expected to strike down the right to an abortion.' And this is what the Supreme Court's
      conservative-theocratic majority indeed did in June 2022 in defiance and violation of
      both the Constitution's protection of personal freedom and right to privacy (under 'lib-
      erty') and disregard and disdain for legal precedent.

ultra-conservative-religious states criminalize abortion by punishing it with life-long and other imprisonment, just as Prohibition and Reaganism did alcohol and drug use, respectively, punishable up to life in prison (and Islamic theocracies do), which indicates a continuity between these conservative-religious Puritan wars. As regards the Supreme Court's violation of its judicial precedents in respect of reproductive freedoms and rights by revoking the constitutional right to abortion in 2022, this reaffirms that its conservative majority post-2016 and even earlier (e.g., its subversion of the 2000 elections) has consistently and ardently enabled and protected the rise of fascism, as well as capitalist dictatorship by pro-capital, anti-labor bias, and theocracy by religious fanaticism against secularism and the separation of church and state. On this account, the post-2016 conservative-dominated Supreme Court actuated by ideological extremism and religious fanaticism has become the fervent and reliable instrument of fascism, capitalist dictatorship, and theocracy in conservative America and to that extent a true national anti-liberal disgrace and shame.[55]

Third, conservative dictatorships in the US, including theocracies and post-2016 fascism, Poland and Hungary tend to be more enduring, persisting, intransigent, and obstinate, indeed claiming to be eternal, than communism that was relatively short-lived and ceased to exist by its own decision through a kind of collective euthanasia. For example, Weberian bibliocracy as evangelical theocracy and in Jefferson's description 'religious slavery' endured in conservative-religious America for centuries since proto-totalitarian and so

---

55 As it stands, the post-2016 Supreme Court and US judiciary overall is dominated by conservative extremists or radical rightists, including fascists and theocrats, as the overwhelming majority, while also including a minority of feminists and members of subordinate ethnicities, but no genuine liberals and secularists. Since the 1980s (or 1992) through the 2000s to post-2016, conservative governments and presidents have typically selected rightist extremists, including fascists and theocrats, for the Supreme Court, while their 'liberal' counterparts usually selecting feminists and members of ethnic minorities regardless of their competence or qualifications rather than true liberals. As a result of such an adverse selection of fanatical conservative extremists and incompetent feminists, there are no longer genuine and competent liberals on the post 2016 Supreme Court in contrast to prior times. No wonder, the post-2016 conservative-dominated Supreme Court has made consistently anti-liberal and anti-democratic, including fascist-style and theocratic, and to that extent disgraceful and shameful decisions, culminating in pro-gun, anti-abortion, anti-church-state separation, anti-climate action, and other rulings in 2022, while the minority's dissent revolving mostly around feminist or racial rather than genuine liberal arguments. On this account, it is hardly an exaggeration to infer that the post-2016 conservative Supreme Court becomes and acts as the chief judicial mechanism of fascism and theocracy in America, resembling its counterparts in Nazi Germany and fascist Europe, as well as neo-fascist Hungary and theocratic Poland today.

proto-fascist Puritanism (as Merton suggests) through its descendant, theocratic evangelicalism and the Bible Belt, claiming to being the eternal 'dominion of God', while communism lasted for around 70 years in the Soviet Union and less than half century in Eastern Europe.

In a digression and extension, the preceding about theocracy in conservative-religious America perhaps need be extended to Western societies generally at least within a certain sociological framework such as that of Pareto. If, as Pareto[56] classically observes, nominal Western democracies effectively evolve in 'demagogic plutocracies', they mutate into or remain substantively, even if not always formally, undemocratic theocracies although in varying degrees, with some, like the conservative-religious pole of America, more and others less. If, in Pareto view, plutocracy becomes the 'ruling power' in Western 'civilized countries', theocracy remains also such, often complementary or allied, power in these societies on account of the continuing high importance of religion in public political and social, even if somewhat declining in private, life. Specifically, just as in Pareto's depiction, being capitalist, as distinct from precapitalist, plutocracies, formal Western democracies are substantively Christian theocracies due to the persistently high importance of the Christian religion in politics and society, although in different degrees and ways, with some of them, above all, conservative-religious America such as the 'Bible Belt', Utah, and similar spaces exemplifying almost 'pure' and total theocracy[57] and others a 'diluted' and limited one, including even Scandinavia mostly retaining a variant of state religion.

The high importance of the Christian religion in Westernpolitics and society persists in that their ruling groups and persons are, as a rule, Christians, a state church/religion still often exists, including in part Scandinavia, religious texts pervade, as an ultimate 'holy' proof, the political process, as with the pervasive use and invocation of the Bible in US politics, dominant and most political parties remain explicitly or implicitly Christian, including 'Christian Democratic Party' in Germany and elsewhere, religious rituals and traditions continue to govern public—and not just private—life and be imposed on non-religious persons, and other deviations from the separation of church and state as the necessary condition of liberal democracy. Regarding the perpetuation and imposition of religious rituals and traditions, public and partly economic life in Western societies virtually comes to a standstill, full stop suspended for almost a

---

56   Pareto (1935, p. 1587) observes that nominal Western democracies 'are tending more and more to become demagogic plutocracies.' Pareto (1935, pp. 1217–20) adds that plutocracy becomes the 'ruling power' in the 'civilized countries of the West'.

57   Sorokin (1970, p. 15) distinguishes 'pure' and 'diluted' theocracy.

month during Christmas to publicly and collectively—not just privately and individually—celebrate the birth of the founder of the Christian religion, as well as for about a week for Easter celebrating the theologically supposed but never empirically demonstrated 'rebirth', as it does at other times in Islamic countries for similar occasions. This overt or subtle forcing of religious beliefs on all society and halting public and economic life for the sake of religious celebrations of a single 'holy' individual happens despite the fact that there are probably many, perhaps hundreds, secular and other historical personalities not associated with founding, spreading, and warring for a religion, notably scientists,[58] artists, philosophers, and the like, who are equally as or even more important for the liberty, prosperity, wellbeing, and progress of these same Western societies and human civilization, from Socrates and other classical Greek figures through Da Vinci and other Renaissance representatives and Copernicus, Galileo, Voltaire, and generally Enlightenment scientific rationalists and liberals to their subsequent and modern heirs in science and society. The fact that even supposedly advanced Western, let alone backward non-Western, societies prefer celebrating the birthday of a founder, spreader, and warrior of a religion from centuries ago to those of a myriad of scientists, artists, and similar figures not playing such religious roles but equally or more crucially contributing to their freedom, prosperity, wellbeing, and progress indicates that they are closer to theocracies or religiously overdetermined social systems rather than to truly liberal-secular, rationalist, and progressive ones contrary to what they hypocritically claim to be, thus substantively, even if not formally, resembling Islamic theocratic regimes. Counterfactually, if Western societies, notably America, were truly liberal-secular, rationalist, and progressive, they would instead celebrate or solemnly mark the birth of some of their many scientists and related non-religious actors contributing equally as or more substantially than any religious founders or prophets to their

---

58   Generally, this is what Saint-Simon (1964, p. 72) in his classic statement that scientists, artists, and similar occupations are 'those who direct the enterprises most useful to the nation, those who contribute to its achievements in the sciences, fine arts, and professions', calling them the 'flower' of the nation that 'would become a lifeless corpse as soon as it lost them.' Saint-Simon (1964, p. 73) suggests 'suppose that [society] preserves all the men of genius that she possesses in the science, fine arts and professions, but has the misfortune to lose in the same day' political rulers (Monsieur the King's brother and 'all the great officers of the royal household, all the ministers'), aristocrats as the first estate (the 'richest proprietors who live in the style of nobles'), so by implication their allies, religious grandees as the 'second estate', and yet 'this loss of individuals, considered to be most important in the State, would only grieve [society] for purely sentimental reasons and would result in no political evil for the State.'

freedom, prosperity, and progress, thus to what they claim to exceptionally, as per 'American exceptionalism', represent in an insidious distinction from unfree, poor, and backward non-Western nations.

At the minimum, if not always, then at least during Christmas and related 'holy' occasions, Western societies manifest themselves as effective theocracies rather than secular democracies, perpetuating and enforcing centuries-old discredited religious rituals and traditions, including theocratic medievalism in the form of the Christian Dark Middle Ages—simply, in such periods peoples in these settings feel like living in a primitive theocracy or 'godly' regime rather than in secular modernity. Minimally, during Christmas and the like, Western societies prove to languish and petrify in pre-Enlightenment and premodern irrational times rather than embodying and implementing the rationalist Enlightenment as the overcoming of the backwardness and darkness of the Christian Middle Ages and its product liberal, secular, and democratic modernity. In other words, at these 'holy' occasions, they, especially conservative-religious America, remain and petrify as 'Christian' and hence primitive, theocratic, religiously nationalist, and exclusionary rather than modern, liberal, secular, and inclusive societies, as they claim to be in an invidious distinction from non-Western nations, thus manifesting their true underlying nature. For instance, America as a 'Christian' society appears as a functional theocratic and so anti-liberal, undemocratic equivalent of Iran, Turkey, and in part Taliban as an 'Islamic' republic or state, thus showing its genuine hidden or latent character, because both represent theocracies even if with differing religious origins, means, and degrees. By definition and in practice, 'Christian' America and the 'Christian West overall is a society in which non-Christians, including both non-Christian believers and non-believers, liberals, and secularists, 'need not apply and indeed exist', just as non-Muslims need not in 'Islamic' republics of Iran, Turkey, and Taliban. This shows that these religious-theocratic societies are functional equivalents despite each claiming to differ from and even oppose, as via wars of religion for global dominance, the other.

The above hence exposes Western societies', especially the American or Anglo-Saxon, tendency to lecture and preach to non-Western countries, including Eastern Europe, the Balkans, China, and Russia, about 'democracy', 'freedom', 'human rights', and 'separation of church and state', as a disingenuous 'cheap talk' and travesty so long as America and the West overall seems no different substantively, even if differing formally, at least during Christmas and similar, especially Bible-invoking American-style, occasions, from the Muslim world, in that both systems exemplify theocracies or 'godly' regimes rather than secular democracies. No doubt, the two differ but theirs are differences in specific ways and means of operation and quantitative, statistical-like degrees of unfreedom or oppression, with Islamic countries being more unfree or oppressive, rather than in quality, substance, or kind that is essentially theocratic or non-secular minimally during Christmas and similar 'holy' times, thus as theocracies. This is what Pareto would likely suggest if he lived at present and witnessed the persistently high importance of the Christian religion in political and social, while by contrast declining in private, life in nominal Western democracies at least during Christmas and similar 'sacred' periods, as of Islam in Muslim countries at other occasions.[59] Notably, he would suggest that while secular aristocracies or elites, including their capitalist and by implication socialist forms, 'do not last' in the long course of history as their 'circulation' and 'graveyard', theocracies tend to perpetuate and petrify themselves as eternal 'in the name of the Divine master,'[60] as their American form from Puritanism to the 'Bible Belt' shows.

Fourth and related, conservative dictatorships, especially theocracies, at least in the US, including post-2016 fascism, Poland, and Hungary, as well as Islamic countries, are more uncompromising, unapologetic, and unrepentant than communism, at least in the above three liberal communist countries. Thus, theocracy, generally conservatism and religion, including post-2016 fascism, in the US never apologizes for its committing various atrocities from Puritanism's proxy-genocide and dispossession of Native Americans, persecutions of dissenters and witch-trials through the invasion and violent conquest of Mexican territories and mistreating South America, Southern slavery and segregation, evangelicalism's coercive Prohibition through wars of aggression, devastation, and torture of Vietnam, Yugoslavia, Iraq, and other countries and peoples, to Reaganism's Puritanical war on drugs and the resulting mass imprisonment of moral sinners and executions of often innocent persons, and

---

59   Indeed, Pareto (2000, p. 86) states that the 'religion of Christ, which seemed especially made for the poor and humble, has generated the Roman theocracy' and suggests that its additional product is the theocracy of Protestantism as in his view even more coercive and total, as with Calvin's Geneva. Regarding the latter, Pareto (1935, p. 1144) observes that life 'at Geneva under Calvin was much less free, much more extensively governed by ultra-experimental considerations, than life in Rome ever had been under the rule of the Popes; and taken all in all, Protestantism was much more narrow-minded, much more oppressive, than the Catholic Church had been in countries where the Reform superseded Catholicism; while Catholicism, on its side, under the impact of the attack upon it became less tolerant, less indulgent, more aggressive.'

60   Pareto (2000, p. 55) recounts that Christian 'warlike prelates donned armor over their stoles and went out to kill in the name of the divine master.'

many other similar acts, while communism apologized for its misdeeds and left the stage by its own choice.

Overall, the collapse of communism in Eastern Europe and the Soviet Union shows that if there is something even more total, enduring, intransigent, unrepentant, briefly worse, then it is conservative or right-wing dictatorship and theocracy ruling and eternalized in America, at least the South qua the Bible Belt, for long, indeed eternally and resurging in other countries like Poland and Hungary, together with fascism rising with the post-2016 US autocratic regime. In this sense, the collapse of communism does not mark the 'end of history' in the sense of ending dictatorship and repression but rather the resurgence and reinvention of conservative dictatorship or right-wing authoritarianism, including fascism and theocracy, as even more totalistic, enduring, and unrepentant from America post-2016 to Eastern Europe like Poland and Hungary. In this regard, the collapse of communism does not usher in true, liberal democracy and free society but instead the rebirth of authoritarian conservatism, the reassertion and perpetuation of theocracy, and as a consequence the new surge of fascism in America post-2016, as well as Poland, Hungary, and beyond.

In any event, the above shows that NATO not only engages in infinite, reckless expansionism and manifests aggressiveness and threat toward non-members from Yugoslavia to Russia, Iran, and conceivably China. To add insult to injury, NATO embraces and adds the WW II Axis of fascist and other authoritarian states in its quest for global military domination in the service of American militarism and imperialism and Western neocolonialism. By so doing, NATO shows its true face and functions as a functional equivalent of the WW II fascist Axis, despite its 'defensive alliance', 'democracy', 'free world' and related deceptions or delusions. This holds true of NATO's 'great' imperial and colonial powers like the US and to some degree Great Britain, France, Italy, and Turkey, and not to its vasal states becoming proxy American colonies or military outposts, such as Eastern and Southern European countries (the Baltics, Poland, Albania, Croatia, Macedonia, Montenegro, etc.).

Namely, during the formation and early stages of NATO, the US allied with such fascist Axis states as Germany, Italy, and Turkey, as well as Nazi-allied Denmark and (Quisling) Norway,[61] together with Japan in the Asian military alliance, and in the later multiple waves of NATO's expansion with other WW II fascist or Nazi-puppet regimes from Portugal and Spain to Albania, Bulgaria, Croatia, Hungary, Slovenia, Slovakia, the Baltics, plus Ukraine and other

---

61   Paxton (2004, p. 40) with reference to the 'themes that appeal to fascists' in various cultural traditions invokes the 'foggy Norse myths that stirred Norwegians or Germans.'

Nazi-ruled parts of the former Soviet Union. So, adding insult to injury, the US government not only formed and expanded NATO despite the non-existence and dissolution of the Warsaw Pact at the points of formation and expansion, respectively, but adopted and included in NATO practically all the fascist Axis or Nazi-puppet states (except for Ukraine for now) from WW II. By allying with these Axis states, the US government effectively allied and to some degree merged with fascism within NATO and related aggressive military alliances in launching and conducting the Cold War against the Soviet Union and intensifying this posture by military confrontation with or provocation of Russia since the 1990s through the 2020s likely eventuating in 'hot' war with a MAD outcome. A related example of this effective alliance and merger with fascism is the US government's recruiting Nazi-era scientists for its missile program during the early 1950s and thus as instruments in its Cold War and religion-style crusade against communism and for global military domination. Another example in this respect is the US government's consistently supporting neo-Nazi secessionist movements and states (Muslim Bosnia, Croatia, and Slovenia) during Yugoslavia's civil war and even allying with them (Kosovo's Liberation Army as a descendent of the pro-Nazi Albanian *Balli Kombëtar* movement from WW II) in attacking the remaining portion of this country. In short, the US government in the Balkans and beyond supported and allied with the same fascist forces that its military fought in WW II. This hence betrays and disrespects those Americans who died fighting fascism and the Axis overall during WW II and hence the Jeffersonian liberal ideals of liberty and democracy as the most effective antidote to the poison of fascism.

To that extent, the above reveals the US government's underlying neo-fascist or extreme-right nature rooted in Puritan theocratic proto-fascism and couched in 'democracy' and 'freedom' slogans, as well as its utter Machiavellian amorality—the depravity of allying and merging with, to use its own terminology, the ultimate 'evil' of fascism (the 'devil') to attain its ends of winning the Cold War and conceivably a real war against its defined 'enemies'. The US government's underlying nature probably expresses the frequent observation that most of America (and the 'American character') is rightist rather than leftist and in that sense closer to fascism as radical rightism than to socialism and liberalism. Of course, this applies to conservative America as the prime source, driver, and epicenter of fascism or radical rightism and the dominant and indeed expanding pole of the US in demographic, geographic, and sociological terms versus liberal America as the secondary, weaker, and diminishing anti-fascist opposite.

The US's creation, perpetuation, and expansion of NATO violates Jefferson-Madison's ideal of non-entanglement also by the 'divide and rule' strategy

especially against non-members and the Warsaw Pact's former members, causing, provoking, or aggravating various wars, such as those between Croatia[62]
and Serbia, Bosnia and Serbia, Kosovo and Serbia, Albanian secessionists and
Macedonia in Yugoslavia, Russia, and Georgia and Ukraine within the Soviet
Union, and so on. By inciting or exacerbating these and other countries to fight
against each other, it replicates the Nazi Balkans and Eastern policy that caused
almost identical wars or animosities, for example, between Croatia and Serbia.
In this connection, an interesting episode is that an American 'evangelist-
methodist' (sic) church, actually a sect (in Weber's sense), has existed in
Macedonia within socialist or communist Yugoslavia since the 1970s and still
exists today, while the US conservative government at federal, state, and local
levels was severely persecuting, discriminating against, or excluding socialists
or communists as 'un-American' from McCarthyism to Reaganism and beyond
up to post-2016/2020. (Some Southern states like Florida and Texas under
conservative-fascist and theocratic rule have even launched new 'red scares'
and 'witch hunts' in the style of McCarthyism after 2020.) Moreover, in a corollary episode, a member of this sect became Macedonia's president in the early
2000s—an equivalent to an irreligious person, communist, or socialist becoming an American President as a supreme taboo, so a reality versus a fiction—
while socialists or communists in the US still being repressed and mistreated
as second-class citizens who 'need not apply' for political position and public
employment or office and subjected to recurring 'red scares' and 'witch hunts'
(as by the federal radical-right government post-2016 and by ultra-conservative
states Florida, Texas, and others after 2020).

These episodes indicate that the US conservative government exported religious fundamentalism and sectarianism to socialist Yugoslavia while banish-
ing and mistreating socialists or communists in America. Apparently, socialist
Yugoslavia was less afraid of and alarmed by religious fundamentalism and sectarianism than the US conservative government was of socialist or communist
and related ideas that it branded 'un-American' in a display of pathological fear

---

62   For instance, during the 1995 Croatian army's attack, reportedly using Germany-provided
     weapons, among others, on the Serbian population, the US ambassador to Croatia stated
     that the US government 'understands' this action and thus effectively supported the mas-
     sacre and massive expulsion of non-Croatian ethnic groups. Such an 'understanding' and
     justification of these atrocities by, to add insult to injury, a government descending from
     the ww II Nazi-puppet (*Ustasha*) state, was in continuity with the 1992 US secretary of
     state denouncing the Yugoslav Federal army intervention against secession in Croatia as
     an 'unjustified attack' as if not knowing or deliberately overlooking that the latter republic
     was a part of Yugoslavia—just as the South was one of the US before the Civil War—thus
     perhaps encouraging its neo-Nazi rulers to perpetrate the above atrocities few years later.

and hysteria as collective madness in the style of Puritan hysterias and witch-trials. This indicates that there was probably more freedom of religion and so liberty of conscience even in socialist Yugoslavia than freedom of opinion and speech in conservative-dominated America as the presumptive leader of the 'free world' since McCarthyism through Reaganism and later. Furthermore, those living under both societal settings and ideologies likely realize after the fact that conservative-dominated America was probably and remains more severe and totalitarian in coercion and repression than socialist Yugoslavia and Eastern Europe (especially Hungary and Poland) and to some degree even the Soviet Union (during Gorbachev), so American conservatism, including fascism or theocracy, reached and sustains at present a higher degree of totalitarianism than communism at least in these Eastern European countries during the 1980s. Thus, the South qua the theocratic 'Bible Belt' from Alabama and Tennessee to Oklahoma and Texas has always been, remains, and even intensifies post-2016 as more severe and totalitarian in conservative-fascist and religion-driven oppression, including mass imprisonment for sins-as-crimes and executions often of innocent persons, than communist Yugoslavia after the 1950s, Hungary and Poland since the 1980s, and even the Gorbachev Soviet Union have ever been.

Notably, this region and conservative America as a whole driven by ideological extremism and religious fanaticism has aways suppressed and still more severely and totally suppresses individual liberty and privacy, including reproductive and sexual freedoms and rights, as well as cultural, intellectual, and religious freedom from coercive religion, than Yugoslavia and these other Eastern European countries have ever done since the 1950s or during the 1980s. (On this account, Orwell's *1984* in which the main actor is executed because of a sexual affair objectively depicts or predicts conservative America such as the theocratic 'Bible Belt' more than Eastern Europe, because the first did and does suppress in Puritanism's style sexual and related individual freedoms and rights more severely and totally than the second.) The preceding only reaffirms that if there has been after WW II a more severe and totalitarian society than socialist Yugoslavia, Eastern Europe (Hungary and Poland), and in part the Soviet Union (Gorbachev's time), it is conservative-ruled America like the 'Bible Belt' and similar regions, so if something worse than communism has existed and still persists, it is American conservatism, including post-2016 fascism and de facto permanent theocracy or religious revolution from Puritanism to evangelicalism (or the Christian Right as a theocratic, anti-democratic evangelical-Catholic alliance).

No doubt, communism in this region at least (China being a more ambiguous case) was bad enough and a dismal failure despite the probably 'good intentions' to create a free, equal, inclusive, and just society, but the anti-communist substitute that American imperialism imposes on or exports to, as a set of 'American values,' to Eastern Europe is essentially no better and even worse in certain economic, political, and other social respects, such as oligarchic control and the slave-like condition of labor, resurgence of anti-democratic conservatism, including fascism and theocracy, suppression of cultural and intellectual freedom, culture irrationalism, and anti-rationalism, Puritan-style religion-driven repression of individual liberties and privacy, and so on. In the economy, American imperialism in the name of 'free enterprise' launched a religious-style crusade against communism as an economic system and yet imposes on or exports to, as 'American values,' to Eastern Europe and beyond unconstrained, antiegalitarian, and coercive anti-labor, including, oligarchic capitalism and to that extent capitalist dictatorship which reduces workers to slave-like conditions by denying basic labor freedoms and rights like unionization, collective bargaining, participation in corporate governance, etc. This exposes the ultimate aim or outcome of American imperialism's crusade against communism as a type of economy—substitution of communist anti-capital dictatorship by capitalist anti-labor dictatorship subjecting labor to slave-style treatment, and not by democratic capitalism with universal freedom ('free enterprise') both for capital and labor. Thus, owing to American imperialism, aside from few exceptions, most of Eastern Europe represents oligarchic capitalism and, in that sense, American-style capitalist dictatorship which weak degrees of basic labor freedoms and rights epitomize, such as low union density and coverage, non-existent or sporadic collective bargaining, absent or minimal labor participation in management, etc. As a result, workers in Eastern Europe under American-style capitalist dictatorship or oligarchic capitalism look less free or have less dignity in and control and security of their economic life than even under communism, especially its liberalized version in Yugoslavia after the 1950s and Hungary and Poland since the 1980s.

In the polity, American imperialism fought in the name of 'democracy' and 'freedom' a religious-like crusade against communism as a political system but imposes on or exports to, as additional 'American values,' to Eastern Europe and beyond extreme conservatism to the point of fascism or radical-right politics post-2016 and theocracy constantly and thus an anti-democratic regime rather than true, liberal-secular democracy and thus universal liberty and rights. This reveals that the underlying goal or effect of American imperialism's crusade against communism as a polity was substitution of communist anti-fascist and anti-religious by fascist or radical-right and theocratic dictatorship committing severe and total repression of political freedoms and rights, and not genuine liberal-secular democracy with universal liberty and rights and inclusion.

Thus, due to American imperialism, apart from few and diminishing exceptions, most Eastern Europe exemplifies ideologically and politically the system of American-style repressive conservatism involving fascism post-2016 or radical-right regimes (e.g., Hungary which US conservatives seek to transplant in reverse as a model for America) and theocracy (Poland) rather than true, liberal-secular democracy, as US and other Western officials promised during the anti-communist revolution they celebrated in an irrational euphoria as the end of history and the beginning of the paradise of liberty. In consequence, people in Eastern Europe under American-style conservatism, fascism, and theocracy do not seem freer or to have more control and power of politics than during liberalized communism, as in the countries mentioned above.

In culture, American imperialism waged in the name of 'freedom' and 'science' a religious-style crusade against communism as a cultural form and yet imposes on or exports to, as other 'American values,' to Eastern Europe and beyond a system of suppression of cultural, including artistic, intellectual, and religious, freedoms and culture irrationalism and anti-rationalism, including religious superstitions and anti-science, rather than freedom and science. This helps uncover the true purpose or result of American imperialism's crusade against communism as a cultural system—substitution of Marxist by religious suppression of artistic, intellectual, and other cultural freedoms (including freedom from coercive religion) and religion-driven perversion of art, science, education, and other culture. Thus, associated with American imperialism, apart from few exceptions, most of Eastern Europe increasingly features American-style religion-driven suppression of cultural, including artistic and academic, freedoms and culture irrationalism and anti-rationalism, including religious superstitions and anti-science (especially theocratic or extremely religious countries like Poland and others). Consequently, people in Eastern Europe under American-style religion-driven suppression of artistic and academic freedoms and culture irrationalism and anti-rationalism like religious superstitions and anti-science appear to be no freer culturally or to have more control of their cultural, scientific, and educational lives than in liberalized communism in which Marxist ideological influences almost disappeared in the countries noted earlier.

In civil society, American imperialism started in the name of 'individual freedom' a religious-style crusade against communism as an (un)civil sphere but imposes on or exports to, as further 'American values,' to Eastern Europe Puritan-style moralistic, religion-driven negation and suppression of individual liberty and privacy and in that sense moral fascism rather than a genuine, liberal civil society respecting and promoting such liberties. This deciphers that that the actual end or product of American imperialism's crusade against communism in civic terms was substitution of non-religious by religious repression of individual liberty and privacy, including religion-driven mass imprisonment, and thus perversion of civil society, rather than protection and promotion of these liberties and rights. Thus, mainly because of American imperialism, apart from rare exceptions, most of Eastern Europe is plagued with American-style Puritanical moralistic and religion-driven suppression of individual liberty and privacy, including reproductive rights in theocracies like Poland, with widespread or growing imprisonment (not yet executions though because of the European Union's prohibition of the death penalty) rather than enjoying a true, liberal civil society. As an effect, people in Eastern Europe under American-style Puritanical moralistic and religion-driven suppression of individual liberty and privacy do not look freer and even look less free in terms of some basic personal freedom and rights like abortion than under liberalized communism in which these were less severely restricted. Taken together, American imperialism launched a religious-style crusade against communism but generates an anti-communist substitute that is in the experience or perception of most of Eastern Europe no much better and even worse in some respects, by involving a set of essential 'American values'.These are, first, capitalist dictatorship through oligarchic capitalism, second, repressive conservatism, including fascism and theocracy, third, religion-driven suppression of cultural freedoms and culture irrationalism and anti-rationalism, and fourth, Puritan-style suppression of individual liberty and privacy like reproductive and related private freedoms and rights.

Overall, most data and rankings in this chapter show that if there is a 'free world' as a Cold-War ideological invidious construction, it is primarily most of Western Europe, notably Scandinavia, and the US does not belong to this setting, let alone being its 'leader', during conservatism and under fascism post-2016. They moreover disclose the US post-2016, namely its conservative-religious pole, as a non- or post-Western society resembling less liberal-secular Western Europe, notably Scandinavia, than third-world illiberal countries, especially Islamic theocracies Iran, Saudi Arabia, Turkey, and Taliban.[63]

---

63   Dawkins (2006, p. 289) points to the Christian 'American Taliban' (also implied in Mansbach 2006) that is especially dominant in the 'Bible Belt' from Alabama and Tennessee to Oklahoma and Texas. In this view, the 'American Taliban' imposes a Christian equivalent of Islamic Sharia law—so made redundant despite religious conservatives' paranoia about 'Sharia law' in America—by numerous suppressions of personal freedoms and rights (including abortion, alcohol, etc.) and Draconian punishments for sins-as-crimes resulting in mass imprisonment and widespread executions, including often of innocent persons yet 'guilty' by association for 'original sin' according to US evangelical theocrats in the South and beyond.

Furthermore, what negates and betrays Jefferson-Madison's independence ideal of the American Revolution is the consequent disrespect of the national independence of especially smaller nations through the US's and NATO's wars of aggression against various countries. They include its UN-unauthorized and so illegal and unprovoked attack on Yugoslavia based on the fabrication of a 'massacre' and allying with Albanian Islamic secessionists and terrorists from Kosovo, the invasion and perpetual occupation of Iraq based on the 'weapons of mass destruction' falsehood, not to mention the Vietnam War as the likely cruelest post-WW II war initiated by similar falsehoods, colonizing the Warsaw Pact's members and parts of the Soviet Union like Georgia and Ukraine, and moving toward Russia's borders as the irrational act of bellicosity with the specter of MAD. Relatedly, a violation of the independence ideal is NATO's incorporating and making, in replication of the Nazi WW II template, smaller countries, such as those in Eastern/Southern Europe and the Balkans, vasal states or proxy colonies and using them as US subservient tools for the sake of confrontation with or provocation of and ultimately wars of aggression against 'enemies' like China and especially Russia, just as Nazi Germany did versus the latter. This tendency results in the US's and NATO's perverting the national independence of smaller members (e.g., Bulgaria, Macedonia, Montenegro, etc.), rather than providing their 'defense' and 'security' from Russian and other foreign 'threats' as deceptive fabrications or ludicrous fictions (e.g., Russia's 'threat' to Macedonia or Montenegro).

In essence, the US/NATO has effectively recolonized or controlled these regions and harnessed them in the service of imperial expansion, conquest, and domination by moving toward and threatening to also colonize or dominate Russia and China through offensive imperial wars that can only terminate in MAD. This recolonizing or controlling tendency violates Jefferson-Madison's independence ideal of the American Revolution and manifests ultimate irrationalism to the point of self-destructive madness caused by the intoxication with supremacist Americanism actuated by 'manifest destiny' delusions or 'superior nation' beliefs.

For example, the US/NATO effectively colonized or controlled and incorporated smaller countries like Bulgaria, Macedonia, Montenegro, and others to use them in its expansion toward and confrontation with their traditional ally Russia rather than to ensure their independence, defense, and security from the 'Russian' threat as a deception and manipulation. Specifically, Macedonia has no border with Russia, so it is ludicrous to claim it is threatened by the latter. The only sensible reason for its NATO application and membership is its protection from NATO itself, especially Albania seeking to create, with the constant and crucial support of the US, a 'Greater Albania' by seizing parts of Macedonia populated by Albanian secessionists whose main supporter are American conservative and other politicians, including Presidents during the 1999 Kosovo War and after 2020. In fact, if Macedonia had a choice, most Macedonians, excluding ethnic Albanians who view themselves as members of some 'Greater Albania', judging by public opinion or private opinions, would probably choose an alliance with Russia perceived as a historical defender rather than with the US/NATO. According to their statements, they have experienced, perceived, and suffered under the latter as an enemy, 'evil' empire, and a protector—as during the 1999 Kosovo War and the 2001 rebellion in Macedonia by Albanian secessionists whom NATO saved from military defeat—of their main existential treat Albania and Kosovo where the US government erected the largest military base in the Balkans, and Albanian separatists and terrorists.

However, they have no such a choice because the US/NATO has effectively recolonized this small country, as most of the Balkans, and recreated a puppet state by actions and threats of economic, political, and military blackmail, threat, and dependency, simply imperialism or neocolonialism. Indeed, most Macedonians and other Yugoslavs, minus neo-Nazi Croat, Slovenian and Bosnian Muslim governments, experience or perceive the US/NATO as an equivalent of Nazi Germany and the Axis by playing a decisive role in the disintegration of Yugoslavia and militarily attacking the rest of the latter on behalf of Albanian secessionists and terrorists, and pursuing the Nazi-style 'divide and rule' policy in the Balkans by pitting one Balkan nation against the other, notably Croatia against Serbia, just as Nazism did during WW II. From their experience or statements, what Pareto remarked about imperial and by implication Nazi Germany applies to the US government after the Cold War: American conservatism, including fascism, 'preaches militarism, war and extermination against the enemies of [America] and also against those who, though not her enemies, refuse to be her slaves.'

For example, in the opinion of most Yugoslavs, the US government driven by imperialism and militarism after the Cold War caused, provoked, or exacerbated and prolonged the various civil wars in their country that led to its disintegration and the death and suffering of its populations, together with secessionist, including fascist, forces. In this opinion, Yugoslavia would have not suffered civil wars and eventually disintegrated without the imperialist activities of the US government in alliance with these secessionist fascist and other nationalist forces. At the minimum, such opinions perceive, rightly or wrongly, the US government as instrumental in causing or aggravating these civil wars and the consequent collapse of this country as were secessionist fascist and other forces in its regions (especially Croatia, Slovenia, Muslim Bosnia, and Kosovo). First, in this view, the American government provoked or aggravated the first civil war in Yugoslavia by denouncing (as by US secretary of state in August of 1992) the counter-secession reactions of the federal government, comparable to condemning the Union's reaction to the Southern Confederacy's secession, while supporting Croatia's violent secession and recreation of a neo-Nazi (*Ustasha*) regime, as well as its atrocities against non-Croatian ethnicities (as by its ambassador's 'we understand' statement in August 1995). Second, in this view, the American government prolonged or exacerbated the second civil war in Yugoslavia by reportedly urging Bosnia's Muslim secessionist forces to reject an early peace agreement (in the Fall of 1992), thus being indirectly responsible for the subsequent death and destruction in this republic. Third, in this view, the American government provoked or aggravated the third civil war in Yugoslavia by US President threatening (in 1992) a military intervention if the Yugoslav federal state reacts to the province of Kosovo's secession, which seems equivalent to the British empire's threat to the Union's reaction to the Southern Confederacy's secession, thus paving the way for the formation of an 'ethnic terrorist army' (Kosovo Liberation Army descending from Nazi-allied Albanian groups) and its protection by NATO's unprovoked bombardment of a country as a classic act of inter-state terror (in 1999). Fourth, in these perceptions, the American government provoked or aggravated the fourth civil war or its proxy in Yugoslavia by continuing to support the operations of the same 'ethnic terrorist army' in Macedonia (in 2001) and indeed NATO rescuing its ally from defeat (as in July of that year) and forcing the Macedonian government to accept the demands of these terrorists (as its secretary generally initially called them) qua 'freedom fighters' as their 'human rights.' (Yet Albanians in Macedonia and Yugoslavia overall had more extensive human rights than in their native country Albania, while showing disloyalty by refusing, especially their secessionist leaders dreaming of the 'Greater Albania', to speak the language of the adoptive country and lawlessness by perverting rule of law through violating laws and committing violent and other mafia-style crimes with impunity, especially after their terrorist insurrection, but still being 'freedom fighters' and 'good guys' for the US government as their main ally and protector, and notably of the neo-Nazi 'Kosovo Liberation Army' and its Macedonian branch. Replicating the divide and rule strategy versus Yugoslavia, the US government has provoked or exacerbated civil wars within the former Soviet Union, such as those between Georgia and Russia and Ukraine and Russia, by arming and instigating anti-Russian, including neo-Nazi, regimes and movements and seeking to incorporate them into NATO and thus convert them into neo-colonial vassal, dependent states in relation to America and the West.) Overall, the US government as a rule did and does support illiberal conservative and undemocratic, including fascist, movements and regimes within Yugoslavia (most egregiously Croatia's and Kosovo's neo-Nazi forces) against their liberal, democratic, as well as socialist counterparts, just as it did in Eastern Europe and the former Soviet Union (including neo-Nazis or nationalist extremists in Ukraine by helping overthrow a democratically elected government in 2014), thus acting consistent with an 'evil empire' in the Balkans. This shows and indeed reaffirms that the US government and hence the nexus of American militarism and imperialism is willing and ready to ally and even merge with fascism in the Balkans, as well as Eastern Europe and the former Soviet Union (e.g., Ukraine), only to attain its supreme end of world domination. This fascist alliance and merger in the former Yugoslavia and beyond demonstrates and confirms the Machiavellian amorality of American militarism and imperialism and exposes its 'higher moral ground' as a deception or delusion, apart from betraying those Americans fighting fascism in WW II.

At the end, owing to NATO expansionism and US imperialism, Macedonia like Bulgaria is vulnerable in case of an imperial offensive war to a retaliatory nuclear strike by its traditional defender Russia, which shows the deadly perversity of the Nazi-style 'divide and rule' policy that the US applies to these fraternal Slavic nations[64] that it made mutual 'enemies.' This holds good for such other Slavic nations as Poland, Czech Republic, Croatia, Slovenia, Slovakia, and the Baltics, plus NATO-aspiring Ukraine, that are also made more vulnerable to such attacks by another Slavic nation, showing the potentially lethal result of the Nazi-style 'divide and rule' policy of NATO expansionism and US imperialism. Overall, the above makes Europe more vulnerable to nuclear retaliation and devastation rather than secure from the Russian 'threat', which indicates the perversity and suicidal irrationalism of NATO expansionism and US imperialism, with the first acting as the military tool of the second and Western neocolonialism.

Further, the US especially under conservatism contradicts and betrays Jefferson-Madison's non-entanglement, independence, and non-militarist

---

64   In passing, the US and Great Britain (plus Germany) denounce or dismiss the actual or potential political solidarity or cultural, including linguistic, commonality between Slavic nations, including Russia, while exalting and promoting that between Anglo-Saxon or English-speaking countries. Thus, Anglo-Saxon countries denounce or suspect such Slavic solidarity or commonality as threatening or cover for the domination of Russia over others. Yet, they approve and support virtually any acts, including the most atrocious, of the US government, as they showed by supporting its invasions, mass killing, and destruction from Latin America and Vietnam to Yugoslavia, Afghanistan, and Iraq, and conversely (as by the US's support of Great Britain's Falkland colonial war) in a display of shared Puritan-style hypocrisy.

ideals by erecting and maintaining foreign military bases in an unparalleled number of countries[65] throughout the world and even beyond NATO. As during the Cold War, the US government continues to use its vast foreign military bases to suppress liberal, democratic, independence, or socialist movements from Europe to Latin America, to sustain capitalist, conservative, religious, and fascist dictatorships in power, and to launch wars of aggression or military interventions, thus in the service of global oppression, militarism, and offensive war. For example, the US government used it military bases in Germany, Italy, Turkey, and elsewhere to launch an illegitimate, unprovoked attack on Yugoslavia in 1999, those in Kuwait, Saudi Arabia, and other Gulf states for its 2003 invasion of Iraq, just as those in Asia for invading Vietnam, and so on. And most Americans, above all conservatives and fascists, are either blissfully ignorant of or assent to support this Leviathan of foreign military bases as tools of global oppression, aggressive war, and imperialism, and hence the warfare state—just as the huge police state at home—while refusing to fund or support, for example, universal health care, welfare assistance, and other facets of the welfare state. In so doing, they legitimize the US government in its impoverishing or keeping impoverished much of the population (almost a fifth judging by the data presented earlier) while spending almost unlimited societal resources on foreign military bases and so on global oppression, offensive war, and imperial domination, which is what, according to what Reagan argued for the Soviet Union, precisely defines an 'evil empire'. Of course, for US conservatives, including false 'libertarians', and fascists, such a Leviathan of foreign military bases, plus the gigantic military industrial complex and limitless military expenditure, hence the warfare state, as well as its twin the pervasive (vice) police state, is a 'limited' government, while the most minimal welfare state in the Western world being 'big' government, which reveals the perversity, deception, or delusion of American conservatism, spurious 'libertarianism', and fascism.

---

65   Steinmetz (2005, p. 361) depicts the US under conservatism as an 'unprecedented empire of bases.' Vine (2015) finds that the US has in more than 70 countries and territories almost 800 military bases belonging to the 'American Empire Project' and harming America and the world. Schaeffer-Duffy (2022) ironically remarks that the 'US, which has military troops and 149 countries, does not consider itself an empire,' thus implying a Puritan-style hypocrisy via deliberate deception or inner delusion. For example, the US government in a typically irrational and self-righteous manner raised alarm about China's opening a military base in some small Islands, its second overall, while itself having and further multiplying 800 bases in 70 countries and territories. So, for the US government another country's just second military base is a graver 'threat' than its nearly thousand bases throughout the globe consistent with its Orwellian eternal war as 'peace' anti-logic.

Therefore, these US most numerous and ever-growing military bases are a syndrome of militarist expansion seeking world domination and resulting in wars of aggression to the no-return point of nuclear war of MAD as the pathological outcome of conservative militarism and bellicose irrationalism rooted in the Puritan 'manifest destiny' delusion and intoxicated by supremacist 'superior nation' Americanism. These military bases virtually in the entire world are an instrument and syndrome of extreme militarism, the blueprint and practice of offensive wars, and imperial conquest and domination rather than the means of national defense and security: they do not serve to defend and secure America but to threaten, attack, and dominate other countries. To that extent, as manifestations and tools of imperialism, such military bases including large troops and destructive weapons in NATO and many other states are consistent with the model of an 'evil' empire. For illustration, the US government has stationed nuclear weapons in dozen NATO European and other countries, manifesting the pattern of aggressiveness and imperialism, including military, political, economic or commercial, and cultural imperialisms, after the model of an 'evil empire', while its defined 'enemies' Russia and China having no such weapons in any foreign locations.

An excursus on economic and cultural imperialism. Concerning American commercial or economic imperialism,[66] it appears that the US government invaded various countries to force them to buy American products that they otherwise would not purchase, likely including notoriously poor-quality cars and other non-quality goods, simply 'lemons', plagued with poor workmanship, that the US economy as a rule produces, aside from a few exceptions, due to its defective model of coercive, predatory, unrestrained capitalism,[67] thus is

---

66   Berger et al. (2013, p. 864) detect American 'commercial imperialism' intertwined with its
      military and political forms, finding that 'US influence raised the share of total imports
      that the intervened country purchased from the US [that is] consistent with US political
      influence being used to create a larger market for US products in the intervened coun-
      try.' Especially, they find that the 'increase in imports from the US was greatest for goods
      which the US had a comparative *dis*advantage in producing. That is, the new goods that
      were shipped from the US to the intervened country were products that US firms were
      less competitive in producing. [So] US influence being used to create a larger market for
      products that firms would otherwise have difficulty selling internationally' (Berger et al.
      2013, pp. 864–5).
67   Relatedly, as a syndrome of a predatory capitalist state, Southern states like Texas have
      laws allowing them to seize individuals' banking accounts if these are inactive for 2 years.
      Thus, these predatory, proto-fascist, and theocratic capitalist states can plunder individu-
      als' assets and violate their property rights while being 'open to business' with capitalists
      that subject their workers to a slave-like treatment by paying them the lowest possible
      wages and suppressing their basic labor rights like union organization. Regarding the lat-
      ter, one needs only to casually observe construction and similar workers—working from

CHAPTER 5

unable to export normally or uncompetitive in the world market. Incidentally, this production of typically non-quality products like cars and others that most countries would not import and their consumers would not buy normally as uncompetitive by their quality-price ratios in the world market is probably a major reason for US persistent and huge trade deficits rather than—as nativist fascists post-2016 and falsely 'free market' conservatives since Reagan's hysteria against Japanese higher-quality car imports, allege—'unfair' competition and trade from other nations and companies. Given the production of typically non-quality products like most cars, home appliances, consumer goods, average homes, and others plagued with poor workmanship and reliability, the reports of the high 'growth rate' of the US economy effectively translate into those of the high growth rate of a junk economy by producing 'lemons' from junk food to junk houses.[68] Overall, considering Reagan's and post-2016 fascist, nativist hysteria against higher-quality car and other imports, Reaganites and other US conservatives-fascists are false 'free market' pretenders so long as there are no free markets without free trade which they overtly or covertly attack, just as do their allies, post-2016 nativist fascists. They do this while preaching 'free market' capitalism that amounts to proxy autarchy, a closed national economy as a long-standing conservative ideal from Hamilton to Reagan and the post-2016 autocracy, and a persistent reality given the comparatively low

---

dawn to dusk (5AM to 9PM summertime) with no uniforms Monday through Saturday (not on Sunday only because of theocratic or religious commandments), minimal pay and no or low benefits, no basic labor rights, no protection under dangerous working conditions, etc.—in Texas and other Southern states to realize that the South has only replaced race-based slavery by a generalized slave-like economy regardless of race. Hence, Texas and other Southern anti-labor rulers invite and entice capitalists tending to threat workers as slaves or servants to move to this region from other parts of the US, notably California. In this regard, Texas' and Southern states' open to business' and similar slogans effectively mean being open to a generalized slave-like economy and to capitalists treating workers as slaves or servants.

68   For example, most houses in the US South are largely made of wood and other cheap, non-endurable, low-quality materials and so are largely wooden houses, even if often disguised as if they were not made of wood, which are usually not deemed 'real' houses constructed almost entirely of concrete, bricks, cement, and other more durable material in Europe and even parts of South America (Colombia), but as auxiliary facilities, just as American 'chocolates' do not qualify as actual chocolates by cacao-content international standards. This wood-based and generally cheap-material construction of houses probably explains why house prices at least in the US South are lower than in Europe. Also, while apartments in shared buildings being smaller, average houses in parts of Europe, for example, Greece and Macedonia, are usually larger, often with 4 or more bedrooms, than in the US, contrary to Americans' uninformed preconceptions of their 'bigger' homes.

share of US foreign trade of GDP, indeed the lowest among Western countries, for example, lower than that of supposedly 'closed' and 'statist' France.

Further, American military, political, and economic imperialisms merge with cultural imperialism through, among other things like religious missionary work, Hollywood-style movies, television shows, and other mass-culture products that are, aside from rare exceptions, servile tools of the overt 'America is the best, strongest' Cold-War and similar imperialist propaganda (a la 'Top Guns' and the like, as is, relatedly, the British James Bond series, and so on). These pop-culture and related products are forces of cultural imperialism by penetrating and dominating, simply Americanizing, other cultures, and usually causing their degradation and figurative poisoning, notably degrading and contaminating art and artistic tastes, by their 'Americanization.'[69] Typically, just as countries subjected to American economic imperialism are inflicted with low-quality, uncompetitive products, so those pervaded by cultural imperialism suffer culture degradation and degeneration, especially of their arts and artistic tastes, due to their penetration by ersatz or low-grade art and culture from the US. While economic imperialism forcing puppet states to buy junk goods, cultural imperialism exports junk cultural products to other cultures and thus perverts or poisons them and artistic tastes. Just as economic imperialism functions as non-quality forcible product importation, cultural imperialism by its effects turns out to be anti-cultural and anti-artistic imperialism and perverts the globalization of culture and art into their Americanization, so essentially their degradation and ultimately poisoning in a figurative sense or degeneration.

Regarding military imperialism, it is notable that the US government reinstalled nuclear weapons in Turkey after secretly withdrawing them following the 1962 Cuban missile crisis, while hiding this withdrawal from Americans

---

69   Scitovsky (1972, pp. 63–4) suggests that the 'fear of Americanization [i.e., uneducated tastes followed the world over] is well founded.' This uneducated 'Americanization' of artistic tastes parallels that of sports through the invention and spread of barbarous, disturbingly violent, including deadly, and extreme gladiator-style sports (e.g., boxing and its variations) and the creation of 'American gladiators', expressing the underlying barbarism and violence of American society, primarily its conservative pole, and showing that the latter has not advanced beyond the violent decay of the late Roman empire. Relatedly, this tendency includes the invention and spread of ludicrous in the infantile sense of *homo ludens* or quasi-tribal sports ('American football', baseball, etc.) that are globally oddities, while resisting their global opposites (football qua 'soccer'), reflecting (to paraphrase Marx's 'idiocy of rule life' statement) the apparent idiocy of American life especially in conservative America and serving to distract Americans from chronic economic, political, health care, and other social problems, thus replicating the deceptive 'bread and circus' formula of ancient Roman dictatorship.

and misleading them by declaring 'victory'. This action displays the mix of aggressiveness and Puritan-style treachery, as does the treacherous reported promise of NATO staying within its original borders and not expanding into Eastern Europe, let alone the former Soviet Union, after the Cold War's end, consistent with the model of an 'evil empire.' In contrast, what Reagan condemned as the Soviet 'evil empire' and later Russa did not reinstall in response nuclear weapons in Cuba; one can imagine the situation if it reciprocated in kind—another Cuban missile crisis and the specter of catastrophic war and MAD due to the American government's militarist recklessness, bellicosity, and Puritanical treachery.

At this juncture, several evident facts emerge and stand out after the end of the Cold War that are generally consistent with those after WW II and which only US conservatives and other Americans intoxicated or deluded by Americanism's claims to the 'Divine mission' to 'lead' the world and supremacy can deny. First, the US government did not withdraw its military forces from NATO and other states, while Russia did withdraw its troops from the Warsaw Pact, such as Eastern Europe and even other parts of the Soviet Union, notably, the Baltics to which it granted independence. Second and related, the US government did not disband NATO even after and despite the Soviet Union disbanding the Warsaw Pact and dissolving itself, thus ceasing to be the cause for NATO's formation and existence, as the latter alleged. Moreover, despite the end of the supposed, now evidently fabricated, cause, NATO expands beyond its original borders to encompass Eastern Europe and even parts of the Soviet Union (the Baltics and conceivably Georgia and Ukraine), thus flagrantly violating its documented promise of non-expansion to the East. Third, the US government's military expenditure becomes nearly 10 times higher (in absolute figures) than that of Russia after the Cold War, higher than those of all its 'enemies' combined from China and North Korea to Cuba and Iran, and nearly equals that of the rest of the world, while further accelerating post-2016 and after 2020 and provoking yet another global cycle of such spending. Fourth and as a result, the US government launches another arms race against its 'enemies' since the early 2000s and post-2016 and after 2020 by multiplying especially 'high-tech' weapons of mass destruction.

Fifth and as another result, the US government maintains the most foreign military bases, even further proliferating them, in the world within and outside NATO, including Eastern Europe (Poland, Romania), and parts of the Soviet Union (the Baltics, possibly Ukraine), despite Russia closing its own in the Warsaw Pact and elsewhere. Further, it continues to use its foreign military bases for the sake of suppressing liberal, democratic, independence or socialist movements, for sustaining capitalist, conservative, religious, and fascist dictatorships in power, and for launching wars of aggression or military interventions against 'enemies'. Sixth and consequently, the US government persists in having the world's largest and further metastasizing military-industrial complex, which is substantially larger than those of its defined 'enemies' from China and North Korea to Russia and Cuba and remains the agent of American militarism, wars of aggression, and imperialism. Seventh, the US government continues to start more wars of aggression against or military interventions in other countries from Panama through Yugoslavia and to Iraq and Libya than any other, including Russia (whose interventions were confined within the former Soviet Union) after the Cold War. Eighth, the US government remains the only one to use unapologetically illegal, prohibited weapons of mass destruction, such as using depleted uranium in the NATO's unauthorized attack on Yugoslavia to protect a 'terrorist army' of Islamist secessionists, just as protecting Islamists like Osama Bin Laden et al. in Afghanistan during the 1980. Lastly, as an aggregate result of the above, the US government is consistently identified by global public opinion such as various surveys as the main threat to world peace and thus human survival after the Cold War. The above clearly reveals that even if the Soviet Union may well have been Reagan's 'evil empire' during the Cold War, the US government has generally assumed this throne afterwards.[70] In light of the above, if Reagan were alive and rational, he might have reconsidered which government to describe as an 'evil empire' after the Cold War, but this is obviously unrealistic given that US conservatives, including fascists, like their role models Puritans, are unable to reason objectively based on facts and act extremely irrational driven by religious fanaticism.

As an aggregate corollary, a betrayal of Jefferson-Madison's non-entanglement and independence ideal is the US's creation and especially perpetuation and expansion eastward, including toward the Soviet Union, of NATO. In retrospect, the creation of NATO by the US and other militarist Western countries like the UK effectively started the Cold War. It looked as if the US, along with the UK, could not wait to start a proxy war against the Soviet Union just a few years after the end of WW II, notably by allying with such former fascist and Axis states as Germany, Italy, Turkey, Japan, and others within NATO and similar military alliances. NATO's creation provoked the reactive formation of the Warsaw Pact and enfolded under the pretext of the 'Soviet threat' despite the lack of evidence that the Soviet Union prepared to attack and conquer the West but sought to defend itself against it given the

---

70   Coatney (2022) admits that since the end of the Cold War 'we [the US] have since become
      the aggressor' and thus by implication an 'evil empire'.

experience and memory of the Western military intervention following the 1917 revolution. Moreover, the perpetuation and expansion of NATO by the US and its allies and satellites after the dissolution of the Warsaw Pact and the Soviet Union and the end of the Cold War causes the latter to perhaps continue and escalate in a 'hot' war via confrontations with Russia or China likely culminating in a nuclear war of MAD.

Hence, beneath the surface of NATO, the latter appears as an extreme emanation of militarism and bellicosity and a lethal, ultimately self-destructive, instrument of American imperialism, in that sense of the 'evil' empire, driven by supremacist Americanism and Western neocolonialism through provocation of, confrontation with, and eventually nuclear war of MAD with its defined 'enemies' like Russia or China. It follows that any action, proclamation, or threat of NATO against enemies from its attacks on Yugoslavia, Iraq, Libya, and Syria to its provocations of and confrontations with Russia and China is best understood and analyzed as its functioning as the tool and in the context of American imperialism and Western neocolonialism.

As it stands, by its threatening movement beyond its borders, such as close to Russia and conceivably but not unrealistically China, the US/NATO looks bent on the path of the madness of mutually assured destruction via wars of aggression, mass death and devastation, and imperial conquest and subjection. At this juncture, if the long-term undoing, or the primary reason for the failure of Russia is the culture and practice of corruption combined with indolence and the lack of a strong work ethic and of organization, that of America is the mix of conservatism, fascism, and religion, including theocracy, allied and ultimately merged with coercive, unrestrained capitalism, as most US capitalists finance extreme conservatives, fascists, and religious extremists or theocrats post-2016 and after 2020 (and since at least the 1930s), just as their German counterparts financed the rise of Nazism and Hitler. This does not signify that corruption is absent in the US—on the contrary, as Michels[71] classically observes noting in the latter corruption on a 'gigantic scale'—but only that it is less visible or more subtle and less socially destructive than in Russia.

---

71   Michels (1968, p. 188) states about a century ago that the 'unrestricted power of capital necessarily involves corruption. In America, however, this corruption is not merely exhibited upon a gigantic scale, but, if we are to believe American critics, has become a recognized institution. While in Europe such corruption gives rise to censure and anger, in America it is treated with indifference or arouses no more than an indulgent smile. [So] if we were to judge the Americans solely by the manner in which they conduct themselves in public life, our judgments would be extremely unfavorable [expressing] a gross and unrefined materialism.'

Since these classic observations apparently of the Gilded Age, the uncon-strained power of capital in America persists or resumes since Reaganism and the post-2016 radical-right regime and continues to generate corruption on a 'gigantic scale', which remains a 'recognized institution' still greeted with indif-ference, indulgence or tolerance consistent with the plutocratic or kleptocratic credo that 'success succeeds' even if through corruption (as Charles Dickens suggests stating that the 'American people will be plundered so long as the American character is what it is; so long as it is tolerant of successful knaves').[72] Concerning Michels' observation of the conduct of American public officials and so ruling classes, for example, most members of Congress or their fami-lies (including the speaker of the House of Representatives) engage in insider stock trading typically with impunity and thus in legalized or tolerated elite corruption widespread in terms of trade participants and costly in amounts traded.[73]

Comparatively, the US and Russia exhibit convergence on chronic, massive corruption–though it seems more pernicious to the second country—just as, for that matter, on their economies mostly manufacturing non-quality, lemon-like civilian products from cars to airplanes (so one hears that mainly American and Russian-made planes crash) in contrast to their producing seemingly 'high-quality' weapons of mass destruction, which shows the shared perversity of high military expenditure, arms races, and overall militarism. In passing, it is not certain that, for example, the lemon-like civilian airplanes of certain

---

72   Cited in Merton (1968, p. 197).

73   At state levels, for example, some Texas ruling hardline conservatives who attempted to subvert the 2020 elections on behalf of the post-2016 fascist autocracy have been under various criminal investigations of corruption for years but have not faced justice appar ently thanks to their power and wealth, while lower and powerless classes, including nonviolent moral sinners like drug users, face what a former state conservative governor exalted as 'swift justice.' So long as this is, as it seems, a pattern of Texas conservative rulers rather than an isolated case and if Michels' diagnosis of corruption in America on a 'gigantic scale' applies regionally, it does to this state. In another instance from a similar state, a Florida former governor and senator was CEO of a hospital company which com-mitted the biggest Medicare fraud in history and moreover received millions of dollars following the fraud. Schultz (2018) remarks that 'when the federal investigation of [sena-tor's] former hospital company became public in 1997, the board of Columbia/HCA forced him out. [He] left with $300 million in stock, a $5.1 million severance and a $950,000-per-year consulting contract for five years.' And in spite and perhaps because of overseeing this historic fraud, Florida's conservatives elected this former CEO twice as governor and then US senator. Generally, Congress pervasive and large insider stock trading formally illegal yet effectively legalized exemplifies and symbolizes corruption on a 'gigantic scale' in America under the unconstrained power of capital and epitomizes what (Pryor 2002, p. 364) denotes American 'mafia capitalism'.

companies in the US or Russia, as exposed in their numerus crashes in recent times, coexist with their 'high-quality' military planes given the congruence and interconnection between various sectors of an economy in terms of product quality or non-quality. This congruence in non-quality products means that their military planes and other weapons of mass destruction may not be 'good enough' to totally extinguish human life and destroy the world, even if they may terminate modern civilization, and hence ironically appears as the sole positive facet of military technical advances as inherently self-destructive according to some opinions.[74]

Nevertheless, if corruption/indolence predicts Russia's failure in economic development, wealth, and defeat in conventional wars with the US and NATO, so its end as a global power, the dominance of conservatism, fascism, and religion or theocracy predestines America to a two-fold self-destructive outcome. First, such dominance is likely to cause another civil war through its warfare against liberalism, or to establish a fascist and theocratic dictatorship like autocracy post-2016 by eliminating liberal democracy and persecuting liberals. In this scenario, civil war may precede such dictatorship by resulting in the latter due to the victory of conservatism, fascism, and religion or theocracy over liberalism. Alternatively, it may result from this dictatorship through the resistance of liberal-democratic forces to fascist or theocratic rulers. Thus, as argued and demonstrated throughout, the post-2016 extreme-right regime at the federal level was essentially a fascist, as well as theocratic, dictatorship sharing the essentials of fascism, just as of theocracy, as were ultra-conservative states in state terms, provoking liberal-democratic resistance, as during the 2020 Presidential elections. Furthermore, after the 2020 elections in spite or precisely because of the extreme-right regime being replaced at the federal level—which is perhaps just a temporary replacement—around 30 or so ultra-conservative states from the South to beyond effectively established fascist-theocratic dictatorships by their intense suppression of social freedoms and rights from labor and voting and political rights to reproductive and other individual liberties and rights to academic and educational freedom. Taken together, the post-2016 radical-right regime and post-2020 ultra-conservative

---

74   For example, if the strikingly poor technical quality (and Puritan dullness and uncreativity) of Dollar banknotes parallels that of the US's weapons of mass destruction, the latter by their breakdowns and failures also paralleling those of civilian goods like cars and airplanes may not be able to totally destroy the world and extinguish human life, as a 'consolation prize' of its extreme military expenditure. Generally, Hicks (1969, p. 99) states that what technological progress 'gives with one hand, it can take with the other [as with] progress in military arts.'

states are in essence national and state fascist-theocratic dictatorships, respectively, which liberal-democratic anti-fascist resistance transiently but not enduringly counteracts, leading to the ever-growing likelihood of a civil war or escalated political, ideological and culture wars. In turn, the likely outcome of these wars is establishing or reinforcing more fascist-theocratic and generally conservative or right-wing dictatorship than liberal-secular democracy. In either case, the dominance of the mix of conservatism, fascism, and religion or theocracy portends the cycle of civil war and fascist or theocratic dictatorship, with the second both causing and resulting from the first, or political, ideological and culture wars.

Second, such dominance through extreme militarism, offensive wars, and imperialism is likely to cause MAD, hence the madness of destruction of America itself, along with its defined 'enemies' like Russia and others. MAD is likely to follow the establishment and imposition of fascist or theocratic dictatorship within America consistent with the pattern of fascism and theocracy launching offensive wars against other societies after the capture and consolidation of power within society. Altogether, if the curse of Russia is the culture and practice of corruption, indolence, weak work ethic, and disorganization, that of America or its nemesis is the socially poisonous mix of conservatism, fascism, and religion or theocracy, allied with coercive, unrestrained capitalism, each causing long-term self-destructive consequences for its society. In this respect, the two countries start from opposite points of social and historical origin and travel different routes to reach the same destination.

Relatedly, US conservative and other politicians and most Americans exalt and oppose America as a democracy and free society to China, Iran, and Russia as autocracies or dictatorships, including, as with the second, theocracies, Thus, they frame the conflicts, disagreements, and tensions between America and these other countries as those between democracy and free society on one hand and autocracy, dictatorship, and authoritarian repression on the other.[75] Contrary to these claims, however, it is not evident and certain that America under conservatism, including fascism post-2016 and theocracy perpetually, is

---

75 Stiglitz (2022) objects that 'US leaders' portrayal of the confrontation as one between democracy and authoritarianism fails the smell test, especially at a time when the same leaders are actively courting a systematic human-rights abuser like Saudi Arabia. Such hypocrisy suggests that it is at least partly global hegemony, not values, that is really at stake.' Moreover, Stiglitz (2022) adds that 'between Donald Trump's election, the attempted coup at the US Capitol, numerous mass shootings, a Republican Party bent on voter suppression, and the rise of conspiracy cults like QAnon, there is more than enough evidence to suggest that some aspects of American political and social life have become deeply pathological.'

more democratic and freer, notably less coercive and repressive, than these defined 'enemies'. First, these claims overlook that America was effectively proxy autocracy and to that extent dictatorship through the rise of fascism post-2016, this authoritarian regime being comparable to and emulating those in China and Russia, as well as that its conservative-religious rulers in the South and beyond consistently move in the fascist or extremely repressive direction after 2020. Second, they ignore the fact that at least half of the US such as the conservative-religious pole of America represented by the South and similar regions has for long been since Puritanism through evangelicalism what Weber connotes bibliocracy, a Biblical form of theocracy commonly named the Bible Belt that eventuates in or intersects with fascism and is almost equivalent or similar to that of Islamic Republic of Iran and Taliban rule. Third, considering its unrivalled suppression of voting freedoms and rights especially but not solely in the South, as the standard indicator of nondemocracy, the US under conservatism, at least the former Southern Confederacy from Alabama to Texas, exposes itself as nearly undemocratic or exclusionary politically as, if not even more so than, China, Iran, and Russia. Fourth, by its unparalleled discrimination against and exclusion of secularists from pursuing and holding political power and favoring religionists especially but not solely in the Bible Belt, the US under conservatism and religion reveals itself as theocratic and so undemocratic or exclusionary as Islamic theocracies like Iran and Taliban rule and even more so on that account than non-religious authoritarian regimes in China and Russia.

Fifth, taking account of the intensifying religion-driven suppression of individual liberties and privacy such as abortion or reproductive rights, the conservative-religious pole of America, notably after the conservative-dominated Supreme Court's revocation of the constitutional right to abortion in 2022, looks as theocratic, illiberal, unfree, and repressive as Islamic theocracies and perhaps even more so in this respect than non-religious regimes in China and Russia, and definitely so than its neighbor Mexico instead institutionalizing such personal freedoms. Sixth, judging by the highest prisoner rate and largest prison population in the world, as the common measure of state coercion, repression and terror, the US since Reaganism and under conservatism overall reappears as coercive and repressive as China, Iran, and Russia (assuming their respective incarceration data are available). Seventh, considering its mass death sentences and executions, as another common measure of state coercion, repression and terror, the US since Reaganism and under conservatism looks more repressive or cruel and inhumane than Russia which does not apply the death penalty after 1996 and comparable to China and Iran supposing that their respective figures are similar. Overall, the preceding suggests the lack of valid grounds for claiming that the US under conservatism, notably theocracy and post-2016 fascism, at least its conservative-religious pole like the former Southern Confederacy or the Bible Belt, is more democratic, freer, or less repressive than China, Iran, and Russia, and that the opposition with the latter is that of democracy and free society versus autocracies or dictatorship and repression. In essence, insofar as the US is ruled by conservatism for long and theocratic religion virtually forever, including post-2016 fascism, it is hardly more democratic, freer, and less repressive than these autocracies or dictatorships, for which its unrivalled suppression of voting rights, combining with suppressing reproductive rights, or its highest prisoner rate and largest prison population in the world, along with the most widespread executions within OECD, is the singular proof or syndrome, among many others.

In sum, returning to Jefferson and Madison in relation to militarism and war, they feared or disapproved the US's 'entanglement' with military alliances as a dangerous and even self-destructive action by resulting in unnecessary and destructive wars. In prospect, they may well prove right so long as the US's 'entanglement' with NATO and the latter's aggressiveness and expansionism inevitably result in a confrontation with other powers like Russia and possibly China and hence in MAD via nuclear and similar war, thus the madness of self-destruction induced by Americanism's claims to 'manifest destiny' as the 'Divine mission' to rule the world and 'superior' American values. Hypothetically, Jefferson and Madison would probably 'turned' in their graves if seeing their government's extreme military expenditure, gigantic, ever-aggrandizing military-industrial complex, repeated arms races, huge standing army, 800 military bases in 70 countries, creation and proliferation of aggressive and expansionist military alliances like NATO and similar others, imperial conquest and domination, and wars of aggression and confrontations with 'enemy' powers ultimately ending in self-destruction. They would likely characterize and experience these processes as symptoms of collective madness or ultimate irrationalism and would not recognize their own nation and would feel deeply betrayed and offended by such extreme militarism, bellicosity, and imperialism betraying and violating their mostly pacifist or non-militarist ideals. In this sense, such militarism, bellicosity, and imperialism primarily under conservatism and fascism post-2016 flagrantly betrays the ideals and aims of the American Revolution.

Taken together, military expenditure in the US especially during the eruption of fascism post-2016 and under conservatism since Reaganism and postwar times is far from being some benign 'defensive spending' in the function of 'national security' but an expression of extreme militarism and bellicosity and an instrument of wars of aggression and imperial conquest and expansion.

The above uncovers the failure of the 'American experiment' in non-military civilian investment and wellbeing, peace, peaceful conflict resolution, and respect for the national independence and freedom of other societies primarily because of conservatism, coercive capitalism, religion, and theocracy, including fascism or right-wing authoritarianism. Relatedly, it discloses the betrayal of Jefferson-Madison's ideal of America as a pacifist society and admonition about the formation of and 'entanglement' in military alliances, by implication NATO as an aggressive alliance, the agent of militarism and offensive imperial war, and a lethal, possible self-destructive and thus MAD tool of American imperialism and Western neocolonialism.

At the end, if MAD through nuclear war happens during the 21st century—as it seems an exponentially growing possibility, indeed a near-certainty while writing these lines—future historians, if any, will probably trace its origin to the US government's rigid intransigence, irrational arrogance, and childish stubbornness[76] to consider Russia's possibly legitimate security concerns

---

76   Coatney (2022) laments that 'by Nuremberg starting/causing a war is the worst war crime of all, begetting all the war crimes which follow. And Biden and Blinken stubbornly and decisively opposing the Russians getting the security treaty they need (and we owe them after our broken promises/agreements) caused this war, making them at least as responsible for any war crimes which have happened.' Coatney (2022) adds that Biden as an ardent and perennial Cold Warrior 'has long wanted [and pushed] for adding Ukraine to NATO.' Further, Coatney (2022) makes this warning of MAD: 'Just as [US/NATO] left [the Russians] with no choice but war, they are now left with no choice but nuclear war.' Coatney probably refers to the President's statement that the US/NATO 'would respond in kind' with 'severe consequences' if Russia used weapons of mass destruction against a non-NATO state like Ukraine. Yet, even by NATO's rules of engagement to respond only to attacks on its members, such a response 'in kind' would amount to an attack and likely provoke an equivalent response, thus escalating into a nuclear war. To that extent, the 'we would respond in kind' statement approaches a declaration of nuclear war and of self-destruction despite the US, along with the other nuclear powers, agreeing that such a war 'cannot be won and should not be fought.' As it stands, this statement is as dangerous and self-destructive as the Soviet Union or Russia—and in a counterfactual NATO—stating 'we would respond in kind' to the US's use of chemical or related weapons (Agent Orange, napalm) in the Vietnam War, depleted uranium in the attack on Yugoslavia, suspect weapons in the Iraq invasion given that all these victimized countries were outside the Warsaw Pact or Russia's bilateral military alliances. Similarly, an ardent Cold-War failed conservative and ultra-religious presidential candidate stated the intent of the US/ NATO 'obliterating' the Russian army, thus overlooking that such obliteration can only be through nuclear MAD, which means 'obliterating' America itself ultimately, as well as forgetting that the 'Biblical sword' American conservatism and extremist religion wields against 'enemies' is double-edged. This confirms what was feared during the 2008-12 Presidential elections, namely, that if elected presidents, such Cold-War bellicose conservatives and ultra-religionists through their intent at 'obliterating' Russia would eventually obliterate America by inflicting it with MAD, killing millions of Americans as sacrifices of

caused by NATO's imperial expansion beyond its original borders to Eastern Europe and even parts of the former Soviet Union (e.g., Ukraine) and thus its potential use of these new territories for wars of aggression in the style of that against Yugoslavia or military preparations and threats. For example, revealing the true aims of its expansionism toward Eastern Europe and the former Soviet Union,[77] the US/NATO's statement that its aim is to militarily 'weaken' Russia to the point of ceasing to be an important military power, if amounting to or being perceived as a declaration of war, may turn out to be an act provoking or a prelude to MAD for future historians.

Historically, Russia's security concerns because of NATO's attempted expansion closer to its borders (Georgia, Ukraine, etc.) look seemingly as legitimate or understandable as those of America due to the Soviet Union's stationing nuclear missiles in Cuba, and the US government's reaction was threatening a nuclear attack, thus self-destructive and utterly irrational. In a way, future historians will likely attribute MAD to the US government's Cold-War mentality and warriors, including the post-2020 president and Congress, persisting and intensifying (because, manifesting schizophrenia, they construe Russia as both a 'threat'[78] and 'weak') as a self-destructive affliction even after the end of the Cold-War.

---

ideological and religious fanaticism hence turned madness reminiscent of Hume's diagnosed 'madness with religious ecstasies' characteristic of Puritanism.

77   The media reported Pope Francis saying that 'NATO barking at Russia's door' was the real 'scandal' causing the 'conflict' that may escalate into a wider and even nuclear war. This implies that 'NATO barking at Russia's door' not only caused a regional military conflict but threatens to escalate it into a wider and nuclear war with the result of MAD.

78   In a way, Russia's supposed 'threat' against countries like the Baltics, Poland, etc. seems virtually non-existent because of both lack of evidence for it and the high probability that the Russian government would not be so irrational to engage in actions that will result in a confrontation and so unwinnable nuclear war with NATO. (In addition, one wonders if the Soviet Union did not invade Poland as a member of the Warsaw Pact, for example, in the 1980s why Russia would do so when this country is part of NATO, and also why it would attack the Baltic states when it let them go free in the 1990s, which shows that this Russian 'threat' looks as manufactured or inflated by the US/West.) Moreover, Russia's 'threat' against these and other NATO countries appears probably weaker than that by American imperialism. Thus, the US conservative, including post-2016 fascist or right-wing, government is more likely than Russia to militarily intervene or engineer state coups in the Baltics, Poland, and other Eastern European countries if liberal-democratic, progressive, secular, as well as socialist forces prevail in these, just as it did in Italy, Greece, and many non-European nations from Iran to South America and Ukraine previously. To that extent, it turns out that the true threat to these countries within NATO, specifically their liberal-democratic, progressive, secular, as well as socialist forces, is the US conservative-fascist government intoxicated and driven by nationalist Americanism and

In retrospect, Cold-War enthusiasm in America and within NATO has always been irrational and self-destructive, but through 'we would respond in kind' and similar statements seems to finally reach the point of no-return—the madness of self-destruction. By threatening to inflict 'severe consequences' for Russia or China eventuating in a devastating nuclear war, these and other US Cold-War, invariably religious fanatics express collectively and perhaps unconsciously (consistent with Mannheim's notion of the 'collective uncon-scious') their religion-based desire to perish as a path to Puritan or Christian 'salvation', 'election', 'rapture', the 'second coming', and the like, a desire which cannot be denied and instead respected to these equivalents of Islamic suicide bombers. The obvious problem with this desire to perish is that these suicide-bombers equivalents will carry with them millions of Americans and others, including those who do not see perishing in nuclear war as a path to salvation and eternal bliss. Relatedly, these Cold-War religious and other fanatics rather than acting as responsible adults behave as immaturely as children incapable of envisioning or predicting the catastrophic consequences of their actions, such as the US/NATO movement toward and confrontation with Russia and wars of aggression.

Relatedly, surviving historians will probably trace the cause of MAD to the US government's incitement and provocation of fraternal wars between Russia and other Slavic nations, such as the Baltics, Poland, and Ukraine, becoming or aspiring to become NATO's vasal members serving the interests of its 'great powers' like America, just as they were satellites relative to the Soviet Union within the Warsaw Pact. On this account, virtually all fraternal wars within Eastern Europe and the Soviet Union, as well as the Balkans like Yugoslavia since the end of the Cold War in the 1990s have been largely the result of the US conservative government's instigation via the 'divide and rule' Machiavellian strategy and bellicosity overall. To use Clausewitz's definition of war, these fra-ternal wars between often identical ethnic groups and/or former members of the same states are the continuation of the US government's policy of 'divide and rule' by other means. (Generally, the US government has started or insti-gated most aggressive wars, from Yugoslavia to Afghanistan, Iraq, and Libya, after the Cold War.)

Further, the US conservative and similar militarist-imperial government by its 'divide and rule' tactic reminiscent of Nazi Germany and the Roman empire not only instigates or aggravates fraternal wars or constant military tensions

---

imperialism rather than Russia so long as the latter is rationally aware that any military action against them leads to a global war of MAD.

in earlier Yugoslavia (Croatia versus Serbia, Muslim Bosnia versus Serbia, Montenegro and Macedonia versus Serbia) and the former Soviet Union (Georgia versus Russia, Ukraine versus Russia, etc.) and Asia (South versus North Vietnam, Taiwan versus China), but does this beyond, virtually in the entire world.

For example, the post-2020 US Cold-War driven President, following its also aggressive predecessor, designated and 'humored' Colombia with a 'special ally' status against, as stated or implicit in any military alliance (which Simmel classically argues), 'enemies' with an overt or implied promise of providing, or the expectation of receiving, arms (the Colombian government shortly afterwards requested tanks to 'rebuild' its military) and against the background of their shared hostility to Venezuela. In this context, as it stands, this action amounts or appears as another overt or covert instigation of a fraternal war in the service of US obstinate Cold-War militarism and imperialism long after the end of the Cold-War. In a related act, instigated by the US post-2016 radical-right regime, the Colombian right-wing government severed diplomatic relations with Venezuela, which may be a prelude to launching an aggressive war, with the promised or expected support of the American military, against its brother nation, as it often happens in such situations of foreign-policy ruptures and consistent with Clausewitz's rule that war is a 'continuation of policy by other means'. Time will tell if this is correct or not (having in mind Colombia's 2022 government change), but if the prior history of US military alliances like NATO provides any lessons, it will be no surprise if Colombia and Venezuela having the same ethnic origin and being formerly parts of the same state eventually find themselves in a fraternal war due or linked to the President designating and 'honoring' the first as a 'special ally' against implied 'enemies.' A fraternal war of Colombia against Venezuela, which the post-2020 US militarist government, continuing the warlike actions of its post-2016 predecessor, apparently instigates, and despite its expectation of defeat of the second and reasserting its imperial control of the region, would be a tragedy for both countries sharing the same national origin, language, and culture, as are all the fraternal wars that American imperialism has overtly or covertly instigated from Vietnam through Yugoslavia to the Soviet Union.

An excursus on American 'commercial imperialism' in Colombia and product quality. Concerning Colombia, as one of those Latin American and other third-world countries directly or indirectly subjected to American 'commercial imperialism' forcing then to buy low-quality, uncompetitive American imports, US firms and products, including junk-food companies and goods, are pervasive while one can hardly find Colombian goods in the US market despite the 'free trade' agreement between the two countries. This suggests that American 'commercial imperialism' in this country and South America overall continues under the guise of 'free trade' agreements and confirms that the US economy remains comparatively closed and protected due to the economic irrationalism of market protectionism and the madness or hysteria of 'buy American' nationalism. Relatedly and perhaps shockingly, in Colombia's economy[79] virtually all products from foods and beverages to home appliances, furniture and apartments and houses are of a higher quality than in the US—everything is simply better. This exposes the ineptness and/or fraud of American capitalism in respect of product quality such as durability, workmanship, and reliability. One can imagine the shock or surprise by Colombians emigrating to or visiting America when they see that, aside from few exceptions, almost everything from foods to homes is of lower quality in the 'promised land' than in their 'third-world' country.

Conversely, Colombians likely experience a shock that, for instance, most apartments/houses in their country are of higher quality, including better workmanship and materials, along with home furnishing and appliances, than those in the 'promised land', such as average houses plagued with poor construction and made of wood and other cheap materials. In another example, they are probably surprised to infer that most retailers in Colombia sell higher-quality products, as well as their stores are cleaner and with more space between isles, than in the US, aside from rare exceptions. Various examples[80]

---

79   Also, the press reported in 2022 with reference to Colombia's presidential elections that 'outgoing conservative President congratulated [the winner] shortly after results were announced, and [the loser] quickly conceded his defeat.' This starkly contrasts with American 2020 presidential elections when the 'outgoing conservative President,' loser, and base refused to concede the defeat and attempted to overturn the results. This sharp contrast makes America, specifically its conservative-religious pole, look after the 2020 (and for that matter 2000) presidential elections more a third-world country or banana republic than the disdained 'third world' and banana republics. It suggests that America in its conservative-religious pole may learn something from other countries, including those classified within the 'third world', in respect of elections and their acceptance and thus democracy rather than lecturing and preaching to them on 'fair and free elections' and 'democracy.' Oppenheimer (2022) remarks that Colombia's government 'deserves credit for holding a peaceful election in a deeply polarized country and respecting its results. On that score, Colombia could teach a lesson in democracy to the United States, where former President Trump still refuses to concede his indisputable loss in the 2020 elections.'

80   And their surprise will increase by concluding that, for example, Carrefour/Jumbo stores in Colombia are probably bigger and definitely cleaner, more spacious, and transparent than most retailers in the US, aside from a few exceptions. To take a relatively trivial but indicative example, these and other retail stores in Colombia feature dozen brands or creative varieties of cultured buttermilk while one can find just 1 or 2 in US retailers, which holds for many other consumer goods like chocolates—not considering

indicate that for many consumer goods not only is product quality lower in the US compared to Colombia but, to add insult to injury, even product variety is narrower. This suggests that American capitalism is inept or unwilling to provide high-quality products, thus indirectly defrauding Americans by selling them mostly 'lemons', or to create new product varieties.[81]

spurious domestic 'chocolates' failing to meet cocoa-content standards and not counting imports—and others. Similarly, Carulla retail stores in Colombia market higher-quality products, are cleaner, more spacious, with their employees wearing more uniforms, than their midsize counterparts inthe US . Trivially but indicatively, even grocery plastic bags are stronger, and soaps and sponges, with most of them made of enduing material hardly ever used for that purpose in the US, longer lasting in Colombian than American retailers, just as electric fans cooling better and being more reliable, and so on. Relatedly, most retailers and restaurants in Colombia, provide complete head-to-foot uniforms to their workers, for example Yumbo and Euro give them company-labelled jeans, sweaters, jackets, and shoes, while their US counterparts providing minimalist uniforms like a shirt passing as a 'uniform' and even none, seeing the spectacle of many restaurant employees serving in their everyday, often unclean or untidy, dress their customers. This indicates that the first enterprises respect and enhance more the dignity and wellbeing of their workers and maintain the hygiene in their facilities than the second. (In a related case, unlike their counterparts elsewhere, but like proverbial barbarians, many US employees, just as Americans generally, do not seem to bother washing their hands in bathrooms, so it is no wonder that salmonella and related infectious outbreaks are a pathological and often deadly regularity in American capitalism.) Overall, this reveals that American unconstrained, predatory capitalism cares neither for the quality of its products nor the dignity and wellbeing of its workers and the hygiene in its enterprises.

81   Some basic but indicative examples of American capitalism's ineptness or unwillingness to provide high-quality products or to create new product varieties include variations of cultured buttermilks and chocolates, long-lasting milk (most of milk sold in US stores not only lasts less than or around 2 weeks but gets soured well before the 'best by' date, which is another form of corporate fraud or ineptness or carelessness), etc. Overall, the quality of most products that US companies produce or sell, including the largest retailers, is so poor that one gets the impression as if they invested maximum efforts and resources in producing or selling goods with the lowest rather than highest possible quality like durability and reliability, an intensification of 'planned obsolescence' into deliberate evanescence. On this account, predatory American capitalism appears as a simulation of production and distribution of products as 'lemons', simply a fake economy in this respect, just as relatedly the quality of democracy/politics especially after the post-2016 rise of fascism, civil society, and intellectual culture like education, so of social life generally, is so low and further deteriorating in America that makes the latter look like a simulacrum ('faking') of 'democracy', 'liberty', 'equality', and 'justice', so the simulated 'land of freedom'. In a way, American capitalism if considered the 'free enterprise' of production and distribution of high-quality products, just as conservative America if deemed the 'land of freedom' and 'freemen', is as real as the Disneyland—a complete delusion and deliberate simulation—and most Americans seem unable or reluctant to distinguish between this pleasant fiction and an opposite social reality.

So, Colombians coming to the US are probably shocked to experience that both consumer product quality and variety are inferior in American capitalism compared to their nominally third-world counterpart. The same applies to most visitors from Europe and elsewhere, so their American hosts probably in embarrassment must explain, if they know, to their visitors why and how virtually all products from foods through cars to houses in America are of lower quality, poorer workmanship, shorter durability, and weaker reliability than in their countries. In turn, Americans need not to go to France or Germany but just to Colombia to find with a surprise that their 'superior' capitalism performs miserably in consumer product quality and variety. In this respect, Americans can see that American capitalism is uniquely inept in comparative terms to provide high and wide consumer product quality and variety or systematically engages in a gigantic fraud by indirectly defrauding Americans through producing and marketing mostly 'lemons',[82] combined with its other

---

82   To take another elemental but indicative example, home plumbing technology in the US is the probably most primitive, backward, or ineffective among Western and other societies (as were, relatedly, washing machines for long) so that one hardly ever experiences in these that dreaded toilet-ball clogging that most American households suffer and creates an entire industry for its resolution, a superfluous 'industry' that is mostly unknown in other economies. This is a typical story of American predatory capitalism and America's economic, specifically consumer, semi-tragedy—an industry persistently and systematically produces defective, poor-quality products ('lemons') and another industry rises to correct such defects forcing consumers to spend extra resources in solving problems like plumbing or car breakdowns. Counterfactually, if US home plumbing technology were more advanced, generally American capitalism instead produced high-quality products, there would be no need for producing and purchasing various devices for solving clogging and other problems. In a way, this primitivism of plumbing technology in American homes, just as the poor quality of domestic cars, home appliances, civilian airplanes, etc., perhaps exemplifies and symbolizes in a semi-grotesque manner the technological backwardness and non-quality of the US economy contrary to the nationalist and ignorant claims of its 'superiority' in this regard. This seems plausible in view of the connection between various sectors of the economy, for example, car, home-appliances, airplane, home-building, and related civilian industries and these with the arms industry, in respect of product quality or rather non-quality within American predatory capitalism. Therefore, the burden of proof lies on those US conservative and other nationalists to disprove this connection and establish some 'disconnection' between primitive and low-quality home plumbing technology and domestic cars and the 'superior quality' of all other products of American predatory capitalism. Moreover, many US manufacturing products are of so poor quality or severe non-quality that they impose large negative externalities on owners, such as the costs of owing junk that often outweigh the benefits. For example, one wonders if it is worth to acquire an American car even at zero or so price given that the costs of its incessant repairs during its lifetime due to poor quality and reliability, not to mention its typical Puritanical aesthetic ugliness or emptiness, may well exceed or equal the benefits of using and owing it. Perhaps only Russian cars are as of poor quality and

direct, Enron-style frauds qua financial and other fraudulent 'innovations' for which it is the global leader and model.

In passing, even in the 'high-tech' banking and other service sector, US banks introduced, for example, chip-reading credit cards several years after their counterparts in Europe and elsewhere, just as US cell-phone makers and networks were lagging for long behind their Chinese competitors in creating 5th generation mobile phones and networks, needing the post-2016 nationalistic government to suppress this foreign competition by banning rivals. (Also, as a trivial but indicative example, banks in Colombia alert customers to take their cards after ATM transactions by AI voice while US banks alerting them by outdating blinking.) This is indicative because it reaffirms that US banks, like most corporations in predatory American capitalism, are more adept in or capable of making spurious financial 'innovations' for extorting or extracting customer money rather than real innovations improving consumer and social welfare. Moreover, they are world 'leaders' in such specious 'innovations' in

---

aesthetically ugly as American ones, showing a curious convergence of US and Russian economies on low-quality automotive products. Like the Russian economy, American capitalism while producing 'high-tech' weapons of mass destruction threatening to extinguish human life is unable to produce quality cars, consumer electronics, home appliances (including micro-ovens, refrigerators, heaters, fans, weight scales, etc.), homes, foods, and other civilian products enhancing human welfare. Yet, humanity can only hope for its survival that, like their Russian forms, US weapons of mass destruction are of such low quality as civilian goods like cars, airplanes, home appliances, foods, homes, etc. so will not be able to extinguish human life via imperial expansion and wars. For example, within the Balkans, their peoples may hope that US weapons of mass destruction are as of poor quality not to extinguish human life as were those American chicken meat products exported to Yugoslavia in the 1980–90s that were of such egregious non-quality that only the poorest would buy and caused common avoidance, bewilderment, and disgust as inferior and uncompetitive to their domestic equivalents especially from Slovenia. Indeed, American commercial imperialism on grounds of helping 'American farmers' regularly includes such inferior chicken products as 'exports' by forcing or persuading various governments from South America to the Balkans to buy US mostly low-quality, uncompetitive goods which they normally would not. This relatively trivial example is indicative in that it exemplifies and symbolizes the comparatively poor quality of most products produced by predatory American capitalism. Overall, most American foods and related products are of such a poor quality—of which Americans' unrivaled obesity is an expression—that they are commonly described as among the worst and, like conservative-religious America, the laughingstock of the world or international disgrace and embarrassment. So, only American commercial imperialism by coercion and blackmail of weaker countries and their resulting economic-financial dependence can force or 'persuade' them to import these low-quality and other products that otherwise they would not, resulting, joined with the spread of fast-food outlets from America to the world, into a global obesity epidemic, among other things.

that many other banks in various countries from South America to Europe adopt these rapacious practices of despoiling customers.[83] In a similar vein, US airlines engage in a myriad of deceptive, predatory 'innovations' from splitting economy class into 'premium' and 'basic' through withdrawing or charging for previously complimentary services like meals to shrinking airline seats and reducing 'legroom', all seeking to extort or extract passenger money, simply 'nickel and dime' passengers. (Literally squeezing most passengers in between seats on planes and thus violating their dignity by US airlines is a picture that illustrates well predatory American capitalism's mistreatment and disregard of Americans as both consumers and workers.) Like banks, US airlines are world 'leaders' in such predatory 'innovations' so that many airlines in other countries also embrace these activities of plundering passengers, thus primarily contributing to the drastic decline of the qualify of air travel worldwide to the point of perverting it from enjoyable experience to disaster and nightmare in recent years. Consistent with the pattern of non-quality in most of the economy, the US private health care system typically ranks among those of the lowest quality in terms of health outcomes like longevity, just as of the narrowest scope in the sense of limited access due to the lack of a universal model, among Western and OECD countries; particularly dental care looks like national disgrace by being among both the worst and the most expensive in the developed world and beyond.

Thus, Americans visiting Colombia may experience the reverse shock seeing that virtually everything from foods to homes is of a higher quality, longer durability, better reliability, and workmanship in a 'third world' country than in their 'superior' nation while born and raised in what appears as an ambiance of non-quality of economic goods and relatedly of politics, art, culture, in part education, and life overall, especially in conservative America like the South. Overall, Americans do not seem to realize the poor quality of products, aside from few exceptions, 'made in the USA', because the US economy is comparatively closed, indeed the least open among Western economies, by the share of external trade, and second, most, especially conservatives, do not travel abroad (and have no passports), except for 'crusade' via missionary work and military-war activities in foreign bases, for example, Germany. Most conservatives Americans get used through (what Weber calls) habituation or

---

83   In this connection, US dollar banknotes are of the probably lowest paper quality and with the weakest protection from counterfeiting among Western currencies, which makes them the main target for forgery, and featuring the Puritanical lack of creativity by the confusing one size-fits-all design, compared to the Euro with its high-quality print and creatively different sizes for different denominations.

are resigned to low-quality products because they are denied access to, or do not know the quality of, non-American goods, except for cars and few others, so their typical nationalist ignorance and contempt of other societies really is blissful. For if US conservatives really possess the knowledge of the comparatively lower quality of most American products, they will hardly make uniformed 'we are the best' Reagan-style claims in this regard and obey 'buy American' nationalist appeals, and instead feel less happy than in the state of ignorance both externally produced by a closed economy and self-inflicted by a distaste to travel to other countries, except for religious and military 'crusades.' Furthermore, most US specially conservatives, seem willing to tolerate and acquiesce as a kind of patriotic duty and act to what most peoples from Europe to Colombia do not—the prevalence of low-quality products and thus actual fraud, ineptness, and carelessness in American capitalism.

Generally and beyond American commercial and related imperialism in Colombia, Venezuela, and the rest of Latin America, the US conservative and other expansionist government's, including presidents', instigation of such fraternal and other wars by 'divide and rule' may be collectively conscious and deliberate driven by militarist and imperialist calculations. Alternatively, they may be an expression of (what Mannheim calls) the 'collective-unconscious' (and Freud might call the collective-subconscious) rooted in the group's quasi-instincts or latent societal impulses and sentiments ('residues', including 'religious ecstasies', in Pareto's words) of 'manifest destiny', the 'Divine mission' to rule the world, and socially inborn and trained supremacist Americanism and conversely (to paraphrase Veblen), the 'trained incapacity' for pacifism or peaceful conflict resolution. Either way, a fraternal war or constant military tension between the above two Latin countries is likely or possible to result from such instigation by the US government's Cold-War 'divide and rule' strategy, thus joining such wars or tensions during and after the dissolution of Yugoslavia and the Soviet Union. If this happens, it will only reaffirm what is abundantly evident already, namely that virtually all fraternal wars or military tensions between countries with same or common ethnical and related roots after the Cold War result from the US conservative government's, including presidents', collectively conscious or 'collective-unconscious' instigation in the function of militarism and imperial expansion and dominance. Critics may lament that it is hard to imagine a more cynical or Machiavellian means to attain ends, but viewed objectively from a historical perspective this has original roots in Puritanism and its proxy-genocide of 'pagan' Native Americans and a long precedent and history in Western, especially British, militarism, colonialism, and imperialism (and the Roman empire), including fascist Italy and Nazi Germany.

Taken together, nuclear MAD seems likely due to the US government's militarism, bellicosity, expansionism, and imperialism under conservatism intoxicated by supremacist nationalism (in 'bipartisan' nationalist consensus[84] on Americanism) and Western neocolonialism of which NATO with its expansion acts as the instrument and its vasal states like former Warsaw-Pact members are made tools too. If so, this would confirm in the most possible sinister way the long-standing perception that the worst enemy of Americans is their own conservative militaristic, warlike, and imperialist, as well as coercive, oppressive, and irrational government, simply their Leviathan-like police-warfare state (a 'limited government' in conservatism's delusions). As it stands, this government not only threatens to terminate Americans' liberties and rights, as under conservatism, theocracy, and fascism since the 1980 and post-2016, including after 2020 with intensifying repression in conservative states, but also ultimately their lives though extreme militarism ('defense spending', 'national security'), imperialism ('American interests'), and wars of aggression as religion-style crusades resulting in destruction and self-destruction. This confirms that conservative-religious rule has always been the curse or nemesis of American society since Puritanism's genocide, persecution, and witch-trials, with MAD due to wars of aggression seemingly reflecting and fulfilling finally the Puritan-evangelical dream of (what Adorno classically diagnosed and probably predicted accurately as) self-destructive annihilation as Christian 'salvation' in the style of Calvinist 'election', 'heaven', 'rapture', 'bliss', etc.

In aggregate, expending near-unlimited social resources on military and war purposes nearly equaling half the world's expenditure while impoverishing or keeping impoverished much of its population, having a Leviathan-like military-industrial complex and so a gigantic warfare (and police) state, the largest standing army or military personnel, holding most foreign military bases, starting constant arms races, launching most wars of aggression or military interventions, installing or supporting fascist, other extreme-right, and theocratic dictatorships across the world, suppressing democratic national movements, using illegal or unconventional weapons of mass destruction, killing millions of civilians in invasions and occupations from Vietnam to Iraq, creating, continuing, and expanding an aggressive military alliance despite the end of its original rationale and beyond its initial borders, confrontations

84   Stiglitz (2022) remarks that 'in Washington, there is a bipartisan consensus that China could pose a strategic threat, and that the least the US should do to mitigate the risk is to stop helping the Chinese economy grow. According to this view, pre-emptive action is warranted, even if it means violating the World Trade Organization rules that the US itself did so much to write and promote.'

with defined 'enemy' states that may ultimately result in MAD—if the state committing the above was called Russia or China, Abracadabra or Nacirema, or a perhaps alien force from Mars, Reagan and other conservatives, including fascists, would definitely condemn it as an 'evil empire'.

Yet, it is the US state controlled by conservatism—in a bipartisan consensus intoxicated by supremacist Americanism so regardless of party affiliation—and fascism post-2016 and is therefore for Reagan and fascists an 'empire for good'[85] or no empire at all refusing to admit imperialism but just 'America and its allies'. In longer historical terms, in addition to extreme military expenditure and its far-reaching pernicious ramifications, committing proxy genocide and expulsion of original inhabitants like Native Americans on the ground of 'manifest destiny' and the 'Divine mission' to rule others, launching violent conquest of other states' territories such as those of Mexico on the same grounds, enslaving and subjugating various racial and religious groups, invading, occupying, and terrorizing the Caribbean and Latin America—if the state perpetrating these acts was called Russia or China, Abracadabra or Nacirema, Reagan et al. would certainly denounce it as a particularly 'evil empire' in world history. However, it is the US state dominated by conservatism (again in a bipartisan consensus on Americanism) and fascism and is hence for Reagan et al. and post-2016 fascists the 'best' nation ever in the history of the world. (The US government typically does not apologize or repent for the above acts and even takes a 'high moral ground' as morally superior to any other in history, which appears as a deliberate deception or what Mannheim would call a collectively unconscious delusion and is continuous with or reminiscent of Puritans' unrepentance and claims to their 'pure' church/morality while committing the most sinister atrocities from the near-genocide or enslavement of Native Americans to the persecution of non-Puritans and dissenters, witch-trials, and pervasive 'holy' terror overall.) On this account, the 'evilness' (to use one of those Puritan-conservative projections of their own traits onto others), including destructiveness and ultimately self- destructiveness, of the American conservative variation of Reagan's 'evil empire' cannot be overstated or exaggerated both historically and comparatively. And if the state featuring or doing the preceding was called Russia or China, Abracadabra or Nacirema, Reagan et al. would definitely make a verdict denying its legitimacy. Yet, it is the

---

85   Critics or cynics may comment that if this is an empire for 'good', then so is Nazi Germany by its imperial conquest and subjugation and are all other Western empires colonizing, enslaving, and terrorizing the rest of the world for centuries and continue to do so in slightly modified ways via the new imperialism and neocolonialism, whose military tool is NATO's expansion and offensive wars.

US state under by conservatism and consequently for Reagan et al. and post-2016 fascists, as well as Bible-Belt theocrats, the 'eternal' nation and empire for 'good' with a self-ascribed 'manifest destiny' qua the 'Divine mission' to 'lead' and dominate the world, especially its defined 'enemies', for the sake of protecting exceptional, superior American interests and values.

In this connection, one wonders if American 'values'[86] are superior and universal why the US government attempts to impose them on other countries form South America through Vietnam and Asia to Yugoslavia and Iraq through wars of aggression and imperial conquest or control rather than leaving them spontaneously assert themselves. Simply, if they were superior and universal, no coercion through wars and conquest would be needed to impose them, and all countries would adopt them effortlessly. Conversely, this implies that by imposing them via militarism and imperialism, the US government somehow admits or senses that especially conservative-religious American 'values' are not really superior and universal. By doing so, this government concedes or feels that they or their outcomes are essentially incompatible with democratic, egalitarian capitalism, liberal-secular democracy, scientific rationalism, and modernity and civilization, as well as particularistic and idiosyncratic not applicable to other societies or applicable only via wars and conquest. For example, such values or their outcomes especially but not solely, include coercive, inegalitarian capitalism suppressing labor freedom, 'faith-based' exclusionary

---

86   Stiglitz (2022) envisages that 'an arrogant and pathological America could lose the new cold war' it started against Russia and China because the 'US says it's fighting for values such as democracy and honor, but America needs to live by those words at home if it wants anyone to stand with it.' Further, Stiglitz (2022) points to the US's 'long history of exploiting other countries.' Stiglitz (2022) adds that 'Europe and America excel at lecturing others on what is morally right and economically sensible. But the message that usually comes through—as the persistence of US and European agricultural subsidies makes clear—is "do what I say, not what I do."' Stiglitz (2022) concludes that especially 'after the Trump years, America no longer holds any claim to the moral high ground, nor does it have the credibility to dispense advice. The US might know how to make the world's best bombers and missile systems, but they will not help us here [and] until we [the US] have proven ourselves worthy to lead, we cannot expect others to march to our drum.' In passing, the statement that the 'US might know how to make the world's best bombers and missile systems' is inconsistent with the evident and enduring fact that American capitalism does not know to make the world's best cars, airplanes, home appliances, consumer electronics, foods, homes, and other civilian goods. This implies that what this statement says is not likely—and for the good of humanity and so America because American bombers, missile systems, and other weapons of mass destruction by probably not being of better quality than civilian 'lemons' may not be able to extinguish human life as rapidly and totally as if they were of a higher quality than other sectors of the economy, an impossibility in view of sectoral complementarities and links in terms of (non)quality.

democracy as de facto theocracy exerting radical-right oppression, including mass imprisonment, widespread executions, police brutality and murder, and other forms of state 'holy' terror, Puritan-style moralistic repression of sinners-as-criminals (drug users), mass gun ownership and gun-driven mass murders, extreme religiosity, beliefs in creationism, flat earth, 'Satan' and other religious superstitions, prohibition of evolution and other natural and social scientific theories, burning or banning books, Puritanical depreciation of aesthetic art, overall cultural irrationalism and anti-science, and so on.

If one wonders about the principal roots or sources of the US state epitomizing Reagan's notion of 'evil empire', they, as the above implies, essentially overlap with, or correspond to the primary causes of fascism, so just a few remarks will suffice. First, conservatism is the principal ideological source of such an 'evil empire' by its inherent militarism, bellicosity, wars of aggression, and imperialism versus other societies, which it inherits from its ideal medievalism or feudalism and then expands and intensifies, just as being the prime cause of fascism as well as theocracy within American society. Second, coercive, unrestrained capitalism is the main economic source of this 'evil empire' through its predatory, rapacious features and actions, such as allying with militarism, supporting wars of aggression, aligning with political (and cultural) imperialism for attaining its ends, and resorting to commercial imperialism by forcing other countries to buy its typically low-quality products.

Third, extremist American religion is the principal cultural, spiritual source of the 'evil empire' by virtue of its religious nationalism and expansionism by alliance with or support of militarism, wars of aggression, and imperialism against other countries, combined with missionary work as the regular ally and 'holy' support of colonialism and imperial conquest or dominance. Specifically, the main historical religious root and inspiration of the 'evil empire' is Calvinist Puritanism due to its original proxy-genocide of Native Americans, which it rationalized by the claim to America's 'manifest destiny' through the 'Divine mission' to rule the world, just as being the remote cause or precedent for fascism within society. If, as Tocqueville famously states in *Democracy in America*, the 'whole destiny of America' is 'embodied in the first Puritan', Puritanism's near-genocide of these 'pagan' tribes predestined the US state to epitomize the 'evil empire' by wars of aggression against and imperial conquest and control of societies from Latin America to Asia and parts of Europe, just as its persecution, 'holy terror', and witch-trials of 'infidels' overdetermined conservative-religious coercion and repression, including fascism post-2016, within society ever since. Overall, Puritanism and generally Calvinism was the most militaristic ('Church militant'), warlike, and imperialist or expansionist branch of Protestantism in relation to other societies, just as the most proto-totalitarian and in that sense proto-fascist within society, with (together with Luther) Calvin and his English-American 'children', Puritans being among the 'greatest haters'[87] of humanity who projected their corresponding traits and behaviors into the 'evilness' of the world. The subsequent and present chief religious source of the 'evil empire' is Protestant evangelicalism as a descendent of Puritanism continuing and expanding religion-driven nationalism and joining (alone or in alliance with its former enemy, dogmatic Catholicism within the Christina Right) or sanctifying militarism, wars of aggression, and joining political (and cultural) imperialism. Particularly, Puritan and evangelical theocracy from New England to the Bible Belt represents the principal specific religious source of the 'evil empire' due to being intensely militaristic, bellicose, launching or consecrating wars of aggression, and pursuing or aligning with political (and cultural) imperialism, just as being the definite 'holy' cause or equivalent of fascism. And fascism as the joint product of the above four factors is consequently the ultimate source of the 'evil empire' due to its compound of intense militarism, extreme bellicosity, wars of aggression, and imperialism which it inherits and reinforces from conservatism, as well as from extremist religion like Puritanism and evangelicalism and Puritan-evangelical and other theocracy.

In any event, the preceding ultimately identifies or implies, if 'Divinely ordained' as necessary in religious terms, the 'mission' to destroy the 'evil' world for its own good in (as Pareto puts it) the 'name of the Divine master' and for the 'glory of God' in Weber's sense of Puritan glorification of the 'God of Calvinism' via theocratic terror and religious war, as the path to 'election'. In short, it yields 'annihilation as salvation', thus acting as or resembling a suicidal cult and sect consistent with its 'in God we trust' credo and 'faith-based' core.

Just as a President alerted to the dangers of the rising military-industrial complex in postwar times, the US's extreme military expenditure and the resulting warfare-imperial state versus 'enemy' societies, entwined with the police state within society, deserves special consideration and attention. This holds because by expressing militarism, perpetuating American imperialism or Western neocolonialism, as via NATO's expansion, and enabling wars of aggression eventuating in global destruction, such military expenditure poses

---

87   Fromm (1941, pp. 82–3) observes that 'Luther and Calvin portray [a] all-pervading hos-
      tility. Not only in the sense that these two men, personally, belonged to the ranks of the
      greatest haters among the leading figures of history, certainly among religious leaders;
      but, which is more important, in the sense that their doctrines were coloured by this
      hostility and could only appeal to a group itself driven by an intense, repressed hostility'
      (see also McLaughlin 1996).

a primary and indeed mortal danger to not just world peace but the survival of civilization, including America itself. Due to its exorbitant military expenditure and so the underlying pathology of militarism, imperialism, and aggressive wars, the US government under 'bipartisan' conservatism seems inexorably, firmly, and obstinately on the path likely ending in MAD—both destruction of its 'enemies' and self-destruction of its 'empire for good.' And aside from a few exceptions (e.g., a single US senator), there hardly exist in America and the West influential contemporary equivalents of Jefferson and Madison to act as voices of reason and pacifism alerting the US government and American society to its self-destructive, collectively suicidal course through extreme military expenditure, militarism, and a warfare-imperial state of offensive wars indicating the end of the Enlightenment's rule of reason and the descent into medieval and conservative-fascist militarist and warlike irrationalism. At this juncture, militarism via unlimited military expenditure and a warfare-imperial state in the US appear as (what Weber may call) an abomination of Jefferson's and Madison's original pacifism or non-militarism, minimal military force for national defense only, non-entanglement in aggressive military alliances, and respect for the independence of other nations, and thus of the American Revolution's ideals, and generally of Enlightenment rationalism. In this sense, it abolishes or deviates from the original ideal and rendition of the American Revolution and Constitution as essentially pacifist or non-militarist, defensive, non-expansionary, and respectful of other nations, for such an 'originalist' interpretation—on which militarist US conservatives adamantly insist—would legally prohibit or question strong militarism via unlimited military expenditure as a betrayal of these revolutionary ideals and unconstitutional. Overall, this deviation from American original pacifism or non-militarism exposes the insistence of US conservatives, such as conservative judges within and outside the Supreme Court, on the 'originalist' interpretation of the American Revolution and Constitution to justify their denying of 'unconstitutional' personal freedoms, privacy, and human rights, including abortion rights, as a deliberate deception hiding their severe repression resulting in fascism or theocracy as in the Bible Belt and beyond. Alternatively, it exposes this conservative intransigence as a self-delusion reminiscent of Hume's diagnosed 'madness with religious ecstasies' of Puritanism and Pareto's detected Puritan moralistic 'insanity'.

Finally, this extensive consideration the US's extreme military expenditure and its actual or potential adverse and ultimately catastrophic consequences for America intends to be positive, pro-American, and patriotic in the sense of pacifist patriotism. It intends to harness pacifism and more broadly cosmopolitanism to save America from the self-destructive tendency of conservative-fascist, religious, and other intense militarism, including extreme military expenditure and a Leviathan-like military-industrial complex, imperialism, a warfare state, and wars of aggression likely ending in MAD, so national suicide. On this account, pacifism, cosmopolitanism, and generally liberalism prove to be more pro-American and patriotic (its 'better angels') than their opposites by saving America from the madness of self-destruction. Instead, militarism, imperialism, and conservatism/fascism overall despite their declared 'Americanism' and 'patriotism' turn out to be extremely anti-American and unpatriotic by threatening to destroy America while destroying the world by wars of aggression causing MAD.

Conclusion

This conclusion offers tentative predictions about the future of America in respect of democracy and generally free society and survival considering the occurrence, expansion, and prospective persistence and dominance of fascism. The 'bad news' is, as its stands post-2016/post-2020, that the future of America in terms of democracy and in extension free society and existence looks generally bleak and hopeless, as does in consequence that of the world, notably the survival of modern civilization.[1] The latter applies given the real possibility of anti-democratic contagion from the 'leader of the free world' and ultimately MAD (mutually assured destruction) through wars of aggression driven by aggressive and self-destructive religious nationalism and militarism qua America's 'manifest destiny' or 'Divine mission' to global domination as 'salvation', superior 'American exceptionalism', or supremacist 'Americanism', reaching the madness of self-destruction as Puritan-style election or salvation.

The bleak and hopeless tentative prediction holds true in view of the explosion and contagion of fascism post-2016 and its inception earlier, such as since the 2010s with the proto-fascist Tea Party, the 1980s with anti-liberal Reaganism, the 1950s with its precedent McCarthyism, and the 1920s (and before) with the Ku Klux Klan as the first proto-fascist movement in America and perhaps the world.

The Jeffersonian Enlightenment-based liberal prospect of America as the 'land of freedom' with universal liberty, equality, and justice 'for all' presently seems dismal, weak, even dead in the sense of democracy dying[2] in the foreseeable future such as few decades due to the exploding and spreading specter of fascism and its destruction of democracy and free society. As it stands during the first decades of the 21st century, Tocqueville's and especially Jefferson's

---

1   As noted, Adorno (2001, pp. 229–30) observes that the 'religious element in American fascist propaganda' derives from the 'Puritan tradition' and ends in 'a delirium of annihilation masked as salvation [i.e.] its self-destructive implications.' He concludes that the 'unconscious psychological desire for self-annihilation faithfully reproduces the structure of a political movement which ultimately transforms its followers into victims' (Adorno 2001, pp. 226–30). He implies that the latter include both the fascist rank-and-file such as the post-2016 autocratic base and ultimately all Americans through internal oppression, murder, and terror by fascism merged with religion and its external offensive perpetual wars resulting in MAD, thus the ultimate madness of self-destruction.

2   This is what Levitsky and Ziblatt (2018) envision in *How Democracies Die*, with special reference to the danger of the dying of American democracy post-2016.

liberal-secular democracy and thus the ideal of universal liberty and free society in America appears less resilient to the illiberal and anti-democratic specter of fascism and thus dictatorship in the form of fascist autocracy, dynasty,
oligarchy, and plutocracy than ever before during its history, specifically since
the Civil War and postwar times. In this regard, American democracy's and
society's celebrated resilience to 'foreign' fascism such as fascist or Nazi-style
autocracy reappears as an illusionary myth or ethnocentric delusion and
exaggeration.

The future of democratic America appears bleak given that fascism not only
rises and spreads post-2016, since what happens during this period involves all
fascist essentials in their almost original purity and so should be denoted by
precisely this term rather than by imprecise or broader terms like 'populism',
the 'far right', 'right-wing', etc. Furthermore, rather than being a one-time random 2016–2020 event, fascism promises or threatens, depending on its adherents or opponents, to continue to rise in America by recurring, persisting,
solidifying, and expanding in the foreseeable future or short to medium terms
through the 2030s. Such an outcome is due to fascism-conservatism's gaining
control of most state powers after the 2020 elections, thus ruling at least for
a decade through voting suppression, partisan gerrymandering, and election
subversion by overturning electoral results to favor fascists and conservatives
united within the larger family of rightism and their political party dominating conservative America like the former Southern Confederacy and beyond.
To that extent, this likely fascist recurrence or persistence portends a bleak
future, truly dark days ahead for America in respect of democracy and free
society in Tocqueville's depiction and especially Jefferson's Enlightenment liberal vision. The future of America in democracy and freedom appears doomed
and gloomy reminiscent, in a reverse form, of Puritan[3] doom and gloom in the
event of fascism's self-perpetuation, expansion, and intensification.

Accordingly, the future of democratic America looks at present bleak
so long as fascism continues to exist and spread by replicating, perpetuating, and consolidating itself post-2016–2020 in continuity with Reaganism/
McCarthyism, the anti-New Deal reaction, and the Ku Klux Klan, as its times of
eruption and initiation, respectively. Fascism will probably continue to recur

---

3 This prediction seemingly resembles but actually reverses Puritan doom and gloom, because
   Puritanism and generally Calvinism envisioned the gloomy future of America and Europe as
   what it condemned as 'godless' Jeffersonian and more broadly Enlightenment-based liberal-
   secular democracy and society superseding its proto-totalitarian theocracy as 'holy' proto-
   fascism that prefigures and inspires fascism proper, including Nazism, as Merton (1939) and
   other sociologists show (e.g., Fromm 1944; McLaughlin 1996; Munch 2001).

in America and via contagion or bellicose imposition beyond—including, intoxicated or deluded by supremacist 'Americanism', its launching of wars of aggression, unilaterally or via NATO expansion, aiming to conquer, rule, and make many societies parts of the American 'empire' and causing global MAD as the madness of religion-style self-destruction—in the foreseeable short- or medium-term future. Crucially, this holds true insofar as fascism's primary social causes continue to prevail, as through 2030 and after, because of the joint fascist-conservative control of most state governments after 2020 enabling its maintenance by voter suppression, partisan redistricting, and overturning election results and thus popular will.

Regarding these causal factors, fascism in America and beyond is just a manifest symptom or aggregate effect that they produce and perpetuate and through their fascist product and alliance eliminate or subvert liberal democracy and its comprehensive and universal liberty. It follows that the prospect of democratic America looks dark so long as the primary causes and predictors of fascism persist, dominate, and operate, causing fascist reproduction in one of the two poles of American society (the 'two Americas'). Recall that the primary causes of fascism in America consist of inherently authoritarian conservatism or rightism, unfettered, coercive, and inegalitarian capitalism, pervasive and repressive religion or religious extremism, and theocracy qua 'faith-based' rule in conjunction and mutual reinforcement. In relation to these causes, fascism in America and elsewhere is just a visible syndrome or compounded outcome that conservatism, unrestrained capitalism, ubiquitous religion, and theocracy jointly generate and sustain and thereby extinguish or pervert liberal democracy.

Consequently, the future of America in democratic terms seems bleak so long as the compound of conservatism, coercive capitalism, omnipresent religion, and theocracy persists and prevails, and hence reproduces fascism in the conservative-religious pole of American society. It turns out that America's democratic future, even its survival, looks doomed and gloomy Puritan-style but for opposite reasons, because of the persistence and prevalence of conservatism, coercive capitalism, repressive religion, and theocracy, as the compounded principal cause and predictor of fascism in American and Western and comparable societies like OECD countries and beyond. Ultimately, the compound of persistent and prevalent authoritarian conservatism, unrestrained capitalism, pervasive religion, and theocracy makes America's future look bleak precisely by generating, sustaining, and rationalizing, or allying and merging with, fascism as their joint product or regular ally. In this regard, fascism in America and beyond via global post-2016 contamination or violent imposition by militarist expansions and offensive wars reappears as the tip of the proverbial iceberg in the 'all-American' exceptional shape of conservatism, coercive capitalism, ubiquitous religion, and theocracy defining 'American exceptionalism'. In short, the likely recurrence of fascism renders America's future bleak due to the joint fascist causation, perpetuation, and justification by conservatism, unrestrained capitalism, religion, and theocracy.

In a counterfactual but realistic constellation, fascism would not have risen, would not recur, and would not render America's future bleak had not the compound of conservatism, compulsory capitalism, religion, and theocracy persisted, prevailed, operated, and thus caused fascist reproduction in one of American society's two poles such as conservative America in the former Southern Confederacy (or the 'Bible Belt'). Simply, the fascist effect would not occur, recur, and extremely darken America's future if the conjoined conservative, unfettered-capitalist, religious, and theocratic cause did not exist and operate to generate and sustain fascism. Taken together, the future of America as democracy and even a viable society appears bleak manifestly if fascism recurs and latently because of the complex of conservatism, unrestrained capitalism, religion, and theocracy jointly causing such fascist recurrence in America and beyond via contagion or imposition by militarist expansions and wars of aggression (unilaterally or under NATO) probably eventuating in the madness of self-destruction, MAD.

First, the future of democratic America looks bleak and dark, almost in the image of the Dark Middle or New Dark Ages so long as intrinsically authoritarian conservatism[4] persists and pervades American society, dominating at least conservative America like the former Southern Confederacy, and thus reproduces fascism in reciprocal relation and intensification with coercive capitalism, omnipresent religion, and theocracy. Generally, conservatism or rightism is invariably the primary ideological-political cause, creator, and predictor of

---

4 Bonikowski et al. (2021, p. 492) alert that extreme conservative 'trends point to the rising demand for radical candidates among Republicans and suggest a potentially bleak future for US politics, as nationalism becomes yet another among multiple overlapping social and cultural cleavages that serve to reinforce partisan divisions and undermine the stability of liberal democratic institutions.' They add that 'if Americans cannot agree on what their country means to them, what lessons to draw from its past, and what core principles should guide its future path, this is likely to further exacerbate zero-sum partisanship—predicated on perceiving the political opposition [liberalism] as fundamentally un-American—that poses a dire threat to the country's liberal democratic institutions' (Bonikowski et al. 2021, p. 503). Specifically, Bonikowski et al. (2021, p. 533) predict that 'in an era of sustained nationalist discord, the Republican Party's active stoking of ethnoracial exclusion and declinist nostalgia will continue to pose a dire threat to the stability of US political institutions [showing] the dangers posed to the future of liberal democracy by the rise of radical [right] politics.'

fascism, including Nazism, that is universally a conservative or rightist effect, creation, and predicted outcome. This yields the empirical generalization and, in that sense, the 'iron' sociological law like Michels' law of oligarchy—'who says conservatism or rightism, says ultimately fascism, including Nazism, all else being equal.' The 'all-American' variation of conservatism or rightism is no exception to this rule, despite its deceptive claims to and delusions of its 'democratic' and 'libertarian' difference or exceptionality from the conservative causation of fascism. Moreover, rather than being an exception in this respect, American conservatism is a strong confirmatory proof and epitome of the conservative 'law' of causing, perpetuating, and allying and merging with fascism as its universal offspring and standard ally.

Therefore, American conservatism or rightism will ultimately generate and perpetuate fascism like neo-fascism or neo-Nazism so long as it continues to prevail over liberalism and to pervade and dominate in America, namely the conservative pole in the South and similar regions. After the 2020 elections, conservatism's political party controls most US state governments and legislatures, enabling it to extend its electoral and political dominance by partisan gerrymandering, voting suppression, and election subversion though overturning electoral results in its favor, perverting elections fascist-style, at least until 2030. In consequence, insofar as the conservative or rightist pole of America solidifies, expands, and reasserts itself against its liberal opposite, it will likely become a neo-fascist subsociety and possibly, via forcible expansion or ideological, political, and media indoctrination, penetrate and shape American society as a whole after conservatism's pattern of reproduction of fascism. Accordingly, democratic America's future appears bleak so long as 'all-American' conservatism persists and prevails over 'un-American' liberalism and conservative America self-perpetuates, grows, and consolidates versus its liberal counterpart post-2016/2020, thus causing, enabling, and sustaining fascism or its religious equivalent like theocracy.

Wherever conservatism petrifies itself after the model of petrified medievalism and reigns supreme, as in conservative America such as the South and similar illiberal spaces, it eventually produces or becomes fascism and thus renders democratic America's future dark after the image of the Dark Middle Ages as the perennial conservative ideal, 'golden past,' and 'paradise lost and found' (as in the 'Bible Belt'). Every persistence, prevalence, and advance of conservatism over liberalism and hence any petrification, predominance, and expansion of conservative America versus its liberal counterpart, as in post-2016/2020 and since the 1980s, is a sure causal path to and a proven recipe for fascism, making democratic America's future bleak.

Second, the future of democratic America appears bleak insofar as unrestrained, coercive, and inegalitarian capitalism perpetuates itself and remains a dominant economic system, thus economically reproducing fascism in interconnection and mutual reinforcement with conservatism, pervasive religion, and theocracy. Such a type of capitalism is the principal economic determinant and predictor of fascism. The latter is in economic terms universally a capitalist phenomenon since fascist Italy and Spain and Nazi Germany, with German capitalists a la Krupp et al. both financing and benefiting from the rise of Nazism, through Chile under neo-fascist dictatorship helped, rationalized, and visited as the 'free market' paradise by 'libertarian' Chicago economics to Hungary under extreme-right rule. This model of capitalism is a proxy for economic 'fascism' and an indirect cause of political fascism in that it eliminates constraints on or regulations of coercion and violent repression, including state murder and terror, of non-capitalist production factors and social strata, such as laborers from the Gilded Age to Reaganism and post-2016. Generally, laissez-faire capitalism constitutes such an economic system and approximates proto-fascism and anticipates fascism and generally authoritarianism— no restraints, rules, and regulations on capital power, control, and domination over labor, with the only rule being the 'law' of the strongest and jungle, and thus 'brute force' from the Hobbesian state of nature and anarchy.

Consequently, so long as 'all-American' unfettered, coercive, and inegalitarian capitalism reproduces itself and prevails over regulated, non-coercive, and egalitarian or welfare capitalism, it will likely economically generate or support and ally with, just as benefit from fascism, including fascist autocracy, dynasty, and oligarchy, and its rise and dominance. Notably, insofar as unrestrained capitalist plutocracy reasserts itself against non-capitalist production factors and social classes, such as repressing labor and its collective organization and action like unionization and collective bargaining, it will likely enable, finance, and ally with, while also benefiting from, fascist autocracy, dynasty, and oligarchy in America, just as major Italian and German capitalists enabled, financed, allied with, and benefited from Mussolini and Hitler's seizure and exercise of absolute power in Italy and Germany. The above suggests that democratic America's future looks bleak so long as American unfettered, coercive, and inegalitarian capitalism continues to prevail over its alternative and thereby generates, enables, and allies, or is essentially compatible with, as well as benefits from, fascism and its capture of power, primarily in conservative America.

Third, the future of America in terms of democracy and freedom looks gloomy so long as omnipresent repressive and exclusionary religion or religious extremism petrifies American society, above all, conservative America, as 'faith-based', and thus religiously grounds, perpetuates, and consecrates fascism

in mutual relation and intensification with conservatism, theocracy, and unrestrained capitalism within the anti-democratic and anti-liberal Christian Right.
Religion, especially its coercive, extremist form, is the major cultural or spiritual source, sanctification, and predictor of fascism that is typically a religious,
'faith-based', 'godly' phenomenon in America and beyond. Despite claiming
'exceptionalism', American religion, particularly religious extremism such as
fundamentalism through Protestant evangelicalism and Catholic dogmatism
united within the Christian Right, is far from being an exception to this pattern.
It is rather the exemplar of the religious causation and consecration of and alliance and merger with fascism, as since the 1980s through post-2016, including
the 2020 elections, when evangelicals overwhelmingly and Catholics largely
embrace and consecrate the rising, persisting, or recurring fascist autocracy
as their 'heaven on earth' and 'savior' 'chosen by God' and 'God's plan' to 'save
America' from its 'enemy' liberalism and liberal-secular democracy.

Consequently, 'all-American faith', particularly religious extremism, will
reproduce, sanctify, or ally and merge with fascism like neo-fascism and
neo-Nazism so long as it persists and prevails over secularism, including the
separation of church and state and the differentiation between religion and
politics, liberalism, and rationalism, and pervades and still dominates in
America, at least the conservative pole. In extension, so long as conservative-
religious, especially evangelical, America qua the 'Bible Belt' petrifies and reasserts itself against its liberal, secular, and rationalist antipode, it will probably
mutate into a neo-fascist subsociety and via coercive imposition or systematic propaganda reshape all American society after extremist religion and its
causation or sanctification of fascism, while expanding beyond via militarism,
'manifest destiny' imperialism perpetuating an 'evil' empire, and offensive war
eventuating in MAD. It follows that democratic America's future looks bleak
insofar as coercive, exclusionary religion,[5] including religious extremism, persists and prevails over secularism and 'faith-based' America petrifies, expands,
and consolidates versus its secular opposite and the world, thus generating,
perpetuating, sanctifying, and eventually blending with fascism.

Fourth and related, the future of America in respect of democracy, free society, and even survival due to the prospect of MAD via offensive war, appears dark
insofar as theocracy persists in American society, above all its conservative-
religious pole like the Southern and other 'Bible Belt', and generates or blends

---

5   Paxton (1998, pp. 3, 23) predicted more than two decades ago that 'religion would cer-
    tainly play a much greater role in an authentic fascism in the United States than in the first
    European fascisms [so that] an authentically popular fascism in the United States would be
    pious.'

with fascism in conjunction and mutual reinforcement with omnipresent religion, conservatism, and coercive capitalism within the Christian Right. Theocracy is the strongest religious determinant or covariate and thus predictor of fascism that is religiously hence, aside from rare and transient exceptions, usually a theocratic or theocentric phenomenon since fascist Italy/Spain and Nazi Germany via the alliance of fascism and Nazism with Catholicism and Protestantism through Chile's neo-fascist dictatorship supported by the Catholic church to Catholic-dominated Poland, plus Islamic-ruled Turkey, Saudi Arabia, etc. Theocracy operates as such a fascist determinant because it represents in a sense 'holy' proto-fascism and generally proto-totalitarianism, simply 'religious slavery' as Jefferson describes it, and thus is fully compatible and profoundly convergent with fascism proper.

Furthermore, theocracy in America and other contemporary societies can be instituted, imposed, and sustained only or primarily through fascism, such as fascist coercion, repression, and counter-state and state violence and terror in combination with religious indoctrination and manipulation. Conversely, fascism in America and beyond can perpetuate and reassert itself and its rulers last and rule in long terms solely or mainly via a theocratic alliance, merger, or support, as within the Christian Right, and generally religious 'holy' consecration and glorification of fascist autocrats and regimes as chosen and instituted by 'God' and 'God's plan'.

As a corollary, so long as theocracy as 'faith-based', 'in God we trust', 'indivisible under God' government ranging from local and state governments to Congress and President and society in America persists and prevails against secular democracy, it will engender, consecrate, and predict fascism. Insofar as the theocratic pole of America like the 'Bible Belt' in the South and beyond petrifies and dominates its weaker secular opposite, it will likely turn into a neo-fascist subsociety and reconstruct entire American society after its theocratic 'divine' design through forcible expansion, religious and culture wars, or 'godly' indoctrination and propaganda, while expanding beyond via offensive war driven by 'manifest destiny' nationalism like supremacist Americanism and likely ending in the madness of self-destruction. Democratic America's future seems dark so long as theocracy couched as a 'faith-based' polity and sanctified as 'God's dominion' over society persists and reasserts itself against democracy, and its theocratic pole in the 'Bible Belt' and beyond (e.g., Utah as a classic theocratic state) petrifies and prevails over its opposite and expands beyond via militarist expansion and wars of aggression with MAD. In short, the result is theocracy's reproduction and consecration of and the alliance and merger with fascism.

In sum, the combination of conservatism with coercive unfettered capital-ism, repressive ubiquitous religion, and theocracy is an existential threat to America as democracy and free and even heathy, normally functioning society by generating and sustaining fascism as the universal poison of all democratic and normal societies. Moreover, this 'all-American' conservatism and such a combination is the most implacable, persistent, and strongest existential threat to democratic and free America by such fascist reproduction, more so than any other 'un-American' or 'foreign' enemies. Home-grown conservatism, combined with coercive capitalism, pervasive extremist religion, and theoc-racy, seems a graver, stronger, and more enduring menace to—or a more cred-ible 'promise' to destroy—democratic, free, and even, by militarist expansion, imperialism, and offensive war with MAD, America itself than Soviet commu-nism, that peacefully ended its threat by a collective euthanasia, and any for-eign enemies were. 'All-American' conservatism develops and operates as the destructive principle of 'live and let die'—as demonstrated by its conduct as an effective death cult during the Covid-19 pandemic, climate change, and wars of aggression—while Soviet communism largely developed or functioned in its later phases as the 'live and let live' tenet of peaceful coexistence (analogous to the behavior of oligopolists in Schumpeter's framework).

As a corollary, 'all-American' conservatism launches and wages a perma-nent literal, including terrorist or violent, January 6, 2021 style, offensive war-fare against liberal democracy and universal liberty in America by causing fascism, while Soviet communism mostly engaged or was forced into a figu-rative and defensive Cold War. Hence, the irony or perverse 'adverse fate' (in Weber's words) is while Americans understandably celebrated the demise of Soviet communism as the termination of an external existential threat to America as democracy and society overall, they did not detect or antici-pate the rise, expansion, and long-standing presence of an internal and more implacable and persistent menace, the conjunction of American conservatism with coercive unfettered capitalism, ubiquitous repressive religion, and proto-totalitarian evangelical theocracy. The end of the Cold War might have been the end of history in the sense of ending Soviet communism as an external existential threat to America as democracy and society. Yet, it was the begin-ning of the even graver, more powerful and perpetual menace by 'all-American' conservatism, combined with coercive capitalism, pervasive religion, and the-ocracy, as the prime generator of fascism. To that extent, America's triumph in the Cold War may prove post-2016 a Pyrrhic victory that becomes an ultimate defeat and destruction of democracy and free society by 'all-American' native conservatism conjoined with unfettered capitalism, ubiquitous religion, and theocracy through the joint reproduction of fascism, even apart from MAD due to militarist (unilateral or within NATO) expansion, imperialism, and offensive war.

The 'good news' is that the future of America as democracy and free society looks less bleak and relatively bright considering the possible demise or decline of fascism and its main ideological and political cause and creator conservatism, together with coercive capitalism, pervasive religion, and theocracy, thanks to the existence and reassertion of countervailing antifascist, nonconservative, and related social powers. The demise of fascism and the decline of conservatism is the categorical imperative or necessary condition for the prevalent democracy and freedom future of America, as it has been of its present and past.

Democratic and free America's future appears less dark and gloomy and instead brighter and more joyous so long as fascism does not recur in the foreseeable future, and thus ceases and desists what it does post-2016 and to some extent since the 1980s or the 1950s and the 1930s. And fascism may not rise again or prevail in America and beyond so long as its countervailing social powers survive, function, and reassert themselves over their fascist and broader conservative opposites. These antifascists and nonconservative factors in America and other Western and comparable societies include liberalism, democracy, secularism, rationalism, progressivism, egalitarianism, universalism, cosmopolitanism, pacifism, and liberal actors. Consequently, the future of democratic, free America, even itself as a viable society, looks less bleak and relatively brighter so long as the complex of liberalism, liberal democracy, secularism, rationalism, progressivism, egalitarianism, universalism, cosmopolitanism, non-militarism, and liberals survives, functions, and prevails over fascism and conservatism and other main fascist causes.

Democratic America's future seems brighter so long as liberalism survives or revives, functions, and reasserts itself against conservatism and thus counteracts the latter's offspring and ally fascism. Liberalism and hence liberal modernity universally is the most effective ideological and generally societal antidote against the illiberal poison of fascism and conservatism and its own source and ideal medievalism or feudalism. This applies to American or, for its conservative-fascist detractors since McCarthy through Reagan et al., 'un-American' liberalism, though the latter has been traditionally secondary to 'all-American' conservatism and occasionally, as in post-2016 and since the 1980s, to the conservative child fascism. In an ironic twist, 'un-American' liberalism proves to be most likely and capable to secure the future of and thus save America in terms of democracy, freedom, and physical survival that conservatism/fascism menaces by wars of aggression with MAD from the lethal danger and nihilistic devastation of fascism (unless conservatives construe the latter, even without using the word, as 'all-American' and 'patriotism', as in post-2016 and since the 1980s).

Consequently, the future of America in democracy, freedom, and societal existence turns from bleak to bright to the extent that liberalism prevails over or counterbalances conservatism as the primary fascist ideological-political source and continues to operate as the strongest countervailing social factor against fascism and thus counters, disables, and possibly defeats the latter. In essence, if sufficiently pervasive and strong, liberalism tends to relegate conservatism to the 'dead past' of its origin medievalism, thus the Dark Middle Ages, and to prevent or overcome its destination fascism as the New Dark Ages. As a corollary, America's future as a democratic, free society, and even surviving entity stands or falls with liberalism and its own standing or falling to conservatism and the latter's product fascism. So long as liberalism stands to and asserts itself against conservatism and fascism, the future of America in this sense changes from dark to light, from the Dark Middle Ages and Puritan-like gloom and doom to Enlightenment-style brightness, joy, and optimism, and from bright to extremely bleak if anti-liberal conservative-fascist forces prevail, as in post-2016 and since the 1980s. In consequence, insofar as the liberal segment of America endures, extends, and becomes stronger in relation to the illiberal conservative section, its future in respect of democracy, liberty, and existence appears bright. In short, liberal America looks as the light future and its conservative pole the dark and 'dead hand of the past', as the former Southern Confederacy shows, in terms of democracy, free society, and survival.

As a corollary, democratic and free America's future looks brighter so long as liberal democracy survives, functions, and reaffirms itself against illiberal conservative and other anti-democratic forces, including fascism or the extreme right. Liberal democracy is the universal and primary countervailing political factor and most efficient remedy against the anti-democratic pathology of fascism and broader conservatism. This holds true for American, or for its conservative-fascist detractors since McCarthy through Reagan et al. 'un-American,'liberal democracy, although the latter has usually been secondary to its ersatz substitute like illiberal, exclusionary, and theocratic or religion-overdetermined 'democracy'. In a corollary ironic twist, 'un-American' liberal democracy is most likely and able to ensure the democratic and free future, indeed survival by refraining from militarist expansion, imperialism, and offensive war with MAD, and thus to act as the savior of America versus its anti-democratic subversion, including fascism's and conservatism's subversion of democracy by voting suppression and overturning elections post-2020.

Accordingly, the future of America in this regard moves from gloomy to joyous so long as liberal democracy survives, continues, and reaffirms itself against illiberal, conservative, and theocratic bogus 'democracy' and counteracts and overcomes fascism by acting as the strongest countervailing anti-fascist political power. Essentially, liberal democracy if sufficiently established and powerful eventually relegates illiberal bogus 'democracy' to its root or precedent the medieval ancient regime of aristocracy and theocracy and rules out or dissolves fascism. As a result, democratic, political America's future and even its survival stands or falls with liberal democracy and its own standing or falling to illiberal conservative and religious ersatz 'democracy' and fascism as ultimate anti-democracy. Hence, the future of America shifts from bleak to bright so long as liberal democracy stands to and reaffirms itself against conservative ersatz 'democracy' and fascist anti-democracy, and vice versa. In consequence, insofar as the liberal-democratic section of America endures and reasserts itself against its non-democratic opposite, its future as democracy and free and viable society changes from dark to light. It is a self-evident inference that liberal-democratic America is the bright future and its non-democratic pole the 'dead past', as the South and similar regions show, for its democracy, freedom, and survival.

Relatedly, the democratic, freedom, and existential future of America seems less dark so long as secularism or secularization continues and reasserts itself against coercive and encompassing religion, especially the perversion of secular democracy, such as the separation of church and state, religious extremism, and theocracy. Secularism or secularization through the functional differentiation between secular and 'sacred' powers and realms universally is the main countervailing social force against the anti-secular pathology of fascism and broader conservatism and its perversion of secular democracy and its religious extremism. Notably, via the institutional separation of state and church, secularism is the most effective antidote to the theocratic poison of fascism and broader conservatism with its underlying system of, or alliance and merger with, theocracy as proto-fascism and proto-totalitarianism overall in the sense of Jefferson's 'religious slavery' by enslaving 'infidels' (a shared Christian-Islamic label). This applies to American, or for its anti-secular and theocratic detractors from Puritanism to Reaganism, the Tea Party, and the post-2016 regime, 'un-American' secularism that hence develops and operates as the counterpoise, conjoined and reinforced with liberalism and liberal democracy, to the anti-secular and theocratic core of fascism and broader conservatism. The above holds true in general and long terms, although American secularism has historically been secondary and subordinate to religion and theocracy qua a 'faith-based', 'indivisible under God', 'in God we trust', 'God's dominion' polity and society from theocratic, proto-totalitarian Puritanism to its descendant evangelicalism eventually allied with dogmatic Catholicism in the anti-liberal, anti-democratic, and anti-secular Christian Right, but with some recent signs of acceleration like the sustained growth of persons with no religion or church ('nones'). These signs are consistent with and follow the accelerating trend toward secularism in other Western societies, notably Western Europe and within it 'post-Christian' (post-Lutheran) Scandinavia. They thus dispel the myth of 'American exceptionalism' that conservatives and rational choice theorists claim in this regard and America's alleged status as a unique counterproof against the 'iron' sociological law or strong empirical pattern of secularization involving the social-structural decline of religion and the demise of theocracy in the West. In another ironic twist, 'un-American' secularism reappears as a social factor securing the democratic and free future of and so saving America from the theocratic destruction of democracy by fascism, conservatism, and extreme religion.

Therefore, the future of America in democratic, freedom, and existential terms changes from bleak to bright so long as secularization continues and reaffirms against encompassing religion and religious extremism, and thus counteracts and transcends fascism by acting as the strong cure against the fascist perversion of secular democracy and its underlying regime of or merger with proto-totalitarian theocracy. If secularization advances sufficiently in America, as in Western societies, especially Western Europe or Scandinavia, versus coercive, encompassing religion and religious extremism, it will probably—aside from relocating faith to the private sphere—relegate the theocratic fusion of church and state to the medieval regime of theocracy that conservatism perpetuated as 'paradise lost and found' since Burke et al., thus overcoming fascism as extreme conservative anti-secularism. As a corollary, America's democratic, freedom, and existential future may change from dark to light, from the darkness of the Middle Ages and Puritan doom and gloom to Enlightenment brightness, joy, and optimism insofar as the secular section continues to grow and reasserts versus its religious and theocratic opposite as the 'holy' treasure of anti-secular fascist energies and forces. In essence, secular, when joined with liberal, America is the light future and its religious and theocratic pole the 'dead past' or 'paradise lost'—a la the 'Biblical Commonwealth' (Puritan theocracy), 'Bibliocracy' (Weber's word), the 'Bible Belt' (in the former Southern Confederacy and elsewhere)—for democracy and free and viable society.

Also related, the future of America in terms of democracy, freedom, and survival shifts from absolute darkness to relative lightness so long as the composite of social, including scientific, rationalism and progressivism reestablishes after its Jeffersonian Enlightenment-based origins and reasserts itself against religious irrationalism, anti-rationalism, and retrogression, in particular superstition and anti-science. In general, Enlightenment-rooted rationalism/

progressivism is universally the strongest countervailing cultural force against the complete irrationalist, anti-rationalist, and retrograde pathology of fascism and broader conservatism. Notably, Enlightenment scientific rationalism and progress acts as the best cure against fascism and other conservatism as the deadly admixture of primeval religious superstition and 'holy' anti-science, including anti-medicine and anti-vaccine, as culminating with mass deadly effects in conservative-religious America during the Covid-19 pandemic, anti-knowledge, and anti-education. This holds true hence for American scientific rationalism and cultural progressivism or 'un-American' for its irrationalist and anti-rationalist detractors from superstitious Puritanism to the anti-science trinity of Reaganism, the Tea Party, and the post-2016 autocratic regime.

The synthesis of rationalism and progressivism proves to be a strong antidote against fascism, even if being weaker than religiously sanctified irrationalism, anti-rationalism, and anti-progressivism, including superstition, anti-science, and obstruction of scientific and medical progress from Puritanism to evangelicalism through anti-evolution 'monkey trials' and to the Covid-19 pandemic. In a further ironic twist, 'un-American' Enlightenment-based scientific rationalism and progressivism that Jefferson et al. imported from Europe, mostly France (Paris salons), turns out to secure America's democratic, freedom, and existential future and thus to rescue it from the irrationalist, anti-rationalist, and retrograde degeneration and destruction of its democracy, polity, and all society by fascism and conservatism. For example, fascism and conservatism, along with omnipresent extremist religion like evangelicalism and dogmatic Catholicism (enemies for long but united finally in the Christian Right) and theocracy qua the 'Bible Belt', threaten such irrationalist, anti-rationalist, and retrograde degeneration and destruction of American democracy and society during the Covid-19 pandemic and climate change, as in all other health, economic, and political crises. By contrast, it is only Enlightenment-based rationalism/progressivism that prevents and remedies such crises by science and scientific, including medical, innovation, knowledge, and progress.

Consequently, the democratic, freedom, and existential future of America becomes brighter so long as rationalism/progressivism prevails over religious and other irrationalism, anti-rationalism, and regression, including superstition, anti-science, and impediment of scientific progress, and thereby counteracts and supersedes fascism and conservatism. If Weberian societal rationalization and progress, especially its scientific form, advances relative to the opposite in America to a level seen in Western societies, this process will likely relegate irrationalism, anti-rationalism, and retrogression, including superstition, anti-science, and blockage of scientific progress, to the Dark Middle Ages as the shared conservative and fascist ideal, and thus will counteract and overcome fascism. America's future in respect of democracy, freedom, and survival turns from medieval darkness to modernist lightness so long as the Enlightenment legacy of reason, progress, knowledge, and science endures, expands, and prevails over that of the Dark Middle Ages, including their Puritan variation through 'witches', witch and monkey trials, and related superstitions a la 'Satan', 'exorcism', and other pre- and anti-science beliefs and practices from 'creationism' to the 'flat earth'.

Accordingly, the future of America in democratic, freedom, and existential terms turns from bleak to bright so long as its rationalist/progressive, notably Enlightenment-based and scientific, enlightened and 'we believe in science' segment transcends and 'enlighten' and educate its irrationalist, anti-rationalist, anti-progressive, particularly superstitious and anti-science, unenlightened, self-destructive, and 'we believe in religion and guns' pole. Hence, Enlightenment/scientific America is the light future in democracy and free society and its medieval-like anti-science pole, consisting of the 'Bible Belt' and similar regions, the 'dead past' or 'paradise lost' of darkness, blissful ignorance, squalor, and self-inflicted death and suffering, as the Covid-19 pandemic, climate change, and other health and social crises show.

Furthermore, the democratic, freedom, and existential future of America turns from bleak to bright so long as the complex of egalitarianism, universalism, and cosmopolitanism or globalism, extends and strengthens versus anti-egalitarianism, anti-universalism or particularism, and anti-cosmopolitanism or anti-globalism. Specifically, this applies insofar as such a complex supersedes or mitigates extreme economic and social inequality, rigid hierarchy, elitism, monopolistic closure, and exclusion, as well as nationalism, nativism, social hatred, xenophobia, and racism. Generally, the complex of egalitarianism, universalism, and cosmopolitanism functions as a countervailing social power to fascism's and conservatism's anti-egalitarian, anti-universalist, and anti-cosmopolitan, particularly hierarchal, elitist, exclusionary, closed, as well as nationalist, hateful, xenophobic, and racist, pathology. This therefore holds true for its American variation, although especially, as for nativist detractors post-2016 and before, 'un-American' cosmopolitanism has always been and remains weaker than and secondary to national exclusion, particularism, and closure via conservative nationalism, social hatred, nativism, xenophobia, and master-race or master-caste racism. In an additional twist of irony and perhaps fate, 'un-American' cosmopolitanism is more likely and capable than its nativist, nationalist or populist, and xenophobic antithesis to sustain the democratic future and in that sense to rescue of America from the anti-egalitarian, anti-universalist, and exclusionary perversion of democracy and society by fascism and broader conservatism into a closed anti-democratic social system.

It follows that America's democratic, freedom, and existential future becomes from bleak to bright insofar as the complex of egalitarianism, universalism, and cosmopolitanism transcends its opposite, including extreme inequality, hierarchy, elitism, closure, and exclusion, as well as nationalism, social hatred, xenophobia, and racism, and hence counteracts, discredits, and supersedes fascism and conservatism. Conceivably, if becoming sufficiently enduring, pervasive, and strong the egalitarianism, universalism, and cosmopolitanism complex could relegate its opposite to the medieval ancient regime of aristocratic/elite and caste inequality, hierarchy, elitism, closure, and exclusion as the common fascist-conservative ideal, thus counteracting and possibly overcoming fascism. In extension, this democratic future turns from Puritan medieval darkness to Enlightenment modernist lightness insofar as the egalitarian, universalist, and cosmopolitan or globalist part of America reemerges and reaffirms in relation to its extremely unequal, hierarchical, particularistic, closed, exclusionary, nationalist, nativist, xenophobic, and racist, opposite, such as the conservative-religious pole. In a word, egalitarian, universalist, and cosmopolitan America is the democratic, freedom, and existential future and its particularistic, exclusionary, nativist, and racist pole is likely to be 'gone with the wind' in the manner of Southern slavery and caste.

Related to especially cosmopolitanism and liberalism, the democratic, freedom future and the survival prospect of America shifts from dark to light so long as pacifism emerges, spreads, and strengthens in relation to militarism, offensive war, and imperial conquest. In general, pacifism is a strong social counterforce against fascism's and broader conservatism's militarist, warlike, and imperialist pathology, notably the most effective peaceful 'soft' antidote to the fascist deadly, destructive, and self-destructive poison of intense militarism and aggressive war. This applies to America's variant that hence operates as such a social countervailing power versus fascism, although American or, for militarist and bellicose qua 'patriotic' detractors from Reaganism to the post-2016 regime, 'un-American' pacifism has been, especially since the post WW II period, weaker than the mostly conservative compound of anti-pacifism, militarism, offensive war, and conquest or imperialism. This implies yet another ironic or indeed fateful twist. 'Un-American' pacifism ensure the future and survival of and thus rescues, by national security minimizing the risk of self-destruction a la MAD, America from the anti-pacifist, militarist, warlike, and lethal degeneration of democracy and society by fascism and conservatism into a Leviathan-like military-industrial complex, exorbitant expenditures for offensive wars, and eternal crusade-style 'holy' war eventuating in collective suicide in the manner of evangelical suicidal cults and sects.

As noted, such American conservative militarism and war globally operate often through NATO as an expression of extreme militarism, an instrument of American imperialism and Western neocolonialism, and an extremely aggressive military alliance expanding beyond its original domain, encircling, provoking, and seeking confrontation directly with Russia and indirectly China. Because such actions can only result in a nuclear war between these nuclear-armed powers with a MAD outcome, NATO acts as an equivalent of a destructive and suicidal club bent on global destruction and ultimately self-destruction. NATO becomes the main and indeed sole militarist and warlike lethal threat not only to world peace but to human life, including the survival of Western civilization whose defender it claims to be, while operating as the tool of continuation and imposition of Western colonialism and imperialism, with incorporation of various small vasal states like former socialist countries and others. Driven by American (and British) conservative militarism, impe-rialism, and wars of aggression, NATO operates as the global instrument of MAD and to that extent as an inter-state analogue of a suicidal cult or sect seeking collective suicide as a path to salvation. Generally, after the Cold War, NATO—not counting its small puppet states like those of Eastern Europe for-merly members of the Warsaw Pact and the Soviet Union, plus the Balkans—epitomizes the law of absolute corruption and arrogance of absolute power at a global level through bellicose expansion and wars of aggression starting with its UN-unauthorized attack on Yugoslavia, with potentially catastrophic consequences of destruction of human life and the end of civilization. The persistence and expansion of NATO as the sole global military alliance turns from the blessing and savior to the curse and suicidal destroyer of Western civilization likely to perish, along with its enemies like Russia and others, in the MAD of its wars of aggression eventuating in an ultimate nuclear catastro-phe ending human life. The only question is when, not if, this catastrophe will happen—in the 21st or the 22nd century and later?—so long as NATO contin-ues on its path of expansion, confrontation, and aggressive war causing the madness of destruction via nuclear MAD.

Against this catastrophic specter and as a corollary of pacifist counterforces, America's democratic-freedom future and survival prospect turns from bleak to bright so long as pacifism becomes more widespread and stronger relative to militarism, offensive war, and imperial conquest, and thereby counteracts and possibly overcomes fascism and conservatism. If it becomes sufficiently extensive and intense as a 'soft' social power in America, as in most of Western Europe, pacifism may relegate militarism, war, and conquest to the oblivion of the militarist and warlike ancient regime of feudalism and warrior nobility as the shared model for conservative-fascist regimes and rulers, thus countering and overcoming fascism. As a regional ramification, America's future/survival seems less bleak and brightens so long as its non-militarist section extends and reaffirms in relation to its militarist, warlike, and imperialist pole that largely overlaps with the conservative, anti-liberal, undemocratic, anti-secular, anti-science, anti-cosmopolitan, nativist, nationalist, xenophobic, and racist part of America which the former Southern Confederacy especially (but not solely) exemplifies. Simply, non-militarist America is the likely future in democracy, freedom, and survival, and its militarist, warlike, and imperialist opposite the 'dead past' or the agent of MAD (together with Western 'great powers' imperialism or colonialism whose persistent militarist instrument is NATO, minus its small vasal members, and its expansion beyond its original borders toward 'enemies' and wars of aggression as effective inter-state terror).

In association with liberalism, the future of America in terms of democracy, freedom, and survival turns bright insofar as liberal actors exist and prevail over illiberal authoritarian personalities as leaders and followers, including sadistic-masochistic characters, repudiate the cult of autocratic rulers, dispel delusions ensuing in collective suicide through a death cult, just as dissolve the mix of morbid gravity and buffoonery. In general, associated with the ideological and sociological impact of liberalism, liberal individual and collective actors are the strongest countervailing socio-psychological forces against fascism's and broader conservatism's authoritarians, sadism-masochism, cult of autocratic rulers by the base, fantasies leading to collective suicide via a death cult, as well as the mix of deadly gravity and ludicrous clownery. This hence holds true for liberal equivalents in America who act as counter-agents to conservative-fascist authoritarians, although American or, for their conservative-fascist detractors from McCarthy and Reagan to Southern anti-liberals and the Tea Party, 'un-American' liberals have been weaker than and repressed by illiberal conservatives since Puritanism through McCarthyism to Reaganism, evangelicalism, and the post-2016 radical-right regime. Ironically but fatefully, 'un-American' liberals embody and ensure the democratic future and survival of and so save America from fascists' and other conservative authoritarians' sadistic-masochistic destruction of democracy and freedom, mix of deadly gravity and buffoonery, cult of autocratic rulers and delusions eventuating in collective suicide via a death cult, as also the Covid-19 epidemic, climate change, and other social crises show.

Therefore, America's democratic, non-authoritarian future shifts from bleak to bright so long as liberal actors survive, increase, and strengthen relative to illiberal conservative-fascist authoritarians with their sadism and masochism, pathological gravity and buffoonery, cults of autocratic rulers, delusions, and collective suicide via a death cult, thus countering and conceivably defeating fascism and conservatism. In socio-psychological terms, the democracy and freedom future, so the fate of America stands or falls essentially with the relative standing or falling of US liberal persons versus illiberal authoritarian personalities like fascist and conservative authoritarians. If liberals stand to and prevail over these fascist-conservative authoritarians, America's democratic future and fate looks brighter than it seems post-2016, including after 2020, and conversely. This confirms what has been evident and known since Jefferson and the Enlightenment. This is that liberal individuals and groups are the most effective antidote to the poison of conservative-fascist authoritarians and the strongest socio-psychological source and defense of democracy and freedom in America, as are in all Western and other societies. In turn, the future of America in democracy and freedom is bleak if liberals become a rare, powerless socio-psychological category by comparison to fascists and other conservatives as illiberal authoritarian, including sadistic, cultish, delusionary, and suicidal, personalities, as in post-2016 and before. Conversely, America's democratic and freedom future appears light if liberals become a prevalent socio-psychological type, redefining the 'American character'. This would redefine the latter as a socially created liberal that Enlightenment-based liberalism and modernity create and cultivate to substitute for the 'natural-born', medieval-rooted authoritarian conservative or right-winger, including the fascist personality erupting and prevailing in the conservative-religious pole post-2016 and since Reaganism and the Tea Party.

In sum, the future of America as a democracy, free society, and even surviving entity looks bleak as long as the principal causes and predictors of fascism surge, persist, and prevail in American society, as in post-2016 and since the 1980s. America's democratic, freedom future and indeed survival prospect seems dark insofar as conservatism, unfettered, coercive, inegalitarian capitalism, pervasive extremist religion, and theocracy resurrect, self-perpetuate, and dominate over their opposites, and thereby in conjunction and mutual reinforcement generate and sustain fascism in America, as in post-2016 and since the 1980s and other societies and times since fascist Europe, including Nazi Germany. America's future/prospect appears like Puritan-style doom and gloom, but for reasons opposite to Puritanism and its fundamentalist ramifications. This holds true as long as its conservative, coercive-capitalist, extremely religious, and theocratic pole petrifies, expands, and prevails over its antipode, and thus mutates into a fascist subsociety that threatens to reconstruct all American society accordingly, as the social system of fascism. Moreover, the future of America as a heathy-functioning and normal polity and society and thus its survival prospect looks bleak as long as conservatism, coercive capitalism, extremist pervasive religion, and theocracy continue to dominate and hence reproduce fascism, and its conservative, coercively capitalist, religious, and theocratic pole petrifies and prevails, and thus mutates into a fascist entity that reshapes American society after its design.

Conversely, the future of America in terms of democracy, free society, and survival presently looks bright as long as countervailing social powers versus fascism and its own causes and predictors develop, endure, and reassert themselves against their opposites, as since the New Deal through the 1970s, aside from some variations, and other societies and times, such as postwar Western Europe, above all Scandinavia. America's democratic and freedom future and survival prospect reappears as light insofar as liberalism, liberal democracy, secularism, rationalism, progressivism, egalitarianism, universalism, cosmopolitanism, pacifism, and liberal actors emerge, survive, and reaffirm themselves against their antipodes, and therefore counteract and eventually overcome fascism. America's future manifests itself as Enlightenment-style lightness and sunshine and for reasons identical to the Enlightenment and its result liberal modernity. This holds true as long as its liberal, democratic, secular, rationalist, progressive, egalitarian, universalist, cosmopolitan, pacifist pole comprising liberal personalities endures, grows, and reasserts itself against its opposite and hence recreates American society accordingly, as the social system of genuine democracy and universal liberty. Generally, the future of America as a functioning polity and society and thus its survival prospect reappears bright insofar as liberalism, liberal democracy, secularism, rationalism, progressivism, egalitarianism, universalism, cosmopolitanism, pacifism, and liberals survive and supersede their fascism-producing opposites, the blend of conservatism, coercive capitalism, pervasive religion, and theocracy. This therefore holds true insofar as the equivalent societal pole of America realizing these liberal and related principles endures, thrives, and prevails over its conservative, rightist antithesis tending to become a fascist subsociety consistent with conservatism or rightism ultimately ending in fascism, including Nazism, as its destination.

As a result, the future of America as a democracy, free society, and surviving entity is Puritan-like bleak and gloom or Enlightenment-style bright and optimism depending on the balance and contestation between the mainly Puritanical causes and predictors of fascism and its Enlightenment-rooted countervailing powers, thus between the setting of the conservative pole involving the first factors and the context comprising the second, namely its liberal antipode. In essence, what determines and predicts America's democratic future and indeed survival is whether the conservative and related causes of fascism and their setting, or its liberal and additional counterpowers and their context, prevail in this contest or warfare that the compound of conservatism/

religion launches and apparently wins against the complex of liberalism/secularism post-2016, including after 2020, and since the 1980s. America's future in this regard may be either a replica and consolidation of the post-2016 victory of the causes of fascism and their setting, or a reversal and triumph by anti-fascist counterpowers and their context. In a way, the conservative and related causes of fascism and their social setting have apparently won the battle, but this does not necessarily rule out that anti-fascist liberal and additional counterpowers and their context may win the war, for the future and survival of America. Taken together, America's future as a democracy and free society and indeed its survival hinges on whether the causes of fascism and their setting, or its countervailing powers and their context will be more pervasive and stronger in prospect—it stands with the second, essentially liberalism and secularism, and falls with the first, basically conservatism and religion, all else being equal.

References

Abbott, Andrew. 2005, Linked Ecologies: States and Universities as Environments for Professions. *Sociological Theory*, 23 (3): 245–274.

Abramitzky, Ran, Leah Boustan, Elisa Jacome, and Santiago Perez. 2021. Intergenerational Mobility of Immigrants in the United States over Two Centuries. American Economic Review, 111 (2): 580–608.

Acemoglu, Daron and James A. Robinson. 2013. *Why Nations Fail: The Origins of Power, Prosperity, And Poverty*. New York: Crown Business.

Acemoglu, Daron and James A. Robinson. 2015. The Rise and Decline of General Laws of Capitalism. *Journal of Economic Perspectives*, 29 (1): 3–28.

Acemoglu, Daron, Georgy Egorov, and Konstantin Sonin. 2018. Social Mobility and Stability of Democracy: Reevaluating De Tocqueville, *Quarterly Journal of Economics*, 133 (2): 1041–1105.

Acemoglu, G Daron, Iuseppe De Feo, Giacomo De Luca, and Gianluca Russo. 2022, War, Socialism, and the Rise of Fascism: An Empirical Exploration. *The Quarterly Journal of Economics*, 137 (2): 1233–1296.

Adorno, Theodor W. 1991. *The Culture Industry: Selected Essays on Mass Culture*. New York: Routledge.

Adorno, Theodor W. 2001. *The Stars Down To Earth And Other Essays on The Irrational in Culture*. New York: Routledge.

Agamben, Giorgio. 1998. *Homo Sacer: Sovereign Power and Bare Life*. Stanford: Stanford University Press.

Akerlof, George A. 2020. Sins of Omission and the Practice of Economics. *Journal of Economic Literature*, 58 (2): 405–18.

Alfani, Guido. 2021. Economic Inequality in Preindustrial Times: Europe and Beyond. *Journal of Economic Literature*, 59 (1): 3–44.

Ali, S. Nageeb, and Roland Bénabou. 2020. Image versus Information: Changing Societal Norms and Optimal Privacy. *American Economic Journal: Microeconomics*, 12 (3): 116–64.

Allcott, Hunt, and Matthew Gentzkow. 2017. Social Media and Fake News in the 2016 Election. *Journal of Economic Perspectives*, 31 (2): 211–36.

Alpers, Benjamin L. 2003. *Dictators, Democracy, And American Public Culture: Envisioning the Totalitarian Enemy, 1920s–1950s*. Chapel Hill: University of North Carolina Press.

Altemeyer, Bob. 2007. *The Authoritarians*. Winnipeg: University of Manitoba.

Altemeyer, R. A. 2010. Comment on the Tea Party Movement. https://www.pdf-arch ive.com/2017/07/29/altemeyer-teaparty2010/ Accessed September 2022.

Alvaredo, Facundo, Anthony B. Atkinson, Thomas Piketty, and Emmanuel Saez. 2013. The Top 1 Percent in International and Historical Perspective. *Journal of Economic Perspectives*, 27 (3): 3–20.

Amiti, Mary, Stephen J. Redding, and David E. Weinstein. 2020. Who's Paying for the US Tariffs? A Longer-Term Perspective. *AEA Papers and Proceedings* 110: 541–546.

Anderton, Charles H., and Jurgen Brauer. 2021. Mass Atrocities and Their Prevention. *Journal of Economic Literature*, 59 (4): 1240–92.

Aneja, Abhay P., and Carlos F. Avenancio-León. 2019. Disenfranchisement and Economic Inequality: Downstream Effects of *Shelby County v. Holder*. *AEA Papers and Proceedings*, 109: 161–65.

Arendt, Hannah. 1951. *The Origins of Totalitarianism*. New York: Harcourt Brace Jovanovich.

Aron, Raymond. 1998. *Main Currents in Sociological Thought*. New Brunswick, Transaction Publishers.

Atkin, David, Eve Colson-Sihra, and Moses Shayo. 2021. How Do We Choose Our Identity? A Revealed Preference Approach Using Food Consumption. *Journal of Political Economy* 129 (4): 1193–1251.

Atkinson, Anthony, Thomas Piketty, and Emmanuel Saez. 2011. Top Incomes in the Long Run of History. *Journal of Economic Literature*, 49 (1): 3–71.

Autor, David, David Dorn, Gordon Hanson, and Kaveh Majlesi. 2020. Importing Political Polarization? The Electoral Consequences of Rising Trade Exposure. *American Economic Review*, 110 (10): 3139–83.

Babb, Sarah and Alexander Kentikelenis. 2021. Markets Everywhere: The Washington Consensus and the Sociology of Global Institutional Change. *Annual Review of Sociology,* 47 (1): 521–541.

Bahr, Peter. 2002. Identifying the Unprecedented: Hannah Arendt, Totalitarianism, And the Critique of Sociology. *American Sociological Review*, 67 (6): 804–31.

Barnett, William and Michael Woywode. 2004. From Red Vienna to the Anschluss: Ideological Competition among Viennese Newspapers during the Rise of National Socialism. *American Journal of Sociology*, 109 (6): 1452–99.

Barro, Robert and Charles Redlick. 2011. Macroeconomic Effects from Government Purchases and Taxes. *The Quarterly Journal of Economics*, 126 (1): 51–102.

Baudrillard, Jean. 1994. *The Illusion of The End*. Stanford: Stanford University Press.

Bauman, Zygmunt. 1997. *Postmodernity and its Discontents*. New York: New York University Press.

Bauman, Zygmunt. 2001. *The Individualized Society*. Cambridge: Polity Press.

Bazzi, Samuel, Gabriel Koehler-Derrick, Benjamin Marx. 2020. The Institutional Foundations of Religious Politics: Evidence from Indonesia, *The Quarterly Journal of Economics*, 135 (2): 845–911.

Beck, Ulrich. 2000. *The Brave New World of Work*. Cambridge: Polity Press.

Becker, George. 1984. Pietism and Science: A Critique of Robert Merton's Hypothesis. *American Journal of Sociology*, 89 (5): 1065–1090.

Becker, Howard. 1945. Interpretative Sociology and Constructive Typology in Gurvitch, Georges and Wilbert Moore (eds). *Twentieth Century Sociology* (pp.77–103). Freeport: Books for Libraries Press.

Becker, Sascha O., Steven Pfaff, Jared Rubin. 2016. Causes and Consequences of the Protestant Reformation. ESI Working Paper 16–13. Retrieved from http://digital commons.chapman.edu/esi_working_papers/178.

Beerli, Andreas, Jan Ruffner, Michael Siegenthaler, and Giovanni Peri. 2021. The Abolition of Immigration Restrictions and the Performance of Firms and Workers: Evidence from Switzerland. *American Economic Review*, 111 (3): 976–1012.

Bell, Daniel. 2002. Afterword in Daniel Bell (ed.), *The Radical Right* (pp. 447–503). New Brunswick: Transaction Publishers.

Bénabou, Roland, Davide Ticchi and Andrea Vindigni. 2015. Religion and Innovation. *American Economic Review*, 105 (5): 346–51.

Bendix, Reinhard. 1984. *Force, Fate & Freedom. On Historical Sociology*. Berkeley: University of California Press.

Benhabib, Jess, Alberto Bisin, and Mi Luo. 2019. Wealth Distribution and Social Mobility in the US: A Quantitative Approach. *American Economic Review*, 109 (5): 1623–47.

Bernstein, Michael A. 2014. *A Perilous Progress: Economists and Public Purpose in Twentieth-Century America*. Princeton: Princeton University Press.

Besley, Timothy and Masayuki Kudamatsu. 2006. Health and Democracy. *American Economic Review*, 96 (2): 313–318.

Besley, Timothy and Torsten Persson. 2009. Repression or Civil War? *American Economic Review*, 99 (2): 292–97.

Berlin, Isaiah. 1990a. Joseph de Maistre and the Origins of Fascism. I. *New York Review* September 27.

Berlin, Isaiah. 1990b. Joseph de Maistre and the Origins of Fascism. II. New York Review October 11.

Berezin, Mabel. 2019. Fascism and Populism: Are They Useful Categories for Comparative Sociological Analysis? *Annual Review of Sociology*, 45: 345–361.

Bergemann, Patrick. 2017. Denunciation and Social Control. *American Sociological Review*, 82 (2): 384–406.

Berger, Daniel, William Easterly, Nathan Nunn, and Shanker Satyanath. 2013. Commercial Imperialism? Political Influence and Trade during the Cold War. *American Economic Review*, 103(2): 863–96.

Biggs, David. 2017. Vietnam: The Chemical War. Biggs https://www.nytimes.com/2017/11/24/opinion/vietnam-the-chemical-war.html.

Bivens, Josh, and Lawrence Mishel. 2013. The Pay of Corporate Executives and Financial Professionals as Evidence of Rents in Top 1 Percent Incomes. *Journal of Economic Perspectives*, 27 (3): 57–78.

Blau, Francine and Lawrence Kahn. 2000. Gender Differences in Pay. *The Journal of Economic Perspectives*, 14 (4): 75–99.

Blau, Francine and Lawrence Kahn. 2017. The Gender Wage Gap: Extent, Trends, and Explanations. *Journal of Economic Literature*, 55 (3): 789–865.

Blee, Kathleen and Kimberly Creasap. 2010. Conservative and Right-Wing Movements. *Annual Review of Sociology*, 36, 269–286.

Blinkhorn, Martin. 2003. *Introduction Allies, Rivals, Or Antagonists? Fascists And Conservatives in Modern Europe.* In Blinkhorn, Martin (ed.), *Fascists and Conservatives: The Radical Right and the Establishment in Twentieth-century Europe* (pp.1–13). London: Taylor & Francis.

Boltanski, Luc and Eve Chiapello.2005. *The New Spirit of Capitalism.* London: Verso.

Bonica, Adam, Nolan McCarty, Keith Poole, and Howard Rosenthal. 2013. Why Hasn't Democracy Slowed Rising Inequality? Journal of Economic Perspectives, 27(3): 103–24.

Bonikowski, Bart and Paul DiMaggio. 2016. Varieties of American Popular Nationalism. *American Sociological Review*, 81 (5): 949–980.

Bonikowski, Bart, Yuval Feinstein, and Sean Bock. 2021. The Partisan Sorting of "America": How Nationalist Cleavages Shaped the 2016 US Presidential Election. *American Journal of Sociology*, 127 (2): 492–561.

Bourdieu, Pierre. 1984. *Distinction: A Social Critique of the Judgement of Taste.* Cambridge, Mass: Harvard University Press.

Bourdieu, Pierre. 1998. *Acts of Resistance: Against the Tyranny of The Market.* New York: Free Press.

Bourdieu, Pierre. 2000. *Pascalian meditations.* Stanford: Stanford University Press.

Bourdieu, Pierre and Hans Haacke. 1995. *Free Exchange.* Stanford: Stanford University Press.

Bowen, Renee, Ying Chen, and Hülya Eraslan. 2014. Mandatory versus Discretionary Spending: The Status Quo Effect. *American Economic Review*, 104 (10): 2941–74.

Brandmayr, Federico. 2021. Are Theories Politically Flexible? *Sociological Theory,* 39 (2): 103–25.

Braverman, Harry. 1998 [1974]. *Labor and Monopoly Capital: The Degradation of Work in the Twentieth Century.* New York: Monthly Review Press.

Broćić, Miloš, and Andrew Miles. 2021. College and the 'Culture War': Assessing Higher Education's Influence on Moral Attitudes. *American Sociological Review*, 86 (5): 856–895.

Brouwer, Steve. 1998. *Authoritarian Democracy.* New York: Henry Holt and Co.

Brown, Courtney. 1987. Voter Mobilization and Party Competition in a Volatile Electorate. *American Sociological Review*, 52 (1): 59–72.

Brubaker, Rogers. 2009. Ethnicity, Race, and Nationalism. *Annual Review of Sociology*, 35: 21–42.

Brubaker, Rogers. 2015. Religious Dimensions of Political Conflict and Violence. *Sociological Theory*, 33 (1): 1–19.

Bruce, Steve. 2002. *God Is Dead: Secularization in the West*. London: Blackwell.

Bruce, Steve. 2004. Did Protestantism Create Democracy? *Democratization*, 11 (4): 3–20.

Brustein, William. 1991. The 'Red Menace' and the Rise of Italian Fascism. *American Sociological Review*, 56 (5): 652–64.

Burawoy, Michael. 2005. For Public Sociology. *American Sociological Review*, 70 (1): 4–28.

Bursztyn, Leonardo, Georgy Egorov, and Stefano Fiorin. 2020. From Extreme to Mainstream: The Erosion of Social Norms. *American Economic Review*, 110 (11): 3522–48.

Caldara, Dario, and Matteo Iacoviello. 2022. Measuring Geopolitical Risk. *American Economic Review*, 112 (4): 1194–1225.

Calder, Ryan. 2020. Halalization: Religious Product Certification in Secular Markets. *Sociological Theory*, 38 (4): 334–61.

Callander, Steven and Juan Carlos Carbajal. 2022. Cause and Effect in Political Polarization: A Dynamic Analysis. *Journal of Political Economy*, 130 (4): 825–880.

Card, David. 2022. Who Set *Your* Wage? *American Economic Review*, 112 (4): 1075–90.

Caren, Neal, Kenneth T. Andrews, and Todd Lu. 2020. Contemporary Social Movements in a Hybrid Media Environment. *Annual Review of Sociology*, 46: 443–465.

Carlson, Jennifer. 2019. Revisiting the Weberian Presumption: Gun Militarism, Gun Populism, and the Racial Politics of Legitimate Violence in Policing, *American Journal of Sociology*, 125 (3): 633–682.

Cassel, Gustav. 1927–8. The Rate of Interest, The Bank Rate, And the Stabilization of Prices. *Quarterly Journal of Economics*, 42 (3): 511–29.

Chrisman, Rick. 2022. If Sen. Paul were in charge of foreign policy, the world would be more peaceful. https://www.yahoo.com/news/sen-paul-were-charge-foreign-124208334.html.

Clark, Bryan. 2022. The new court's absurd inhumanity: To preserve procedure, an innocent man must die. https://www.yahoo.com/news/court-absurd-inhumanity-preserve-procedure-100000629.html.

Clark, Colin. 1957. *The Conditions of Economic Progress*. London: Macmillan and Co.

Clawson, Dan and Alan Neudstadt. 1989. Interlocks, PACs, and Corporate Conservatism. *American Journal of Sociology*, 94 (4): 749–773.

Coatney, Lou. 2022. Russia Now Left With No Choice But Nuclear War. May 3. https://www.yahoo.com/news/lou-coatney-russia-now-left-18401930.html.

Cohen, Daniel. 2003. Our Modern Times: The New Nature of Capitalism in the Information Age. Cambridge, Mass. MIT Press.

Cohen, Daniel, and Olivier Jean Blanchard. 1988. What Caused the Rise of Conservatism: A French View. *Economic Policy*, 3 (6): 196–219.

Colantone, Italo, and Piero Stanig. 2019. The Surge of Economic Nationalism in Western Europe. *Journal of Economic Perspectives*, 33 (4): 128–51.

Collins, Randall. 2012. C-Escalation And D-Escalation: A Theory of The Time-Dynamics of Conflict. *American Sociological Review*, 77 (1): 1–20.

Cooney, Mark and Callie Burt. 2008. Less Crime, More Punishment. *American Journal of Sociology*, 114 (2): 491–527.

Dahrendorf, Ralph. 1979. *Life Chances. Approaches to Social and Political Theory.* Chicago: Chicago University Press.

D'Ammassa, Algernon. 2022. Does verbal slip reveal anything George W. Bush would like to confess about Iraq? https://www.yahoo.com/news/does-verbal-slip-reveal-anything-120102316.html.

Dawkins, Richard. 2006. *The God Delusion.* New York: Bantam Books.

Dell, Melissa and Pablo Querubin. 2018. Nation Building Through Foreign Intervention: Evidence from Discontinuities in Military Strategies, *The Quarterly Journal of Economics*, 133 (2): 701–764.

Dewey, John. 1940. *Freedom and Culture.* London: Allen & Unwin.

Dickinson, Tim. 2022. 'Fight the Barbarians': The MAGA Movement Lays Out a Warpath at CPAC. https://www.yahoo.com/entertainment/fight-barbarians-maga-movement-lays-110058533.html.

DiPrete, Thomas A., Andrew Gelman, Tyler McCormick, Julien Teitler, Tian Zheng. 2011. Segregation in Social Networks Based on Acquaintanceship and Trust. *American Journal of Sociology*, 116 (2): 1234–83.

Djelic, Marie-Laure and Sigrid Quack. 2018. Globalization and Business Regulation. *Annual Review of Sociology*, 44: 123–143.

Domhoff, William. 2013. *Who Rules America? Power, Politics and Social Change.* New York: McGraw Hill.

Dorn, David, and Josef Zweimüller. 2021. Migration and Labor Market Integration in Europe. *Journal of Economic Perspectives*, 35 (2): 49–76.

Dube, Arindrajit, Ethan Kaplan, and Suresh Naidu. 2011. Coups, Corporations, and Classified Information. *Quarterly Journal of Economics*, 126 (3): 1375–1409.

Duggan, Mark. 2001. More Guns, More Crime. *Journal of Political Economy*, 109 (5): 1086–114.

Dunn, Charles and David Woodard. 1996. *The Conservative Tradition in America.* Lanham, MD: Rowan & Littlefield Publishers, Inc.

Durkheim, Emile. 1966 (1895). *The Rules of Sociological Method.* New York: Free Press.

Edwards, Sebastian. 2019. On Latin American Populism, and Its Echoes around the World. *Journal of Economic Perspectives*, 33 (4): 76–99.

Einolf, Christopher. 2007. The Fall and Rise of Torture: A Comparative and Historical Analysis. *Sociological Theory*, 25 (2): 101–121.

Elliott, Thomas, Jennifer Earl, Thomas V. Maher, and Heidi Reynolds-Stenson. 2022. Softer Policing or the Institutionalization of Protest? Decomposing Changes in Observed Protest Policing over Time. *American Journal of Sociology*, 127 (4): 1311–1365.

Enke, Benjamin. 2020. Moral Values and Voting. *Journal of Political Economy*, 128 (10): 3679–3729.

Esping-Andersen, Gosta. 1990. *The Three Worlds of Welfare Capitalism*. Princeton: Princeton University Press.

Esping-Andersen, Gosta. 2003. *Social Foundations of Postindustrial Economies*. Oxford: Oxford University Press.

Fajgelbaum, Pablo D, Pinelopi K Goldberg, Patrick J Kennedy, Amit K Khandelwal. 2020. The Return to Protectionism, *The Quarterly Journal of Economics*, 135 (1): 1–55.

Ferguson, Thomas, and Voth Hans-Joachim. 2008. Betting on Hitler: The Value of Political Connections in Nazi Germany. *Quarterly Journal of Economics*, 123 (1): 101–37.

Fischer, Stanley. 2003. Globalization And Its Challenges. American Economic Review 93 (2): 1–30.

Flaaen, Aaron, Ali Hortaçsu, and Felix Tintelnot. 2020. The Production Relocation and Price Effects of US Trade Policy: The Case of Washing Machines. *American Economic Review*, 110 (7): 2103–27.

Formisano, Ronald. 2015. *Plutocracy in America: How Increasing Inequality Destroys the Middle Class and Exploits the Poor*. Baltimore: Johns Hopkins University Press.

Frank, Robert. 2007. Plutonomics. https://blogs.wsj.com/wealth/2007/01/08/plutonomics/.

Friedland, Roger. 2002. Money, Sex, and God: The Erotic Logic of Religious Nationalism. *Sociological Theory*, 20 (3): 381–425.

Friedman, Milton and Friedman, Rose. 1982. *Capitalism and Freedom*. Chicago: University of Chicago Press.

Fromm, Erich. 1941. *Escape from Freedom*. New York: Holt, Rinehart and Winston.

Fromm, Erich. 1991 [1955]. *The Sane Society*. London: Routledge.

Galbraith, John Kenneth and Richard Parker. 2017. Economics in Perspective: A Critical History. Princeton: Princeton University Press.

García-Jimeno, Camilo, Angel Iglesias, and Pinar Yildirim. 2022. Information Networks and Collective Action: Evidence from the Women's Temperance Crusade. *American Economic Review*, 112 (1): 41–80.

Gastil, Raymond D. 1989. *Freedom In the World: Political Rights and Civil Liberties 1988–1989*. New York: Freedom House.

Gauchat, Gordon. 2012. Politicization of Science in the Public Sphere: A Study of Public Trust in the US, 1974 to 2010. *American Sociological Review*, 77 (2): 167–187.

Gersbach, Hans. 2020. History-Bound Reelections. *American Economic Journal: Microeconomics*, 12 (3): 33–75.

Gethin, Amory, Clara Martínez-Toledano, Thomas Piketty. 2022. Brahmin Left Versus Merchant Right: Changing Political Cleavages in 21 Western Democracies, 1948–2020, *The Quarterly Journal of Economics*, 137, (1): 1–48.

Gibney, Mark, Linda Cornett, Reed Wood, Peter Haschke, Daniel Arnon, Attilio Pisanò, and Gray Barrett. 2019. *The Political Terror Scale 1976–2018*. Data Retrieved, from the Political Terror Scale website: http://www.politicalterrorscale.org.

Gibson, David. 2011. Avoiding Catastrophe: The Interactional Production of Possibility during the Cuban Missile Crisis. *American Journal of Sociology*, 117 (2): 361–419.

Giddens, Anthony. 1979. *Central Problems in Social Theory. Action, Structure and Contradiction in Social Analysis*. Berkeley: University of California Press.

Giddens, Anthony. 1981. *A Contemporary Critique of Historical Materialism*. Berkeley: University of California Press.

Giddens, Anthony. 1991. *The Consequences of Modernity*. Cambridge: Polity Press.

Glaeser, Edward. 2004. Psychology and the Market. *American Economic Review*, 94 (2): 408–13.

Glaeser, Edward, Giacomo Ponzetto, and Jesse Shapiro. 2005. Strategic Extremism: Why Republicans and Democrats Divide on Religious Values. *Quarterly Journal of Economics*, 120 (4): 1283–1330.

Go, Julian. 2008. Global Fields and Imperial Forms: Field Theory and the British and American Empires. *Sociological Theory*, 26 (3): 201–229.

Go, Julian. 2020. The Imperial Origins of American Policing: Militarization and Imperial Feedback in the Early 20th Century. *American Journal of Sociology*, 125 (5): 1193–1254.

Gorman, Brandon and Charles Seguin. 2018. World Citizens on the Periphery: Threat and Identification with Global Society. *American Journal of Sociology*, 124 (3): 705–761.

Gorski, Philip and Ates Altınordu. 2008. After Secularization? *Annual Review of Sociology*, 34, 55–85.

Gorski, Philip and Gülay Türkmen-Dervişoğlu. 2013. Religion, Nationalism, and Violence: An Integrated Approach. *Annual Review of Sociology*, 39: 193–210.

Gross, Bertram. 1980. *Friendly Fascism*. Boston: South End Press.

Gross, Neil, Thomas Medvetz, and Rupert Russell. 2011. The Contemporary American Conservative Movement. *Annual Review of Sociology*, 37: 325–354.

Guriev, Sergei. 2018. Economic Drivers of Populism. *AEA Papers and Proceedings*, 108: 200–203.

Gusterson, Hugh and Catherine Besteman. 2019. Cultures of Militarism. An Introduction to Supplement 19. *Current Anthropology* 60 (S19): S3–S14.

Habermas, Jurgen. 1975. *Legitimation Crisis*. Boston: Beacon Press.

Habermas, Jürgen. 1989. *The New Conservatism: Cultural Criticism and the Historians' Debate*. Cambridge: MIT Press.

Habermas, Jürgen. 2001. *The Postnational Constellation: Political Essays*. Cambridge: MIT Press.

Habermas, Jürgen, Cronin, Ciaran, De Greiff, Pablo. 1998. *The Inclusion of the Other: Studies in Political Theory*. Cambridge: MIT Press.

Hahl, Oliver, Minjae Kim, Ezra W. Zuckerman Sivan. 2018. The Authentic Appeal of the Lying Demagogue: Proclaiming the Deeper Truth about Political Illegitimacy. *American Sociological Review*, 83 (1): 1–33.

Harris, Sam. 2005. *The End of Faith: Religion, Terror, and the Future of Reason*. New York: W. W. Norton.

Harrod, Roy. 1956. *Towards a Dynamic Economics*. London: Macmillan.

Harrold, Frederick C. 1936. The Nature of Carlyle's Calvinism. *Studies in Philology*, 33 (3): 475–486.

Hayek, Friedrich. 1960. The Constitution Of Liberty. South Bend: Gateway Editions.

Head, Keit, and Thierry Mayer. 2021. The United States of Europe: A Gravity Model Evaluation of the Four Freedoms. *Journal of Economic Perspectives*, 35 (2): 23–48.

Hechter, Michael. 2004. From Class to Culture. *American Journal of Sociology*, 110 (2): 400–45.

Hedges, Chris. 2004. The Christian Right and The Rise of American Fascism. www.theocracywatch.org (Nov 15).

Hedges, Chris. 2006. *American Fascists: The Christian Right and The War on America*. New York: Free Press.

Heiberger, Raphael H., Sebastian Munoz-Najar Galvez and Daniel A. McFarland. 2021. Facets of Specialization and Its Relation to Career Success: An Analysis of US Sociology, 1980 to 2015. *American Sociological Review*, 86 (6):1164–1192.

Helm, Paul. 2008. *Calvin: A Guide for The Perplexed*. London; New York: T & T Clark.

Herman, Finer. 1945. *The Road to Reaction*. Boston: Little, Brown and Co.

Hicks, Alexander. 2006. Free-Market and Religious Fundamentalists versus Poor Relief. *American Sociological Review*, 71 (2): 503–510.

Hicks, John. 1969. Preface—And a Manifesto. In Kenneth Arrow and Tibor Scitovsky (eds.), *Readings in Welfare Economics* (pp. 95–99). London: Allen and Unwin.

Hirschman, Daniel. 2021. Rediscovering the 1%: Knowledge Infrastructures and the Stylized Facts of Inequality. *American Journal of Sociology*, 127 (2): 739–786.

Hirschman, Albert. 1994. Social Conflicts as Pillars of Democratic Market Society. *Political Theory*, 22 (2): 203–19.

Hitchens, Christopher. 2009. *God Is Not Great: How Religion Poisons Everything*. New York: Twelve Books imprint of the Hachette Book Group USA.

Hodgson, Geoffrey. 1999. *Economics and Utopia: Why the Learning Economy Is Not the End of History*. New York: Routledge.

Hodgson, Geoffrey M. 2002. *How Economics Forgot History: The Problem of Historical Specificity in Social Science*. London: Routledge.

Horkheimer, Max and Adorno, Theodor W. 1993. *The Dialectic of Enlightenment*. New York: Continuum.

Huber, Kilian. 2021. Are Bigger Banks Better? Firm-Level Evidence from Germany. *Journal of Political Economy*, 129 (7): 2023–2066.

Huber, Kilian, Volker Lindenthal, and Fabian Waldinger. 2021. Discrimination, Managers, and Firm Performance: Evidence from Aryanizations in Nazi Germany. *Journal of Political Economy*, 129 (9): 2455–2503.

Hume, David. 1983 (1778). *The History of England from the Invasion of Julius Caesar to the Revolution in 1688*. Indianapolis: Liberty Fund.

Johnson, Dale L. 2017. *Social Inequality, Economic Decline, and Plutocracy: An American Crisis*. Palgrave Macmillan.

Jouet, Mugambi. 2017. *One Nation, Divisible: Exceptional America*. Berkeley: University of California Press.

Juergensmeyer, Mark. 1994. *The New Cold War?: Religious Nationalism Confronts the Secular State*. Berkeley: University of California Press.

Juergensmeyer, Mark. 2003. *Terror in The Mind of God*. Berkeley: University of California Press.

Kaltwasser, Cristóbal. 2018. Studying the (Economic) Consequences of Populism. *AEA Papers and Proceedings*, 108: 204–07.

Kapur, Ajay, Niall Macleod, and Narendra Singh, 2005. Plutonomy: Buying Luxury, Explaining Global Imbalances, New York: Citigroup, Equity Strategy, Industry Note: October 16.

Kettler, David and Volker Meja. 1984. Karl Mannheim and Conservatism: The Ancestry of Historical Thinking. *American Sociological Review*, 49 (2): 71–85.

Keynes, John M. 1960 (1936). *The General Theory of Employment, Interest and Money*. London: Macmillan.

Kimeldorf, Howard. 2013. Worker Replacement Costs and Unionization: Origins of the US Labor Movement. *American Sociological Review*, 78 (6): 1033–1062.

King, Ryan, Michael Massoglia, and Christopher Uggen. 2012. Employment and Exile: US Criminal Deportations, 1908–2005. *American Journal of Sociology*, 117 (6): 1786–1825.

Kinloch, Graham. 1981. *Ideology and Contemporary Sociological Theory*. Englewood Cliffs: Englewood Cliffs.

Knight, Frank H. 1967. Laissez Faire: Pro and Con. *Journal of Political Economy*, 75 (6): 782–795.

Kranton, Rachel E. 2016. Identity Economics: Where Do Social Distinctions and Norms Come From? *American Economic Review*, 106 (5): 405–09.

Krasa, Stefan and Mattias Polborn. 2014. Social Ideology and Taxes in a Differentiated Candidates Framework. *American Economic Review*, 104 (1): 308–22.

Lamont, Michèle. 2018. Addressing Recognition Gaps: Destigmatization and the Reduction of Inequality. *American Sociological Review*, 83 (3): 419–444.

Lemert, Charles. 1991. The End of Ideology, really. *Sociological Theory*, 9 (2): 164–72.

Levitsky, Steven and Daniel Ziblatt. 2018. *How Democracies Die*. New York: Penguin Random House.

Levy, Roee. 2021. Social Media, News Consumption, and Polarization: Evidence from a Field Experiment. *American Economic Review*, 111 (3): 831–70.

Levy, Gilat, and Ronny Razin. 2017. The Coevolution of Segregation, Polarized Beliefs, and Discrimination: The Case of Private versus State Education. *American Economic Journal: Microeconomics,* 9 (4): 141–70.

Levy, Gilat, Ronny Razin, and Alwyn Young. 2022. Misspecified Politics and the Recurrence of Populism. *American Economic Review*, 112 (3): 928–62.

Lipset, Seymour. 1996. *American Exceptionalism: A Double-Edged Sword*. New York: Norton.

Lloyd, Richard. 2012. Urbanization and the Southern US. *Annual Review of Sociology*, 38, 483–506.

Lundberg, Shelly and Robert Pollak. 2007. The American Family and Family Economics. *Journal of Economic Perspectives*, 21, (2): 3–26.

Manent, Pierre. 1998. *Modern Liberty and Its Discontents*. Lanham: Rowman & Littlefield Publishers.

Mann, Michael. 2004. *Fascists*. Cambridge: Cambridge University Press.

Mannheim, Karl. 1936. *Ideology and Utopia. An Introduction to the Sociology of Knowledge*. New York: Harcourt, Brace & World.

Mannheim, Karl. 1986. *Conservatism*. London: Routledge and Kegan Paul.

Mansbach, Richard. 2006. Calvinism as a Precedent for Islamic Radicalism. *Brown Journal of World Affairs*, 12: 103–115.

Manza, Jeff and Brooks, Clem. 1997. The Religious Factor in US Presidential Elections, 1960–1992; *American Journal of Sociology*, 103 (1): 38–81.

Margalit, Yotam. 2019. Economic Insecurity and the Causes of Populism, Reconsidered. *Journal of Economic Perspectives*, 33 (4): 152–70.

Marks, Gary, Heather Mbaye, and Hyung Min Kim. 2009. Radicalism or Reformism? Socialist Parties before World War I. *American Sociological Review*, 74 (4): 615–635.

McDermott, Monica and Frank Samson. 2005. White Racial and Ethnic Identity in the US. *Annual Review of Sociology*, 31, 245–61.

McElhattan, David. 2022. The Proliferation of Criminal Background Check Laws in the United States. *American Journal of Sociology*, 127 (4): 1037–1093.

McLaughlin, Neil. 1996. Nazism, Nationalism, and the Sociology of Emotions: Escape from Freedom Revisited. *Sociological Theory*, 14 (2): 241–261.

McMurtry, John. 1999. *The Cancer Stage of Capitalism*. London: Pluto Press.

Mencken, H. L. 1982. *A Mencken Chrestomathy*. New York: Vintage Books.

Merriman, Ben and Josh Pacewicz. 2022. The Great Interstate Divergence: Partisan Bureaucracies in the Contemporary United States. *American Journal of Sociology*, 127 (4): 1221–1266.

Merton, Robert K. 1939. Review Of *the Protestant Crusade, 1800–1860*. By Ray Allen Billington. *American Sociological Review*, 4 (3): 436–438.

Merton, Robert K. 1968. *Social Theory and Social Structure*. New York: The Free Press.

Michels, Robert. 1968 (1911). *Political Parties. A Sociological Study of the Oligarchical Tendencies of Modern Democracy*. New York: The Free Press.

Milanovic, Branko. 2014. The Return of Patrimonial Capitalism: A Review of Thomas Piketty's Capital in the Twenty-First Century. *Journal of Economic Literature*, 52 (2): 519–34.

Miliband, Ralph. 1969. *The State in Capitalist Society. An Analysis of The Western System of Power*. New York: Basic Books Inc. Publishers.

Miller, Jon D., Eugenie C. Scott, And Shinji Okamoto. 2006. Public Acceptance of Evolution. *Science* 313 (5788): 765–766.

Miller, Sarah, Norman Johnson, and Laura R Wherry. 2021. Medicaid and Mortality: New Evidence from Linked Survey and Administrative Data, *The Quarterly Journal of Economics*, 136 (3): 1783–1829.

Miller, Joanne, Kazimierz Slomczynski, and Melvyn Kohn. 1987. Authoritarianism as Worldview and Intellectual Process. *American Journal of Sociology*, 93 (2): 442–4.

Mises, Ludwig Von. 1951. *Socialism: An Economic and Sociological Study*. New Haven: Yale University Press.

Mitchell, Wesley C. 1917. Wieser's Theory of Social Economics. *Political Science Quarterly*, 32 (1): 95–118.

Mooney, Chris C. 2005. *The Republican War on Science*. New York: Basic Books.

Mueller, Dennis. 1996. *Constitutional Democracy*. New York: Oxford University Press.

Mueller, Dennis. 2007. Democracy, Rationality and Morality. Max Planck Institute of Economics. The *Papers on Economics and Evolution*, edited by the Evolutionary Economics Group, MPI Jena.

Mueller, Dennis. 2009. *Reason, Religion, and Democracy*. Cambridge: Cambridge University Press.

Mueller, Dennis 2013. The State and Religion. *Review of Social Economy*, 71 (1), 1–19.

Mueller, Julia. 2022. Kissinger: US foreign policy 'very responsive to the emotion of the moment.' https://www.yahoo.com/news/kissinger-us-foreign-policy-very-133058692.html.

Munch, Richard. 1994. *Sociological Theory*. Chicago: Nelson-Hall Publishers.

Munch, Richard. 2001. *The Ethics of Modernity: Formation and Transformation in Britain, France, Germany, and the United States.* Lanham: Rowman & Littlefield.

Murray, Joshua. 2017. Interlock Globally, Act Domestically: Corporate Political Unity in the 21st Century. *American Journal of Sociology*, 122 (6): 1617–1663.

Myrdal, Gunnar. 1953 (1930). *The Political Element in The Development of Economic Theory.* London: Routledge and Kegan Paul.

Naidu, Suresh and Noam Yuchtman. 2013. Coercive Contract Enforcement: Law and the Labor Market in Nineteenth Century Industrial Britain. *American Economic Review*, 103 (1): 107–44.

Newhouse, Joseph P. 2021. An Ounce of Prevention. *Journal of Economic Perspectives*, 35 (2): 101–18.

Nisbet, Robert. 1966. *The Sociological Tradition.* New York: Basic Books Publishers.

Noakes, Jeremy. 2003. *German Conservatives and The Third Reich: An Ambiguous Relationship.* In Blinkhorn, Martin (ed.), Fascists and Conservatives: The Radical Right and the Establishment in Twentieth-century Europe (pp. 71–97). London: Taylor & Francis.

Nordhaus, William. 2019. Climate Change: The Ultimate Challenge for Economics. *American Economic Review*, 109 (6): 1991–2014.

Nyhan, Brendan. 2020. Facts and Myths about Misperceptions. *Journal of Economic Perspectives*, 34 (3): 220–36.

Olesen, Thomas. 2021. Democracy's Autonomy Dilemma: Whistleblowing and the Politics of Disclosure. *Sociological Theory,* 39 (4): 245–264.

Olick, Jeffrey. 1999. Collective Memory: The Two Cultures. *Sociological Theory,* 17 (3): 333–48.

Olson, Mancur. 2000. *Power and Prosperity: Outgrowing Communist and Capitalist Dictatorships.* New York: Basic Books.

Oppenheimer, Andres. 2022. Colombia's New Leader Petro Will Push Latin American Further To The Left—But Not Too Far. https://www.yahoo.com/news/colombia-leader-petro-push-latin-231700509.html?.tsrc=fp_deeplink.

Panunzio, Costantino. 1945. Italian Sociology. In Gurvitch, Georges and Wilbert Moore (eds). *Twentieth Century Sociology* (pp. 638–652). Freeport: Books for Libraries Press.

Pareto, Vilfredo. 1935 [1916]. *The Mind and Society. A Treatise on General Sociology.* New York: Dover Publications.

Pareto, Vilfredo. 2000 [1901]. *The Rise and Fall of Elites: An Application of Theoretical Sociology.* New Brunswick: Transaction Publishers.

Parsons, Talcott. 1949. *Essays in Sociological Theory.* New York: The Free Press.

Parsons, Talcott. 1951. *The Social System.* New York: The Free Press.

Patriotic Millionaires. https://patrioticmillionaires.org/about/.

Paxton, Robert O. 1998. The Five Stages of Fascism. *The Journal of Modern History,* 70 (1): 1–23.

Paxton, Robert O. 2004. *The Anatomy of Fascism*. New York: Alfred A. Knopf.

Perelman, Michael. 2000. *Classical Political Economy and the Secret History of Primitive Accumulation*. Durham: Duke University Press.

Perla, Jesse, Christopher Tonetti, and Michael E. Waugh. 2021. Equilibrium Technology Diffusion, Trade, and Growth. *American Economic Review*, 111 (1): 73–128.

Pfeffer, Fabian T., Paula Fomby, Noura Insolera. 2020. The Longitudinal Revolution: Sociological Research at the 50-Year Milestone of the Panel Study of Income Dynamics. *Annual Review of Sociology*, 46: 83–108.

Pfister James W. 2022. American Interference and Vietnam, Ukraine and Taiwan Cases. https://www.yahoo.com/news/american-interference-vietnam-ukraine-tai wan-080005091.html.

Phillips, Kevin. 2006. *American Theocracy: The Peril and Politics of Radical Religion, Oil, and Borrowed Money in the 21st Century*. New York: Penguin Group.

Piketty, Thomas. 2014. *Capital in The Twenty-First Century*. Cambridge: Harvard University Press.

Piketty, Thomas. 2020. *Capital and Ideology*. Cambridge, MA.: The Belknap Press of Harvard University Press.

Piketty, Thomas, Emmanuel Saez, Gabriel Zucman. 2018. Distributional National Accounts: Methods and Estimates for the United States, *Quarterly Journal of Economics*, 133 (2): 553–609.

Piketty, Thomas, Emmanuel Saez, and Gabriel Zucman. 2019. Simplified Distributional National Accounts. *AEA Papers and Proceedings*, 109: 289–95.

Plotke, David. 2002. The Success and Anger of The Modern American Right. In Bell Daniel (ed.), *The Radical Right* (pp. vi–lxxvi). New Brunswick: Transaction Publishers.

Portes, Alejandro and Erik Vickstrom. 2011. Diversity, Social Capital, and Cohesion. *Annual Review of Sociology*, 37: 461–479.

Pryor, Frederic. 2002. *The Future Of U.S. Capitalism*. New York: Cambridge University Press.

Rajan, Raghuram and Luigi Zingales. 2004. *Saving Capitalism from the Capitalists*. Princeton: Princeton University Press.

Ramirez, Steven A. 2013. *Lawless Capitalism: The Subprime Crisis and the Case for an Economic Rule of Law*. New York: NYU Press.

Rawls, John and ebrary, Inc. 2010. *A Brief Inquiry into The Meaning of Sin and Faith: With On My Religion*. Cambridge, Mass: Harvard University Press.

Ray, Rebecca and Schmitt John. 2007. No-vacation nation USA–A Comparison of Leave and Holiday in OECD Countries. *European Economic and Employment Policy Brief* No. 3–2007.

Redbird, Beth and David B. Grusky. 2016. Distributional Effects of the Great Recession: Where Has All the Sociology Gone? *Annual Review of Sociology*, 42: 185–215.

Richards, Zoë. 2022. House GOP candidate called Hitler 'the kind of leader we need' in 2021 remarks. https://www.yahoo.com/news/house-gop-candidate-called-hitler-232944131.html.

Riley, Dylan. 2005. Civic Associations and Authoritarian Regimes in Interwar Europe: Italy and Spain in Comparative Perspective. *American Sociological Review*, 70 (2): 288–310.

Riley, Dylan, and Juan J. Fernández. 2014. Beyond Strong and Weak: Rethinking Postdictatorship Civil Societies. *American Journal of Sociology*, 120 (2): 432–503.

Rodrik, Dani. 2014. When Ideas Trump Interests: Preferences, Worldviews, and Policy Innovations. *Journal of Economic Perspectives*, 28 (1): 189–208.

Rodrik, Dani. 2018. Is Populism Necessarily Bad Economics? *AEA Papers and Proceedings*, 108: 196–99.

Rogers, Joel and Wolfgang Streeck. 1995. *Works Councils: Consultation, Representation, and Cooperation in Industrial Relations*. Chicago: University of Chicago Press.

Romero, Mary. 2020. Sociology Engaged in Social Justice. *American Sociological Review*, 85 (1): 1–30.

Rose, Evan K. and Yotam Shem-Tov. 2021. How Does Incarceration Affect Reoffending? Estimating the Dose-Response Function. *Journal of Political Economy*, 129 (12): 3302–3356.

Rosenfeld, Jake 2019. US Labor Studies in the Twenty-First Century: Understanding Laborism Without Labor. *Annual Review of Sociology*, 45 (2): 449–465.

Rousseau, Peter L. 2021. Jackson, the Bank War, and the Legacy of the Second Bank of the United States. *AEA Papers and Proceedings*, 111: 501–07.

Rydgren, Jens. 2007a. The Sociology of the Radical Right. *Annual Review of Sociology*, 33, 241–62.

Rydgren, Jens. 2007b. The Power of the Past: A Contribution to a Cognitive Sociology of Ethnic Conflict. *Sociological Theory*, 25 (3): 225–244.

Sadler, Evan. 2020. Diffusion Games. *American Economic Review*, 110 (1): 225–70.

Saez, Emmanuel, and Gabriel Zucman. 2020. The Rise of Income and Wealth Inequality in America: Evidence from Distributional Macroeconomic Accounts. *Journal of Economic Perspectives*, 34 (4): 3–26.

Saint-Simon, Henri de. 1964 [1816–18]. *Social Organization, The Science of Man and other writings*. New York: Harper Torchbooks.

Satyanath, Shanker, Nico Voigtländer, and Hans-Joachim Voth. 2017. Bowling for Fascism: Social Capital and the Rise of the Nazi Party, *Journal of Political Economy*, 125 (2): 478–526.

Savelsberg, Joachim 2006. Religion, Historical Contingencies, and Institutional Conditions of Criminal Punishment: The German Case and Beyond. *Law and Social Inquiry*, 29 (2): 373–401.

Savelsberg, Joachim and Ryan King. 2005. Institutionalizing Collective Memories of Hate: Law and Law Enforcement in Germany and the US. *American Journal of Sociology*, 111 (2): 579–616.

Schaeffer-Duffy, Scott 2022. No Excuse for Russian Invasion Of Ukraine, But Americans Must Remember … https://www.yahoo.com/news/scott-schaeffer-duffy-no-exc use-090429932.html.

Schelling, Thomas. 2006. An Astonishing Sixty Years: The Legacy of Hiroshima. *American Economic Review*, 96 (4): 929–937.

Schultz, Randy. 2018. Gov. Rick Scott took responsibility? No, he took $300 million https://www.sun-sentinel.com/opinion/fl-op-col-rick-scott-medicare-fraud-20181 002-story.html.

Schumpeter, Joseph. 1950. *Capitalism, Socialism and Democracy*. New York: Harper and Brothers.

Schumpeter, Joseph. 1991. *The Economics and Sociology of Capitalism*. (Edited by Richard Swedberg). Princeton: Princeton University Press.

Scitovsky, Tibor. 1972. What's Wrong with the Arts Is What's Wrong with Society. *American Economic Review*, 62 (1): 62–69.

Sen, Amartya. 1977. Rational Fools: A Critique of The Behavioral Foundations of Economic Theory. *Philosophy And Public Affairs*, 6 (4): 317–44.

Simi, Pete, Kathleen Blee, Matthew DeMichele, Steven Windisch. 2017. Addicted to Hate: Identity Residual among Former White Supremacists. *American Sociological Review*, 82 (6): 1167–1187.

Simmel, Georg. 1955 [1923]. *Conflict. The Web of Group Affiliations*. New York: The Free Press.

Simons, Marlise. 2001. Radiation from Balkan Bombing Alarms Europe. https://www .nytimes.com/2001/01/07/world/radiation-from-balkan-bombing-alarms-eur ope.html.

Simpson, Herbert D. 1934. The Problem of Expanding Governmental Activities. *American Economic Review*, 24 (1): 151–160.

Slater, Dan and Nicholas Rush Smith. 2016. The Power of Counterrevolution: Elitist Origins of Political Order in Postcolonial Asia and Africa, *American Journal of Sociology*, 121 (5): 1472–1516.

Slattery, Cailin, and Owen Zidar. 2020. Evaluating State and Local Business Incentives. *Journal of Economic Perspectives*, 34 (2): 90–118.

Smeeding, Timothy. 2006. Poor People in Rich Nations: The US in Comparative Perspective. *Journal of Economic Perspectives*, 20 (1): 69–90.

Smelser, Neil. 1997. *Problematics of Sociology: The Georg Simmel Lectures, 1995*. University of California Press.

Soehl, Thomas, and Sakeef M. Karim. 2021. How Legacies of Geopolitical Trauma Shape Popular Nationalism Today. *American Sociological Review*, 86 (3): 406–429.

Solow, Robert, Alan Budd, and Christian von Weizsacker. 1987. The Conservative Revolution: A Roundtable Discussion. *Economic Policy*, 2 (5): 181–200.

Sorokin, Pitirim. 1970 [1957]. *Social & Cultural Dynamics*. A Study of Change in Major Systems of Art, Truth, Ethics, Law and Social Relationships. Boston: Porter Sargent Publisher.

Spenkuch Jorg L., and Philipp Tillmann. 2017. Elite Influence? Religion and the Electoral Success of the Nazis. Northwestern University Analysis Group.

Squicciarini, Mara P. 2020. Devotion and Development: Religiosity, Education, and Economic Progress in Nineteenth-Century France. *American Economic Review*, 110 (11): 3454–91.

Steinmetz, George. 2005. Return to Empire: The New US Imperialism in Comparative Historical Perspective. *Sociological Theory*, 23 (4): 339–367.

Steinmetz, George and Eric Olin Wright. 1989. The Fall and Rise of the Petty Bourgeoisie: Changing Patterns of Self-employment in the Postwar US *American Journal of Sociology*, 94 (5): 973–1018.

Stiglitz, Joseph. 2010. *Freefall: America, Free Markets, And the Sinking of The World Economy*. New York: Norton.

Stiglitz, Joseph. 2012. *The Price of Inequality*. New York: W. W. Norton & Company.

Stiglitz, Joseph E. 2022. Opinion: How an arrogant and pathological America could lose the new cold war. https://www.marketwatch.com/story/how-an-arrogant-and -pathological-america-could-lose-the-new-cold-war-11655483678?siteid=yhoof2.

Stivers, Richard. 1994. *The Culture of Cynicism. American Morality in Decline*. Cambridge: Blackwell.

Tetlock, Philip E., Barbara A. Mellers, and J. Peter Scoblic. 2017. Sacred versus Pseudo-sacred Values: How People Cope with Taboo Trade-Offs. *American Economic Review*, 107 (5): 96–99.

Throsby, David. 1994. The Production and Consumption of the Arts: A View of Cultural Economics. Journal of Economic Literature 32 (1): 1–29.

Tocqueville, Alexis De. 1945 [1835]. Democracy in America. Vol II. New York: Knopf.

Torche, Florencia, and Tamkinat Rauf. 2021. The Political Context and Infant Health in the United States. *American Sociological Review*, 86 (3): 377–405.

Tuğal, Cihan. 2021. Populism Studies: The Case for Theoretical and Comparative Reconstruction. *Annual Review of Sociology*, 47 (1): 327–347.

VanHeuvelen, Tom. 2020. The Right to Work, Power Resources, and Economic Inequality. *American Journal of Sociology*, 125 (5): 1255–1302.

Vásquez, Ian and Tanja Porčnik. 2019. T*he Human Freedom Index: A Global Measurement of Personal, Civil, and Economic Freedom*. The Cato Institute, the Fraser Institute, and the Friedrich Naumann Foundation for Freedom.

Vine, David. 2015. *Base Nation: How US Military Bases Abroad Harm America and the World*. New York: Henry Holt and Co.

Volscho, Thomas and Nathan Kelly. 2012. The Rise of the Super-Rich: Power Resources, Taxes, Financial Markets, and the Dynamics of the Top 1 Percent, 1949 to 2008. *American Sociological Review*, 77 (3): 679–699.

Wagner, David. 1997. *The New Temperance: The American Obsession with Sin and Vice.* Boulder: Westview Press.

Wang, Tianyi. 2021. Media, Pulpit, and Populist Persuasion: Evidence from Father Coughlin. *American Economic Review*, 111 (9): 3064–92.

Weber, Max. 1976 [1904]. *The Protestant Ethic and the Spirit of Capitalism.* New York: Charles Scribner's Sons.

Wieser, Friedrich. 1967 [1914]. *Social Economics.* New York: A. M. Kelley.

Williams, Christine. 2021. Life Support: The Problems of Working for a Living. *American Sociological Review*, 86 (2): 191–200.

Wimmer, Andreas and Yuval Feinstein. 2010. The Rise of the Nation-State across the World, 1816 To 2001. *American Sociological Review*, 75 (5): 764–790.

Young, Alex. 2022. Roger Waters Calls Biden a "War Criminal," Defends Russia and China in CNN Interview. https://www.yahoo.com/entertainment/roger-waters-calls -biden-war-144920102.html.

Index